For Patrick Fox,

I truly hope you enjoy the book!

Very Best Wishes,

Ian Parshall

Shattered Sword

The Untold Story of
The Battle of Midway

Jonathan B. Parshall • Anthony P. Tully

Potomac Books • Washington, D.C.

Published in the United States by Potomac Books, Inc. All rights reserved. No part of this book may be reproduced in any manner whatsoever without written permission from the publisher, except in the case of brief quotations embodied in critical articles and reviews.

Library of Congress Cataloging-in-Publication Data

Parshall, Jonathan, 1962–
    Shattered sword: the untold story of the Battle of Midway / Jonathan Parshall and Anthony Tully.
        p. cm.
    Includes bibliographical references and index.
    ISBN 1-57488-923-0 (hardcover : alk. paper)
    1. Midway, Battle of, 1942. 2. World War, 1939–1945—Naval operations, Japanese. 3. World War, 1939–1945—Naval operations, American. 4. World War, 1939–1945—Aerial operations, Japanese. 5. World War, 1939–1945—Aerial operations, American. I. Tully, Anthony, 1961– II. Title.
D774.M4P37 2005
940.54'26699—dc22

2005011629

Printed in Canada on acid-free paper that meets the American National Standards Institute Z39-48 Standard.

Potomac Books, Inc.
22841 Quicksilver Drive
Dulles, Virginia 20166

First Edition

10   9   8   7   6   5   4   3   2   1

Jon Parshall dedicates this book to

Margaret, Anna, and Derek,

and to
the late Dr. David C. Evans, whose kindness
and collegiality rekindled a young man's dormant
interest in the IJN and set him on this path.

Tony Tully dedicates this book to

Dan, Kay, and Matt Tully, Heather Cooper,
and his nieces and nephews, who speak of their "writer" uncle,

and to
the late Walter Lord, whose careful sifting of facts
and rich narrative inspired my own style and love of history,
and whose help honored our work.

Contents

List of Figures

Acknowledgments

Tony and I fortuitously have found ourselves at the center of a nexus of technology, friends, and community created in the late twentieth century, and are profoundly grateful to all three. The advent of the Internet, and the spontaneous creation of globe-spanning communities of interest it fostered, truly revolutionized the way we were able to approach and assemble this book. By leveraging the Web, we were able to identify and then contact the right people to elucidate almost any arcane matter. Not only that, but the answers to questions that would have taken months to retrieve "back in the old days" of, say, a decade ago often came back to us within hours. We both consider ourselves extremely fortunate to have ridden on the cusp of such a providential technological transformation.

Of course, the people we met during the process of creating *Shattered Sword* were ultimately far more important than the communication medium that connected us to them. It has been our privilege to have widened our circle of associates enormously during this endeavor and to have made many genuine friends along the way. It is no exaggeration to say that this book is, in a sense, a vast collaborative effort on the part of the wider Japanese naval history community. The research and insights of many extraordinary people on both sides of the Pacific can be found within these pages. We are profoundly grateful to them for agreeing to let us benefit from their acumen and apply the fruits of their hard work. It is appropriate, therefore, that we acknowledge their efforts first and foremost.

At the top of the list stands historian John Lundstrom, whose fine books on the Pacific war have been mainstays of its students for twenty-five years. This could easily have been John's book, had he chosen to write it. Instead, he gave openly and generously from his vast store of wisdom on the topic of the Pacific war in general, and Midway in particular. He has been our tireless advocate, adviser, and friend—always pointing out new sources we might have overlooked, new perspectives we might not have considered. This book literally would not have been possible, let alone had the depth of insight it seeks to deliver, without John's selfless collegial efforts and constant encouragement. We are deeply in his debt.

Noted aviation historian Tagaya Osamu, despite his hectic professional schedule, gave liberally of his time to review and critique our manuscript. Sam's intimate knowledge of Japanese naval aviation, and his detailed, well-considered comments, saved us from numerous factual errors, gaffes in Japanese terminology and pronunciation, and other problems that would have damaged the credibility of this work. Sam's father, Tagaya Yoshio, a former Imperial Japanese Navy technical officer, likewise made helpful suggestions for the kanji on the book's section headers.

James Sawruk is known to serious students of the Pacific air war as the undisputed master of the Japanese operational records. Jim generously translated the carrier air group records for both Midway and the Aleutians operations, which appear here in English for the first time. Jim also provided numerous insights into Japanese aviation technique, as well as American aviation operations. His information provides an important cornerstone of the operational bedrock on which our account is based.

Mark Peattie, coauthor of two groundbreaking studies of the Imperial Navy, has been a firm friend since 1996. The work I did for Mark on *Sunburst* served as my "apprenticeship" in this trade, and Mark has taught me much of what it means to be a good scholar and a good colleague. Mark's gentle comments on the initial manuscript, much like Sam Tagaya's, were instrumental in channeling the enthusiasm of my initial prose into a style more likely to weather the test of time, for which I am grateful.

David Dickson, perhaps the foremost Western expert on Japanese naval doctrine and carrier design, provided us with a constant stream of ship plans, doctrinal tracts and other documents and, most important, his well-honed comments. David might well have been a coauthor of this work had not other commitments intruded, but he has been a first-rate collaborator regardless. In the same vein, J. Michael Wenger, noted expert on both Pearl Harbor and the Indian Ocean battles, aided us with his consummate knowledge of Japanese carrier operations and his deep understanding of the Japanese source materials. Mike also provided many of the pictures that grace this volume. Eric Bergerud, author of several well-received volumes on the Pacific war, similarly lent his advice and encouragement and was a sounding board during many pleasant evenings spent at my home.

Mark Horan, coauthor of *A Glorious Page in Our History,* augmented and synthesized Jim Sawruk's operational information and added to it with his extensive interviews of the American Midway aviators. Mark's detailed knowledge of the American side of the battle greatly informed our interpretations and graphics for the various American aerial attacks at Midway. Tony is particularly grateful for Mark's discussion of interviews that provided clues for reconstructing the Japanese formation at various times during 4 June. Likewise, Robert Cressman, Mark's coauthor and historian at the Naval Historical Center, imparted his wisdom on many issues, as well as giving the entire manuscript a very thorough going over, thus eliminating many errors of fact and terminology. Special notice must be taken of the late, widely respected Walter Lord, who in his last years graciously agreed to contribute important unpublished original interviews and notes from his own Midway research. Our thanks likewise go Mr. Lord's personal secretary, Lillian Pacifico, who conscientiously and efficiently arranged for copying and forwarding these materials to us.

Richard Wolff, author of a forthcoming study of carrier *Taihō,* contributed his insights on Japanese carrier design and contributed to fact-checking in the carrier data appendix. Lars Ahlberg helped translate the Japanese carrier crew rosters and also tracked down the internal plans of *Sōryū*. The source of those plans, Endo Akira, publisher of the fine private ship magazine *Senzen Senpaku*, graciously provided additional carrier plans. My good friend Yoshida Akihiko, former Japanese Maritime Self Defense Force captain and expert on the Imperial Navy, spent many hours translating those plans into English, as well as providing a lively, informative correspondence on many matters pertaining to this book over the years. To Captain Yoshida we are indeed very grateful.

Newspaper reporter Takashi Koganemaru of the *Sankei Shimbun* in Tokyo, spent many hours providing translations of several key survivor accounts, as well as materials from Hyōdō Nisohachi. Hyōdō-san, an expert on Japanese naval aviation and military technology in general, graciously prepared a set of manuscripts pertaining to Japanese flight deck and arming operations that confirmed and elaborated on a great deal of what we had previously uncovered in the extant English-language sources.

Finding new Japanese survivor accounts was a difficult proposition, and in this we were aided by Yoshida Jiro, who helped arrange interviews with *Hiryū* survivor Arimura Yoshikazu. Mr. Arimura filled in a number of missing details for us. His friend, fellow Midway veteran Maeda Takeshi, also supplied us with his personal remembrances of several of *Kido Butai*'s senior officers. Likewise, Ron Werneth, author of a forthcoming book of first-person accounts of Japanese naval aviators, not only supplied us with portions of his account, but also put us in contact with *Kaga* survivor Yoshino Haruo. Mr. Yoshino's comments regarding *Kaga*'s scuttling were most helpful. Noted dive-bomber pilot Abe Zenji likewise provided a wealth of details of both Japanese operational technique, as well as insights into the personalities of several of the senior officers at Midway.

A number of skilled translators helped us along the way. Tony's longtime translator, Inoue Hirokuni, did his usual exacting work on our behalf. Mr. Inoue's knowledge and ability to translate older Japanese texts proved invaluable. Further translation help was provided by Quinn Okamoto, Tennessee Katsuta, Alan Clarke, and Ricardo Jose. We are particularly appreciative of Jean-Francois Masson's insights into Japanese naval officers and casualties, developed from his forthcoming translation of the Japanese Naval Officer registers.

Photographs for this volume involved the labors of many individuals, including the indefatigable Mutsuo "Mucho" Uchiyama, Hajime Maejima, Todaka Kazushige (curator of the Kure Maritime Museum), Uchida Katsuhiro, Tohru Kizu, Ono Noriko of KK Bestsellers, and Asano Kiyoshi. In America, Dr. Linton Wells III, Edward Miller, Steve Ewing, Dr. Ellen Schattschneider, Dr. Donald Goldstein, Tom McConnell and his wife Leslie Berger, and Paul Wilderson (formerly of the Naval Institute Press) all provided assistance. Dave Jourdan of Nauticos kindly provided rights to the pictures of *Kaga*'s wreckage. Finally, Charles Haberlein, curator of the photographic section of the U.S. Naval Historical Center in Washington, D.C., provided not only photographs, but also ship plans, insights into ship construction and damage control, and a kindly interest toward our project in general.

I am fortunate to have been capable of producing my own illustrations and maps, but I was very happy to have "outsourced" one piece of artwork—the kanji for the book's section headers—which show the beautiful calligraphy of Yuko Kajiura Smith. Likewise, our good friend Richard Wolff very kindly produced the computer-generated kanji used in the carrier illustrations and in my other artwork concerning the battle.

We are also thankful to the following individuals for their contributions: David Aiken, Allan Alsleben (regarding tail codes and Japanese industrial production figures), Warren Bailey, Jim Broshot, John Bruning Jr. (for providing numerous first-person accounts from Japanese aviators and for being encouraging in general), Chris Carlson, Midway fighter pilot Thomas Cheek, Robert Dulin, Richard Dunn, William Garzke, Chris Hawkinson, 1st Lt. Matthew Jones of the U.S. Army (for his very timely assistance checking our order of battle appendix), Cdr. John Kuehn of the U.S. Navy (for his insights into strategy and modern U.S. carrier doctrine), James Lansdale, Ed Low, Jeff Morris, the entire crew at Nauticos, Allyn Nevitt—a key combinedfleet.com contributor in his own right, who provided important materials regarding destroyer operations, Dennis Norton (for catching a potentially embarassing map typo at the 11th hour), Andrew Obluski (for work on biographies of senior ship's officers), Okazaki Masao, Nathan Okun (the acknowledged expert in all things having to do with external ballistics, armor penetration, and World War II U.S. naval ordnance), William O'Neill (for his help in acquiring sundry source documents, as well as his well-considered insights into the feasibility of Japanese amphibious operations directed at Midway), Jeff Palshook (for his unparalleled knowledge of U.S. submarine operations at Midway), good family friend Marcia Pankake of the University of Minnesota library (who assisted us in acquiring microfilms from various private collections), Dave Pluth (owner of www.j-aircraft.com and breakfast companion of long standing), Clay Ramsey, an Asiatic Fleet enthusiast (for reading chapters and providing key suggestions), Carlos Rivera (for his generosity with Japanese-language sources), Brooks Rowlett, Daniel Rush of the U.S. Navy, William Schleihauf, C. Raymond Smith, H. P. Willmott, and, last but not least, Alan Zimm, for his insights into Japanese logistics and floatplane operations. If I have forgotten anyone, please forgive my unintended oversight. Tony and I, of course, take full responsibility for any omissions or factual errors in this work—they would have been much more numerous but for the good efforts of the people just mentioned.

Quinn Bracken, my longtime accomplice in crime at my Web site on the Imperial Navy, www.combinedfleet.com, deserves credit for keeping the site alive while I was busy writing. And writing. Similar kudos go to Robert Hackett and Sander Kingsepp, who contributed the majority of the site's new content during that time. In addition to Tony's discussion list on combinedfleet.com, the very lively message boards on www.j-aircraft.com have provided Tony and me with a congenial, supportive, and infinitely interested and interesting community surrounding all things having to do with the Imperial Navy. We heartily salute all the "regulars" on these boards, as this book represents a positive example (we hope) of what collaborative research can achieve. By the same token, I am grateful to the members of the Midway Roundtable (www.midway42.org), whose enthusiasm and collective knowledge has been tempered with patience for my somewhat iconoclastic views. Anyone interested in learning more about the battle would do well to consider joining this group.

Don McKeon of Potomac Books was our worthy editor and grappled gamely with a manuscript that was rather longer than originally promised. We are grateful for his forbearance and help. Likewise, we wish to thank our copy editor, Gary Kessler, and John Church, Sam Dorrance, Dana Adams, Katie Freeman, Claire Noble, and the other good people at Potomac Books for their efforts. Finally, our agent, Jim Hornfischer, himself a naval historian of note, was our tireless advocate, helping us navigate the publishing world, and liberally dispensing good advice along the way.

The families and confidants of authors are never unaffected by their undertakings, and in recognition of that we would like to close with some personal acknowledgments of their support.

Tony: A work of this scope does not come into being with just the assistance of those familiar with the subject. It also relies on the encouragement and support of family and cherished friends. To that end I wish to extend profound gratitude to my family—parents Dan and Kay Tully, brother Matt, sister Heather, and their families. They have been able to see this work grow out of an elementary student's freehand drawings of warships into the present work. Special friends and confidants on this journey include James Moore, whose literary roundtable fueled the muse, whose keen suggestions sharpened my thoughts, and whose jesting kept everything in perspective; to Janice Malmgren, whose loving counsel never ceased to inspire; and to Jeff Gilchrist, without whose principles of self-management this work that fulfills a long-held dream might not have found expression. The role they played will always be treasured.

Jon: My parents, Peter and Carol, are to be commended for having supported their son's interests: first dinosaurs, then tanks, then ships—never truly realizing, I suspect, that things might eventually get to their present state of affairs. Even more bravely, my father, a former college English professor, acted as my surrogate target audience for this work and has read the manuscript in its many stages more often than any person besides Tony and me. His constant stream of positive and well-considered suggestions for restructuring and rewording have been of immeasurable value. Finally, of course, I am permanently in debt to my beloved wife, Margaret. Her good-natured jibes and amused eye rolling at her frequently preoccupied spouse have been a much-needed tonic for the preternatural intensity that has consumed me on far too many late evenings (and early mornings) over these past five years. I *promise,* Honey, I'll fix the ceiling in the playroom now. The same goes to my children, Anna and Derek, who have now spent more than half their lives watching their "geek dad" write this thing, and who have wisely adopted their mother's bemused tolerance of his idiosyncrasies. You three make it all worthwhile.

Foreword

In June 1942, Admiral Chester W. Nimitz's United States Pacific Fleet surprised and decisively defeated Admiral Yamamoto Isoroku's Imperial Japanese Combined Fleet during its attempt to capture tiny Midway atoll in the Central Pacific Ocean. Described variously in American histories as a "miracle" and an "incredible victory," the Battle of Midway is considered a paradigm of the spectacular reversal of military fortune by the weaker force. The tale possesses all the elements of a Greek epic poem, or tragedy, if one considers the Japanese viewpoint. In this most extraordinary of naval battles, there were plentiful instances of hubris and courage, complacency and guile, calculation and sacrifice, disaster and enduring success. Fortune's favors flitted from one side to the other as if the fickle gods actually controlled events, until the four aircraft carriers of the Japanese striking force suffered the ultimate penalty. The myths that arose after the battle from both defeated and victor were also exceptionally powerful and have obscured the whole truth for more than sixty years.

The Pacific portion of the Second World War opened on December 7, 1941. Hitherto vastly underestimated by the Western Allies, who were preoccupied with Nazi Germany, the Imperial Japanese Navy crushed the Pacific Fleet's battleships at Pearl Harbor. That staggering blow opened the way for Japan to conquer Southeast Asia and the Philippines. Moreover, the Japanese achieved their signal triumph through a new form of sea power. Yamamoto's unprecedented concentration of naval airpower in the form of the six mighty aircraft carriers of Vice Admiral Nagumo Chūichi's *Kidō Butai* ("Mobile Force") created a task force against which no opponent could stand and survive. In the next five months, Japan triumphed in East Asia. Spearheaded by a few carriers of its own that missed destruction at Pearl Harbor, the Pacific Fleet nevertheless confined its raids to places where it was known the Japanese carriers would not be. By spring 1942, Japan's strategic successes had come so effortlessly that the Imperial Navy was momentarily at a loss over what to do next. Debate raged at the highest level whether to seek the isolation of Australia by seizing several island bases in the South Pacific or to do what Yamamoto desired and finish what was begun at Pearl Harbor. Yamamoto sought to use the assault on Midway to draw the remnants of the Pacific Fleet into decisive battle and destroy them. In the end, the Imperial Navy opted for compromise. A limited move against the periphery of Australia would take place in early May with the seizure of Port Moresby in New Guinea. Then massive offensives against Midway and also the western Aleutians would follow in early June. Thereafter, in triumph, the Combined Fleet would regroup at Truk and that summer complete the isolation of Australia by taking New Caledonia, Fiji, and Samoa. The famous Doolittle raid in April 1942 only hardened Japanese resolve to get the job done and end any threat to the homeland. Assaults against the outer islands of the Hawaiian chain would begin possibly in the fall of 1942. Either the discouraged Americans would submit to a negotiated peace or dash themselves against an impregnable defensive perimeter that barred the way into the western Pacific.

Far from cringing in desperation as the Japanese imagined, the Pacific Fleet grew in confidence and strength in early 1942. Nimitz benefited from the increasing excellence of his radio intelligence, which began forecasting broad Japanese strategic moves with remarkable accuracy. That allowed him to position his forces in threatened areas ahead of time and thus negate the Japanese advantages of interior lines and holding the initiative. In April 1942, Nimitz resolved to meet the Japanese in battle in the South Pacific, where he thought the main thrust would come. In the first wave of the defense, two carriers under Rear Admiral Frank Jack Fletcher checked the Japanese advance in the Coral Sea and saved Port Moresby. Fletcher sank or disabled three carriers for the loss of one of his own. By failing to capture Port Moresby, Japan suffered its first strategic setback of the war. All three carriers sent against Port Moresby had also been earmarked for the Midway offensive. The U.S. carriers had shown up in the Coral Sea earlier than expected and fought well, but Yamamoto did not care, for he believed both U.S. carriers had succumbed there. Nagumo's four remaining carriers were sufficient for victory. The main difficulty at Midway seemed to be to induce the Americans to come out of Hawaii and actually fight.

Even while the Battle of the Coral Sea raged, Nimitz learned of indications the Japanese would soon attack Midway and even possibly Oahu. He redeployed his carriers northward from the distant South Pacific and made ready to defend Midway against strong odds. Nimitz's decision to fight is dramatically portrayed as a desperate gamble where the outnumbered Pacific Fleet could only hope to sink its weight in Japanese ships before going down fighting. Yet, he had strong reasons for optimism at Midway, because the situation certainly warranted taking a "calculated risk." To advance to Midway, Japan must expose its precious carriers to several forms of counterattack strongly abetted by the element of surprise. The U.S. carriers would finally enjoy a "fairly strong" land-based air umbrella to report and engage the enemy, whereas the Japanese carriers lacked similar support. An admiral who wore the dolphin insignia, Nimitz anticipated a stellar performance by his submarines. Moreover, he, unlike the historians, did not realize the full weight of the resources arrayed against him. A persistent Midway myth is that the intelligence picture was so perfect, like reading the actual Japanese operation order, that even the day and time of the initial attack on Midway was known well beforehand. In truth, Nimitz worked only from a broad outline of Japanese intentions and partial order of battle, absolutely invaluable as they were. The odds still favored Japan, but he had devised a careful plan and knew victory would pay enormous dividends. It did, but no one could have ever imagined how that victory would actually be achieved.

The U.S. carrier attacks on the morning of 4 June certainly succeeded beyond reasonable expectation. Three of four of Nagumo's carriers sustained mortal damage before they could respond in kind. Even the trade of the carrier *Yorktown* for the fourth carrier did not affect the outcome of the battle. Midway truly was an "incredible victory," but (with apologies to the late Walter Lord, a fine gentleman as well as a superb scholar) not so much, as commonly thought, in terms of the overall disparity of odds. Instead, "incredible" better described the chances of such a poorly framed U.S. attack succeeding so brilliantly. The U.S. carriers were extremely fortunate to defeat a foe, who with a few telling exceptions handled his aircraft far better than they did. The Achilles' heel of Japan's carrier force was defense, primarily from the lack of radar and adequate shipboard antiaircraft guns. The American nemesis was teamwork above the squadron level. Fletcher and his principal subordinate, Rear Admiral Raymond A. Spruance, had the right to expect, once having maneuvered their task forces within striking range, that the carriers could accomplish their prime mission of delivering an effective attack and afterward retrieve their aircraft. Yet, only Fletcher's flagship, the highly innovative *Yorktown* (best of all the U.S. carriers in 1942), had contrived to get all her strike planes simultaneously to the target. Spruance's main effort, upon which so much depended, proved very nearly a shambles. Most of the *Hornet* planes never even laid eyes on the enemy, and at the outset the *Enterprise* group fragmented into three widely separated elements. Glorious success arose from individual initiative on the part of a few splendid leaders, the heroic sacrifice of the Midway attackers and the carrier torpedo planes and the dazzling skill of some of the dive-bomber pilots.

More books have been written about Midway than any other single naval battle of the Second World War. What is fascinating is that, in the West, the earliest scripted version of Midway came virtually to be set in stone. The near-unanimity of historical interpretation stifled the posing of new questions and reexamination of events from different perspectives. I found this to be true in 1984 when I wrote *The First Team: Pacific Naval Air Combat from Pearl Harbor to Midway,* which challenged certain widely held beliefs about Midway.

The same stubborn orthodoxy of thought prevailed in Western interpretations of the Japanese side of Midway, which largely stemmed from Fuchida Mitsuo and Okumiya Masatake's *Midway: The Battle that Doomed Japan* (1955) and Gordon W. Prange's 1983 *Miracle at Midway.* Thus it was for me a great surprise and pleasure six years ago to make the acquaintance, via the Internet, of Jon Parshall and Anthony Tully, and learn of the revolutionary new ideas they were developing on the Battle of Midway. Moreover, I was delighted to be invited to join in discussions of this newly emerging evidence, and along with other Midway experts such as Mark Horan and James Sawruk, to offer my two cents' worth on a host of amazing new ideas and interpretations. I was truly shocked to learn from Jon and Tony that much of what Fuchida wrote about the Battle of Midway (and some on Pearl Harbor for that matter) has been debunked in Japan, where a whole corpus of historical thought on Midway remained untapped in the West. One of the many achievements in this book is the bridging of these two hitherto isolated historical traditions. *Shattered Sword* is without doubt the most significant and balanced treatment of the Japanese side of the Battle of Midway and is likely to remain so for the foreseeable future.

John B. Lundstrom

Introduction

The Battle of Midway has rightly remained one of the most important and widely studied engagements in naval history. It is, in the eyes of many, the quintessential contest between Japan and America—*the* decisive naval battle in the Pacific war. This is understandable, since Midway contains all the timeless elements that define a classic clash of arms—an apparent mismatch in the strength of the combatants, a seesaw battle with the initiative passing back and forth, acts of tremendous heroism on both sides, and an improbable climax. It is a battle that has rightly captured the imagination of subsequent generations seeking to understand both the engagement itself and its effects on the course of the greater conflict of which it was a part.

By any measure, June 4, 1942, was a watershed date, after which the Pacific war entered an entirely new phase. For the Japanese, Midway abruptly rang down the curtain on a triumphant first six months of war and largely destroyed Japan's ability to initiate major new offensives in the Pacific. The destruction of the Imperial Navy's four finest aircraft carriers—*Akagi, Kaga, Hiryū*, and *Sōryū*—forever ruined the world-class naval aviation force with which it had opened hostilities. While the imperial fleet remained a force to be reckoned with, it never regained the combination of material and qualitative superiority that made it so feared during the initial phase of the conflict.

For the U.S. Navy, the Battle of Midway marked a reprieve; a chance to gather itself and turn to new tasks. If Midway checked the ambitions of Japan and signaled the destruction of its primary means of naval offense, it foretold just the opposite for the Americans. The battle of 4 June meant that the Japanese and U.S. navies would fight on roughly equal terms for the remainder of 1942. American commanders, for the first time since their humiliation at Pearl Harbor, could now legitimately contemplate offensives of their own against the enemy. It is no exaggeration to say that only a victory at Midway could have created the moral and material basis for the crucial American campaign at Guadalcanal. And if Midway itself did not harm Japan's military in absolute terms as much as the following year's worth of warfare in the Solomons would, it clearly opened the gates to this hellish attritional cycle.

For naval historians, particularly those interested in the Pacific war, Midway has lost none of its fascination over the intervening sixty years. Indeed, particularly for the authors, both of whom have been captivated by the Imperial Navy since childhood, this battle encapsulates both the most laudable, as well as the most frustrating aspects of the imperial fleet. It is not a stretch to state that in June 1942 Japan possessed the most powerful navy in the world in many respects. The Navy had opened the war with a stunning attack on Pearl Harbor, followed up two days later by the shocking destruction of the British capital ships *Prince of Wales* and *Repulse,* and then proceeded to systematically crush the Allied flotillas in the Philippines and around Java. Powerful raids against Port Darwin in Australia and then into the Indian Ocean had cemented *Nihon Kaigun*'s fearsome reputation.

Japan's carrier force in particular was truly without peer. At Pearl Harbor it demonstrated a level of sophistication that the U.S. Navy would not be able to replicate for another two years. Whereas the Allies were still using their flight decks singly or in pairs, Japan had used *six* fleet carriers to sweep American airpower aside and smash a major naval base in broad daylight. In terms of their ability to use massed airpower, the Imperial Navy had no rival. Japan's pilots were war hardened, supremely aggressive, and highly skilled. Likewise, Japanese carrier aircraft—epitomized by the marvelous Mitsubishi Zero—were in many cases superior to those used by the U.S. Navy at this stage of the war.

And yet, despite these formidable strengths, at Midway the imperial fleet committed a series of irretrievable strategic and operational mistakes that seem almost inexplicable. In so doing, it doomed its matchless carrier force to premature ruin. Before it even arrived off Midway, the Japanese Navy had frittered away its numerical advantage through a hopelessly misguided battle plan. During the battle itself, the Japanese in many cases performed sloppily, almost haphazardly—a far cry from the elite force that had opened the war. The reasons why this happened are manifold and complex and defy easy explanation.

All great battles develop their own unique mythos. That is to say, they become wrapped in a set of popular beliefs—"the common wisdom"—that interprets the battle and its meanings. In many cases, this mythology centers on a pivotal event— some noteworthy occurrence that captures the imagination, thereby crystallizing what the battle was all about. History is replete with such defining moments—the breaking of the French Imperial Guard at Waterloo, Pickett's Charge at Gettysburg, the siege of Bastogne during the Battle of the Bulge. They are timeless events, and not to be reinterpreted lightly. Yet, it is imperative that such momentous happenings be understood properly, for if these are the lenses through which we perceive great battles, then it stands to reason that any flaws in these crystals must necessarily distort our perception of the battle as a whole.

This has certainly been true of Midway, whose defining moment will always be the devastating and seemingly last-minute attack of American dive-bombers against the Japanese carrier task force at 1020 on the morning of 4 June. The image of American Dauntlesses hurtling down from the heavens to drop their bombs on helpless Japanese carriers, their decks packed with aircraft just moments away from taking off, has been emblazoned on the American consciousness since the day the battle was fought. Yet, this precise version of the events surrounding the decisive attack—a rendition that would be accepted in any contemporary history book—is but one, and perhaps not the greatest, of the misconceptions surrounding Midway. In fact, the 1020 attack did not happen in this way, in that it did not catch the Japanese in any way ready to launch their own attack. Others myths of the battle include:

- The Americans triumphed against overwhelming odds at the Battle of Midway.

- The Aleutians Operation was conceived by Admiral Yamamoto, the commander in chief of Combined Fleet, as a diversion designed to lure the American fleet out of Pearl Harbor.

- During the transit to Midway, Admiral Yamamoto withheld important intelligence information from Admiral Nagumo, the operational commander of the carrier striking force. As a result, Nagumo was in the dark concerning the nature of the threat facing him.

- Had the Japanese implemented a two-phase reconnaissance search on the morning of 4 June, they would have succeeded in locating the American fleet in time to win the battle.

- The late launch of cruiser *Tone*'s No. 4 scout plane doomed Admiral Nagumo to defeat in the battle.

- Had Admiral Nagumo not decided to rearm his aircraft with land-attack weapons, he would have been in a position to attack the Americans as soon as they were discovered.

- The sacrifice of USS *Hornet*'s Torpedo Squadron Eight was not in vain, since it pulled the Japanese combat air patrol fighters down to sea level, thereby allowing the American dive-bombers to attack at 1020.

- Japan's elite carrier aviators were all but wiped out during the battle.

All of these are fallacious. All are either untrue, or at least require careful clarification. Some of these ideas have been implanted in the Western accounts as a result of misunderstandings of the records of the battle. Some have resulted from a faulty understanding of the basic mechanics of how the battle was fought. Some are misrepresentations of the truth that were deliberately introduced by participants in the battle. And each has caused lasting distortions in Western perceptions of the reasons for victory and defeat. Correcting these distortions is the overriding goal of this book.

How could such misconceptions creep into the historical record? It is fundamentally because the study of Midway in the West has been conducted primarily on American terms, from American perspectives, and using essentially American sources. "Winners write the history books" is certainly true in this case. The fact that the winners of Midway by and large also had no ability to read the loser's history books certainly didn't help matters. As a result, the majority of the English-language accounts written about this pivotal battle have been built around a trio of translated Japanese sources. These are the after-action log of Admiral Nagumo ("The Nagumo Report"), which was captured on Saipan in 1944 and later translated; the interviews with Japanese naval officers conducted immediately after the war by the United States Strategic Bombing Survey ("USSBS"); and Fuchida Mitsuo's book, *Midway: The Battle that Doomed Japan,* which was originally published in Japan in 1951 and then translated and republished in the United States in 1955. These three sources, augmented by survivor accounts and other fragmentary records, have formed the backbone of the Japanese account for fifty years.

Unfortunately, one of these sources—Fuchida's *Midway*—is irretrievably flawed. The effects of Fuchida's misstatements, which have lain undetected until recently, are manifold. In essence, every single Western history of the battle has passed along Fuchida's untruths to at least some extent, because his errors pertain to very important facets of the engagement: Nagumo's intelligence estimates, his search plan, Japanese flight deck operations, and the nature of the decisive American dive-bomber attack. Fuchida's are not minor errors of omission—they are fundamental and willful distortions of the truth that *must* be corrected. Intriguingly, Fuchida's account has been overturned in Japan for more than twenty years. Yet, in the West, he has remained as authoritative as on the day his book was first published.

This book builds a new account that not only corrects these errors, but also broadens our understanding of the Japanese side of the battle. In this, we employ three new approaches that have yet to be used extensively in any prior study of Midway. The first is a detailed understanding of how Japanese aircraft carriers operated. Carriers, of course, formed the very heart of the battle. And in this context, seemingly trivial technical details—the configuration of the ship's command spaces and flag accommodations, the arrangement of the hangar decks, the relative speed of a ship's elevator cycles—could have important implications for how a carrier performed its mission. These details are anything but dry—taken together, they help bring the tangible personalities of these warships more clearly into focus.

In addition to the details surrounding the carriers, we also draw heavily on the Japanese operational records of the battle. While it is true that the logs of the individual Japanese vessels at Midway were destroyed after the war, the air group records of the carriers survived. The tabular data contained in these reports (known as *kōdōchōsho*s) has been used in some newer works to supply such details as the names of individual Japanese pilots. Yet, these records have never been used in a systematic way to understand what the carriers themselves were actually doing at any given time. For instance, knowing when a carrier was launching or recovering aircraft can also be used to derive a sense for the direction the ship was heading (into the wind), and what was occurring on the flight decks and in the hangars. Thus, we use the *kōdōchōsho*s as tools to understand the carrier operations of 4 June in more detail than has been attempted previously.

Third, we apply an understanding of Japanese naval doctrine—in particular their carrier doctrine—to analyze how and why the Japanese operated as they did. Heretofore, American authors trying to put themselves in Nagumo's shoes had to make the assumption that Japanese carriers and air groups functioned pretty much as did their American counterparts. In fact, though, because of differences in both ship design and doctrine, the Japanese operated very differently from the U.S. Navy. Worse yet, many earlier authors didn't really have a grasp of how *American* carriers operated, either. The result has been that many of the criticisms of Admiral Nagumo's actions during the battle have proceeded from a flawed basis, leading to equally flawed conclusions.

It is only recently that information on Japanese doctrine has begun to be employed in the study of the Pacific war. Works like John Lundstrom's *First Team* series contained the first solid information on Japanese air group operations and doctrine. These were augmented in 1997 by the publication of David Evans and Mark Peattie's landmark study *Kaigun: Strategy, Tactics and Technology in the Imperial Japanese Navy,* and Peattie's subsequent *Sunburst: The Rise of Japanese Naval Aviation.* The latter, in particular, supplied sufficient information on Japanese carrier operations to form the basis for this book.

We expand on these earlier works by drawing on additional Japanese sources particular to the battle. The core of these is the official Japanese war history series— the various volumes of the *Boeicho Boeikenshujo Senshibu* (often referred to as "BKS," or *Senshi Sōsho*). Compiled by the War History Section of the Japanese Defense Agency, these studies are highly regarded for their comprehensive treatment of individual campaigns, as well as their general lack of bias. The Midway volume, *Midowei Kaisen* (Battle of Midway), was published in 1971 and remains the authoritative Japanese work on the topic. Beyond *Senshi Sōsho,* we also have used never-before-translated Japanese primary and secondary sources, including monographs on Japanese carrier and air operations, as well as accounts of various Japanese survivors.

Taken together, any reader of this book will emerge with a fuller understanding of how and why the Japanese Navy, and its carriers in particular, operated as it did. In the process, we hope to give our readers a better flavor of what it was like to be a sailor serving aboard an imperial warship. And while this is neither a technical design study nor a treatise on Japanese carrier doctrine, we also necessarily seek to relate (with the least pain possible to the reader) the critical points regarding Japanese weaponry, doctrine, and carrier operations that shaped the outcome at Midway.

While our work is intended as a new, comprehensive, and clarified history of the Japanese Navy at Midway, it is also a very tightly scoped work. For instance, although we are keenly interested in the carrier operations and command decisions of the Americans during the battle, we do not seek to address comprehensively all aspects of the American account. Much of this has already been covered by such works as Walter Lord's *Incredible Victory,* Gordon Prange's *Miracle at Midway,* and two other fine, but underappreciated volumes—H. P. Willmott's *The Barrier and the Javelin,* and Robert Cressman et al.'s *A Glorious Page in Our History.* Likewise, we do not deal exhaustively with such topics as American cryptography—we have nothing to add in these matters that hasn't been previously covered by works such as the late Admiral Edwin Layton's *And I Was There.* Nor do we seek to be the final word on the air combat of the battle—John Lundstrom's account holds that honor for the foreseeable future. This is not to say that nothing new remains to be done on the American side of the battle. However, we choose to focus primarily on the Japanese history, since there are clearly important new aspects of the tale that need to be clarified here.

The work is divided into three main sections. The first—Preliminaries (*Joshō*)—is an examination of the strategic context of the engagement, including its origins, and the political machinations that led to the creation of the disastrous Japanese plan of battle. The second section—Battle Diary (*Sentō Nikki*)—is a detailed narrative of the battle itself, from the morning of 4 June until the final return of the Japanese fleet to home waters on 14 June. The third section—Reckonings (*Kessan*)—analyzes why the Japanese lost at Midway, as well as what it meant to lose this particular battle within the larger context of the Pacific war. The book closes with a reexamination and clarification of some of the myths of Midway mentioned previously.

Throughout the book, our narrative perspective is almost wholly that of the Japanese. Furthermore, during the description of the actual battle of 4 June, the book is almost exclusively carrier centric in its viewpoint. Except in those cases where crucial context is required to understand the events at hand, we deliberately relate the battle's narrative in terms of what would have been either directly visible or otherwise known from the bridges of the Japanese carriers themselves.

Some might question the validity of adopting a "carrier-centric" narrative viewpoint for a battle as large as Midway. Yet, this approach lends itself well to re-creating the "fog of war," which is crucial to understanding the handicaps under which Admiral Nagumo had to labor in making his command decisions. It was on board the Japanese aircraft carriers that most of the crucial decisions of the day were made. It was the destruction of the Japanese carriers that brought the battle to an effective close, even though the bulk of the imperial fleet involved in the overall operation remained unengaged. And it was on board the carriers that the vast majority of Japanese casualties were suffered. Thus, the story of *Akagi, Kaga, Hiryū,* and *Sōryū,* in many ways, *is* the Japanese story at Midway.

This method also has merits from a strategic perspective, because it was around the operational realities of the carrier weapon system that strategy necessarily had to be crafted. Understanding the strengths and limitations of their own carrier force in early 1942 should have had a dramatic impact on the Japanese operations that unfolded during that time frame. Not only that, but as we will show, the number and strength of the carrier force in itself should have imposed a logic on Japan's strategic calculus in terms of target selection and operational timetables. Contrary to outside appearances, the truth was that, after six months of war, Japan's naval aviation arm was already balanced on a knife's edge in terms of its men and matériel. The carriers and crews were tired and badly in need of refit and repair. In the same vein, Japan's naval air groups, though still highly proficient, needed to be replenished with new aircraft and pilots.

Yet, we argue that these realities were not understood by the men vying over the right to decide Japanese naval strategy. These were Admiral Yamamoto Isoroku, commander in chief of the Imperial Navy's Combined Fleet, and his various foes in Naval General Headquarters. Their political wrangling, complicated still further by the baleful influence of interservice rivalries with the Imperial Army, badly warped the process of strategy formulation. Likewise, the morally dishonest methods Yamamoto employed to ensure his victory in this process, and employed again during the operational planning phase, ensured that the Midway battle plan was flawed from the outset. Worse yet, during this same period, and despite the fact that any rational analysis should have shown that *all* of Japan's fleet carriers would be needed at Midway, Naval GHQ continued to insist that these irreplaceable combat assets be doled out to subsidiary operations in penny packets, thereby exposing them to unacceptable dangers.

These mistakes belie an unpleasant truth, that despite the Imperial Navy having opened the Pacific war with one of the most daring military feats of all time—the massed carrier attack on Pearl Harbor—neither Yamamoto nor Naval GHQ truly comprehended the strengths and weaknesses of the world-class weapons system they possessed. As a result, they unwittingly consigned Japan's finest fleet—the product of untold years of industrial and organizational toil—to its premature doom off Midway. To have lost this magnificent force in such a miserable—and wholly preventable—fashion, was one of the greatest of Japan's failings as a modern nation. For Yamamoto personally, the defeat at Midway utterly eclipsed his very real achievements in the first six months of World War II.

At a deeper level, though, it is important to clarify that the defeat at Midway was not just the product of flawed decisions by a handful of men at the top. Likewise, Admiral Nagumo's command decisions on the day of the battle, which have widely been held up as having been the reason for Japan's defeat, were not solely to blame, either. Instead, we will show that Yamamoto, Nagumo, and indeed all the Japanese forces involved, suffered from deep-seated flaws that were a product of the Imperial Navy's strategic outlooks, doctrinal tenets, and institutional cultures. This is not to say that individual mistakes were not made, but these mistakes must be understood within the proper context. In fact, contrary to the prevailing wisdom, the seeds of Japan's defeat at Midway were not planted in the six months of easy Japanese victories that led up to the battle, but had instead been sown in the very earliest days of the Imperial Navy's development.

The Battle of Midway loses none of its grandeur when retold from a different perspective. Instead, the fundamentals of the battle's greatness remain the same. Midway is, and always will be, a tale of confusion and difficult decisions, of tremendous bravery, and of furious combat to the death. Yet, inevitably the Japanese story is also that of a mighty force brought low and contains all the grief and human suffering that characterize the losing side of any great conflict. These aspects bear retelling. Indeed, they warrant amplification from new sources. An accurate account of the Japanese travails of June 4, 1942—of what it meant to be trapped on board a burning vessel for hours on end, of the horrendous conditions encountered by the men of the Imperial Navy as they fought their own personal battles aboard their doomed warships, and of how the survivors ultimately managed to come through their ordeal—deserves to be related, for it is a tale that transcends nationality. It reminds us that all warfare, in the final analysis, boils down to a lowest common human denominator. All parties to a great battle—winner and loser—can benefit from greater knowledge of the other's story in this respect. Particularly in an age where aerial warfare is often strangely antiseptic, and where violence is inflicted from great distances and seemingly omnipotent heights, we would do well to remember what the ultimate, intimate results of such activities are.

PART I
Preliminaries

1

Departure

The Inland Sea of Japan was still veiled in darkness when the anchorage at Hashirajima began to awaken. On board the aircraft carrier *Akagi,* white-clad crewmen, ghostly in the deep twilight on the forecastle, began raising the ship's anchors. The clatter of the capstan was overlain with the bright sound of spraying water as the foredeck gang played hoses along the dripping anchor chains, washing them clean of the harbor's black mud. All around *Akagi,* just barely discernable in the gloom, lay dozens of great gray warships, many of them weighing anchor as well. Nautical twilight was at 0437. But the dark waters of the bay, sheltered by the mountainous islands, would remain shrouded in gray until well after sunlight dappled the hilltops. *Akagi* would sortie around dawn. The date was 27 May 1942.

Those in the deck gang chatted in tight little knots as they worked. The topics of conversation were the age-old harps of all sailors—wives and girlfriends, home, and what was likely to be on today's menu. Hopefully, this morning's fare would be something soothing to the stomach, as many of the men were rather hung over. The drinking on board *Akagi* the previous night had started early and ended late. The crew on the foredeck knew this much—as tedious as raising anchor could be, duty on the foredeck was still vastly to be preferred to the job of cleaning out the lavatories this morning. Only the bravest (or most coerced) of men would venture into those spaces after the excesses of the night before.

By far the prevalent topic of conversation, though, concerned the operation ahead. Something was up; the activity in Hashirajima this morning made that much clear. It was known that a large banquet had been held on board Combined Fleet's flagship two nights previously for the fleet's commanders. The top brass didn't throw parties just for laughs. *Akagi* was headed somewhere important. Where to was anybody's guess, though. Many of the men still sported suntans from their recent operations in the South Pacific, and it was possible they might be headed there again, either to Truk, Japan's great sanctuary in the Carolines, or perhaps Singapore. They might even be returning to Staring Bay in the Celebes, which had been their base of operations for much of March. Others didn't think so. The scuttlebutt around the fleet was that some of the ships provisioning at Kure lately had been fitted for cold-weather duty. That meant *Akagi* could be headed north. Having attacked Pearl Harbor in December, the crewmen knew that the North Pacific was no joke—the weather

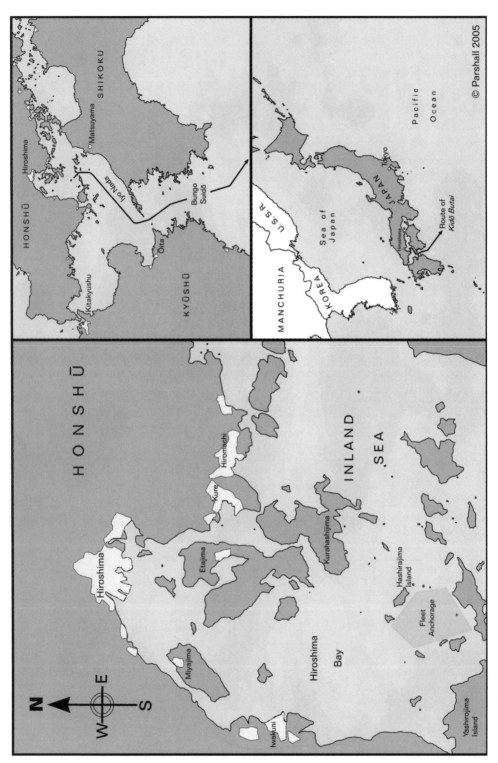

1-1: Hashirajima Bay, situated near Hiroshima and Kure, was Japan's most important naval anchorage. The route of *Kidō Butai*'s exit from the Inland Sea is shown.

© Parshall 2005

had been atrocious, and high seas had washed several men overboard. Hopefully, though, the weather in June would be a little more forgiving.

Located in the seclusion of Hiroshima Bay, the fastness of Hashirajima was perfectly situated to give access to the open ocean within a few hours' steaming. It was Japan's equivalent of Britain's Scapa Flow or America's Hampton Roads—a vast anchorage, where the entire fleet could be safely sheltered close to its logistical centers and the sea, and yet protected from snooping enemies. It was ringed with antiaircraft weapons, interdicted by antitorpedo netting, and ceaselessly patrolled by smaller warships. Phone lines laid to the main mooring buoys meant that the fleet's flagships enjoyed secure communication back to Naval General Headquarters in Tokyo.

Hashirajima lay just twenty-two nautical miles from the lively port city of Hiroshima. Closer yet, sixteen miles to the northeast, lay the great naval arsenal and shipyard of Kure. Kure had built an appreciable portion of the Japanese Navy. It was also close to the Naval Academy, which was located just west of the yard on the island of Etajima. It was here, in the red-brick buildings built in deliberate imitation of the British Royal Navy, that the emperor's naval officers were trained. The combination of Kure's yards, Etajima's academy, and Hashirajima's anchorage made this area of the Inland Sea the very cradle of the Japanese Navy.

From where she lay, *Akagi*'s crewmen could see the battleship anchorage near Hashirajima island. There lay the seven great dreadnoughts of First Fleet, the symbols for the last twenty-five years of Japan's undeniable status as a major navy. At their head was the largest battleship ever built, the 69,000-ton *Yamato*, which had become operational just two days earlier. Flagship of Combined Fleet and home to its commander, Admiral Yamamoto Isoroku, her bulk overshadowed every other warship in the bay.[1] For many officers in the Navy, her enormous guns still represented the apotheosis of naval power. Bristling with weapons, her girth made her appear almost like a mountain rising out of the still waters. Yet her swept-back stack, undulating deck, and streamlined superstructure lent her a grace that seemed curiously out of place on such a behemoth.

The battleships wouldn't be sailing this morning. No surprise there, joked *Akagi*'s crewmen—they hadn't done anything during the entire war. For them the battleships were irrelevant, nothing more than a symbol of a bygone era. Worse yet, in the workaholic culture of the Imperial Navy, which, popular lore had it, operated eight days a week, the battleships were seen as slackers. While *Akagi* and her companions had been winning unprecedented victories, the battleships had largely lain at anchor, leaving only to conduct gunnery practice in the nearby Iyo Nada waterway, and earning in the process the unwanted sobriquet of the "Hashirajima Fleet." Only the four fast battleships of Battle Division 3 (hereafter rendered as BatDiv 3), which had been stalwart companions of *Akagi*'s for the last six months, were excluded from the scorn heaped on the slower battlewagons. *Yamato* might be pretty to look at, but *Akagi*'s men knew, and everyone else in the anchorage knew, that the carriers, in particular *these four carriers*, were the Imperial Navy's superstars. They were the Navy's samurai sword, the gleaming blade that had humbled Japan's enemies at Pearl Harbor and across the breadth of the Pacific; the finest naval aviation force in the world.

1-2: Aircraft carrier *Akagi* in Sukumo Bay, April 1939. (Naval Historical Center)

Akagi was flagship of Carrier Division 1 (*Dai-ichi Kōkū Sentai,* referred to hereafter as CarDiv 1).[2] She flew the flag of Vice Admiral Nagumo Chūichi, commander of First Air Fleet and its tactical incarnation, the First Mobile Striking Force (*Dai-ichi Kidō Butai*).[3] *Akagi* was enormous, at 855 feet the longest carrier in the Imperial Navy, displacing more than 41,000 tons. Her architecture immediately betrayed her as a hybrid—a carrier constructed on top of what had originally been intended as a capital ship. Her lower hull was all sleek battle cruiser, its most prominent feature being her massive, rakish bow. It was a bow built for speed, not seakeeping—a huge meat cleaver of a prow. Near the stern lingered another vestige of her original design; six casemated eight-inch guns, set three to a side down near the waterline. Constructed at a time when no one was sure how carriers would operate with the battlefleet, these weapons had been intended to help *Akagi* fend off enemy cruisers. Now, they were simply wasted displacement.

Above the main deck, her clean lines quickly gave way to a crazy quilt of upper works enclosing her hangars. Her clifflike sides sported a maze of catwalks, huge grills covering engine ventilator intakes, and a forest of slanting supports for her walkways, gun galleries, and fire-control equipment. A gargantuan downswept funnel sprouted from the ship's starboard side. Her improbably high flight deck towered six stories above the ocean's surface. Yet, despite the mishmash appearance, she had a curious balance and power in her lines. She wasn't a pretty ship, but she wasn't to be trifled with, either.

It was *Akagi*'s thirty-one-knot speed that had first recommended her to the Japanese as a carrier. When the Washington Naval Treaty of 1922 was signed, *Akagi* was still on the building ways. Instead of being scrapped, she and her sister, *Amagi,* had been slated for conversion to carriers in much the same fashion that the Americans had converted battle cruisers *Lexington* and *Saratoga.* Both navies had tentatively decided—through the operations of their respective carrier prototypes,

Hōshō and *Langley*—that they needed larger carriers than they currently had, with bigger flight decks and a healthy margin of speed. Battle cruisers, with their size and swiftness, were perfect for the job.

As a result, work on *Akagi* had been stopped long enough to redraw her plans. What emerged was almost bizarre—a design with three flight decks forward to allow simultaneous takeoffs of multiple types of aircraft, supported by three separate aircraft hangars. Her conversion also proved enormously expensive—at ¥53,000,000 ($36.45 million), she was by far the most costly warship the Imperial Navy had ever built.[4] Not only that, but within eight years of her commissioning, it had been decided that her original triple flight deck configuration was unusable, owing to the ever-increasing weight (and hence takeoff room required) of modern carrier aircraft. She reentered the yards in 1935 for another expensive refit.

She emerged in 1938 with a full-length flight deck and an island on her port side. *Akagi* and *Hiryū* were the only carriers in the world whose islands were located to port. This unorthodox configuration had come about as the result of design studies in the mid-1930s that had suggested that turbulence over the flight deck aft (which affected aircraft during landing) could be reduced by moving the island away from the ship's exhaust gases. In the event, the port-side arrangement actually made things somewhat worse, but there was no helping that now.

This was not to say that *Akagi* hadn't been useful during her first eight years—far from it. It was on board her and *Kaga* that Japanese naval aviation had largely been created. Japanese carrier doctrine had been predicated on *Akagi*'s capabilities; she was the first Japanese vessel that possessed the size, speed, and aircraft-handling facilities to justify being called a true carrier. Even now, as the oldest of the four carriers in harbor,[5] she was arguably still the most useful—fast enough to keep up with almost any battle force, yet larger and better protected than her smaller compatriots in Carrier Division 2 (hereafter CarDiv 2). Only the spanking new *Shōkaku* and *Zuikaku* clearly eclipsed her.

As it happened, *Akagi* would be sailing under a new skipper for this operation. The tall and angular Captain Hasegawa Kiichi, veteran of the Pearl Harbor attack, had been relieved by Captain Aoki Taijirō, fifty-two. Aoki was a spare, compact man who sported a trim little mustache. Most recently he had been the commander of a floatplane training squadron—not exactly a glamorous assignment—although he had commanded the seaplane carrier *Mizuho* previously. This was his first combat posting, making him the only carrier commander in *Kidō Butai* with no battle experience.

However *Akagi*'s crew was well stocked with experienced officers. Undoubtedly the most important of these as far as the flight operations was concerned was her air officer (*hikōchō*), Commander Masuda Shōgo. The *hikōchō* was in charge of orchestrating both the flight deck and the hangar decks. He also directed the ship's combat air patrol aircraft when they were aloft. It was his job to ensure that the ship was capable of carrying out the captain's orders—to arm, launch, and recover aircraft when required. Masuda, the father of four daughters, was not a flamboyant individual, but he was highly capable, having been with the ship since the beginning of the war.

Akagi's sistership, *Amagi,* had never joined the fleet. She was wrecked on the ways during the Great Kanto Earthquake of 1923. Lacking any further battle cruiser hulls,

1-3: Aircraft carrier *Kaga*, post-reconstruction. (Photo courtesy Michael Wenger)

the Navy had selected a battleship hull scheduled to be scrapped under the Washington Naval Treaty. *Kaga* was thus saved from the scrapyard and towed instead to Yokosuka to be completed as a carrier. The same lengthy building time (and astronomical cost) as *Akagi* had preceded her commissioning in March 1928.

Kaga, too, had initially been designed with triple flight decks, but she lacked *Akagi*'s speed—her twenty-five knots was barely sufficient to hold station with her faster division mate. By 1934 it was clear that she was the least serviceable of the pair, and she went into the yards for a refit. In the process, Yokosuka's yard workers ripped the guts out of her propulsion plant and completely re-engined her. She emerged in 1935 with better hangar facilities but still far from speedy, although new engines and a slight lengthening of her hull had raised its speed another three knots. Her flight deck, though, was generously sized, towering above the water much like *Akagi,* and making for a wide, dry platform for takeoffs and landings. All in all, *Kaga* had an appealing, homey dumpiness about her. She was, by all accounts, a happy ship to serve on board.

Kaga's commander, Captain Okada Jisaku, was forty-eight years old, the same age as the skippers of both *Sōryū* and *Hiryū*. A severe, comely man, he had been associated with aviation for much of his career. Starting as a squadron commander, he later rose to command seaplane carrier *Notoro* and later the light carrier *Ryūjō*. Following a posting as a commander in the Navy Technical Department (*kansei honbu*), he came on board *Kaga* in September 1941.

Okada had just inherited a new *hikōchō,* Commander Amagai Takahisa, who had been carrier *Hiryū*'s *hikōchō* since the outbreak of hostilities. Amagai was apparently something of a bumpkin. One fighter pilot who knew him described him as both artless and rather sloppy in appearance.[6] For all that, though, his simplicity of character made him approachable, and he was always happy to talk with anyone and everyone.

Further off, but still easily visible from the flight decks *Kaga* and *Akagi,* were the two ships of CarDiv 2—*Hiryū* and *Sōryū*. Whereas the ships of CarDiv 1 were both

1-4: Aircraft carrier *Sōryū* at Kure, 29 December 1937. This shot, not published before in the West, offers a fine study of *Sōryū*'s port side on her commissioning date. Note the sailor engaged in maintenance work hanging silhouetted under her flight deck forward, near one of the flight deck supports on the ship's bow. (Photo courtesy KK Bestsellers)

notable for their size, CarDiv 2 was characterized by speed. *Sōryū,* the elder of the pair (having joined the fleet in 1937), was the progenitor of Japan's standard fleet carrier design. Built around a cruiser-style hull and power plant, which generated a prodigious 152,000 shaft horsepower, she was capable of cranking out thirty-five knots. She was the fastest aircraft carrier in the world when she was launched. In fact, she could outrun *Kaga* at only 40 percent power.[7]

Unlike CarDiv 1's ships, *Sōryū* had been designed from the keel up as a carrier. Her hangar decks, instead of simply being plopped down on top of an existing hull like *Akagi*'s and *Kaga*'s, had been smoothly faired into the structure of the hull itself, making her profile lower, her lines cleaner, and her flight deck unfortunately wetter. *Sōryū* seemed almost out of place next to the hulking members of CarDiv 1—she was small, lean, almost elegant. However, her diminutive size and delicate features betrayed her weaknesses—light construction, and a near-total lack of armor. Thus far, though, her defensive characteristics had never been tested.

Sōryū was commanded by Captain Yanagimoto Ryūsaku. Yanagimoto was an intensely handsome man, possessing high cheekbones, a delicate mouth, and wide-set, intelligent eyes. His credentials were equally impressive, having previously served as a naval attaché, a Naval War College instructor, and as head of the intelligence section of the Naval General Staff. His reputation in the fleet was that of both a gentleman and a warrior. He was revered for his self-confidence, fairness, and courteous manners to both peers and underlings alike—no small feat in a navy ruled by iron discipline. He and his *hikōchō,* Commander Kusumoto Ikuto, had been with *Sōryū* since before Pearl Harbor, making them unquestionably the most experienced air operations duo in the fleet.

Sōryū's compatriot, *Hiryū,* was really only a stepsister. Entering service in 1939, she shared much of *Sōryū*'s general layout, but with some notable differences. Her hull was a bit wider, and her island was located to port like *Akagi*'s. Her bow had been plated up an extra deck, flattening her sheer forward. As a result, she had boxier, more

1-5: Captain Yanagimoto Ryūsaku, the highly popular commander of carrier *Sōryū*. (Photo courtesy Michael Wenger)

severe lines than *Sōryū,* although she shared her sister's speed. *Hiryū* was currently the flagship of the fiery Rear Admiral Yamaguchi Tamon, commander of CarDiv 2. Until a month earlier, he had flown his flag in *Sōryū,* but in early May Yamaguchi had decided to avail himself of *Hiryū*'s more commodious command spaces. Her bridge was the largest and most modern of the four carriers, and therefore more convenient for housing the admiral's staff.

Hiryū was commanded by Captain Kaku Tomeo. Kaku, like *Kaga*'s Captain Okada, was an early proponent of airpower. As early as 1927, he had been participating in the development of the Navy's air doctrine, first as a student at the Naval War College, and later as an air group commander and ship's captain. Kaku had the distinction of being the only aviator among the four carrier commanders in *Kidō Butai.* He was an intimidating figure; a burly man whose mouth fell naturally into a ferocious scowl. Kaku's new *hikōchō* was Commander Kawaguchi Susumu, a former fighter pilot.

In addition to *Akagi, Kaga, Sōryū,* and *Hiryū,* two other carriers ought to have been sortieing this morning as well—the brand new *Shōkaku* and *Zuikaku* of Carrier Division Five (hereafter CarDiv 5). CarDiv 5 was an integral part of *Kidō Butai,* having been incorporated into Nagumo's battle force upon *Zuikaku*'s commissioning in September 1941. Though they were inexperienced vessels, their large size and excellent aircraft-handling facilities had made them indispensable for December's Pearl Harbor operation.[8] Under the command of Rear Admiral Hara Chūichi, they had operated with *Kidō Butai* continuously since then. However, in mid-April, CarDiv 5 had been detached to support the Japanese landings against Port Moresby in New Guinea, slated for early May. There, on 7–8 May in the Coral Sea north of Australia, they had been put through the wringer. An American carrier force had appeared unexpectedly, and in the ensuing battle, the two yearlings had suffered heavily. *Shōkaku* had sustained three bomb hits, knocking her out of the battle. *Zuikaku* had escaped physical damage, but her air group had been shredded. Both carriers were now at Kure. *Shōkaku* had made port on 17 May, having run a gauntlet of American submarines (and very nearly capsizing in the process as a result of the rough treatment on her damaged bow). *Zuikaku* had docked four days later. *Shōkaku* would ultimately spend the latter half of June in dry dock. *Zuikaku* was nominally operational, but her air group was not and would not be fully reconstituted for months. Thus, both carriers were out of the picture for the current operation.

1-6: Aircraft carrier *Hiryū,* 5 July 1939. This photo, not seen widely in the West, shows *Hiryū* on the date of her commissioning. Note the large retractable crane raised on her flight deck aft—a feature not often seen in photos of these vessels. (Photo courtesy KK Bestsellers)

If the rank and file on board *Kidō Butai* were worried about this diminution of their strength, they weren't showing it. Why should they? Nagumo's remaining carriers were an elite formation with or without CarDiv 5. *Kidō Butai* had ranged across the Pacific Ocean during the first six months of the war, wreaking havoc, running up a nearly unbroken string of victories, and humiliating Allied naval forces. During *Kidō Butai*'s opening assault on Pearl Harbor, they had sunk or disabled the better part of the U.S. Pacific Fleet's battleship force and crushed U.S. airpower on Hawaii. Shortly afterward, *Sōryū* and *Hiryū* had provided air cover for the second invasion of Wake Island.[9] Following this, *Kidō Butai* refitted briefly in Japan before moving into southern waters to cover operations in Malaya and the Indies. On 19 February 1942, as part of the opening moves against Java, the Striking Force had launched a major raid against the northern Australian harbor of Port Darwin, causing heavy damage and effectively shutting down the port.

In early April 1942, *Kidō Butai* (composed of *Akagi, Sōryū, Hiryū, Shōkaku,* and *Zuikaku*)[10] raided the Indian Ocean. The Japanese carriers launched attacks against the British bases of Colombo and Trincomalee on Ceylon. Colombo was hit on the morning of 5 April, causing heavy damage to its port facilities. More important, in the afternoon the Japanese located the heavy cruisers *Dorsetshire* and *Cornwall* fleeing the scene of the action southward. The Japanese quickly dispatched these vessels with a devastating dive-bomber attack. Nagumo's force had retired briefly to the east, returning on 9 April to attack Trincomalee. In the process, they caught the carrier *Hermes* and a destroyer and dispatched them in similar fashion before retiring. These raids exposed the enormous gap between Japanese and British naval aviation. For the first time in centuries, the Royal Navy was impotent in the face of a foe that had clearly moved ahead of British practice in a crucial area of naval combat.[11]

1-7: Captain Kaku Tomeo, *Hiryu*'s skipper. (Photo courtesy Michael Wenger)

Kidō Butai then returned to Japan for much-needed rest and refitting. Nagumo's ships had been in near-constant operations for four and a half months and had traversed nearly a third of the globe. Though aircraft losses had been relatively light by the standards of a global conflict, they had still been a serious drain. New replacements needed to be integrated into the air formations and trained. Similarly, the carriers needed dry-dock time and maintenance. However, if the crews were looking forward to a leisurely period of R&R in the delightful city of Hiroshima, they were gravely disappointed. Returning to Hashirajima on 22 April, the carriers had immediately been plunged into frantic preparations for the next sortie. Each ship had been taken in for a quick refit, and then began reprovisioning. There had been precious little time for the men to enjoy liberty, though the ferry ride was short, and Hiroshima well liked for its May flower festival, not to mention its tasty food and pretty girls. Now, a scant month after returning, they were getting ready to leave again. The Navy's work was never done, the men joked.

At 0600, *Akagi* raised her ensign and signaled—"Commence sortie as scheduled." One by one, *Kidō Butai* fell into line and began parading through the anchorage. Light cruiser *Nagara* headed the column, leading her destroyer squadron. Cruiser Division 8's (hereafter CruDiv 8) flagship, *Tone*, followed, with sister ship, *Chikuma*, next, followed by battleships *Haruna* and *Kirishima*. At the end of the proud line came *Akagi, Kaga, Hiryū,* and *Sōryū.*

Coincidentally, 27 May was also Navy Day, the anniversary of Admiral Tōgō Heihachirō's spectacular victory over the Russians in 1905—a good omen for victory if ever there was one. Across Japan, the morning dailies were already trumpeting the accomplishments of the Imperial Navy. The English edition of the *Japan Times and Advertiser* proclaimed that "this year, Navy Day is not a day of mere remembrance, not a mere reminder; it is a day of fulfillment. The Japanese Navy has not only duplicated the exploits of 37 years ago, it has repeated it [*sic*] time and again and in an unbelievably greater scale. Navy Day this year is the climax for which all Navy Days of past years have been in preparation." The article concluded that "Japan stands today as the premier naval power of the world. It may well presage the rise of Japan in the future history of the world to a position comparable to that which Britain has occupied in the past."[12] It was a heady vision. Indeed, no newspaper reporter who might have had the privilege of witnessing this morning's sortie would have faulted the splendor of the spectacle spread before him. On the decks of every ship in the bay, white-clad crewmen packed the railings. The men on board the warships still at anchor cheered lustily as Nagumo's force promenaded in slow splendor. *Kidō Butai* cheered them back. Though most of them had no idea of the particulars of what was afoot, Operation MI, the assault on the island of Midway, was now under way.

On *Akagi*'s bridge stood the man on whom the weight of command for the mission was laid. Vice Admiral Nagumo Chūichi, commander of the First Mobile Striking Force, was small, gruff, and fifty-five years of age.[13] A sailor's sailor, he had held numerous seagoing commands on his way up through the ranks. A torpedo expert by training, as a young officer, he had garnered a reputation for dash and intelligence and was considered a rising star within the Navy. Somewhere along the way, though, his earlier drive had been leeched away. Perhaps it was simply the onset of premature old age—once an avid kendo fencer, bouts of arthritis now left him in considerable pain. He wore the command of *Kidō Butai* uneasily. An official photograph, taken of him in a dress uniform dripping in medals, seems to reveal a man distinctly uncomfortable with the image of an admiral, staring with muted supplication at the camera. Perhaps he simply longed for the simpler days, when he was a lower-level commander and spent his time at sea, out of the limelight. The complexity of the new mode of aerial warfare clearly was beyond his ken.

Nagumo's true personality is difficult to pin down. It is probable that he, like many men, had different faces for different audiences. His youngest son remembered him as a serious, somewhat brooding father. His ambitions to have his two sons follow him into the Navy were destined for disappointment. Nagumo was all business and rarely joked at home, seemingly always consumed with the concerns of a career Navy officer. He was often at sea, leaving his three children for long periods of time. To his junior officers, he often appeared friendly, evincing the sort of fatherly familiarity that his own son apparently rarely saw. He was always willing to lend them a helping hand and provide advice. He was also given to delegating responsibility to younger men, sometimes too much so. His peers in the admiral's ranks apparently considered him a mixed bag at best; competent, but given to drunken bravado. The mercurial Admiral Ugaki Matome, chief of staff for Combined Fleet, disliked Nagumo intensely, and in the privacy of his diary ascribed to him all manner of mental shortcomings, from panics and nerves to simple stupidity.

It is unlikely that Nagumo had friendly relations with his chief, Admiral Yamamoto. Yamamoto was a noted member of the faction within the Navy that had supported the Washington Naval Treaty. Nagumo had been a member of the militaristic Fleet Faction, which opposed the treaty as if it were a national hemlock. Given that Yamamoto's life had been threatened by extremist members of the Fleet Faction, it can be safely speculated that each man loathed the other.

Yamamoto could not have been happy that it was Nagumo who was put in charge of First Air Fleet when it was formed in April 1941. This new entity, which concentrated all the large flight decks in the fleet into a single tactical unit, needed to be commanded by a vice admiral. Unfortunately, the more air-minded Vice Admiral Ozawa Jisaburō, who had been one of the primary advocates behind First Air Fleet's

1-8: Vice Admiral Nagumo Chūichi, commander of First Mobile Striking Force. (Naval Historical Center)

creation, had just been assigned to a different post, leaving Nagumo next in line. According to the Navy's strict rules of seniority, he was given a command for which he was basically ill suited. It wasn't that Nagumo was a bad officer. Rather, he was largely passive and not terribly innovative, at a moment in history when adaptability would be key to the Navy's fortunes. Nagumo had no real affinity for the supremely powerful weapon that was thrust into his hands.

However, by the time of Midway, Nagumo's name was also inextricably linked to the successes of *Kidō Butai*. Though Yamamoto had rebuked him over his performance at Pearl Harbor, he wasn't in any position to remove him from command. When such an action had been suggested by a member of Yamamoto's staff, he had replied that such an action would "be the same as killing him. It would be the same thing as asking him to commit hara-kiri." Besides, such an action would have had to be ratified by the Naval General Staff in any case, and it was known within the circles of Combined Fleet that Naval GHQ could not and would not approve such an action.[14]

It's possible, too, that Nagumo's passivity may have been somewhat appealing to the commander in chief. Admiral Yamamoto was used to having his way and already had had plenty of internal battles to fight with the Navy establishment in 1941 when trying to get approval for Pearl Harbor. Having a strong-willed commander presiding over the primary implement of that strategic vision could have been quite inconvenient. Yamamoto liked original thinking, as long as it was his, or if it emanated from individuals he could directly control. In Nagumo he found a commander who, though grudging, was at least not inclined to resist his orders. Nagumo grumbled, but he did what he was told.

1-9: Rear Admiral Kusaka Ryūnosuke, First Air Fleet chief of staff. (Photo courtesy Donald Goldstein)

That *Kidō Butai* had won, and won big, for the first six months of the war was no real indication of Nagumo's prowess or growth as a carrier commander. At the beginning of the Pacific War, the Japanese Navy had found itself within the happy confluence of three key forces—weak opponents, possession of a superior weapon system (in the form of high-quality, massed naval airpower), and an effective doctrine for its employ. None of *Kidō Butai*'s foes had an effective reply to the challenge posed by six carriers and some four hundred aircraft that could appear and disappear at will. Japanese planes and pilots were so markedly superior that apparently nothing could stand before them. But if Nagumo used this honeymoon period to gain a deeper understanding of the workings of carrier warfare, it does not show in his subsequent actions. Nagumo was merely the ringleader of this traveling circus; he had hardly anything to do with its success.

Nagumo's right-hand man was his chief of staff, Rear Admiral Kusaka Ryūnosuke. Originally a gunnery officer, he had been posted to Kasumigaura Air Group in 1926, whereupon his career became totally devoted to aviation. Though not a flier himself, he had commanded both the *Hōshō* and *Akagi* before being promoted to rear admiral in 1937.[15] Kusaka was, by all accounts, devoted to his chief and became something of an apologist for him after the war.[16] They were both cautious by nature, although Kusaka's personality was more placid and philosophical than that of his dour commander. A Zen Buddhist, he was apparently a skilled negotiator and conciliator. However, there is little to suggest that he possessed an incisive mind. His lectures on aerial tactics at Kasumigaura were remembered by the aviators there as being not so much on aerial tactics as on "aerial philosophy."[17] He was, in short, something of a dilettante—a man who recognized the potential of naval aviation and wanted to be associated with it, but whose training and personal insights into airpower were limited. That, in combination with his rather laid back personality, meant that he was unlikely to take bold actions when the need arose.

1-10: Rear Admiral Yamaguchi Tamon, commander of Carrier Division 2. (Photo courtesy Donald Goldstein)

Kidō Butai's other ranking carrier admiral was Rear Admiral Yamaguchi Tamon. The commander of CarDiv 2, Yamaguchi was a much different man than his superior. Five years younger than Nagumo, he seemed ages more youthful and energetic. Photographs of Yamaguchi reveal an odd mixture of features, with high eyebrows, close-set eyes, and an almost feline appearance. He was widely seen within the fleet as being the logical successor to Admiral Yamamoto. He had an impeccable pedigree for higher command—a Naval Staff College graduate, schooling abroad at Princeton University, and extensive sea service. Yamaguchi had worked his way up through command of light cruiser *Isuzu,* heavy cruiser *Atago,* and eventually battleship *Ise.* He had been a member of Japan's naval delegation to the London Naval Conference in 1929 and had also served as naval attaché in Washington, D.C. During the conflict in China, he had commanded the Navy's First Combined Air Group and directed its bombing campaign against central China. Though not a pilot, he was respected in the aviation community and had been a vocal supporter of its growth.

Yamaguchi appears to have been quite social, which may have furthered his career. An American naval officer who met Yamaguchi in 1923 when he was still a lieutenant, observed that he appeared "to prefer pleasure to work." Yamaguchi was quite enthusiastic about his American alma mater, Princeton, where he apparently preferred "horses, tennis, golf and liquor to study." The American went on to observe that Yamaguchi "did not give the impression of being well founded professionally, but would be better suited [to diplomacy.]"[18]

Yet, despite what his vitae or American social acquaintances might have said, in the final analysis, Yamaguchi fell into the category of man that Chihaya Masatake, himself a commander in the Imperial Navy and a shrewd observer of its failings, would later term the "Oriental Hero Type"—"rough-hewn, [and] lacking precision of thought and a clear-cut sense of responsibility in the western sense of the word."[19] He was, in short, the epitome of the traditional samurai—hot tempered, aggressive to a fault; a man who valued honor as the ultimate virtue.

It is clear that Yamaguchi had misgivings about his more passive superior, and indeed of First Air Fleet's staff in general. Admiral Ugaki recorded in his diary that Yamaguchi had complained to him on several occasions that "First Air Fleet headquarters had never taken steps to expand its achievement in battle, grasping an opportunity to do so, or to cope with a change of circumstances." He confided to Ugaki that what was missing in First Air Fleet was leadership: "The commander in chief [Nagumo] doesn't say a word, and both the chief of staff [Kusaka] and the senior staff officer [Captain Ōishi, Kusaka's right-hand man] lack boldness."[20] In his complaints, Yamaguchi found a receptive ear, for Ugaki was hardly impressed with Nagumo himself and urged Yamaguchi to continue recommending his views as much as possible in the future."[21]

1-11: Commander Genda Minoru, staff air officer of First Air Fleet. (Author's collection)

If true brilliance was to be found in *Kidō Butai*, it lay further down the chain of command. Nagumo's air officer, Commander Genda Minoru, was commonly recognized as the house genius. Like his commander, he wore his mantle somewhat uneasily, but for entirely different reasons. There was no questioning his air credentials. Genda had first made his name as a highly skilled fighter pilot, eventually going so far as to organize a naval acrobatic team to tour Japan. After his run with the "Genda Circus" (as it came to be known), he had served as an air staff officer in China, flight instructor, and an assistant naval attaché for good measure. Genda was gifted, insightful, and had a firm grasp over the workings of carrier warfare. Indeed, he was largely responsible for creating and shaping the force now under Nagumo's command. He had been handpicked by Yamamoto for his position, and thus far in the war he had performed well. It was Genda who had been the architect of massed naval airpower within the fleet, and it was his and Vice Admiral Ozawa's constant nagging of the top brass that had finally prompted Yamamoto to officially create the First Air Fleet.

Nagumo, with his penchant for delegating to talented juniors, essentially let Genda run the show when it came to planning air operations. As far as Genda was concerned, this was a mixed blessing. While he was confident in his abilities (to the point of arrogance, according to Kusaka), he was also aware of his limitations.[22] Nagumo rarely critiqued his plans. Genda would have preferred having someone supervising him to ensure that he didn't overlook the obvious. Unfortunately, there was no one else with the necessary insight into aerial matters to do so. The net result was that air operations for *Kidō Butai* were disproportionately the responsibility of a single individual.

Nagumo's warships left Hashirajima traveling south, passing between the islands of Yashirojima and Nakajima before turning into the broad Iyo Nada waterway. The heavily cultivated islands of the Inland Sea are verdant and steep sided, rising spectacularly from the blue waters. Fishermen in their boats paused to wave at the grim warships as they cruised along. *Kidō Butai* made its way toward the north entrance of the Bungo Suidō, the key waterway that separates Shikoku from the southern island of Kyūshū. Entering the narrow channel in single file, the force plowed south-southeast toward the open ocean, clearing Bungo Suidō around noon.

Kidō Butai's screening vessels began shaking themselves out into an alert cruising disposition. Nagumo's escorts for this mission were well known to the force as a whole. The fast battleships *Haruna* and *Kirishima* (the second section of BatDiv 3) were along to provide whatever heavy gunfire might be needed. Both ships were old but had been refitted several times during their long lives. Originally constructed as battle cruisers, they could still crank out thirty-one knots, and as such were perfect heavy escorts for *Kidō Butai*'s carriers. Each mounted eight fourteen-inch guns and relatively heavy antiaircraft armament as well. They were in no way equivalent to a modern fast battleship but could certainly stand up against a heavy cruiser, which was their primary screening role. They could also be called on to initiate a night action against any American forces that might be in the neighborhood, if the situation required it.

Nagumo's screen commander, Rear Admiral Abe Hiroaki, flew his flag in the heavy cruiser *Tone*. Both *Tone* and *Chikuma* had been built as adjuncts to the carrier forces. Each mounted their eight eight-inch guns in four twin turrets forward, leaving the entire rear deck available for floatplane operations. Each ship normally carried five aircraft, although on this occasion *Tone* was missing one of hers.[23] The role of these cruisers was to act as scouts for the fleet, through their floatplanes, thereby freeing up the carrier aircraft for offensive operations.

The light cruiser *Nagara*, flagship of Rear Admiral Kimura Susumu, commander of Destroyer Squadron 10, directed a screen of eleven destroyers—*Arashi, Nowaki, Hagikaze, Maikaze, Kazagumo, Yūgumo, Makigumo, Isokaze, Urakaze, Hamakaze,* and *Tanikaze. Nagara* was an older 5,500-ton cruiser and wasn't much help in a fight. But her role was to act as flagship for the destroyers in her charge, which is where the real surface combat power of the force lay. Each of the destroyers was a new fleet unit, and all of them were armed to the teeth with five-inch guns and the feared Type 93 torpedo.

Nagumo's force settled onto a course taking it southeast into the broad Pacific. They would continue in this fashion for the rest of the day before turning east that night and heading toward the objective. The coastline of Shikoku was fading into the distance. Tsuchiya Ryōsaku, a 3rd class seaman from Shizuoka province, still four months shy of his sixteenth birthday, may have had a chance to look over *Akagi*'s railing one last time as the shore vanished behind him. Fifty-seven-year-old Hōdate Ken, a lieutenant commander from Kagoshima, might well have done the same from *Sōryū*'s bridge.[24] They were destined to be, respectively, the youngest and oldest of the 3,057 Japanese who would never see their homeland again as a result of Operation MI.[25] Within ten days, they and the proud carriers they served on would be lying at the bottom of the cold Pacific.

2

Genesis of a Battle

Whereas the spectacle surrounding Nagumo's sortie six hours earlier had been gala, the mood among his senior officers was quite the opposite. This was not a popular operation, particularly among the staff members of *Kidō Butai,* who worried that Combined Fleet's planning staff was sending them on a fool's errand. Nagumo had been withdrawn and apathetic during the planning phase.[1] Admirals Kusaka, Yamaguchi, and Kondō, along with Captain Kaku of *Hiryū* had all been downright hostile to it almost from the outset.[2] Commander Genda, for his part, while not opposed to seeking a decisive battle with the Americans off Midway, also felt that the mission's operational planning left much to be desired. Indeed, to many fleet officers, Operation MI, and its concurrent northern counterpart, Operation AL (aimed at the occupation of the Aleutian Islands), appeared to have been simply thrown together. Appearances, in this case, were not deceptive.

Operations MI and AL were the unhappy outcome of a lack of real strategic direction on the part of the Japanese military, and the Imperial Navy in particular, in early 1942.[3] To a large degree, these difficulties stemmed from Japan's unforeseen successes during the first four months of war. By March 1942, Japan had either attained all of her initial objectives or was in sight of doing so. Malaya had already been captured, after a brilliant campaign that had seen the fall of the great British bastion of Singapore on February 15, 1942. The Dutch East Indies, including the rich resources of Borneo and Java, had survived less than a month longer. The key to securing the Indies had been a series of savage naval battles near Java. There, the Imperial Navy had crushed the combined squadrons of the American, British, Dutch, and Australian Navies (the ill-starred ABDA command) and then hunted down their fleeing remnants. In addition to capturing the oil and rubber that had been the reason for going to war in the first place, Japan had also ripped apart the last line of defense in front of Australia. The Imperial Navy's fleet was now in a position both to raid Australia's northern coast and to make moves into the Indian Ocean.

Similarly, the Japanese campaign in Burma was well in hand and would see the expulsion of the British by the end of April. In the Philippines, the initial landings had gone smoothly, and Manila had fallen on January 2, 1942. American and Philippine forces had retreated to the Bataan Peninsula and were still holding out, but the outcome was a foregone conclusion, because the U.S. Navy was in no position to

2-1: The Japanese Empire and the Battle of Midway. This map shows the extent of Japanese conquests as of approximately March 1942, as well as the outlines of Yamamoto's decisive battlefield.

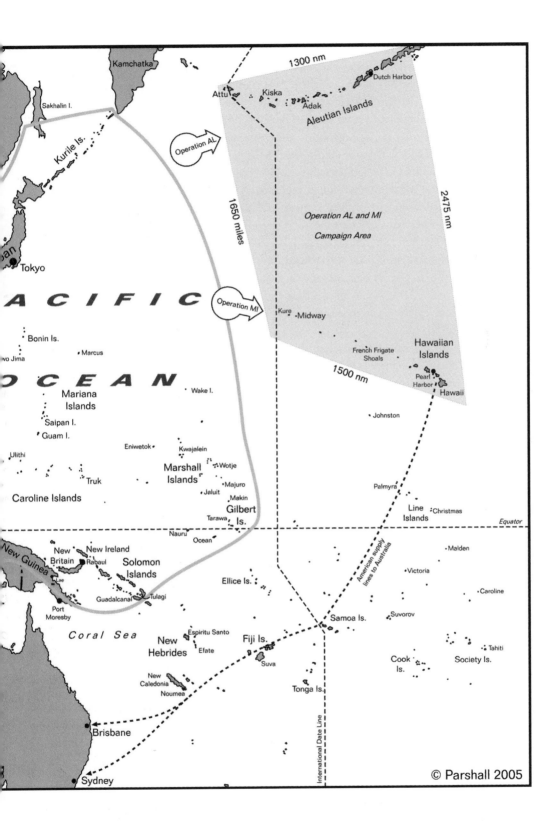

© Parshall 2005

relieve the siege. The entirety of the west central Pacific basin, including the American possessions of Guam and Wake, had fallen in the opening weeks of the conflict. Further south, the Japanese had secured the important port of Rabaul (located on the northern tip of New Britain) in January. From there, they threatened to make further inroads into New Guinea and ultimately to develop offensives to the south and east that could potentially cut communications between Australia and the United States.

Thus, on the face of it, Japan had all but achieved all of the goals that she had gone to war for. She had expelled the white colonial powers and secured the southern resource areas in the Indies that would, in time, supply her with all the oil and strategic minerals that her new Pacific empire required. With her earlier conquests in China, she now had under her control a vast territory, stretching from Manchuria in the north, through central China and French Indochina into Malaya and Burma in the southwest. From there, her possessions ran eastward down the line of islands stretching from Sumatra all the way to Rabaul, and proceeded north from there through the stronghold of Truk all the way to the Kuriles. In the space of a few short months, the Japanese had thus secured for themselves one of the largest empires in the history of mankind.

Japan now stood temporarily supreme in the Pacific. Dutch and British naval power had for all intents and purposes been eliminated from the area, with the Royal Navy having retreated to Ceylon and India. The U.S. Navy had been humbled at Pearl Harbor and bloodied again in the Philippines and around Java. Though unbeaten, it had been incapable of disrupting Japanese offensive actions in the Pacific and was currently able to do little more than conduct hit-and-run raids against Japanese outposts. It had not yet recovered the ability to launch strategically meaningful operations of its own—it could only react to Japanese moves. The Japanese held the initiative everywhere.

The logical question that arose in the ranks of the Japanese military's planners as a result of their success was how to use that initiative. It was to this strategic debate that Japan's leadership turned its attentions, beginning as early as January 1942. As it developed, there was widespread disagreement over this subject, not only between the Army and Navy, but within the Navy itself as well. But Admiral Yamamoto Isoroku, the commander in chief of Combined Fleet, was determined to have the final say in Pacific war strategy.

Yamamoto, the most controversial and important figure in the history of the Japanese Navy, was a man who defies easy description.[4] He was widely portrayed during the war both at home and abroad as a brilliant commander. However, his reputation within the fleet itself was less clear-cut, despite his considerable prewar achievements. Born to humble origins, he combined intelligence with an intense drive to better his circumstances. Along the way he had acquired a taste for the creature comforts of rank, which he would retain until his death. Charismatic and capable, he was also an ambivalent husband and father, enjoying gambling and spending time with geishas instead. Taken together, he was a man of notable strengths and weaknesses, though his personality flaws were not those that would have been detrimental within the social organization of the Navy.

2-2: Admiral Yamamoto Isoroku, commander in chief, Combined Fleet. Ambitious and politically adroit, he was determined to have the final say in Japanese naval strategy formulation. (Author's collection)

What is surprising about Yamamoto is that he had managed to rise nearly to the pinnacle of his profession despite having been a standard-bearer for some very unpopular causes. He was a supporter of the Washington and London Naval Treaties, within a Navy whose majority considered those agreements to be a slap in the face of national pride, because they pegged Japan's naval forces at a level below those of the United States and Great Britain. He was an advocate of naval aviation at a time when the Navy still worshipped at the temple of the big-gun warship. Finally, he was an opponent of Japan's alliance with Nazi Germany, whose martial prowess and antipathy toward the Soviet state were widely admired throughout the Japanese military. Given these facts, two general conclusions can be reached about Yamamoto. First, he must have combined a high degree of confidence and competence along with the survival skills necessary to have reached his present position. Second, he had undoubtedly made a lot of enemies. The forthcoming strategic planning process would swell their ranks still further.

Assuming command of Combined Fleet in 1939, Yamamoto had imposed his stamp on it in a way that no commander had done since the days of the revered Admiral Tōgō. To his detractors, it must have seemed that Yamamoto was determined to make Combined Fleet his own personal fiefdom. His staff became a haven for unorthodox thinkers, including many of the airpower supporters within the Navy. This was a mixed blessing. On the one hand, it is undeniable that Yamamoto's advocacy had brought about a greater reliance on naval aviation within the fleet, which had subsequently served Japan well. On the other hand, Yamamoto and his staff saw themselves engaged in a perpetual struggle against the naval establishment.

Not surprisingly, he and his officers were unpopular at Imperial General Headquarters (IGHQ) in Tokyo, which thought (somewhat justifiably) that Combined Fleet's commander and cronies had a bit of an attitude problem. Worse was yet to follow. As war approached, Yamamoto laid the groundwork for what was in effect a coup against IGHQ over who was to set strategic direction for the fleet. In so doing, he sowed the seeds of future military defeat by destroying the checks and balances within the Navy's policymaking processes.

Yamamoto had insisted in 1941 that if Japan chose to capture the resources of the south through war, that war also had to include the United States. Furthermore, he believed that the U.S. Navy had to be dealt a crippling blow at the outset so as to buy time for Japan to carry out its operations in the southern campaign areas without opposition. In this view, he was opposed by several senior members of the Naval General Staff, including its head, Admiral Nagano Osami. Nagano was of the opinion that the United States would find it very difficult to go to war if Japan refrained from an outright attack. He reasoned (correctly) that President Franklin D. Roosevelt would have a difficult time rallying sufficient support for a *causus belli* based only on Japanese attacks against British and Dutch colonial holdings, as American popular opinion was decidedly ambivalent about defending such interests.

Nagano had eventually lost the debate, even though his basic reasoning was sound. Yamamoto had won on the basis of both his personal reputation, and his willingness to use inelegant means to get his way. In the midst of the Pearl Harbor debate, he had let it be known that he and the entire staff of Combined Fleet were prepared to resign if his views were not confirmed.[5] Nagano, given the choice between acquiescing or confronting his wayward subordinate, had backed down. In so doing, he essentially let Yamamoto hijack the Navy's strategic planning process and place it under the purview of Combined Fleet. Yamamoto would later remark to his cohort Ukagi that, in his opinion, naval headquarters seemed to have "no definite ideas" as to how to carry out the war. Indeed, during a meeting in Tokyo on 5 December to brief the emperor, Yamamoto had gone so far as to tell the chief of the Naval General Staff, as well as the Navy minister, "not to interfere too much and thus set a bad precedent in the navy."[6] This was, bluntly, a rather incredible state of affairs for any military organization.

The Pearl Harbor attack (*Hawaii sakusen*) proved a spectacular success, at least superficially. Although it had left some notable loose ends in its wake—including the failure to sink any American aircraft carriers—it had resulted in enough damage to the

U.S. Navy that the Japanese greeted it as a great victory. As a result, Yamamoto's political clout within the Navy was considerably enhanced, especially as one Japanese success piled on the next in the heady first months of war. Wherever the Navy had gone, Yamamoto's name by default had gone with it. By early 1942, he was associated by the Japanese public with all the fruits of victory that the Navy had won for the nation.

Having taken control over naval strategy, Yamamoto had no intention of relinquishing his new perquisite. The Naval General Staff in Tokyo, of course, had other ideas. Consequently, strategic formulation concerning future operations was accompanied by a tug of war between Hashirajima and Tokyo. However, Yamamoto already knew two things. First, his threat to resign had already been effective once. Second, his own political clout had increased dramatically since the inception of the war. Naval GHQ held no such cards.

A fractured internal policymaking process was only the first hurdle to the Navy's being able to fashion a reasonable set of follow-on operations in 1942. The second major problem was that the Navy itself did not have unilateral say in such matters. Any further territorial expansion required ground forces to capture and garrison the conquests. The Navy had too few troops to do any real "heavy lifting" of its own and therefore had to rely on the Army if it wanted to secure important objectives. The Army recognized that it had an important say in such matters, and it intended to use this leverage. Unfortunately, whereas most nations' interservice relationships range from bad to worse, Japan's were mired at the dysfunctional end of the spectrum. The Imperial Army and Navy loathed each other, their interchanges being marked by suspicion, pettiness, and outright hostility. Admiral Nagano's penchant (real or feigned) for conveniently falling asleep during joint Army/Navy liaison conferences was indicative of the overall level of civility that prevailed between the two services.[7]

The Army was still largely focused on its private quagmire in China, which had consumed the vast majority of its forces since July 1937. Furthermore, given the Army's heavy defeat at the hands of the Soviets during a series of violent border clashes in Manchuria in the summer of 1939, it felt compelled to maintain substantial forces in the area. Thus, it had been parsimonious in relinquishing forces for the initial stage of war operations in the Pacific.

In fact, only a shade over eleven divisions had been required to conquer the entirety of the new Japanese empire. This represented perhaps a fifth of the Army's total manpower. Given that stinginess had apparently paid for itself in the opening campaign, it was loath to release any more forces than it had to for future operations. It was also determined to resist any operational concepts that created open-ended manpower commitments.

In fairness to the Army, it rightly wanted to preserve its strength for further actions against the Russians in Manchuria. Despite the mauling the Japanese had been subjected to two years earlier, in late 1941 it looked as if the Russians themselves were being overwhelmed. The Red Army had been continually beaten by the *Wehrmacht* during the previous summer, and to all outward appearances the Soviet Union was on the verge of collapse. This reversal of fortunes for the Soviet colossus meant that there might exist real opportunities for the Japanese to seize more of Manchuria. But the net result was that the Army's attention was not fully engaged by the Pacific.

This tendency reflected fundamental differences between the Army and the Navy about how the war was to be brought to a close. The Navy was steeped in a tradition of seeking decisive battle with its foes. It believed that landing a single roundhouse blow, if sufficiently powerful, would bring hostilities to a close. It was the Navy's fervent hope, therefore, that the war could be concluded in 1942. The Army, however, held no such illusions, particularly against an opponent as powerful as the United States. Instead, the Army was girding itself for a protracted struggle. It was deeply suspicious of any attempts to increase the size of Japan's territorial holdings in the largely empty wastes of the Pacific, knowing it didn't have the strength to garrison every outpost. Instead, the Army wished to fortify an outer shell as strongly as possible, preparing to make the Americans pay an unacceptable price in blood when their inevitable counterattacks began. As a result, the Army consistently resisted any notions that looked likely to increase its troop commitments in the Pacific.

Thus, when the Navy began floating trial balloons during a series of joint service consultations in the early part of 1942, the Army held important trump cards. Lacking naval transport, it could not unilaterally initiate actions against Americans. But by the same token, neither could the Navy, in that the Army had no qualms in vetoing strategic avenues that appeared too risky or that created open-ended commitments. This, then, was the treacherous landscape across which Japan's military leadership groped for a solution to their strategic dilemmas. In such a poisonous political atmosphere, it is hardly surprising that Japan put its carrier force to little strategically meaningful work during the months of March and April 1942. While the internal debate over second-stage war policy raged, the only operations that could be countenanced for *Kidō Butai* were by definition those that did not tread too decisively down any strategic avenue. Thus Japan was guilty of wasting its most important strategic asset at a time when it was largely unchallengeable in the Pacific.

In the eyes of the Imperial Navy, Japan had an array of strategic options open to it at the beginning of 1942. Not all of these alternatives were recognized or developed simultaneously. The sine qua non of success for any of them, though, was the presence of the Navy's fleet carriers. Of course, there were only so many flight decks to go around. As will be seen, the Navy ultimately ended up committing its carriers in support of more operations than they could handle, with disastrous consequences. The circuitous path by which it shouldered these disparate and contradictory commitments was a misadventure of truly epic proportions.

The first strategic option was switching over from an offensive to a defensive stance. Rear Admiral Kusaka, Nagumo's chief of staff, was one of the leading proponents of this vision.[8] At this point in the war, Japan had conquered but it had not really consolidated its gains. It needed time to toughen up its defensive shell and begin preparing for when America would counterattack. Obviously, this could not be accomplished while the defensive perimeter was still being pushed outward. Shifting to a defensive stance would give the fleet time and breathing room to replenish its aircraft and pilots, which were already showing the deleterious effects of an all-out war.

Kusaka had a legitimate point, but he was the wrong man to present such a plan.[9] Both he and his superior, Nagumo, had been opposed to the attack on Pearl Harbor.[10] As a result, *Kidō Butai*'s two senior officers paradoxically had very little cachet within the fleet. Not only that, but such an approach seemed too passive to be countenanced by a service as habitually aggressive as the Imperial Navy. If a legitimate combat leader had agitated for the same proposal, it might at least have been debated. But coming from a paper pusher like Kusaka, it was dead on arrival.

The second option envisioned occupying some or all of Australia. On the face of it, given the size of the objective, this was an outrageous proposal. Yet it actually offered a number of attractions. Though large, Australia was sparsely inhabited and could muster no more than a handful of divisions in its own defense. Its very size meant that the Japanese could be reasonably assured of getting ashore *somewhere,* since the Australians could not adequately cover their coastline. Even securing the northern portion of the country would create a beachhead on the Allies' most important remaining bastion in the South Pacific. The Japanese were well aware that Australia figured prominently in America's calculations. There were indications that the United States intended to use it as a jumping off point for operations in the south. Capturing their base would preempt these operations. Indeed, Admiral Nagumo's raid against Darwin was launched partly with such a goal in mind. Attacking Australia was supported by the Plans Division of the Naval General Staff, which was headed up by Rear Admiral Fukudome Shigeru, and ably assisted by his right-hand man, Captain Tomioka Sadatoshi.[11] It was also advocated by the fiery Vice Admiral Inoue Shigeyoshi, an airpower visionary and now the current commander of the Navy's Fourth Fleet (headquartered at Truk), which had authority over operations in the southern region.

However, the Army quickly nixed this proposal, arguing correctly that it would take a minimum of ten to twelve divisions to execute.[12] Australia was just the sort of open-ended manpower sump that the Imperial Army wanted at all costs to avoid. Thus, while agreeing that there were benefits to undertaking its conquest, the Army asserted that the troops and transports were simply unavailable. Worse, it tweaked the Navy's nose by suggesting that an extension of Japan's campaign this far south would create a theater of operations that was beyond the nation's logistical capabilities. That the Army was wholly justified in its assessment of Japan's already slender logistical base did not help the Navy's temper.

A fallback option to an Australian invasion was cutting its line of supply with the United States. To do so, Japan would attack to the southeast, through the length of the Solomon Islands. From there, advances would be made into the New Hebrides, New Caledonia (with its important port of Noumea), Fiji, and finally Samoa. By doing so, Japan would sit astride Australia's communications lines, preventing any American buildup. This alternative was seen as less desirable by both Tomioka and Inoue, but they were open to considering it in the event an Australian invasion was dismissed.

At the same time, though, Combined Fleet had been quietly contemplating conducting second-stage operations not in the south, but in the Central Pacific. Initial support for this approach came from Vice Admiral Hosogaya Moshirō, the commander with responsibility for guarding Japan's seaward approaches in the north—the path by which an American carrier force could gain easiest access to the Japanese homeland.[13] It was Yamamoto and his staff, though, that were its most forceful proponents. Yamamoto had been haunted by the cardinal disappointment of Pearl Harbor—the failure to sink the enemy flattops that by rights should have been moored at Ford Island on the morning of the attack. Instead, for all his efforts, the American carriers had yet to be brought to battle. Yamamoto was determined to destroy them. Knowing that their primary base was Pearl Harbor, Yamamoto believed it only made sense to precipitate a battle somewhere near their lair.

Given Pearl Harbor's outcome, Yamamoto had been considering the Central Pacific almost from the inception of the war. On December 9, 1941, he had ordered Admiral Ugaki to reexamine the notion of an invasion of Hawaii.[14] Ugaki was actively working on this by early January 1942.[15] Included in this early operational plan was the concept that a direct invasion of Hawaii would be used to precipitate a decisive battle with the Americans.[16] However, Ugaki admitted to himself shortly afterward that Hawaii's native strength made fighting a battle there extremely risky.[17]

It is important to clarify the role of an invasion in these schemes, however. It has commonly been supposed that any successful Japanese operation in the Central Pacific would automatically have culminated in an invasion of Hawaii. Certainly this is what Yamamoto had in mind. However, like the notion of operations in the Central Pacific itself, an invasion of Hawaii was by no means accepted within the Navy as a whole, much less by the Army. Admiral Yamamoto and his staff had been contemplating such a venture since the summer of 1941, but few others had contemplated such a notion.[18] During the planning for the attack on Pearl Harbor, the idea had briefly been floated that a simultaneous invasion also occur against Oahu.[19] However, such an attack was judged by Naval GHQ as being far too risky. In September 1941 the notion was dropped, though it was not forgotten by Combined Fleet. Thus, during the strategic debate that reemerged in early 1942, Yamamoto and his staff found themselves rolling not one, but two rocks uphill.

It didn't take long for both Naval GHQ and the Army to get wind of Combined Fleet's ambitions in the Central Pacific, whereupon Naval GHQ moved aggressively to put a stop to them. On 16 December, HQ sent Captain Tomioka down to Hashirajima to meet with Ugaki and discuss follow-on operations. While there, Capt. Kuroshima Kameto, Combined Fleet's "God of Operations," briefed Tomioka on operations aimed at seizing Palmyra, a tiny atoll that lay halfway between Hawaii and Samoa. Tomioka initially believed that this move was designed to help support follow-on operations into Fiji and Samoa, which was Tomioka's own favored axis of attack.[20] Upon returning to Tokyo, Tomioka relayed the results of his meeting to both his boss, Fukudome, and to Fukudome's counterpart on the Army General Staff, Lt. Gen. Tanaka Shinichi. Tanaka saw immediately that Tomioka had been misled and that invading Palmrya was intended as a move into the Central Pacific and a stepping stone toward Hawaii, not Fiji or Samoa. He told Tomioka bluntly that the Army viewed any enlargement of the defensive perimeter as dangerous and unnecessary.[21]

Captain Tomioka was now on his guard. Highly intelligent and capable (some said arrogant as well), he was not a man to be trifled with.[22] In reaction to General

Tanaka's misgivings, he shortly had Capt. Miwa Yoshitake of Combined Fleet staff come up to Tokyo to report further on Combined Fleet's plans. Miwa dutifully arrived on 27 December, 1941, and delivered a briefing on what was coming to be known within Combined Fleet as "Eastern Operation"—the invasion of Hawaii.[23] Tomioka, alarmed, saw that he had indeed been given the wrong impression about Combined Fleet's schemes. He thereupon tasked one of his subordinates, Capt. Kami Shigenori, to prepare a logistical study of the proposed operation. Kami dutifully complied, and by 11 January Tomioka had all the ammunition he needed to shoot Combined Fleet's proposal down. While capturing Hawaii might be feasible, the logistical problems associated with keeping the islands' large civilian population supplied were substantial. Hawaii was not even remotely self-sufficient in basic foodstuffs. These necessities, in addition to the needs of the large garrison Japan would have to post there, would require at least sixty transport loads per month—a figure beyond Japan's meager resources.[24] It was obvious that in the face of likely resistance from American submarines, these basic figures would need to be even further expanded.

While Kami was preparing his report, Tomioka was simultaneously working his superiors. At an Army/Navy conference in Tokyo on January 10, 1942, Admiral Nagano discussed the notion of Hawaiian operations with General Sugiyama Gen, head of the Army General Staff. Sugiyama and Nagano agreed that a direct attack on Hawaii was impossible, and that operations into the Fiji/Samoa area made better sense.[25] General Sugiyama liked this option, because it would require less of a commitment from his branch of the service. Nagano liked it, because it was at least an indirect move against Australia.

Into this lion's den of stacked-deck politics walked Commander Sasaki Akira, a relatively junior member of Combined Fleet staff, to deliver yet another briefing to Naval GHQ on January 13th.[26] His comrade, Miwa, not having gotten a strong negative reaction to "Eastern Operation" on his previous trip up to Tokyo, Sasaki was undoubtedly expecting smooth sailing as well. Instead, he was treated to Captain Kami's damning logistics study, followed by the Army's flat refusal to sanction an invasion of Hawaii, and topped off with the announcement of Nagano and Sugiyama's joint accord to proceed into the Fiji/Samoa region instead. Sasaki thereupon retreated to Hashirajima to relay the news to Combined Fleet staff.

Yamamoto and Ugaki were understandably furious at this turn of events, but they had little choice but to temporarily turn their attention to the operational concepts favored by Tokyo. Yamamoto instructed his chief of staff to flesh out the Fiji/Samoa operation.[27] Ugaki complied, although both he and his staff were unenthusiastic. It is apparent, too, that the notion of operations in the Central Pacific may have been temporarily banished from consideration, but it was never far from either Ugaki or his superior's minds. Indeed, Ugaki's diary makes it clear that both he and Kuroshima continued batting the idea around internally for the next several weeks.[28]

However, it was at this junction that a fifth strategic option began its brief rise to ascendancy. Just two weeks after Commander Sasaki's demoralizing trip to Tokyo, Ugaki privately confided to his diary that immediate actions against Hawaii were probably impractical anyway, because of its inherent airpower, and broached the notion that operations aimed at the Indian Ocean might offer better results.[29] Under this scheme, Japan would move against the British in India, attempting to pry India from British rule by a combination of military action and (it was hoped) a rebellion on the part of the indigenous population. Success in this theater raised the possibility of effecting a linkup with Japan's Axis partners through the Middle East, thus creating a corridor of fascism across half the globe. It also had the added bonus of being in accord with popular sentiment in Japan, whose press was calling for just such a world-spanning Axis hegemony.[30]

By early February, Combined Fleet's staff invited both Naval HQ as well as Army representatives to attend a series of Indian Ocean war games to be held on board *Yamato* on 20–23 February. The results were mixed at best. Ugaki noted in his diary that "The idea of the operation in the Indian Ocean was not good."[31] The exercise suggested that it would be difficult to locate the enemy's fleet and that enemy airpower would badly hinder operations. However, the results of the war gaming were apparently good enough to continue studying the operation, with increasing attention given to the capture of Ceylon. For the time being, the Army was going along with the concept, and it seemed to be interested in expanding operations along the Indian front in the near future.[32]

However, within a matter of a few weeks, the bloom was apparently off the rose. Indeed, just five days after the exercises on *Yamato* wrapped up, no mention was made of such operations at a high-level liaison meeting in Tokyo.[33] Part of this resulted from the continuing reluctance on the part of the Army to open a new theater and thereby commit ground troops (planning estimates had called for a minimum of five divisions) for garrison duties in places like Ceylon. Not only that, but the Army began to become suspicious that by committing substantial numbers of new troops to any coming Indian Ocean venture, it would undermine its previously successful strategy of being able to veto any new operation on the basis of troops simply "not being available." The Army suspected that the Navy might get it to commit to the Indian Ocean and then pull a bait and switch back to the eastern operational front while simultaneously demanding to use forces that were now known to be available. Given this possibility, however far-fetched, the Army apparently judged that a return to sophistry was the less risky strategy.[34]

A further complicating factor was that by mid-March the Army was beginning to face up to the fact that operations in Burma were going to require more support than had been anticipated. With Rangoon having fallen on March 8th, the Army was shortly to turn north to chase the British out of Burma and into India, requiring a long advance up the Irrawaddy River into very inhospitable terrain. Logistically, the Army was getting near the end of its rope. The later construction of the infamous Burma Railroad was but one indication of the difficulties Japan faced in keeping pressure on India via this axis of advance. The addition of Ceylon would have vastly complicated these problems.[35]

Finally, matters were not helped by Germany's signaling that it would not carry out operations in the Middle East aimed at securing their portion of the land bridge to

Asia. This weakened the overall rationale behind an adventure in the Indian Ocean, at least from the standpoint of generating propaganda.[36] Taken together, this option was dead by the end of March. Other than Nagumo's coming April raid—an operation that had been in the works for some time—no further moves were anticipated.

So far as Army and Naval GHQ knew, the only strategic alternative now left standing was the Southwest Pacific. On 13 March, Naval GHQ and the Army formally ratified the notion of operations against Fiji and Samoa.[37] In this, they were further supported by Admiral Inoue, who had recently suffered two setbacks that argued for more attention being paid to this theater. The first was an abortive raid on Rabaul on 20 February by an American carrier, *Lexington,* under the command of Vice Admiral Wilson Brown. During the course of this action, the Americans had taught the Japanese a painful lesson concerning the vulnerability of both their aircraft and their defensive perimeter as a whole.

Brown's intention was to launch a hit-and-run attack. However, his task force had been detected while still too far away to launch its aircraft. Rabaul was hardly undefended, and the base air commander had dispatched his entire group of seventeen Type 1 land-attack aircraft (later code-named "Betty" by the Allies) from the recently activated 4th *Kōkūtai* against the American carrier. The ensuing engagement was a minor disaster. Fifteen of the squadron's bombers had been shot down, with no damage against the enemy to show for it.[38] This was an ominous development indeed. Rabaul was an important installation and ought to have been able to defend itself from such a raid. That it could not cast a pall over one of Japan's basic strategic premises, namely, that a perimeter buttressed by bases such as Rabaul could be defended against American incursions.[39]

Then, barely a month later, on 10 March, came a second stunning reversal. American carriers had again appeared in southern waters and launched surprise attacks against Japanese forces making landings against the towns of Lae and Salamaua on the northern coast of New Guinea.[40] Two American carriers (*Lexington* again, along with *Yorktown,* both under Vice Admiral Brown) had launched 104 aircraft within sight of New Guinea's southern coast. From there, the Americans had flown across the towering Owen Stanley mountains and then down upon the Japanese invasion forces, which were taken completely unawares. The material effects were dramatic—two thirds of the invasion transports were either damaged or sunk. The only thing that had prevented more Army casualties was the fact that many of the transports had been close to shore when the Americans attacked, allowing several of the ships to beach themselves.

In psychological terms, this raid had an even larger impact than had the 4th *Kōkūtai*'s mauling. The Army, for its part, was horrified at the prospect of similar attacks. Likewise, Vice Admiral Inoue immediately discerned that the days of easy pickings were over in his theater of operations. Allied resistance was stiffening, enemy air activity was on the rise, and the Americans were clearly willing to employ their carriers to contest Japanese moves in the region. Shoestring operations were no longer viable in the face of such opposition. If Inoue was to complete the southern defensive perimeter, he needed help from Combined Fleet to augment his tiny forces. Inoue was supported in his views by the Naval General Staff.

In light of these unwholesome developments, Inoue invited a member of Combined Fleet's staff to confer with him at Truk. His goal was to lobby for more support from Yamamoto. The well-traveled Captain Miwa, arriving on 13 March, agreed with Inoue that more support was needed.[41] But the Navy's fleet carriers were currently unavailable, because they were about to enter the Indian Ocean. However, Miwa assured Inoue that a carrier division could be freed up to assist him within about a month. Inoue was encouraged by Miwa to write up a proposal and submit it to Combined Fleet. Thereupon Miwa departed. What Inoue discovered upon submission of his proposals in early April, though, was that he had been sold a bill of goods. No carriers were forthcoming, as Yamamoto had already earmarked them for operations in early June—operations aimed at the Central Pacific!

During March, unbeknownst to anyone else, Yamamoto and Ugaki had begun turning their attentions back to the Central Pacific. In the opinion of Yamamoto, the fact that American carriers had recently shown an interest in Inoue's theater was less important than the simple fact that the Americans still *had* carriers at all. As such, interdicting Australian supply lines in Fiji was secondary to eliminating the naval strength that underwrote the safety of those supply lines. Consequently, Japanese operations should be aimed at their destruction. In fact, this was exactly the same objective that Yamamoto's opponent, Admiral Chester W. Nimitz, intended to achieve as well. Since Yamamoto held the initiative, though, it was up to him to create the conditions whereby the Americans could be brought to battle.

At this point in the war, Japan believed that the U.S. Navy had probably been reduced to a quartet of fleet carriers in the Pacific. *Lexington* was believed to have been sunk early in the war by submarine attack.[42] This left *Saratoga* and the three *Yorktown*-class carriers (*Yorktown, Enterprise,* and *Hornet*) available in the Pacific. The location of the remaining American carrier, *Wasp,* was unknown.[43] The smaller *Ranger,* which the Japanese factored into their calculations, was believed to be in the Atlantic.[44] This meant a theoretical maximum of five American carriers to deal with. However, since it was (presumably) unthinkable that the Americans would have a clear sense for Japanese intentions, it was considered equally unlikely that all five would be in the same location when the Japanese attacked. Yamamoto was confident that with all six of his large carriers, Nagumo could deal with any enemy force he encountered.

It is perhaps not surprising that the destruction of America's carriers had taken on such a heavy dose of symbolism in Yamamoto's eyes. The mere existence of these vessels—effective or not—illustrated the absurdity of the war Japan had gotten itself into. While Japan's initial victories had been spectacular, they had also been ultimately empty, in that the war-making potential of the United States remained intact. It was true that America had been expelled from its Pacific dominions and that its Navy had been battered and humiliated at Pearl Harbor. But the Americans were still willing to fight and had declared that nothing short of total victory would satisfy their war aims against Japan.

Herein lay the fundamental strategic conundrum that now faced the Japanese—how to force to the negotiating table an enemy who, although wounded, was both vastly more powerful in the long term, and in the short term had demonstrated a furious disinclination to bargain? Likewise, Japan had to grapple with the question of how to secure, once and for all, the economic underpinnings of its new empire against an enemy whose economy was not only much larger but also largely untouchable. Clear-cut as these problems may have been, the potential solution was far from obvious. In fact, it probably didn't exist. Having initiated the war with a surprise attack, it was almost certainly beyond her means to cajole the Americans to the table, no matter what military setbacks she subsequently foisted on her adversary. Given the lack of readily identifiable exit strategies, Admiral Yamamoto's answer—to continue offensive operations aimed at the destruction of the American fleet—was predictable, and yet ultimately empty.

Yamamoto was convinced that the best way to lure the American carriers out was to attack an objective the Americans could not relinquish without a fight. As related previously, his first notion had been to attack Hawaii directly.[45] But American strength on the Hawaiian Islands had ballooned since the time of December 7, and the seas and skies around them were now too heavily patrolled to allow a repeat visit from Nagumo on anything like the favorable terms he had achieved in December.[46] Yet, Yamamoto reasoned that an attack against an intermediate objective that placed Hawaii in danger would be met with a vigorous American response. At the same time, the objective needed to be outside the range of U.S. airpower stationed in Hawaii, thereby curtailing its ability to intervene directly in the battle.

The place of attack he selected was the island of Midway. Aptly named, it sat in the middle of the Pacific at the far tip of the Hawaiian chain, some 1,300 miles northwest of Oahu. On the face of it, Yamamoto's objective hardly seemed worth a good bar fight, let alone a decisive sea battle. Midway was a tiny atoll, composed of two islands—Sand and Eastern—surrounded by a coral reef. Both islands together comprised less than two square miles of real estate. Eastern Island, the smaller of the two, was almost totally covered by the three crisscrossing landing strips of an American airbase. Japanese intelligence estimated that fifty-odd aircraft were operating from it.[47] Sand Island held the majority of the shore facilities, barracks, and the new American seaplane base. This installation, which the Americans had completed just prior to the war at the then-staggering cost of $20 million dollars, hosted a number of Catalina PBY flying boats that patrolled the seas in all directions. However, given the diminutive size of Midway itself, there was little chance that the Americans could operate a very large air group there no matter how much money they poured into its facilities.

The value of Midway lay not in the intrinsic value of its facilities, but rather in its location. Capturing Midway would allow the Japanese to establish themselves within the Hawaiian Islands. Midway could theoretically be used as a springboard for future operations aimed at the conquest of Hawaii itself, although its practical value as an advanced base was limited. However, holding Midway would enable the Japanese to intercept American raiding forces operating in the empty expanse of waters north and west of the Hawaiian islands. It would also prevent the island being used by

2-3: Map exercise held by the staff of Naval General Headquarters, 1942. Admiral Nagano is visible second from left, Rear Admiral Fukudome is third from left (with mustache), Captain Tomioka is in direct center, next to the table and Fukudome. (Author's collection)

the Americans for attacks against Wake.[48] As such, Yamamoto reasoned that the Americans would be compelled to fight for it.

Given that the Naval General Staff was still behind the Fiji/Samoa option, and Combined Fleet supported the Central Pacific option, things were bound to come to a head once GHQ became aware of Yamamoto's rekindled intentions. A series of staff meetings in Tokyo during April 2–5, 1942, was the venue for the showdown between the two camps. The battle was fought by proxy, with both sides using staff officers to duke it out, while Yamamoto remained sequestered on board *Yamato* at Hashirajima.

At Naval GHQ, Yamamoto's errand boy, Captain Watanabe Yasuji, laid out Combined Fleet's proposal to the assembled officers. Yamamoto's scheme was immediately taken under fire by Admiral Fukudome's three top planners—Captain Tomioka and his two leading subordinates, Commanders Yamamoto Yūji and Miyo Tatsukichi. Commander Miyo, himself an air officer and classmate of Watanabe's from Staff College, was particularly well suited to commenting on Admiral Yamamoto's plan. He promptly meted out a withering criticism.

Miyo's critique was based on three fundamentally sound objections. The first was that in attempting to attack Midway, the Navy would be reversing the formula that had worked so well during the previous months. In the opening operations of the war, the Japanese had advanced under the cover of land-based airpower, quickly establishing themselves at captured bases and moving the air umbrella forward. In this new operation, though, they would be attacking across the Pacific without such support. By the same token, Midway was itself an outpost of a far-larger enemy bastion, Oahu, which could support it with relative ease. Midway was within range of American heavy bombers but was too far from Hawaii to allow Japanese fighter aircraft to extend their own sphere of influence over the main islands.

It is important to recall that at this stage in the development of naval aviation, conducting extended carrier operations in the face of enemy land-based airpower was infeasible. *Kidō Butai* couldn't stand off a hostile enemy base and hope to wear it down through attrition. This capability, the very definition of the true carrier task force, would not be created until later in the war when the U.S. Navy brought its vastly superior logistics capabilities to bear. *Kidō Butai,* although powerful, was a raiding force, and this is exactly how the Japanese understood its usage. Once Midway was captured, Nagumo would be forced to retire and replenish. At that point, Midway would be on its own, exposed to Hawaii-based air and sea power.

This led directly to the second point: even if Midway was captured, it was unlikely that it could be supported, particularly in the face of concerted enemy submarine attack. The Japanese merchant marine was already overtaxed. Japan had begun the war at a disadvantage in that many of her imports had previously been carried in either neutral or Allied ships. When war was declared, Japan in effect lost millions of tons' worth of shipping overnight. These difficulties were compounded by the need to support the military's troop transport missions, which pulled more tonnage out of service to the civilian economy. Unnecessarily impacting this already overstretched network was to be avoided at all costs.

The truth was that every mile that Japan's defensive perimeter expanded placed an additional *two* miles of burden on the nation's shipping, because ships not only had to go *out* to the newly captured base, but also had to *return*. Given that there was nothing on Midway even vaguely worth transporting home, those ships would return empty. Every mile traveled in ballast, of course, lowered the overall efficiency of Japan's merchant marine still further. As a result, shipping difficulties increased at a geometric rate in relation to the distance of the defensive perimeter from the Home Islands. Whether or not Miyo understood this problem in precisely this fashion is unlikely, but he and his fellow staff officers could tell instantly that keeping the island in supply would be exceedingly difficult.

Miyo also correctly pointed out that Midway itself was tiny, and could only support a small air group, thus mitigating its usefulness as an advance base to be used against the hundreds of American aircraft known to be on Hawaii.[49] Yet, even keeping a diminutive air group operating in the face of such opposition would be difficult. Midway was so small that dispersing aircraft would be impossible. This raised the specter of suffering outsized aircraft losses on the ground in the event of American bombing. Miyo knew that aircraft shortages were already a serious problem in the fleet—how did Yamamoto propose to keep Midway supplied with aircraft given the likely attrition rates it would suffer? In the same vein, Miyo doubted that sufficient aviation gasoline could be provided. Japan's stock of tankers was small, and most were already tied up supporting the fleet or transporting crude oil from the southern resource areas back to the Home Islands. Keeping aircraft operating on Midway would require a major logistics effort, a fact that Yamamoto's proposals ignored.

Miyo's third and final critique was that attacking Midway would not provoke the type of reaction from the Americans that Yamamoto blandly assumed. In Miyo's opinion, Midway was superfluous to the ultimate defense of Hawaii for the very reasons just laid out. The Americans could afford to cede their outlying outpost and then reclaim it whenever the Japanese logistical thread showed signs of fraying. In the meantime, Japan's ownership would not jeopardize Hawaii's position in the slightest. Why, Miyo asked, would the Americans react as violently as Yamamoto assumed they would over such an insignificant speck of land?

In Miyo's opinion, and that of the Naval General Staff, launching operations that severed American communications with Australia were far more likely to provoke the needed reaction. If the Americans were serious about using Australia as a base for future operations—and their recent commitment of carriers to this area indicated that this was so—they could not help but respond vigorously to any threat to its supply lines. Furthermore, a campaign in this region of the Pacific, while distant from Japan, would at least place an equal burden of distance on the Americans. Precipitating combat near Hawaii handed the Americans the advantage of fighting from interior lines.

It seems clear that Watanabe found himself in an unenviable position. Unable to counter Miyo's arguments, he was on the verge of angry tears.[50] The truth was that Miyo's critique was far better thought out than Yamamoto's plan. Despite being flustered, though, Watanabe refused to be lured into an argument against Miyo's well-reasoned objections. Instead, he simply restated Combined Fleet's position by rote, presenting its arguments as incontrovertible fact. This inability to engage Yamamoto's lackey in any form of rational discourse soured Tomioka and Miyo's moods still further.

In the end, under increasing pressure from GHQ, Watanabe was forced to appeal to his chief to intercede. Placing a call to *Yamato,* Watanabe asked Yamamoto to comment on Miyo's alternative proposal for actions in the southwest Pacific. Yamamoto replied that the most effective way of severing the American lines of communication was to destroy the means whereby these lines were maintained, namely, their carriers. He also argued that in the unlikely event that the Americans did not bite at Midway, Japan would win a bloodless victory there that extended the defensive perimeter outward.[51]

Yamamoto, in other words, was unmoved. Furthermore, the manner of his delivery, and his unflinching support for an aide who had just been logically dismembered made it clear that he was prepared, once again, to resign unless he got his way.[52] The Naval General Staff, having already lost this game once, was in a much worse position to call Yamamoto's bluff this time, particularly in light of Yamamoto's successes over the previous months. Predictably, when push came to shove, the Naval General Staff caved in once more. The men in a position to actually do something about Yamamoto's near insubordination—Fukudome and Nagano—apparently did nothing to defend their subordinates against what was, in essence, a coup against their own authority. Nagano thereupon grudgingly ratified Yamamoto's basic operational plan on 5 April.[53] All that remained now was for Yamamoto's staff to work out the details.

As one historian has noted, this was a disgraceful way of conducting a war.[54] Nagano and Fukudome had essentially ceded all responsibility for planning to Combined Fleet and had elevated Yamamoto's writ to law. No one was now in a position to challenge his authority. Yamamoto had also demonstrated precisely what sort of leader he was—one who ruled through intimidation rather than reason and who was not prepared to accept criticism.

However, Yamamoto's victory came at a price. In return for GHQ's grudging adoption of Midway as the objective of the next operation, Yamamoto was shortly forced to accede to first one, and later a second of the Naval Staff's demands. The first, which greatly affected Yamamoto's operational planning for his decisive battle, was an agreement to incorporate an attack on the Aleutian Islands into the overall scheme for June's operations.[55] The second concession, as we shall see shortly, would be a decision to support a limited incursion into the Southwest Pacific *prior to* the attack on Midway. Thus, a strategic formulation process that should have logically reached a final decision in favor of a unified strategy with a single near-term objective, in fact resulted in de facto support for *three* objectives in two theaters, none of which was mutually reinforcing. Nothing better illustrates the depths to which Japan's policymaking had sunk on the eve of its great battle.

An attack into the Aleutians had not originally been part of Yamamoto's vision. Rather, it was an idea that had been kicked around by lower-level officers within Army and Naval GHQ.[56] Capturing the Aleutians was seen as a means of forestalling U.S. offensives (both by air and naval forces) toward northern Japan. In Naval GHQ's conception, Operation AL would have been conducted at the very beginning of the second-phase operations, before any of the major offensives were opened. However, during the heated April exchanges, it was decided to attack both Midway *and* the Aleutians in early June. This was agreed to by Nagano on 5 April as well, and orders were issued to that effect on 16 April.[57] Thereafter, Yamamoto handed off the detailed planning to Captain Kuroshima.

The inclusion of the Aleutians widened the overall scope of planning enormously. The area of campaign now encompassed a trapezoidal area bounded on the north and south by the 1,500-mile lengths of both the Aleutian and Hawaiian island chains and spanning the 2,400-odd miles in between. This represented an area of nearly four million square miles, or roughly 2 percent of the surface area of the globe, most of it composed of the stormy waters of the North Pacific. It was an outsized battlefield, to say the least.

Even with the ambitious inclusion of the Aleutians into the overall scheme, follow-on operations against Hawaii had *not* been authorized, because Army ratification would be required for such an undertaking. Indeed, at this point, the Army had not yet even agreed to contribute forces to securing Midway, let alone the divisions that would have been required for Hawaii. Unfortunately for the long-suffering Captain Tomioka, now that Admirals Fukudome and Nagano had given their assent (thereby making it the *Navy's* plan, rather than just Combined Fleet's), it fell to *him* to sell the idea to the Army. Though he doubtless viewed the task ahead with a distaste bordering on nausea, on 12 April he dutifully met with General Tanaka.[58]

The meeting did not go well. The general was a sharp customer, and though Tomioka did his level best to deliver a version of the plan that would deflect criticism, Tanaka immediately realized that Midway necessitated a substantial enlargement of the defensive perimeter. More important, Tanaka correctly divined that capturing

Midway represented Combined Fleet's first step toward an eventual operation aimed at Hawaii. He was strongly opposed to both notions, even going so far as to declare that an Hawaiian invasion would undermine the empire's entire war effort.[59] In the end, Tanaka flatly refused to contribute troops to either Midway or the Aleutians.

Despite this rather sharp dismissal, Tomioka had little choice but to proceed with the wholesale gulping down of Yamamoto's plans, culminating in his penning a naval staff document entitled "Imperial Navy Operational Plans for Stage Two of the Great East Asia War." Within its pages, the notion of an operation aimed at the Indian Ocean was officially relegated to secondary status. An advance against Fiji and Samoa was dropped altogether (although only for the moment, as we shall see). In lieu of Army forces, naval landing troops would be employed against Midway.[60] After the seizure of Midway, Johnston and Palmyra would be taken, setting up an invasion of Hawaii. Despite Tanaka's rebuff, the Navy's plan optimistically anticipated that this operation would be launched in cooperation with the Army. It was this plan that Admiral Nagano personally submitted to the emperor on 16 April. Also present was General Sugiyama Gen, the Army's chief of staff, who raised no objections. Perhaps he was waiting for a more opportune time to make the Army's counterarguments. As events were to prove, though, this was the Army's last opportunity to stop the forthcoming operation. Just two days after the audience with the emperor, the Americans would seal Yamamoto's political victory.

3

Plans

To all outward appearances, during the first four months of 1942 the Americans were losing the war in the Pacific in a truly spectacular fashion. The raid on Pearl Harbor had shaken the self-confidence of the U.S. Navy to its foundations. America's battleship force—the core of its naval power for decades—had been crippled at the outset, meaning that there was no hope of defending the Philippines when the Japanese simultaneously launched operations there. Nor could it do more than offer token forces to the defense of Java and Sumatra. The Americans were forced to watch as the Japanese offensive unfolded with a speed and precision that no one had thought possible. If the U.S. Navy's material losses had been, in absolute terms, marginal to its overall strength, the blows to its pride had been real enough.

By April the strategic position of the Allies in the Pacific had been reduced to a shambles. Java and Sumatra had fallen, with almost the entire U.S. Asiatic squadron destroyed in the process. The Japanese were now in a position to threaten Australia directly. The Philippines were completely isolated, and the bulk of General Douglas MacArthur's forces there, though gallant, would surrender on 9 April.[1] Malaya and Burma had fallen under the aggressor's boot, and the British would shortly find India directly threatened as well. The picture was one of utter calamity. However, the disasters of the previous four months had resulted in several key realizations on the part of the Americans.

First, it was clear that the battleship was no longer a weapon of decision. If the war was to be won, America would have to rely on aircraft carriers for power projection and submarines for destruction of enemy shipping. For the U.S. Navy, this was a simple matter of finding virtue in necessity. The preservation and augmentation of its carriers, and the destruction of the enemy's, were the overriding goals of the U.S. Navy from the time the smoke cleared over Pearl Harbor.

Second, if a successful defense against the Japanese was to be made, it would hinge primarily on the abilities of the U.S. military. The tiny Dutch forces had been annihilated. More important, British strength had evaporated to the point that the Royal Navy was in no position to leave the Indian Ocean, even in direct defense of Australia and New Zealand. This was a shocking state of affairs, but the weakness of Britain's position was plain for all to see. For their part, Australia and New Zealand, though possessed of first-rate militaries, had neither the population nor the economic basis to guarantee their own defense, let alone carry the war to Japan. If the war in the Pacific was to be won, the United States would have to shoulder the majority of the burden.

Third, in light of these considerations, it was vital that the Americans immediately guarantee the security of those Pacific bases that were essential to the long-term prosecution of the war. In an immediate sense, these were Pearl Harbor and the Panama Canal. The loss of either would have been catastrophic. The Panama Canal was so remote that its outright capture was almost inconceivable, and hence it required little garrisoning. Hawaii was quite another matter, however, and the Americans moved quickly after 7 December to beef up Oahu's defenses, as well as those at outlying bases such as Johnston Island and Midway. By April of 1942, the garrison in Hawaii had already increased to nearly 70,000 combatants (up from about 30,000 in October 1941), and was projected to grow to 115,000 in short order.[2] If not absolutely guaranteeing the security of the islands, the size of the American garrison certainly presented the Japanese with formidable obstacles to conquest.

However, by the same token, if the United States was ultimately to be successful in carrying the war to the enemy, Australia had to be defended as well. By February the Japanese were already threatening its northern frontiers. Worse yet, several of the Aussie's splendid infantry divisions were still deployed in the Middle East with the British Army. At this critical juncture, President Franklin D. Roosevelt had personally assured Australia's prime minister, John Curtin, that at least one division of American troops, and perhaps more, would be sent to ensure Australia's security.

Such a promise was logical, but it generated additional requirements beyond the direct commitment of American forces. To support ground troops, it would also be necessary to defend the communications lines to Australia. This meant that several important island groups—including the Fijis, New Caledonia, and Samoa—would need to be fortified more strongly. The Australian and New Zealand garrisons already in these areas were pitifully understrength. Accordingly, the Americans lost little time in scrambling to send substantial combat contingents to these potential hot spots.

Thus, the Americans in short order found themselves moving regiments and divisions to places that many U.S. officers wouldn't have been able to find on a map just six months earlier. This led directly to the fourth American realization—if the Pacific was to be defended, the notion of a "Germany First" strategy had to be flexible enough to accommodate the immediate needs of the Pacific. In practical terms, this meant that the prevailing notion of an invasion of the European continent as early as mid-1942 had to be put on ice. In hindsight, attacking Germany directly in 1942 was completely unrealistic in any case. Nevertheless, this temporary reordering of military priorities in favor of the Pacific represented a dramatic modification of prewar strategy.

The man upon whom command in the Pacific fell was Admiral Chester W. Nimitz, commander in chief of the Pacific Fleet. Nimitz had taken charge on 31 December 1941, after the disgraced Admiral Husband E. Kimmel had been relieved following the attack on Pearl Harbor. Nimitz was by all accounts an excellent officer. Instead of sacking Kimmel's staff, his first act was to retain them amid assurances of his utter confidence in their abilities. This had the effect of steadying the morale of a command that had been badly shaken. Likewise, the new commander in chief was a sound judge of men, knowing who to promote and who to lateral into positions that

3-1: Admiral Chester W. Nimitz. Shrewd and insightful, Nimitz provided the U.S. Pacific Fleet with a winning combination of calculation and boldness. (Photo courtesy John Lundstrom)

better fit their abilities. He delegated authority easily and knew how to get the best out of his subordinates. Levelheaded, Nimitz was apparently immune to panic and retained at all times a shrewd ability to assess odds and likely outcomes. His calculating nature was complemented, though, with boldness and an aggressive spirit. Nimitz was determined to destroy the main force of the Japanese Navy as soon as was practical, and he knew that his carriers would be the centerpiece of any such action. Even in the face of the near hysteria of the early war months, when the exploits of Japan's warriors had given them the aura of invincibility, Nimitz was confident that his sailors and aviators were fully the equal of their opponents.

For the moment, though, Nimitz had little choice but to react to Japanese moves. He did not yet have anything resembling the material preponderance that he would need to win the war. He was outnumbered in fleet carriers, the *Saratoga* having been heavily damaged in January by an enemy submarine. The newer, but smaller *Wasp* was still in the Atlantic. This left four carriers—*Saratoga's* sistership, *Lexington,* and the

Enterprise, Yorktown, and their newly commissioned sistership, *Hornet,* which had just reached the Pacific in March.

Throughout the first months of the war, Nimitz gamely employed his carriers in a series of raids against exposed enemy outposts. Although these minor actions had little material impact on the war, they did have the positive effect of hardening the American carrier air groups. However, by April, reacting to pressure from Washington that the Navy do something positive to boost the morale of the American public, two of Nimitz's carriers participated in a far more audacious carrier raid, one that ultimately produced outsized results.

On the morning of 18 April, just two days after Admiral Nagano had presented the Midway plan to the emperor, sixteen American twin-engined medium bombers appeared as if by magic over Tokyo and half a dozen other cities. Commanded by Army Air Force Lieutenant Colonel James Doolittle, these aircraft had been launched some 400 miles off of the Japanese coastline by the carrier *Hornet.* She, along with her consort *Enterprise,* had penetrated the Japanese defensive lines in much the same way that Japan had opened the war against the United States—by traversing the desolate wastes of the northern Pacific.

Given the scarcity of carriers, Admiral Nimitz had been reluctant to authorize such an operation. But he had no choice but to comply with his superiors' wishes and ordered the newly arrived *Hornet* to participate. At Alameda Air Station in California, *Hornet* had duly stowed Doolittle's B-25s on the after end of her flight deck and then set off directly across the Pacific for what the majority of her sailors thought was an aircraft ferrying mission. It was only after being joined by Vice Admiral William F. Halsey Jr.'s *Enterprise* in mid-ocean that the nature of the mission was fully revealed.

Such a raid had not been unanticipated by the Imperial Navy—Ugaki had remarked on the danger of such attacks in his diary as early as 2 February, 1942.[3] To safeguard against these threats, the Japanese had placed a ring of picket boats 700 miles off the shore of the Home Islands to detect the approach of enemy task forces. A pair of these sentinels had, in fact, sighted the American task force in time to warn Tokyo before being sunk by the Americans. However, the Japanese had not anticipated the American innovation of using longer-ranged Army bombers launched from a carrier. Normally, an enemy flattop would have been obligated to close to within about 200 miles (the extreme range of U.S. carrier-based aircraft) in order to attack. Upon being sighted, however, the Americans had simply let fly with their B-25s and then promptly headed for the exits.

The Imperial Navy tried to redeem the situation. Coincidentally, Nagumo and his five carriers were making their way back to Japan from their raids against Ceylon when Doolittle attacked, and *Akagi, Sōryū,* and *Hiryū* were sent charging eastward from Mako (Taiwan) in pursuit of the American flattops. But the Americans were not waiting around to receive Japanese retribution for their insolence. *Akagi* and company had found nothing but empty ocean and were obliged to return to Hashirajima empty-handed.

Strictly speaking, the military results of the Doolittle raid were so minimal as to be laughable—a few bombs sprinkled in desultory fashion over various targets and the light carrier *Ryūhō* slightly damaged on the building ways in Yokosuka. But the psychological impact of the attack was enormous. Admiral Nagano, having personally heard the explosions in Tokyo, reacted to news of the attack with stunned disbelief, muttering, "This shouldn't happen. This just should not happen."[4] Yamamoto took ill and retreated to his cabin for an entire day.[5] Like all the Navy's upper command, he felt a deep obligation to safeguard the nation from attack. More particularly, the thought that the emperor had been personally endangered filled Yamamoto with an unquenchable remorse. He knew, and his peers knew, that such a raid could never have materialized if the American carriers had been sunk outright in Hawaii at the beginning of the war. The fact that not a single American plane had been brought down by Japanese defenses only made the whole episode even more mortifying.

This American pinprick had the effect of cementing the strategic debate in favor of Yamamoto and winning the Army over regarding operations in the Central Pacific. Until the American carriers were safely in their graves, the homeland could never be completely protected from their attacks. After April 18, their destruction had been raised to the status of an axiomatic good.

The day after Doolittle's raid, General Tanaka privately told Captain Tomioka that he was rethinking his reservations regarding Operation MI.[6] On the 20th, Tanaka not only formally approved of Operation MI, but also committed the Army to supplying troops for the assault.[7] Even more intriguing, he informally asked Tomioka for more details on "Eastern Operation," which marked something of a watershed in the Army's appreciation for the scheme. The Army initially assented to Operation MI on the explicit understanding that it not be dragged into operations aimed at Hawaii.[8] However, within a month, the Army had done an about-face on this matter, too. On 25 May, just days before the Nagumo force was slated to sail for Midway, the Army issued orders to several units to begin preparing for an amphibious attack against Hawaii. Training for the assault was to be completed by the end of September.[9] Thus, against great odds, Yamamoto had achieved his goal—operations in the Central Pacific aimed at the destruction of the American fleet and the subsequent capture of Hawaii.

It is necessary now to turn to an examination of Yamamoto's operational plan as it emerged in its final form, a task for which the reader would be well advised to pour a rather tall glass of spirits beforehand. The first order of business involves clarifying the exact relationship between the operations aimed at the Aleutians (AL) and those centered on Midway (MI). Western accounts of the battle have generally characterized Operational AL as being an elaborate diversion in support of Operation MI.[10] According to this interpretation, AL was designed to lure the U.S. fleet out of Pearl Harbor such that it could be intercepted and engaged north of Hawaii as it moved to relieve the Aleutians. However, this rendering of Japanese intentions is incorrect. In fact, Operation AL was an entirely separate endeavor that was never designed to impact the conduct of operations around Midway.

The debunking of the "diversion" myth is supported by numerous Japanese sources. Prominent among these are a pair of monographs prepared by Japanese naval officers for the Military History Section of U.S. Army Forces Far East immediately after the war.[11] According to one of these reports, the April 5 compromise between Nagano and Yamamoto led to "a revision of the [operational] plan to allow for conducting the Midway and Aleutian Invasions *simultaneously* in early June [emphasis added]."[12] The second monograph confirms that Operation MI was to be carried out "nearly simultaneously with the Aleutians Operation."[13] In neither of these monographs is mention made of Operation AL being a feint or diversion to be launched before Operation MI or of its being intended to draw the Americans north out of Pearl Harbor. It's worth noting, too, that the main battleship groups for the two operations—Yamamoto's Main Body and Takasu's Guard Force—sortied *together* from Hashirajima and simply diverged thereafter.

Admiral Nagumo's official report on the battle similarly makes no mention of the Aleutians operations being a diversion. Indeed, it doesn't describe the Aleutians as being related to the action off Midway in any way whatsoever. Similarly, the postwar interview of Commander Watanabe Yasuji—Yamamoto's staff officer—is completely silent on the topic.[14] One would have supposed that such a prominent feature of the plan would have been pointed out by Watanabe, making this omission curious indeed. The interview of Admiral Nagano as well (despite Nagano's spurious disavowal of his staff's role in creating the Aleutians operational concept) makes no mention of AL being a diversion. Watanabe and Nagano, of course, were both present at the 2–5 April staff discussions that led to Operation AL's incorporation into the overall battle plan and were clearly in a position to have pointed out this facet of the operations.

The second objection to be raised is simply one of common sense. For a diversion to have lured the Americans from Pearl Harbor, an attack in the Aleutians would have needed to take place not one, but several days before the Japanese showed their hand at Midway. This was absolutely necessary in order to give the U.S. fleet time to react to the perceived threat and begin steaming north to the Aleutians. Even had they responded quickly, on only a day's notice, the Americans would still have been well south of Midway when Nagumo attacked. Indeed, as will be shown, Yamamoto never considered that the enemy would move directly north toward the Aleutians. Rather, he envisioned U.S. forces sailing *west* from Oahu and then giving battle to the southwest of Midway.[15] This was hardly the course of action one would expect of a force being deliberately lured toward the Aleutians.

The final piece of the puzzle is to be found in the Japanese official war history. In its final form, Yamamoto's plans all fundamentally revolved around "N-day," 7 June (Tokyo time, 6 June local), when Midway was to be invaded and captured.[16] As mentioned, offensive operations would open several days beforehand, on day N-3 (4 June Tokyo, 3 June local). On this day, as set forth in the *original* Japanese plan of operations, Dutch Harbor and Midway were *both* to have been attacked.[17] Indeed, this was the plan up until shortly before Nagumo actually sailed.[18] Thus, the idea of the Aleutians being a feint is clearly untrue.

For the most part, Operation AL was simply an expedient landgrab, to be executed while the U.S. Pacific Fleet was busy elsewhere. Its goal was to push Japan's defensive perimeter outward. More precisely, AL's object was "to capture or demolish points of strategical [*sic*] value on [the] western Aleutian Islands in order to check the enemy's air and ship maneuvers in this area."[19] By doing so, air and surface patrols "would provide a perfect shielding opportunity for Japan. . . . Potential incursion from the north, and communication links between the United States and Russia would then be obstructed." This latter was a very important point, given the quantity of American supplies being sent to Russia via the Barents Sea. Furthermore, Japanese possession of the Aleutians was "conceived as a flanking movement to protect . . . Midway from a possible attack from the north," once the island was secured.[20]

It is clear from the foregoing that the Japanese held an exaggerated opinion of the utility of the Aleutians as a possible path for launching either an invasion or strategic bombing attacks against the homeland. The weather conditions in the Aleutians (as the Japanese were shortly to discover) were routinely awful. The islands themselves—small, mountainous, and devoid of any ground cover or building materials—made the archipelago useless for staging any offensive action larger than an occasional narwhal hunt. Yet, such were the defensive goals with which the Japanese went forth.

The second major clarification regarding AL regards how it was to unfold. Despite being almost a sideshow in comparison to the operations off Midway, Operation AL's order of battle was perhaps more complex than that of Operation MI. Yamamoto's plan considered three distinct phases of operation, each of which anticipated major reshufflings of the naval formations involved. This has the effect of greatly complicating any discussion of the anticipated movements of warships during the operation. The three phases, known as "Distributions," were detailed in Northern Naval Force Order No. 24, issued on 20 May.[21] Their goals and timing were as follows:

- The First Distribution encompassed the initial approach to the objective and operations up to the point where the immediate landing objectives were achieved (i.e., approximately 8 June, 1942).
- The Second Distribution pertained to operations designed to consolidate Japan's hold on the area and would continue until such time as the threat of counterattack by the enemy had been largely nullified.
- The Third Distribution defined reallocation of ships to guard the northern area. This was to be in effect by 20 June, 1942.[22]

The three Distributions, and their effects on the forces assigned to Operation AL, are described in tabular format in Appendix 11.

Yamamoto envisioned opening Operation AL with an attack on Dutch Harbor on 4 June (three days before the planned invasion of Midway itself). This would nullify American naval and airpower at their only major base proximate to the western end of the Aleutians archipelago. Attacks would continue as needed, followed by landings on the islands of Kiska and Adak on the 6th. An optional landing on Attu was scheduled for the 12th. The landing at Adak was to be temporary, lasting only as long as it took to destroy the American facilities that were feared to be there. Although the capture of Dutch Harbor was not contemplated at this time, the Japanese felt it was important to secure bases from which patrols could be mounted against it. Doing so would forestall the feared development of Dutch Harbor as an air and submarine base that threatened the north Pacific.

To accomplish these aims, an Army force of 1,143 troops was slated to land on Attu and Adak, carried by a single transport. Guarding it would be light cruiser *Abukuma,* four destroyers, and a minelayer. Meanwhile, Kiska would be assaulted by 550 troops from the Navy's Maizuru Third Special Pioneer Force (known in the West as Special Naval Landing Forces, or SNLF), accompanied by a construction battalion.

The Navy troops were to be carried in two transports guarded by the light cruisers *Kiso* and *Tama* and three destroyers, accompanied by an armed merchant cruiser and three minesweepers.[23]

Overall command of the Aleutians operation was to be vested in Vice Admiral Hosogaya Moshiro's Northern Force Main Body, which during the First Distribution would consist of heavy cruiser *Nachi,* two destroyers, two oilers, and three supply ships. Also under Hosogaya's control was Rear Admiral Yamazaki Shigeaki's force of six submarines, which were to scout ahead of the landing forces and screen the surface forces behind them.

The real striking power of the Aleutians operation was centered on Rear Admiral Kakuta Kakuji's Second Mobile Striking Force. *Dai-ni Kidō Butai* bore little resemblance to its more illustrious cousin. It consisted of Carrier Division 4 (hereafter CarDiv 4), composed of the converted carrier *Junyō* (which had just been commissioned) and the light carrier *Ryūjō.* They were an odd pair. *Junyō* was larger and had better aircraft-handling facilities, but she was hampered by her low speed of twenty-five knots. This meant that she was not considered capable of operating torpedo aircraft, because in light wind conditions she wasn't fast enough to create the relative wind over her bow necessary to launch them. Kakuta's flagship, *Ryūjō,* was faster, but she was plagued by small elevators, meaning that she could not operate the burly Type 99 dive-bomber.[24] Thus, neither of these ships was as useful as a true fleet carrier alone, and they were only marginally more useful in tandem. Kakuta's command was filled out by heavy cruisers *Takao* and *Maya,* three destroyers, and an oiler.

A small independent Seaplane Force, composed of the seaplane tender *Kimikawa Maru* and a destroyer, was responsible for cooperating with the landing operations as well as locating enemy ships.[25] In a similar vein, the 22nd Picket Boat Squadron would provide a defensive perimeter around the operation. The Aleutians Base Air Force, consisting of four transports and six large Type 97 flying boats from the *Tōkō* air group, would provide scouting support.

In distant support of Kakuta's force was the Aleutians Screening Force under Vice Admiral Takasu Shirō, who hoisted his flag on battleship *Hyūga.* The core of his force was BatDiv 2, composed of *Hyūga*'s sistership, *Ise,* and the dowager battleships *Fusō* and *Yamashiro.* These were the four oldest battlewagons in Japan's inventory and were roughly equivalent to the aged American battleships sunk at Pearl Harbor. Screening these heavy units were light cruisers *Kitakami* and *Ōi* and twelve destroyers. Two oilers accompanied them. However, Takasu's dreadnoughts were not officially part of Operation AL and were only mentioned tangentially in the original Japanese planning documents. They would sail with Yamamoto's Main Body and thereafter place themselves in a position to provide support to the Aleutians forces if "events warranted."[26]

Once the Aleutians were captured, the Second Distribution would bring about a large-scale reshuffling of Japan's warships. The Attu-Adak and Kiska invasion force would be dissolved and its vessels incorporated into other formations, notably the Main Body. This beefed-up unit would be retained for "support of the entire Aleutian Operation."[27] Meanwhile, Kakuta's Second Mobile Striking Force would be augmented by light carrier *Zuihō* and a quartet of destroyers drawn from the various Midway forces. Kakuta's goal remained the same—the annihilation of any American vessels encountered. In support of this, the Submarine Force would be more than doubled by the addition of another seven boats that had been under maintenance in Japan at the time the operational orders were issued (20 May). The Seaplane Group, reinforced with *Kamikawa Maru* (again drawn from the Midway forces), would continue its scouting mission, as would the Base Air Force.[28] On both Kiska and Attu, the land forces would begin deploying for defense.[29]

The Third Distribution anticipated yet another major reshuffling, aimed at the long-term defense of the newly won territories. The Main Body would be reduced, though its support-oriented mission would remain. Two new support formations would be formed, each centered on a pair of fast battleships from the BatDiv 3 and augmented by heavy cruisers and destroyers, in many cases newly released from the forces clustered around Midway. At the same time, Kakuta's Second Mobile Striking Force would be heavily reinforced and divided into two separate raiding groups. The first group would essentially consist of the forces he had begun the battle with— CarDiv 4 and their escorts. Meanwhile, *Zuihō* would be split off into the 2nd Raiding Group, joined by the *Zuikaku,* which was expected to be ready for operations by this time.[30] Both raiding groups were to be under Kakuta's overall command. However, no specific missions for either group were defined, and it is difficult to see what these forces would have been able to accomplish in such latitudes.

Operation AL's three Distributions ultimately expected to call on the services of more than eighty vessels at one time or another, including eight battleships out of the Imperial Navy's inventory of eleven, four of her eleven carriers, and thirteen submarines. By itself, the Aleutians plan represented a larger commitment of forces than any operation the Japanese had embarked on thus far in the war. Far from being a sideshow, AL actually represented a sizable drain on the Imperial Navy's already-scarce resources.

It is interesting to note that nowhere in the Aleutians battle plan was there apparently any provision for Kakuta's Second Striking Force to be in any position to support Nagumo's operations to the south after its initial attacks against Dutch Harbor were concluded. If anything, the flow of forces was in reverse, in that many of the vessels slated for inclusion in AL's later phases were to come directly from the Midway forces. Indeed, some of them, including four destroyers from Nagumo's own screen, were scheduled to arrive soon after 8 June. Presumably these vessels would be detached and head northward immediately after the conclusion of operations in the vicinity of Midway.

All in all, Operation AL reflected the larger problems inherent in Yamamoto's battle plan. It anticipated using widely separated forces and putting a great number of warships into northern waters, many of which weren't accomplishing anything terribly important. At the same time, AL's force structure for its later Distributions actually anticipated siphoning off units that were being used near Midway, which was ostensibly the center of strategic gravity in the entire Pacific Ocean. These requirements directly contributed to the clockwork rigidity of the planning for Operation MI itself. It is difficult to escape the conclusion that all the time and energy that went into Operation AL might have been better spent focusing on operations to the south. Operation AL's flaws, though, paled in comparison to the errors Yamamoto would commit in his schemes aimed at Midway.

Operation MI would begin at the same time that Kakuta opened his attacks on Dutch Harbor: N-3 day (4 June Tokyo time, 3 June local). Nagumo's force—six fleet carriers (CarDivs 1, 2, and 5), two fast battleships from BatDiv 3, two heavy cruisers, and eleven destroyers with their light cruiser flotilla leader—would approach Midway from the northwest. On the morning of the 4th (Tokyo time), *Dai-ichi Kidō Butai* would be in position to strike. It was believed that a single attack would be sufficient to destroy the American airbase and its aircraft.[31] The Japanese presumed that they would have the element of strategic and tactical surprise on their side, because offensive activities would be opened concurrently with Operation AL. Thus, Nagumo's carriers would simply sweep in unannounced and deliver a death blow against American airpower on the island.

Day N-2 (5/4 June) would see additional air strikes, with the Japanese turning their attention toward reducing the island's defenses in preparation for the coming amphibious operation. While it was understood that Nagumo would have to deal with any American carriers that ventured north from Pearl Harbor to contest the Midway invasion, it was anticipated that the Americans would not be able to steam the distance between Hawaii and Midway in any less than three days. This being the case, Nagumo would only have to attend to one thing at a time. Nagumo's force would also use ten of its Type 97 carrier attack planes for scouting purposes. Each of these aircraft would search out to a range of 400 miles to help provide early warning of the American fleet.[32]

Ground operations would begin on the morning of N-1 day (6/5 June). The Japanese would land on Kure Island, a tiny islet sixty miles west of Midway. Rear Admiral Fujita Ryūtaro's Seaplane Tender Group would secure this objective with a small contingent of troops. It was then to be put into operation as a seaplane base for use against Midway itself. On the morning of N-Day (7/6 June), Midway would be assaulted by a mixed group of both Navy and Army units. The landing would be carried out by barge, known in the Imperial Navy as *Daihatsu,* each of which could carry about 100 soldiers as far as the reef.[33] From there, the men would have to wade the remaining 200 or more yards, through the lagoon, and onto the beaches by foot. The Navy's 2nd Combined SNLF, consisting of some 1,500 soldiers, would be landed on Sand Island. Eastern Island would be invaded by the 1,000 men of Colonel Ichiki Kiyonao's regiment, named the Ichiki Detachment after its commander. Both forces would be landed on the southern shores of the islands, where the reef was less of an obstacle to amphibious movements.[34] An additional landing on Sand Island's northwest corner was also planned, if necessary.

Accompanying the combat troops were two construction battalions (some of which were equipped with American construction material captured at Wake Island) and other auxiliary personnel necessary to repair Midway and turn it into a frontline air base, bringing the total ground forces to over 5,000. The transports would also be hauling along ninety-four cannon, forty machine guns, six Type A midget submarines, five motor torpedo boats, and all the accoutrements to develop Midway into a major outpost. Additional midget submarines, as well as land-based torpedo tubes and a dozen 20-cm guns, were slated for delivery in mid-June.[35]

In a fashion that was typical of Japan's interservice cooperation, the Army troops would sail separately from Yokosuka, while the SNLF troops would sail from Kure. Both the Army and Navy had their own separate transports, and neither service was willing to accommodate the other aboard their own ships. Both private fleets would rendezvous at Saipan and thereafter would sail together under the command of Rear Admiral Tanaka Raizo's Transport Group. This force consisted of the light cruiser *Jintsū*, ten destroyers, three patrol boats, twelve transports, and several oilers.

In relative proximity to Tanaka would sail Vice Admiral Kurita Takeo's Close Support Group, which was centered on the four powerful heavy cruisers of CruDiv 7—*Kumano, Suzuya, Mikuma,* and *Mogami*. This quartet's forty eight-inch guns were to provide fire support for the landing. However, the Imperial Navy's raison d'étre was engaging enemy warships, not supporting landings. The Navy had never spent much time developing any sort of formal approach for spotting and coordinating gunfire ashore for troops. In hindsight, there is a very real question as to how effective CruDiv 7 would have proved to be in this role had it actually been put to the test. Kurita was accompanied by two destroyers and an oiler. Also near to hand, but sailing separately, was a minesweeper group consisting of three minesweepers, three subchasers, and an ammunition ship.

Somewhat farther away would be the Invasion Force Main Body, under the command of Vice Admiral Kondō Nobutake. It consisted of the other two members of BatDiv 3—*Hiei* and *Kongō*—under Rear Admiral Mikawa Gun'ichi. Four heavy cruisers—*Atago, Chōkai, Haguro,* and *Myōkō*—also accompanied the force. The screen for this powerful unit was commanded by Rear Admiral Nishimura Shōji aboard the light cruiser *Yura*, which led seven destroyers. Also included in this group was the fine new light carrier *Zuihō* and her plane guard destroyer. All three of these formations—Tanaka's, Kondō's, and Kurita's—were to approach Midway from the west-southwest.

Midway was scheduled for capture on the 5th (local time), leaving a day for the base to be put back into operation in advance of the expected sea battle with the Americans. During this time, Nagumo's carriers would be supporting the invasion and simultaneously moving to the northeast of the island in preparation for the naval battle. His force was expected to be in position to support Kondō from the north-northwest by the end of the 6th. Kondō, for his part, would keep his battleships ready to deliver backup fire support against Midway if stiff resistance was encountered.[36]

The backstop to both Kondō's and Nagumo's forces was Yamamoto himself and his Main Body. Centered on BatDiv 1—*Yamato, Nagato,* and *Mutsu*—this force contained the largest guns in the fleet. It was to follow behind Nagumo during the initial phase of the operation. Within this force would be several smaller formations that could maneuver independently if need be. One of them, the Special Group, consisting of seaplane tenders *Chiyoda* and *Nisshin*, which were carrying midget submarines and motor torpedo boats, respectively, to reinforce Midway once it was captured. The second special formation, the Carrier Group, consisted of the ancient light carrier *Hōshō*. Around all of the elements of the Main Force would be Rear

Admiral Hashimoto Shintaro's Screening Force, consisting of light cruiser *Sendai* and eight destroyers. Three oilers accompanied the group. Once Midway was secured, the Main Body would be in position to support Kondō should the need arise.

It was strongly believed that after six months of war, the Americans were now sufficiently weakened and demoralized that they would only sortie from Pearl Harbor with some coaxing.[37] Kondō was the bait. Among other things, his flotilla contained a pair of capital ships (*Hiei* and *Kongō*), which made it a force worth attacking. At the same time, his two battleships were fast enough to extricate themselves from trouble if need be. Yamamoto apparently did not want to tip his hand by revealing his Main Body too soon, in the belief that such a massive array of firepower would induce the Americans to stay home. In other words, Yamamoto's dispersal of forces was purely an attempt at deception—his killing force would not enter scouting range of Midway until after the Americans had themselves sortied from Pearl. In a way, his plan was almost reminiscent of the usage of cruiser forces by both the German High Seas Fleet and the Royal Navy in World War I to lure the enemy into range of the main battle squadrons.

Not surprisingly, having current intelligence on the American units that would presumably be walking into the trap was crucial to the operation's success. Yamamoto would be aided in these efforts by a special mission designed to assess the status of the American fleet at Pearl Harbor. Referred to as Operation K, the Japanese would employ flying boats operating out of the islands of Jaluit and Wotje to overfly the American fleet base on 31 May, just before the commencement of the fleet actions.[38] Kawanishi Type 2 four-engined flying boats had performed this same mission twice before in early March. On the first occasion, a heavy overcast on 3–4 March had made reconnaissance impossible. During the second, on 9–10 March, American fighters from Midway had intercepted and destroyed the Japanese plane. Yet, despite the negative results from these two missions, not to mention the evidence that this particular gimmick might be wearing a bit thin, Yamamoto didn't waver from trying a third time.

The catch to Operation K was that no Japanese aircraft, even the big Kawanishis, had the range to fly all the way to Pearl Harbor and back without refueling. A flying boat, however, could make good this deficiency by stopping at some secluded place along the way to refuel. The chosen stopover had been an uninhabited islet known as French Frigate Shoals, which lay between Midway and Hawaii. In March, the Navy had used a submarine there to refuel the Kawanishis, which then proceeded to Hawaii. The same approach was to be used again on 31 May.

In addition to aerial reconnaissance, two picket lines of submarines would be positioned across the presumed line of advance of the Americans. The southern cordon ("A"), and northern cordon ("B"), were each composed of seven fleet boats. However, the submarines of both groups were assigned fixed positions, rather than being placed in patrol boxes in which they could operate freely. Worse, the patrol lines did not have overlapping fields of vision, making them porous indeed. This static mode of employment (which was typical of Japanese submarine operations throughout the war) meant that the big Imperial Navy boats could not be concentrated on enemy units with anything like the flexibility that the Germans were currently employing in the Atlantic.[39]

The decisive battle, as Yamamoto envisioned it, would be fought somewhere off Midway, with the main Japanese forces arrayed so as to intercept the oncoming Americans. After pounding Midway, Nagumo would withdraw and wait some five hundred miles north-northeast of Midway, with Yamamoto's Main Body supporting him three hundred miles to the west.[40] Takasu's battleship force would come down from its position in the north Pacific to hover five hundred miles north of Yamamoto. Second Mobile Striking Force, with its two carriers, would perform a similar maneuver to position itself three hundred miles to the east of Takasu. Kondō's force would supply the bait to draw the Americans out of hiding at Pearl Harbor and lure them north, with the Japanese heavy forces lurking out of range of American reconnaissance aircraft and submarines.

If all went according to plan, the Americans would appear off Midway after the landings had taken place. Yamamoto presumed that the Americans would sortie west from Oahu and then head north so as to be able to ambush the exposed Kondō as he trailed his coat near the island. Interestingly, it appears that Combined Fleet's opinion was that the Americans would bring not only their carriers, but also their few remaining battleships to the fray.[41] It was further assumed that the carriers would operate separately from their battleship-centric Main Body, screening them from the west-northwest. This was a fairly doctrinaire interpretation of how the Americans would maneuver their forces, with the carriers presumably governed by the movements of the slower battleship force operating in the rear. In other words, it assumed that the Americans thought their battle squadrons were capable of making a meaningful contribution to a modern carrier battle, as Yamamoto believed his own could.

In this, the Japanese were projecting their own beliefs on their opponent, a classic failing of many military plans. Having manufactured roles for their own battleships, the Japanese believed that the enemy would do likewise. However, what the Japanese couldn't know was that the Americans had by now totally discarded the idea of using their older battlewagons in conjunction with fast carriers. Yamamoto had only himself to blame for this radical transformation of American naval thought, as his triumph at Pearl Harbor had demonstrated unequivocally to his enemies the total vulnerability of such forces in the face of modern airpower.

Once the Americans were detected, Takasu's battle group would move south to join Yamamoto. On the eastern flank, Nagumo would move south to engage the American fleet as well. It was expected that attrition from the submarines, coupled with air strikes from the carriers, would weaken the Americans sufficiently that they could be engaged and annihilated by the Japanese battleships. In a sense, Yamamoto's plan represented a curious reversion to a more gunpower-oriented philosophy, relegating Nagumo's carriers to an attritional role on par with the submarine force.

Taken together, Operations AL and MI represented the commitment of almost the entirety of the Imperial Japanese Navy—all of its carriers, all of its battleships, all but four of its heavy cruisers, and the bulk of its lesser combatants. Twenty-eight admirals would lead these forces into battle, and they would log more miles and consume more fuel in this single operation than was normally used in an entire year.[42]

It was planned that once the battle was won, Nagumo's carriers would retire to Truk between 16 and 20 June.[43] The battleships would return to home waters, or head north to assist Operation AL. Thereafter, operations would be launched to consolidate the fruits of victory. Truk would be the jumping-off location for further planned incursions into the southwest Pacific, with New Caledonia, Fiji, and Samoa slated for occupation in July. In other words, in the interval between 5 April, when Admiral Nagano had acceded to Yamamoto's plans (and the Southwest Pacific had been ostensibly removed from consideration), and early May (when the detailed battle plan was to be war-gamed), Naval GHQ's preferred strategic option had once again been reintegrated into the Navy's overall strategic plan, albeit as a follow-on operation. August was to see the occupation of Johnston Island, as well as the first invasions of the Australian landmass itself. Last to go would be Hawaii, now shorn of any sort of mobile support, and increasingly isolated by Japanese outposts. It was a breathtaking vision indeed. Yet its grandeur was betrayed by fundamental flaws in planning.

Readers may be pardoned at this juncture if they are somewhat dizzied by the array of geographic objectives, formations, admirals, and ships that paraded through the schemes for Operations AL and MI. Indeed, this is the first and most obvious drawback to the plan drafted by Kuroshima and ratified by Yamamoto—it was almost incomprehensibly complex. More than a dozen different surface formations, and numerous groups of submarines, were expected to participate in this tightly scripted operation. However, the expectation that these formations could coordinate their actions in such a fashion was ill founded.

Byzantine intricacy was a trademark of prewar Japanese naval strategy. Fleet exercises often featured exquisitely coordinated maneuvers on the part of the Imperial Navy being met with conveniently inept countermoves by the oafish Americans, who never failed to go lowing obediently to their choreographed slaughter.[44] Yamamoto, far from having steered his way clear of this strategic dreamland, had instead erected a monument to it. He concocted a plan that dissipated his own superiority of numbers such that the essential core of the operation—the neutralization of Midway—was to be performed by a mere twenty-two warships.[45] This was about a tenth of the total number of vessels he envisioned scattering across the breadth of the Pacific in pursuit of various objectives, many of which were completely irrelevant to the success or failure of the centerpiece of the plan.

The Aleutians operation stands at the top of this list of frivolous goals. By anyone's measure, the reduction of Dutch Harbor was a poor excuse to send the fifty-odd warships of the First Distribution to the north Pacific. In light of the fact that Operation AL was not even intended as a feint, it is difficult to understand devoting *any* resources to such a strategic irrelevancy. If the American carriers were destroyed off of Midway, then the Aleutians could be captured at will. If Nagumo failed, however, then in the long run the Aleutians could not be defended even if captured. As it developed, Attu and Kiska were to be the trifling consolation prizes for the failure of Operation MI. Their loss meant almost nothing to the Americans. Indeed, when he was informed of Attu's fall after the Battle of Midway had already transpired, U.S. Navy secretary W. Frank Knox offered a pithy indictment of Yamamoto's plan by remarking that "Japan was either unable to understand modern war or not qualified to take part in it."[46]

It must be emphasized that blame for this strategic faux pas must be shared by not only Yamamoto, but by Naval GHQ as well. It was GHQ that appended the Aleutians concept to Yamamoto's offensive as the price for his ill-won gains in the realm of planning prerogative. If Yamamoto's downstream planning was flawed, Admiral Nagano and company had only themselves to blame for demanding that he throw good assets at a fundamentally bad idea. Yamamoto, though, apparently didn't put up much of a fuss at the notion, such was his confidence in his ability to beat the Americans.

The larger issue of dispersal of Japan's forces—of which Operation AL was only a symptom—has, of course, been minutely examined in earlier histories of the battle. Certain points bear repeating here, though. As was mentioned, the prevailing opinion within Combined Fleet, and a belief that Yamamoto apparently shared, was that the American fleet was a beaten, demoralized outfit that would need to be coaxed toward its own annihilation. The corollary to this was that the need for deception outweighed the need for placing forces where they could be mutually supporting. Only by using deception would Yamamoto be able to bring his array of warships to battle without spooking the Americans into remaining in Hawaii.

In this age of unquestioned American military hegemony, it is difficult to understand how any nation could have characterized the U.S. Navy in such a fashion. Yet, it must be remembered that in 1942 Japan had only a very limited context for judging the character of America's fighting forces. Indeed, in Japan's two previous wars—against the Chinese and Russians—it had been up to the Japanese to precipitate many of the naval encounters, despite being the underdog. The Imperial Navy was thus used to being the aggressor against reluctant opponents.

The first four months of the Pacific conflict had confirmed certain aspects of this Japanese self-image. The Allies had been handed an unbroken string of defeats since the inception of hostilities. If their bravery was not in question, it was apparent to all that their equipment, doctrine, and training were in many ways not equal to Japan's. And while American morale had never broken, there was no question that American military prowess to date had been somewhat lacking. Given the beating the U.S. Navy had taken thus far, it was hardly surprising that the Japanese might have thought the Americans would be reluctant to fight them on the high seas. Faced with such a foe, Yamamoto might well have thought that he was emulating the ancient Chinese military sage Sun Tzu's ninth maxim concerning weaknesses and strengths: By making his dispositions "Subtle and insubstantial, the expert leaves no trace; divinely mysterious, he is inaudible." Yamamoto would have been well advised to read ahead to the chapter's thirteenth maxim, which his opponent Nimitz would adroitly use to destroy him in the coming days: "If I am able to determine the enemy's dispositions while at the same time I conceal my own, then I can concentrate and he must divide. And if I concentrate while he divides, I can use my entire strength to attack a fraction of his."[47]

This points to the first in the catalog of Yamamoto's flaws as a commander—his inability to correctly fathom the true nature of his enemy. He had already failed in this regard once before, at Pearl Harbor. There, his passion for disabling the American fleet with a swift strike at the outset of hostilities had blinded him to the fact that attacking Hawaii by surprise would guarantee the implacable hatred of America. Now, during the planning for Midway, he likewise failed to discern the moral character of the enemy and its willingness to fight. Had Yamamoto correctly gauged the will of his foe, he might have realized that what was called for was less subtlety and more in the way of brute strength.

Yamamoto then compounded this error by creating unnecessary subsidiary missions within the overall battle plan. One cannot fail to get the impression that many of the forces involved in both AL and MI seemed to have been put there almost out of a simple desire to find something for them to do. In fact, this may not be far from the truth. Admiral Ugaki remarked in his diary on 3 March that he feared that "the morale of the Main Body is stale after a long stay in home waters. I have encouraged them, but we must . . . engage in some operational action."[48] Given this situation, Yamamoto may well have felt that make-work was better than no work at all. Yet of the eleven battleships deployed, only the four fast battleships in Nagumo's and Kondō's forces would actually be providing any real support to the crux of the operation. And as it developed, Kondō's pair would never really be involved in any meaningful way. This left the seven remaining slower battlewagons to provide "distant cover" for other groups.

This was neither the first nor last time that the notion of distant cover would rear its misshapen head in Japanese battle planning—indeed, it plagued their operations throughout the war. As it turned out, "distant" too often meant "nonexistent," in that the forces meant to be covered were too remote to be succored when needed. This had very nearly proven the Japanese undoing at the Battle of Java Sea in March, where a Japanese cruiser force supporting an invasion convoy had been caught out of position by an Allied squadron. Only the speediness of Japan's cruisers had saved the day, allowing them to make up time on their slower charges. Likewise, the same notion of distant cover was to cost them the services of the light carrier *Shōhō* in the not too distant future.

It would be tempting to point to the Aleutians Force Main Body as being another poster child for this concept. Hosogaya's anorexic formation—whose warships were outnumbered by noncombatant vessels five to three—could barely fend off an attack on itself, let alone pull anyone else's bacon from the fire. However, it must be recalled that, according to the First Distribution of Operation AL, the Main Body was little more than a placeholder for a larger force that would come into being in the Second Distribution.

Takasu's Aleutians Screening Force, centered on BatDiv 2, was perhaps a more appropriate target for this criticism. With the four oldest battleships in the Japanese inventory "covering" the two misfit carriers of *Dai-ni Kidō Butai,* Takasu's force could not by itself provide a credible threat to any American carrier task force that somehow ranged into northern waters. Nor, with a top speed of around twenty-four knots, could it run away quickly enough to save itself should the wolf show up at its own doorstep. Had he encountered American carriers, Takasu would have suffered the same fate as the Pearl Harbor battleships, the only difference being the greater depth and lower ambient temperature of their respective watery graves. Of course, it was Yamamoto's intention that they never be brought to battle in northern waters at all. The fact that Takasu's group was not even administratively attached to Operation AL in a formal manner reinforces this impression.[49]

It is difficult to understand why Yamamoto didn't simply put Takasu's battlewagons in the Main Body and have done with. As it was, Takasu was poorly positioned to unite with the Main Body when the main battle began. The fact that Takasu was hundreds of miles north necessarily limited Yamamoto's speed of reaction if and when the Americans were detected. Should the Americans deviate from their script, Yamamoto might be forced to go into battle without BatDiv 2's gun power. By standing equidistant between two friendly forces, Takasu in essence supported neither.

Yamamoto's own Main Body, despite its much heavier gun power, lay in a similarly poor position to provide support if called upon. With at least six hundred miles between him and Nagumo's fleet carriers (according to the original plan), he would be at least two days steaming away from any trouble they might run into. However, in Yamamoto's mind, the likelihood of this was low. Nagumo's opponent in the opening round of the battle would be solitary and static—namely, Midway Island. Obviously, dictating the range to an island was much easier than doing the same with an enemy task force. If Nagumo got in trouble, he could always fall back on the Main Body—Midway wasn't going anywhere.

Not surprisingly, many postwar commentators have criticized Yamamoto's placement of the Main Body relative to Nagumo. However, the remedy proposed by these same commentators—the direct integration of the Main Body with the Striking Force—would actually have made little operational sense, even if Yamamoto had decided to dispense with subtlety. *Yamato,* at twenty-seven knots the fastest of the Main Body's three battleships, would perhaps have been able to keep up with *Kidō Butai* during a battle, although she was a full knot slower than the slowest carrier in the group (*Kaga*). However, *Nagato* and *Mutsu* were two knots slower than *Yamato,* and almost ten knots slower than *Hiryū* and *Sōryū.* As such, they would have been more of a hindrance than a help in any situation where the ability to maneuver rapidly was called for. Thus, direct integration of the two forces was not the right answer.

Had direct support of Nagumo's carriers with heavy gunfire been needed, it would have made much more sense to have maintained the Main Body as a separate formation, but also to have kept it close to Nagumo. Yamamoto could have trailed Nagumo at a short distance, so as to be partially shielded by Nagumo's own combat air patrol (CAP) from American air attacks coming from the island. Alternately, and more boldly, the Main Body could have been placed in advance of the carrier force, providing the Americans with a tempting target, and thereby providing an airpower sump for the enemy.

All of these musings, however, miss the real point. In truth, supporting Nagumo was strictly secondary to the Main Body's intended mission of destroying the American fleet during the later stages of the battle. This, in turn, points to a central truth about Yamamoto's planning. If the premise is accepted that the Americans would have to be lured from Pearl Harbor in order to create the needed battle, there was *no way* to construct an operational plan whose distribution of warships was *both* deceptive *and* mutually supporting. The two goals were antithetical. Yamamoto knew he couldn't have it both ways, and he willingly sacrificed mutual support to the perceived need for stealth. In a very real sense, this one assumption about the nature of the enemy doomed the battle plan from the start.

Notwithstanding Yamamoto's penchant for strategic deception, the arrangement of the various invasion forces approaching from the southwest is also difficult to understand. All were ultimately intended to arrive at roughly the same time off of Midway, albeit with Kondō's more powerful group heading up the van during the final approach. Thereafter, Kondō would head southeast without his weaker charges. For all this labor, all four groups could just as easily have sailed together from either Saipan or Truk and spared themselves the difficulty of coordination while simultaneously providing a greater degree of mutual protection.

Likewise, directly incorporating the four fast, powerful cruisers of CruDiv 7 (*Mogami, Kumano, Suzuya, and Mikuma*) into Nagumo's force would have greatly increased his odds of success at little increased risk. Operating directly with *Kidō Butai*, CruDiv 7 could have contributed greatly enhanced antiaircraft and surface gun power during the actual battle and still have been easily detached to bombard Midway when the time came. More important, the dozen or so long-range scout aircraft carried by these cruisers would have improved Nagumo's scouting capabilities immensely.[50] Including CruDiv 7 would have made it possible to more than double the number of scout aircraft that were fated to be used on the morning of 5 June and commensurately increased the number of aircraft in reserve for following up enemy contacts. Clearly, too, stripping CruDiv 7 from the immediate vicinity of Tanaka's invasion convoy hardly exposed the latter to greater danger, as *Kidō Butai* was the final guarantor of its safety in any case.

A commander's job is to orchestrate and direct the three major dimensions of combat—space, time, and force. From the preceding remarks, it can be seen that Yamamoto's plan failed to address the concept of space in a flexible manner. In his attempt to be "divinely mysterious," he had rendered much of his fleet purposeless through dispersion. Many of his forces were positioned in such a way that they could accomplish nothing more meaningful than parading about in the Pacific in lieu of fighting. If they were called on to react to unforeseen developments, they could not do so.

What, then, of the other two dimensions—time and force? In these as well, Yamamoto's plan suffered from alarming deficiencies. Nagumo's schedule required him to begin subduing Midway on the 4th, support landings on Kure on the 6th, followed by more landings on Midway on the 7th, and then be ready to fight a major fleet engagement immediately thereafter. In the course of these operations, Kure was to be placed in operation as a seaplane base within a day of its capture, and Midway restored to fighting order the day after that to be ready to support Nagumo on the 8th. This was, to put it mildly, cutting things a little fine.

Kure Island would have been relatively easy to put back into service—seaplanes require less in the way of facilities for operation. But Midway's airstrip was a completely different matter. Given that Nagumo was to conduct air raids against it from the 4th through the 6th; it hardly seemed likely that the strip would be captured intact or even in working order. This was doubly true if CruDiv 7's guns were actually needed to support the landing operations. The Americans could also be expected to sabotage whatever they could before the island's capture. At the very least, the aviation fuel stores would be torched, and without them, there would be no flight operations from Eastern Island. All in all, despite construction workers accompanying the combat troops, the odds of Midway being transformed literally overnight into a workable base were remote.

In addition, by the very strictures of the timetable being imposed on him, Nagumo's freedom of movement was grossly degraded. There was little possibility of his being able to meet unforeseen contingencies while still maintaining the strict tempo of operations the plan called for. No admiral would want to see his options limited in this fashion. Worse yet, the tight timing of Yamamoto's plan was predicated on the belief that the Americans were unaware of Japanese intentions. If that precondition did not hold up, Nagumo's might be in trouble. And despite all the power arrayed around him in "distant support," he would be essentially on his own to deal with whatever problems arose. However, with six carriers, Nagumo was assumed to have the capability to deal with any American force that appeared—freedom of movement would simply be compensated for by superior numbers of aircraft.

This, then, was the linchpin upon which the entire operation hung: force. For all of Yamamoto's defective planning—his obsession with concealment and deception, shotgun approach to objectives, frivolous distribution of assets, and rigid timetable—his operational scheme could probably still have been made good so long as he retained his final trump card: a fully constituted *Kidō Butai,* with all six of its fleet carriers. In the final analysis, since no one was in a position to support them anyway, these were the only ships in the entire operation that really mattered. But with six flattops at hand, it would have been difficult for Nagumo to lose. The Americans would have been hard-pressed to assemble sufficient numbers of aircraft to oppose them, even with Midway's thrown into the mix. The three Japanese carrier divisions between them would bring more than 350 planes into the battle, the equivalent of about five American carriers.[51] It was known that the Americans could barely match that number of flight decks in April 1942, even if *Wasp* were in the Pacific. Even in the unlikely event that the Americans *were* able to bring all their carriers together, they had never operated them as a group before, whereas the Japanese had extensive experience fighting together as a unit. As long as this final variable in the equation held up, Nagumo would have been in a very good position to emerge victorious.

However, shortly after having won the April staff battles, Yamamoto had altered his basic operational designs in a way that jeopardized his final trump card. Apparently as yet another quid quo pro to the Naval General Staff for his having run roughshod over them, Yamamoto agreed to lend significant naval support to 4th Fleet's plans for operations in the southwest Pacific. Admiral Inoue was still determined to capture Port Moresby in New Guinea, as was Naval GHQ. Yamamoto wasn't in favor of Operation MO (as it was known), but he reasoned that if Port Moresby were captured in early May, whatever carriers were used there could still be returned in time for Nagumo's complete force to be reassembled in home waters by mid-May. If so, they could still sally forth on Nagumo's designated sortie date for Midway, which had been set for 26 May.[52]

At first, Combined Fleet was of a mind to send just *Kaga* southward. Having missed the Indian Ocean operation because of the need to repair hull damage suffered in a mooring incident in Palau, she was already in home waters and had just been refitted. This would give Inoue a total of about one and a half carriers, since he already had the brand-new light carrier *Shōhō* under his command.[53] Inoue, however, raised strenuous objections to this. The Japanese did not know that the Americans had used two fleet carriers in their 10 March raids against Lae and Salamaua—they suspected that they had been attacked by a combination of *Saratoga*'s air group and land-based air operating from Australia. However, whatever the makeup of the enemy's forces, it was apparent that the Allies now had substantial air forces in the area. It was unlikely that the veteran *Kaga* and a rookie lightweight like *Shōhō* could face up to serious opposition if it should materialize again. As a result, Combined Fleet relented and on 12 April issued orders telling CarDiv 5 to proceed via Mako to Truk at the termination of their Indian Ocean sortie. They would be ready to participate in Operation MO thereafter. Yamamoto reasoned that *Shōkaku* and *Zuikaku* probably couldn't get themselves into too much trouble by participating in Inoue's sideshow and might even garner some additional training in the process. In the event, they got quite a bit more than they bargained for.

The utter illogic of Yamamoto's 12 April decision has been commented on before, but it bears repeating here. By any rational standard, it was absolutely essential to have CarDiv 5 in Nagumo's force if it was to be assured of material superiority at Midway. In effect, the feasibility of Operation MI now depended on whether or not Operation MO came off without CarDiv 5 suffering significant losses. Taking this gamble was a huge mistake, as it held the more important of the two operations hostage to the subordinate's success. What this suggests is that Yamamoto had not so much won the right to set the Navy's strategy as simply to have his plan go first, and even then with provisos. In effect, none of the competing strategic options that he had supposedly suppressed had actually been removed from the mix—they had merely been shoved to the end of the line in terms of timing.

Though no one in the fleet would have been willing to admit it, CarDiv 5, despite its relatively junior status, represented Japan's current margin of superiority over the American Navy. No more real fleet carriers were slated to be delivered to the Navy until *Taihō*, then building, was completed in 1944.[54] In other words, the Japanese carrier force was fixed for the foreseeable future. The Japanese believed they currently outnumbered the U.S. Navy eleven carriers (six heavy and five light) to six (five heavy and one light).[55] If the Imperial Navy was to preserve for itself the freedom of action that had thus far characterized its operations, it was essential to also conserve its numerical superiority, particularly in heavy carriers. Every senior Japanese officer knew that this current numerical ascendancy was bound to be transient. The Americans were known to have more than a dozen *Essex*-class fleet carriers building, in addition to several light fleet units comparable to *Shōhō* and *Zuihō*. Japan could not hope to match this output. Therefore, Japan's naval leadership needed to manage its window of opportunity so as to maximize the utility of its assets while this superiority lasted. Such was Japanese confidence in the proficiency of their military, though, that they apparently felt no pangs of uncertainty in committing CarDiv 5 to the south.

What the Japanese failed to realize was that "maximizing utility" did *not* mean splitting up one's forces. Attempting multiple operations simultaneously held out the hope of more rapid conquest. But it was also very risky, because it opened the door to the possibility of one of the smaller formations being destroyed by a locally superior

American force. If that happened, Japan's advantage in carriers would be prematurely destroyed as well. And once the Imperial Navy lost numerical superiority *it could never regain it*. Maximizing utility, then, really involved applying the intellectual rigor necessary to determine which operations were truly worth conducting. Unfortunately, intellectual honesty and analytic exactitude were characteristics notably absent from the strategic discourses within the Imperial Navy at this time.

Taking these observations regarding CarDiv 5 to their logical conclusion, Yamamoto should have realized that there were, in fact, precisely *two* types of objectives in the Pacific—those that were worth attacking with *all six* of Japan's fleet carriers, and those worth attacking with *none*. Until the enemy's carriers were destroyed, there was no middle ground on this matter. Japan, which had opened the war with a massed carrier strike across unprecedented distances, certainly ought to have been cognizant that the same trick could be played in reverse. The American carriers—*all* of them—had already demonstrated that they could appear practically anywhere on the perimeter of the empire. There were no "safe" missions such as Combined Fleet envisioned Operation MO to be. If the Americans were operating in force in the area, then CarDiv 5 and Operation MO would be placed in jeopardy, which in turn placed Operation MI in jeopardy as well. By the same token, if Operation MO was truly important enough to support with all of *Kidō Butai,* then the overall operational schedule needed to be adjusted to reflect these realities. It was imperative that the Japanese carrier force applied its strategic potential at maximum strength everywhere it went. This meant accepting an operational tempo that afforded the carriers time between missions to rest and refit. In essence, the Japanese needed to recognize that their real problem was not one of resource allocation between multiple objectives, but rather scheduling multiple operations around a single, *finite* resource. Neither Yamamoto nor Naval GHQ apparently ever apprehended this logic. Or if they did, they were so overconfident that they simply failed to notice their peril. Either way, the Imperial Navy was now attempting too much in too many places, and with too few assets.

4

Ill Omens

If the Doolittle raid had a positive effect on American morale, it also soaked up the services of half of Admiral Chester W. Nimitz's available carriers at a time when events in the South Pacific were coming rapidly to a head. American intelligence had become aware of Inoue's forthcoming operation in the Coral Sea, and Nimitz had to scramble to meet this new threat.

The foundation for Nimitz's forthcoming deployments was a major intelligence coup, one that would influence the course of the entire Pacific war. Unbeknownst to the Japanese, the Americans had broken the Imperial Japanese Navy's (IJN's) most important operational code—known as JN 25—in late March 1942. As a result, American cryptanalysts were becoming more successful in deciphering enough of the IJN's operational signals traffic to discern the overall intent of the Imperial Navy's plans.

The nature of American code breaking was not such that the U.S. Navy could simply read complete messages at will. They could only siphon a small number of transmissions from the veritable river of coded Japanese traffic. On an average day, the Americans were only intercepting around 60 percent of the Imperial Navy's transmissions. Of those, only about 40 percent of the messages could be analyzed, because of lack of time and human resources. And even then American cryptographers were rarely able to make out more than 10–15 percent of the code groups within any given transmission.[1] Thus, code breaking in itself, though a vitally important advantage, was hardly a panacea. However, when coupled with traffic analysis—the art of deriving operational intelligence by deducing the identity of enemy call signs and then monitoring the pattern and extent of their radio transmissions—the Americans had gained a good sense for which messages were most likely to be important.

As early as 9 April, American intelligence noted the recent transmission of orders to *Kaga* instructing her to be in the New Britain area by the end of the month.[2] The following day, they deduced that another carrier (misidentified as *Ryūkaku*)[3] was to be used in the operation as well. Additional information suggested an accumulation of shipping and air assets at Truk and Rabaul. As a result, the Americans began to suspect that something was afoot in the South Pacific. In the opinion of the analysts, the strategic town of Port Moresby, located on the southern coast of New Guinea, was the likely objective.

On the basis of this information, Nimitz decided to dispatch *Lexington* to the South Pacific in mid-April to back up *Yorktown,* which was already there. The problem was that with *Hornet* and *Enterprise* committed to Doolittle's operation, he had too few carriers to oppose a major Japanese offensive, should all of *Kidō Butai* be present. However, the fall of Port Moresby would place northern Australia in immediate peril, and Nimitz was determined to defend his southern communications lines. By 1 May, both *Yorktown* and *Lexington* were on station in the Coral Sea, with *Hornet* and *Enterprise* slated to join them by 14–16 May.[4] But for the Doolittle raid it is likely that the Japanese would have found CarDiv 5 opposed by not two, but four American carriers. Had that occurred, it is possible that the Japanese would have been presented with an altogether more decisive battle than they had envisioned.

Meanwhile, at Hashirajima, events rapidly moved forward. The capstone to the planning process took place on 1 May on board the battleship *Yamato.* She was to play host to a series of war games designed to solidify the operational aspects of MI. Here, in a series of map exercises conducted until the 5th, the operational plan was put to the test in front of the command staffs of the various task forces. The forward mess spaces were cleared of their normal furnishings, and a large table surrounded by chairs was put in place.[5] Individual cabins around the ship were used as command posts for the operational staffs involved in the actual operation. At each, the unit's commander or chief of staff behaved as if he were standing on the bridge of his respective flagship, issuing orders that were relayed by runners to other commands in mimicry of radio communications.[6]

War gaming is an old and respected adjunct to the formulation of military planning, allowing participants to explore issues and make revisions to their plans accordingly. Whatever rules are used, the emphasis during gaming is supposed to be on honestly identifying and correcting errors in operational concepts and preparing contingency plans. Yet from the get-go, the farcical nature of Operation MI's games was apparent to everyone present. Yamamoto clearly intended this conference not so much as a true exercise, but as a rubber stamp.

During the games, Yamamoto's chief of staff, Admiral Ugaki, frequently played the role of umpire. In that capacity, he consistently passed down rulings that glossed over the difficulties encountered by the Japanese. In this effort, Ugaki was aided by a lack of preparation for the exercise on the part of the various staff commands. The planning for the operation had proceeded at such a speed in April that proper briefing documents had only lately been distributed to the participants. Thus, the officers now on board *Yamato* had had very little opportunity to do their homework beforehand. Whether this was a deliberate maneuver on the part of Yamamoto and Ugaki, or simply a reflection of MI being thrown together too quickly, is unknown. The practical effects, however, were identical—the staff officers of the subordinate commands were in an inherently weaker position to criticize the plan's basic assumptions. As a result, they mostly went along with what they were told.

The attitude of many of the participants, moreover, was that this exercise was little more than a formality. In contrast to the assiduous studies before Pearl Harbor, these games revealed a certain sloppiness. In the words of Nagasawa Kō, who went on to become a rear admiral in the Japanese Naval Self-Defense Forces after the war, the general tenor of the games was one of "This is a necessary drill, but don't worry, we'll take care of anything that comes along."[7] An attitude of bored indifference permeated the various commands, most notably that of First Air Fleet.[8] Nagumo opposed the operation but felt powerless to stop it. At a wedding that May, he remarked to a friend that his superiors "spoke ill" of him already and that if he actively opposed the operation his bravery would be called into question. All things considered, he went on to say, he "would rather go to Midway and die than be branded as a coward."[9]

What Nagumo thought of the proceedings on board *Yamato* is not recorded, which is in itself interesting. As "point man" in the operation, he would have been within his rights to ask the sharpest questions of anyone. Yet, he apparently voiced no concerns whatsoever. It must be recalled, though, that Nagumo was in a weak position to object to Yamamoto's plans in any case. He had been upbraided by his superior for his perceived lack of aggressiveness at Pearl Harbor. And he was clearly out of his element in discussing the complexities of air operations—Genda had to handle these questions for him.

If Nagumo was guilty of being withdrawn, it shortly became clear that Yamamoto and his staff were engaged in being actively disingenuous. The character of the games was established early on when an officer in charge of playing the Red forces (representing the American Navy) submitted a course of action that closely resembled the tactics that would be used by the Americans in the actual battle. Having shown up sooner than anticipated, while the invasion of Midway was in process, Red proceeded to attack Nagumo's flank. The Japanese carriers were heavily hit, and the invasion was placed in great difficulties. At this juncture, the table judge demurred, asserting that such American tactics were impossible, and reversed the damage to three Japanese carriers. Despite the emotional supplications of the Red player, his plea was overturned and his tactics were recast along lines more in keeping with Yamamoto's vision as to when and where the foe should show himself.[10]

In a second incident, the Japanese side was playing through the ramifications of an attack by American land-based aircraft against Nagumo's force. The table judge for the event, Lt. Commander Okumiya Masatake, rolled dice to determine that nine hits had been scored, resulting in both *Akagi* and *Kaga* being sunk. Ugaki then personally intervened to revise the number of hits downward to three, leaving *Kaga* the sole victim of the American attack. Later in the exercise, *Kaga* was allowed to reappear as a participant in the follow-up operations against Fiji and New Caledonia.[11] Both of these events reinforced the opinion of many of the assembled officers that the operation was fundamentally flawed. However, it was clear that the commander in chief was not prepared to listen to reason on these matters.

Interestingly, near the end of the exercises Yamamoto himself asked what Nagumo would do if an enemy carrier force appeared on his flank while he was engaged in operations against Midway. All eyes turned to Air Officer Genda, whose internal reaction might well have been, "If that happens, we're in terrible trouble." But what he uttered instead was a famous Japanese military phrase: "*Gaishu Isshoku* (One touch of the armored gauntlet!)," meaning roughly "We'll wipe them out!"[12] Captain Miwa then rose to declare that, because Japanese defensive power was "unbreakable," the matter was of small concern.[13] Coming from two officers in a Navy whose renunciation of all things defensive bordered on the fanatical, these fanciful answers put a capstone on four days of scripted silliness and underlined the air of unreality that pervaded the operational planning as a whole.

Yamamoto was apparently somewhat put out that First Air Fleet's staff didn't have a credible answer to his question. But as another student of the battle has pointed out, he had little grounds to be upset at the failure of a subordinate to supply an original answer in the midst of an exercise that had been so heavily choreographed as to be meaningless.[14] Having done his best to quash all criticism, Yamamoto had thrown honesty and creative thinking out the window as well. Yamamoto did take this opportunity, though, to interject an instruction to Nagumo and his staff that they should reserve at least half of *Kidō Butai*'s attack aircraft in readiness for an antishipping strike should the need arise.[15] However, these orders were verbally transmitted to First Air Fleet; nothing was ever put in writing. At the time, the instructions seemed clear enough.[16] As events would prove, though, their intent would be far from clear-cut a month later.

At the end of the exercise, the situation remained much as before—Yamamoto's battle plan was unchanged in almost all particulars. The games had served as a monologue. There had been no intellectual discourse, no learning; the entire affair had been a mockery of professional staff work. The net result was that Nagumo would go to battle armed with practically nothing in the way of realistic contingency plans. Whatever difficulties arose would be his to handle, alone.

Only two days after the games concluded, word came back from Admiral Inoue and CarDiv 5 that a pair of American carriers had been engaged in the Coral Sea. The initial assessment of the battle's results was mixed. Light carrier *Shōhō,* operating separately from the fleet carriers, had been attacked and sunk by American naval aircraft. In the exchanges that followed, the Japanese had attacked both American flattops, which they identified as *Yorktown* and *Saratoga*. It was believed that they had been left in a sinking condition. However, there was no positive confirmation of these losses. As it developed, *Lexington* had indeed been sunk. But *Yorktown,* despite heavy damage, was able to escape.

In return for these successes, the costs to CarDiv 5 had been high. *Shōkaku* was badly hit by three bombs, which wrecked her flight deck, started several fires, and killed 108 crewmen. The Japanese were fortunate that she was not only one of the sturdiest Imperial Navy warships afloat, but also that she had few aircraft on board at the time of the attack. Nevertheless, she could no longer conduct flight operations and was forced to retire. *Zuikaku,* though undamaged, was effectively rendered hors de combat by aircraft losses. Worse, the operation to secure Port Moresby had to be abandoned, much to the disgust of Combined Fleet's staff, who wanted the operation to continue despite CarDiv 5's losses.

As cooler heads prevailed and more information came in regarding the encounter, Yamamoto and Ugaki took stock of the situation. Ugaki noted certain disquieting implications of the battle for future operations. In his diary entry for 7 May, he wrote: "A dream of great success has been shattered. . . . When we expect enemy raids, can't we employ the forces in a little more unified way? After all, not a little [of the present setback] should be attributed to the insufficiency of air reconnaissance. We should keep this in mind."[17]

Prophetic words indeed. Yet, Ugaki and his chief on board *Yamato* apparently missed the larger implications of Coral Sea, namely, that the last shred of operational legitimacy underpinning Operation MI plan had just been destroyed. Nagumo would no longer have his trump card to play should the need arise. Even assuming, as the Japanese did, that both the American carriers had been sunk at Coral Sea, the U.S. Navy could still potentially have as many as three more available to them in the Pacific—*Enterprise, Hornet,* and *Wasp.* Indeed, it was clear from the Doolittle raid that the Americans had been operating at least another pair of flight decks besides the ones encountered in the Coral Sea. *Kidō Butai* would no longer be bringing six carriers to Midway, although it was not clear that *Zuikaku* would be unable to participate in the coming operation until she reported her air group losses more fully on 14 May. Given that the Americans might have as many as three fleet carriers and Midway's air complement at the scene of the forthcoming battle, this meant that there could be no guarantee of numerical superiority for *Kidō Butai.*

This should have been of grave concern to Combined Fleet, but evidently it was not. In fact, Combined Fleet's staff, notwithstanding having received word that *Shōkaku* and *Zuikaku* had been damaged in what was supposed to have been a sideshow, bitterly condemned Inoue and the commander of the carrier striking force (Vice Admiral Takagi Takeo) for failing to continue offensive operations despite the very real possibility of losing its two newest fleet carriers. Such a reflexive inclination toward the offensive points again to a complete lack of perspective within the Imperial Navy. It was as if the mere act of attacking was more important than fighting in a manner that held out the best possibility of success.

For their part, the men of CarDivs 1 and 2 were treating Coral Sea as a victory, as the superficial evidence suggested it was. If CarDiv 5 had been handled a bit roughly in the process, it could be chalked up to its relatively junior status. The joke in the wardrooms ran that "if the sons of the concubine [meaning *Shōkaku* and *Zuikaku*] could win the victory, the sons of legal wives should find no rivals in the world."[18] This revealed a rather condescending, and wholly unwarranted, view of the relative skill of CarDiv 5, not to mention a misreading of the true importance of the losses *Kidō Butai* had just suffered.

With *Shōkaku* and *Zuikaku* out of the picture, a serious reappraisal of Operation MI was called for. Yet nothing of the sort occurred. Ugaki's diary reveals no mention of concern that his superior's designs might have been somehow awry now that a third of Nagumo's airpower had suddenly been rendered unusable. When *Shōkaku* limped into Kure on 17 May, Admiral Ugaki went on board to visit the wounded. He commented on his feelings of pity for the men, many of whom were terribly burned. He might well have reflected on what CarDiv 5's experiences portended for Midway.

In all truth, the results at Coral Sea should have given Ugaki and Yamamoto all the warning they needed that this was not the same war as five months ago, or even *one* month ago. Indeed, a perceptive observer would have noticed a number of worrying trends revealed by the battle of 7–8 May. For one thing, American carriers had been lurking when no one expected them to be there. With their unwelcome appearance, Japan's dispersal of forces in the face of a mobile enemy had just been shown for what it was—an invitation to piecemeal destruction of valuable assets. In this case, the asset in question had been a light carrier, which hardly constituted a crushing setback. But the amount of American ordnance that had hit *Shōhō* would have sent any *two* Japanese fleet carriers to the bottom in short order, had they been present to receive it.

Equally ominous was the fact that American carrier pilots had been shown to be qualitatively different from much of the opposition the Japanese had faced thus far. American naval aviators didn't shy away from combat. They flew aggressively and were certainly more skillful than many of the Allied aircraft over Borneo, Java, and Malaya had been. The U.S. Navy's primary carrier fighter, the F4F Wildcat, wasn't a match for the Zero, it was true. And the Americans' main torpedo plane, the TBD Devastator, was well past its prime. But the SBD Dauntless had been shown to be a fine dive-bomber, capable of lugging a heavy bomb load and delivering it with accuracy. Likewise, American dive-bomber pilots had been proficient enough to score three solid 1,000-lb bomb hits on *Shōkaku,* despite her being one of the fastest, toughest carriers in the fleet. The hapless *Shōhō* had been smashed by as many as eleven bomb hits and five torpedoes. Taken together, the bloom was distinctly off the rose in terms of Japanese carriers somehow being immune to damage. Before Coral Sea, not one had been so much as scratched by the enemy. One look at *Shōkaku*'s shattered bow and flight deck should have given Ugaki all the evidence he needed to begin revising his opinion of the Americans and what it would be like fighting them.

Yamamoto, however, was in no mood to recast his plans or move the dates of the operation backward in order to wait for CarDiv 5's reconstitution. From all appearances, *Shōkaku* would be months in the yard.[19] However, the landing operations against Midway required a full moon, which meant that if the troops were not landed before 8 June, the whole operation would have to be moved back a month. Furthermore, the weather in the Aleutians was awful most of the year, and if landings were to be made on Kiska and Attu, they needed to be made before June was out. In other words, if Operation AL was to be carried out at all, it needed to occur as Combined Fleet had ordained.[20] Yet again, the timetable for a strictly subordinate operation—in this case in the Aleutians—was helping drive the primary operational plan.

At the very least, the Japanese might have tried to reconstitute *Zuikaku*'s air wing in time to participate in MI. Unfortunately, the organization of Japanese carrier air groups hampered them in this respect. Unlike American carrier squadrons, which were independent (and interchangeable) units that shifted from carrier to carrier at need, Japanese groups were organic to the ship itself. As such, if either the carrier or the air unit was mauled in the course of combat, both components were withdrawn until they could be reconstituted. This was an inherently less flexible organizational arrangement than that of the Americans.[21] But if ever there was a need for some enlightened improvisation on the part of the Japanese, it was now.

If *Zuikaku*'s air group was to be resurrected for this operation, both aircraft and pilots would need to be scraped up. But they appeared to be available. When *Zuikaku* returned to Kure, she carried her own aircraft as well as refugees from *Shōkaku*. These totaled twenty-four Zeros, nine dive-bombers, and six torpedo planes operable. An additional Zero, eight dive-bombers, and four (later raised to eight) torpedo planes were believed repairable.[22] That gave a maximum of fifty-six aircraft to work with, which totaled twenty-five Zeros, seventeen dive-bombers, and fourteen torpedo planes. This was seven aircraft short of *Zuikaku*'s nominal establishment of sixty-three but was still roughly equivalent to the totals being carried by the carriers of CarDiv 1 and 2 at this time. Admittedly, this force would have been composed of aviators who had not flown together before. But if there was one thing the Japanese Navy had going for it, it was a remarkably high degree of tactical homogeneity. Events later in the war were to show that IJN "pickup" teams could operate together successfully.[23] It is hard to escape the conclusion that *Zuikaku* could have been made available if her presence had been considered vital.

However, Yamamoto apparently did not feel any sense of urgency regarding her. In light of having supposedly sunk two enemy flattops in the Coral Sea, Japanese intelligence estimates now suggested that the Americans had only two or three carriers in the Pacific—two of the *Yorktown* class, and perhaps the *Wasp*.[24] In addition, it was felt that the Americans might have two or three "converted carriers," but they were judged by the Japanese to be unfit for active duty with the carriers.[25] Thus, in the matter of fleet carriers, Nagumo should have an edge of four to three in the worst case. The consensus among Combined Fleet's staff officers was that this seemed good enough.[26]

If this was the depth of Combined Fleet's strategic calculus, it represented a pretty shallow level of analysis indeed. For one thing, American carrier air groups were larger than their Japanese counterparts. And while current intelligence placed only about fifty aircraft on Midway,[27] it was also recognized that the island could be rapidly reinforced with large numbers of aircraft from Hawaii.[28] It was obvious that holding an advantage of a single carrier did not constitute a reasonable margin of superiority over the possible laundry list of opponents, even if they were encountered sequentially (as Yamamoto's designs intended). Should the unthinkable happen, and Nagumo have to combat both threats simultaneously, he would be operating at bare parity in aircraft. *Zuikaku* could have given him a crucial edge.

And yet on the eve of what Yamamoto conceived as the decisive battle—the battle that was supposed to determine the fate of the war, and whose cardinal importance had been ingrained in every Imperial Navy sailor for the last twenty years—the Japanese were evidently unconcerned enough with the outcome that working *Zuikaku* back into the mix wasn't deemed worth the effort. This stands in stunning contrast to the Herculean efforts the Americans were shortly to perform between 27 and 30 May in patching up *Yorktown* in time for her own rendezvous with destiny off Midway. In sports parlance, the only conclusion that can be reached is that the Americans simply "wanted the win" more than their opponents. The U.S. Navy was willing to adapt to changed circumstances, was willing to put in the hard work it took to overcome the obstacles to success. The Japanese were disinclined to go to the same lengths to secure the fruits of victory. If this was symptomatic of "victory disease"—as some writers have ascribed the mental complacency and sloppiness in early 1942 that led to Japan's forthcoming defeat—then it was a malady that sapped the imagination and diligence of those afflicted. In contrast to the unstinting efforts that had characterized earlier Japanese victories, Combined Fleet was sleepwalking into its most important battle ever.

This same haphazardness was being felt all the way down the line. The general shape of the battle had been sent to operational commands as part of Naval GHQ's Navy Order Number 18 on 5 May. Initial operational orders were issued on 12 May that began moving units toward their assembly points.[29] However, given the tight time frames, the final operational orders for the lower-level commands were not cut until 20 May.[30] Likewise, the fleet was finding it difficult to distribute the new codebooks needed to support the operation, having delayed its changeover from JN25-B to the new JN-25V variant from 1 May to 27 May in the scramble.[31]

At the same time, several of the needed ships were still undergoing repairs. Carriers *Ryūjō* and *Junyō,* cruisers *Takao* and *Maya,* as well as several destroyers assigned to the northern operations, were all in maintenance. The same was true of the bulk of 20th, 24th, and 27th destroyer squadrons assigned to the Midway Invasion Force. Destroyers *Ushio, Oboro,* and *Akebono,* which had just returned from the Coral Sea operation, were shunted north to Ominato for use in Operation AL. They arrived one day before the Aleutians forces were scheduled to sortie.[32]

As a result, preparations and training for battle were skimpy at best. Lower-level map exercises were hastily convened, but in many cases not all the officers who were to participate in a given operation were physically present, because their ships had yet to arrive at their respective marshaling places. Similarly, the Army's North Sea Detachment was first organized on 9 May at Asahikawa and then shipped out less than two weeks later to Ominato. Once there, they and the Maizuru SNLF troops participated in a single practice-landing exercise on the 25th.[33] Overall, the units involved were simply going to have to draw on past experience to do the best they could in the coming operation.

The final episode in this rather shabby tale of Japanese preparations played itself out on the very eve of Nagumo's sailing. In a final conference held on board *Yamato* on 25 May, war games again pointed to the possibility of flaws in Yamamoto's operational scheme. During this exercise, the Red player promptly sortied to the west from Oahu and then headed north at high speed. During the subsequent fray, Japan suffered one carrier sunk and two damaged, while Red lost both of its carriers. It was pointed out after the exercise that if Red forces appeared south of the Hawaii/Midway axis, there would be a gap in the air search pattern for the fleet. It was also noted that coordinating the widely separated friendly forces would be quite difficult under conditions of strict radio silence. Some of the officers were of the opinion that the Main Body was positioned too far from Nagumo's carriers to be able to provide effective support. Yamamoto again asked First Air Fleet staff about their ability to repel an attack should the Americans appear unexpectedly off Midway and was

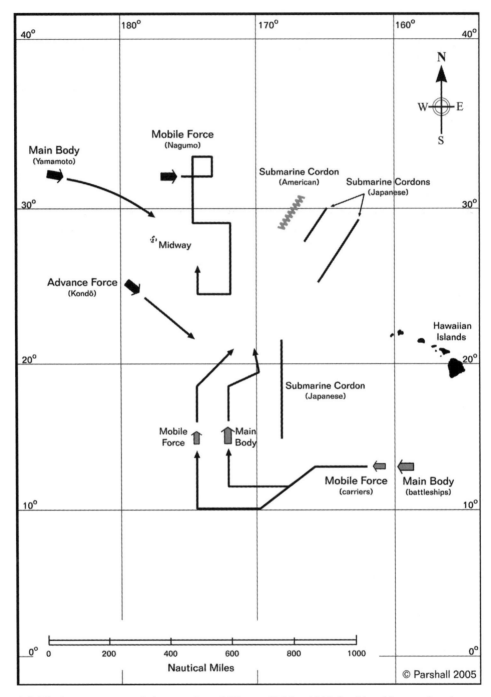

4-1: Final war games carried out on board *Yamato,* 25 May 1942. In this table exercise, the American forces exploited an air search gap to the south of Midway and inflicted heavy losses on the Japanese carrier force. (Source: *Senshi Sōsho,* p. 117.)

once again given bland assurances by Nagumo and his subordinates that they were prepared for such a contingency.[34]

During the same exercise, Admiral Nagumo dropped a bombshell—*Kidō Butai* would not be able to sortie the following morning (26 May) as planned.[35] His carriers needed more time for provisioning and other preparations.[36] Nagumo asked that the timetable for the entire operation be pushed back a day. Other lower-level commands, under strain to get their units prepared in time to sortie, supported his request. They also wanted the ability to change some of the assembly points for their forces, because there had been problems supplying all the ships with necessary oil.[37]

Yamamoto demurred. If Nagumo couldn't sail, so be it. But the operational imperatives remained the same. The tides around Midway weren't going to accommodate Nagumo's tardiness or that of the other units—the landings had to take place as scheduled. Nagumo would simply have one less day to knock the island out. In so doing, Yamamoto explicitly acknowledged that Nagumo's new timetable meant that Tanaka's invasion convoy and its covering forces would in essence be a day ahead of where they were supposed to be relative to *Kidō Butai*. As such, they would be exposed to detection and attack before Nagumo could deal with the threat from the island. However, this was a calculated risk that Yamamoto was prepared to take.[38]

The incredible part of this episode is not so much that Nagumo couldn't sail on time, although that was bad enough. Rather, it was the fact that no shred of the operational plan was adjusted to accommodate the new sortie date. Yamamoto may well have been right that the overall timetable was essentially driven by tidal forces and that the schedule for invasion was therefore immutable. But at the very least some contingency plans, even of a verbal sort, ought to have been put in place to deal with the likelihood that Tanaka and Kurita's invasion forces would be detected prematurely by the Americans. Yet nothing of the sort apparently occurred. Neither Nagumo nor Yamamoto could have left the 25 May conference in good temper.

All in all, as one Japanese naval officer later remarked, "for a naval force which was the protagonist in the most ambitious plan of the Imperial General Headquarter in the war, this was a precarious situation."[39] At the end of nearly three months of top-level bickering, the fleet was shortly to head out on a mission whose goals were questionable at best. The operational plan was impossibly complex, its disposition of forces mutually nonsupporting, and its timetable overly rigid. Compounding these basic operational problems were errors in execution as well. Any staff officer worth his salt could tell that Operation MI hadn't been war-gamed properly, and there had been too little time for training. The plan hadn't been revised to accommodate the unexpected absence of two crucial flight decks, nor in light of the other developments in the Coral Sea. Nagumo's late departure, coupled with yet another wholly predictable failure to revise the positions of the invasion units or the operation timetable, had been the icing on the cake. Chihaya Masatake perhaps summarized these multiple failures most succinctly when he wrote later of Combined Fleet, "It could not be said of them, 'Everything was done that was humanly possible.'"[40] It was under this cloud of ill fortune that *Kidō Butai* sailed to meet its fate two days later.

5

Transit

After exiting the Inland Sea on the afternoon of 27 May, Nagumo's force proceeded through the night on a southeasterly heading. They woke to a brilliant sun rising over the bows of the ships. Now swinging due east, they cruised along at fourteen knots. The men, as usual, rose at sunrise, with breakfast being served about an hour thereafter. The crews then got down to business—cleaning the ship, tending the machinery, and participating in combat drills. For all the men, though, there were ample opportunities for recreation. Indeed, steaming to battle often afforded more such occasions than their normal peacetime routine did.[1] The pilots amused themselves by playing card games or *shōgi* (Japanese chess), loafing in the ready room, or sunning themselves on the flight deck near the island. Others read the popular novels that passed around endlessly through the ranks or played musical instruments. Some of the men had learned from their experience in the South Pacific to bring folding wooden chairs with them, so that they could recline at their ease on the decks.

Every afternoon after lunch, the crews were assembled on deck to exercise and sing martial songs. This was designed to keep morale up and imbue the men with fighting spirit. Some of the officers, however, let the men mix up the musical fare with more popular and less militaristic numbers from back home—it was important to get the younger sailors' buy in on such matters to get their full participation.[2]

Conditions on the ships quickly became somewhat squalid. Fresh water was limited, particularly on longer cruises. The destroyers, whose tankage space was much more limited, suffered more in this regard. As a result, bathing was held to a minimum. This was a deprivation; the evening bath is a Japanese ritual. Since showers were unknown in their warships, the men were limited to washing their hands and faces before meals.[3] As a result, the crew had to ventilate the ship to ensure that the air did not become foul. This was done throughout the day, with the men opening groups of portholes (even during battle-steaming conditions) under the supervision of the officers.

On a war mission, the cooks made special efforts to ensure that the men were given tasty rations. The crews were indulged with fresh fruit and delicacies such as *ohagi* (sugar and red bean rice cake) and *shiruko* (red bean soup with rice cake in it).[4] Overall, the mood in the rank and file appeared relaxed, as if they were simply on a pleasure cruise. However, overnight on the 27th–28th at least one bad omen had befallen the task force. Commander Fuchida Mitsuo, the leader of *Akagi*'s air group, had fallen ill. Already feeling under the weather at the time of the force's departure, he had doubled over during the evening. He was diagnosed with acute appendicitis. Fuchida pleaded in vain to postpone the inevitable, but *Akagi*'s surgeon overruled him and operated immediately.[5] For the air groups, this was disheartening. Fuchida was a popular commander, and the men would miss having the Pearl Harbor attack leader in their ranks during the battle.

John Keegan, in his book *The Face of Battle,* noted that battle is neither "'strategic,' nor 'tactical,' nor material, nor technical." Rather, what battles have in common "is human: the behavior of men struggling to reconcile their instinct for self-preservation, their sense of honour and the achievement

5-1: Commander Fuchida Mitsuo, *Akagi* air group *hikōtaichō*, leader of the Pearl Harbor strike force, and subsequent author of a prominent book on Midway. (Photo courtesy Michael Wenger)

of some aim over which other men are ready to kill them." The study of battle is therefore "necessarily a social and psychological study." More important, though, "Battles belong to finite moments in history, to the societies which raise the armies which fight them, to the economies and technologies which these societies sustain."[6]

Keegan's words pertain precisely to the study of naval combat as well. Indeed, they are perhaps even more pertinent in a nautical setting, for the study of naval warfare (more than any other form of combat) holds the potential to completely subordinate the human element to the weapons themselves. Naval combat is conducted almost exclusively by means of machines—machines that are in many cases so huge and grand that they often seem to take on a life and personality of their own that transcend the tiny figures that inhabit them. Yet, in the final analysis, it is men who live in the ship, command and fight the ship, and often die in the ship. Their story, no matter how seemingly eclipsed by the great vessels they serve in, is still the fundamental story to be related.

Any study of the First Mobile Striking Force, no matter how technically grounded, to some degree must also be a study of the Japanese Navy in a social sense. The Battle of Midway was fought by Japanese men, who were the products of an intensely disciplined, patriarchal, militarized, and above all, Eastern society. Understanding the battle without comprehending their emotional and cultural outlook is pointless. Of course, any Occidental portrayal of an Oriental society, especially at the space of several decades remove is (to say the least) fraught with peril. Yet despite this, it is necessary to draw together an honest picture of the Japanese that is comprehensible to a Western reader. Who, then, were the men of *Kidō Butai*?

The first thing that must be recalled pertains not only to the Japanese psyche, but that of Asia as a whole. It is simply this—that for more than a century preceding the Pacific war, to be born almost anywhere in Asia was to be born the chattel, either explicit or implied, of a white colonial government. Colonial interests directed every facet of economic and political life in Asia. Asians were not allowed to choose their own governments, their affairs being presided over by administrations whose rule ran the gamut from largely benign to hideously inept and downright cruel. The colonies' economic raison d'être was to feed low-priced raw materials and local trinkets to their masters and consume manufactured goods in return, often at disadvantageous financial terms. As part of this general subjugation, Asians were almost universally regarded as moral, intellectual, and social inferiors by whites.

Only in Japan did these general conditions of servility not pertain. And the only reason the Japanese had not shouldered their own yoke was that they had armed themselves to the teeth with modern weaponry. This process had begun in 1853 with the descent of Admiral Matthew Perry's jet-black warships on the Japanese coast, thereby "opening" Japan to the West (an event characterized more in terms of rape by those who had been "opened"). This traumatic and unwilling entrance onto the stage of world politics had triggered the social tumult of the Meiji Restoration, which had led to the establishment of a new national government in 1868.

Thereafter, the Japanese had, by a combination of cunning policy, ruthless implementation of a national industrialization plan, and frantic effort and sacrifice on the part of the populace, begun transforming their nation into a modern industrial state. Within forty years, Japan was a major regional player; within forty more she was a world power. The breathtaking scope of this accomplishment had impressed the Japanese as being proof of their own moral superiority. Simultaneously, it had reinforced the inescapable social message that national security was the product of unstinting labor, limited internal dissent, and a plenitude of modern military hardware.

Along the way, of course, it had been necessary for Japan to visibly demonstrate that it would not be pushed around by the colonial powers. The object of this exercise had been Czarist Russia, which the Japanese had shrewdly assessed as being the most proximate, least militarily capable, and most domestically unstable of its potential opponents. The stunning Japanese military successes achieved during the Russo-Japanese War of 1904–1905, including the annihilation of a large Russian fleet during the Battle of Tsushima, had served notice that an Asian power had arisen that was not to be trifled with. At the same time, though, Tsushima planted the seeds for Japan's defeat in World War II by creating a warped perception within the Japanese Navy regarding the importance of winning decisive battles. In the prescient words of Chihaya Masatake, "Dazzled by . . . brilliant victories, [the Japanese Navy] concluded erroneously that victory was brought about solely by the single stroke of a decisive engagement." Chihaya labeled this "a blind belief that spelled disaster."[7]

That disaster, however, lay thirty-seven years in the future. The immediate importance of Tsushima in a geopolitical sense was both positive and undeniable. While the colonial powers had occasionally suffered local and largely temporary reverses at the hands of "the natives" on *land,* no white nation had ever had its *navy* beaten by an indigenous force. Particularly since the advent of steam power, the idea was simply unthinkable. For the Japanese to have then followed this achievement by forcing Russia to sue for peace after defeating its army in the field put the capstone on a shocking war. The fact that the conflict had, in fact, nearly bankrupted Japan, and had exposed to the perceptive observer the still-fragile infrastructure of Japanese industrial power, was overshadowed by the dramatic changes in the regional security picture that resulted from her victories. From this moment, the Japanese had a sense of having arrived on the world stage and believed (with some justification) that the white nations should accord them the same respect they accorded one another. That they did not, rankled Japan greatly.

This frustration was compounded by a deeply held belief on the part of the Japanese that they were part of a unique, and uniquely *superior* ethnic group. The Japanese were certainly not alone in the early part of the century in considering their own race better than the next, but the Japanese version of this social ill was perhaps more clannish than most. The Japanese harbored the belief that their society was possessed of an unusual cultural homogeneity. Perhaps this notion was driven by their exceptional racial uniformity and homogeneity—even today, Japan's population is still 99 percent native Japanese. Whatever the reason, to the Japanese, being Japanese meant a lot more than simply living in one country with people that looked the same. It meant being a part of a group that shared a common culture, a set of mutual beliefs, a uniform heritage and language, and supposedly a common outlook on life.

Venture much farther down the path of what it truly means to be Japanese, and the line between rational and semimystical inevitably begins to blur. The Japanese people, it was said, were all one race, embodied in the person of the emperor. The emperor himself was held to be divine, a direct descendent of the semimythical First Emperor Jimmu who had reigned around 600 BC, and who was in turn supposedly a descendent of the Sun Goddess Ameterasu herself. With such an impeccable pedigree, who could doubt that this one true race—the "Yamato race," imbued with the "true Japanese spirit"—was a people of destiny? To a Westerner, particularly Americans raised in a nation where diversity, fractiousness, and individuality are a part of the basic social fabric, such flowery notions of a "true" Japanese race are preposterous at best, downright dangerous at worst. Yet it must also be recalled that Japan was not alone at this time in harboring ethnocentric outlooks, many of which were a good deal less poetic in nature.

During the decades leading up to the war, this belief in Japanese racial unity, of being a part of a divinely purposed people, had been reinforced by the rhetoric of nationalism until it had become the central pillar around which the tent of Japanese militarism was pitched. To this mix were added legitimate and reinforcing grievances against the racism and asymmetrical economic advantage that Western colonialism had created throughout Asia. What emerged was a twisted pseudonationalist mythos that promised only ill for Asia and ultimately the Japanese themselves. By divine right, Japan would be the instrument that lifted the hated yoke of white oppression from all of Asia. The Asian peoples would naturally come under the aegis of Japanese society. It was a heady mission indeed. "One hundred million hearts advancing as one!" was a common exhortation of Japanese wartime propaganda, and it roughly fit the image that the militarists wanted to project to the public and the world—that of a dynamic race fulfilling its noble destiny with a single, almost telepathically felt purpose.

The militarists' concept of "liberation" ultimately proved to be little more than the bodily shoving aside of the white powers so that the Japanese might themselves swill at the trough of economic exploitation. However, that apparently did not sully the underlying purity of this grand vision in their eyes. Neither did Japanese resentment of racist inequality from the West stop it from foisting an equally virulent form of oppression on its own Asian neighbors. To all the internal contradictions of their Pan-Asian mission the Japanese turned a blind eye. Wrapped in the cloak of heaven-sent purpose, Japan had ultimately moved, perhaps inevitably, first from border fracases and provocations into a state of "Special Undeclared War" in China as the 1930s wore on.

To the average Westerner, steeped in the winner's history of World War II, any attempt to justify Japan's war in terms of Pan-Asian liberation is simply so much hogwash. The Japanese were aggressors, the Allies liberators, and everything from a moral standpoint has been very much cut and dried for half a century. The prevailing American attitude toward the war was crystallized as soon as the first Japanese bomb fell on Pearl Harbor. Yamamoto's "sneak" attack simply put an exclamation point on the writ of contemporary American moral outrage over previous Japanese aggressions in Asia.

Yet, despite the fundamental validity of these Western views, it is important to recall that at some level the Japanese people sincerely believed they were fighting for a larger cause, whose intrinsic good was undeniable. If they were also capable of ignoring the social injustices and outright atrocities—which were many and sordid— that accrued under this banner, then that sublimation came about from a conviction that achieving the larger goal of destroying Western colonialism somehow justified the means employed. This long-standing rationalization lies at the core of Japan's inability to examine and condemn its own wartime actions with anything approaching the sincerity and candor that its victims feel is required.

Given the transparent nature of the seemingly lofty ideals accompanying the creation of the Greater East Asian Co-Prosperity Sphere, it is ironic that Japan's destruction of the existing colonial system was perhaps the only goal Japan actually attained during her ruinous war. Whatever the conflict's ultimate outcome, the humiliating defeats inflicted on the Dutch and British during 1941–42 irrevocably destroyed their ruling legitimacy. Within a decade of the end of hostilities, white colonialism would be banished from Asia. Of course, it is doubly ironic that this goal was accomplished in a manner that none of Japan's military leaders would have appreciated. Indeed, instead of lording over all of Asia, Japan herself was burned down to cinders for inflicting "liberation" on her neighbors.

Toward America the Japanese reserved a very particular animus, one based on a long history of Yankee mistreatment that was hardly imagined. From blatantly unfair immigration quotas on the West Coast, second-class treatment of Japanese émigrés, and the economic and social repression of the very sizable Japanese population on Hawaii, the Japanese could point to a long list of grievances against their powerful Pacific neighbor.

To this general list the Japanese Navy added a complaint of their own—a long resentment against what they felt were unfair and insulting provisions in the naval treaties that governed all the world's major navies during the 1920s and 1930s. The Washington Naval Treaty of 1922, and its successor the London Naval Treaty of 1930, had established caps on major categories of warships. In each case, the Japanese received a lesser tonnage quota than either the Royal Navy or U.S. Navy. The treaties were a slap in the face of the Imperial Navy's self-perception as a world-class force. Worse yet, they placed Japanese quotas of warships at a level that conventional naval strategy of the time pegged as being insufficient for the defense of the Home Islands.

In reality, of course, by signing these treaties, the Japanese were able to avoid an impending arms race against America, which, with their much less developed economy, they could not have hoped to win. The act of placing an artificially low ceiling on America's enormous industrial capacity was a far more effective defense than attempting to match American output. The treaties thus protected Japan against American aggression better than the imperial military could have done on its own.

These brutal economic realities were readily apparent to the more perceptive thinkers within the Imperial Navy. Admiral Yamamoto had been a delegation member to the Washington Naval Treaty negotiations and shared the vision of the chief of the naval delegation, Admiral Katō Tomosaburō. Katō argued that Japan's security vis-à-vis the Americans necessarily rested on diplomacy, at least for the foreseeable future. However, the so-called Fleet Faction was violently opposed to the treaties (and those who supported them). Eventually, the heat of nationalist fervor overcame the cold logic of economics, and Japan announced that it would withdraw from the London Treaty in 1937.

Unpopular naval treaties could be renounced with relative ease; the grim truth of the economic gap that existed between Japan and her potential American opponent could not be dispelled so simply. On one side of the Pacific lay Japan, an island nation with few natural resources. She was completely dependent on the trade of other nations to supply her factories with raw materials and her military with oil. On the other side lay the United States—enormous and self-sufficient in practically everything she needed. Even when mired in the midst of the Great Depression, the United States still possessed an economy that was some seven times larger than Japan's. The inherent and largely intractable "unfairness" of this situation (in Japan's eyes) inevitably placed the empire in an inferior bargaining position. America knew she was in a position to dictate; Japan was expected to listen. The seeds of the coming war lay in America's misreading of Japan's long-term willingness to be dictated to, coupled with Japan's own inability to completely recognize the implications of these military/economic realities should she decide to go to war against her powerful opponent.

When the United States began applying economic pressure to first curtail and then roll back the empire's gains in China, the emotional concoction that had been brewing for decades finally came to a boil. With the Japanese occupation of Vichy French Indochina, America had reacted by imposing a total embargo on oil in July 1941. Piled on top of previous curtailments of iron ore, scrap metal, and strategic minerals, the West was using every economic weapon at its disposal to bring the empire to its knees. Japan seethed; to finally strike back, even if doing so meant a ruinous war, was the wish of the entire country.[8]

What was even more remarkable was that this emotional fervor was generated in a country that was already heartily sick of its war in China. The public perceived (correctly) that the war against the Chinese tar baby was stalemated and could not be brought to a successful resolution. The Japanese public felt powerless and detached from their own domestic politics, viewing the machinations of the Army and Navy, the assassinations of government officials by members of the armed forces, and the other unsavory political acts of their own military with a jaundiced eye. That the prospect of fighting an *additional* war against the most powerful economy on earth, with the British and Dutch Empires thrown in for good measure, could bring a sense of elation to the Japanese public demonstrates the depth of its resentment against white imperialism in general, and America in particular. It also illustrates the extent to which nationalist fervor had apparently detached the nation's leadership from any ability to engage in a cool, reasoned appraisal of the likely nature and outcome of such a gargantuan conflict.[9]

The military culture of the Imperial Navy was the natural result of these powerful and sometimes contradictory societal reactants. Its men were, above all things, intensely motivated to succeed. Duty—duty to one's country and one's family—looms large in the Japanese consciousness, and the Imperial Navy's fleet raised this ethos to standards few navies have seen. Perhaps the first thing that an American sailor might have noticed upon strolling about a Japanese man-of-war would have been the seriousness with which the average sailor performed even the least of his shipboard affairs. The Japanese are notable for their earnestness, which to many Westerners comes across as almost mawkish, and perhaps even contrived. Contrived it most certainly is not—Japanese society places a premium on conformity, discipline, and a deeply felt need to fulfill one's obligations. Failure to act correctly in the eyes of society results in shame, and shame is to be avoided like the plague, as it attaches itself not only to the individual, but also to one's family, friends, neighbors, and ultimately even the emperor and the entire Japanese people. When used as the basis for indoctrination in the self-referential confines of a military institution, the result was a group of fighting men who feared the shame of ignoble failure more than death itself.

Another thing an American would have quickly noticed was the harsh discipline meted out to the enlisted men. To strike a man was nothing; it happened all the time in response to even the most trivial infractions. In the words of one veteran, the Navy appeared to "put almost superstitious faith in the belief that brutality and physical punishment made better sailors."[10] As part of that iron discipline, every Japanese military man was expected to conform instantly to orders. Naval pilot Sakai Saburō, who entered the Navy as a seaman recruit, remarked that his petty officers in training were "absolute tyrants" and "sadistic brutes of the worst sort." While his training as a recruit had been brutal enough, shipboard life was, if possible, even more violent. The effect, in Sakai's words, was to reduce the men to "human cattle," who never "dared to question orders, to doubt authority, to do anything but immediately carry out all the commands of our superiors."[11]

Yet insubordination was not at all unknown within the military, though curiously it often manifested itself in the officer corps. Junior officers in both the Army and Navy had a reputation for violence, even against their superiors. Ultraright junior officers had assassinated several prominent political figures—including Japan's prime minister during a brief mutiny in February 1936—for trying to curtail the military's budgets and activities. In like fashion, a group of relatively junior Army staff officers, led by the infamous Lt. Col. Ishiwara Kanji, had fomented the Mukden Incident of September 1931. This became the pretext for Japan's invasion and consolidation of Manchuria. In 1937 junior staff officers of the Kwantung Army essentially started the current conflict against China on their own initiative, betting correctly that their superiors in Tokyo would be reluctant to rein them in and thereby lose face.

Likewise, while the Navy liked to think of itself as the more educated and world-wise of Japan's two services, violence was hardly unknown even within the ranks of its flag officers. When the planning for Pearl Harbor had been in full swing, Admiral Yamaguchi had learned of a version of the attack plan that scratched his CarDiv 2 from the operation. Accounts of the ensuing incident vary, but all agree that a highly intoxicated Yamaguchi essentially assaulted Nagumo, placing him in a Judo headlock and demanding that he relent and include *Sōryū* and *Hiryū* in the operation.[12] Kusaka apparently intervened and separated the two. For his part, a similarly intoxicated Nagumo had threatened to knife Admiral Inoue at a garden party being held by no less personage than Prince Fushimi, the emperor's uncle.[13] Many saw Yamamoto's appointment as head of the Combined Fleet as an effort to remove him from the very real threat of assassination in the politically charged snake pit of Tokyo. Yamamoto, like Inoue, opposed the powerful Fleet Faction, and it was felt that he would be safer in Hashirajima. Thus, despite the rigid discipline inherent in the service, violent outbursts (often abetted by alcohol) were apparently within the norms of acceptable behavior.

This, then, was the character of the Navy that fought at Midway—a military force perhaps more definable by its contrasts than anything else. It was an organization that was both ferocious and sentimental, where extreme loyalty and discipline were matched by an equal aptitude for brutal behavior toward the rank and file, and a callous disregard for the lives of its men. As events were about to prove, it had put in the hard work necessary to be technically and tactically astute. But it had not matched those efforts with the mental exertion needed to operate at the higher strategic levels required by a global war.

At 1430 on the 28th, Nagumo's force sighted ships on the horizon. This was *Kidō Butai*'s supply unit, consisting of the oilers *Kyokutō Maru, Shinkoku Maru, Tōhō Maru,*

Nippon Maru, and *Kokuyō Maru.* They were escorted by destroyer *Akigumo.* As soon as these ships integrated themselves into the formation, Nagumo ordered a course change to the east-northeast. Things began to settle into a routine. Cruising speed was maintained at fourteen knots, in consideration of the fuel needs of the force's escorts, as well as the somewhat slower speed of the oilers.[14] Destroyers were notorious fuel hogs, and when conducting high-speed operations, their consumption rates could jump by a factor of ten or more. Therefore, all commanders took pains to ensure that their escorts were topped off as close to the battle site as possible. Each ship refueled at least twice en route.[15] The destroyers did so almost every day. The Japanese Navy wasn't as proficient in underway replenishment as the U.S. Navy was, and, as a result, their refueling operations were slower and more cumbersome. Larger ships used the less-efficient astern refueling method, wherein a six-inch hose was passed aft to a warship trailing the oiler. Destroyers sometimes did so as well, but more often they refueled side by side with the tanker.[16] These evolutions went on almost continuously as the fleet headed east.

Each day during the transit, one of the four carriers was designated the duty ship for the force.[17] *Sōryū* had the first watch on the 27th. As such, she was responsible for keeping a small combat air patrol contingent above the fleet at all times during daylight hours. In addition, the duty carrier worked with the cruisers and battleships to maintain antisubmarine patrols. ASW watches usually amounted to no more than two Type 99 bombers at any time. The duty carrier typically kept a small number of aircraft (either fighters or Type 99s) on the flight deck and warmed up during these hours. Patrols lasted two hours, although the Zeros could stay aloft much longer than this if need be.[18] Being the duty carrier meant a constant hum of low intensity flight operations continuing throughout the day, with remunitioning and refueling taking place in the hangars constantly. On the "off-duty" carriers, the crews devoted themselves to routine maintenance and training.

At this point in the war, the Japanese Navy relied on three types of carrier aircraft. The first was the famous Mitsubishi Type 0 (A6M2) carrier fighter (in Japanese, *kanjō sentōki,* often referred to by its abbreviated form *kansen,* or "fighter"). A small, highly streamlined airplane, the Zero had first won renown over the skies of China and then during the opening campaigns of the Pacific war. It was the epitome of the Japanese Navy's offensive spirit, combining extraordinary maneuverability and good firepower delivered by two 7.7-mm machine guns in the front cowling, and two 20-mm cannons in the wings. Optimized for low- to mid-altitude aerobatics, the Zero was perfect for dogfighting and complimented the *samurai*-like temperaments of its owners splendidly. In the hands of an expert pilot, it could fly rings around any Allied fighter.

The Zero was built around the Sakae-12 radial engine, which developed 950 horsepower at takeoff. Though not a particularly powerful engine by contemporary standards, it benefited from the Zero's lightweight construction and provided the plane with good wing loading and climb rate. When fitted with a drop tank, which the Japanese used routinely, it was also an extraordinarily long-ranged fighter, capable of operating as much as 300 miles from the carrier. However, it was also lightly built, almost totally unarmored, and did not possess self-sealing fuel tanks. It was, in short, a

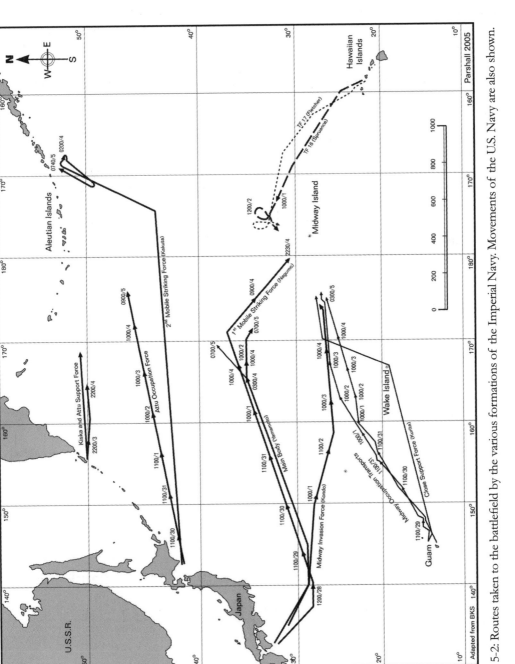

5-2: Routes taken to the battlefield by the various formations of the Imperial Navy. Movements of the U.S. Navy are also shown.

Adapted from BKS   Parshall 2005

very easy machine to be killed in if the enemy managed to get a good shot, as the pilot was exposed to gunfire and vulnerable to fires and explosions as well. Thus far, however, the Allied fighters hadn't been able to get the measure of the Zero in combat.

The Navy's dive-bomber was the large Aichi Type 99 (D3A1) carrier bomber (in Japanese, *kanjō bakugekiki,* referred to by its abbreviated form *kanbaku*). These powerful aircraft were notable for their spatted landing gear and graceful, elliptical wings. A two-seat plane (pilot and radio operator/rear gunner), they were ruggedly constructed to survive the rigors of screaming down at steep angles and high speeds. Their armament was either a 250-kg (550-lb) armor-piercing bomb, or a 242-kg (532-lb) high-explosive weapon. The Japanese had already demonstrated that their pilots were some of the best in the world, capable of hitting fast-moving warships routinely. If the Type 99 had one drawback, it was the weight of its payload—its opposite number in the U.S. Navy, the SBD Dauntless, was capable of carrying a 1,000-lb bomb. Still, the Type 99 had proven itself a worthy airplane in all theaters of combat and was rightly to be feared for its accuracy.

The third major plane in the Navy's carrier inventory was the Nakajima Type 97 (B5N2) carrier attack aircraft (*kanjō kōgekiki,* or just *kankō* for short.) The Type 97 was a dual-role aircraft and could perform both level bombing as well as torpedo attacks. In the first role, it could be armed with up to 800 kg (1,760 lb.) of bombs. In its antishipping role, it was armed with a Type 91 torpedo instead. Manned by three crewmen (pilot, observer/bombardier, radio operator/tail gunner) the Type 97 was a solid performer. It was markedly superior to its counterparts in the U.S. Navy in terms of speed, as well as the altitude and speed at which it could release its torpedo.[19] This last advantage was more the function of the ordnance than the plane, as the Japanese Type 91 torpedo was a much more reliable and robust weapon than its American equivalent.

In addition to these three proven mainstays, Operation MI would also witness the debut of a new carrier aircraft. *Sōryū* had on board her at least one, and likely two, prototypes of the much-anticipated successor to the Type 99 dive-bomber, the Yokosuka D4Y1 *Suisei* ("Comet"). These preproduction models had been modified for reconnaissance work, because they had good range and high cruising speed.[20] Having been worked up by two of *Sōryū*'s Type 99 crews, they were now along in place of two of the eighteen *kanbaku* normally carried by the carrier.[21] They would be used in a scouting role if necessary.

The basic tactical building block of every aircraft formation was the three-plane *shōtai.* Led by a *shōtaichō,* the *shōtai* was roughly equivalent to a section or element in a Western air force.[22] A *shōtai* typically flew in an inverted "V" pattern, with the lead aircraft slightly below the two trailing aircraft. The formation was looser than the old-style British three-plane "Vic," and somewhat more flexible. The Japanese had not yet picked up on the more useful four-plane formations that now dominated aerial tactics in the European theater and that had already been copied by the Americans.

A group of two or three *shōtai* composed a *chūtai* (equivalent to a division). At the beginning of the Pacific war, all carrier aircraft used a nine-plane *chūtai* organization. However, around March 1942, the *kankō* groups had begun shifting over to six-plane *chūtai,* most likely because it provided more flexible target selection capabilities for the

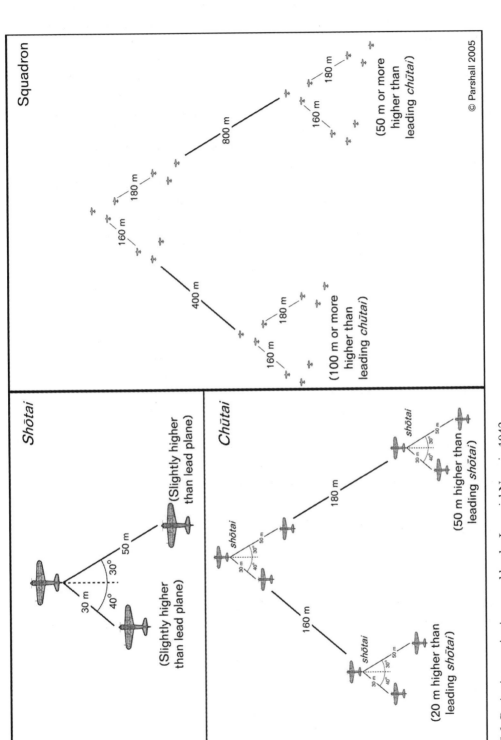

5-3: Basic air organizations used by the Imperial Navy in 1942.

squadron as whole.[23] Dive-bombers, however, still used nine-plane *chūtai* at Midway, as did the fighters. In the case of fighters, the *chūtai* formation was not really used tactically, the Zero pilots reverting to the three-plane *shōtai* formation during the heat of combat. Bombers, though, tended to maneuver and attack by *chūtai*. The leader of the *chūtai* was typically a lieutenant, designated the *buntaichō*.

The entire ship's establishment of a given type of aircraft was typically composed of two or three *chūtai*. Each squadron was designated according to the type of plane composing it. Thus a *kanjō kōgekikitai* was a torpedo bomber squadron, whereas a carrier's Zero unit was the *kanjō sentōkitai*, and so on. The squadron was led by the senior *buntaichō* among the two or more *buntaichō* that served in it. When operating with another carrier's matching *kitai*, the senior *buntaichō* among the two groups would lead the composite unit. The combination of all three of an individual carrier's squadrons resulted in the *hikōkitai*, or carrier air group. Commanded by either a lieutenant commander or commander (known as the *hikōtaichō*), the *hikōkitai* was referred to by the ship's name, for example, *Akagi hikōkitai*.

However, unlike the U.S. Navy, which at this point in the war did not actively employ a tactical organization higher than the individual carrier air group, during the China war the Japanese had taken the concept of massing airpower one step further by combining the air establishments of a carrier division (*Kōkū Sentai*) into a virtual combat organization of its own. To the Japanese, the carrier division, not the individual carrier, was the fundamental operational grouping, and naval air doctrine was centered on combined strikes using these groups. *Dai-ichi Kidō Butai* had been employing this practice since the beginning of the war, wielding a minimum of two and often three carrier divisions.

Having discussed Japanese aircraft and air unit organization, it is necessary to turn to a brief discussion of Japanese carrier doctrine and organization. Most readers of military history don't understand doctrine and don't want to, because it has no place in the tales of individual soldiers or great military leaders that they are used to. Indeed, doctrine is often seen as an unnecessary encumbrance that loses battles and gets in the way of exercising creative command. This is ironic, in that one of the prevalent goals behind doctrine is the simplification and streamlining of command, precisely so that commanders can fashion appropriate solutions during battle.[24]

Much of this disinterest in doctrine, particularly in the United States, stems from two factors. The first probably has much to do with the American temperament, which has always placed a premium on allowing talented individuals the freedom to "do things their own way." American civilian culture emphasizes individuality and the ability to improvise successfully under challenging circumstances. Along with this comes a unique American mistrust of dogma of any kind—religious, political, or cultural—on top of which is sprinkled a profound societal suspicion of overly professional militaries. Not only that, but doctrine itself is just impossibly dull for the average reader (and isn't noticeably livelier for the professional, for that matter). It is not surprising, therefore, that works on military doctrine have hardly been best sellers in the United States.

The other factor is that few devotees of military history actually know precisely what doctrine *is* or understand its purpose in battle. Doctrine is just, "Procedures you've got to follow." Yet, while it is true that doctrine does contain a mandatory element, this does not satisfactorily answer why militaries have doctrine. It also must be admitted that the basic criticism of amateurs—that doctrine atrophies the ability of commanders to reason critically—contains a kernel of truth. Doctrine *does* have a potential downside, in that it can stifle creativity if it is applied in an unthinking manner.

At its simplest, doctrine is the body of formal knowledge that tells a fighting force how it is expected to fight. Strictly speaking, doctrine is bigger than tactics, in that doctrine encompasses not only the means for actually handling forces in battle, but also augments it with a command structure and communications procedures that ensure that its directives are carried out. Wayne Hughes, whose book on naval tactics is probably the best modern offering in the field, describes doctrine as the intellectual glue that holds tactics together. It is more than what is written in the manual; it is the corpus of "guiding principles that warriors believe in and act on."[25]

The development of doctrine is the natural imperative of any military trying to rise above the level of being merely an armed mob. It is an essential means by which militaries compensate for the negatives of warfare by building a certain measure of automatic behavior into the organization. Indeed, in the terrible crucible of combat, under the enormous pressures created by mass violence, doctrine is sometimes the only thing that holds forces together and allows them to continue fighting. By setting out a coherent set of tactical goals, units can continue to operate even if the chain of command is disrupted or destroyed.

From the perspective of command, doctrine pays dividends in that it allows the commander to focus on "The Big Picture." Leaders can be secure in the knowledge that their forces will, to a certain extent, be able to "think" for themselves and thereby behave with some manner of predictability. The ability to impose *any* sort of predictability on the chaos of warfare is a commodity to be treasured. It is for this reason that militaries pour huge amounts of time and money into creating combat doctrine and training their forces to follow it. The Japanese were certainly no different from their foreign contemporaries in this respect.

Why does this matter to a study of the Battle of Midway? Because without understanding a Navy's doctrine, how and why it fights the way it does cannot truly be understood. Indeed, a great many retrospective questions along the lines of, "Why didn't Admiral So-and-So just do such and such?" can often be answered, "Because it wasn't part of their doctrine." Going against doctrine is almost always a dicey proposition within a military culture. Doctrinal innovators, even if they win the battle, will still be riddled with second-guessing regarding their approach, as if the victory were somehow tainted by heterodoxy. Worse yet awaits the commander who violates doctrine and loses.

Unfortunately, for the past sixty years, almost every Western historian who has written on the Battle of Midway has made the assumption that Japanese carriers and naval aviation forces behaved pretty much like their Western counterparts. In fact, in many respects they did *not*. The reasons the Japanese operated differently stemmed from a host of factors—starting with cultural and strategic imperatives, but also including technology and warship design. A grounding in Japanese doctrine is therefore a prerequisite for evaluating the performance of Nagumo's force during the battle. Fortunately, these principles, although poorly understood in the West until recently, are relatively simple to relate.

The fundamental principle that informed all Japanese doctrine was the need to offset the advantages of the United States, an opponent whose industrial base was incomparably stronger than Japan's and whose Navy was mandated by the Washington and London Naval treaties to be more powerful. The Japanese were thus caught in the intellectual vise of trying to devise the means to fight the Americans on a geopolitical landscape that guaranteed them fewer military assets at the outset and no hope of procuring long-term economic superiority. The result of these pressures were manifold and affected everything from the formulation of national strategy down to the level of tactics and equipment.

In terms of Japanese naval doctrine, there were two chief effects. First, the overriding need to compensate for numerical inferiority resulted in a tactical doctrine that elevated the principle of using coordinated, massed firepower to the status of divine law. Likewise, striking first, at longer range and with more powerful weaponry, was seen as the only possible antidote to American numerical preponderance. This was a rather archetypal "quality versus quantity" response, and the Japanese pursued this goal with a single-mindedness that would have been laudable had it not been so narrow-minded.

Before the war, it was presumed that the likely venue of Japan's superior firepower would be a decisive battle fought in the Western Pacific. Here, the Japanese would draw the American battle line to its eventual doom, relying first on coordinated night torpedo attacks delivered from cruisers and destroyers to whittle the American force down to size. Once the American battle line had been damaged and disorganized, a more conventional surface battle would be joined. In that culminating fight, devastating long-range gunfire from the Japanese battle line would complete the victory. It was for this battle that the Japanese Navy trained, to the exclusion of almost all else. As is often the case, though, overemphasis on one mission was detrimental to the balance of the force as a whole, as well as its thinking processes. Put simply, Japanese doctrine was warped. It placed an unrealistic emphasis on one type of battle and largely ignored the other traditional missions of great navies—sea control, amphibious power projection, and the protection of the nation's seaborne commerce. The result was that by the late 1930s, Japanese tactical doctrine was an almost Baroque ode to the principle of the offensive. And while it contained many elements that would serve the Japanese well during the first part of the Pacific war (superior night-fighting capabilities being a notable example), it was not an honest intellectual basis on which to build a successful war-fighting approach.[26]

The second major manifestation of the pressures placed on the Japanese Navy was to be found in its weapons systems. In a certain sense, warships and aircraft can be viewed as physical manifestations of doctrine. This only makes sense—weapons systems *should* be designed to operate in the fashion in which a navy as a whole intends to fight. Budgetary pressure and politics being what they are, most designs are usually modified away from the purely doctrinal requirements that spawned them. However, the warships and aircraft of the Japanese Navy as a whole represented a fairly congruent implementation of the Navy's intended approach to fighting a war. Japanese warships emphasized speed and offensive firepower, elements that suited the tactical homogeneity the Japanese always sought. These same general tenets were reflected in the Navy's aircraft, with their preference for range, firepower, and maneuverability. Conversely, Japanese warships placed less importance on structural strength, stability, protection, and damage control. Likewise, Japanese planes were built to dish it out but weren't really intended to take it. They tended to amplify the advantages of a superbly trained pilot but neglected the preservation of that pilot's life. Both Japanese ships and aircraft were more suited to a short naval conflict, where loss of human capital was less critical. They were not the calling cards of a navy with true staying power.

It can be argued that Japan's naval aviation forces were slightly more immune to the creeping orthodoxy that was slowly choking the Navy's ability to think creatively. This had more to do with the newness of naval aviation technology than anything else. By the 1930s, the battleship was a known commodity, a relatively "mature" technology. Such technologies tend to develop in a more incremental fashion, and their mode of employment is typically well understood. Indeed, apart from the longer range of the weapons, the commander of a battleship at Jutland would not have been impossibly out of his element standing twenty years later on the bridge of *Yamato*.

The aircraft carrier, in contrast, was the Wild West of the world's major navies. It was an immature weapons system, being created in front of everyone's eyes out of whole cloth. Nobody knew how carriers were supposed to fight or how they would be integrated within their respective naval forces. Both the ships and their aircraft were undergoing frantic, almost frightening technological changes, and their capabilities were improving at phenomenal rates. This, in turn, continually opened up new tactical and operational possibilities. Under such circumstances, carrier doctrine was a slate that had to be constantly written, erased, and then rewritten as new technological imperatives outmoded yesterday's beliefs. Not surprisingly, this dynamic environment attracted individuals who were comfortable with a certain degree of ambiguity and who had the ambition to put their stamp on the emerging air arm. Simply put, there was more room for innovation in the area of naval aviation than perhaps anywhere else within the Japanese Navy.

However, despite the influence of mavericks like Yamamoto and Genda, naval aviation could not help but be influenced by certain tenets of Japanese naval thought. The principle of delivering integrated, massed firepower against an objective was an idea that flowed naturally out of the "Gun Club" and into the carrier force. Mass has always been a cardinal military principle, and it was this desire for mass that ultimately led to the establishment of the world's first true carrier striking force—First Air Fleet (*Dai-ichi Kōkū Kantai*)—in April 1941.

The basic idea for this formation had apparently been Genda's.[27] According to him, he had been watching a movie newsreel, wherein the U.S. fleet was briefly featured. There, he had caught a glimpse of the U.S. fleet's *Lexington* and *Saratoga* parading in company with *Yorktown* and *Enterprise*. To Genda's way of thinking, massing carriers could be used for much more than simply making a good-looking film clip. It suddenly became clear to him that carriers could be grouped for tactical purposes, using hundreds of aircraft to project large bursts of devastating firepower. It took some doing, but eventually Genda persuaded Rear Admiral Ozawa Jisaburō, who in turn went directly to the Navy minister to ensure the formation of the organization Genda envisioned.[28]

First Air Fleet's establishment was a truly revolutionary development. For the first time in history there existed an agglomeration of naval air assets (ships, planes, pilots, and doctrine) that had the potential to create strategically meaningful results on the battlefield. The British and American navies had clearly influenced this development (the Japanese were keenly aware of the British carrier operation against the Italian fleet at Taranto, for instance). But it was the Imperial Navy that first established massed naval airpower at an operational level. By doing so, it had moved naval aviation out of its previous scouting/raiding role and transformed it into a decisive arm of battle.

The attack on Pearl Harbor represented the first clear-cut triumph of this new mode of warfare. And it is a simple statement of fact that in 1941 no other navy in the world could have implemented such a daring aerial assault—*Kidō Butai* alone possessed the combat assets and abilities to do so. Pearl Harbor demonstrated irrefutably that the Imperial Japanese Navy was no longer beholden to the West. It had clearly eclipsed the Royal Navy in terms of naval aviation and was in some ways more advanced than the U.S. Navy as well. This was particularly true with regards to integrating multiple aircraft carriers into a cohesive fighting force.

Massing and coordinating multicarrier air groups was something that the Japanese did exceedingly well. When employed in this way, Japanese doctrine prescribed attacking targets with groups of aircraft containing elements of all three disciplines—fighters, dive-bombers, and carrier-attack planes (acting in either a torpedo- or level-bombing capacity). In multidivision attacks, an entire carrier division would contribute matched air groups to the overall effort, launching both of its dive-bomber units (for instance), while a second division would launch its two carrier attack bomber units. These four squadrons—seventy or more combat aircraft—would be escorted by fighters contributed by all four carriers. On follow-up strikes, the air group compositions would be reversed, with the first division sending up its torpedo bombers and the second contributing the dive-bombers. The result was that Japanese carriers could launch large, well-balanced strikes against their enemies.

To support this favored mode of attack, the Japanese evolved a practice known as "deckload spotting," wherein a carrier would launch about half of its air group at any one time—a complete attack unit of some sort (torpedo- or dive-bombers) and usually a *chūtai* of fighters. With this initial force launched, the carrier would still retain half of its striking power for follow-up operations. This practice probably grew out of the impracticality of launching the carrier's complete air group. Such a group would need to be spotted and launched in two separate deck cycles, thus keeping the first half of the strike package waiting in the air over the force (and burning precious fuel) while the second portion was spotted and launched—an operation that could take at least half an hour to complete. With a deckload strike, though, the Japanese launched a group that fit comfortably on the flight deck and still had sufficient tactical weight. Indeed, the smaller carriers like *Hiryū* and *Sōryū* would have had difficulty in spotting a larger force in any case, because their decks would not accommodate the extra aircraft and still leave enough run-off room forward for takeoff.[29] Deckload strikes had worked well for the Japanese thus far in the war, because they left little question as to each carrier's contribution and lent themselves well to aggregating aircraft for an initial strike. Interestingly, this practice stood in direct contrast with how the U.S. Navy ran its carriers. U.S. flattops could, and occasionally did, send their entire air group aloft, although the complications this introduced into the deck cycles of their carriers would plague them throughout the coming battle.[30]

Having worked well for the Japanese, the practice of using deckload strikes was apparently no longer questioned. Herein lies the cardinal issue that any analysis of Japan's options at Midway revolves around—above all things, the Japanese believed in massing airpower, since delivering concentrated firepower at range was considered the most effective way of attacking the enemy. In the words of Ugaki, "This concentrated use of carriers has advantages, making it possible to command them so that their movement can be concealed, combined defense against an enemy attack is facilitated, and a combined simultaneous attack can be launched."[31] As a result, Japanese carrier commanders tended to look for tactical solutions that allowed airpower to be deployed in an integrated, multidivisional fashion.[32]

The weakness of this approach is apparent to anyone who has studied military affairs, namely, that in combat there are other factors worth considering besides mass, most notably speed. Thus far in the war, the Japanese had never been presented with a situation where the speed of their spotting and launching activities might well be more important than the combat mass delivered thereby. It remained to be seen whether Japanese air doctrine could react appropriately to such circumstances should they arise.

As his ships steamed eastward on the 29th, Nagumo took the opportunity of conducting limited air group training. After the battle, Nagumo would be bitter in his assessment of his fliers' deficiencies.[33] Carrier landings, torpedo and bombing attack, air combat, and practically every other index of air group efficiency came in for scathing treatment from *Kidō Butai*'s chief. However, upon closer examination, it is likely that these shortcomings were less real than that they were simply sour grapes on the part of Nagumo.

There's no question that the carriers of *Kidō Butai* had not had a lot of formal training during the previous six months. Torpedo practice, which was typically carried out on well-marked ranges at major bases, was certainly lacking. Training ranges were required because aerial torpedoes were a precious commodity. It was therefore important to have the necessary facilities to retrieve, refurbish, and then reissue them to the air units. Yet, except for a short sojourn in home waters immediately after Pearl Harbor, and again in May when *Kidō Butai* returned to Japan, the carriers had spent most of their time in remote waters with relatively primitive facilities. Anchorages like

Staring Bay were precisely that—a protected place to drop anchor, but hardly "bases" in the operative sense of the word. There were no torpedo or bomb ranges readily available in these locations. There were also usually no large airfields nearby that could accommodate the air groups from as many as six carriers at a time, meaning that even if training was attempted, it could only be done sporadically or in smaller groups. The only large-scale training undertaken before May was around Kendari during late March, in preparation for the raids in the Indian Ocean.[34] During this time, the fliers had drilled in large groups and had sought to implement new tactics learned as a result of battle lessons. It would appear that the Kendari sessions were more than just "brush-ups"; they were formally intended to maintain, and even improve, the proficiency of the air units through a brief regimen of intensive training. Thus, when Kidō Butai engaged in combat in the Indian Ocean in April, its overall efficiency appears to have been good.

Upon returning to the Inland Sea, the carrier air groups had been split up and sent to various land installations. Akagi's group was at Kagoshima in the extreme southern tip of Japan. Hiryū's was some eighty miles northeast at Tomitaka, near Saeki. Kaga's hikōtai was based about twenty-five miles southeast of Kagoshima at Kanoya, with Sōryū's close by at Kasanohara. Some of the bomber leaders were sent to Iwakuni (located just west of Hiroshima). Even with this distribution, the majority of the aircraft were within eighty miles of each other, which was a fairly easy distance as far as coordinating group exercises was concerned. It is true that the training undergone by the air units immediately before Midway was not satisfactory in all respects. For one thing, the majority of the carrier training had to occur on Kaga, because the other three carriers were in and out of dry dock and provisioning at Kure during this time. As a result, the majority of the exercises necessarily had to be done from the land bases, because Kaga could only handle a limited number of aircraft during this time.

However, the bottom line was that Kido Butai was still a very proficient force. The intensive workups before Pearl Harbor had already honed these men to a high degree of readiness, and despite the operational losses and transfers that had occurred since then, there were still a very large number of these senior aviators left. Thus, Nagumo's comments regarding the bare margin of proficiency of his "young fliers" in such basics as carrier landings seem a bit disingenuous, because by and large these were the same men who had been performing carrier landings routinely for the last six months in combat conditions. Because of Kidō Butai's heavy schedule, all of its aircraft had been constantly in use—fighters for combat air patrol, dive-bombers for ASW patrols, and kankō for long-range scouting around the fleet—meaning that stick time for the pilots was hardly a problem.

Nagumo's comments regarding his aviators are further laid bare by a detailed examination of the composition of his air group personnel in June 1942. Fully 70 percent of the pilots in Kidō Butai's four dive-bomber units were Pearl Harbor veterans.[35] The situation in the kankō groups was even better, with 85 percent of the pilots being Pearl Harbor alumni. Every single pilot in Akagi's kankōtai had been with the ship in December 1941.[36] Furthermore, many of the new pilots in the air groups were senior petty officers who had most likely been culled out of shoreside training commands and other billets. Thus, even the replacement aviators very often also were experienced men. Furthermore, they had been introduced into the air units in dribs and drabs over the course of the previous six months, meaning that they had had plenty of time to adjust to their units and get to know their shipmates.

It is true that the aircrews may have been employing their weapons less frequently, particularly their torpedoes. For instance, it is unlikely that *any* of CarDiv 1's or 2's *kankō* squadrons had dropped a torpedo in anger against an enemy target since Pearl Harbor. It is possible, therefore, that torpedo proficiency in the *kankōtai* may have been reduced. Yet, this was but one index of air group readiness. And in a broader sense the evidence seems to indicate that the aircrews still retained proficiency in the employment of their ordnance. In the Indian Ocean, the dive-bombers had demonstrated on two separate occasions that they were perfectly capable of attacking fast-moving warships. Even the relatively junior carriers of CarDiv 5 had performed credibly during the recent battles in the Coral Sea. It is hard, therefore, to discredit the quality of the aviators in *any* of Japan's fleet carrier divisions at this point in the war. Thus, in the final analysis, the comments in Nagumo's report must be taken with a large grain of salt.

A much more clear-cut problem was the number of planes in Nagumo's air groups. The truth was that when it came to aircraft complements throughout the fleet, things weren't just fraying around the edges, they were downright awful.[37] The Pearl Harbor operation had resulted in aircraft being stripped from other units to beef up *Kidō Butai*. After the operation had concluded, some of those units had been returned, but many of the smaller carriers were still little better than paper tigers. These flattops were flying fewer aircraft than they could carry and in several cases were being forced to use planes that weren't fit for frontline service. Japan had not started the war at a running start in terms of aircraft production, either. Of the major manufacturers devoted to carrier aircraft production—Mitsubishi, Nakajima, and Aichi—only Mitsubishi's fighter line was running well. Rumor in the fleet had it that there were production problems back at the other two, because carrier attack aircraft in particular were in short supply.[38]

In fact, Nakajima had stopped production of the Type 97 altogether in anticipation of fielding the new *Tenzan* torpedo bomber and had to be asked to restart production to meet war needs. Aichi, the builder of the D3A Type 99 dive-bomber, was in the same position. It was focusing all of its efforts on ironing out the production issues associated with the new D4Y and was neglecting production of the older platform. Consequently, by the middle of 1942, production of carrier bombers and attack aircraft had temporarily ground to a near halt and was completely insufficient to replace ongoing combat and operational losses. Japan would produce just fifty-six carrier attack aircraft during all of 1942—a pathetically low figure. Thus, even though Japan had won a string of stunning victories and its combat losses had been extraordinarily light for the territory it had gained, Japan's aircraft industry was not keeping up with even these modest demands. The result was a dramatic shortage of aircraft making their way to the fleet.[39]

Here at the edge of the sword in Nagumo's own force the effects were obvious. When the war had opened, *Kidō Butai*'s air groups had been full strength, although without as many spare aircraft as would have been optimal. But by June 1942, the situation had deteriorated. At the time of Pearl Harbor, *Akagi* had carried sixty-six aircraft; now she had just fifty-five. *Kaga* had been cut from seventy-five to sixty-three. *Sōryū* and *Hiryū* had come down from sixty-three apiece to fifty-four apiece.[40] Nominally, each squadron (fighter, bomber, and torpedo bomber) should have been allotted three spare aircraft, for a total of nine per ship. None were now carried by any ship in *Kidō Butai,* and *Kaga* was the only ship that still retained an oversized squadron of twenty-seven torpedo bombers. The rest of the ships were all operating eighteen aircraft squadrons, with no spares. In a nutshell, each of the *Kidō Butai* carriers had suffered a 16 percent decrease in their fighting power since December. Any casualties to the operating air groups, even damaged aircraft, would immediately impact the tactical cohesion of the air units, since there were no spare aircraft to feed into the formations.

Kidō Butai's carrier air groups at Midway were as follows:[41]

	Fighter	Dive-Bomber	Torpedo Attack	Total
Akagi	18	18	18	54
Kaga	18	18 + 2 spare[42]	27	63 + 2 spare
Sōryū	18	16 + 2 recon[43]	18	52 + 2 recon
Hiryū	18	18	18	54
Total	72	70 + 2 spare + 2 recon	81	223 + 2 spare + 2 recon. Total: 227 aircraft in the ships' organic *hikōtai*.

5-4: *Kidō Butai*'s carrier air groups at Midway.

However, in addition to the organic air strength of the carriers themselves, *Kidō Butai* also had guests along for the operation. Each carrier in the force was ferrying Zeros of the 6th Air Group (6th *Kōkūtai,* often abbreviated simply 6th *Kū*), which were intended as the future garrison of Midway. Twelve of these fighters were on board *Junyō* with the Second Carrier Striking Force, but the remainder were assigned to Nagumo's carriers. *Akagi* carried six, spacious *Kaga* hosted nine, and *Hiryū* and *Sōryū* carried three apiece.[44] These aircraft were stowed fully assembled, because the reduction in *Kidō Butai*'s own air groups had made space available in the hangars. The 6th *Kū* aviators had been welcomed warmly. Some of them were carrier-qualified pilots who could participate in combat activities in a pinch.[45] Nagumo thus had a grand total of 248 aircraft aboard his ships. By way of comparison, *Kidō Butai*'s six carriers had brought around 412 aircraft to the Pearl Harbor operation.[46] Nagumo was thus fighting the decisive battle with only 60 percent of the airpower he might reasonably have expected to use as recently as May.

If the aircraft situation was threadbare in the frontline carriers, it was far worse in the second-line carrier divisions. They were scraping up pilots and aircraft in any way they could to try and cobble together air groups, yet in most cases were falling short. *Junyō*'s case is illustrative. Recently commissioned, she was designed to carry fifty-four aircraft. Her dive-bomber group seems to have been reasonably intact and was composed of fifteen Type 99 aircraft. Her fighter group, however, was another matter. It was still in the midst of being activated and was in complete disarray. Twelve of the eighteen Zeros on board ship were actually aircraft from the 6th *Kū*. Yet 6th *Kū* was itself three planes and several pilots short of its nominal thirty-six plane establishment (the remaining twenty-one aircraft being with Nagumo). Not only that, but 6th *Kū* apparently didn't have enough aviators to man its own aircraft. Nor could *Junyō*'s aviators fill all the gaps. Indeed, *Junyō*'s air group for the battle contained only five of its own pilots. The remainder were four 6th *Kū* pilots, a trio of aviators (one of whom was fresh out of flight school) on temporary attached duty (TAD) from *Shōkaku*, and two more TAD fliers from *Ryūjō*![47] At the same time, though, *Junyō* had sent one of her own fighter pilots TAD over to *Sōryū*. Taken together, this meant that *Junyō* probably only carried thirty-three aircraft into battle.[48] The point to be made is obvious—not only was *Junyō* understrength, but also her fighter group at least was composed of men who did not know each other and who had never exercised together even once. The same was true for all the second-line carriers. *Ryūjō* was carrying thirty aircraft of her forty-eight nominal,[49] *Zuihō* twenty-four out of thirty,[50] and *Hōshō* a mere eight obsolete biplanes.

In a word, after six months of war, the Japanese carrier force was tired. It needed rest, refit, and replenishment of its air groups. It needed additional training. Above all, it needed time for the anemic Japanese aircraft industry to catch up to the demands of a full-scale war. For a Navy supposedly on the top of its game, the air groups were going into the decisive battle in a decidedly shabby fashion—fatigued and desperately short of aircraft. Yet the men were counting on playing the same game they had played against the Allies for the first six months of the conflict—using their own superb aviators against inferior enemy pilots and planes. It had always worked before; why not now as well? The problem, as some of the men must have suspected, was that they might be going back to the well once too often, and with too small a bucket.

After 29 May, the Japanese air groups did not participate in any further training. The *hikōtai,* other than patrol aircraft from the duty carriers, were stood down for final maintenance. The weather had been good for the first several days, and the eastward passage had been generally bland and unhurried. But as 1 June wore away, the weather began to turn, and Nagumo's force headed into hurrying clouds and a gray overcast.

6

Fog and Final Preparations

An observer hovering high over Midway on the morning of 2 June 1942, would have beheld a fascinating sight. Swarming over the horizon to the west and northwest were numerous Japanese naval task forces, most of which were converging on the tiny atoll below. Foremost among these was Nagumo's task force, followed at a distance of several hundred miles by Yamamoto's Main Body. The Aleutians forces were already headed into the seemingly never-ending fog and overcast that surrounded their objectives. Almost due west of Midway, Tanaka's invasion force was flanked by Kondō and Kurita's battle groups. Ahead of them, the individual submarines of the cordon lines were picking their way toward their posts in solitary stealth. As far as the Japanese could tell, despite Nagumo's late departure, all was still going according to Yamamoto's design. Yet a further glance over the shoulder would have revealed a shocking sight. Three American carriers—*Enterprise, Hornet,* and *Yorktown*—had already sailed from Pearl Harbor and were even now poised for battle to the northeast of Midway.

The events that led to the disclosure of Japan's designs at Midway to the enemy need only a brief retelling here. Just as American cryptographic prowess had allowed the U.S. Navy to thwart Inoue's thrust into the Coral Sea, so too it had revealed Yamamoto's intentions concerning Midway. As a result, Admiral Chester W. Nimitz was given enough warning, just barely, to assemble his forces in time to defend the island. It was a near-run thing, but the Americans showed great ingenuity and determination in using their more-limited assets to the greatest possible effect.

Nimitz had no clear idea as to Japanese intentions until very late in the game. It was not until 9 May that American intelligence began suspecting that operations might be afoot in the Central Pacific, perhaps in the form of a raid against Hawaii.[1] Around the same time, the American code-breaking station in Hawaii (known as HYPO) became aware of a "forthcoming campaign" that would demand the services of many battleships, carriers, and screening destroyers.[2] Furthermore, after the mysterious operation, these forces were going to be reassembled at Saipan, which in turn indicated that the preceding operation would occur in the Central Pacific.[3] At the same time, traffic analysis was recording an increase in message traffic between *Akagi* and subordinate commands like BatDiv 3. In the eyes of HYPO, Midway became the logical place for such an operation.

Nimitz himself was playing a dangerous game with his own superior, the demanding Admiral Ernest J. King, commander in chief of the U.S. Fleet. King remained nervous about a renewed Japanese offensive in the South Pacific, which his own intelligence chiefs were convinced remained the main objective of the Imperial Navy. Even before the Battle of Coral Sea, he had ordered Nimitz to commit *Enterprise* and *Hornet* to the region. Now, with *Lexington* sunk and *Yorktown* damaged, he wanted to keep them there. Nimitz, however, had confidence in the analysis of his intelligence staff and was determined to bring his carriers back to Pearl. In a daring move, Nimitz ordered Vice Admiral William Halsey, in an eyes-only communiqué to the latter aboard *Enterprise,* to deliberately expose his force to the Japanese. On the morning of 17 May, Task Force 16 was sighted by a Japanese flying boat operating out of Tulagi.[4] HYPO duly intercepted Japanese messages raising the alarm about American carriers, allowing Nimitz to use Halsey's manufactured sighting as reason to cancel his current mission and order *Enterprise* and *Hornet* back to Hawaii.

Meanwhile, Nimitz and HYPO still needed a breakthrough that would definitely confirm Midway as Japan's near-term objective. Nimitz's cryptographers devised an ingenuous stratagem to divine the location of the attack. On 19 May, on instructions from HYPO, Midway's radio station broadcast in clear that the island's desalinization plant had broken down.[5] Just one day later, the Americans broke a Japanese message giving the objective's call sign (MI) and indicating that a water ship should accompany the occupation forces. The Americans now definitely knew that Midway was the target of the forthcoming Japanese offensive. While the timing of the operation was still in doubt, the first cornerstone of Yamamoto's plan—the element of strategic surprise—had been irretrievably lost.

Another of Yamamoto's fundamental assumptions—that the U.S. Navy would need to be coaxed into battle—was erroneous as well. In fact, Nimitz was spoiling for a fight. His beliefs mirrored Yamamoto's in at least one regard—the most effective way to win the war was to bring the enemy's carriers to battle and defeat them. Nimitz's willingness to fight rested on two assumptions.[6] First, he was convinced that his commanders and crewmen, as demonstrated in the Coral Sea battles, were the match of their Japanese opposite numbers. Second, Nimitz believed that his advantage in strategic intelligence would allow his forces to ambush *Kidō Butai.* Now, his only problem was finding the necessary numbers of carriers.

HYPO's estimates indicated that the Japanese would launch their attack with four or five flattops, probably operating in two groups. Nimitz had to figure out how to roughly match their numbers.[7] The U.S. Navy had begun the war with seven carriers. One of these, *Ranger,* was no longer deemed fit for frontline service. This left six fleet units—*Lexington, Saratoga, Yorktown, Enterprise, Hornet,* and *Wasp.* The *Lexington* had been sunk at the Battle of Coral Sea. *Wasp* was currently engaged in the Mediterranean, ferrying British Spitfires to Malta, although she had been ordered to move to the Pacific immediately thereafter. *Saratoga,* having been torpedoed by a Japanese submarine on 11 January, had been repairing and refitting on the West Coast, and as of the end of May was still furiously putting together her air group and collecting enough escorts to sail. She would not be able to reach Pearl Harbor until 7 June. American intelligence estimates had the Japanese opening operations against Midway as early as 2 June, meaning that their own carriers would need to be in position off the island by the 1st.[8] *Saratoga* was therefore out of the picture. This left the *Yorktown*-class carriers available to contest Japanese moves.

Unfortunately, *Yorktown* herself had been badly damaged by bombs during the same battle that had claimed the *Lexington* at Coral Sea. Trailing a slick of oil from storage tanks that had been cracked as a result of a near miss, she had limped back to Pearl Harbor, arriving the same day Nagumo had sortied. Yet her presence in the coming Midway operation was absolutely vital. Although Nimitz was willing to do it, he knew that pitting just two American carriers against four of their Japanese opposite numbers was an extremely risky proposition, even with Midway-based aircraft backing them up. But with the addition of a third flight deck, the U.S. Navy could match the Japanese in total numbers of aircraft. It was essential that *Yorktown* be returned to working order as soon as possible.

In contrast with the Japanese lack of urgency about getting *Zuikaku* back into action, the Americans had moved heaven and earth on *Yorktown*'s behalf. Returning to Pearl Harbor on 27 May, she had first entered the repair basin, where 1,400 workmen had clambered on board and gotten to work.[9] She was then into dry dock on the 28th.[10] Realistically, *Yorktown* needed a three-month refit. Instead, she would receive slightly more than forty-eight hours of emergency repairs. It was an all-hands, around-the-clock effort, with some of the personnel simply working straight through without sleep. At the same time, *Yorktown* received replacements of three of her squadrons. *Saratoga*'s Bombing Three (VB-3) took the place of *Yorktown*'s Scouting Five (VS-5), which had suffered heavy casualties at Coral Sea. Likewise, Fighting Three largely replaced VF-42,[11] and Torpedo Three replaced VT-5. The fact that the Americans could insert replacement air groups into a carrier that they had never served aboard, while the Japanese hadn't even attempted a similar operation with the surviving aircraft from *Shōkaku* that had already been sitting in *Zuikaku,* gives testimony to the superior organizational skills that the U.S. Navy was already beginning to draw upon in the conflict.

By 0900 on 30 May, *Yorktown* headed back to sea, forming the core of American Task Force 17. She carried seventy-six aircraft—twenty-five F4F fighters, thirty-seven SBD dive-bombers, and fourteen TBD torpedo bombers.[12] With *Yorktown* went two heavy cruisers—*Astoria* and *Portland*—and five destroyers—*Hammann, Hughes, Morris, Anderson,* and *Russell.*

Yorktown's two sisterships, *Enterprise* and *Hornet,* had sortied the day before as Task Force 16. *Enterprise* carried seventy-eight aircraft (twenty-seven F4F fighters, thirty-seven SBD dive-bombers, and fourteen TBD torpedo bombers); *Hornet* carried seventy-seven (twenty-seven F4F fighters, thirty-five SBD dive-bombers, and fifteen TBD torpedo bombers).[13] Around them were the heavy cruisers *New Orleans, Minneapolis, Vincennes, Northampton,* and *Pensacola,* and the brand-new light cruiser *Atlanta.* A screen of nine destroyers—*Phelps, Worden, Monaghan, Aylwin, Balch, Conyngham, Benham, Ellet,* and *Maury*—completed the force.

Rear Admiral Frank Jack Fletcher, flying his flag in *Yorktown,* would have tactical command of the carrier striking forces, as well as direct control over TF 17. He was a veteran of much action already in the war, having been at sea since the commencement of hostilities. Fletcher was a careful commander and certainly somewhat more cautious than his counterpart, Halsey. He had been taught some lessons in this regard at the Battle of Coral Sea just prior. Much like Admiral Takagi, the American commander had struck an aggressive blow against what he presumed to be the main Japanese task force, only to discover that he had launched an all-out attack against the light carrier *Shōhō*. While sinking her was useful, it had been something of a waste and had left Fletcher's own forces exposed. It was an error he did not intend to repeat.

6-1: The experienced Rear Admiral Frank Jack Fletcher, commander of the American carrier forces. (Photo courtesy John Lundstrom)

By rights, Fletcher's senior officer in Task Force 16 should have been Vice Admiral Halsey, who had commanded the forces centered on *Enterprise* since the beginning of the war. However, Halsey had recently contracted shingles, making it impossible for him to sleep. As a result, upon returning to Pearl he was immediately placed on medical leave, leaving a gap in the command structure. Nimitz asked Halsey for his recommendation for a replacement, and to Nimitz's great surprise, he nominated his cruiser commander, Rear Admiral Raymond A. Spruance. Spruance was not a carrier man and had never commanded a mixed task force before. Nevertheless, Halsey had such complete confidence in his abilities that Nimitz was persuaded that Spruance would make a sound choice.

It is ironic that the hot-tempered and profane Halsey had such utter faith in a man so completely his opposite. Spruance was a very cool customer. A man defined almost totally by his intellect, he was articulate, careful, methodical, and extremely attentive to detail. Upon assuming command of Task Force 16, he wasn't overawed by his own lack of knowledge regarding naval aviation. But he also had the intellectual honesty to be aware of his shortcomings, and he took rapid steps to fill in the gaps. As events were to prove, he was also aggressive, calculating, and a commander who would not panic in adversity.

Altogether, the American carriers brought 233 aircraft to the fight, just fifteen fewer than Nagumo's carrier force. However, the American carriers had much less experience in joint operations than did the Japanese. Furthermore, Task Force 16 and 17 intended to fight separately, often out of eyesight of each other, making coordination problematic. It was hoped, however, that dispersal would make it more difficult for the

6-2: Rear Admiral Raymond A. Spruance, commander of Task Force 16. (Naval Historical Center)

Japanese to detect and attack all of the American carriers simultaneously.

Nimitz had not been idle in reinforcing Midway's own air strength. Commanded by Captain Cyril T. Simard, Midway was currently operating four squadrons, composed of thirty-one PBY Catalina patrol planes. These planes were aggressively pushing reconnaissance flights out to 700 miles from the atoll. By 4 June Eastern Island's airstrip was stuffed to the rafters with another ninety-six aircraft of all sorts, including Navy, Marine Corps, and Army Air Force attack planes. There was a squadron of seventeen B-17 heavy bombers, as well as a foursome of B-26 medium bombers fitted for carrying torpedoes. The Marines had contributed a squadron of twenty-one old Brewster F2A Buffalo fighters and seven F4F Wildcats, and a squadron of nineteen SBD dive-bombers and twenty-one older SB2U scout bombers. The Navy brought in a detachment of six brand-new TBF torpedo planes and a light utility plane. In all, 127 U.S. aircraft were temporarily calling Midway home. The increase in the numbers and range of patrols, as well as the much larger air group at the base meant that by 1 June the base's aviation fuel consumption had exploded to 65,000 gallons daily, against a total of about 150,000 gallons of avgas storage on the island.[14] Keeping the air station supplied with fuel was quickly becoming a problem.

Nimitz placed his forces brilliantly, ordering Fletcher to hold his carriers some 300 miles to the northeast of Kidō Butai's anticipated axis of advance. From this otherwise indistinguishable spot of ocean, named "Point Luck" (32N, 173W), his carriers would be in a position to ambush the Japanese after the enemy launched their aircraft against Midway. By steering clear of the waters south of the island, he was well positioned to avoid any possible entanglements with the various advancing Japanese formations. Here, the Americans were more exposed to attack, but they were also in a better position to launch their own surprise assault on the Japanese flank. Nimitz didn't know the exact composition of the enemy forces, but he was confident that he could give battle under favorable terms as long as he retained the element of surprise. He had also deployed a strong group of twelve American fleet boats around Midway itself, which would hopefully weaken any Japanese force and open it up to attack.

Despite the boldness of his plan, Nimitz felt no need for a do-or-die effort in defense of the atoll. He expected his carrier admirals to attack aggressively but judiciously, seeking opportunities to inflict maximum damage at the minimum cost in what was termed "strong attritional tactics." Under no circumstances were the carriers to be sacrificed unnecessarily. If the situation became untenable, they were to back off and let the Japanese attempt an invasion. Nimitz understood the logistical situation of the atoll better than the Japanese did themselves, knowing that he would be in a better position to retake the islands than the Japanese would be to defend it. As a result, preserving the three American flight decks was more important than preserving the Marine garrison there.

However, the Marines had taken their own measures to ensure that if it ever came to a fight, they would be able to face the Japanese on the best terms possible. Their Sixth Defense Battalion, under the energetic leadership of Col. Harold D. Shannon, had been stiffened by the addition of two companies of elite Marine Raiders. A platoon of light tanks had been sequestered in the tiny pine forest at the center of Sand Island. The men had engaged in a frenzy of defensive preparations—digging multiple lines of emplacements, hardening heavy weapons sites, and clearing fields of fire across the beaches. They had laid thickets of barbed wire around their perimeters and entrenched their communications lines. And they had improvised an array of lethal explosive booby traps and mines to strew across the beaches and landing approaches. Midway's two islands now bristled with defenses. Even a heavily supported Japanese landing would have found the going very difficult. (See Appendix 5 for an analysis of the likely outcome of such a landing operation.) Thus, by 1 June, after weeks of frantic work, everything was coming together for the Americans.

The same was hardly true of the Japanese. Indeed, an omniscient observer would also have noticed that by this time the Japanese strategic scouting plan for Operation MI had fallen completely to pieces. The submarine cordon lines, upon which Nagumo was counting for early warning of northward-advancing Americans, were tardy in taking their positions, having left Kwajalein late. But even had they left on time they would have missed the American carriers. By the time Cordon A and B were established, the Americans had already slipped past it.

The reasons for the failure of the submarine picket lines, which were not properly understood until after the war, verge on the scandalous.[15] The commander of Sixth Fleet, Japan's submarine forces, was Vice Admiral Marquis Komatsu Teruhisa, the cousin of the empress of Japan, and a close personal friend of Emperor Hirohito. The marquis was a great fan of Yamamoto's and had such confidence in the Midway operation that in his opinion the battle was as good as won. So much so, in fact, that he was already preoccupied with follow-up plans to attack the Panama Canal and terrorize California. He thus paid little attention to the nuts and bolts of the deployment against Midway. While he was supposed to be at the staff planning sessions held on board *Yamato*, Komatsu did not attend, sending his staff instead.[16] Furthermore, according to Gordon Prange, the submarine cordon details "never appeared in the official orders for Operation MI. Writing up the submarine portion of such orders was a normal responsibility of Commander Arima Takayasu, Yamamoto's submarine officer. But for some reason, Captain Kuroshima told Arima that he had no need to do so."[17] This rather incredible oversight meant that the Japanese boats were committed to action without a workable operational plan.

Furthermore, the boats that were tasked for the operation—the older vessels of SubRon 5—were far from ideal for the mission. None of them could dive safely past 200 feet,[18] and all of them were under refit during the April–May period, with the intent of being shortly moved into the reserve fleet and relegated to training purposes. Not surprisingly, Commander Iura Shōjirō of Naval GHQ's submarine staff protested to Admiral Fukudome that the boats were too slow and balky to get on station in a timely manner, nor could they cope with air attacks and patrols once they got there.[19] His protests fell on deaf ears.

As matters developed, Iura was completely correct in his estimation of SubRon 5's weaknesses. Their overhauls took too long, and the boats were late in leaving Kwajalein, departing between 26 and 30 May. Worse yet, the long daylight hours, coupled with intensifying American patrol activity, meant that the boats had only limited time during the night to transit on the surface. During the days they were often forced to dive to avoid Catalinas, creeping forward submerged as best they could. The result was that while the boats were scheduled to be in place by 1 June (local), some of them didn't reach their stations until 3 June, by which time the American carriers had already passed through.[20] Had the American task forces been sighted in the vicinity, Yamamoto and Nagumo would have had both actionable information and the time to make last-minute adjustments to their operational plans. As it was, they received neither.

This would have been bad enough, but even worse was the fact that Admiral Komatsu was fully aware that his force had taken up their stations late, but did not relay this up the chain of command. On or about 3 June, Komatsu notified Admiral Yamamoto of the failure of Operation K (described shortly).[21] However, he did *not* call Yamamoto's attention to the fact that his picket submarines had arrived late on station. Obviously, this was a serious oversight, if oversight it was. The net result was that not only did Yamamoto and Nagumo not know whether the American carriers had sortied toward Midway or not, they weren't even *aware* that they didn't know. In fact, they didn't know that there was any problem with their scouting arrangements at all.

It would appear that because of Komatsu's membership in the imperial family, he was never held to account for this crucial failure. As one observer later noted, "Japanese historians in later years would allude to [the event] only obliquely, and American historians . . . would [necessarily] follow the lead of the Japanese."[22] One example of such an oblique reference is supplied by Admiral Ugaki, who remarked after the battle in his diary that "we failed to make good use of subs in reconnaissance," despite having ordered the cordons in place to prevent the very sort of ambush that in fact occurred.[23]

Komatsu's oversights, though, might have been made good, if the Japanese were willing to put some of the other pieces of the puzzle together. Indeed, as the Japanese advanced, they began receiving evidence that the Americans were wise to at least some of Yamamoto's initial deployments. On 30 May, shortly after Admiral Tanaka's Invasion Force sortied from Saipan, an American submarine dead ahead had been overheard broadcasting a long coded message of an urgent nature.[24] Given that Tanaka's force was on course almost directly for its ultimate objective, it would not take much for the Americans to figure out where he was headed. In addition, the Japanese had noted via radio intercepts that an increased number of American submarines were operating in the mid-Pacific and Aleutians.[25]

Closer to the battle area, Operation K, the seaplane scouting effort aimed at assessing the status of Pearl Harbor, had had to be aborted on the 31st. One of the Japanese refueling subs, the *I-121,* approaching French Frigate Shoals on the 27th, had found that the previously isolated islet had now become the abode of an American seaplane tender and her destroyer consort. The Japanese submarine was shortly joined by her sister, *I-123,* but the Americans showed no signs of departing. On the 30th, *I-123* reluctantly radioed headquarters at Kwajalein regarding the setback. Operation K was postponed for twenty-four hours in the vain hope that the Americans would move on the following day. However, the next morning American flying boats were now seen moored in the lagoon. French Frigate Shoals was clearly an operational American seaplane base. Attacking their ships would only bring attention to the area, but without them gone, there was no way that the huge Kawanishi flying boats could refuel. Operation K had to be scrubbed, thus depriving Nagumo of any intelligence regarding the American's main fleet base.

Submarine *I-168,* meanwhile, had been scouting Midway itself. Her captain, Lt. Commander Tanabe Yahachi, submitted a comprehensive report on 2 June concerning the activities he had observed there. The atoll was mounting an average of nearly 100 flights daily. The seaplanes were gone much of the daylight hours, meaning that they were patrolling aggressively out to great distances. At night, blazing work lights indicated that construction was proceeding around the clock.[26] Midway did not appear to be a sleepy backwater unaware of its approaching fate. On the contrary, the atoll had every appearance of an outpost doubly on its guard. Commander Tanabe's reports were duly sent up the chain of command but apparently didn't make much of an impression.

Japanese radio intercept stations in Japan, Truk, and Saipan had also noticed that American radio traffic emanating from Hawaii was up.[27] Additionally, many of the orders being sent by Nimitz to his subordinates were tagged "Urgent." Taken together, Japanese traffic analysis seemed to indicate that American heavy forces were probably operating at sea, rather than sitting in Pearl Harbor.[28]

The question is, how much of this information actually came into Nagumo's hands as he sailed toward battle, and did he act on it? The conventional wisdom, as promulgated by Fuchida Mitsuo's postwar account, *Midway: The Battle that Doomed Japan,* is that Nagumo was completely in the dark regarding all of these matters except the failure of Operation K.[29] Nagumo's own report states flatly that the Americans were not aware of Japanese plans and that his forces were not discovered until the morning of 5 June (4 June Midway time).[30] Fuchida blamed this failure in part on Combined Fleet staff's decision on board *Yamato* to not transmit information forward to Nagumo, and also on *Akagi*'s poor communications capabilities, resulting from her allegedly small island and limited number of radio aerials.[31] However, neither of these excuses really stands up to scrutiny.

First of all, *Akagi*'s problems with communications, if there were any, likely had less to do with the number or quality of her aerials than it did with their height above

6-3: Battleship *Haruna,* flagship BatDiv 3 (Second Section). (Photo courtesy Todaka Kazushige)

the surface of the ocean. All Japanese carriers suffered from this problem, in that they had relatively small bridge structures and mainmasts. Consequently, there were few places high in the ship to place an aerial, which in turn explains their location on the sides of the flight decks. When flight operations were under way, they were cranked into their horizontal positions, away from the flight deck and any potential accidents, thus lowering them further and hampering their use for communications. This was a known weakness of making an aircraft carrier a flagship, yet the Japanese accepted these drawbacks to exercise better local control over the task force's various air groups.[32] However, despite these shortcomings, it is equally clear that *Kidō Butai's* communications did not rely solely on *Akagi's* equipment.

The Japanese communications plan for Midway called for each ship's wireless receivers to be continuously manned and tuned to the broadcast of the First Communications Unit in Tokyo, which was responsible for relaying all messages received from units of Combined Fleet back out to the forces at sea. Each of Nagumo's twenty ships, plus the six ships of the Supply Unit, were thus continuously on the alert for communications from Tokyo and would relay such information first to their respective unit flagships and then on up to the force flagship (*Akagi*) as the need arose. In addition to listening for Tokyo's broadcasts, every vessel in *Kidō Butai* that had sufficient receivers was also listening to enemy frequencies, hoping to intercept enemy aircraft and submarine transmissions.[33] This latter function was the responsibility of each ship's radio direction finding (RDF) unit, such equipment being carried by all of the larger ships.

Both *Haruna* and *Kirishima* had communications facilities befitting a capital ship, including radio aerials mounted high atop their towering mainmasts. It is known that one of BatDiv 3's vessels (most likely *Haruna*) was officially designated as a backup battle force communications facility in the event of an emergency.[34] The brand-new cruisers *Tone* and *Chikuma* also had quite modern facilities.[35] Even old *Nagara's* RDF and radio outfit had been upgraded in 1936.[36] All in all, *Kidō Butai* seems to have been well equipped to receive instructions from either Tokyo or Combined Fleet Headquarters (*Yamato*). It also mounted adequate equipment for intercepting and localizing enemy radio transmissions. Indeed, the overall problem with Japanese communications had less to do with their inability to receive information than it did with Japanese emphasis on radio silence, as well as commanders' tendencies to gloss over or equivocate regarding transmitting bad news. Without a willingness to evaluate and *act* on information, all the radio equipment in the world wasn't going to help Nagumo.

The radio reports surrounding the failure of Operation K illustrate how the system was supposed to work. *I-123*'s messages regarding French Frigate Shoals were broadcast upward to her headquarters at Sixth Fleet in Kwajalein. Kwajalein, in turn, was required to keep Saipan, Truk, Wake, Combined Fleet HQ (at sea), and (most important) the First Communications Unit at Tokyo in the loop. First Communications Unit was then responsible for rebroadcasting pertinent information back out to the various fleet commands. This is exactly what happened on the 31st with *I-123*'s reports. Both Fuchida and Ugaki acknowledge in their accounts that the Main Body received these messages.[37] In other words, the system (with its very centralized control of communications) was working. It was successfully passing information from low-level units up the chain of communications and then back out to the various commands (although it is unclear whether *Yamato* received *I-123*'s initial message, Sixth Fleet's report of the incident to Tokyo, First Communications Unit's rebroadcast, or some mixture of these three sources).[38] *I-168*'s report on the 2nd regarding enemy activity at Midway was similarly received on *Yamato*.

It is true that even with modern facilities, *Kidō Butai* might well have suffered a communications breakdown. Merely having radios tuned to the right frequency was no guarantee that Nagumo was actually receiving the information he needed. Indeed, such failures plagued both the Japanese and Americans during the early portions of the war. However, *Akagi*'s air group report provides compelling evidence that the admiral and his staff were much better informed on the matter of American activities than the common wisdom would have us believe. *Akagi*'s report specifically notes increased patrolling by American aircraft operating out of Midway starting around 29 May. It also cites the increased presence of enemy submarines whose goal was apparently reconnoitering the Japanese forces. Crucially, both of these items were described as having been derived from either radio intelligence and/or Japanese reconnaissance aircraft. More important, the report further indicates that "According to Naval General Staff service message radio intelligence of 31 May, for the last several days there has been a tendency for the number of enemy vessels participating in the Pacific Air Base Communications System and the General Ships Communications System centered at Honolulu to increase."[39]

Several aspects of *Akagi*'s report bear elaboration. First, it is specific that the information in hand had been derived from other units, not *Kidō Butai*. Second, the fact that it describes the conditions of the enemy on both 29 and 31 May means that this information was received by *Akagi* *after* she sailed from Hashirajima. If so, then she had to have received messages from the First Communications Unit. Ugaki's diary makes mention of the very same data being received on board *Yamato* on the 29th as well, indicating that *Akagi* and Nagumo were receiving Tokyo's transmissions just fine.[40] Finally, the fact that *Akagi*'s report describes these three pieces of intelligence information under the heading of "Enemy Situation before the Battle" clearly implies that Nagumo had received this data *prior* to the engagement.

The matter of the transmitting American submarine off of Saipan is interesting as well. Fuchida's account asserts that it was the radio intercept unit aboard *Yamato* that detected the American boat. However, Admiral Ugaki, who was actually on board *Yamato* at the time, mentions only that the submarine's messages had been intercepted, not by whom. Given the proximity of land-based radio equipment at the fleet base at Saipan, and the fact that *Yamato* had barely cleared the coast of Japan at the time the intercept was made, it would appear much more likely that *Yamato*'s interception (if it occurred at all) was merely a supplement to a detection by Saipan's own RDF unit. Such a radio intercept would have been communicated directly to Tokyo by the Fifth Communications Unit at Saipan, and thence back out to the fleet, where Nagumo would likely have received it as well. In sum, it appears likely that Nagumo was less in the dark about the Americans' alertness than has been believed. If he did not have the complete puzzle in hand, he at least had a number of the important pieces.[41]

Taking *Akagi*'s report at face value, Nagumo should have known three things. First, that American patrol aircraft out of Midway were operating far afield and that the risk of detection was high. This placed the invasion forces to his south at particular risk, because Nagumo's tardy departure had, in essence, placed Tanaka one day ahead of where he should have been relative to *Kidō Butai*. This, in turn, meant that Nagumo could not count on the timing of the battle unfolding as planned. Second, given the increase in enemy signal traffic, it was likely that the American fleet carriers were engaged in urgent operations *somewhere* in the Pacific. Third, with the failure of Operation K, he was now completely devoid of any credible intelligence on the enemy's strength and movements. The American carriers could literally be anywhere. Given no clear-cut evidence for either an optimistic or pessimistic estimate of the enemy's dispositions, a prudent commander should have planned for the worst case.

The question is, why did he apparently not bother to recast his plans? At the very least, why did he not make arrangements to beef up his scouting assets, so as to completely assure himself that there would be no surprises? There are a number of explanations for this. The first probably hinges on the lack of any direct information from Komatsu's tardy submarine picket line. Another factor is the general contempt in which the American forces were held at this time by the Japanese. Despite the setback at Coral Sea, the fact remained that the Japanese had reeled off an almost unbroken string of victories in the first six months of the war. Tired air groups and aviators notwithstanding, the Japanese, and especially the members of Combined Fleet staff, believed that they were better than the Americans: no matter where, when, or under what circumstances they met. Admiral Ugaki, commenting on the possibility of Tanaka's transport force having been detected sooner than planned off of Saipan, remarked in his diary that "its premature discovery might lead to a showdown with the enemy force, which is rather welcome."[42] Such an attitude of supreme confidence bespoke the general attitude throughout the fleet—simply showing up was apparently all that was required for Nagumo to secure the victory.

Whatever his faults, though, Nagumo does not come across as an arrogant man, nor does he seem to have been rash, as the following anecdote illustrates. Following the return of *Kidō Butai* to Kyūshū after its sortie into the Indian Ocean in April, a technical research conference was held at Kanoya air base to begin planning for the development of the Zero fighter's successor. Present were representatives from *Kōku Hombu* (the Navy Air Technical Bureau) and the Yokosuka Air Group (which was the Navy's test pilot squadron). Representatives from *Kidō Butai,* including Nagumo, were there to provide the latest in direct combat experience. Mitsubishi's Horikoshi Jiro, the famed designer of the Zero, was present, as was Lt. Cdr. Nagamori Yoshio, who represented the fighter airframe section from *Kōku Hombu.* Both men later report that the mood of overweening self-confidence among the airmen was palpable, especially among the fighter pilots. Any attempt at cautious analysis or measured debate tended to get pushed aside by their unlimited exuberance.

After the conference, the participants attended a dinner hosted by Nagumo. The admiral dutifully made the rounds, exchanging toasts of sake with everyone present. When he came to Nagamori, Nagumo sat down on the *tatami* mat and crossed his legs in front of the young lieutenant commander. According to Nagamori, Nagumo said to him, quite emphatically, "Don't take what the men of the fleet tell you at face value. At times we tend to be swayed by emotion and give opinions based on the momentum of the moment. Your job is to take all factors into consideration and reach a cool and balanced conclusion."[43] This was not a reckless individual, nor one given to being dismissive of the enemy.

If true, though, what are the reasons for Nagumo's lack of initiative in terms of incorporating current intelligence into his operational planning? First of all, it is not clear that Nagumo's orders allowed him to improvise if the need arose. All the senior officers in the fleet knew that Yamamoto had not been inclined to change even the tiniest details of his grand scheme at any point during the previous two months of planning. Having been previously castigated by the commander in chief over his performance at Pearl Harbor, Nagumo would hardly be inclined to take matters into his own hands unless the situation clearly warranted it. The intelligence he had may have been worrisome, but that was about it. Without concrete information to act on, Nagumo may have simply judged that the wisest course was to continue with what he was doing and attend to any unpleasant realities as they arose.

This rather passive, fatalistic outlook was further compounded by an institutional weakness on the part of the Japanese military toward improvisation. The truth of the matter was that an inability to change their plans in midstride was endemic to the Japanese military as a whole. Nagumo was emotionally and by training a creation of this military tradition. He didn't know how to improvise, and he didn't want to try. But really, why would anyone expect him to be otherwise? He was the product of a military that placed obedience above all other virtues, a military that had succeeded in snuffing out the flame of individuality in the majority of its officers, a military that for four years would send men to their deaths in the blindest, most stupid ways imaginable. For a Western historian, this is one of the most maddening aspects of the Japanese Navy to contemplate: that in many cases the Japanese almost seemed to view defeat and their own deaths as the easier option to take, rather than shouldering the mental burden of having to reason their way out of unanticipated problems. Nagumo, despite his exalted position and responsibility, in the final analysis behaved as he ought to have behaved—by acting as the unquestioning tool of a supreme commander who was himself a demonstrated autocrat. Whatever Nagumo's failings as an operational leader, the final responsibility for his unwillingness to improvise must be laid firmly at the feet of the man whose flawed strategic outlook had created the mess in the first place, and the military culture that had let all of this occur.

On the morning of 2 June (1 June for the American forces), the weather around *Kidō Butai* began to worsen noticeably. By 1000, the force was beset by fog, which worsened through the day, until by evening Nagumo's ships were shrouded in an impenetrable white cloud. The situation was no better on the morning of the 3rd. All the ships streamed buoys aft, so that the vessels following them would be able to determine if they were overhauling a hidden ship in front.[44] Yet the ships still had to attempt to zigzag, and keeping station was a nightmare.[45] *Akagi*'s navigator, Commander Gishiro Miura, was a bundle of nerves but tried to affect a casual air by padding about the bridge in his slippers.[46] His tiny three-by-four-foot map table was now the center of *Akagi*'s world, as he strained to keep the flagship heading in the right direction while fretting about what the other ships might be doing out there in the gloom.

On the right side of the bridge, clustered around the fifteen-centimeter spotting glasses, Nagumo and his staff tried to stay out of the way. Nagumo stared out the windows into the opaque white walls surrounding him. Occasionally, one of the force's escorts would heave momentarily into view at the apex of a zigzag but then was almost immediately lost to sight again. Nagumo's anxiety was high. He was scheduled to change course southeast this morning to begin the final approach to the objective. In normal conditions, this would be executed with ease, but visual communications were now almost out of the question. Waiting until the appointed hour arrived and then trusting that every ship in the task force would simply execute a smooth turn to starboard was a fool's hope—a collision was almost guaranteed. Some sort of positive action had to be taken to assure the coordination of the force, or *Kidō Butai* might not make its designated flying-off spot in time. However, the fleet was currently steaming under a formal state of absolute radio silence (Condition "*Te-Se-Ka*"). As such, radio transmission was only authorized in emergencies where operations required it. Under this condition, Nagumo alone was empowered to make decisions regarding the usage of the fleet's radios.[47]

On the bridge, the situation was tense, as Nagumo and his staff debated what to do. Kusaka's deputy, Captain Ōishi, was in favor of sticking to the schedule.[48] But in the next breath he noted that the entire invasion schedule was dependent on attacking Midway on 5 June. Nagumo finally came down in favor of venturing a radio transmission. At 1030, the order was given over *Akagi*'s medium frequency

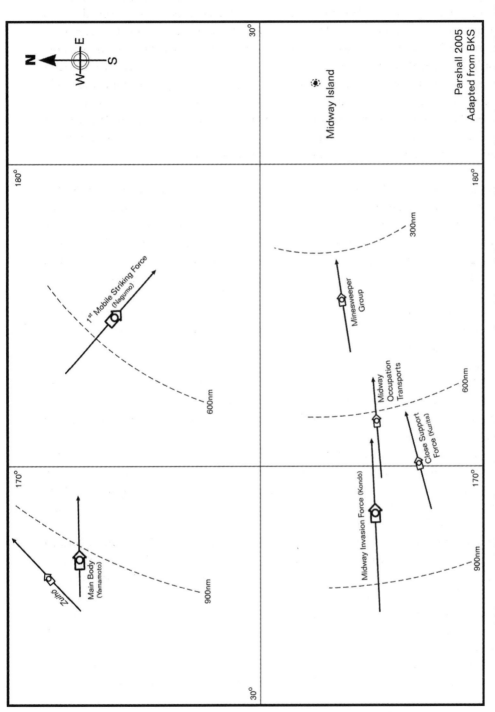

6-4: Situation on 4 June (Tokyo time). This map shows the relative movements and positions of the various Japanese formations during 4 June. Of particular importance is the relatively forward deployment of the various invasion forces—a result of Nagumo's delayed departure from Hashirajima. (Source: *Senshi Sōsho*, p. 242)

set: "At 1200 hours, change to course 100 degrees."[49] Nagumo and First Air Fleet staff fervently hoped that the Americans would not be the wiser to their low-power broadcast. There was no way of telling, of course, whether the enemy was now alerted to their plans.[50]

At noon, Nagumo's force made its appointed turn. Almost immediately, as if in mockery, the weather began to clear. *Kidō Butai*'s thirsty destroyers, which had been forced to suspend fueling activities the previous day, at once began sidling up to their designated oilers. Fueling went slowly, and the force still encountered heavy intermittent fog banks. Nevertheless, it seemed that the worst of the weather was behind them.

Meanwhile, far to the south, this day had not been without complications for Tanaka's invasion force, as the Americans had become aware of his approach. At 0843 on the 4th, a PBY Catalina had stumbled across Captain Miyamoto's Minesweeper Group. About forty-five minutes later, a different PBY had sighted Admiral Tanaka's group, which was at that point almost 700 miles due west from the atoll. Initially misidentified by the American pilot as the Japanese Main Body, it took until nearly 1100 for Midway's air commander to satisfy himself that Tanaka's force did not, in fact, contain the Japanese heavy units. Nevertheless, it was a significant enough force to be worth attacking. Accordingly, nine B-17s from the 431st Bombardment Squadron were dispatched against Tanaka shortly after noon.

The bombers took more than four hours to reach Tanaka, arriving overhead at 1623. For all the formidable reputation that Japanese lookouts were to develop in subsequent engagements, this one did them little credit, because the Americans were able to set up their initial runs at altitudes between 8,000 and 12,000 feet without the transports arrayed neatly below them apparently being aware of their presence. Only at the last minute, with bombs exploding around them, did the Japanese vessels realize their peril and begin jinking to avoid the incoming ordnance. As luck would have it, no hits were scored on any of Tanaka's charges. The Japanese force quickly put up a hasty, heavy antiaircraft barrage, but it did no good. After about ten minutes overhead, the American aircraft withdrew. Tanaka promptly radioed news of his encounter out to Combined Fleet.

The morning of 4 June had also seen the detachment of the Supply Force from *Kidō Butai*. The five oilers concluded their refueling activities at 0307 (roughly 0507 local), and they and destroyer *Akigumo* departed the formation, steaming south at twelve knots. Thereafter, *Kidō Butai* kept ready-duty fighters on deck, because they were now within range of American patrols. Two and a half hours later, *Akagi*'s signal lamps began blinking out the following day's strike mission to the force, which called for Midway to be struck at dawn. At 1025 ship's time,[51] Nagumo followed up with orders concerning the fleet's anticipated movements after the strike force was in the air. Shortly afterward, the force increased speed to twenty-four knots. They would steam at high speed for the rest of the day and through the night to close on the objective in time for the following morning's launch. Finally, at 1530 ship's time, Nagumo blinkered detailed signals to the fleet regarding the search activities to be undertaken on 5 June.

The reconnaissance program as conceived by Commander Genda was simple and direct. Seven aircraft would fly a series of spoke-shaped searches out from the fleet, principally on the exposed eastern and southern flanks. The No. 1 and No. 2 search lines (being 181 and 154 degrees) were to be flown by torpedo aircraft from *Akagi* and *Kaga*, respectively. Heavy cruiser *Tone*'s aircraft were tasked with searching down lines No. 3 and No. 4 (123 and 100 degrees). To do this, she would use two E13A1 Type 0 reconnaissance seaplanes. In addition, she would contribute an E8N2 Type 95 to the task force's antisubmarine patrol. *Chikuma* would do likewise with one of her Type 95s and use two more Type 0s to search lines No. 5 and No. 6 (77 and 54 degrees, respectively). Line No. 7 (31 degrees) would be run by a Type 95 seaplane from *Haruna*. Each of the recon planes except *Haruna*'s was assigned to fly their line for 300 miles before making a port turn for sixty miles. At the completion of the dogleg, each plane would return to the task force. *Haruna*'s Type 95 seaplane would only search out for 150 miles before making its 40-mile dogleg and then homing.

The primary criticism leveled against Genda's search plan—that it was more of a rubber stamp than an honest attempt to assess if an enemy was truly at hand—is certainly warranted. This is a point that has been hammered home in every Western book on the battle, though it was first brought to light by Fuchida. His views on the topic are worth stating at length, since they comprise the bulk of an argument that has been picked up on by historians ever since:

Although the coverage appeared adequate, I still felt that a two-phase search would have been wiser. A single-phase search might be sufficient if we wished only to confirm our assumption that no enemy fleet was in the vicinity. However, if we recognized the possibility that this assumption might be wrong and that an enemy force might be present, our searches should have been such as to assure that we could locate and attack it before it could strike at us. For this purpose a two-phase dawn search was the logical answer.

As the term indicates, a two-phase search employs two sets of planes which fly the same search lines, with a given time interval between them. Since our planes were not equipped with radar at this time, they were completely reliant on visual observation and could search effectively only by daylight. Consequently, to spot an enemy force as soon as possible after dawn, it was necessary to have one set of planes, (the first phase) launched in time to reach the end of their search radius as day was breaking. This meant that the areas traversed in darkness on their outbound flight remained unsearched. Hence a second-phase search was required over these same lines by planes taking off about one hour later.

Men assigned to the first phase of such a search obviously had to be well trained in night flying. Nagumo had such pilots and could have used this method, but it would have required twice as many planes as a single-phase search. Despite the importance of conducting adequate searches, our naval strategists were congenitally reluctant to devote more than a bare minimum of their limited plane strength to such missions. Ten percent of total strength was all they were willing to spare for search operations, feeling that the rest should be reserved for offensive use. But such overemphasis on offensive strength had proven detrimental to our purposes before this, and it would again.

Naturally enough, Admiral Nagumo was eager to devote maximum strength to the Midway attack and did not want to use any more planes for search than seemed absolutely necessary. Since he had no reason to suspect that presence of an enemy force in the area, he was satisfied that a single-phase search was adequate precaution against the unexpected.[52]

Fuchida's diagnosis of the problem is largely correct, but his prescription—a two-phase search—is based completely on hindsight derived from later war experience. In fact, at this stage in the conflict, a two-phase search was totally unknown, and single-phase searches were the only kind of search plans there were.[53] It would not be until May 1943 that Combined Fleet would formally incorporate two-phase searches into its doctrine, largely as the result of lessons learned at Midway and in the Solomon Islands.[54] For Fuchida to assign blame to Nagumo and Genda for somehow failing to apprehend an (ostensibly) obvious solution that was not even a part of contemporary Japanese naval doctrine is clearly unfair.

A truly honest assessment of the Japanese reconnaissance plan must begin by discarding this non sequitur and analyzing what could reasonably be accomplished within the framework of the doctrine, search assets, and meteorological conditions that pertained on 5/4 June 1942. Fuchida is correct in pointing out that Japanese carrier doctrine, like their naval doctrine as a whole, was almost purely offensive minded. Any reduction of the carrier attack squadrons to perform scouting missions was ipso facto looked upon as something of a waste. As such, Japanese carriers had no formally established search units on board. Conversely, of course, the Japanese clearly needed to make sure that their offensive firepower was being fully employed against the right targets, thereby making sound scouting essential to the success of the operation.

On the face of it, it would appear that the reconnaissance effort could have been undertaken without the carriers' help. After all, battleships *Haruna* and *Kirishima,* heavy cruisers *Tone* and *Chikuma,* and the light cruiser *Nagara* all carried reconnaissance floatplanes. In fact, the Japanese had developed heavy cruisers like *Tone* and *Chikuma* precisely for the purpose of off-loading scouting duties from the carriers. Unfortunately, the majority of the floatplanes in the fleet were actually ill-suited for long-range reconnaissance. *Tone* and *Chikuma* nominally carried five aircraft apiece— three Type 0 floatplanes and two Type 95. The two battleships of BatDiv 3 were equipped with three Type 95s as well. *Nagara,* in her role as a destroyer flotilla flagship, was most likely carrying one of the rather rare Aichi E11A1 night reconnaissance seaplanes.[55] Unfortunately, whereas the newer Type 0 floatplanes had a range of over 1,100 miles, the Type 95 was limited to 485. Developed in the mid-1930s, it was really more of a spotting plane—used for correcting the fall of shot from a battleship or heavy cruiser—than a true search aircraft. At the time it was designed, carrier-borne aircraft barely had the ability to strike over the horizon. Now, they could attack from more than 200 miles away. The Type 95 simply did not have the range necessary to detect enemies before they were within striking distance. Similarly, *Nagara*'s plane was intended for night work and wouldn't have been used during the day in any case. Thus, the Type 0 floatplanes were the only decent reconnaissance floatplanes in the fleet, and only five of these appear to have been available.[56] If carrier aircraft weren't used, Nagumo's scouting assets were slim indeed.

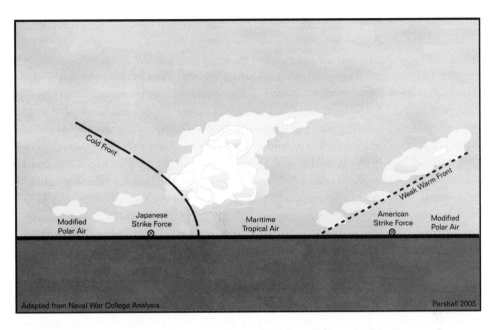

6-5: Schematic of weather conditions pertaining 0100 June 5/June 4. This diagram shows the relative positions of *Kidō Butai* and the American striking force in the vicinity of Midway. (Source: U.S. Naval War College Analysis of the Battle of Midway, p. 84, plate 11)

The other factor to consider was the weather and the size of the battle area. If a rectangle were laid over the extremes of the Japanese search plan, it would cover more than 176,000 square miles, an area larger than Sweden. The weather conditions would not be uniform across this space, meaning that each aircraft's sighting range would vary. Come the morrow, *Kidō Butai* would be trailing just behind the leading edge of a strong cold front moving down from the northwest. The front would be demarcated by lines of cumulous clouds, squalls and showers. The heavy weather and fog that Nagumo's force had plowed through on the 2nd and 3rd was now behind them, but it was also continuing to follow them down from the northwest. The weather to their north and northeast was therefore likely to be poor for scouting. Furthermore, as the front moved down, it was pushing scattered clouds into the area in a broad east-west band that would gird the middle of the battlefield, making scouting to the east more challenging as well. Only to the south was the weather likely to open up a bit.

At *Kidō Butai*'s launch position, the conditions were a mixed bag. Behind the front, they would be sailing beneath bands of broken clouds, with ceilings of between 1,000 and 3,000 feet. This offered the force excellent concealment. However, as events would prove, more clouds than sky would be visible, making detection of incoming aircraft more difficult.

Before the days of radar, scout aircraft (on both sides) flew at relatively low altitudes, typically between 1,000 and 1,500 feet. There were several reasons for this.[57] First, it was difficult to spot submarines at higher altitudes, and spotting submarines was an important part of any scout's job. Second, staying low gave the scout a better chance to evade hostile aircraft, because it could dive for the deck and thereby avoid being attacked from below. Third, and most important, scouting at low altitude allowed the horizon to be used as a mechanism for scanning for ship profiles. In fact, flying at high altitude was often counterproductive for spotting ships below if patchy cloud conditions were prevalent. Whereas breaks in the clouds allowed good visibility directly under the aircraft, those gaps disappeared toward the horizon as the angle of view from the aircraft became shallower, making even patchy cloud cover appear to be an unbroken blanket at longer ranges.[58] The end result was that scout aircraft had visual ranges that were relatively limited to begin with because of their altitude and that could be impacted significantly by local weather conditions.

With the above in mind, it is clear that Genda's plan suffered from a twofold failure. The first had nothing to do with the hypothetical phasing of the search. Rather, it was the sheer number of aircraft being devoted to the initial sweep. Put simply, seven planes could not reconnoiter an area the size of Sweden. By way of comparison, the U.S. Navy was not only planning on devoting the thirty-one PBYs based at Midway for scouting duties, but could call on three squadrons of armed Dauntless dive-bombers (fifty-six aircraft in all) from their carriers in an armed scout role as well.[59] The PBYs by themselves would outnumber Japanese scout aircraft by more than four to one.

Genda wrote postwar that "it has to be admitted that the planning of the air searching was slipshod."[60] Although the plan was a repeat of the search missions used at Pearl Harbor and Indian Ocean, Genda went on to elaborate that this plan "involved a defect of leaving an uncovered space in the search area, especially when an enemy force moved across or slant-wise of the planned search arc. The search plan should have been made more mathematically and precisely."[61] Genda might have also added the word "flexibly" to his list of desirable attributes. Mathematically precise or not, the search scheme was completely divorced from the realities of the weather conditions that would likely pertain on 5 June. Having just traversed a front of very bad weather, it should have been apparent to Nagumo's staff that more aircraft would be needed. When the likely spotting ranges of the Japanese aircraft are superimposed over the tracks that they (nominally) flew, the basic problem is immediately apparent— there were serious gaps in the coverage. As such, it might have been wise to hold a few aircraft in reserve to blanket those vectors with lower visibility conditions.

The success of Genda's plan depended on having decent weather everywhere, alert crews, and nearly perfect timing on the part of all the planes involved to ensure that their very tightly defined routes were adequately reconnoitered. If these arrangements were thrown off in any way, then detection of the enemy might be tardy. Genda, better than anyone in the fleet, had a sense for what *Kidō Butai*'s operational cycles were like. As events were to prove, the First Carrier Striking Force possessed many laudable military assets, but operational flexibility did not figure prominently in its portfolio of strengths. Genda should have had a sense that, faced with a suddenly emerging threat, the Japanese carrier force would not be able to simply drop what it was doing and turn to face the new opponent, particularly if it was already heavily

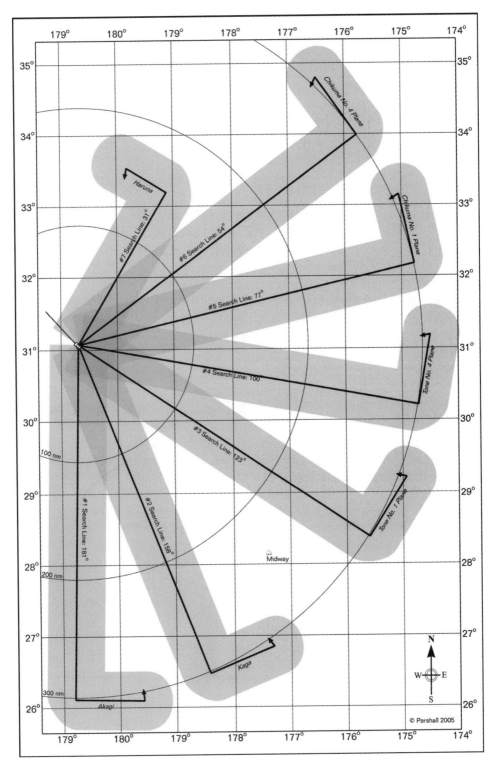

6-6: *Kidō Butai*'s planned single phase search pattern with nominal twenty-five-mile search ranges superimposed. (Adapted from *Senshi Sōsho,* p. 286)

engaged against Midway. It was absolutely critical to ensure that the force had the time necessary to react.

If that meant making a down payment of striking power, and devoting *Kaga*'s extra *chūtai* of nine Type 97 *kankō* to the problem of covering the eastern flank of the force, then so be it. Even an extra three aircraft on that flank could have changed the aspect of Genda's search from Swiss cheese to at least a medium cheddar. But Genda didn't think he'd need these extra aircraft. Instead, he opted to cut his scouting margin to nothing and reserve as much offensive firepower as he could. Here is where the false economy of Genda's plan is made clear. By not being willing to sacrifice a fairly marginal number of aircraft for scouting duties, Genda had implicitly forfeited the fleet's ability to buy time for itself.

As for the dawn strike against Midway itself, it was to take off at 0430 and comprise 108 aircraft total. CarDiv 2 would contribute its entire contingent of thirty-six Type 97s acting as level bombers. These planes would lead the attack from the east and thereby gaining the advantage of having the sun at their backs. *Hiryū*'s aircraft were tasked with bombing Sand Island's facilities; *Sōryū*'s would attend to Eastern Island and its airfield. Once the initial wave of high-level attacks was concluded, the dive-bombers would move in. CarDiv 1 would contribute thirty-six bombers from both of its flight decks. *Akagi*'s eighteen were slated to attack Eastern Island, with *Kaga*'s hitting Sand Island. The remainder of the attack force, a strong contingent of thirty-six Zero fighters, had a twofold mission. The first, obviously, was to safely shepherd the attack aircraft to the target and destroy or disperse any enemy fighters that got in the way. Then, having achieved air superiority over the objective, the Zeros would strafe any enemy aircraft on the ground.

On the face of it, this was a fairly powerful strike force, but, in fact, it was marginal to the task at hand. Midway, for all its diminutive size, actually possessed an aircraft contingent nearly as large as the attacking Japanese force. Not only that, but its base facilities were strongly defended. The thirty-six Zeros in the fighter escort could provide little in the way of real offensive firepower to neutralize these objectives, meaning that the four attack units would have to take them all out. Seventy-two aircraft were simply insufficient to accomplish this in the course of a single strike. High-level bombing was not all that accurate an attack technique. It was performed by six-plane *chūtai* flying in formation and dropping together on command, the basic rationale being that if one dropped six large bombs on something fairly large itself, perhaps one or two might actually do some damage. For this reason, level bombing was used against large targets such as runways or shore installations. This left just thirty-six dive-bombers to get at the meat of the matter—the antiaircraft defenses, command and control installations, and other hardened targets that composed the guts of Midway's defenses. Clearly, thirty-six medium-sized bombs weren't going to get the job done. It was almost guaranteed that a second strike would be needed to degrade the atoll's ability to defend itself.

In fact, all indications are that Nagumo's staff fully expected a second strike to be required. This had become something of a de facto pattern of the Striking Force over the last several months. The operations in the Indian Ocean had been executed in a similar fashion—an initial strike launched, with a reserve force held in readiness, followed by the rearming of the reserves for land attack in a subsequent wave. The fact that a second strike would be required wasn't a problem in and of itself, but it pointed to a lack of offensive firepower on the part of the force as a whole. If there were American carriers nearby, *Kidō Butai* didn't really have sufficient firepower to deal with both threats in a timely manner. This indicates a fundamental misapprehension on the part of Combined Fleet's staff of the type of operation it was actually undertaking. They were treating the operation like a raid, à la the attacks made thus far on Pearl Harbor, Port Darwin, Colombo, and Trincomalee. But Midway wasn't a raid; it was an invasion. And conducting a proper invasion carried with it an implicit commitment to sustainable action in the face of the enemy. *Kidō Butai* was short on staying power in several key dimensions—logistical support, heavy gun power (if it got involved in a surface action), and particularly numbers of aircraft.

Given that a second strike would most likely be required, the question remained as to which aircraft would undertake the action. It will be recalled that during the May war games, Yamamoto had issued verbal orders to First Air Fleet staff to maintain at least half of the striking power of the fleet armed for antiship missions. However, it is unclear from the record as to what exact time frame or contingencies the orders pertained. How, and when, were these reserve aircraft to be used in the (likely) eventuality that there were no American fleet units present next morning? Was it truly Yamamoto's intent to permanently divide Nagumo's operational aircraft into two halves—a ground-attack half and an antiship half? Or were his orders merely given to remind Nagumo that the threat of American naval resistance was not to be underestimated? What, really, were his priorities—attacking Midway, or attacking warships should he encounter them? In the lack of written orders, it is impossible to know, although common sense would dictate that any enemy naval force had to be given priority. The overall effect of Yamamoto's instruction, though, was to add another element of inflexibility and uncertainty into the following day's operations.

By the time Nagumo issued his morning's orders, it is likely that he (like the Main Body steaming behind him) had received news of Tanaka's being discovered and then attacked. Admiral Kusaka later stated that they received the communiqué.[62] This was yet another clue that the enemy was fully alerted to the impending Japanese operation. But still nothing was done to alter the instructions just issued to *Kidō Butai* regarding the coming operations.

As the day crept toward evening, the level of tension began ratcheting up a notch. At 1630 cruiser *Tone* opened fire with her main battery in the direction of what appeared to her to be multiple enemy aircraft bearing almost due south. A *shōtai* of fighters took off from *Akagi* a minute later but found nothing. At 1640 a chagrined *Tone* reported that it had lost track of the enemy aircraft. Skepticism reigned on *Akagi*'s bridge—everyone was simply getting a little edgier as the morning of battle drew closer.

The men went to General Quarters a half hour after nightfall to change over to nighttime steaming formation.[63] The fleet loosened its columns and moved the carriers into a box. Meanwhile, *Haruna* moved to the fore, so as to have some heavy gun power in the van in the event of an unexpected night fight. Around midnight, shadowy American aircraft would twice be reported by *Akagi*'s jumpy lookouts. Belowdecks, the majority of the crews had long since gone to bed—adequate sleep time was enforced after lights out.[64] Everyone, from Nagumo down to the lowliest crewman, knew that tomorrow would be busy.

The final act of the evening played out far to the south, where Tanaka's Invasion Force had its own encounters with shadowy enemy aircraft that turned out to be all too real. Determined to get another blow in against the Japanese as soon as possible, the American air commander, Captain Simard, had ordered four radar-equipped Catalinas sent out for a night torpedo attack. Dropping torpedoes was hardly stock in trade for PBYs at this point in the war, but the crews were game for giving it a try. One of the aircraft ran into bad weather and was forced to turn back, but the remaining trio made it to the Japanese convoy by about 0130. Tanaka's charges were plodding ahead in two columns surrounded by the screen. None of the ships were taking evasive maneuvers, and all were neatly silhouetted by the moon as the Americans attacked sequentially from out of the gloomy northeast.

The Japanese were caught flat-footed and were slow to react with either helm or antiaircraft fire, although the latter strengthened noticeably as the attack continued. Two of the PBYs missed, but the third plane—piloted by Ensign Gaylord D. Propst—managed to put a torpedo into the port bow of the oiler *Akebono Maru* at 0154 (local), killing or wounding twenty-three men. Propst didn't know it, but his jury-rigged Catalina had just pulled off the only successful American torpedo attack—aerial or submarine—of the entire battle. *Akebono Maru,* though damaged, shortly rejoined formation and continued on. That ended the night's excitement for Tanaka. Within an hour, the Nagumo force would begin rousing from its slumber to begin preparations for the coming dawn.

PART II
Battle Diary

7

Morning Attack—0430–0600

Thursday, June 5/4[1] began with *Dai-ichi Kidō Butai* doing what it had been doing regularly since the start of the Pacific war—arming, fueling, lifting, and positioning (spotting) its aircraft for a strike. The outcome of these tasks—putting planes in the air—is so familiar to any reader of World War II naval history that the precursors are largely taken for granted. This is what carriers are meant to do, after all—launch and recover aircraft. Yet sixty years of separation have left the details of exactly how the Japanese operated their carriers so poorly understood that the way they actually fought is no longer entirely understood either. As a result, historians have been in the unenviable position of trying to analyze the Japanese circumstances on 4 June in terms of analogs based on Western practice. In fact, Japanese carriers did things their own way, which is crucial to understanding how *Kidō Butai* fought and died this day.

To be ready for takeoff at 0430, the day's work had to begin well before dawn.[2] It would involve the prodigious labor of thousands of well-trained crewmen, the majority of whom were not aviators. Indeed, the pilots were still sleeping at around 0230 when the order "*Seibiin-okoshi* (Wake up the crew)" was issued for the aircraft mechanics.[3] Stumbling out of their hammocks and narrow bunks deep in the crew spaces, they dressed, stowed their bedding, breakfasted quickly, and then made their way to the hangars. Many of the men, not having had a change of uniform in some while (again, because of freshwater concerns), changed into fresh clothes, believing that the code of chivalry required clean clothing for combat.[4] Some of the officers were dressed in blue winter uniforms (Admiral Ugaki had postponed the normal June 1st switch to summer uniforms until "further notice").[5] Many of the crewmen, however, were likely in uniform whites or in the cooler "South Seas uniform" of khaki shorts, shirts (or sometimes just their white undershirts), and floppy hats beloved by Japanese sailors. It wasn't hot now, but they knew it would be later, and there wouldn't be an opportunity to change again during the day's duties.

The aircraft—dark green, buff and black—sat in the harsh electric glare of the hangars. Some of them sported elaborate camouflage patterns or the bright horizontal tail bands indicating *shōtai* and *chūtai* leaders. Many of these aircraft were veterans of the Pearl Harbor attack, not to mention the other strikes that *Kidō Butai* had launched across half the breadth of the Pacific. Not surprisingly, some of them were beginning to display the weather-beaten look seemingly universal among well-used naval aircraft

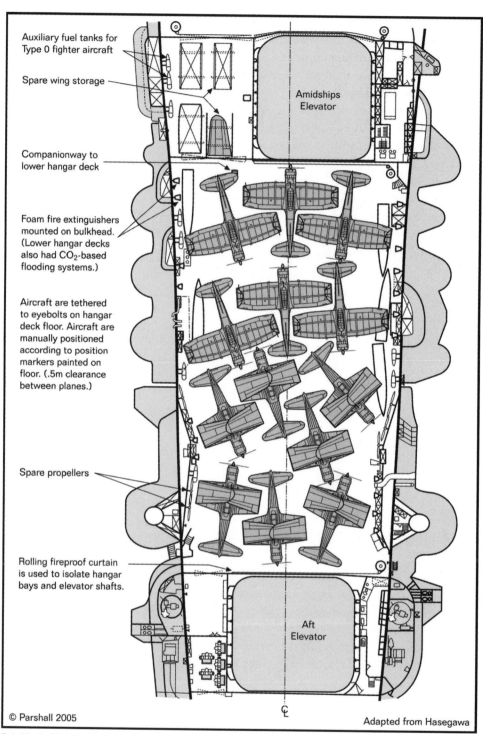

Auxiliary fuel tanks for Type 0 fighter aircraft

Spare wing storage

Amidships Elevator

Companionway to lower hangar deck

Foam fire extinguishers mounted on bulkhead. (Lower hangar decks also had CO_2-based flooding systems.)

Aircraft are tethered to eyebolts on hangar deck floor. Aircraft are manually positioned according to position markers painted on floor. (.5m clearance between planes.)

Spare propellers

Rolling fireproof curtain is used to isolate hangar bays and elevator shafts.

Aft Elevator

© Parshall 2005

Adapted from Hasegawa

7-1: Typical hangar deck interior. The extremely tight packing of the ship's aircraft can be seen, along with the complexity of equipment to be found on the hangar.

of all nations—worn and chipped paint, dripping hydraulics, and a certain level of idiosyncratic crankiness that persisted in spite of the care they were given. All were now empty—unarmed and unfueled.

There were more than sixteen hundred mechanics on board Nagumo's four carriers. These men, like the pilots of *Kidō Butai,* were among the very best practitioners of their craft in the world. They had worked together for years and were intimately familiar with their charges. Unlike America, where almost every young man had at least a passing acquaintance with internal combustion engines, Japan was far less industrially developed. In 1940 Japan manufactured only one-*eightieth* the number of automobiles that were produced in the United States.[6] Agriculture was still largely performed by hand. As a result, Japanese mechanics did not grow on trees. These men, whether they had been plucked from the *inaka* ("the sticks") or had grown up in the teeming coastal cities, had been trained from the ground up over the course of years.

Each mechanic was assigned to a specific plane, just as in the USN, and labored under the watchful eye of the plane's maintenance petty officer (*seibichō*). Unlike American carriers, the Japanese normally did not stow their aircraft on the flight deck in a deck park when not in use.[7] Instead, the hangars were always stuffed. The aircraft were crammed in practically touching each other, with each plane's location in the hangar indicated by symbols painted on the deck. Each was secured by tether wires to tie-down points arranged in a 1.5-meter grid across the deck.[8] Chocks were also placed under the wheels. The hangars smelled strongly of the exotic mix of grease, oil, paint, and all the chemicals and lubricants that go along with the operation of aircraft. No amount of white-gloved fastidiousness was sufficient to remove the odor.

On board CarDiv 2, the division's attack planes needed to be fueled and armed before being moved topside. The crewmen began unrolling metal hoses to the aircraft and pumping fuel into them. Along the hangar walls, a seventy-three-gallon drop tank for each Zero was unfastened from brackets on the bulkheads, attached, and then fueled. Each plane required between 180 and 235 gallons of fuel, and gassing the aircraft (as well as the Zero's drop tanks) took several minutes apiece. Unlike American carriers, the Japanese hangars were entirely enclosed from the elements. As fueling continued, the faintest hint of aviation gasoline could be detected, mingling with the predominant aroma of paint and motor oils. Overhead, on the port side of the hangar spaces, ventilation systems noisily blew new air in, while the starboard-side vents mounted at deck level labored to suck the noxious fumes away.

Simultaneously, armorers were beginning the arduous task of affixing their deadly wares to the attack aircraft. For the initial attack against Midway, CarDiv 2's planes would be armed with Type 80 800-kg land-attack bombs. Deep below the waterline, in the bomb storage rooms of *Hiryū* and *Sōryū,* the men used overhead block and tackle to wrestle the gray-painted weapons onto the lifts that carried them up to the hangars. The bomb lifts terminated on a platform set a meter above deck level. This arrangement prevented deck-hugging gasoline vapors from seeping down the lift shafts and into the magazines. The platform also provided a more convenient means for loading the weapons onto the carts that would carry them to the waiting planes.

Each aircraft carrier was equipped with special carts for moving ordnance around. One variety was used for the 242-kg and 250-kg bombs that were carried by the dive-bombers. A second, much heavier cart was used to carry both the Type 80 bombs, as well as the 850-kg weight of the Type 91 Mod. 3 torpedoes. Typically, each carrier had enough ordnance carts to rearm one-third of their respective *hikōtai* at a time, meaning six carts for each type of ordnance (and nine for the twenty-seven-strong wing of torpedo bombers on board *Kaga*).

One by one, the nine-foot-long weapons came up the bomb lift. One by one, they were secured to overhead tackle and deposited on the waiting bomb carts. Then *Hiryū* and *Sōryū*'s men rolled their three-ton packages of cart and bomb from the loading platform to their assigned planes, wending their way through the jammed hangars. Once there, they began the five-minute process of hoisting the heavy weapon up into place and securing it to the plane's curved ordnance holding brackets (*tokaki*).[9] Each Type 97 had a hand crank in its starboard wheel well for the plane's ordnance winch. In conjunction with the jacks on the carts, this equipment was used to lift the bomb into the *tokaki*. Once in place, a carrying harness was attached to the weapon, along with the release and safety wire mechanisms. Next, the bomb's nose and tail fuses were set by an armorer. The weapon was now live, although it couldn't detonate until the tiny fuse propellers had rotated a certain number of times during the weapon's free fall after release. At the completion of this exercise, the arming crews pushed their carts back to the ordnance lift to get another bomb. Three times they repeated this process before the bombers were ready to be taken up to the deck. They probably started doing this sometime after 0330.

The Zeros were being armed as well. Belts of 7.7-mm ammunition were fed into each pair of nose-mounted machine guns, while sixty-round canisters were crammed into the wing spaces for the two 20-mm cannons. Additional boxes of ammunition were set out for the day's combat air patrol fighters—there would be many sorties this morning, and each of them would need to be refueled and rearmed as soon as they returned to the mother ship.

Meanwhile, on *Akagi* and *Kaga,* the process had gone somewhat differently. Unlike torpedo bombers, dive-bombers were normally armed on the flight deck.[10] The spotting process thus started immediately after the aircraft were fueled. Of all the Japanese carrier planes at Midway, the Type 99 dive-bomber was undoubtedly the most difficult to deal with belowdecks. A large, powerful airplane, it had to be robust enough to survive the harrowing near-vertical dives and gut-wrenching pullouts that were the trademark of expert pilots. Because of the placement of the Type 99's control surfaces and dive brakes, not to mention its need for structural strength, Aichi's designers had decided not to place a folding mechanism too near the center of the wing. Instead, the Type 99's wings folded very near the tips, making it difficult to stow, tricky to maneuver through tight spaces, and a hog of precious parking "real estate."[11] The large fixed wingspan also meant that the Type 99 was too big to fit on the diminutive aft elevators of *Akagi, Kaga,* and *Sōryū.* As a result, dive-bombers were stowed amidships, closer to the larger elevator there. The Type 97 torpedo bombers, although about the same size and weight as the dive-bombers, had wings that folded much more compactly, allowing them to use the smaller elevators on the carriers, and so were stowed at the aft end of the ship. Zeros were stowed forward.

Spotting a strike for launch was a complex operation, requiring both hard physical labor and quite a bit of precision.[12] Each aircraft had to be individually extracted from the hangars. There wasn't a lot of room to work. The first step was for the crewmen to untether the aircraft and remove its wheel chocks. Then each fully armed and fueled plane, in some cases weighing more than four tons, was pushed through the hangar deck and onto an elevator. A team of a dozen or more plane handlers was required to move each aircraft. The trip to the elevator could be several hundred feet in length if the plane had been stowed in the middle of the deck. In the heat of the hangar, such extended pushes were exhausting.

When the time came, each plane was shoved onto the elevator as quickly as possible. For the Type 99s, this had to be done very precisely, as they only barely fit on even the larger elevators. During this process, the crew chief intoned the proper commands to ensure the exact positioning of the aircraft—"*Migimae-e* (Forward right)," "*Hidarimae-e* (Forward left)," "*Yōsorō!* (Hold steady!)." The crew then rode on the elevator together with their plane up to the flight deck to complete topside preparations.

Elevator cycle times were crucial to the efficiency of the entire operation, because elevator moves had to be performed sequentially. The problem was aggravated by the Japanese use of dual hangars (one atop the other), necessitating a trip of thirty-plus feet (equivalent to a three-story building) each way when lifting an aircraft from the lower hangar deck. Even on the newer carriers like *Shōkaku*, a round-trip to this deck could take as much as forty seconds,[13] including the time necessary to muscle the plane on and off the elevator. On the older *Akagi* and *Kaga,* whose elevators were slower, the cycles were even longer.[14]

Often, if space was sufficient, the plane's wings were manually unfolded by the pusher team while still on the elevator.[15] Once the plane reached the flight deck, it was rolled by the crew into its place in the spot.[16] This again necessitated pushing a multiton aircraft over a considerable distance. Once the aircraft was in position, the wheels were chocked, and the wings retethered. The planes were arranged in three staggered columns down the length of the flight deck, with the bombers in the rear and the fighters in front. The lead fighter was roughly abreast *Akagi*'s bridge.

Had the plane pushers been aware of what was going on around them, they would have seen that *Kidō Butai*'s nighttime cruising formation was changing for conducting flight operations. At the head of CarDiv 2, *Hiryū* was edging off to port. The rearmost ships, *Kaga* and *Sōryū,* were peeling out of formation to starboard and port, respectively, to open the distance between their divisional mates. *Kidō Butai*'s formation was becoming a much looser square, with as much as 8,000 meters between the carriers. The evidence suggests that BatDiv 3 formed in column abreast the port flank of the box, while CruDiv 8 did the same to starboard. *Nagara* remained in the van, and the destroyers spread out as far as 20,000 meters from the carriers. BatDiv 3 and CruDiv 8 were themselves as much as 8,000 to 10,000 meters abeam the carriers. For this reason the ships of CruDiv 8, as we shall see, were almost always the first main units to sight approaching enemy aircraft.[17]

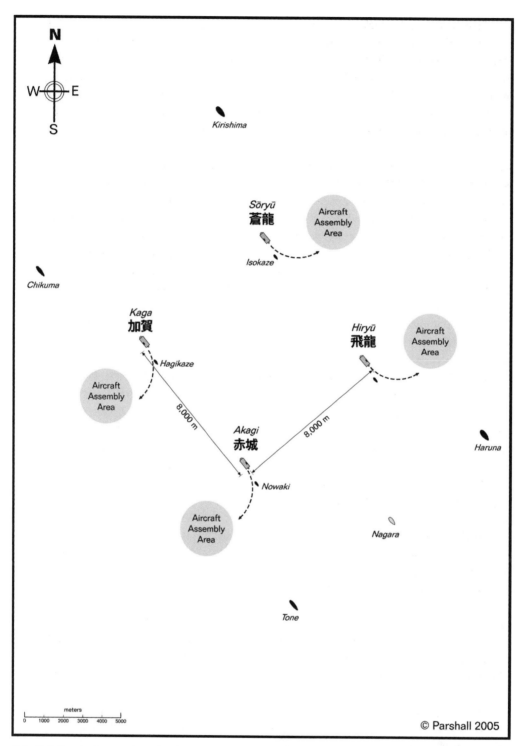

7-2: *Kidō Butai*'s formation, 0430. The fleet's carriers operated in a fairly dispersed manner, allowing free operations and ease of maneuver, while still retaining the ability to easily mass the fleet's offensive airpower.

Around the flight deck, the ship's radio aerials were being winched down from their vertical positions into the horizontal mode used during flight operations. These forty-foot masts normally towered over the deck, but they were set on a rotating base that allowed them to be rigged outboard over the water, so as not to impede landing operations. In the adjacent gun tubs, the antiaircraft crews were being assembled and were checking their weapons and ammunition in anticipation of a busy day. All around the deck the mood was one of bustling optimism.

The weather, which had been bad the night before, was still rather dreary. The sea was somewhat rough, and low broken cumulus clouds scudded over the force at between 2,000 and 5,000 feet.[18] The Nagumo force had emerged from the front of the storm system that had bedeviled it previously, and the weather promised to improve the farther south the fleet traveled. However, the broken cloud cover was at best a mixed blessing, because it could conceal the lurking enemy aircraft as well as the fleet.[19]

With the carriers done maneuvering, their designated plane guard destroyers took up their stations. *Akagi*'s bridge crew watched as *Nowaki* edged into a spot some 700 meters ahead and slightly to starboard of *Akagi*'s bow. She was now in position to perform *tonbo-tsuri* ("dragonfly-fishing")—the rescue of crewmen from any aircraft that suffered a mishap during takeoff.

On *Akagi* and *Kaga*'s flight decks, the dive-bombers were now in place and being armed from carts. For the morning strike, each would carry a 242-kg Type 98 No. 25 bomb. These high-explosive weapons were designed for use against land targets. *Kaga* had a bomb lift next to the midships elevator forward that ran all the way to the flight deck, so she loaded her bomb carts on deck. *Akagi,* whose bomb lift terminated on the lower hangar deck forward, was forced to load her carts belowdecks and then bring them to the flight deck using the forward aircraft elevator. As with the torpedo planes below, this was accomplished in shifts of six planes at a time.

It was now 0400. Over the carrier intercoms, a trumpet blared, calling the crew to general quarters. Looking out over the water, *Akagi*'s deckhands and gunners could barely make out the outlines of the other three carriers in the gloom, but they blinkered their progress to the flagship at intermittent intervals. Even before arming of the dive-bombers was complete, the task of warming up aircraft engines began.[20] Because of their internal hangars and lack of natural ventilation, Japanese carriers had no choice but to warm their planes up on the flight deck.[21] This was not an exercise that could be slighted. Radial aircraft engines were complicated, powerful, and built to very tight tolerances. Takeoff required the application of full military power, which placed a great strain on a plane's power plant. Engine failures routinely caused aircraft to abort their missions and either crash or return to base. It was imperative to detect and prevent as many engineering-related aircraft scratches as possible while still on the deck of the carrier, rather than risking the plane and its crew with a hasty takeoff.

On each plane, a deck crewman scrambled into the light gray-green cockpit, while another of the deck crew waited at the right side of the engine. Clustered around the plane were damage control personnel with fire extinguishers. On signal, the crewman below cranked the engine with a hand crank. The engine's internal flywheel began groaning and gaining speed. The cockpit man shouted *"Mae-hanare!* (Get away from the front!),", and his crewmate retreated from the danger zone of the propeller. With another shout of "*Kontaaku!* (Contact!)," he engaged the prop with the flywheel. Upon startup, a special mixture of 91-octane starter fuel was fed to the engine to initiate combustion. Coughing white smoke, the strike force's engines roared one by one to life.

For several minutes the power plant was idled at between 1,000 and 1,500 RPM, as hydraulic pressure, oil pressure, fuel pressure, and temperature built up to proper levels. Establishing nominal oil pressure was critical. When a radial engine was shut down, oil tended to collect in the lower cylinders, leaving the upper cylinders "dry" when the engine was restarted. A proper warm-up was necessary to ensure that oil was flowing correctly to the upper cylinders before full power was applied. During this process, the magnetos (right and left) were switched back and forth and the propeller pitch control moved from low (fully feathered) to high ("full increase RPM"). The fuel mixture control was run from lean to rich and back again.

When the temperatures and pressures were within proper ranges, the engine would be opened up fully. With the engine at maximum manifold pressure, RPM, and full rich fuel mixture the gauges were monitored for at least a minute. On land this required real physical leg strength to accomplish, as the brakes had to be held firmly to keep the plane from moving. On the flight deck, of course, the wheels were still chocked. If the final full power check was done before the engine was properly warmed up, it could blow the engine outright. During this time the radios and surface controls (rudder, ailerons, horizontal stabilizer, and flaps) were also checked. The whole process took no less than fifteen minutes and might take more if the air or engine was particularly cold. Only now was the aircraft finally ready for the rigors of takeoff.

During engine warm-up, the flight crews finally made their appearance. Rousted out of bed at around 0245, they had proceeded to their briefing room (*tōjōin taikisho*).[22] There, the men had received their breakfasts from the stewards and consumed it in their seats. The loudspeakers in the ready room blared "*Tōjōin seiretsu!* (Airmen line up!)," and the men began climbing the companionway up to the flight deck. Garbed in their heavy brown cotton flight suits and helmets, they emerged into the morning air. They were already sweating. The aviators then crowded round the large blackboards attached to the side of the islands.

At around the same time, Commander Fuchida, *Akagi*'s air group leader, decided that he could no longer lie abed in the sick bay, where he was still recovering from his appendectomy. Rising painfully to his feet, he began picking his way through the gray-painted maze that was *Akagi*. The ship was now in watertight condition, and he had to undog numerous hatches as he made his way, sometimes crawling, through the vessel. The process left him exhausted and shaking by the time he finally reached the bridge.

Shortly after Fuchida's arrival, Commander Genda, who had come down with a virus in the last few days, also appeared. Visibly ill, he clambered painfully up the ladders from the air platform.[23] Nagumo was particularly touched to see his staff air officer, still dressed in his pajamas, as he entered the tiny command space. Putting his arm around Genda, Nagumo made small talk with him as the bustle of launch operations continued below on the flight deck.

On board each carrier, the air groups were now being briefed by their respective *hikōchō*. The weather was expected to be moderate, with broken cloud cover that should not impede the planned attack sequence. It was known that Midway hosted a formidable air group. But it was expected that the strike force's thirty-six-plane-strong fighter escort would sweep enemy fighter opposition aside, as they had during every other operation during the war.

Once the attack force was launched, according to the attack plan, Nagumo's carriers would maintain their present course for the next three and a half hours at a speed of twenty-four knots. Thereafter, as the wind was basically from the east, the fleet would come to course forty-five degrees and steam at twenty knots, allowing the attack force to home on *Kidō Butai* and land sometime after 0830. If these arrangements needed to be changed, a ship would be sent to the locale of the original landing zone to redirect the aircraft.[24]

7-3: Lt. Tomonaga Jōichi, *Hiryū* air group *hikōtaichō*, leader of the Midway attack force. (Naval Historical Center)

The conclusion of the briefing was usually an opportunity for the ship's air officer to issue a ringing exhortation to the men to do their best. Regardless of the manner of delivery, the crews implicitly understood the importance of the coming action. Each man knew the level of effort and sacrifice that was required of him. After a pause, the *hikōchō* barked out, "*Kakare!* (Get to it!)." The men broke into a run for their planes. As they did so, the deck crewmen set the throttles at 1,000 RPM and cleared the waiting aircraft. Simultaneously, each carrier's deck was illuminated in preparation for takeoff. The centerline and edges of the flight deck were indicated by rows of specially hooded white lights designed so that they only shone inward, not outward, where hostile eyes might be watching. The fantail was similarly lit in red, allowing a landing aircraft to judge where the aft end of the flight deck lay.[25]

In the absence of Fuchida, overall command of the morning's attack had fallen on *Hiryū*'s *hikōtaichō*, Lieutenant Tomonaga Jōichi. He was a handsome, serious man with high cheekbones and forehead and piercing dark eyes. Somewhat aloof, and known as a hard drinker, he was a recent addition to *Hiryū*'s air unit, although he was a veteran of the air war over China. This was, however, his first combat sortie against the Americans. He mounted plane BI-310, along with his observer, Lt. Hashimoto Toshio, and radioman PO1c Murai Sadamu.[26] The complete roster for the morning's first launch was as follows:

Carrier Division 1	Carrier Division 2
Akagi	*Hiryū*
18 Type 99 carrier bombers	18 Type 97 carrier attack aircraft
(Lt. Yamada Shōhei)	(Lt. Tomonaga Jōichi, Midway striking force
1 Type 97 carrier attack aircraft	commander)
(reconnaissance— WO Nishimori Susumu)	9 Type 0 carrier fighters
9 Type 0 fighters	(Lt. Shigematsu Yasuhiro)
(Lt. Shirane Ayao)	3 Type 0 carrier fighters
3 Type 0 fighters	(combat air patrol l—Lt. Mori Shigeru)
(combat air patrol l—PO1c Tanaka Katsumi)	
Total: 31 aircraft	*Total: 30 aircraft*
Kaga	*Sōryū*
18 Type 99 carrier bombers	18 Type 97 carrier attack aircraft
(Lt. Ogawa Shōichi, Midway striking force dive-	(Lt. Itō Tadao)
bomber group leader)	9 Type 0 carrier fighters
1 Type 97 carrier attack aircraft	(Lt. Suganami Masaji, Midway striking force
(reconnaissance—Lt. Yoshino Haruo)	fighter group leader)
9 Type 0 carrier fighters	3 Type 0 carrier fighters
(Lt. Iizuka Masao)	(combat air patrol l—PO1c Harada Kaname)
2 Type 0 carrier fighters	
(combat air patrol—PO1c Yamamoto Akira)	
Total: 30 aircraft	*Total: 30 aircraft*

7-4: Roster for *Kidō Butai*'s 0430 launch against Midway.

The pilots began checking their mounts: the engine's condition, and the movement of the flaps, rudder, and stabilizers. One by one, each man raised his hand, shouting "*Yōsorō!* (OK!)" to the deck crewmen still huddled about. The drone of the engines grew louder as throttles were boosted. The deck launching officer (*shō-hikōchō*), a subordinate to the carrier's *hikōchō*, who was in charge of flight deck operations, was making the rounds of the strike aircraft, checking each individual plane to make sure that all was in readiness.

Akagi's *hikōchō*, Commander Masuda, watched from the air control station on the aft portion of the island. He could see his *shō-hikōchō* running back to the air station, and as he did so, Masuda barked into the voice tube up to the bridge that all was in readiness for takeoff. *Akagi* was steaming at battle speed 3 (twenty-two knots).[27] At that moment, the wind was from 160 degrees at two meters per second (four knots).[28] One by one, in the dim light of dawn, each carrier in the force raised her *seibiki* (service flag) and simultaneously signaled to *Akagi* via blinker that all was in readiness. *Akagi*, in turn, raised signal flags and blinkered to the force, indicating "*Kōgekitai hasshin junbi yoshi* (Attack force ready to launch)."

7-5: A classic shot of preparations for takeoff on board *Akagi,* taken during the attack on Pearl Harbor. This strike is evidently still several minutes away from launch, judging by the large number of erect deck crewmen on the flight deck and the fact that the aircraft wings are still tethered. The engines are in the process of being warmed up. (Photo courtesy Michael Wenger)

At the head of *Akagi*'s deck spot were the nine Type 0 fighters commanded by Lt. Shirane Ayao. The son of an important politician, Shirane had been with *Akagi* since the first day of the Pacific war. Now, upon seeing the signal flags being raised, he looked over his shoulder at the planes packed behind him. He could see the other eight pilots in his own *chūtai,* as well as the three combat air patrol fighters. Right aft of them was *Akagi*'s full complement of Type 99 bombers, under Lt. Yamada Shōhei. He could see all the pilots had their hands raised, indicating readiness. He responded by turning on his wing lights. The other aircraft immediately followed suit.

Akagi now signaled to the other ships "*Hasshin yōi* (Prepare to launch)." Some of the remaining deckhands untethered the wings of each plane and then ran for the crew shelters, leaving a pair of crewmen under each plane, tending the wheel chocks. Their white uniforms were buffeted in the cool, blustery propwash, yet all the men kept their eyes on the *hikōchō.*

Now, nearly two hours after the crew had first gotten to work, all was finally in readiness. On *Akagi*'s bridge, Nagumo looked to Genda, who returned his gaze solemnly, then nodded. This was it. Nagumo then gave the order, "*Kūchū kōgekitai wo hasshin seyo* (Launch the air attack force)," which Genda immediately relayed via the speaker tube to Masuda at the air station. Simultaneously, *Akagi*'s signal lamps began blinking to the other ships, instructing them to begin launching.

Masuda now ordered the steam jet at *Akagi*'s bow turned on to indicate the wind direction to the pilots. From his Zero's cockpit, Shirane could see the white vapor streaming down the flight deck. A glance up over his left shoulder at the wind sock flying from *Akagi*'s mainmast confirmed his impression. It was stiffly aligned almost fore and aft. *Akagi*'s 41,000-ton bulk was charging ahead, her massive bow kicking up sheets of white water as her engines thrummed. In the east, the sky was beginning to lighten. It was 0426.[29]

On the flight deck, the *shō-hikōchō* blew a whistle, then swung his red lantern in a great circle. On the bridge, Masuda used a signal lamp to alert all the planes on the deck to begin taking off. Simultaneously, another officer on the air platform began vigorously waving a white flag toward the direction of the bow. Having retreated to the side of the flight deck, the *shō-hikōchō* then signaled to the deck crewmen to remove the wheel chocks, which they did before scurrying to the deckside shelters.

Making a last-minute check behind him again, Shirane upped his throttle and yelled, "*Ikimasu!* (I'm going!)." His plane surged forward as Shirane gunned it. Within a few meters his tail came off the deck and he charged ahead on his main gear alone. Some eighty meters later his plane left the deck and hurtled into the air with a growl. Along the length of the deck, the crewmen in their shelters shouted encouragement and waved a veritable blizzard of white caps, wishing him good luck. Unlike Western navies, once the takeoff signal was given, it was up to the individual pilots to determine when to begin their own takeoff runs. One by one, each of Shirane's fighter division pilots repeated his maneuver, the outboard planes angling in to the centerline and then gunning it down the deck. It only took ten to fifteen seconds apiece.[30] *Akagi* had begun launching first, at 0426. *Hiryū* followed suit at 0428, with *Kaga* and *Sōryū* beginning operations at 0430.

On board *Hiryū*, attack leader Lieutenant Tomonaga watched as her nine escort fighters departed, led by the athletic and energetic Lt. Shigematsu Yasuhiro. Right after them, three Zeros under Lt. Mori Shigeru, whose *shōtai* was leading the morning's first combat air patrol watch, departed with similar alacrity. Getting Tomonaga's *kankō* in the air, however, was a different story altogether. Fully loaded, his plane weighed more than four tons, almost 400 pounds more than a dive-bomber, and more than a ton heavier than a Zero. Yet his horsepower-to-weight ratio was the lowest of the three types of carrier planes in the fleet. In a word, the Type 97 was a pig. He would need every ounce of power to make it off the deck.

The compound wind over *Hiryū*'s flight deck generally needed to be around thirteen meters/second (twenty-six knots) to launch aircraft, but Tomonaga's Type 97s really were better off if the relative wind was closer to fifteen meters/second (thirty knots). This created problems for the older *Kaga*, whose top speed of twenty-eight knots (on a good day) meant that she could barely launch her Type 97s if there was no wind. Too much wind, though, could be a problem in itself—at speeds above twenty-five meters/second the planes were impossible to control on the flight deck. On *Hiryū*, creating relative wind wasn't an issue—Yamaguchi's flagship had plenty of speed. But even under ideal conditions, Tomonaga's heavily laden bird still needed around 120 meters to make it into the air. On the shorter flight decks of *Hiryū* and *Sōryū* this was problematic, particularly for the lead strike aircraft spotted at the head of the pack.[31] Tomonaga's nose was almost atop the central elevator. From here it was 135 meters to the forward end of the flight deck—doable, but hardly comfortable.[32]

Under the circumstances, the only thing Tomonaga could do was jam his throttle all the way to the stops, pop the brakes, and hope for the best. If worse came to worst and he went into the drink, hopefully *Hiryū* wouldn't run over his plane. Then the guard destroyer would pluck him and his men to safety. He gunned his engine. His *kankō* began plodding down the deck, gaining speed with agonizing slowness. He could see his plane coming up on the white-painted wind gauge and the steam jet at the forward end of the flight deck—it was happening all too quickly. Then, seemingly at the last second, his plane nosed up and lifted grudgingly from *Hiryū's* deck. Cheers rang out again from the crew galleries. Tomonaga immediately began circling to port, putting his plane into a waiting pattern as the rest of his squadron took off. One by one, *Hiryū's kankōtai,* clutching their deadly cargoes to their bellies like great, green dragons, lumbered into the air. Across the water, the other carriers were doing the same—sending their heavy attack planes up into the growing light. The last to leave the decks were a Type 97 *kankō* apiece from *Kaga* and *Akagi.* These two planes were slated to join the search missions that were already getting under way from the cruisers and battleships. The carriers completed launching their aircraft within about seven minutes.

Climbing upward, the various unit commanders gathered their forces together, merging them into a cohesive whole. Meanwhile, the patrol fighters and recon flights headed off to their respective tasks alone or in small groups. At 0445 the strike force turned as one and headed southeast toward Midway at 125 knots—108 aircraft all told. Had the Americans been able to observe this spectacle, they might well have been envious of the prowess of their foes. At this point in the war, the U.S. Navy still struggled to mount a coordinated attack from a single flight deck, as the events of this day would soon demonstrate. The Japanese, by contrast, were able to launch and assemble a synchronized strike from as many as six carriers as a matter of course. They thought nothing of creating combat units assembled from physical elements of several carriers—an escort fighter group from all four carriers led by *Kaga's* senior fighter commander, a combined-arms attack force (level and dive-bombers) led by Tomonaga. It was a testament to the skill and training of the Japanese that they could accomplish such an impressive feat of arms.

Nagumo stood watching his attack force depart. Once they were out of visual sight of the task force, they would be completely beyond his control. Radio silence would be maintained until the attack against Midway had actually been carried out and the flight leader's radioman had the chance to tap out a brief preliminary report on his radiotelegram. Nagumo wouldn't really know the particulars of the strike results until Tomonaga and the others landed and were debriefed. Until then, his intelligence on the state of Midway would remain spotty. Such were the vagaries of command on board a 1940s carrier—the strike force, once launched, was on its own, and so, too, was Nagumo.

Overhead, the combat air patrol (CAP) of eleven fighters were fanning out to cover the fleet. Each *shōtai* took a different quadrant of the sky; two *shōtai* at 2,000 meters, the other two at 4,000.[33] All in all, this was a fairly skimpy force to protect a fleet as large as Nagumo's. Yet Commander Masuda was already preparing *Akagi*'s next deck spot. This time around it wouldn't be attack planes, but fighters. They would be needed for patrol operations as long as the air threat from Midway remained. A *shōtai* of three CAP fighters had already gone up with the first attack wave. Another *shōtai* was scheduled for launch within an hour. *Kaga, Hiryū,* and *Sōryū* had already contributed two, three, and three planes, respectively, to the CAP force as well. Up from *Akagi*'s forward elevator came a brace of nine fighters.[34] Across the water, Commander Masuda could see the other carriers following suit, spotting and warming up additional fighters so they would be available at short notice. Even with all of the flight deck to work with, these aircraft were spotted well aft, to give the pilots as much runoff room to work with as possible. *Hiryū*'s fighter contingent had to be rolled out of the way almost immediately after being spotted, though, as Yamaguchi's flagship sighted one of her own planes in difficulty. Ensign Akamatsu Saku's torpedo bomber had developed engine trouble, and had to abort. He came limping back and was recovered without further incident.[35]

Meanwhile, in the forward magazines of *Akagi* and *Kaga,* armorers had begun dragging seventeen-foot-long torpedoes from their stacked storage racks in order to arm the reserve strike aircraft. The Type 91 Mod. 3 was the latest addition to the aerial arsenal of a Navy that had elevated torpedo attack into an art form. Each carrier stowed around thirty-six of these lethal fish, which had just been introduced in the previous few months. Torpedoes were (and still are) complex, finicky beasts. Yet they were worth their high cost and maintenance headaches because of their capacity to inflict enormous damage on an enemy ship. The new Type 91 packed a powerful 140 horsepower engine into its 17.7-inch diameter frame, along with guidance gyroscopes, depth-keeping gauges, steering motors, and a dozen other highly technical pieces of equipment, not to mention a 529-pound warhead. It was capable of reaching speeds of forty-two knots over a 2,000-yard range—substantially better performance than its American counterpart.[36]

The Type 91 had a reputation of being extremely reliable if it was taken care of, and the torpedo handlers in CarDiv 1 were experts at this. Each fish had been scrupulously maintained, having been checked the day before to ensure that it was topped off with distilled coolant water, kerosene fuel, and engine oil.[37] Their air flasks had been charged to 2,560 PSI on a special compressor that ran off an imported German two-cycle diesel in the torpedo maintenance room just forward of the magazine.[38] Now the men performed last-minute checks to ensure that the detachable wooden tail fins and rubber nose cap—both of which shattered on impact and thereby absorbed the shock from a high-altitude launch—were securely in place. Finally, the running depth of each torpedo was set at a relatively deep five meters. If any enemy forces were detected, it was assumed that they would contain capital vessels, and with torpedoes it was best to hit the target as low in its hull as possible.[39] One by one, the gleaming, greasy fish were secured by their attachment lug to the overhead tram, wrestled onto the ordnance lift, and sent up to the hangars.

Once there, the torpedoes were trundled out to CarDiv 1's Type 97 aircraft, using the same sort of carts that had been employed earlier in the morning to load the heavy Type 80 bombs. However, the Type 97 used different *tokaki* mounting brackets for a torpedo than the 800-kg bomb—a fact that would have important implications later in the day. The torpedo *tokaki* had been attached the previous day to the aircraft of CarDiv 1. Meanwhile, on board CarDiv 2, the dive-bombers were fueled and had their machine guns munitioned, but were left otherwise unarmed. They would be armed on the flight deck as usual when spotted. Until that time, the entire reserve strike force on all four carriers would be kept below in the hangars.

This last point is an important one and is contrary to the common wisdom that has been passed down from Fuchida's book to innumerable Western texts on the battle. At no time during the morning prior to 1000 was the reserve strike force ever spotted on the flight decks. Spotting the reserve force at 0500 or so would have required breaking the spot once the initial CAP fighters began returning to their ships around 0700. Getting the aircraft back off the deck would require between twenty and thirty minutes, representing a needless decrease in the flexibility of the flight decks, as well as a colossal waste of labor.[40]

Everyone in the hangar crews sincerely hoped that if the Americans *were* sighted this day, that there would be no repeat of the rearming snafus that had plagued *Kidō Butai* in the recent Indian Ocean operation. While leading the aerial attack force home after bombing Colombo on the morning of April 5, Commander Fuchida had recommended to Admiral Nagumo that the reserve aircraft be readied for a follow-up strike against the same target.[41] But those second-wave planes had already been armed for antiship duties, just as today. Nagumo had gone ahead and ordered the changeover at 0853 that morning, and it had been nearly complete by the time the initial strike waves were landed at 0948.

Then, at 1000, a sighting report had come in advising the fleet of the presence of two British cruisers (*Dorsetshire* and *Cornwall*) heading southwest away from Ceylon at high speed. After some deliberation, at 1023 Nagumo had given the order to rearm the reserve aircraft with antiship weapons once again. The armament shuffle had not gone smoothly among the force's torpedo planes. Finally, in exasperation, CarDiv 2 went ahead and launched its force of dive-bombers against the British warships at 1200, a full two hours after the initial sighting report. Even then, the Type 97s aboard *Shōkaku* and *Zuikaku* still had not been ready. In the event, it hadn't altered the outcome a whit—CarDiv 2's dive-bombers had sunk the two British cruisers with dispatch—but Admiral Nagumo had been understandably livid at the delays.[42]

However, on this morning in June, the men had complete confidence in the reserve strike force—they were in every sense of the word Nagumo's "A-team." CarDiv 1's torpedo aircraft were nominally led by Fuchida, but in his absence they would be commanded by Lt. Cdr. Murata Shigeharu. Murata was one of the finest torpedo bomber pilots in the entire Navy, and a veteran of Pearl Harbor. A training fanatic, it was Murata who had perfected the techniques needed to use torpedoes in the shallow waters of the Hawaiian operation. He had then molded the *kankōtai* of *Kidō Butai* into a battle implement that could habitually achieve the tight launch parameters required for such a daring operation.[43] During the attack itself, he had personally led his team in delivering the devastating torpedo attacks against Battleship

Row that had sunk *Oklahoma, California,* and *West Virginia.* Murata's opposite number on *Kaga,* Lt. Kitajima Ichirō, led a similarly experienced group of pilots.

On board *Sōryū,* CarDiv 2's dive-bomber contingent was led by the famed Lt. Cdr. Egusa Takashige, universally acknowledged as the leading dive-bombing ace in the entire Navy. Possessed of a flamboyant personality, Egusa was regarded by Genda as a "god-like" combat leader.[44] He and his men had terrorized their opponents with their startling prowess in the difficult art they practiced. It was Egusa's *kanbaku* team that had crushed the *Cornwall* and *Dorsetshire* in April, sinking both cruisers in five minutes flat and scoring an unprecedented percentage of hits against the veteran warships. Egusa's counterpart on *Hiryū,* Lt. Kobayashi Michio, was another well-respected veteran. If trouble arose, Nagumo clearly had a crack aerial team to deal with it.

In contrast to the relatively smooth flight operations on the carriers thus far, the cruisers *Tone* and *Chikuma* were having a rough morning. Both cruisers were supposed to have gotten their aircraft (three apiece) into the air at 0430 along with the morning strike force. In the event, neither of them had been able to do so. Of the two, *Chikuma* at least had the good sense to launch the scout planes for lines Nos. 5 and 6 first (at 0435 and 0438, respectively) but then had taken another twelve minutes getting her antisubmarine patrol plane in the air. *Tone* had not fared even this well. Her initial plane (the antisubmarine scout) had been launched at 0438, and the scout plane for line No. 3 had gone off at 0442. However, getting the No. 4 scout plane launched took until 0500, a delay that smacked of incompetence on someone's part.

This plane, piloted by PO1c Amari Hiroshi,[45] had experienced difficulties in getting off the catapult, as the result of circumstances that remain murky.[46] Perhaps he had engine problems, or an issue with the catapult itself. Floatplane takeoffs were more dangerous than a carrier launch. Even with engines running full out, the plane still had to be hurled off the end of the catapult by an explosive charge, accelerating it to sixty-two MPH within the space of fifty feet. At such whiplash-producing accelerations, even the slightest pilot miscalculation or mechanical mishap meant instant death.[47] If there were some sort of mechanical fault evident, Amari probably wouldn't have wanted to take off until all systems had checked out fully.

However, others have suggested, including *Chikuma*'s *hikōchō,* Lt. Kuroda Makoto, that the orders for getting the floatplanes aloft were simply not forthcoming, keeping the pilots waiting on board ship past the appointed hour. Kuroda then went to the bridge to see what was going on. However, *Chikuma*'s commander, Captain Komura Keizō, had not the "slightest recollection about reasons why their departure was delayed."[48] *Tone*'s assistant communications officer recalls the pilots simply waiting around for orders to depart, not any equipment failure. Indeed, other sources have suggested that *Tone*'s catapult officer was unfamiliar with the equipment and took longer than he should have to get the launch under way.

According to both Genda and Kusaka, no communications apparently passed between the cruisers and the fleet flagship apprising Nagumo of the delay.[49] Perhaps in the context of a four-hour recon mission, thirty minutes either way didn't really matter to either Admiral Abe or Nagumo. However, on board *Hiryū* it was a very different story, because both Admiral Yamaguchi and Captain Kaku were exceedingly

7-6: Heavy cruiser *Tone*: This picture, taken in early 1942, shows *Tone* weighing anchor. She is carrying a total of four reconnaissance floatplanes: three Type 0 and one Type 95. This photo seems to confirm that *Tone*'s nominal complement of aircraft—five—may have already been below strength (four aircraft instead of five) before the Battle of Midway. (Photo courtesy Todaka Kazushige)

vexed at the various delays and decried the apparent incompetence of CruDiv 8.[50] Whatever the reason for the delay, the effect was to further degrade the efficiency of an already porous search pattern.

As has already been related, Nagumo probably had never been under any illusions about the ability of Tomonaga's force to neutralize Midway with a single strike, particularly in the absence of CarDiv 5's attack squadrons. At 0520 he issued orders to the fleet to be prepared to launch a second strike: "Unless unforeseen changes in the situation occur, the second attack wave, in Organization #4 (under command of Air Officer on *Kaga*) . . . will be carried out today." This merely confirmed what the armorers on *Akagi* and *Kaga* already suspected—at some point later in the morning, it would be necessary to replace the torpedoes on the Type 97s with land-attack bombs. For the time being, however, there was nothing to do but wait.

However, only ten minutes later, about 0532, a number of flies began appearing in the ointment. First *Nagara,* and then *Kirishima,* in the front of the formation, began laying down a smoke screen, an indication that their lookouts had seen something. An enemy flying boat had been sighted bearing 166 degrees, forty kilometers away.[51] The force had now been located for certain. Even now, enemy aircraft might be on their way in. Fighters already in the air scurried to drive the intruder away. Then, at 0545, *Tone*'s No. 4 plane radioed to announce that at 0520 it had sighted not one, but two surfaced American submarines on the outward bound leg of its search, just eighty miles from the force. *Kidō Butai* began thickening its combat air patrol. *Hiryū* had already added a trio of Zeros at 0525, and *Akagi* followed suit with three more at 0543. At 0555 *Tone*'s No. 4 search plane initiated the day's air actions when he radioed: "15 enemy planes are heading towards you!"[52]

Unbeknownst to Nagumo, the Americans had not been idle this morning. Given their sighting of Tanaka's force the day before, they were now confident that their intelligence on Japanese intentions was correct. However, Capt. Cyril Simard was equally concerned that the Japanese might try to hit his base at dawn on 4 June. Accordingly, he had elected to steal a march on his opponents and begin flight operations before first light. Commencing at 0350, he began launching a dawn CAP of Wildcats to cover the takeoff of the base's bombers and search planes. Twenty-two Catalina PBYs had subsequently taken off from the lagoon and Eastern Island at 0415 to search radially all around the island. Shortly thereafter, fifteen B-17s had been sent aloft with instructions to hit Tanaka's convoy again, but to be ready to be redirected to the north if Nagumo's carriers were detected.[53] The rest of the island's aircraft were kept on the ground—armed, fueled, and manned.

As for the American carriers, they had commenced air operations at roughly the same time as their Japanese counterparts. TF 17 and *Yorktown,* the northernmost of the two American task forces, was slated to search the northern flank, although Frank Jack Fletcher was relying on Midway to perform most of the reconnaissance work this day. At 0420 *Yorktown* sent aloft ten of her SBDs for this purpose. However, these aircraft were slated to search out to only 100 miles and to return within two hours. *Yorktown* also sent up six CAP fighters at this time. Ten miles to the south, TF 16 had eschewed a CAP of its own, instead spotting *Hornet*'s and *Enterprise*'s strike aircraft on the flight deck in readiness for any sighting reports that might arrive.

By 0500 a temporary lull had settled over Midway and the American carriers. For the island, though, all that had changed in short order. Lt. Howard P. Ady's PBY had detected Nagumo's carriers at around 0530 and broadcast as much at 0534.[54] Shortly thereafter, another PBY, flown by Lt. William A. Chase, sighted Japanese aircraft inbound and radioed in plain at 0544 "Many planes heading Midway."[55] Chase subsequently sighted the Japanese fleet as well, transmitting at 0552 "Two carriers and battleships bearing 320 distance 180 course 135 Speed 25." Crucially, Chase only reported seeing two Japanese flattops.[56] In fact, this would set the pattern for every American sighting report of the day. Given the broken cloud cover, and *Kidō Butai*'s dispersed formation, almost no American aircraft would report seeing more than two carriers at any given time.

Ady and Chase's report, while electrifying, created difficulties for Admiral Fletcher. He had been apprised by Chester Nimitz that the Japanese might be operating their carriers in two groups. If the PBYs had only seen two carriers, that might mean that another Japanese task force lay still undetected somewhere to the west or southwest. As such, Fletcher believed it would be wise to withhold some of his striking power to deal with the second group if and when it was located. It was essential, though, to attack the first Japanese task force as expeditiously as possible. Accordingly, he ordered Raymond Spruance at 0607 to "Proceed southwesterly and attack enemy carriers as soon as definitely located."[57]

As for his own force, *Yorktown* was committed to recovering the morning search SBDs in short order and was heading east into the wind to do so, thus moving him away from the Japanese. As such, it would take TF 17 some time to make up the lost ground to be in a position for launching his own strike. Fletcher informed Spruance that TF 17 would follow TF 16 to the southwest as soon as his search aircraft were recovered. If another Japanese carrier group was detected during the interim, Fletcher would retain enough firepower to deal with at least one additional enemy flight deck, even if Spruance had already fully committed his aircraft to destroying the first group. If, however, no further enemy carrier groups were detected, Fletcher would be able to back up Spruance's initial strike.

For his part, Spruance wanted to attack as soon as was practical, per Fletcher's orders to close and strike. However, he would have to wait a bit. According to his calculations, and those of his staff, he was approximately 175 miles from the reported position of the Japanese carriers. His shortest-ranged aircraft, the TBD torpedo planes and the Wildcats, both had about a 175-mile combat radius, theoretically putting the Japanese within striking distance. However, two factors militated against an immediate launch.

First, Fletcher and Spruance couldn't be certain that Chase's spotting reports were accurate regarding their positions. In fact, Chase's report placed the Japanese only 200 miles from the American carriers, when *Kidō Butai* was, in fact, more than 200 miles distant.[58] Nor could the Americans be certain of what the Japanese fleet's movements would look like during the time Spruance's aircraft were heading toward the target. If the Japanese weren't exactly where expected, the attackers would have to perform additional searches to find them, burning more precious fuel. That might force some aircraft to drop out, weakening the overall impact of the attack.

Second, the breeze was light this morning, meaning that when he turned into the wind to launch, he would have to ring his ships up to twenty-five knots to generate sufficient wind over the bow. TF 16 would thus be moving tangentially to the target at a high speed throughout the entire launch cycle, increasing the range still further. For both these reasons, launching now meant leaving no margin for error for his strike aircraft. Basic mathematics dictated that the most prudent course of action was to delay until Spruance had closed the range somewhat. He set 0700 as the fly-off time for both *Enterprise* and *Hornet*.

Ady's and Chase's reports had spurred Midway into furious activity, which was compounded when the island's own radar detected Tomonaga's formation shortly thereafter. By 0600 every available American aircraft had been scrambled. An odd-lot assemblage of twenty Brewster Buffalo and four Grumman Wildcat fighters started climbing to intercept the incoming Japanese. Meanwhile, Midway's attack aircraft stayed low and headed northwest, intending to discover Nagumo's carrier force. Behind them, Col. Harold Shannon's Marines readied every antiaircraft weapon at their disposal. The rest of the American defenders braced themselves for the inevitable attack, the first of the day's desperate pitched battles. Its results would be known to the Americans as they happened. For the Japanese commanders of *Kidō Butai,* however, the full details surrounding Tomonaga's mission would remain unknown for almost another three hours.

8

A Lull before the Storm—0600–0700

Back on board *Kidō Butai*, the possibility of imminent air action had spurred *Sōryū* into launching three fighters to augment the combat air patrol (CAP) at 0600. *Hiryū* followed suit at 0612. Lookouts now scanned the sky intently. Unlike the American ships, none of the Japanese ships at Midway had radar. This fundamental fact vastly complicated the ability of the force to defend itself against American air attacks. At this point, the Japanese Navy was at least two years behind the U.S. Navy in development in this critical field and was only just beginning to deploy its first operational sets to the fleet. The test beds for this new technology, the battleships *Ise* and *Hyūga*, had had experimental sets installed just a week before the sortie of Takasu's force for Operation AL.[1] However, none of the Midway ships carried such devices.[2]

To detect incoming aircraft, the Japanese still completely relied on the Mark 1 eyeball, with all of the vagaries and stress-induced phantasms that it was prone to. Japanese lookouts, at least when it came to surface warfare and spotting enemy ships, were better than most. But the broken cloud cover this morning made for a frustrating exercise, because aircraft could use it to their advantage. The burden of aircraft detection fell primarily on the escort destroyers, which had been deliberately pushed far enough away from the carriers that they could provide some modicum of early warning.

Once an incoming raid was spotted, the question remained how to communicate that information to the CAP fighters. The aircraft radios carried on the Zero fighter were of inferior quality and of limited range and power and were difficult to use. As a result, while all carrier Zeros had radios, pilots rarely relied on them.[3] Not only that, but communications with all aircraft aloft—CAP, reconnaissance, and strike forces—was apparently conducted via a single radio frequency, making it difficult for the various formations to be fed just the information that was pertinent to them.[4] Shipboard fighter control was haphazard at best—there was no such thing as a combat information center (CIC) in the sense of a centralized facility responsible for pooling and coordinating CAP assets and vectoring them onto their targets. Each carrier's *hikōchō* was nominally responsible for controlling his CAP fighters. In the absence of any practical means for doing so, however, and burdened by running the flight deck as well, it was impossible for the *hikōchō* to dedicate the sort of undivided attention to the CAP that it required.

As a result, the CAP pretty much ran itself, attacking anything that came within visual range. When a ship spotted an incoming raid, it was standard practice to begin laying smoke to attract the attention of the aircraft above, as well as blinkering an alert to the carriers in the center of the formation. Sometimes the ship would also fire a few salvos from its main battery in the direction of the enemy to generate splashes, which would in turn draw the attention of the fighters overhead.

The weakness of these command arrangements (if they can be called that) are readily apparent. The Japanese CAP was more of an "understanding" than a true system for air defense. It worked only so long as the enemy did not saturate the ability of the lookouts to detect them and the fighters to self-direct their formations to the attack. Against attacks that materialized sequentially, this approach worked moderately well. As events would show, however, against a multivector, multialtitude threat, the Japanese system proved too brittle and slow to react. Worse yet, it relied far too much on the discipline of the individual fighter pilots (who could only rarely see the "big picture") to somehow maintain an optimum distribution of fighters around the fleet. In fairness to the Japanese, both of the other carrier navies (U.S. and Great Britain) were still groping their way through these same issues. Even with radar, the Americans still didn't have a good approach to handling fighter direction yet. But the fact remained that Japanese fighter defenses, while formidable, could be beaten.

Beyond the primary protection that the fighters provided, there were three other factors that influenced the air defenses of the task force—the fleet's formation, the individual handling of the ships within that formation, and the lethality of the ship's antiaircraft guns. The Japanese differed from the U.S. Navy in their approach to all three areas, sometimes drastically.

The fundamental issue of whether to disperse or concentrate one's carriers in the face of the enemy had been hotly debated on both sides of the Pacific during the years leading up to the war. Dispersal of flight decks into widely separated task forces held out the promise of reducing potential losses if one of the groups was attacked. However, dispersal also carried with it attendant problems of coordination—how, in conditions of radio silence, could one reasonably assure that the task forces could launch and attack an enemy together? Concentration, conversely, made coordination much easier, but it inevitably placed all of the force's eggs in one defensive basket.

The Japanese had initially been champions of dispersal, and most of their war gaming and staff workup until 1937 had supported this viewpoint. However, the China war had conclusively demonstrated two things to the Japanese. First, bombers could only achieve decisive results if they were employed en masse, and second, that bomber formations were inherently vulnerable to enemy fighters and therefore required strong escorts in order to achieve their missions. These factors, which were the foundation of their ability to mass offensive airpower as well as they did, began to move the Japanese away from the view that dispersal was the best way to employ their carriers. This movement was confirmed in fleet maneuvers carried out in 1939–40, which demonstrated the difficulties of offensive coordination between dispersed assets—a fact that the Americans would learn to their cost on this very day.[5]

By the time First Air Fleet was formed, the idea of operational dispersal had essentially been abandoned. The basic carrier formation that was eventually adopted by First Air Fleet, and used by *Kidō Butai* during most of the engagements of the war thus far, was a box. At Midway, this basic configuration remained in place. With 8,000 meters between ships, this was very loose formation, allowing the carriers a good deal of sea room to operate. Intriguingly, too, other than the individual plane guard destroyers, there were no escorts anywhere near the flattops. Thus, it was up to the carriers to fend for themselves against air attacks.

It should be noted, too, that contrary to some Midway accounts that describe the Japanese escorts as being in a ring around the carriers, this is not strictly correct. At this point in the war, the concept of a tight ring formation optimized for antiaircraft screening (i.e., the active defense, via combined gun power, of a capital ship), was unknown to the Japanese. While both the U.S. and Royal Navies were already using such defensive alignments, ring formations did not appear in Japanese doctrine until mid-1943.[6] During the course of 4 June, those destroyers that were not assigned as plane guards were pushed out to the extreme perimeter of the formation to act as air-raid warning pickets. Thus, while the formation might have appeared as a ring from the air, the escorts on the perimeter were there for different purposes than an American ring formation and were much farther out from the high-value vessels.

On the face of it, dispersing the escorting vessels might be considered poor doctrine on the part of the Japanese. But as we will see, the majority of the defensive firepower in the formation actually resided with the carriers themselves. Given this, the placement of the destroyers on the perimeter made good sense, because it bought time for the CAP to react to incoming threats. As much as possible, the Japanese wanted to reduce the number of times the carriers had to engage aircraft with their guns to an absolute minimum.

Akagi's antiaircraft outfit was the weakest of the four. Her heavy AA armament had yet to be upgraded to the more modern five-inch/40-caliber guns that were now prevalent throughout the Navy. She was still equipped with older 4.7-inch/45-caliber weapons, which possessed neither the rate of fire nor the maximum elevation of the newer gun. In fact, *Akagi* was slated for an overhaul that would have upgraded her fire-control equipment and replaced her mounts with the newer five-inch model as soon as she returned from Midway.[7] Not only were her guns outdated, but the sky arcs for her 4.7-inch battery were bad as well. Instead of having her heavy mounts distributed around the four quadrants of the ship, they were grouped amidships and relatively low on the hull. She had no means to bring large-caliber fire to bear either directly forward or aft. On the port side, the island blocked the forward arcs of the port battery even further. If a target dove from directly overhead, particularly from the region of the port bow, the 4.7-inch guns would have a very difficult time aiming at it, meaning that only the 25-mm weapons would be able to fire. This made *Akagi* particularly vulnerable to dive-bombers.

Kaga had her own difficulties in the gunnery department. While she sported the newer five-inch/40 gun, her fire control system was the older Type 91 model, rather than the Type 94 that was used on the other three carriers.[8] "Fire control," the rather arcane science of how a ship's guns are aimed at a target, is often neglected in favor of focusing on the raw characteristics of the weapons themselves. This is understandable—such factors as the rate of fire of a gun and the size of the shell it

8-1: A fine study of *Akagi*'s port 4.7-inch AA battery, taken from the aftmost mount looking forward toward the bridge. Note low placement of the batteries, the generally poor sky arcs (i.e., the restricted firing areas resulting from obstacles, like the bridge, being in the way), and the inability to fire across the flight deck. (Photo courtesy Michael Wenger)

fires make intuitive and quantitative sense, whereas the relative merits of relying on barrage fire versus having a fully tachymetric director are less obvious. However, a weapon itself has no intrinsic usefulness unless it can hit its target, and in this rather vital respect *Kaga* was sadly lacking.

The Type 91 *kōshaki* (director), which was first deployed in 1931, was a slow, manually trained model lacking many of the power-assisted features that helped Type 94 maintain a bead on a fast-moving airplane. Type 91 was designed at a time when combat aircraft did not exceed speeds of 200 mph and dive-bombing was still in its infancy. In the early 1930s, it was still thought that the greatest danger to a ship came not from dive-bombers or torpedo aircraft, but from level-bombers attacking at high altitudes. Aircraft attacking a ship in this manner were obligated to fly straight and level in order for their bombsights to make an accurate fix on the target. Unfortunately, in the intervening decade, aircraft performance, as well as dive-bombing technique, had improved enormously. Flying straight and level, as any of *Kidō Butai's* own dive-bomber pilots would readily have attested, was a charming anachronism rarely witnessed in modern combat. Contemporary aircraft, when piloted by skilled men, maneuvered constantly and made their attack runs at frightening speeds.

Against these targets, Type 91's only recourse was to direct the guns to fire a barrage. Contrary to the popular lexicon, in which the word "barrage" implies "firing roughly that-a-way with everything you've got," barrage fire has a very precise meaning in the parlance of the gunnery officer. Placing a barrage means creating an imaginary box in the sky at some preset range and altitude, and then pumping shells into the box as quickly as possible. The effect is to create a zone of exploding flak through which an enemy plane must fly on its way to the target. The advantages of this method are that it doesn't take much time or thinking to create a good barrage—all the shell fuses are set to a given range, and the guns are shooting at an unmoving point. Over a short period, this method can deliver impressive output from the guns. However, barrage fire also has a crucial drawback, in that once a plane has made it through the barrage, it is effectively home free. A barrage is a one-shot deal. If it fails, the target vessel can be reasonably assured that enemy ordnance will soon be incoming.

Even the newer Type 94 systems on *Akagi, Sōryū,* and *Hiryū* were scarcely better able to defend their ships against dive-bombers. Type 94 was a fully tachymetric system, meaning that it was designed to track and aim against individual targets moving in three dimensions. It was theoretically capable of tracking a plane moving at 500 knots, but in reality, the system was not nearly fast enough to engage such a target. Dive-bombers, for instance, hurtled downward at 225 knots, shedding appalling chunks of altitude as they went. In the process, they created large vertical-rate changes that made life very difficult for an opposing fire-control director. Not only that, but while the nominal range of the five-inch/40 weapon was about 20,000 meters, in actual use the Japanese figured it was only good out to about 7,000 meters, with a useful ceiling of about 3,000 meters. This meant that under normal combat conditions, even the five-inch weapon had difficulty engaging a dive-bomber before it reached its pushover point. Once it reached that point, it would deliver its ordnance in under a minute.

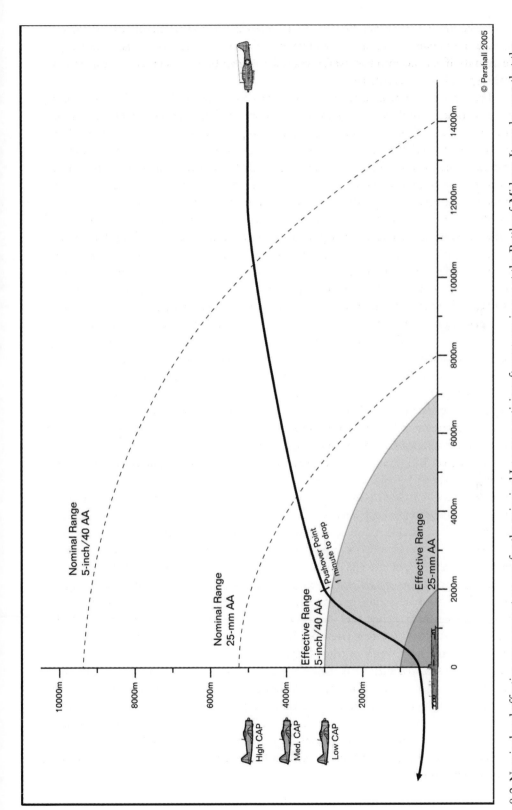

8-2: Nominal and effective engagement ranges for the principal Japanese antiaircraft weapons in use at the Battle of Midway. It can be seen that the Japanese antiaircraft weapons did not have the ability to effectively engage a dive-bomber before it reached its pushover point.

Nominal Range
5-inch/40 AA

Nominal Range
25-mm AA

Effective Range
5-inch/40 AA

Pushover Point
1 minute to drop

Effective Range
25-mm AA

High CAP

Med. CAP

Low CAP

© Parshall 2005

10000m
8000m
6000m
4000m
2000m

0   2000m   4000m   6000m   8000m   10000m   12000m   14000m

It wasn't that Type 94 was a bad system. It was roughly on par with the U.S. Navy's basic Mk. 37 director (although when the Mk. 37 was paired with radar inputs, its effectiveness was greatly enhanced).[9] Being fully tachymetric, Type 94 was certainly better than anything the British currently used. In fact, it was probably the best AA fire-control system deployed on *any* Axis warship at this time. But it couldn't cope with a dive-bomber. Even with an experienced crew, it took Type 94 a minimum of ten seconds, and often as long as twenty, to establish a fire-control solution for the target.[10] Obviously, if a ship was caught unaware, spending the first twenty seconds of a minute-long engagement window waiting for the computer to generate a solution was hardly conducive to its survival. The end result was that a dive-bomber, once it reached pushover, was an almost insuperable weapon system.

At shorter ranges, of course, ships also relied on their machine guns to provide additional defensive fire. Light AA weapons compensated for their relatively crude fire-control arrangements by simply putting a large number of bullets in the air and hoping something hit. The Japanese were no exception in this regard—their light AA fire-control system (the Type 95 *kōshaki*) was essentially a glorified telescope with an etched-glass ring sight that transmitted training and elevation data to the guns it nominally controlled. It was then up to the gun crews to follow the pointer of the director and hose down the target.

The standard Japanese light AA weapon was the Type 96 25-mm automatic gun. It was a copy of a French Hotchkiss design and had been in licensed production in Japan since 1936. Most of the 25-mm mounts in the fleet were twin-barrel models, although *Hiryū* had a number of the newer triple mounts. It was generally well liked by the Japanese, but it suffered from some important drawbacks. First off, its rate of fire was badly hampered by its ammunition supply, which came in a fifteen-round box. These clips had to be changed frequently, chopping the gun's nominal rate of fire in half to only about 130 rounds per minute. With a full clip, the 25-mm had around a four-second burst before it needed to be reloaded. As a result, it was standard Japanese practice to fire only one barrel of a double or triple mount at a time. In this way, the gunner was able to put sustained fire on a target while the other barrels were being reloaded.[11] Obviously, this was a poor substitute for being able to blaze away with full firepower when it really counted. It must be noted, though, that against a dive-bomber, the target might not be within the 25-mm's effective range long enough for the problems of changing out magazines to be terribly pertinent in any case—the engagement window against such targets was very small.

This points out another flaw of the 25-mm weapon, namely, that it didn't have the range or hitting power it needed. While nominally effective out to 8,000 meters, Japanese gunners routinely held their fire until the target was within 2,000 meters. Against a torpedo airplane the 25-mm could be an effective weapon. Given their need to launch their weapons below a given altitude, torpedo planes were inherently more constrained in their vertical movements. This eased the gunner's problem by making his fire-control solution much more two-dimensional. However, against a dive-bomber, the equation was more complicated, because the target was moving in all three dimensions—and much more rapidly to boot.

In the case of both heavy and light guns, a single director controlled a "battery" composed of between two and four weapon mounts. On the Midway carriers, the heavy AA batteries were grouped port and starboard into batteries of three or four twin mounts apiece.[12] With the lighter guns, *Sōryū*'s and *Hiryū*'s 25-mm mounts were grouped into five batteries—two on each side and one at the bow. *Kaga*'s and *Akagi*'s automatics were subdivided into six light batteries, three per side. The important point here is that the total number of aircraft that could be engaged at any one time by a carrier was really *not* equal to the number of gun mounts, but rather to the number of fire-control directors, and hence the number of batteries. Thus, seven or eight aircraft composed the theoretical maximum that any of the carriers could protect itself against at any one time. In practice, this number was actually much lower, as multiple 25-mm batteries tended to be concentrated against a single target. Consequently, even a large ship's defensive systems could be swamped fairly easily if the CAP fighters didn't thin out the attackers beforehand. AA was therefore really only useful for stopping "leakers."

The other major defense the Japanese carriers had against their attackers was the ship's helm. The Japanese viewed maneuver as a primary mechanism to defeat incoming aircraft. This approach had pros and cons. A skilled skipper could usually make life very difficult against a slow attacking aircraft, such as a torpedo plane. Particularly against the Americans, where both components of the weapon system (torpedo and plane) were subpar in terms of speed, simply executing a sharp turn to place the aircraft astern could complicate their attack greatly. Such a maneuver presented the plane with a markedly longer approach and lengthened its exposure to fighters and AA fire accordingly. American airborne torpedoes, with a top speed of only thirty-three knots, were in roughly the same predicament. Both *Hiryū* and *Sōryū* could outrun the American "fish" outright, and even against *Kaga* and *Akagi* they had little chance of hitting unless the Americans laid down a perfectly timed attack from several directions.

However, using violent maneuvers to throw off attackers had its downsides as well. In the first place, it made it very difficult for any escorting ship to stay close enough to the carrier to add effective firepower to her defense. The chances of collision with one's charge were very real under such circumstances, and destroyers knew they had to keep their distance, although with the bulk of the Japanese destroyers pushed out to the perimeter of the formation on 4 June, this was less of a problem. However, radical maneuvers also badly degraded the ability of a fire-control system to hit its target. Fire-control computers were essentially mechanical slide rules that accepted numerous inputs such as target speed, target course, ship's own speed and course, and other variables. These were fed into the computer by a gang of crewmen (sometimes as many as a dozen manned the computer alone) via dials and knobs. The result was then mechanically generated, displayed, and fed back to the guns. Putting the ship's helm over hard introduced rates of change into the system of several degrees per second for at least one crucial variable (known as "ship's own course"), making it very difficult to generate a meaningful solution for the guns. In fact, it was generally acknowledged that performing a radical turn threw the solution right out the window.

Both the Japanese and American Navies recognized this problem, but each adopted a different approach to it. The Japanese accepted the fact that fire control against aircraft was exceedingly difficult and continued to rely on the helm to evade attack throughout the war. Even as late as 1944, Japanese doctrine prescribed that, "In AA combat the normal procedure will be to maneuver at long range avoiding as much as possible any reduction in the effectiveness of fire. When the enemy tries to attack at close quarters, the required evasive maneuvers will be executed, if necessary, without regard to development of firepower."[13]

This de-emphasis on firepower in preference for the helm was in marked contrast to American practice. American capital ships, knowing that they were closely surrounded by escorts that were actively contributing to their defense, tended to maneuver in such a way as to maximize the aggregate firepower of the group. Unless they were absolutely forced to, American vessels avoided radical maneuvers. U.S. doctrine in 1944 noted that while individual ships were allowed to maneuver to avoid a specific threat, "This doctrine does not constitute an unrestricted license to individual maneuver. Lack of restraint exacts heavy penalties. Ships become scattered. Mutual support is lost. Risk of collision is added to the dangers of enemy weapons."[14]

The USN's approach would certainly make more sense by 1943, when the massed firepower from five-inch, 40-mm Bofors and 20-mm Oerlikons (coupled with radar direction) mounted on its warships would fill the air with almost impenetrable curtains of fire. In June 1942, though, the "correct" answer to the question of whether or not to maneuver was far less obvious. For one thing, at this stage of the war, firepower from both side's escorts was minimal. The average destroyer in 1942 sported only a handful of light automatic weapons. Japanese "tin cans" often carried little more than a pair of twin 25-mm mounts. Not only that, but their low-angle five-inch guns, which were optimized for surface fighting, were practically useless as antiaircraft weapons. They could neither elevate high enough, nor train quickly enough to engage a fast-moving airplane. Consequently, the Japanese destroyers didn't have a lot to contribute in the way of screening fire.

An examination of *Kidō Butai*'s aggregate AA firepower makes this fact clear. The four carriers between them mounted more than half the total usable AA barrels in the formation. In terms of "throw weight"—the actual weight of shells that could be fired within a given amount of time—the carriers accounted for nearly 60 percent of the force's total. Each of the carriers *individually* had twice the throw weight of light cruiser *Nagara* and all eleven of the force's destroyers *combined*. The only other ships in the force with any meaningful AA firepower were the two battleships and the heavy cruisers *Tone* and *Chikuma*. However, unlike a destroyer, the handling characteristics of these large vessels made them less useful for taking up station close to a carrier, even if they had wanted to. To add to this basic problem, *Tone*'s and *Chikuma*'s duties as floatplane mother ships, as well as indicating incoming raids to the CAP by firing their main batteries at intruders, meant that they had their own matters to attend to. The battleships were high-value targets in themselves and maneuvered independently. The result was that the only help that each carrier could likely expect in the event of an attack would come from its division partner, assuming it was close by.

Given this state of affairs, preferring maneuver over firepower may well have been the "right" answer for the Japanese in mid-1942. However, it was hardly an answer derived from a position of strength, and the results of the coming battle would reflect this. Of the 146 American aircraft lost to all causes on 4 June, only two would be confirmed victims of Japanese antiaircraft fire.[15] To this total can perhaps be added some of the aircraft written off as constructive losses by the Americans after the battle, but the point must also be made that these were aircraft that had lived long enough to deliver their ordnance and then make it home. Indeed, more American aircraft were lost in landing accidents than from Japanese flak.[16]

The final point that must be made about Japanese antiaircraft procedures is that the Japanese themselves probably did not know just how weak their defenses actually were. Except for an isolated incident in the Indian Ocean, *Kidō Butai* had never really faced a concerted air attack. There, on 9 April, a flight of nine British Blenheim bombers operating out of Ceylon had managed to penetrate the Striking Force's CAP without being detected. *Hiryū* had observed the incoming enemy but had inexplicably failed to pass along a warning to the rest of the force.[17] The first indication that anyone on *Akagi* had that something was amiss was when waterspouts off the flagship's starboard bow announced the thundering arrival of nine sticks of bombs dropped from an altitude of 10,000 feet. Scrambling fighters had then pursued the attackers, eventually shooting down all but four of the bombers.[18]

By all accounts, *Kidō Butai* was somewhat chastened by this lesson. The official Japanese war history, *Senshi Sōsho,* notes that "the fact that the carrier strike force, with a combat patrol overhead was bombed without being aware of it was an extremely serious matter."[19] *Hiryū*'s battle report for the mission noted that it was an absolute priority to improve detection facilities to deal with these threats. Having some of the world's foremost practitioners of the art of naval dive-bombing on board, it should have been apparent that if the Blenheims had been Dauntlesses, and not level-bombers, *Akagi* might well have been critically damaged or even sunk.

Yet, there are no indications that any concrete measures had been taken by the Japanese to counter the threat posed by such attacks. For one thing, the Japanese may well have had too little experience with live firing their antiaircraft weapons against enemies to have drawn any lessons. For another, they may simply have dismissed the enemy's ability to hit their ships. By the time American carrier pilots demonstrated conclusively at Coral Sea that they could hit anything that moved, it was a little late for the Japanese to reflect on these lessons before sortieing for Midway. In the absence of any better arrangements, the only thing the Japanese could do under the circumstances was simply try harder not to be caught with their pants down.

Nagumo had more to fret over than just the threat of incoming aircraft. He was also worrying about his own attack force—Tomonaga should have been approaching Midway about now. Finally, at 0616, *Akagi* overheard a message. Tomonaga's radio operator, PO1c Murai, was tapping out a message from the *Hiryū* strike commander to his force: "Assault Method No. 2; wind 90 degrees, nine meters, approach course 270 degrees." As anticipated, Tomonaga was attacking out of the east, so as to have the sun at his back. Apparently the wind over the target was gusty. Four minutes later,

Tomonaga was overheard giving the order to the formations to assume their attack positions.[20]

Another empty fifteen minutes followed. Nagumo knew that his air forces were in battle to the south, but he knew absolutely nothing of the tactical situation over Midway and could do nothing to intercede. After the morning's discovery by the American PBYs, the question of surprising the base seemed moot, but how many enemy aircraft were still there? How stiff had their antiaircraft defenses been? Had Suganami's fighter escort been sufficiently powerful to brush aside their American opposite numbers? It was one of the most frustrating aspects of exercising command over a force that fought well beyond visual range—the powerless waiting, devoid of all but the most cursory information on the circumstances of battle, the supply of actionable battle data choked down to the anemic transmission rate of the force's radiotelegraphs. The man commanding the most powerful carrier force in the world could do nothing but wait for the message orderlies. Every so often one of them would run up to the bridge from *Akagi*'s radio room and deposit the scanty fruit of Murai's telltale tapping. In the interim, Nagumo had little to do but stare out the bridge windows.

Nothing further was heard until 0636, when Tomonaga radioed another message to his entire force: "Assume penetration formation." This was an indication that Tomonaga wanted the various *chūtai* and *shōtai* (particularly the dive-bombers, which necessarily had been scattered by their individual attack runs) to begin regrouping into an orderly formation—one that could defend itself. The actual bombing attack on Midway—save for the fighters strafing the target—was now almost over, and the tedious process of rounding up the stragglers had begun. Nine minutes later, at 0645, Tomonaga sent out his first message to the Mobile Striking Force: "We have completed our attack and are homeward bound."

In the meantime, *Akagi* was setting up to cycle her CAP fighters. Lt. Ibusuki Masanobu and his *shōtai* of three Zeros were warming up on the flight deck. They were sent aloft at 0655, and the deckhands immediately prepared to take aboard PO1c Tanaka Katsumi and the other two fighters that had flown the morning's first CAP watch. These were brought down starting at 0659. *Hiryū* was starting to do the same, preparing to land Lt. Mori Shigeru and his two wingmen.

By around 0630, out of sight and out of mind, Nagumo's meager scouting arrangements had quietly gone to hell. The *Chikuma* aircraft flying the sixth search line (along bearing 54 degrees) had radioed Nagumo at 0649 that, because of bad weather, he was returning to base. The timing of his message indicates that he would only then have been reaching the outer end of his first search leg. Further south, flying the 77-degree search line, *Chikuma*'s No. 1 plane was apparently hotdogging it. Instead of flying below the cloud cover that dotted its route, this plane was flying above weather and merely peeking down through the clouds as the opportunity afforded itself. Either that, or it was badly off course. One of these explanations must be true, else by all rights it should have detected Task Force 17 sometime during its outbound leg.

South of *Chikuma* No. 1, *Tone* No. 4 was continuing on its way along the fourth search line (down the 100 degree bearing). However, in retrospect it seems almost

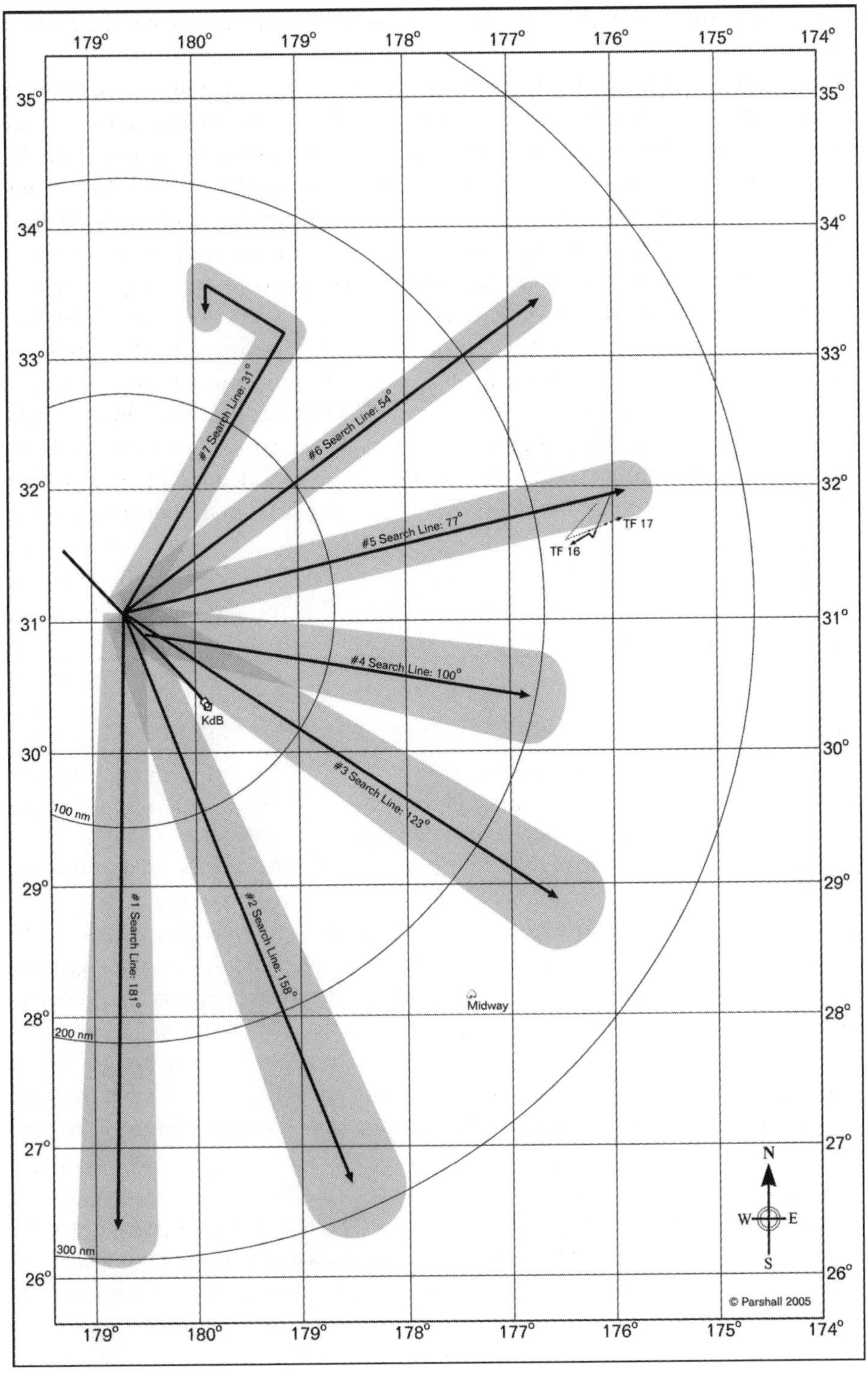

179°
180°
179°
178°
177°
176°
175°
174°
35°
34°
33°
32°
31°
30°
29°
28°
27°
26°
#7 Search Line: 31°
#6 Search Line: 54°
#5 Search Line: 77°
#4 Search Line: 100°
#3 Search Line: 123°
#2 Search Line: 158°
#1 Search Line: 181°
TF 17
TF 16
KdB
Midway
100 nm
200 nm
300 nm
N
W
E
S
© Parshall 2005

8-3: State of Japanese search arrangements at approximately 0630, with nominal search ranges superimposed. *Chikuma* plane No. 1, flying the No. 5 search line, should have detected TF 17 at about this time, but failed to do so.

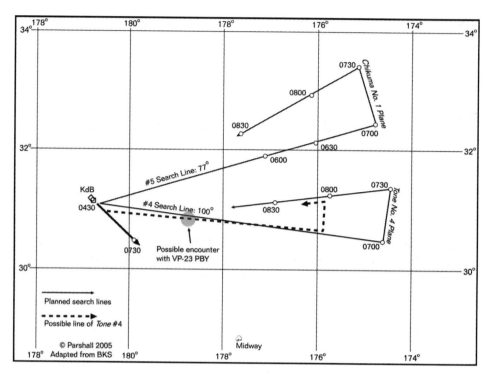

8-4: Planned course tracks of *Chikuma* No. 1 and *Tone* No. 4 search planes, with the speculative course track presumably flown by *Tone* No. 4. (Source: *Senshi Sōsho*, p. 309)

certain that this aircraft was not flying along its intended route. Having started a half an hour late, Petty Officer Amari may have been intending to save *Tone* the trouble of doing a late recovery and was simply cutting his route short so as to make his appointed return time.[21] Furthermore, there are indications that he may have had a run-in with an American PBY.[22] Whatever the reason, though, instead of flying out to the full 300 nautical miles of his intended search, Amari was apparently either pushed off course, and/or made his dogleg at about 220 miles.[23] Had he not done so, he would not have been in position to spot the Americans shortly thereafter. Neither Amari nor any of his crew were to survive the war, and the truth is that no one knows exactly what route he flew that day or why he did so, leaving his movements open to speculation.

Nagumo was aware of the return of *Chikuma*'s No. 1 scout plane as a result of weather conditions, but he had no way of knowing that the other two aircraft were not doing their jobs. All he knew for certain was that he had heard no tidings at all from his disengaged flank. So far as he and his staff were aware, everything was going pretty much according to plan. Within an hour, though, he would be disabused of that notion in the most inconvenient way imaginable.

9

The Enemy Revealed—0700–0800

At precisely 0700, *Akagi* finally received word from Tomonaga regarding the outcome of the morning's strike when another decoded transmission was brought up to the bridge. The strike leader's message was blunt enough: "There is need for a second attack wave." Around the bridge, mental shoulder shrugging was the order of the day—no big surprise there. Seventy-odd bombers had, indeed, been insufficient to put Midway out of business, just as many of the staff had foreseen. Now the question was what to do about it?

The manner with which Tomonaga transmitted his message, which was clearly noted by the American signals intelligence unit on Hawaii, also supports the picture of a force that knew all along that it would have to strike Midway again this day.[1] Tomonaga's message—a single code group repeated three times: "KAWA KAWA KAWA 0400"[2]—was strongly reminiscent of the famous "TORA TORA TORA" signal used at Pearl Harbor, and is indicative of a prearranged message format. No matter what Yamamoto's instructions had been regarding only needing to hit Midway once, it seems clear that Nagumo's staff had arranged prior to Tomonaga's departure that the strike leader should have this certain code group in his back pocket if need be. Having sortied a day late, with less time to reduce the island before the landings, it is little wonder that *Kidō Butai* had anticipated hitting the place more than once this day and had planned accordingly.

While Nagumo pondered Tomonaga's signal, *Akagi* prepared to reinforce the combat air patrol still further. As soon as Tanaka's previous threesome of Zeros had been brought on board and stowed down the forward elevator, the same elevator began bringing up more fighters. The next group of five aircraft to go up would include three from the 6th *Kōkūtai*, under the command of Lt. Kaneko Tadashi. Kaneko, a fine pilot, who would go on to make ace, was just itching to get into action.[3] Commander Masuda, *Akagi*'s *hikōchō*, had seen no reason not to use the "cargo" aircraft in this fashion. Spotting began a little before 0700. *Sōryū* was spotting three fighters of her own. Both ships sent their Zeros up at 0710, just as the first real American attack developed.

Japanese lookouts on *Akagi* spotted enemy planes coming in low at 0710. Captain Aoki turned the flagship to head into them. Probably none of the men on the bridge recognized these particular aircraft. They were, in fact, six of the American's new TBF

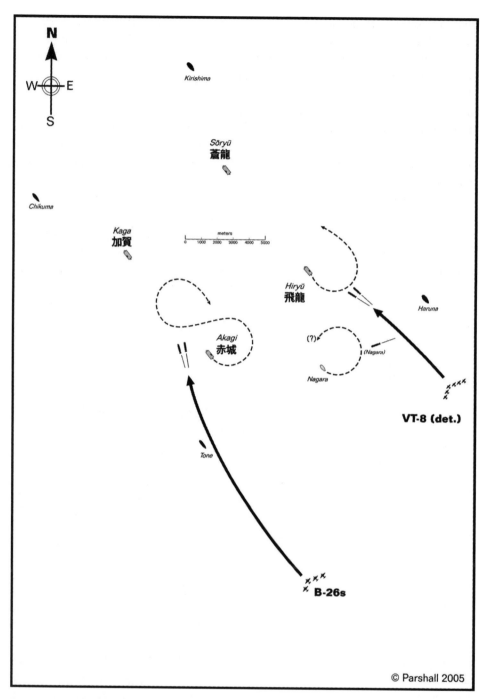

9-1: 0710 attack on *Kidō Butai*. This initial set of attacks nearly resulted in a successful suicide attack on *Akagi*.

Avenger torpedo planes and four twin-engined B-26 Marauder medium bombers. Neither had earned much of a reputation in the Pacific war thus far. In fact, this was the first combat mission ever for an Avenger. Both types were big and robust, and the B-26 was blazing fast as well. The two American formations were coming in on the bows of the lead carriers. As far as the Japanese could tell, they were attempting a version of an anvil attack, except that instead of targeting a single ship on either bow (which might have produced results), they unwittingly chose to divide their attentions between the two division flagships—*Akagi* and *Hiryū*. This was hardly surprising, given that one flight was manned by U.S. Army aviators, the other by Navy fliers, neither of whom had had any opportunity to coordinate their attacks with their opposite numbers. Their near-simultaneous arrival at their objective was wholly intentional.

Akagi had several CAP fighters up, including a *shōtai* led by WO Ono Zenji, a second under Lt. Ibusuki Masanobu, and now Lieutenant Kaneko's still-launching formation.[4] Kaneko headed straight toward the B-26s along with the rest of the flagship's complement. At the same time, *Hiryū*'s fighters also swung into action. She had seven in the air, including a *shōtai* apiece under PO1c Hino Masato and WO Kodama Yoshimi. The seventh plane was that of PO2c Sakai Ichiro, the final plane from *Hiryū*'s first CAP watch that had gone up at 0430. His flight mates—Lieutenant Mori and wingman PO2c Yamamoto Tōru—had already landed at 0700, but Sakai had not yet made it down and apparently decided to peel out of his landing approach to join in the fray.

Sōryū's and *Kaga*'s fighters also contributed, although it is likely that they played more of a role in the latter stages of the action. *Kaga*'s first CAP watch of two planes under the very senior PO1c Yamamoto Akira, and her second watch of five planes, under Ens. Yamaguchi Hiroyuki, both made their presence known. *Sōryū*, likewise, sent at least two *shōtai* in to the attack, including PO1c Harada Kaname's trio and the newly launched Lt. Fujita Iyozo and his two wingmen. Thus, *Kidō Butai* dispatched a total of over thirty fighters to destroy the ten American warplanes of this first raid.

The American aviators quickly discovered that Japanese carrier fighter pilots were every bit as good as their reputations made them out to be. *Kidō Butai*'s fighters set upon the interlopers like wolves. For their part, though, the Japanese found the B-26s speedy and difficult to bring down. Not only that, but the sleek American bombers had decent defensive armament as well. *Akagi*'s PO3c Hanyu Tōichirō discovered this fact to his cost, killed by a Marauder's fire during the engagement. The Avengers, too, exacted a price, splashing the late-landing Sakai within sight of his ship.

Yet the Zeros methodically slashed at the bombers with well-timed runs, culling them out of their groups and bringing them down. They hurled at least one of the Marauders flaming into the sea, probably at the hands of the skilled Lieutenant Kaneko.[5] To the north, Lieutenant Fujita's fliers began scoring heavily on the Avengers.[6] The Americans could do little but grimly hang on, boring in low and fast. The Avengers were savaged, all but one of them eventually being destroyed. The few American aircraft that managed to remain aloft were in tough shape as well—all of them holed dozens or even hundreds of times. Yet despite the prodigious punishment they meted out, the CAP couldn't bring all of the attackers down before they reached their drop points.

On board *Hiryū*, 2nd Lt. Nagayasu Yasukuni, commander of her starboard five-inch guns, gave the order to commence firing. *Hiryū* cranked up to flank speed, thirty-four knots, and turned hard to port to unmask her starboard batteries.[7] Across the way, *Akagi* was doing the same, and *Tone*, *Chikuma*, and *Nagara* were all blazing away as well. Finally, under heavy attack, several of the planes launched their torpedoes.

To the cool eyes on board the carriers, it was clear that the Americans weren't very good at this sort of thing. They had dropped their fish much too far away. Yet, drop them they did, and their targets had no choice but to react. *Nagara* had been targeted by an Avenger pilot who had dumped his torpedo at whatever ship was closest, thinking his badly shot-up plane was about to go in the drink.[8] *Hiryū* simply ran away from the pair that had been launched against her. Meanwhile, Captain Aoki first threw his big ship into a looping port turn to avoid the torpedoes being aimed at *Hiryū* by the Avengers, then executed a neat one-eighty back to starboard to avoid the fish dropped by the surviving B-26s. In the process, *Akagi* received a strafing from one of the Marauders as it roared overhead after its attack. The flagship's No. 2 machine-gun mount suffered some minor damage, and two men were killed.[9]

The American aircraft were suddenly gone—except for one. This particular B-26, having been hit by *Akagi*'s automatic weapons, made no effort to pull out of its run. Instead, he bored in directly at *Akagi*'s bridge, where Nagumo and his staff stared wide-eyed back at their assailant. The plane was either unnavigable, or the American pilot, knowing his life was forfeit in any case, had decided to sell himself dearly.[10] The bridge watch were stunned—Americans weren't supposed to show this sort of bravery. Then reflexes took over and the men ducked as the American plane barreled in—there was no chance of it missing now. But instead of an explosion, the green bomber somehow flashed past the top of the island and cartwheeled into the sea. Nagumo and his staff let out a collective shout of relief—how it had missed, no one knew, but that had been too close by half!

If Tomonaga's message fifteen minutes earlier hadn't already decided matters for Nagumo, the determined self-sacrifice of this particular Marauder may well have done so. Having just evaded torpedoes, been strafed, and then nearly been turned into a bomber hood ornament, Nagumo's blood was up. Enough was enough. It was clear that Midway was still full of fight, and until the island was neutralized it would be a threat. The Americans had not been terribly skilled, but everyone on the bridge had just witnessed firsthand how important luck was in combat. Had the American plane been ten feet lower, *Akagi*'s island would have been given a daisy cutter, and the staff of First Air Fleet would have all been killed outright. It was time to put the American base out of business. However, attacking Midway in an effective manner meant disobeying direct orders from Yamamoto that the Striking Force keep its reserve aircraft armed for antiship operations.

Nagumo has been endlessly pilloried for deciding to violate this order. Yet, very few people have reflected on the practical implications of *not* doing so, or on whether Yamamoto's order was sound in the first place. Had Nagumo rigidly adhered to his superior's wishes, what were his realistic options for beating down the island's defenses? Was he simply to let Tomonaga's men go back out later in the day to finish the job? Nagumo, after all, had absolutely no detailed information regarding the state of the island after Tomonaga's attack. All he knew was that his flight leader had thought a second strike necessary. Relying on only half of his force to single-handedly bring about Midway's destruction, even over the course of multiple attacks, really didn't make much sense. Tomonaga's air group was bound to take losses in the process, and as it did so, it would become weaker even if the enemy was correspondingly weakened as well. Yet, Yamamoto's orders presumably would have kept Egusa and the rest of the "A-team" sunning themselves on the flight decks while Tomonaga and his men beat themselves bloody. The whole idea was simply asinine.

Genda certainly agreed with this assessment, remarking after the war that Yamamoto's instructions were "inflexible." He added that if the order had been adhered to, "one-half of the attack force would be kept idle unless a suitable enemy target [was] located. A decision should [have been] made depending upon the circumstances."[11] Kusaka, too, felt that it was "intolerable for the commander at the front to keep [his] half strength in readiness indefinitely only for an enemy force which might not be in the area after all."[12] Both men were absolutely correct in their judgment.

The job of Admiral Nagumo and his staff was to craft timely, appropriate responses to the conditions then pertaining. Regarding Midway, one approach that strongly recommended itself at this juncture was reducing *Kidō Butai*'s own casualties by bringing overwhelming power to bear on the enemy—an approach to warfare that has been highly regarded since mankind first started sharpening sticks. If no American warships were nearby, it clearly made sense for Nagumo to attack Midway with as large a follow-up strike as possible in order to force the (presumably) depleted enemy into an even more unfavorable attritional spiral.

There was another practical reason for violating the order—that of time. Regardless of what condition Tomonaga's group came home in, it would be a matter of several hours before they could be turned around for another attack. Planes had to be refueled and rearmed, damaged aircraft patched up, and the pilots debriefed and fed. Replacement aviators would need to be slotted in for the crewmen who had been wounded. A new mission plan would have to be created, the pilots briefed, and then the attack force armed, fueled, spotted, and launched. This probably could not have happened before the early afternoon. Giving the enemy more time to lick his own wounds and recover made no sense whatsoever—it was far better to hit the Americans again as quickly as possible, preferably while their aircraft were on the ground and being refueled.

Here, in the cold light of combat on the morning of 4 June, Yamamoto's earlier order was revealed for what it was—twaddle. Concocted in the unreal atmosphere of May's war games, his instructions contained no operational parameters and no indications as to when Egusa's force could be considered available for land attack operations. Was Nagumo to reserve these aircraft until the outward-bound legs of the recon flights were completed, or until the scouts returned to *Kidō Butai,* or simply forever? Apparently, no one knew. Yamamoto's order, if literally interpreted,

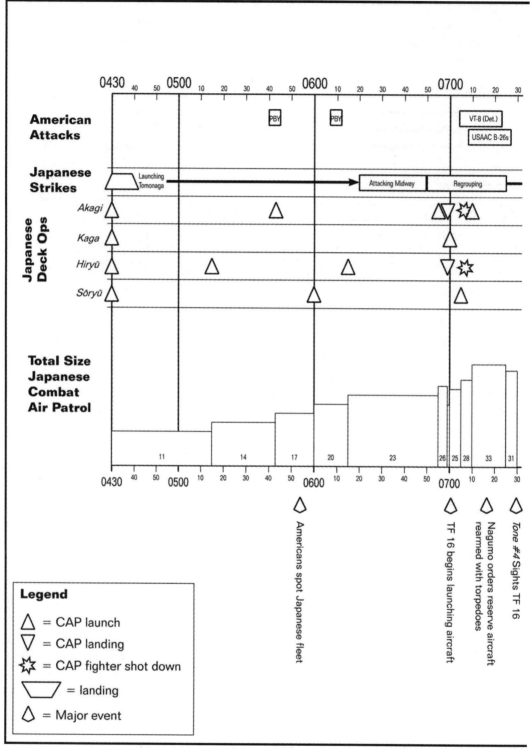

9-2: Air operations time line. This schematic shows the tempo of air operations on board the four Japanese carriers on the morning of 4 June, as well as the American attacks against them.

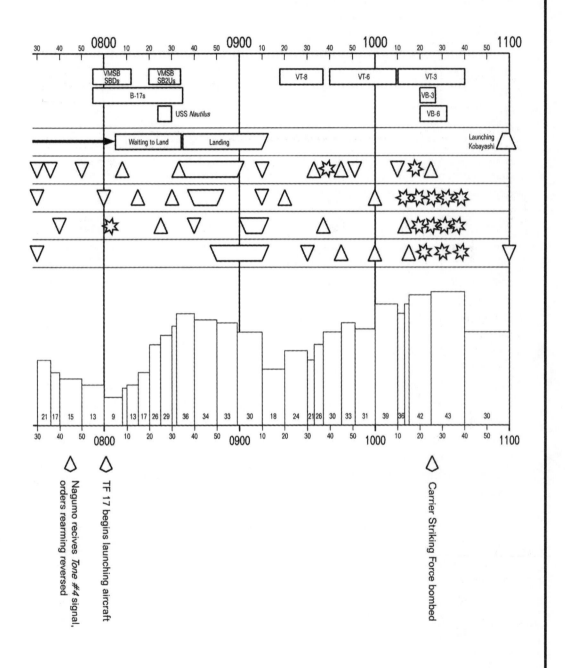

© Parshall 2005

essentially condemned Nagumo to fight with one hand tied behind his back—pitting Tomonaga's strike group against Midway in a pathetic race to see who limped to impotence first. Had Yamamoto truly been concerned about the U.S. Navy making its presence felt in the initial phase of operations, he should have backed up his reserve strike concept with requirements for a realistic scouting scheme and other contingency plans, so as to guarantee Nagumo's ability to deal with one opponent at a time. Instead, he had delivered a single flippant order—verbally, almost casually, and without any set of guiding particulars or modifying conditions. When viewed in this light, it is almost impossible to anticipate Nagumo *not* making the decision to hit the island again with his reserve force at some point during the morning.

Nagumo has also been castigated for not waiting to rearm his reserve aircraft until the morning's reconnaissance searches were completed. This criticism hits nearer the mark, in that (as will be seen) his relatively speedy decision to commence rearming deprived the force of vital time when a valid scouting report actually arrived. However, it should be remembered that by 0715, the meaningful portions of the morning's searches *were* completed for all intents and purposes. The scout aircraft had now been aloft for nearly three hours. They had already run their outbound routes and were currently halfway through their left-hand doglegs as well. Within fifteen minutes, all of them would be turning for home. As soon as that occurred, the symmetry of the search pattern would break down as the search planes began individually converging on *Kidō Butai*. It was probably never expected that anyone would find anything on the *inbound* leg in any case.

In the midst of these goings-on, Nagumo had been handed a message that had just been forwarded from *Kaga*. *Kaga*'s *hikōchō*, Cdr. Amagai Takahisa, had apparently received a message regarding the effects of the Midway attack from *Kaga*'s dive-bomber leader (Lt. Ogawa Shōichi) at 0640. Ogawa reported that Sand Island had been bombed and "great results obtained."[13] Nagumo had only to recall the American Marauders boring in a few minutes previously to put Ogawa's optimistic assessment into proper perspective. Accordingly, at 0715 Nagumo sent the following message to the fleet: "Planes in second attack wave stand by to carry out attack today. Reequip yourselves with bombs."

At 0720 *Akagi* took on board a single Zero. This plane, piloted by PO1c Iwashiro Yoshio, had been airborne a grand total of twenty-five minutes. His *shōtai* leader, Lt. Ibusuki Masanobu, was still aloft with the CAP. His wingman, Hanyu, was already dead. Iwashiro was likely out of cannon ammunition, having just experienced firsthand the amount of punishment American bombers could take (and dish out) before folding. This would become a common occurrence during the morning, with several Japanese fighters going up and coming right back down again after an attack. With sixty rounds of cannon ammunition for each of the Zero's two cannons, they weren't good for more than a few firing runs. Iwashiro's plane was quickly struck below.

Down below, the hangar crews were beginning to carry out the rearming order issued five minutes previously. As will be recalled, the reserve strike aircraft had not been on the flight decks yet this morning.[14] Consequently, there had been no need to send these aircraft back below to be worked on. Within the hangars, the forty-three carrier attack planes on board CarDiv 1 were currently armed with torpedoes.[15] These would need to be changed to Type 80 land bombs for the attack against the atoll. However, on board CarDiv 2, the thirty-four *kanbaku* were still *unarmed* at this point, because that normally occurred on the flight deck during spotting. Thus, none of them needed to be rearmed, either. Nagumo's orders really only pertained in an immediate sense to the Type 97 aircraft on board *Akagi* and *Kaga*. Until CarDiv 1 had completed rearming, CarDiv 2 would wait to begin its spot. This represents a rather different vision of the rearming situation than has been portrayed in most texts on the battle, which have all four carriers engaged in frantic rearming activities at this time.

On board CarDiv 1, though, the activity was real enough. Changing from torpedoes to bombs was no simple matter. Not only did it require removing the torpedo from the aircraft, it also entailed changing the mounting hardware (*tokaki*) on the belly of the aircraft. Unlike the dive-bombers, whose main payloads were roughly the same size and shape whether they were high-explosive or semi-armor-piercing, the Type 97 aircraft carried ordnance that differed wildly in shape, requiring differently shaped mounting brackets as well.[16] Thus, rearming with new ordnance was a complex, multistep operation.

In *Akagi,* armorers pushed their six heavy carts out to the waiting *kankō* and began the process of detaching the torpedo-carrying harness. They then lowered the torpedo onto the cart via the plane's winch. Once it was down, a team of handlers began pushing it gingerly through the crowded hangar and back to the ordnance elevator to take it back below. However, once the men arrived, they found the elevator already in use hauling Type 80 bombs up to the hangar deck. Indeed, the bomb handlers in the magazines quickly let it be known that they had their hands full just getting the bombs out of storage and not to send anything down to them yet.[17] The armorers on the hangar deck had little choice in the matter except to deposit their loads in the holding racks next to the ordnance elevator. Each carrier had sets of curving brackets attached to the hangar bulkheads near the bomb lift for temporary storage of ordnance in just such situations. One by one the torpedoes were secured to the racks using block and tackle, and then the men moved the cart back to the elevator to receive the bomb. As always, the bombs came up in pieces. They would need to be assembled before they were attached to their planes.

Meanwhile, back at the aircraft, another group of men was sweating to remove the old *tokaki* and get the new hardware screwed into the plane. This operation took some twenty minutes to perform amid the clatter of wrenches and the grunts of the armorers. *Kaga* was going through the same motions. She had a larger *kankō* squadron, but she also had nine ordnance carts, as opposed to *Akagi*'s six. The net result was that the time needed to change *Kaga*'s squadron over was identical—the limiting factor in the operation was not the number of aircraft, but rather the 1:3 ratio of carts to planes.

All in all, it took around half an hour to rearm a *kankō,* the bulk of the time being spent in changing the mounting hardware and assembling the bomb. Despite the portrayals of the entire hangar buzzing with activity, in truth the action was rather localized. While the first *chūtai* was attended to, the maintenance crews for the other twelve *kankō* of *Akagi's* group simply idled—their mounting hardware couldn't be switched until the torpedoes were off, which in turn required a cart. With only six carts to go around, it was a long process, one marked by tedium for the crews waiting to get one, followed by frantic labor as they tried to replace the *tokaki* as quickly as possible.

Armed with this information, we can make some fairly accurate estimates concerning what Nagumo's options were at any given time during the morning. The math is reasonably straightforward—half an hour to rearm a single *chūtai,* three *chūtai* per carrier, and only one *chūtai* can be rearmed at a time—hence an hour and a half to rearm the lot.[18] Once complete, about forty-five minutes were then required to lift, spot, warm up, and launch the attack group. For dive-bombers, a few minutes longer would probably be added on the flight deck for arming. All in all, it would not be unreasonable to assume that two and a half hours would be required before the force could be completely rearmed, spotted, and warmed up for launch. This meant that at a bare minimum, with no interruptions, the reserve strike force would not be ready much before 0930. This time estimate stands in contrast to estimates put forth in earlier Western tracts that suggest that an hour and a half might have been sufficient for sending off the second strike. Furthermore, it is clear from the foregoing that attacking Midway two and a half hours from when the order was given with full deckload strikes from all four carriers was *only* achievable if everything went smoothly, above decks and below.

This projected launch time obviously depended heavily on the speediness of the forthcoming recovery operations. Tomonaga's planes would begin orbiting the carriers at around 0815, while rearming was still going on in the hangars of CarDiv 1. If the reserve strike was to be spotted starting at 0845 (i.e., an hour and a half from the time the rearming order was given), all of Tomonaga's strike aircraft would need to be recovered and stowed below to clear the flight deck for spotting. In the days before modern angled flight decks and deck-edge elevators, carriers could do only one thing at a time on their flight deck—spot aircraft, launch aircraft, or recover aircraft. For all practical purposes, one operation could not be started until the other was complete.

It is true, of course, that if Nagumo had given the word to attack promptly at 0715, he could probably have struck Midway with just the dive-bombers from CarDiv 2. These aircraft were as yet unarmed. They could have been spotted, armed, and launched by about 0800. However, this would have meant scrapping the idea of a coordinated strike with the First Carrier Division's *kankō,* which were to operate in a level-bombing role. Japanese doctrine, as we have seen, vastly preferred the idea of launching balanced deckload strikes, thereby gaining the benefits of combined arms. Consequently, a partial strike would probably not have been considered as an option at 0715. This made perfectly good sense—Midway wasn't going anywhere, and there were no indications as yet that there would be any difficulty in sending off a second strike after Tomonaga landed.

Apparently in anticipation of needing the decks cleared for Tomonaga's return, several of the carriers began cycling their CAP fighters. *Kaga* recovered three planes from her second watch at 0730, while across the way, *Sōryū* simultaneously brought down all six aircraft from her first two CAP watches. At 0736 *Akagi* landed another lone Zero, while *Hiryū* brought on board two fighters at 0740. At the end of these operations, *Kidō Butai* had only fourteen fighters aloft, down from the thirty-one it had up between 0710 and 0725. *Akagi* landed an additional plane at 0740, but it wasn't a fighter, but rather WO Suzuki Shigeru's Type 97 reconnaissance aircraft that had been launched with the morning strike. This aircraft had patrolled the No. 1 search line, flying almost due south. It had detected nothing.[19]

By about 0740, the rearming operations had been under way for about half an hour. *Kaga* and *Akagi*'s first *chūtai* of Type 97s (nine and six planes, respectively) were both nearing the end of the rearming process—leaving two more *chūtai* to go on each ship. Both ships of CarDiv 1 were also currently holding a course into the wind in order to bring on board additional fighters. Suddenly, in the midst of these proceedings, came a bolt from the blue.[20] *Tone*'s No. 4 scout plane sent the following report: "Sight what appears to be 10 enemy surface units, in position bearing 10 degrees distance 240 miles from Midway. Course 150 degrees, speed over 20 knots." This was a stunning development, because it stood every assumption of Yamamoto's plan on its head. Nagumo and his staff quickly huddled to discuss the implications.

It is important to clarify the exact delivery time of *Tone* No. 4's message to the bridge of *Akagi*, because this matter has been subjected to great scrutiny. Nagumo's composite log indicates that the original signal was transmitted to *Tone* at 0728.[21] It may well be that Amari had spotted the Americans sometime before this. It was the practice of Japanese search aircraft to work their way around the perimeter of an enemy formation before transmitting. Doing so would hopefully confuse the enemy as to the actual bearing back to the carrier force once the scout breached radio silence. As a result, we cannot know the exact time that Amari actually sighted the American force, only when he transmitted.

It has generally been supposed that Amari's transmission made it up to *Akagi*'s bridge sometime before 0745, because Nagumo's battle report logs an order at that time to reverse the earlier rearming order and to "leave torpedoes on those attack planes which have not as yet been changed to bombs."[22] However, at least one contemporary historian, Dallas Isom, has asserted that Nagumo actually did not receive Amari's transmission until 0800 or later.[23] As part of this theory, it has been proposed that Nagumo's orders to reverse arming may have been misrecorded in the composite log that forms the basis of the Nagumo Report. This notion is vaguely supported by Nagumo's own statement in the summary section of his report that *Tone* No. 4's message was not received until "about 0800," and is repeated in other Japanese materials as well.[24]

However, in this particular case, it is clear that Nagumo *did* receive Amari's transmission about the same time it was logged in the Nagumo Report. Furthermore, Nagumo thereupon acted on this information with great alacrity. This is confirmed not by Japanese sources, but by those of the enemy. At 0740 American radio intelligence logged Amari's third message of his flight thus far, reporting the initial sighting of

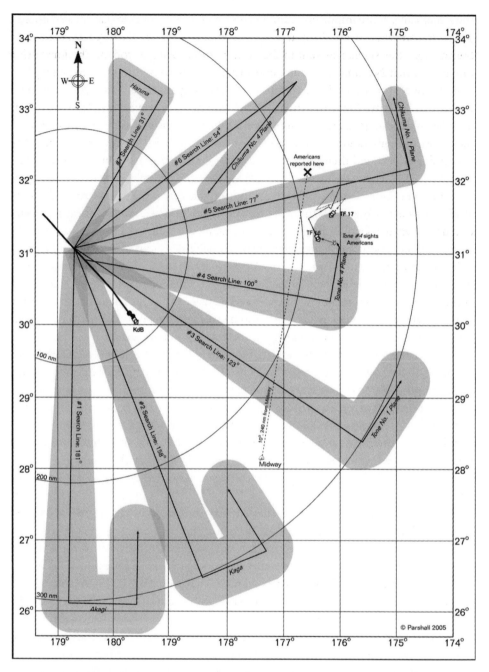

9-3: 0728 Sighting report from *Tone* No. 4. The likely search route of *Tone* No. 4 is indicated, as well as likely nominal visual detection ranges. (Source: *Senshi Sōsho*, p. 309)

the Americans. More important, American signals intelligence on Hawaii also noted a return transmission from *Akagi* at 0747, requesting that *Tone* No. 4 "retain contact."[25] Surprisingly, this signal was sent in the clear, without being encoded. The impression one gets is that Nagumo was quite concerned at Amari's sighting report, enough so that the need for a speedy response to his scout apparently outweighed any need for signals security. Thus, the theory that Nagumo experienced a delay in receiving *Tone* No. 4's message cannot be supported. Likewise, it is clear that Nagumo did not dawdle in his deliberations—upon receiving Amari's message he immediately reversed his arming orders and then promptly asked for clarification from his scout regarding what had been seen.

However, Isom is quite correct in noting that *Tone* No. 4's detection of TF 16 at 0728 was actually one of the few pieces of *good* luck that Nagumo was to receive this day.[26] On the face of it, this seems an incredible statement. After all, *Tone* No. 4's tardiness in taking off has commonly been held up as one of the crucial Japanese failures during the battle. Yet, a careful examination of the American course tracks overlaid by the original Japanese search pattern provides an important revelation. Had Amari been launched promptly at 0430 and actually flown his route as prescribed in the original search plan, he would have flown well south of both American formations on his outbound route and would not have detected them until the *inbound* leg. This would have delayed his likely detection time until at least 0800, meaning that Nagumo, in turn, would probably not have had an initial report in hand until closer to 0815 or later. Not only that, but had Amari actually flown his prescribed route *after* his delayed launch, the situation would have been made worse still. It was only Amari's unauthorized truncation of his search pattern, or perhaps muddled navigation, coupled with his apparent decision to dogleg north at around 0645 that put him in a position to make his initial sighting report—badly flawed though it was.

The question then remains: what should Nagumo have done at this time? Finding the "right" answer to Nagumo's conundrum—if such even exists—has consumed endless gallons of ink over the years. Much of it, regrettably, has been spilled to little purpose. For without having a clear grasp of what the actual state of the Japanese force was, and what was (and was not) possible for their carriers in the way of operations, a meaningful analysis of Nagumo's options cannot be constructed. Since this was perhaps *the* critical point in the battle for Nagumo, it's worth spending the time to lay these issues out in detail.

Nagumo's command decisions were governed by three primary constraints. The first was time. It's worth remembering at this juncture, reading at our leisure decades later in the quiet of a library or our own home, that Nagumo had approximately fifteen minutes to find the correct solution to a set of operational problems whose outlines—because of the spotty intelligence endemic to this morning's actions—he only partially grasped.

The second constraint was the physical arrangement of *Akagi*'s bridge. Unlike us, Nagumo wasn't parked in an easy chair. Indeed, a factor that has been entirely overlooked until now is the nature of *Akagi*'s command facilities and the effect these likely had on the admiral's ability to reason clearly. *Akagi*'s bridge was a tiny trapezoid, some fifteen feet wide and twelve feet long. Containing little more than a small map table, a chart locker, and several sets of pedestal-mounted spotting binoculars, it was extraordinarily cramped. In this tiny space stood at least five officers—Nagumo, Kusaka, Genda, Captain Aoki, and *Akagi*'s navigator, Commander Miura. In addition, if Fuchida's account is to be believed, several other individuals were present at least some of the time as well—Captain Ōishi (Kusaka's senior staff member), Lt. Cdr. Ono (staff intelligence officer), Lt. Cdr. Nishibayashi (staff flag secretary), Commander Masuda (*Akagi*'s *hikōchō*), and Fuchida himself. Of these, Ōishi and Ono appear to have been present at all times. Fuchida apparently came and went at various points during the morning, and Nishibayashi was likely doing the same. Commander Masuda would perforce have been spending much of his time on the air-control platform on the aft end of the island, one level lower, but would have been coming up to the bridge periodically to report to Captain Aoki on the state of air operations. In addition, a minimum of several enlisted personnel were required on the bridge for lookout duty and running messages. Taken together, it's difficult to imagine that there were fewer than a dozen individuals in the command spaces almost constantly. The men had to have been standing practically shoulder to shoulder, with Nagumo and his staff crammed into the starboard half of the bridge.

Nagumo was unlikely to be able to give or receive candid opinions from his staff in such a setting. The Japanese as a rule do not like interpersonal confrontations and tend to shun uncomfortable social situations. Kusaka and Genda were undoubtedly sensitive to the fact that Nagumo was not as well versed in naval aviation matters as he needed to be. Yet, in such a setting, they probably would have been unwilling to make the full extent of their own knowledge known, because that would risk embarrassing their commander in front of Captain Aoki and the ship's crew. Nagumo, for his part, would certainly not have wanted to reveal his own shortcomings in these matters. In such a setting, it's difficult to construct a scenario wherein a truly fluid exchange of information was possible. Worse yet, there was no place Nagumo and his staff could retreat for some temporary privacy and still be in proximity to *Akagi*'s command and communications equipment—*Akagi*'s island was simply too small.

These miserable arrangements stand in stark contrast to the facilities on board WWII American carriers, which were made possible by the American vessels having much larger islands. On each of the *Yorktown*-class ships there was a separate bridge for both the captain and the admiral. The ship's captain was not even allowed inside the admiral's bridge without an invitation from the flag. As such, an American admiral was free to discuss, debate, or flat out argue with his staff members behind closed doors. They were shielded from the distracting hubbub of the ship's helm and watchmen, allowing them to focus strictly on the management of the battle. The admiral had a sea cabin located in the island, allowing him to take naps if needed in order to maintain his alertness. In addition, American admirals often had their own separate radio facilities located nearby in the island as well.[27] All of these were luxuries Nagumo could only have dreamed of in the Spartan and completely public setting of *Akagi*.

It should be noted, too, that during much of the morning, *Akagi* was either being directly attacked or was under threat of same. During these periods, the ship was frequently maneuvering at high speeds. Nagumo had nearly been killed by a B-26 forty minutes earlier and would shortly witness several new attacks requiring additional defensive gyrations from his flagship, accompanied by CAP actions and heavy antiaircraft fire. *Akagi* was also conducting flight operations with some frequency. Stuck as he was in a cramped fishbowl, it's likely Nagumo spent a fair amount of his time looking out the window at these various happenings and trying to gauge their importance. In other words, the situation on the bridge was uncomfortable, noisy, and distracting in the extreme. Kusaka noted that even the ship's public address system was barely audible above the din.[28] It's hardly surprising that in such a setting Nagumo found it difficult to reason either quickly or clearly.

Nagumo's third major constraint revolved around his deck operations. A solution for Nagumo had to proceed on the basis of what was actually possible on the flight decks. Down through the years, numerous commentators on the battle have offered facile "solutions" for Nagumo's conundrum that have ignored these very real limitations. For instance, why could not the Japanese have moved their strike force to the flight decks and then rolled the strike aircraft forward of the crash barriers to warm up while the morning strike was recovered? Then, after recovering Tomonaga's aircraft and striking them below, why couldn't the strike aircraft (now presumably warmed up and ready for launch) be rolled back to the rear of the flight deck for spotting?

The answer to questions like these is that some of these operations *might* have been technically possible, but the Imperial Navy had never tried doing any of them before. 0800 on 4 June was a lousy time to try to figure out how. Militaries fight as they train. They absolutely have to, or they would descend into utter chaos when confronted by the enormous pressures of battle. Any attempt to monkey with fundamental activities as complex as deck operations was guaranteed to lead to confusion, wasted time, and a degraded operational tempo. This was precisely what the Japanese did *not* need at this time. Consequently, whatever Nagumo decided to do needed to be crafted from operational building blocks that were known commodities to the ship's crews.

Finally, it must be recognized that even if there was a "right" solution for the situation Nagumo found himself in, odds were that it would not be easy to implement, risk free, or even likely to forestall all of the horror and misery destined to descend on the Japanese this day. At this point in the battle, with the basic logic of the operational plan revealed as nonsense, the scouting plan in a shambles, and an unforeseen enemy suddenly on their flank, there was no magic solution that was going to transform the battle's outcome. Errors in strategy as grievous as the Japanese had inflicted on themselves are rarely reversible. Instead, the best that could really be hoped for was finding an approach whereby *Kidō Butai* had a reasonable chance of coming away with some of its carriers intact, or at least having extracted a heavy toll from the Americans.

What, then, did Nagumo have to work with in the way of actionable information? The answer is: not much. In fact, there were *three* worrisome aspects to *Tone* No. 4's sighting report. First, the enemy's position as given by Amari just didn't make any sense at all. If *Tone* No. 4 had indeed sighted American surface ships where he said he did, then he had encountered them well to the north of his appointed outbound search route. Indeed, the Americans appeared to be in the search sector of *Chikuma*'s No. 5 search line—so why hadn't that plane spotted the Americans first? Either Amari was out of place, or the enemy force wasn't where he had reported it to be. In fact, Amari's initial report placed the Americans some sixty miles north-northeast of their actual location. Indications are that Nagumo knew that scout aircraft sometimes took great liberties when "working" a contact and therefore doubted some aspects of Amari's report. Yet he had little choice but to take it at face value in terms of the reported location of the Americans.[29]

Second, *Tone* No. 4's report was miserably bereft of any indication as to what sort of American warships were out there. "Ten enemy surface units"—just what did that mean? Within minutes of the message's receipt, Nagumo sent a signal back to *Tone* No. 4 to ascertain the American ship types. Yet, despite the absence of positive confirmation that a carrier was with the enemy force, the presence of ten warships of any kind should have been highly suspicious. The American task force, if it could attack with aircraft, was ideally located to ambush Nagumo's carriers. Indeed, as one historian of the battle has noted, there was no point in *any* enemy task force being where Amari said it was unless it *could* attack with aircraft.[30]

Third, upon closer examination, the fact that the enemy was steering a course of 150 degrees was ominous in itself. The prevailing winds of the morning had been from out of the southeast (although they were presently shifting around to the northeast in the area near *Kidō Butai*). Such a course track could well be indicative of an enemy task force launching aircraft.[31]

It would seem that the significance of some or all of these clues was not lost on Nagumo and his staff. Kusaka was apparently of the opinion that "there couldn't be an enemy force without carriers in the area reported."[32] If *Senshi Sōsho* is any indication, this appears to have been Nagumo's belief as well. However—and this is a critical point—both the admiral and his staff came to the conclusion that whatever enemy force was out there was most probably a *surface* force.[33] The Americans may have had at least one carrier in attendance with that force, but it was not viewed as a carrier force per se.

Despite these ambiguities, there were several pieces of information that could be used to craft an operational plan. First, it was now clear that the Americans had a naval force in the area, and prudence would dictate that it be treated as if it contained a carrier until proven otherwise. Second, given that Nagumo's approximate location had been known to the enemy for almost two hours, he had to assume that any enemy carrier in the neighborhood would be in receipt of sighting reports. That meant that they could have launched against him by now. Consequently, Nagumo had every reason to expect further attacks, this time by carrier aircraft, which could arrive at any time. Third, *Kidō Butai*'s own geographic position was far from optimal—it was essentially located on the horns of a dilemma. There was no question that the horn to the northeast (the enemy naval force) was potentially the more dangerous of the two and would have to be attacked as soon as was practical. However, as part of his reaction to this new problem,

Nagumo needed to consider maneuvering his force in such a fashion as to minimize the impact of potentially being caught between two enemies.

Nagumo basically had two options—to try and mount an immediate attack against the newly detected American force before Tomonaga returned, or to stand pat and attack after Tomonaga had been recovered. Obviously, all things being equal, attacking sooner rather than later would generally have been preferred. However, there were numerous problems with such a course of action. First of all, Nagumo was rightly cautious about launching a strike against the enemy force before conclusive ship identifications had been provided to him. He knew, and everyone on *Akagi*'s bridge knew, what had happened to Rear Admiral Takagi when he had been placed in a similar situation just a month earlier. During the preliminaries at Coral Sea, the commander of CarDiv 5 had launched a powerful group of his aircraft against an American naval target based on what had turned out to be faulty spotting information. As a result, instead of attacking a "carrier," the Japanese had wasted their strength sinking an American oiler and destroyer.[34]

The second obstacle, of course, was that Nagumo had *nothing* in the way of strike aircraft ready to go at 0745. No aircraft were currently spotted on his flight decks. The spate of CAP fighter landings on all four carriers from 0730 to 0740 is proof positive of that—for fighters to have landed at that time the decks absolutely had to be clear astern. Thus, striking "immediately" could not happen in less than the time it actually took to spot, warm up, and launch a strike. This meant a minimum of forty-five minutes from now, that is, at about 0830 at the earliest.

However, Tomonaga's returning force was expected to begin orbiting Nagumo's carriers around 0815, meaning that an immediate strike would need to be launched in time for the morning strike force to land. Tomonaga's group undoubtedly contained damaged aircraft and wounded airmen. They would have been airborne for almost four hours by that time and would soon be running low on fuel, particularly on those aircraft that had suffered battle damage to their wings.[35] It would be imperative to get them down as quickly as possible, and the carrier *hikōchō* would have been keenly aware of this need. As we will shortly see, landing the Midway force—including not only the time to recover aircraft, but also the time needed afterward to clear them off of the flight deck and stow them below—was a process that could not help but take about twenty minutes per carrier. In the event, it was actually to take from around 0837 to 0912 to completely land Tomonaga and his men on all four carriers.

The clever reader will immediately have noticed that since Tomonaga's force was not to be recovered until 0912 in any case, could not Nagumo have anticipated this and intentionally kept Tomonaga orbiting long enough to launch a full-blown strike with all his aircraft? Working backward from a hypothetical final recovery time for Tomonaga of around 0915 proves an illuminating exercise. If all of Tomonaga's aircraft were to be recovered by then, then they would need to *start* recovering by about 0845, or perhaps a bit later. This meant, in turn, that the reserve strike force would have to be launched (and the decks clear) by this time. Again working backward, that implies an initial spotting time of about 0800 *at the latest* for the reserve strike force, meaning that rearming would need to be complete by then as well. In other words, if

Nagumo was to launch anything before Tomonaga *had* to come down, he had to begin his spotting almost immediately. Time was, indeed, a very precious commodity.

By 0745 one *chūtai* of Type 97s on *Kaga* and *Akagi* had already been rearmed with 800-kg bombs. Had Nagumo *immediately* given the order to stop rearming with bombs at 0745, as it appears he did, he *might* possibly have caught the armorers in time to prevent them from beginning the switch out of the second *chūtai*'s torpedoes. This would have allowed CarDiv 1 to each begin spotting *two* of their three *chūtai* of torpedo-armed aircraft by about 0800. But in no case would Nagumo have been able to send up his entire reserve force of Type 97s before Tomonaga had to land—the *chūtai* on each carrier that had already been rearmed with Type 80 bombs simply couldn't be switched back in time.

In terms of force, then, the difference between spotting now or waiting for the *kankō* squadrons to be completely rearmed essentially boiled down to about fifteen aircraft. If Nagumo waited, his available forces would be as follows:

Akagi: eighteen *kankō* (three six-plane *chūtai*)
Kaga: twenty-six or twenty-seven *kankō* (three nine-plane *chūtai*)[36]
Hiryū: eighteen *kanbaku* (both of her nine-plane *chūtai*)
Sōryū: sixteen *kanbaku*[37] (both of her nine-plane *chūtai*)
Total: seventy-eight or seventy-nine attack aircraft

Conversely, if Nagumo decided to spot immediately, the strike assets we can be reasonably sure were available were:

Akagi: twelve *kankō* (two of her total of three six-plane *chūtai*)
Kaga: eighteen *kankō* (two of her total of three nine-plane *chūtai*)[38]
Hiryū: eighteen *kanbaku* (both of her nine-plane *chūtai*)
Sōryū: sixteen *kanbaku* (both of her nine-plane *chūtai*)
Total: sixty-four attack aircraft

Clearly, even without the full torpedo plane complements from *Akagi* and *Kaga,* Nagumo had the potential to launch a powerful, well-balanced strike package. The sixty-four attack aircraft he had available immediately were easily capable of sinking two American carriers outright if properly employed. In fact, this group of aircraft represented more than twice the aggregate firepower that the Japanese would actually manage to throw at the American carriers during the day's later actions. However, such a strike would have broken the organizational symmetry of CarDiv 1's *kankō* groups by leaving a *chūtai* apiece of semi-armed planes sitting in both *Akagi* and *Kaga*'s hangars, a move that no doctrinaire Japanese commander would have viewed with a favorable eye.

A second alternative, and one which better preserved the fleet's organizational integrity, was to go with a more-limited immediate strike and just send out CarDiv 2's thirty-four *kanbaku*. This would have left Nagumo with another strike force in the process of arming (CarDiv 1's *kankō*) that could be launched shortly thereafter, and with Tomonaga's group to follow up later in the morning after they were recovered.

The downside of this approach, though, was twofold. First, it reduced the power of the initial strike by reducing the sheer number of aircraft attacking. Second, it lowered the theoretical effectiveness of the strike by presenting the enemy with a one-dimensional threat, that is, no torpedo aircraft coming in at low altitude to stretch the enemy CAP while the dive-bombers attacked. Doctrine frowned on both of these sacrifices.

Most likely, these were the only two options Nagumo and his staff considered in terms of launching an immediate attack. From the standpoint of postwar carrier operations, though, there were probably several more possibilities available to *Kidō Butai*. If the enemy's southeast course heading *was* indicative of their conducting flight operations, then *Kidō Butai* needed to consider its defensive needs as well. In light of this requirement and the technical and doctrinal imperatives at work, an approach that suggests itself is one wherein CarDivs 1 and 2 operated independently. Fuchida suggested something similar in the postmortem analysis of his account, where he advocated attacking with only a single carrier division at a time while holding the other in reserve.[39] However, it is clear that in making this suggestion, Fuchida, like Nagumo and his staff, was strictly thinking in terms of how best to deliver *attacks* against the enemy. The fleet's defense didn't figure into Fuchida's calculus, nor (apparently) that of any Japanese officer this day. Admiral Yamaguchi, too, was opposed to operating independently for the moment,[40] although, as we shall see, as the day wore on, his CarDiv 2 operated in an increasingly detached manner from CarDiv 1.

A slightly different approach might have been to effect an actual split along *functional* lines, with one carrier division attending to the fleet's offensive chores, the other to the defensive. This is precisely what modern carrier divisions often do.[41] This same concept, in fact, had already been cooked up by the Yokosuka squadron but had yet to be formally implemented in the Navy's doctrine. If such were attempted, the logical division of labor would have had CarDiv 2 launching an immediate attack against the Americans, while CarDiv 1 was tasked with air defense. This would have conferred a number of advantages on the Japanese.

From an offensive standpoint, using only CarDiv 2's dive-bombers for an initial attack obviously meant that the force would not benefit from combined arms. Nevertheless, it placed the attack force in very capable hands. It was commonly acknowledged that CarDiv 2's strike units were the best of the best. With the famed Commander Egusa leading the counterstrike, the Japanese could be confident of scoring against the enemy. This approach also obviated the need to shut down all of *Kidō Butai*'s flight decks simultaneously upon Tomonaga's arrival. *Akagi* and *Kaga*'s strike planes could have been recovered almost immediately, thereby keeping only *Hiryū*'s and *Sōryū*'s morning strike planes circling, while Egusa's force was spotted and launched.

An even more esoteric approach might have attempted roughly the same functionalized arrangement of offensive/defensive duties, but with *Sōryū* and *Akagi* designated as the CAP carriers, and *Hiryū* and *Kaga* the attack carriers. In this way, a total of thirty-six strike aircraft (eighteen *kanbaku* and eighteen *kankō*) could be spotted immediately. In other words, this arrangement would not only split *Kidō Butai* into two roles, but also would split the divisional structure in allocating those roles. The benefit of such an approach would be in allowing *Kidō Butai* to launch an immediate strike package that also benefited from combined arms.

However, it is clear that Nagumo and his staff were hamstrung by Japanese naval doctrine in terms of considering such options. In fact, it is unlikely that either of the "functionalized" approaches outlined above would have even occurred to them, particularly since the fruits of Yokosuka's research had yet to be harvested. In 1942 Japanese doctrine was strictly offensive, and its prescription for practically any tactical situation was to attack the enemy with a full-strength combined arms strike—period. Nagumo's needs for a more flexible approach were therefore negated by the Imperial Navy's doctrinal emphasis on mass. In the end, as he saw it, he had only one option— to attack with everything he had, regardless of how long it took to make the necessary arrangements.

Regardless of the composition of the strike force, another question that needed solving was the matter of providing a fighter escort for the attack. Fuchida later asserted that providing Zeros in the 0800 time frame would have proven impossible, as the second wave fighters had already been sent aloft to reinforce the CAP. This meant that CarDiv 2's *kanbaku* would have to go in unescorted, a prospect that no one relished.[42] This factor has been cited by many postwar scholars as being a determining factor in Nagumo's decision.[43]

A detailed examination of *Kidō Butai*'s flight records, though, reveals an entirely different situation. As mentioned, the four carrier *hikōchō* had anticipated Tomonaga's return and apparently tried to proactively manage the impending shutdown of the flight decks by ratcheting down the CAP from about 0730. As a result, by about 0800 *Kidō Butai* had the following fighters available in the hangars: *Akagi*, twelve; *Kaga*, eighteen, *Hiryū*, eight, *Sōryū*, nine; for a total of forty-seven. Thirty-five of these Zeros had been on board their respective ships for at least half an hour and could thus be reasonably assured of being fueled and munitioned. This was a powerful escort force, especially given the demonstrable superiority of Japanese fighter aircraft and pilots over their American counterparts.

However, committing this body of fighters en masse to a strike against the Americans meant that *Kidō Butai* would have almost *no* fighter reserve to reinforce the CAP, which by now was down to just nine fighters. If Nagumo chose to launch with both CarDiv 1 and 2, this rather pitiful CAP would have to *stay* aloft for the duration of the spotting and launch process. Thereafter, they would need to be replenished and reinforced. Clearly, the number of fighters that would escort this second strike of the morning would have to be fewer than the thirty-six sent out with Tomonaga. However, it is equally clear that Nagumo could have provided his force with at least some escort. Indeed, an escort of a dozen Zeros could have easily been sent, and twice that many would probably not have been out of reach.

The final factor Nagumo had to consider was how to maneuver his force. *Kidō Butai* currently found itself between two enemies. Worse, Nagumo only really knew the location of one of these foes—Midway itself. Until *Tone* No. 4's position report was independently confirmed, he was dealing in vagaries as far as the American fleet was concerned. Knowing that he wanted to attack the American carrier, it made good sense to move away from Midway for the time being. Indeed, it may have even made sense to temporarily move away from the American naval force as well. In retrospect, Nagumo's subsequent decision to change course to the northeast and close the American force without first having sound knowledge of its composition and exact whereabouts was ill conceived. It not only increased his danger from the American carriers, but it also had the effect of leaving Midway near to hand upon his southern flank.

Nagumo was certainly well within his rights to maneuver freely. Frankly, by 0800 it should have been clear to everyone on *Akagi*'s bridge that Yamamoto's battle plan needed to be summarily consigned to the ash can. Absolutely nothing was going according to plan this morning. Yet Nagumo still possessed some important advantages. For one thing, Japanese attack aircraft were somewhat longer ranged than their American counterparts. Taking a northwest course would have fulfilled his need to strike while employing his longer reach. He knew that the weather to his north wasn't good. If he could get back underneath the cold front he had come through on the previous day, he could use it to shield his movements. From there it might have been possible to work around the Americans' northern flank. Nagumo might have suspected that the Americans were covering this quadrant with their own search aircraft (as indeed they were), but at least from that direction he could deliver attacks against them without fear of direct interference from Midway, which would be far to the south of where Nagumo would have hoped to develop the follow-on battle. Furthermore, he also could have used the time he spent maneuvering northward to call for reinforcements (in the form of Kakuta's Second Mobile Force) and start bringing them down from the Aleutians.

Students of the battle will note that withdrawing to the north or northwest in the 0800–0900 time frame most likely would not have resulted in *Kidō Butai* being missed altogether by the incoming American strike aircraft. *Enterprise*'s dive-bomber group eventually overhauled *Kidō Butai* from the southwest and might also have detected a force lying directly to their north. Likewise, *Kidō Butai* might have encountered *Hornet*'s strike force as well. Thus, any maneuver Nagumo attempted in that direction would probably have exposed the fleet to a strike of some sort. However, this would potentially have had its benefits. Instead of facing attack groups from both *Yorktown* and *Enterprise* coming in simultaneously from several points on the compass, *Kidō Butai* might have encountered these strikes sequentially, and from a single direction, thereby making detection and interception much easier. The Japanese CAP had already demonstrated that it could deal with a single-vector threat if it was given sufficient warning.

However, maneuvering in this fashion would cause problems, in that it necessarily meant throwing the entire operation's timetable completely off kilter. This would undoubtedly have drawn fire from Yamamoto. Even if he were inclined to do so, Nagumo would have needed to begin coordinating not only the activities of his own vessels, but also helping reorient the various invasion and support forces as well. There was, in other words, a formidable level of "plan inertia" that would need to be overcome at an operational level. It wouldn't have been enough for Nagumo to simply radio Admiral Tanaka and say, "Stay where you are and I'll let you know when it's safe to invade." Any hint of discarding the commander in chief's precious timetable would need to be backed up by mental toughness, sound logic, and the ability to supply Combined Fleet staff with reasonable estimates of when the job would be completed.

Taking all together, and admittedly operating with the benefit of hindsight, the "right" answer to Nagumo's conundrum probably should have emphasized maneuver, offensive speed in preference to mass, and passive damage control. With fifteen minutes in which to act, he didn't really have time to implement anything terribly fancy. But he could have helped himself immensely by *immediately* spotting *every* strike airplane in his hangars, whether they were armed or not, and launching them at the Americans. The sixty-four armed aircraft he had in hand were perfectly capable of doing enormous damage to his enemy. And by emptying his hangars, he removed the single greatest danger to his carriers—the presence of fueled and armed aircraft within them.

However, even as Nagumo was considering these options, a new hurdle emerged. At 0753 *Kirishima* was seen to lay down smoke—another American air raid was coming in. As we shall see, within a matter of just a few minutes, Nagumo would be under assault yet again. Launching an attack before Tomonaga returned was now going to be doubly difficult, in that he would need to spot aircraft in the face of an ongoing American attack. No right-minded *hikōchō* was going to be happy spotting aircraft while the force was being bombed. With the ships engaged in high-speed maneuvering, pushing aircraft across an exposed flight deck and into their spots would have been hideously dangerous. Plane handlers could be maimed or crushed by an aircraft that got out of control—a very real possibility if the flight deck suddenly canted to one side. In fact, one of *Zuikaku*'s plane handlers had been killed under similar circumstances at Coral Sea, and a plane lost overboard as a result.[44] Furthermore, having the armed and fueled aircraft on deck directly exposed them to strafing attacks. Pressing home a spot, and then launching under such circumstances, would require both steady nerves and a steely resolve. Yet, a truly insightful commander would have pointed out to his balking captains and *hikōchō* that keeping armed and fueled aircraft *inside* the ship during an American attack was, if anything, more dangerous than getting them airborne as quickly as possible, even in the face of enemy fire.[45]

The bottom line is that Nagumo chose not to attempt an attack at this time, most likely for a host of reasons. In the first place, he probably judged that trying to shoehorn an immediate strike in before Tomonaga landed was probably going to be too difficult to deal with, particularly with a new American attack rolling in. He might also have been concerned, too, that *Tone* No. 4's position report appeared to be bogus, meaning that further scouting work would be necessary to locate the enemy.

Furthermore, while we know in hindsight that the fighter situation was not as dire as Fuchida later made it out to be, both Genda and Kusaka were apparently worried about finding enough escorts for the attack force at this time.[46] They may not have known how far along the rearming activities had progressed within *Akagi*'s hangars, nor what the status was of the fighters aboard the other ships in *Kidō Butai*. And while it is not documented in the available sources, it is likely that both Genda and Kusaka disliked the idea of distorting the symmetry of *Kidō Butai*'s air groups by sending out a partial strike unit. Breaking the attack squadrons apart at this time meant trying to figure out where to integrate the remainder into strikes later in the day, if indeed the physical constraints of the force's flight decks would allow the leftovers to be spotted with Tomonaga's force later on. A partial strike now portended more mess and less efficiency later.

It must be emphasized, too, that Nagumo's course of action was doctrinally correct. It favored mass and held out the promise of a fully integrated strike. Right now, the choices available to Nagumo were all tough calls between various half measures. But by waiting a bit, he might not have to make the tough choices and would be able to strike with his full force. Many critics of his performance—Japanese and American alike—have neglected to acknowledge that he at least acted in a fashion that was doctrinally coherent.

Indeed, if Nagumo had actually been fortunate enough to attack with *Kidō Butai*'s complete reserve strike force, it would have unquestionably been the most powerful, best-coordinated strike launched by either side during the day. Unlike their American counterparts, Japanese torpedo aircraft were fully capable of delivering telling attacks. Furthermore, the Japanese were well versed in coordinating simultaneous dive-bomber and torpedo strikes against moving targets. Any American flattop on the receiving end of such an assault would have found itself in the most dreadful peril. Indeed, a full strike by all four of Nagumo's flight decks had the firepower to sink every American carrier in the battle, had they been caught operating in proximity.

However, the most important factor is that Nagumo probably felt little real urgency to strike at this moment. Hitting the American task force was clearly the highest priority mission at hand. Having only sighted ten warships, though, he apparently judged the enemy to be rather weak. Indeed, it was possible, albeit unlikely, that a stray American carrier had simply been in the area, delivering aircraft or some such, and had moved toward Midway as a result of the actions on 3 June. No matter where it came from, there were no real indications at the moment that *Kidō Butai* would have any problem attacking it in due time. Given the very real difficulties inherent in trying to put together a strike force before Tomonaga's imminent homecoming, the path of least resistance was simply to accept the slight delay in counterattacking. Nagumo would use the time gained during recovery operations to complete the rearming of CarDiv 1's *kankō* and then launch a full-blown strike force later in the morning.

This perception of American weakness clearly influenced his subsequent decision to close the enemy. Indeed, before the strength of American airpower made itself calamitously known, Nagumo would issue orders to his fleet at 0930 that his intention was to destroy the enemy in a "daylight engagement," in other words a *surface* action.[47] Apparently, Nagumo judged the American fleet to be weak enough that if need be he could dispatch it with his own rather light screening forces (albeit stiffened by two fast battleships). Such an order would telegraph the unconscious message to the Japanese forces that there was no need to wait until after dark to employ the Imperial Navy's vaunted night battle techniques against this particular enemy. They could be mopped up right now, in broad daylight. Thus, for the next three hours, Nagumo treated this force as an enemy that was first to be attacked from the air, and then annihilated by his destroyers and battleships on the surface.

Much like his earlier decision to authorize attacking Midway with his reserve aircraft, Nagumo's decision to delay attacking the American task force has been mercilessly criticized. Fuchida remarked:

> Looking back on this critical moment, which ultimately was to decide the battle, I can easily realize what a difficult choice faced the Force Commander. Yet, even now, I find it hard to justify the decision he took. Should he not have sacrificed every other consideration in favor of sending the dive bombers immediately against the enemy ships? Should he not have dispatched the torpedo bombers also, even though armed with bombs? He could have launched them to orbit until enough fighters could be recovered refueled and launched again to provide escort. The planes back from Midway could have been kept in the air at least until the bombers had cleared. Damaged planes, if unable to remain aloft any longer, could have crash-landed in the sea, where destroyers would have rescued the crews.
>
> "Wise after the event," the saying goes. Still, there is no question that it would have been wiser to launch our dive bombers immediately, even without fighter protection. In such all-or-nothing carrier warfare, no other choice was admissible. Even the risk of sending unprotected level bombers should have been accepted as necessary in this emergency. Their fate would probably have been the same as that of the unescorted American planes which had attacked us a short while before, but just possibly they might have saved us from the catastrophe we were about to suffer.[48]

Fuchida's comments require careful analysis, because they contain important grains of truth, but also some stunning misstatements. Fuchida was correct to say that if at all possible it *was* desirable to attack the Americans quickly. This was clearly a time when The Book needed to be tossed aside in favor of haste. He was also right in pointing out that the fewer planes in the hangars, the better. Whether Fuchida truly apprehended this during the battle, or only upon reflection afterward, the truth remains that the best thing that Nagumo could have done to augment his force's survivability was to get as many aircraft out of his hangars and up in the air as possible, whether they had anything useful to do up there or not.

Fuchida was wrong, however, on three crucial points. First, of course, was his deliberate neglect to mention that Nagumo could actually launch nothing at 0745, because all of the force's reserve strike aircraft were in the hangars. Second, whatever the need for a speedy attack, that imperative absolutely had to be balanced against the need to preserve the combat power of the force as a whole. In other words, Nagumo needed to minimize unnecessary losses (through deliberate ditchings and so on) among Tomonaga's force, if at all possible. *Kidō Butai* was now confronted by not one, but two enemies. Without aircraft, Nagumo's carriers could neither attack nor defend themselves. Responding to a suddenly augmented estimate of enemy firepower with a knee-jerk reaction that deliberately subtracted from one's own inventory of this vital commodity hardly made good sense. In a war that was to be filled with examples of needless sacrifices of Japanese forces, Nagumo is to be applauded for electing to preserve Tomonaga's assets at this juncture, rather than simply squandering them. Instead, he has been unfairly pilloried for his prudence.

However, the most important criticism of Fuchida's comments stems from his ignoring a vital piece of information that his postwar account should have had ready to hand. What Fuchida almost certainly knew in 1951, but Nagumo could only suspect on 4 June 1942, was that even as the commander of *Kidō Butai* was mulling his options on the bridge of *Akagi,* the bulk of the American carrier aircraft that would ultimately destroy his force were either already taking to the air, or were shortly to do so. In a nutshell, whether or not Nagumo launched a counterstrike before Tomonaga returned, he was still likely to be on the receiving end of a very heavy American attack at some point in the morning.

It will be recalled that Admiral Fletcher had ordered Spruance to attack the Japanese as soon as practicable, and Spruance had duly headed southwest to close on *Kidō Butai's* reported position. He had set 0700 as the time to launch both *Hornet's* and *Enterprise's* air groups, and precisely at the appointed hour they had begun doing so. However, their subsequent flight operations were notable for a lack of coordination and poor organization. No plan was in place to use the two carrier's air groups en masse. Rather, American doctrine dictated that each carrier's group was an independent entity. Furthermore, Spruance's air adviser, Cdr. Miles R. Browning, neglected to issue detailed instructions to *Hornet,* thus leaving it to her skipper, Captain Marc A. Mitscher, to issue orders to his air group as to their outbound route. Furthermore, the method by which the two American carriers spotted their respective strike forces was left strictly up to their captains as well.

Both skippers understandably wished to strike with every attack plane at their disposal. However, given the number of aircraft they would send up, they would need to first launch one portion of the strike, respot the decks, and then launch the remainder. During the respotting process, the aircraft already aloft would need to circle overhead, waiting for the complete strike to come up.

Capt. George D. Murray, *Enterprise's* skipper, chose to send up CAP fighters and his longer-ranged SBDs in his first spot, followed by his shorter-ranged fighters and TBDs in the second package. This plan made a good deal of sense, in that it kept the shorter-ranged aircraft on deck until last, thus providing them with the best possible amount of actual flying time toward the objective. In the event, though, because of mechanical issues and other problems, *Enterprise* took an immensely long time to spot her second deck load after the first was launched. Furthermore, in the middle of the protracted spot, TF 16 had become aware of *Tone* No. 4's presence, in the form of its intercepted 0740 transmission to Nagumo, which to *Enterprise's* radio intelligence officer looked conspicuously like a sighting report. Desperate to get things moving, Spruance informed *Enterprise's* dive-bombers to proceed on their assigned mission without waiting for the follow-up fighter escort or TBDs. Worse yet, when these second-wave aircraft were finally launched, they chose a different outbound route from the dive-bombers. Thus, *Enterprise's* strike had already been split into two components, each of which was proceeding independently.

Hornet's performance was even worse. Captain Mitscher, despite his experience, inexplicably decided to position his fighters in the front half of his first spot, followed by the SBDs and then half of the TBDs. Once these aircraft were aloft, the remainder of the torpedo planes would be spotted and launched. Forty-five minutes later, this is exactly what had transpired, leaving the fighters with just that much less combat radius. *Hornet*'s strike departed at 0755.

The subsequent movements of *Hornet*'s air group remain somewhat mysterious to this day. Some accounts maintain that the air group commander, Lt. Cdr. Stanhope C. Ring, flew a southwest course after being launched, and thereby ultimately missed *Kidō Butai* by flying to the *south* of it. However, we hew to the interpretation that *Hornet*'s group actually flew almost due west from their launch point and thereby flew to the north of Nagumo. Why Ring made the decision to take his group west, rather than southwest toward the location of the initial PBY spotting reports, remains unclear. But the result was that only a single squadron of *Hornet*'s air group would ultimately get into the fight this morning, and then only as the result of the most bizarre circumstances.

The contrast between these rather benighted deck operations and those of the Japanese could not be more striking. Whereas Tomonaga's 108 aircraft had taken just seven minutes to send aloft, *Hornet* and *Enterprise* labored for an hour to launch their own strikes, which totaled only eight aircraft more—twenty fighters, sixty-eight dive-bombers, and twenty-nine torpedo aircraft, for a total of 117.[49] Not only that, but instead of getting a coordinated strike from their two carriers, they had gotten three separate air groups heading in three different directions. As events transpired, some of the aircraft that set off together would not stay together long, leading to a further dispersion of power. Thus, the American aircraft, even if they reached the Japanese fleet at all, would be forced to attack in squadron-sized parcels. Nevertheless, by around 0800, the fates of Nagumo and *Kidō Butai* were already sealed to a certain degree.[50] The Americans had a fairly good idea of where the Japanese lay, and they had managed to put enough firepower in the air to be reasonably assured of causing the Japanese force great harm—*if* they could find *Kidō Butai*.

This fact places the questions surrounding Nagumo's options in a completely different light. Whether *Kidō Butai* struck back before or immediately after Tomonaga came home to roost, the Americans had still taken the initiative away from the Japanese. If Nagumo was to have attacked the Americans in time to forestall their strikes against him, he needed information from *Tone* No. 4, or somebody else, *much* earlier in the morning. In fact, working backward from when the American carriers launched their respective strikes, it is possible to determine when spotting information ceased to be actionable in a preemptive sense.

The slowest Japanese strike aircraft, the Type 97 *kankō*, cruised at 138 knots. They would take about an hour and a half to cover the roughly two hundred miles to the American task force.[51] But in the best of circumstances, attacking even the *Yorktown*, which (as we shall see) would start sending her own planes aloft at 0838, meant that Nagumo would have had to have his own aircraft *in the air* by around 0715 in order to hit the Americans first. That, in turn, means that Nagumo needed to have begun spotting his strike no later than 0630. Worse yet, hitting *Enterprise* and *Hornet* before *they* began launching would have required having a strike in the air no later than 0530. Thus, by the 0745–0800 time period, when Nagumo was actually debating the information he had in his hands, the Americans could no longer be forestalled. Nothing Nagumo could do at this point could entirely unmake the morning's events.

This, in turn, shifts a hefty share of the day's blame away from *Tone* No. 4 and onto *Chikuma*'s No. 1 aircraft, which had flown the No. 5 search line. As bad as Petty Officer Amari's subsequent navigation would prove, the critical reconnaissance failure really lay here. *Chikuma* No. 1 was the only plane that could have gotten timely information into Nagumo's hands. Had this plane flown its route correctly, and closer to the surface, it almost certainly should have detected the American task force between 0615 and 0630, that is, within the time frame (barely) needed to act decisively. Its failure cost Nagumo more than an hour of reaction time. It was this failure, not *Tone* No. 4's late launch, that set in motion a veritable avalanche of negative tactical consequences.

Chikuma No. 1's gaffe was indicative of a larger failure, however, for it was here that the paltry number of aircraft devoted to the morning's search really hurt Nagumo's chances. No properly conceived search program should have been completely compromised by the failure of a single asset. There should have been more aircraft devoted to the search. Some would point to *Chikuma* No. 1's inability to sight the Americans as somehow supporting the notion that the weather was so bad on Nagumo's eastern flank that no number of additional scouting assets in the area would have rectified the situation.[52] However, this makes no sense. The failure of one scout plane in one location, for whatever reasons of local weather conditions, poor navigation, and/or improper scouting technique, says nothing about the odds of another nearby plane—in slightly different weather, with different sight lines, and performing its search in a disciplined manner—to detect the same enemy. There can be no denying that more search assets would have significantly bettered Nagumo's odds. But Japanese doctrine, and its offensive-minded outlook, precluded this. As it was, Genda's reconnaissance scheme was essentially a roll of the dice, and Nagumo had crapped out hours ago.

10

Trading Blows—0800–0917

*K*irishima's warning smoke at 0753 presaged the arrival of a series of nearly continuous enemy attacks over the next forty minutes delivered by three separate American formations. The first was a group of sixteen dive-bombers under Major Lofton R. Henderson that were approaching *Kidō Butai* from the southeast. His Marine pilots, members of VMSB-241, had taken off just after Midway's B-26s and TBFs. However, owing to the slower cruising speed of his SBDs, as well as having taken a more northerly course, they had been later in spotting the Japanese force.

Henderson's men were some of the rawest fliers on the American side of the battle. Most of them had never flown an SBD until a few days previously, and more than half had only been with the unit for a few days. In their commander's opinion, his unit did not yet have the skills needed to execute a true dive-bombing attack. Instead, Henderson led his flight in from an altitude of 9,500 feet, hoping to survive long enough to execute a shallower glide-bombing attack against the two flattops he saw on the port side of the Japanese formation—the wildly maneuvering carriers of CarDiv 2. Henderson's men had just started their gradual descent toward the target when the Zeros hit them.

The Japanese CAP fighters tore into Henderson's formation with merciless precision. *Akagi*'s Lieutenant Ibusuki and his two remaining 6th *Kū* pilots were joined by *Hiryū*'s 3rd patrol, a pair of Zeros led by WO Kodama Yoshimi, as well as *Sōryū*'s 3rd patrol *shōtai*, under the redoubtable Lieutenant Fujita. This was, in fact, the entirety of the Japanese CAP, as *Kaga*'s four remaining fighters were already lining up for recovery. Nine fighters wasn't much with which to tackle a full squadron of enemy dive-bombers, but, in the event, they proved deadly effective.

Six U.S. aircraft went flaming down into the ocean almost at once. Major Henderson was one of the first, trying to hold his plane and his formation steady until the end. Henderson's death would lead to his name being used for a captured airfield on Guadalcanal, which would earn one of the most glorious names in American military history. However, there was nothing glorious about the predicament his surviving men found themselves in. They had little choice but to hold formation and continuing boring in toward the target, firing back as best they could. Somehow in the process, the American radio gunners managed to send *Hiryū*'s Kodama to his demise.

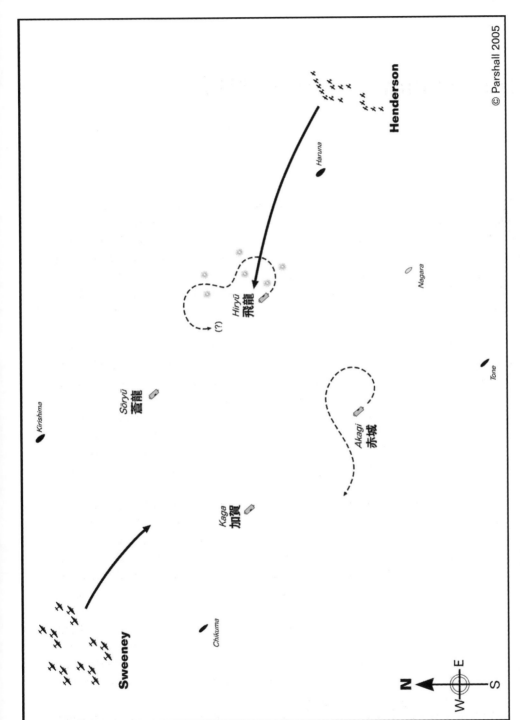

Sweeney

Chikuma

Kaga
加賀

Kirishima

Sōryū
蒼龍

Akagi
赤城

Hiryū
飛龍

(?)

Haruna

Nagara

Tone

Henderson

N
W · E
S

© Parshall 2005

10-1: Attacks against *Kidō Butai*: 0753–0815.

Finally, Henderson's wingman (Capt. Richard E. Fleming) led the shredded squadron into their glide-bombing attacks. Below them, Gunnery Lieutenant Nagayasu on *Hiryū* again ordered his batteries into action, adding to the general noise and confusion and making the American attack runs all the more difficult. They were coming in from all sides now, their formation shattered. The 25-mm mounts that lined *Hiryū*'s flight deck spat out strands of incongruously pretty tracer shells. To the Japanese watching from *Akagi*, it was obvious that the Americans were poorly trained—no self-respecting dive-bomber pilot would have attempted to bag a carrier with such an anemic attack. Glide bombing was the worst of both worlds. It eschewed the slender advantage of hugging the deck, while accruing neither of the twin benefits gained from a high-angle attack—accuracy and near-invulnerability to return fire. Yet, the results of the American attack were spectacular, if utterly ineffective.

Despite the hell they had just come through, Fleming's men managed to bracket *Hiryū* with numerous near misses between 0808 and 0812, some as close as fifty meters from the ship. These bombs raised such waterspouts that Yamaguchi's flagship was momentarily hidden from the eyes of the rest of the fleet. Nagayasu and his men in the gun tubs were drenched with seawater. Yet in the end, *Hiryū* emerged unscathed from the gray-white plumes that had erupted around her. Once again the Americans had paid prohibitively for no result, and the Japanese combat air patrol thereupon hounded the surviving SBDs out of the area.

One portion of this rather sorry episode has been overlooked, namely, that even against poorly trained American pilots attacking in a highly vulnerable fashion, *Hiryū*'s antiaircraft failed to account for a single enemy aircraft that we know of, despite Nagayasu's own belief that his "very fierce" fire had been responsible for the Americans' poor aim.[1] *Hiryū* should have been able to bring a half dozen five-inch and a dozen or so 25-mm barrels to bear on almost any broadside bearing. This was hardly an insignificant amount of firepower. Yet she apparently hit nothing. Indeed, American strafing killed more of her crewmen than she claimed in return. If this was how Japanese AA performed against opponents who were hardly the varsity, it did not bode well if the Americans' "A-team" should suddenly appear.

Yet, for all the Japanese knew, this *was* the enemy's best. They had seen three different American attacks thus far, the last of which had been flown by carrier-type aircraft (although the Japanese did not know that Henderson's squadron was land based). Yet, in each case, the performance of the Americans had been subpar. They were clearly brave, but they had come in dumb—unescorted and attacking poorly. If these were the same caliber of pilots who had managed to send *Shōkaku* limping back to the yard, then CarDiv 5's lowly status within *Kidō Butai* was well deserved.

However, almost simultaneously with Henderson's gallant but futile effort, another American attack began materializing. At 0754 Japanese lookouts spotted aircraft at high altitude, which quickly revealed themselves to be a dozen four-engined American bombers. This was the B-17 force of Lt. Col. Walter C. Sweeney, which had been sent aloft at 0430 to attack Tanaka's transports, only to be redirected north by Midway as soon as the Japanese carriers had been detected. They were very high up, over 20,000 feet. The Zeros were going to have a devil of a time reaching them all

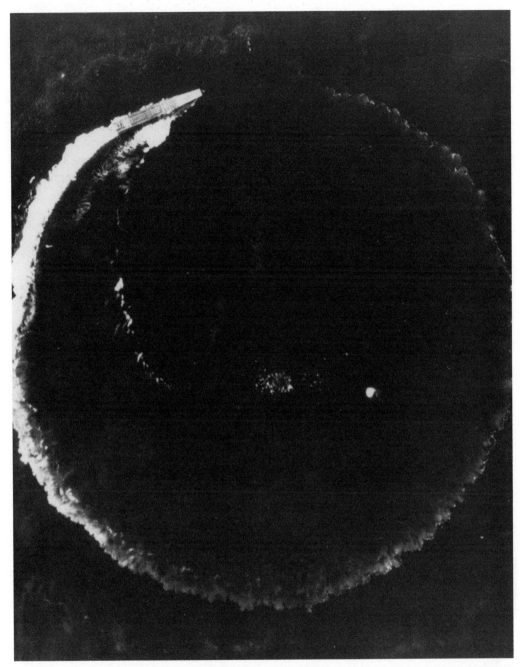

10-2: *Sōryū* evading B-17 attack at high speed. Putting the helm hard over was a standard Japanese technique for avoiding attacks. In the case of the B-17s, the Japanese could wait until the planes had dropped their weapons before committing to an evasive maneuver. *Sōryū* had a reputation for quick response to the helm and rather violent handling, because of her inclined twin rudder configuration. Note the complete absence of planes on deck. (Naval Historical Center)

the way up there. Not only that, but the entirety of the CAP was already engaged in repulsing Henderson's attack in any case.

The bombers split into three groups and went after *Akagi, Sōryū,* and *Hiryū* in an almost leisurely fashion. The Japanese began banging away with their heavy AA guns, but the Americans were never in any great danger. Having attacked Tanaka's invasion force the previous day from medium altitudes, Sweeney's men, upon further reflection, had judged their approach rather too low. This morning, against more heavily armed warships complete with fighter cover, they had decided to stay higher up. It was a sound decision, as the Japanese antiaircraft fire was none too good. The Americans noted that the Japanese shells seemed to be fused to detonate at the right altitude, but consistently exploded well behind them.[2]

Altitude, however, worked both ways. Down below, the Japanese captains watched as the bombers came into their runs. Coolly, they waited until each element had dropped, then put the helm over into radical evasive maneuvers. Whether the Americans dropped promptly or even on target was largely irrelevant. The pirouetting warships below still had a good thirty seconds' worth of air time to play with, meaning that they could be a quarter of a mile in nearly any direction when the bombs finally landed. Even by dropping a "stick" of a dozen or more 500-lb weapons at a time, the odds of securing a hit weren't good. Not only that, but the cloud cover over *Kidō Butai* frustrated several of their attacks, forcing some aircraft to make numerous runs before finally dropping. Yet, the Americans almost got lucky. In the course of the twenty-minute-long series of runs, both *Hiryū* and *Sōryū* were bracketed by near misses, to the consternation of the Japanese. In the end, though, the American heavies scored no damage.

In the midst of all this mayhem, at 0758 *Tone* No. 4 sent a message apprising Nagumo that the enemy task force had changed course to 080. Nagumo sent a terse communiqué back: "Advise ship types." Course information was not what was required at this point—he needed the enemy force's composition as quickly as possible. It seems almost certain that Nagumo signaled to *Sōryū* around this time to make her special reconnaissance aircraft ready for launch. This was a perfect mission for the new D4Y, where its great speed could hopefully make up for some of the force's lost time.

Given that both Henderson's and the B-17 attacks were getting under way by 0800, the men of *Akagi* had been somewhat incredulous to observe *Kaga* holding her course into the wind long enough to bring on board the last of her four CAP fighters.[3] *Kidō Butai* was vulnerable, with only nine fighters overhead. Not surprisingly, *Akagi* had already been warming up a replacement *shōtai. Kaga,* as soon as she had recovered her foursome, immediately spotted another seven for warm-up and launch, even as the B-17s droned away overhead. In fact, intermittent CAP launches from all the carriers would punctuate the breaks in the action—clearly, each carrier's captain was feeling the need to augment the CAP. Whether they were operating independently or under orders from the flagship, we cannot know. But the net effect was that the flight decks were in near-constant use by small groups of aircraft at this time.

10-3: *Akagi* evading attack by B-17s. Already in a shallow starboard turn, she has just executed a much harder turn to starboard. The broken cloud cover over the Japanese force is evident in this photograph. The destroyer following *Akagi* is probably *Nowaki,* her plane guard destroyer. No fighters are evident on deck, and her forward elevator is in the down position. *Akagi* launched fighters at 0808 and again at 0832. It is likely that this photograph was taken immediately after the launch of the first *shōtai,* and that the carrier was in the process of bringing up the second to the flight deck. Note also the large *hinomaru* (Rising Sun emblem) on her flight deck forward. (Naval Historical Center)

Such was the spectacle that Tomonaga and his returning force beheld when *Kidō Butai* heaved into view at about 0805. On the northern horizon ahead of them, their carriers bobbed and weaved beneath the American heavy bombers. *Hiryū* described a series of "S"-shaped maneuvers as sticks of bombs landed on either side. *Sōryū* was resorting to the simple expedient of putting the helm hard over to starboard and carving an enormous donut in the ocean.

Seeing the retreating American SBDs from Henderson's savaged flight coming toward them on the deck, one of Tomonaga's *Akagi* Zeros took this opportunity to join the CAP. He was joined by six of *Kaga*'s *kanbaku* as well.[4] The Type 99 was a maneuverable airplane once it had shed its bomb, and some of CarDiv 1's drivers may have judged that they could take on their opposite numbers in the apparent absence of any American fighters. At the same time, seeing their mother ship under heavy attack, all nine of *Sōryū*'s strike fighters pitched into steep climbs to engage the B-17s overhead. For his part, Tomonaga and the rest of the *kankō* and *kanbaku* simply

10-4: This famous photograph shows *Hiryū* under attack by B-17s between 0800 and 0830. A stick of 500-lb bombs has just landed off her starboard quarter. The *shōtai* of three Zero fighters spotted near the bridge is Lt. Mori Shigeru's CAP patrol No. 4, indicating that this picture was taken before their takeoff at 0825. Note that these fighters had eschewed using maximum runoff room and were simply pushed back from the forward elevator as far as the bridge for takeoff. Time apparently was of the essence. Also of interest is *Hiryū*'s *hinomaru,* which clearly shows the carrier's white deck stripes painted over the top. *Hiryū*'s *kana* "HI" identification symbol (a white-painted, open-sided box) is visible on the flight deck aft, as well as the red and white alternating stripes painted across the aft end of the flight deck. (Naval Historical Center)

eased down to 400 meters and circled at a distance, waiting to commence landing. Until the American attacks cleared up, the carriers below had no ability to take their aircraft on board. Waiting with them was WO Yoshino Haruo, the recon flight leader from *Kaga*. Yoshino, who had joined the Navy because all the marching in the Army seemed like way too much work, took a while to find *Kaga* amidst the chaos—the fleet was all spread out as a result of the attack. When he did find her, *Kaga*'s flight deck was already closed for business, and not receiving aircraft.[5] Instead, Yoshino loitered nearby with *Kaga*'s *kanbaku*.

Akagi had turned into the wind briefly at 0808 to launch a flight of three fighters under WO Ono Zenji. *Kaga* followed suit at 0815, sending up a group of five Zeros under Ens. Yamaguchi Hiroyuki. Given the threat of attack, the carriers weren't bothering holding a steady course into the wind for their launches; they were simply bringing their bows momentarily close enough to it that the Zeros could dash down the deck and into the air. Between these two launches and the fortuitous addition of the returning strike fighters, *Kidō Butai* was now finally beginning to put sufficient air cover up to beat off the ongoing American attacks.

However, the B-17s overhead proved to be tough customers. *Kaga*'s Yamaguchi immediately took two of his wingmen up in pursuit of them, joining *Sōryū*'s Zeros. However, the attacks by both groups of fighters were desultory at best. They managed to damage a few of the Flying Forts, but none seriously. Lt. Col. Sweeney's pithy summation afterward was that "their heart was not in their work."[6] This was probably simply confirmation of what everybody in the force below already knew—the Zero was no great shakes at high-altitude combat. Not only that, but after four hours in the air, *Sōryū*'s fighters were almost at the end of their tether in terms of fuel and ammunition.

At 0811, just as *Hiryū* was being bracketed by Henderson's attack, *Tone* No. 4 signaled back to Nagumo that "The enemy is composed of 5 cruisers and 5 destroyers." On *Akagi*'s bridge, a momentary sense of relief washed over Nagumo's staff—perhaps there was not as much to worry about as had previously been feared. If the Americans had only surface ships, and no carriers, then they were well outside the range where *Kidō Butai* needed to worry about them for the moment. The critical question of why the enemy would be where he was without having carriers was apparently not explicitly asked, although Kusaka remembered in retrospect that he was still suspicious. "One message alone," in his opinion, "couldn't make it clear that no enemy carriers were there. Nor could there be an enemy force without carriers in the reported area under the prevailing circumstances."[7]

Sure enough, ten minutes later, at about 0820, a third message from *Tone* No. 4 came back to *Akagi* that permanently dispelled Nagumo's temporary sense of security: "The enemy is accompanied by what appears to be a carrier." Nagumo's exact reaction has not been recorded, but there couldn't help but have been great consternation on *Akagi*'s bridge. Now, beyond all doubt, the admiral and his staff knew that their original battle plan was out the window. The American Navy was present in force. Destroying the enemy flight deck was absolutely the highest priority at hand.

A justifiable question at this point would be why it took *Tone* No. 4 as long as it did to discern a carrier in the midst of the enemy formation. Indeed, one recent historian goes so far as to assert that the reason Amari didn't see the carrier initially is because it wasn't operating directly with its escorts.[8] However, this position really isn't sustainable. First of all, this simply isn't how escorting vessels behave. More important, it is completely unsubstantiated by the American ship records. The most likely explanation continues to be a combination of variable visibility conditions and/ or haphazard spotting on the part of Amari.

At the moment, however, nothing could be done, as Tomonaga was still orbiting the fleet. On board *Akagi, hikōchō* Masuda was dying to begin recovery operations. But the American B-17s continued loitering overhead, making it impossible. In addition, *Akagi* now had yet another group of fighters warming up on its deck, a quartet of Zeros under PO1c Taniguchi Masao. *Kaga,* having sent aloft Yamaguchi's *shōtai* at 0815, had another trio on deck getting ready as well. Its *shōtaichō,* PO1c Yamamoto Akira, would be flying for the second time this morning. *Hiryū* was in the same boat and was at this very moment sending aloft a threesome under Lt. Mori Shigeru, who was taking his second shift aloft as well. Meanwhile, on *Sōryū,* preparations to launch the D4Y reconnaissance plane were well advanced, with the spanking new bomber warming up on the flight deck.

At 0824, in the midst of these CAP preparations, several ships within the force sighted a submarine periscope smack in the middle of the formation. This was *Nautilus,* which had been skulking around at periscope depth on an intercept course from the southwest. She had previously spotted *Kidō Butai* at 0710, sighting the "smoke of bombing and AA-fire beyond the horizon" to the northwest. Her skipper, Lt. Commander William Brockman, had promptly changed course to close the target and gone to battle stations.[9]

Brockman was rewarded at 0755 when he sighted masts on the horizon. However, a sharp-eyed CAP Zero spotted him in return and made a quick strafing run. Brockman took his boat down to 100 feet and continued closing. As he did so, the sounds of Japanese sonar could be heard ahead. At 0800 *Nautilus's* skipper was pleased to sight four vessels, one of which appeared to be a battleship of the *Ise* class, one a light cruiser of the *Jintsū* class, and the last two apparently cruisers of the *Yūbari* class. All were headed westerly on course 250 at twenty-five knots.[10]

Naturally, Brockman decided to attack the battleship and changed his course to draw ahead of her. However, at this moment, his periscope was again spotted by an alert Japanese aircraft, most likely a Type 95 floatplane aloft on antisubmarine patrol. This time, Brockman was greeted not with a strafing, but with a bomb deposited next to his boat. Worse yet, the enemy light cruiser bored in with at least two other escorts, pinging as they came. Despite the risks, though, Brockman boldly remained at periscope depth and continued to work closer to his quarry.

Nautilus had, in fact, stumbled onto *Kidō Butai* as it temporarily reversed course westward, bringing it directly toward the American submarine. The battleship he had sighted was most likely *Kirishima,* now leading the heavies westward after the formation's reversal. The "*Jintsū*-class cruiser" was obviously *Nagara,* while the two

"*Yūbari*-class cruisers" were actually *Kagerō*-class destroyers, their larger forward stacks perhaps being the reason for Brockman's misidentifying them. Interestingly, *Kirishima* appears to have been well in advance of Nagumo's flattops at this time, because Brockman did not sight any of them.

Despite Brockman's boldness, the Japanese knew he was coming. At 0810 *Nagara* dropped five depth charges near the sub, just as *Nautilus* was getting set up for her final attack run. At 0817 six more depth charges came crashing down. Things were getting a bit too hairy for even the gutsy Brockman's tastes, and he eased his boat down to ninety feet to avoid the wary eyes of both the buzzing CAP and the Japanese lookouts. *Nagara* and her consorts promptly dropped nine more depth charges. Brockman, though, popped back up to periscope depth as soon as the attack ended. Raising his periscope, he recalled that, "the picture presented . . . was one never experienced in peacetime practices. Ships were on all sides moving across the field at high speed and circling away to avoid the submarine's position. Ranges were above 3,000 yards. The *Jintsū*-class cruiser had passed over and was now astern. The battleship was on our port bow and firing her whole starboard broadside battery at the periscope!"[11]

Brockman, though, was having problems setting up his attack. One of his torpedoes was running hot in its tube, having had its retaining pin sheered away during the depth charging. It was making a hellacious racket, and Brockman was certain that the Japanese escorts could hear its banshee wailing. Nagumo's fleet—what little Brockman could see of it—was still on a westerly heading when *Nautilus* fired at 0825. His target was *Kirishima*. Taking aim at her starboard side, Brockman let fly with two torpedoes at a range of 4,500 yards. Or at least he thought he did—he found out later that one tube did not fire, leaving only one fish streaking toward the target.

Kirishima evaded this threat by executing a sharp turn to port, heading south and directly away from the torpedo. Whether *Kirishima* even saw *Nautilus* is open to debate—her "firing" at the sub's periscope may in fact have been directed at a fresh set of American planes that were attacking her about this time. Whatever the reason, though, her neat turn away was exactly what was needed to spoil Brockman's attack. Not only that, but *Nagara* once again sighted the sub and charged in to renew her attack. Brockman quickly dove to 150 feet just as another round of depth charging began at 0830.

As soon as *Nautilus*'s scope was seen on the western edge of the force, Nagumo's carriers made tracks to get away by heading back east. The fact that *Nagara*'s persistent attacks had forced the American boat to dive again was comforting for the Japanese, at least as far as it went. However, the knowledge that an American submarine was lurking near at hand undoubtedly notched the pressure on the Japanese up still further. Not only that, but nearly simultaneous with *Nautilus*'s appearance, yet another American air attack—the third in the last thirty minutes—began materializing. This was a force of eleven old Marine SB2U Vindicator scout bombers—the second half of VMSB-241—led by that unit's executive officer, Major Benjamin W. Norris. His aircraft had followed Henderson's flight in at some distance. Captain Aoki, seeing this new threat, at 0827 turned *Akagi* sharply away from the Americans.

Fortunately for *Akagi,* she had just launched fighters, or she would have been sorely beset. As it was, though, these new additions, as well as some of the Zeros that had just beaten off Henderson, were able to assemble in time to deflect this new blow. *Akagi*'s hard working Lieutenant Ibusuki was present, along with the two 6th *Kū* pilots still in the air. They were joined by WO Ono Zenji's trio. *Hiryū* contributed the two remaining members from her third watch. And *Sōryū*'s Lieutenant Fujita and his three-plane *shōtai* also charged back in to the attack.

Norris's command, though, benefited from the rather hasty nature of the defense thrown up in front of the force's two flagships. The Americans lost no inbound aircraft this time, though several were badly shot up. Whether by prudence, or simply judging that *Akagi* and *Hiryū* were too far away to be attacked effectively, Norris decided to focus his efforts on the battleship *Haruna.* She was on the edge of the main body, and as such was easier to get to. In the face of the battleship's AA, they began tilting into their dives. *Haruna*'s skipper, Rear Admiral Takama Tamotsu, wasted no time in demonstrating that he knew how to drive his ship. The big battlewagon slithered through a series of evasive turns, neatly threading the needle between the Vindicators' attacks. Although *Haruna* was bracketed by five or six near misses, the bombs didn't damage her a whit. At the conclusion of the attack, *Kidō Butai*'s Zeros harried the Americans off to the southwest, eventually claiming a pair of dive-bombers.[12]

The reader is forgiven for being confused by the rather bewildering welter of goings-on at this juncture, but that is precisely the point that needs to be made. The situation *was* confusing, no less to the contemporary historian trying to pick apart the exact sequence of events ex post facto than to the men standing on *Akagi*'s bridge. The American air attacks, while materially ineffective, were nearly constant. As a result, *Kidō Butai* was having no luck getting into any sort of a rhythm; it was operating reactively. Worse, its various responses, at least in terms of air defense, do not appear to have been centrally coordinated. The rather precipitous drop in CAP assets at around 0800 had been followed by something of an overreaction on the part of the individual *hikōchō*s as they stoked the CAP back up. There does not appear to have been anyone within the force looking down the road and assessing what was really needed. Instead, as the American attacks rolled in, the Japanese responded almost reflexively, sending up *shōtais* piecemeal.

It's not hard to see how this might have happened. Nagumo was stuck on board a wildly maneuvering carrier, watching his other vessels running pell-mell in all directions. Every time it looked as if things were settling down a bit, another air raid warning would come in. Nagumo can hardly have known where all his *ships* were at any given time, let alone have had an appreciation of what his aggregate CAP strength was.

Here is where the Japanese lack of early-warning radar materially damaged their chances in the battle. Radar was like a crystal ball—in effect, it allowed the commander to look a certain distance into the future, see developing threats, and plan accordingly. As it was, though, the CAP battle was being directed by four air officers on four separate ships, who could barely communicate with each other, or their forces aloft. Without the ability to prognosticate what was pending in the way of attacks, the predictably human response to the question of "How much CAP is enough?" was "Just a little bit more."

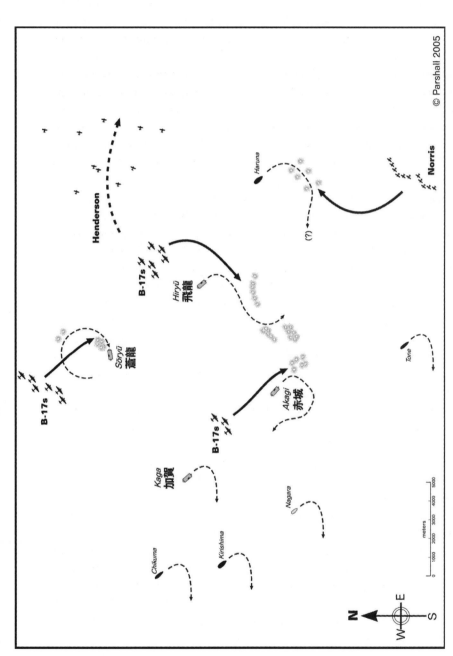

10-5: Attacks against *Kidō Butai*: 0815–0840. Scale and movements are approximate. This phase of the battle is extremely difficult to depict accurately, because of the large number of individual attacks and the evasive maneuvers undertaken by the carriers. However, it is clear that *Nagara* and *Kirishima* were somewhat out of place in the formation as a whole, as they were subsequently to become involved with *Nautilus* on the western flank of the formation. It is also known that by about 0830, the fleet was briefly headed westward to avoid Norris's incoming attack. Shortly afterward, however, *Kidō Butai* would be headed east once again.

Lack of radar also reduced the effective distance at which the CAP fighters could engage the Americans. Early warning for the Japanese force was provided by its outlying cruisers and destroyers. Yet these pickets could only be pushed out so far from the force before they, too, would be beyond visual range of the carriers. As a result, the CAP was frequently engaging the Americans fairly close to the Japanese carriers. In many cases, the Zeros pursued fleeing Americans through the midst of the force itself. Not only was this dangerous, but it also meant that in many cases the CAP wasn't being given the space it needed to operate most efficiently. Many of the American attacks would have probably been even more badly chewed up had they been detected farther away.

Having radar might not have been a panacea for the Japanese, though. As the Americans could testify, learning to use this new technology was no cakewalk. Effective use of radar had already driven the Americans to make the conceptual leap toward the centralized coordination of air defense assets from many ships via a single location—the combat information center (CIC). The first prototype CIC had been installed aboard *Hornet* when she was commissioned in October 1941. Even later in the war, having had radar on their ships for two years, the Japanese would never manage to make this leap. Above all, effective use of radar required adequate communications to the individual CAP elements. The Japanese, operating as they were on a single radio frequency for all of their aircraft,[13] and having faulty radios in their Zeros, met neither of these prerequisites. Thus, even if the Japanese had had radar at Midway, its use might have been limited.

By around 0830, the American attacks were finally starting to wind down, and the Japanese were beginning to think about landing the Midway attack force. Admiral Yamaguchi, however, was probably concerned by having been on the receiving end of an attack by what had appeared to be carrier-type aircraft. Apparently exasperated by the inability to strike back, he had a message flashed from *Hiryū* to *Akagi*'s plane guard destroyer *Nowaki*. She, in turn, dutifully relayed the admiral's message to Nagumo—"Consider it advisable to launch attack force immediately."[14] Nagumo's mood upon receiving this entreaty from his brash subordinate has not been recorded, but it hardly could have been charitable. By any rational standard, the time for launching a strike against the Americans was long past, and Yamaguchi should have known it. Indeed, the force was even now scrambling in preparation for bringing Tomonaga down.

More important, of course, was the fact that at 0820, Nagumo still had no ability to strike "immediately." The photographs taken by American B-17s during this interval make it perfectly clear that no strike aircraft were on the Japanese flight decks. Thus, Yamaguchi's entreaty really was tantamount to suggesting that Tomonaga's flight be ditched en masse in preference for an immediate spotting and subsequent launch at perhaps 0915. Coming from a man who had suggested during the planning for Pearl Harbor that the solution to *Hiryū*'s and *Sōryū*'s shorter range was to abandon them off the Hawaiian Islands after the completion of the operation, this simply was not a serious proposal. Nagumo didn't even bother replying.

At the same time Yamaguchi was venting spleen, *Akagi* sent aloft PO1c Taniguchi's *shōtai* of Zeros at 0832. *Kaga* did the same with PO1c Yamamoto's threesome. To the rear, *Sōryū* sent up her Type 2 recon aircraft, with explicit orders to find the American task group and send back a definitive position fix. The D4Y buzzed off to the east. None too soon, as at 0834 Petty Officer Amari radioed Nagumo that *Tone* No. 4 was homeward bound. This announcement was not greeted with joy on *Akagi,* and Amari was told in short order to stay where he was.

Besides his admiral's displeasure, Amari was beginning to have difficulties of his own. His fuel was starting to run low. Worse, the Americans were now aware of his presence, having detected him on radar at around 0815.[15] On several occasions during the morning, flitting about just above the southern horizon, he was hunted by enemy CAP fighters. Amari's pilot, though, skillfully ducked into clouds when pressed.

Relatively near at hand to *Tone*'s elusive scout, Frank Jack Fletcher's *Yorktown* was about to get into the action. Having charged down from the northeast after recovering her search aircraft, she was now within range to launch. Fletcher had hoped that further reports from the PBYs would clarify the enemy situation somewhat during the interim. However, no new information on any additional Japanese carrier groups was forthcoming, and in the end Fletcher ordered *Yorktown* to begin launching at 0838.

Unlike her sisterships, *Yorktown* managed to launch a well-coordinated strike. She sent up a total of thirty-five aircraft—six fighters, seventeen dive-bombers, and twelve torpedo planes, in two deckloads. The SBDs went first, followed by the TBDs, the latter heading off immediately to the southwest at 2,500 feet. A quick spot and launch then sent up the shorter-ranged Wildcats. The SBDs and fighters soon followed after the slower TBDs. The entire formation was in the air by 0906.[16] *Yorktown*'s second dive-bomber squadron (VS-5) was left on board as a reserve, much to the collective disgust of its pilots.

Fletcher's plan was fairly simple. He and his staff had mapped out a course to an intercept point where they expected Nagumo's fleet would be at 0900. They knew they had to allow for the fact that the original Japanese sighting reports were now several hours old. Further, while they were convinced that Nagumo would roughly hold his course, they also assumed that he would not approach Midway too closely.[17] Therefore, Fletcher judged the most likely position of the Japanese carriers to be 30-00'N, 179-00'W, which at 0900 would place them at a bearing of 240 degrees, 150 miles from TF 17. *Yorktown*'s planes would fly a course straight to that point. If they did not spot the enemy, they would turn northwest and fly up the enemy's line of advance, before turning at last for the northeast leg back home. With such an approach, Fletcher's staff believed they would be able to come across the Japanese no matter which way they maneuvered.[18]

It is worthwhile noting the differences between the staff and air operational work aboard TF 16 and 17. Whereas TF 16's launches had devolved into almost a shotgun approach to the problem, *Yorktown*'s entire group was directed along a single bearing toward a single point on the ocean. This meant that if *Yorktown*'s group found the enemy, it would be in a much better position to deliver a well-coordinated attack. Not

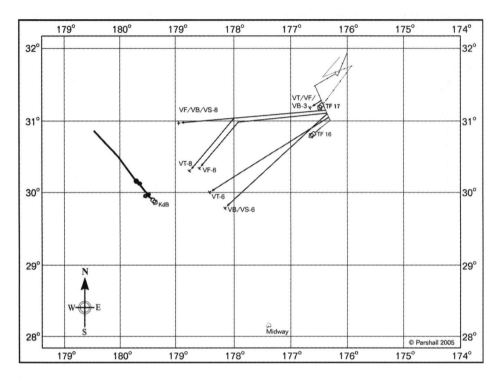

10-6: American air operations, circa 0900. This shows the relative positions of the various American air groups at 0900, immediately after the launch of *Yorktown*'s strike package.

only that, but since TF 17's departure was almost an hour later, her air group would benefit from changes in weather conditions and visibility as they flew their route. With *Yorktown*'s launch, the Americans now had a total of 151 carrier aircraft in the air.[19] The question was, could they find the Japanese?

At the very moment Fletcher was sending the last of his aircraft up, Nagumo was bringing the bulk of his down. Finally at 0837, *Akagi* hoisted a white flag with a black ball, indicating that her decks were "open for business." Underneath the landing ensign were two numeric flags giving the wind velocity in meters per second.[20] Still circling overhead, Tomonaga's force no doubt breathed a collective sigh of relief to see these welcome signals come fluttering up the carriers' yardarms. Now came the tricky part.

In the intervening four hours since Tomonaga's launch, *Kidō Butai* had moved farther away from the descending cold front. As the force had traveled southeast, the wind direction had gradually shifted around until it was now coming out of the east-northeast at about three meters/second.[21] Contrary to most maps of the battle that show *Kidō Butai* steering a southeastern course at this time, it is far more likely that the carriers were now all steering roughly east. This is supported by *Akagi*'s log entries in the Nagumo Report and is consistent with a carrier force landing aircraft.[22] Furthermore, we know from the postwar testimony of several of *Kidō Butai*'s carrier officers that the carriers moved in unison when performing large takeoff or landing

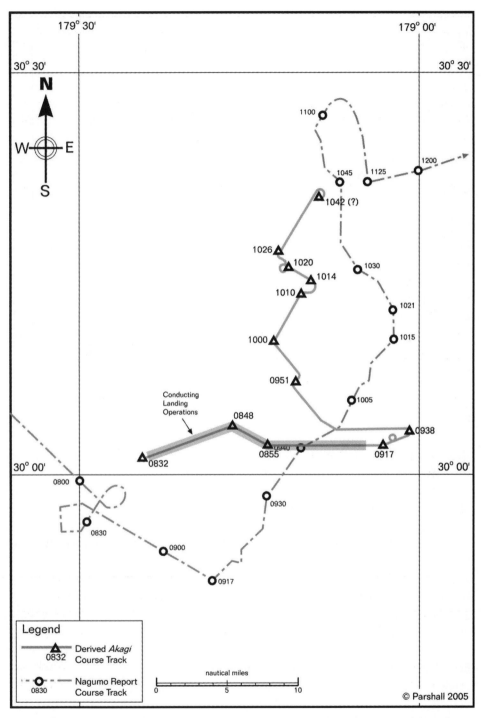

10-7: Revised track chart. This diagram shows *Akagi*'s reconstructed movements from the log entries in the Nagumo Report, superimposed on the report's track chart. *Akagi* commenced recovery operations to the northeast of *Nagara* at 0837, while the latter was busy hunting *Nautilus*. The derived course indicates that *Kidō Butai*'s carriers moved east during recovery operations.

operations.[23] Thus, we can presume that all four carriers were headed roughly east at this time.

The other effect that the eastward turn had was to place CarDiv 2—*Hiryū* and *Sōryū*—in the lead of the formation. Whereas formerly the two divisional flagships had taken the fore, now the fleet had essentially turned on its heels, with each ship turning individually to take up the new heading. Nagumo didn't have time for niceties now—dressing his formation for parade would have to wait. It seems likely, though, that *Sōryū* used her superior speed to catch up to *Hiryū* somewhat, keeping her divisional flagship off her starboard beam. Thus, *Kidō Butai*'s carriers were no longer in a box formation, but were gradually elongating into something of a trapezoid. The position of the escorting heavy units is more difficult to ascertain, and it is probable that they were in various sectors of the formation during different times of the day. However, it seems likely that BatDiv 3 was in column on the port side of the formation, with *Haruna* in the lead. Likewise, Abe's flagship, *Tone,* led *Chikuma* on the starboard side. *Nagara* was in the center van, leading the carriers.[24]

The positions of many of the Japanese destroyers are almost totally unknown, other than the fact that the majority of them were acting as air-raid pickets. The rough whereabouts of *Arashi* we know about only because she was busy dealing with *Nautilus* for a portion of the morning. We have consistent evidence that *Nowaki* was *Akagi*'s plane guard destroyer, and *Isokaze* was *Sōryū*'s. We can presume that *Hagikaze* was likely acting in the same role for *Kaga*. But the specific location of the others is unknown, and in the absence of their logs, will likely remain so. In truth, they probably varied wildly as the morning's attacks unfolded. *Nagara,* as squadron flagship for the destroyers, most likely tried to maintain a position at the head of the formation, but it would appear that she may have roamed about as well, particularly in response to *Nautilus*'s earlier attack.

Landing an airplane on a carrier is perhaps the most difficult challenge faced by any pilot, and Tomonaga's men had to do it under more stressful circumstances than normal. The morning mission had been a long one, and everyone was hungry and tired. Their aircraft were low on fuel, and the landing had to be conducted under the threat of enemy attack. They needed to get down as quickly and precisely as possible. Unfortunately, given the damaged condition of many of the airplanes, just getting them on the deck in one piece was going to be a challenge. Indeed, Fuchida's rather glib statement that "with the veteran fliers we had at this time, speedy recovery operations on board the carriers even under stringent battle conditions were little more than child's play," is clearly an oversimplification of the situation facing Tomonaga's fliers. His quip both understates the inherent dangers of landing operations and simultaneously heaps further discredit on Nagumo's moanings regarding his pilots' training.[25] In fact, both men were wrong—Nagumo's pilots *were* well trained, but carrier landings were a very delicate business even for experienced aviators.

The aircraft began forming clockwise holding patterns outboard of their home carriers. Each was readily identifiable by the configuration of their island and deck features, but each also had a large white *kana* symbol painted on the flight deck aft

10-8: This shot, taken from a 25-mm gun tub looking forward, shows *Kaga*'s starboard aft green landing light array. The array of four lights is mounted atop a triangular support brace, which is attached via a hinge to another 25-mm gun tub. (Coincidentally, this is the same light array and gun tubs that were found on the sea bottom off Midway in late 1999.) When flight operations were not under way, the array could be winched parallel to the flight deck. Note also the radio aerials in their lowered horizontal position, as well as the deck-edge nets designed to prevent aircraft from rolling over the side of the flight deck. (Photo courtesy Michael Wenger)

for identification—"A" for *Akagi,* "Ka" for *Kaga,* "Hi" for *Hiryū,* and "Sa" for *Sōryū.*[26] Planes with mechanical problems or wounded crewmen were moved to the heads of queue. One by one, each plane broke out of the holding circle, crossed the bow of the carrier some ways ahead, and flew down its opposite side. Once behind the ship, each turned inward to line up their final approaches. This took them practically over the top of the carrier's plane guard destroyer, which was stationed 700 to 1,000 meters astern. From there, they could rescue any downed aviators who fell short of the fantail or went over the side. If all was normal, the aircraft would turn in so as to be about 700 meters behind the carrier, at 200 meters altitude.

Just as with takeoffs, the decision-making authority for landing was vested almost solely in the pilot. The Imperial Navy had no comparable officer to the U.S. Navy's Landing Signal Officer (LSO). No one on board the carrier was charged with actively directing the planes, although a signals *seibiin* under the command of the *hikōchō* could wave off a plane if it was judged to be in a blatantly unsafe approach, or if the deck was fouled.

Once in the final approach, the pilot established his glide slope. However, the Japanese also had a unique landing aid (*chakkan shidōtō*—"landing guidance lights") to assist the pilot in setting up a safe approach. Originally, it had been intended for night landing purposes, but it had proven so useful that it was used in daytime as well. This device consisted of a bank of two red lights set at the level of the flight deck and a similar bank of four green lights set some 10–15 meters forward. First developed in 1932, each of the one-kilowatt lights was variable in intensity and equipped with a mirror so as to emit a very narrow cone of illumination.[27] Matched arrays were located on opposite sides of the ship.

The angle of the lights was adjusted for each type of airplane. Attack planes typically came in at around a five-degree slope; fighters perhaps a half degree steeper than that. As the pilot descended, he attempted to make the lights line up so that the green lights were positioned immediately above the red. If the pilot could only see the red lights (i.e., he had fallen out of the cone of green light), he was below the correct slope. If the red lights were over the green, he was coming in so low that he would probably hit the ship's fantail. Likewise, if the green light was positioned far above the red, the pilot was coming in too high.[28]

As the plane approached the flight deck, he would eventually lose sight of the rear edge of the flight deck. However, Japanese carriers had white or red-and-white-striped outrigger platforms near the aft end of the flight deck. These platforms helped the pilot gauge the orientation of the flight deck even if the deck was obscured by the nose of the aircraft.[29] At any point in the approach, the *seibiin* could signal the pilot as to his condition. A red flag from the *seibiin* signaled that the pilot should go around again; a white flag with an "H" meant that the aircraft's hook was not lowered.[30] Each pilot aimed to keep his airspeed about ten knots above stalling. For most aircraft, this meant maintaining between seventy and seventy-five knots.[31] Lining up the final few seconds of the approach required excellent reflexes. In any sort of a crosswind, even a second's worth of inattention could mean putting the plane over the side and into the heavy steel netting that lined the flight deck. But if everything went properly, the pilot would cut his engine just before reaching the brightly painted fantail and then catch one of the arresting wires with his hook.

Snagging the arresting wire was hardly a restful way to come to a halt, but it was not nearly as violent as the deceleration found on a postwar carrier jet. The Kure Type 4 arresting gear used at Midway had an induction coil drum below the flight deck, around which the arresting wires were spooled. The wires were held about eight inches off the deck by a support that could be lowered flat when not in use. The Type 4 could stop a four-ton aircraft traveling at a speed of sixty knots in less than forty meters, applying about 2Gs of deceleration in the process.[32]

As the first aircraft began approaching, the deck crewmen crouched in their tubs alongside the flight deck. This was where things could get really exciting. Landing accidents were not uncommon even under peacetime conditions, and with damaged aircraft and wounded pilots, the odds were good that somebody was going to crack

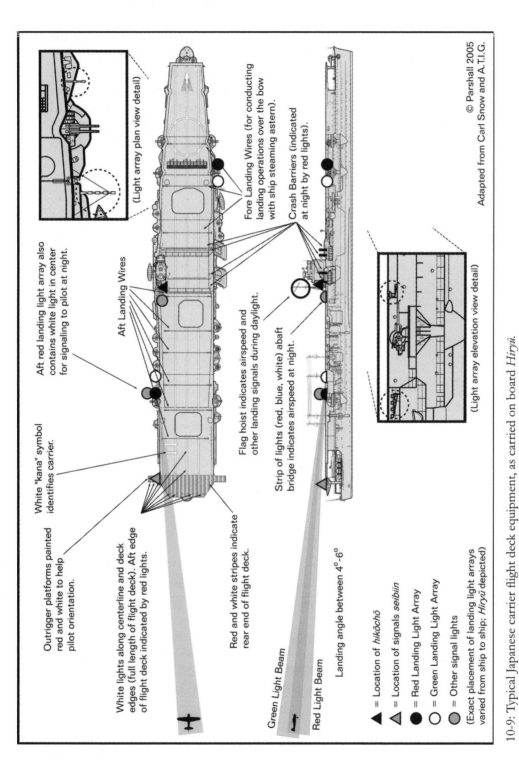

Outrigger platforms painted red and white to help pilot orientation.

White "kana" symbol identifies carrier.

Aft red landing light array also contains white light in center for signaling to pilot at night.

Fore Landing Wires (for conducting landing operations over the bow with ship steaming astern).

Crash Barriers (indicated at night by red lights).

(Light array plan view detail)

Aft Landing Wires

White lights along centerline and deck edges (full length of flight deck). Aft edge of flight deck indicated by red lights.

Red and white stripes indicate rear end of flight deck.

Flag hoist indicates airspeed and other landing signals during daylight.

Strip of lights (red, blue, white) abaft bridge indicates airspeed at night.

(Light array elevation view detail)

Green Light Beam

Red Light Beam

Landing angle between 4°–6°

▲ = Location of *hikōchō*

△ = Location of signals *seibiin*

● = Red Landing Light Array

○ = Green Landing Light Array

◐ = Other signal lights

(Exact placement of landing light arrays varied from ship to ship; *Hiryū* depicted)

© Parshall 2005

Adapted from Carl Snow and A.T.I.G.

10-9: Typical Japanese carrier flight deck equipment, as carried on board *Hiryū*.

up this morning. The most common mishap was the pilot missing the deck astern. Damaged landing gear from hard landings, hitting the island with a wing, and going over the side were not unheard of either.[33] Another common accident was a barrier crash, wherein a plane would miss the landing wire and go hurtling into the crash barrier.

Like the Americans, the Japanese used barriers to separate the after end of the flight deck (where landings were taking place) from the forward portion. If aircraft were parked forward, there would almost certainly be one or more barriers in place between them and the fantail, because a crash into a group of parked aircraft could have disastrous consequences. A typical crash barrier consisted of three athwartships steel cables (upper, middle, and lower) spanning the width of the flight deck. These were supported by poles that could be raised or lowered by compressed air in a matter of a few seconds. Such a barrier could stop a four-ton aircraft traveling at a speed of fifty feet per second in a distance of less than twenty-five feet.[34] Obviously, hitting the barrier at 4Gs was hardly a love pat, and it often led to unpleasant consequences for the plane and pilot. Still, it was better than plowing into one's squadron mates.

As the planes came down, the deck crew prepared to receive them. Men with fire extinguishers were standing by, and any damaged plane could be swarmed almost instantly by dozens of rescuers. Japanese records do not record how many deck accidents occurred during the Tomonaga force's landings, but there must have been some. According to Fuchida, a *kankō* is known to have landed on one wheel on board *Hiryū,* which would have left the plane out of commission for certain. And a mortally wounded fighter pilot from *Kaga,* PO1c Tanaka Yukuo, most likely crash landed his as well. He died before he could be removed from the cockpit.[35]

Most of Tomonaga's men, however, landed successfully. The Japanese were certainly aided by the easy landing characteristics of their carrier aircraft, which had low stall speeds and forgiving handling. Not surprisingly, the Zero retained its responsiveness even at low speeds. But even the lumbering Type 97 (in the opinion of one British test pilot who later flew it) "had a docile stall, and thus could be flown to its maneuver limits with impunity."[36] All three aircraft also had good visibility over the nose, making control of the plane during the final approach much easier.

As soon as each plane had been brought to a halt, deck crewmen rushed out to begin the stowage process. The pilot (or in the case of the *kankō* and *kanbaku,* the observer) would already be releasing the hook,[37] and the crash barriers would be lowered on command from the *hikōchō.*[38] By now, the deck crew had reached the plane, and begun folding its wings. Time was of the essence; already the next plane would be moving into position to land. The entire final approach, from the time of turn-in to landing on the deck, had taken about twenty seconds so far, and further time was needed to move the plane forward off of the arresting wires. During normal operations, the Japanese were able to land a plane every twenty-five to forty-five seconds.

As mentioned earlier, the Japanese avoided deck parks whenever possible. They believed that the hangar afforded more protection to the plane and crew. During landing, the Japanese shoved the newly landed aircraft forward of the crash barrier in preparation for taking the next one on board. Then, as soon as landing operations were completed, all planes were stowed below. It is likely that aircraft whose hangar

10-10: Taking on board a Type 97 during the Pearl Harbor operation, as seen from the top of *Akagi*'s island. The signals officer (*seibiin*) can be seen standing on the flight deck. The crash barrier, which can be seen just aft of him, is lowered flush with the deck. The landing wires are clearly visible. Also visible (though somewhat obscured behind the signal lanyards running vertically through the picture) is *Akagi*'s plane guard destroyer, steaming astern and almost directly in line with *Akagi*'s port deck edge. (Photo courtesy Michael Wenger)

locations were ahead of the barrier (such as fighters) were simply wheeled forward and stowed below immediately. However, for the *kankō* in particular (whose typical storage spots were in the rear of the hangars), striking below had to wait until all aircraft were recovered. This technique (called *renzoku shūyō*—"continuous recovery") of temporary deck parks and immediate stowage had been a feature of Japanese carrier operations since the mid-1930s. However, this fixation on hangars had a definite downside, in that the stowage process was governed by elevator cycles. This necessarily retarded Japanese carrier flight operations in comparison to those of their American opposites who, in general, performed most refueling and rearming functions right on the flight deck. Not only did this restrict the flexibility of Japanese flight operations, but it also restricted the Japanese to performing dangerous rearming procedures within the confines of the ship. The practical consequences of this approach would become apparent in about an hour and a half.

As *Akagi*'s aircraft now came on board, the talk on her bridge was all about what to do after landing operations were completed. Nagumo had already sent word out at 0830 that the force's dive-bombers should equip themselves with 250-kg (i.e., semi armor-piercing) bombs.[39] Having committed to dispatching the enemy task force, Nagumo chose to close with the enemy so as to ensure that *Kidō Butai*'s strike would be within range when his strike was prepared. Nagumo's decision may have also been informed by the desire to keep the wind on his bow. A northeastern course would allow him to conduct flight operations without breaking away from the enemy.

At 0845, *Tone* No. 4 sent a new report: "Sight what appears to be two additional enemy cruisers in position bearing 8 degrees, distance 250 miles from Midway." Nagumo apparently did not apprehend the true nature of this signal—Amari had sighted the fringes of a second American carrier group. *Tone* No. 4 did not know it, but they were observing Task Force 17. Coincidentally, at the same time that Amari's signal came in, Admiral Abe on board *Tone* signaled Captain Komura of *Chikuma* to send another Type 0 recon floatplane to Amari's position. It was clear that Amari was not sending information along quickly enough.

At 0850 *Tone* No. 4 again repeated that he was homeward bound, only to be told at 0854 that not only was he to stay where he was, but he was to activate his radio receiver and keep it on so that the fleet could home in on him for direction-finding purposes. What Amari thought of this order cannot be known, but it should have been apparent that Nagumo wasn't pleased with his performance thus far. The fact that he was now being expected to broadcast his position, which the Americans could pick up just as easily as his compatriots, could not have been a welcome order. However, he quickly acknowledged its receipt at 0855 and added that ten enemy torpedo aircraft (*Yorktown*'s newly launched strike force) were headed toward *Kidō Butai*.

At 0855 Nagumo finally decided to apprise Admiral Yamamoto of the situation he had been grappling with for the last hour and a half, signaling "Enemy composed of 1 carrier, 5 cruisers, and 5 destroyers sighted at 0800 in positions bearing 10 degrees, distance 240 miles from Midway. We are heading for it." By any measure, this was a very sparse communiqué regarding the current situation. It made no mention of what *Kidō Butai* had been doing since the sighting nor of Amari's recent report hinting at additional enemy vessels.

In fact, though Nagumo could not know it, Yamamoto was already well aware of the presence of the enemy, having intercepted a number of the previous transmissions between *Tone* No. 4 and *Kidō Butai*. Incredibly, the unexpected presence of the American carrier apparently did not disturb Yamamoto and his staff in the slightest. Captain Kuroshima asked if they should order Nagumo to attack the Americans, but almost immediately vacillated by reminding the commander in chief that Nagumo was to have kept half of his aircraft in reserve for just such a contingency. Yamamoto let the matter drop.[40] His leadership at this moment was nothing short of nonchalant—a far cry from the heavy-handed rigidity he had shown a mere two months earlier.

At the same time Nagumo was sending his situation report, cruiser *Chikuma* was recovering two of her search planes. It was standard operating procedure for the planes to land in the wake of their mother ship, so as to receive the benefit of the relatively calm water there. As soon as they set down, the cruiser would execute a ninety-degree turn, usually through the wind, so as to create an area of stiller water on the lee side of her hull. The plane would then taxi up to the ship to be winched on board by the ship's crane. At 0855 *Chikuma* was dead in the water and recovering her aircraft. This made her vulnerable to submarine attack, but there was no other practical way of retrieving her planes. By 0902, having recovered a Type 95 and a Type 0, she began working herself back up to rejoin the formation.

Submarine attack was a very real possibility, as *Kidō Butai*'s old nemesis, *Nautilus*, was still in the neighborhood. With *Kidō Butai*'s carriers more or less holding their respective courses during landing operations, Lieutenant Commander Brockman picked this inopportune moment to put in a third appearance. Poking his periscope up at 0846, he saw that his original group of ships and the target battleship were all well out of range except for the "*Jintsū*-type cruiser," whose echo ranging was "still quite accurate."[41] *Nautilus* headed back down for a bit. Then at 0900 Brockman raised scope again, and was thrilled to sight a "*Sōryū*-class" carrier off his starboard bow, heading east at twenty-five knots, some 16,000 yards distant. She was apparently undamaged but was firing her AA guns at something and "changing course continuously." Brockman was on a converging course, but once again *Nagara* ruined his approach. Brockman noted that "while making this observation [of the carrier], the *Jintsū*-type cruiser began to close again at high speed."[42] Admiral Kimura was handling his flagship with dash and aggressiveness.

This time Brockman resolved to go after the pesky cruiser instead of firing a single torpedo at the zigzagging target at 0910. The range was close, just 2,600 yards. But *Nagara* changed course, the torpedo missed, and Brockman had no choice but to go deep as quickly as possible. He rigged for depth charging and didn't have long to wait, as the Japanese shortly dropped a brace of six of them on his boat, followed by another eight over the next twenty minutes.

Interestingly, if *Nagara* noticed the fish being fired at her, she did not report it. One of her consorts, though, the destroyer *Arashi,* noted receiving the attack, indicating that she must have been in proximity to *Nagara* at the time. In any case, either on his own initiative, or perhaps as ordered by *Nagara,* Cdr. Watanabe Yasamusa of *Arashi* decided to remain behind and pin *Nautilus* down. The Japanese probably didn't know that thus far they had had three visits from the same submarine, but the fact remained that there had been too many of them poking their noses out this morning. It was time to let *Kidō Butai* get far enough ahead of this one that it wouldn't be a problem anymore.

Throughout these happenings, the carriers were still bringing down strike aircraft. The landing process had not proceeded in a uniform fashion across the fleet. *Kaga* recovered all of her aircraft by 0850. *Hiryū* had apparently not yet even begun recovering hers by that time, for reasons unknown.[43] *Akagi* completed recovery at 0859, some twenty-two minutes after she began. The carriers of CarDiv 2 both completed their landings by 0910. Immediately thereafter, *Akagi* recovered a lone CAP fighter, and *Kaga* brought down five more of her own Zeros from her third watch.

Once landing operations were complete, the deck crews lost no time moving the strike aircraft below to the hangars. Many of the flight crews had already made their way to their ready rooms for debriefing. This would be the first chance that the ship's officers had to get a detailed picture of what had occurred over Midway more than two hours earlier. Yet, the normal debriefings apparently did not take place immediately. Everyone was too busy with preparations for the coming strike![44] This was unfortunate, because some valuable information could have been learned from the returning airmen, particularly regarding the defensive firepower of the Americans. For one thing, it would have helped explain why there were so many faces missing in the ready rooms of CarDiv 2.

The first part of the morning mission had gone well, with Tomonaga leading his force southward into ever-improving weather conditions. Yet, despite radio silence on their part, the Japanese had found Midway alerted to their coming when they sighted the island at 0615, some forty miles distant. Tomonaga hadn't known, of course, that *Kidō Butai* had been detected by an American PBY less than an hour after his force's departure. All he knew was that all of the enemy's aircraft had been airborne.

By 0617 the Japanese formation had closed up in preparation for attacking, just in time to have numerous undetected American fighters make diving runs on their formation at 0621. *Hiryū* had lost three *kankō* in the first pass before Suganami's fighters had been able to react. Two were from the tail end of the first *chūtai*. The third was the leader of *Hiryū's* second *chūtai*, Lt. Kikuchi Rokurō. Kikuchi's plane was so badly hit that he was forced to ditch near Kure Island, though he and his crew survived the crash.[45] PO1c Maruyama Taisuke, commander of a plane in the second *chūtai*, had looked across to the first *chūtai* in horror, as PO2c Miyauchi Masaji's *kankō* was hit in the fuel tank by one of the Wildcats. Mortally wounded, the torpedo bomber began blazing up. To Maruyama, Miyauchi's plane seemed so close he could almost reach out to it. He could see the struggling faces in the cockpit, as Miyauchi bravely held his formation. But as Maruyama watched, the flames consumed the cockpit, and the *kankō* nosed over for the sea below.[46] Another first *chūtai kankō* joined Miyauchi in a similar death dive, that of PO1c Toba Shigenobu. On his opposite side, Maruyama could see *hikōtaichō* Tomonaga's Type 97 blowing gasoline vapor out of a hole in its wing. The commander's plane briefly caught fire, but the flames later died out. Further off, a Type 97 from *Sōryū* also fell to the enemy fighters.

After the Wildcats had expended their initial attacks, though, Suganami's men had largely had their way with them. The enemy's fighters were no match for the Zero, nor for the superior experience of the Japanese aviators. Those who had tried dogfighting with the Japanese had simply died, as their slower, clumsier aircraft were out-turned and then shot down in flames. One *Akagi* aviator aptly summed up the situation in response to Fuchida's subsequent inquiry: "Enemy fighters are lousy indeed. I think they were almost wiped out."[47] And indeed, most of the American fighters had been slaughtered or driven away in short order. Thereafter, the attack force had continued to the target unhindered.

Tomonaga had approached Midway from the north but then circled east. CarDiv 2's level-bomber formations led off, approaching the island from the northeast at 150 knots at an altitude of 11,000 feet. In this way, *Hiryū* and *Sōryū's* level-bombers would fly down the long axis of each island, including the length of one of the runways on Eastern Island. The force's monolithic formation likely began slipping apart into component *chūtai*, as each formation selected targets and began its attack run.[48]

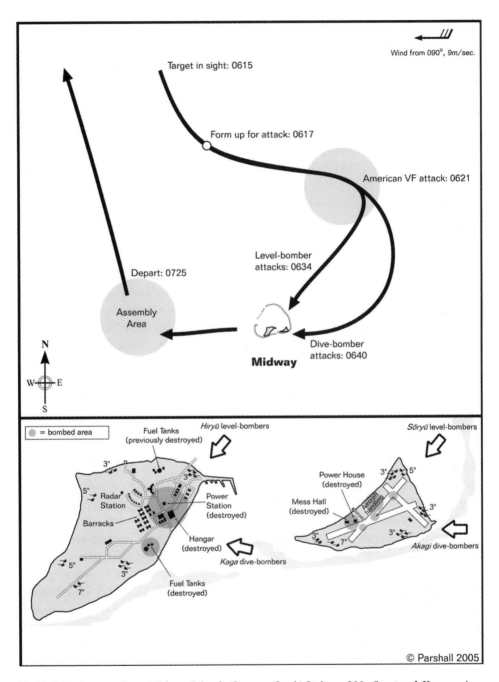

10-11: Morning attack on Midway Island. (Source: *Senshi Sōsho*, p. 300; *Sōryū* and *Kaga* carrier action reports)

Any belated hopes the Japanese might have had of finding the atoll's defenses weak or surprised had vanished in short order, as a storm of flak rose to greet them. The first bursts exploded behind the formation, but the defenders quickly corrected their aim. The Marines' heavy antiaircraft guns had made the most of the target presented by Tomonaga's stately procession. The Americans had zeroed in and continued firing rapidly. Soon, Tomonaga and his flight found themselves clawing their way through thick, evil clouds of exploding shells. Their aircraft had been buffeted by black shell bursts, and several planes had been hit. One of *Hiryū*'s second *chūtai* aircraft, that of PO1c Sakamoto, had been fatally damaged and fell into the lagoon short of Sand Island. To Tomonaga, the flight over the island had seemed interminable. Yet, finally they had been able to drop their ordnance, their planes surging upward as the heavy bombs were released. Being able to finally leave the island's defenses behind had been the purest joy.

Next it had been the dive-bombers' turn. They had loitered to the north, watching the level-bomber assault. Now, under *Kaga*'s *buntaichō,* Ogawa Shōichi, they had come in from the east. Visibility before the attack had been excellent, but that was before the mayhem that the level-bombers had unleashed. The wind was gusting to almost eighteen knots, which had the effect of blowing smoke from the first hits west over the islands, obscuring the targets for the following aircraft. The wind also promised to degrade the accuracy of the dive-bombers. However, the worst impediment to conducting a smooth attack had again been the islands' defenses. Against the dive-bombers, the Americans had not been restricted to using heavy flak—numerous automatic weapons had opened up on the *kanbaku.*

To say that the Japanese were disagreeably surprised by the power of American antiaircraft fire badly understates the case. The islands had fired back with everything at their disposal, transforming their perimeters into twin rings of fire. *Hiryū*'s report noted that, "Around the entire circumference of Eastern and Sand Islands there are many dual purpose anti-aircraft emplacements of the latest equipment. These . . . guns seem to make use of a director . . . the accuracy is excellent, and the anti-aircraft fire is intense."[49] Lieutenant Tomonaga himself had never been exposed to American antiaircraft fire before, though the rumors in the fleet said that during the attack on Pearl Harbor, despite the element of surprise, the Americans had responded with very heavy fire in a matter of minutes. Tomonaga could well believe it. This morning they had certainly staked their claim to having some of the finest flak in the world.

The dive-bomber attack lasted about three minutes, with individual aircraft making their exits on the deck at high speed to avoid return fire. After they left, the fighters continued strafing shore installations and hunting down whatever stray American aircraft they could find. Meanwhile, the attack aircraft had proceeded to the assembly point located west of the island. There they had waited for another forty minutes before the fighters and stragglers had rejoined them before turning for home at 0725.

It was difficult for the debriefers back on the four carriers to assess the damage inflicted on Midway, as the pilots claimed a wide range of results. *Akagi*'s report stated that "the total results of the strike were assessed as small fires being started at three places among the land installations; heavy losses appear to have been inflicted on installations and personnel." It further stated that, "Major fires were started in oil tanks, barracks and various seaplane sheds."[50] Upping the ante, *Kaga*'s report claimed "nine direct hits with No. 25 [high-explosive] bombs on Sand Island seaplane sheds causing heavy damage and fires; seven direct hits with No. 25 bombs on Sand Island Officers and Enlisted Men's quarters, causing heavy damage and fires; Sand Island oil tank was left on fire."[51] *Sōryū*'s report trespassed into the realm of fantasy, recording that her first high-level *chūtai* had "attacked Sand Island dual purpose batteries; all bombs were hits; silenced one emplacement; heavy losses inflicted." Indeed, the tally for her second and third *chūtai,* which had both attacked the Eastern Island airfield runways, enumerated the same supposedly perfect accuracy.[52] Perhaps merely striking the ground was sufficiently accurate to judge a bomb a hit. However, the scarcely diminished antiaircraft fire of the Americans must have sounded a cautionary note to these claims. Indeed, *Hiryū*'s report was more restrained than her division mate: "The First *chūtai* scored a hit on a fuel tank in the vicinity of the NE cape on Sand Island. The tank burned. The Second *chūtai* destroyed part of a dual purpose gun emplacement on the east shore of Sand Island. The Third *chūtai* covered [*sic*] flying boat and seaplane ramp at Sand Island and demolished it."[53]

In actuality, Tomonaga's assault had done fairly serious damage to the atoll's installations but had hardly sufficed to put the place out of business. On Eastern Island, bombs had demolished the power plant and the gasoline lines supporting the aircraft servicing areas. This meant that refueling on the airstrip would have to be accomplished by hand. Bombs had hit near the sick bay and had destroyed the command post. The mess hall and post office had been flattened. Another bomb had hit one of the rearming pits near the airstrip, setting off several bombs and killing four men. Several bombs had cratered the runway, although the damage to the strip was relatively minor overall.[54]

On Sand Island, bombs had hit the water lines, as well as a trio of oil storage tanks, which were left burning heavily. Various base facilities on the eastern side of the island near the seaplane facilities—the laundry, dispensary, Navy mess hall and galley, brig, and contractor's buildings—had all been destroyed. The torpedo and bombsight maintenance sheds had both been blown apart. Several of the barracks were badly damaged, and the seaplane hangar had been burned down to a bare steel skeleton.[55] The island had been surmounted by a heavy column of black smoke when Tomonaga's men had left.

The various staff officers probably perceived that Tomonaga's initial terse radio report had gotten closer to the nub of the matter than any of the wildly optimistic reports emanating from *Sōryū*'s squadron room. The enemy's fighter power had been badly shattered, but his strike planes had already left to attack *Kidō Butai* before the morning raid had hit home. Not only that, but until the American antiaircraft weapons were destroyed, delivering effective tactical support to the Army and Naval landing forces on N-Day would be next to impossible. A second strike was clearly going to be needed to accomplish the goal of neutralizing the target's defenses. All of that, though, would have to wait until the enemy task force was destroyed.

Unfortunately, Tomonaga's losses had been heavy, making the job in front of *Kidō Butai* even more difficult. *Hiryū*'s attack unit had suffered the worst of all the carriers. Her fighter group had returned all nine planes, though two of them were deemed unfit for service. Her *kankō* squadron, though, had been decimated. Of the seventeen planes in the group (after PO1c Takahashi Toshio's abort), two had been shot down outright by fighters, and another by AA over Midway itself. A fourth had disappeared en route home.[56] WO Nonaka Satoru's *kankō* couldn't quite make it back to the ship, ditching near a cruiser, though he and his crew were recovered. Five more aircraft had been shot up so badly as to be unserviceable. These included Tomonaga's plane, which had sustained a hit in one of her wing fuel tanks during the initial fracas with the American fighters. Every one of the remaining aircraft had been hit as well, though their damage was minor. In total, this left precisely eight serviceable aircraft (including Takahashi's) in *Hiryū*'s inventory. *Hiryū* had also taken on board a straggler from *Sōryū* piloted by PO2c Tanabe Masanao. His *kankō* had only barely made it back to the fleet and had set down on the closest flight deck he could find, after which it had been written off.

Hiryū's division mate *Sōryū* had fared better, though probably more by luck than anything else. Besides Tanabe's battered *kankō,* the group had lost one plane shot down over Midway, and two more had ditched near destroyers after struggling back to the fleet. The ditched crews were both rescued. Of the remaining fourteen *kankō* that landed on the carrier, four were judged out of commission. This left ten for future operations, although all of these had been damaged to some degree as well. Her nine fighters, amazingly, had returned completely unscathed.

In CarDiv 1, *Akagi* had lost a fighter shot down by AA over Eastern Island. Three more Zeros had been damaged to some degree. All of her dive-bombers had landed safely, though one was so badly damaged as to be out of commission, and four more were damaged to some extent. *Kaga*'s fighter unit had been knocked about as well. One plane had been shot down over Midway. And even despite PO1c Tanaka gallantly managing to land his plane before he died, his bird was too badly damaged to be usable. *Kaga*'s *kanbaku* squadron had lost a single bomber shot down over Sand Island.

The total casualties to the Midway strike force was eleven aircraft lost, with another fourteen heavily damaged, and twenty-nine more shot up to some degree. Fully half the aircraft involved had been hit. Counting missing aircraft and those rendered out of commission, the mission had lost 23 percent of its strength in about thirty minutes of combat. Twenty aviators were dead or missing, and several more had been wounded. The *kankō* crews on board CarDiv 2 must have been stunned. Between the American fighters and the flak, their formations had been decimated. Four had been shot down, four more damaged so badly they had to ditch, and another nine put out of commission after they made it back. Every other *kankō* in CarDiv 2 had been damaged to some extent. In the ready rooms, the talk was grim. If this sort of defensive fire (and casualty rate) was going to be the norm when flying against the Americans, the carrier attack squadrons would be totally annihilated in the course of a couple more strikes. This did not bode well for coming operations.

11

Fatal Complications—0917–1020

At 0917, with the strike aircraft being struck below, Admiral Nagumo altered his course slightly to 070, still at battle speed 3 (twenty-two knots), to close the enemy, which he believed lay directly ahead. The sky had now been clear of enemy aircraft since about 0840. If that happy state of affairs continued, it would soon be possible to start spotting the counterstrike. It seems almost certain that this is what Nagumo had in mind. It is quite probable that CarDiv 2 began bringing at least some 242-kg high explosive and 250-kg semi armor-piercing bombs out of the magazines at this time, so as to have them near to hand when the dive-bombers were finally spotted.[1] On *Sōryū,* it would have been possible to bring this ordnance all the way to the flight deck, but there is no evidence that this was done. It is more likely that *Hiryū* and *Sōryū* both simply brought their ordnance to the hangars in anticipation of spotting.

Most accounts of the battle hold that rearming activities were still continuing on CarDiv 1 at this time. Because of this, Fuchida later claimed that the force would not have been ready to launch before 1030.[2] The Nagumo Report anticipated that CarDiv 1 would be ready to go by 1030, and CarDiv 2 sometime between 1030 and 1100.[3] Upon closer examination, it is difficult to support the notion that rearming CarDiv 1 would have taken so long. It was now almost an hour and a half since the order had been issued to countermand the thirty to forty-five minutes' worth of rearming that had occurred before 0800. Even despite the occasionally violent maneuvers the ships had participated in, it is difficult to imagine that rearming had not been fully completed, and that all of CarDiv 1's Type 97 aircraft were now armed with torpedoes. Thus, Nagumo ought to have had sufficient armed and fueled aircraft to attack the enemy with all four of his carriers, *if* he could find the time to spot them.

However, no sooner had *Kidō Butai* changed course than a new flight of enemy aircraft was sighted at 0918, coming in fine on the port bow. Nagumo's reaction to the new aircraft sightings is not recorded, but it cannot have been a happy one. Fuchida speaks of the mood on the bridge suddenly losing its optimism, but one can't help but imagine a singularly more negative scene unfolding on *Akagi*'s bridge: one of enormous frustration that events were conspiring against them.

Both *Tone* and *Chikuma* immediately began laying smoke. The fleet increased speed and readied itself for AA action, although the enemy was still some thirty-five kilometers away. The CAP force, having surged briefly to thirty-six fighters, was back down to eighteen Zeros. *Kaga,* however, had two *shōtai* warming up on deck under the command of Lt. Iizuka Masao and promptly sent them aloft at 0920. *Akagi* was in the process of spotting five more Zeros, which would go up at 0932, and a further foursome at 0937.

This new attack was being delivered by the fifteen torpedo bombers of *Hornet*'s VT-8, under Lt. Cdr. John C. Waldron. These were the only aircraft from *Hornet* that would make it into the fight this morning. As was related previously, rather than flying directly toward the last-known position of the Japanese, *Hornet*'s planes had flown west after takeoff, on the decision of their air group leader, Commander Stanhope Ring (commanding VS-8, VB-8, VF-8, and VT-8). However, Waldron—an intense, hard-driving commander, whose men revered him despite the hard work he put them through—was certain that the Japanese lay to the southwest. He had remarked to one of his men before launch to "Just follow me. I'll take you to 'em."[4] That was precisely what he was doing now.

Waldron hadn't been happy with Ring's flight plan from the get-go, and he had not been long in challenging Ring's outbound route. Waldron had broken formation at around 0825, banking left, and leading his squadron away independently.[5] The fact that Waldron subsequently closed *Kidō Butai* from almost dead ahead (i.e., from the northeast) is further indication that Ring's flight path was headed due west, and thus missed Nagumo to the north.[6]

Whether by his part-Cherokee intuition or just a fine appreciation of the enemy, Waldron's instincts were spot on. Waldron seems to have flown a course of 246 degrees, which led almost straight to Nagumo once the latter came to 070. Waldron's flight had traversed the 140-odd miles to *Kidō Butai* "as if connected by a plumb line."[7] However, while Waldron's instincts were to be lauded, in leaving Ring's command behind, he discarded any hope of direct fighter support. In so doing, he unknowingly signed his own death warrant—and that of every man in his command save one.

As Waldron's planes bored in, *Kidō Butai*'s carriers began swinging to port, turning westward. This had the effect of putting their sterns to the enemy's line of approach, a maneuver they would use time and again when faced with torpedo attacks. When VT-8 began its attack, the carriers were still turning, and their starboard beams were exposed. Three carriers were directly in front of Waldron, what his squadron report would later characterize as an "*Akagi*-class" type on the right and the left, with a "*Sōryū*-type" in the middle.[8] Waldron headed for the center flattop.

The *Sōryū*-class carrier in the center was none other than *Sōryū* herself. She was at this very moment bringing on board a *shōtai* of fighters, and was thus relatively vulnerable. However, the Zeros aloft at this moment contained a veritable murderer's row of hot pilots. *Akagi*'s Ono Zenji had just returned to the flagship to replenish his bird, but his two wingmen from the fifth watch were still airborne. Joining them was *Akagi*'s sixth watch—a pair of two-plane *shōtai* led by two first-class petty officers: Taniguchi Masao and Iwashiro Yoshio. Taniguchi was destined to become a notable ace, with fourteen kills by the end of the war.[9] *Kaga* now had nine planes in the air, including her fourth watch under PO1c Yamamoto Akira. Yamamoto was one of the most senior NCO pilots in the fleet and would go on to claim thirteen enemy aircraft during the conflict.[10] In addition, *Kaga*'s fifth watch had just been launched—a double-fisted pair of *shōtai* under the overall command of Lt. Iizuka Masao, who was to command several squadrons during the war. Iizuka's *shōtai* also contained PO1c (later WO) Suzuki Kiyonobu, another highly experienced NCO and instructor pilot. A decorated veteran of the China conflict, Suzuki would be credited with nine planes shot down before his death at the Battle of Santa Cruz later that year.[11]

Sōryū had her own fighters up as well; a trio of Zeros from the morning strike that had yet to land.[12] Likewise, *Hiryū* also had Lt. Mori Shigeru's *shōtai* aloft. In all, the Japanese sent twenty-one fighters tearing toward the Americans, with *Akagi* and *Hiryū* spotting a further nine between them to be launched shortly. Not only was *Kidō Butai*'s CAP relatively sizable to the task, but it also had been alerted in plenty of time. Worse yet for the Americans, their TBD aircraft were underpowered and barely able to break 100 knots while lugging a torpedo.

The results reflected these realities. VT-8 was completely annihilated. Initially, Waldron split his force into two divisions, one under himself and the other led by his XO, Lt. James C. Owens Jr. However, immediate pressure from the Japanese CAP forced the two groups of American planes back together in short order, with Zeros attacking from all sides.[13] By all accounts, Iizuka's *shōtai* (containing Suzuki), Yamamoto's trio, and Taniguchi's quartet literally tore the American force apart in a series of vicious close-quarter attacks, sending the lumbering bombers blazing down to the ocean below.[14]

The Japanese fleet had turned and was running west, so as to place VT-8 at a further disadvantage. As a result, the American run-in lasted perhaps fifteen minutes, which was an eternity for the plodding TBDs. Three of them, however, eventually managed to get close enough to *Sōryū* to oblige her to make a sharp turn to starboard, into the teeth of the American attack.[15] In the midst of this turn, the CAP nailed two more of the Americans, leaving a single damaged plane aloft. This lone aircraft bored in and made its drop against *Sōryū*'s port bow at about 800 yards, then banked to hop over the carrier. *Sōryū*, though, managed to dodge the incoming fish. On the other side of her, the lone Devastator ran headlong into *Akagi*'s newly launched seventh patrol, led by Lt. Shirane Ayao. With the odds five on one, the enemy torpedo plane was quickly shot down almost in the middle of the formation. The pilot, Ens. George H. Gay, was the sole survivor of the squadron. His backseat gunner had been killed by machine-gun fire, and he clambered out of his sinking aircraft as it skidded into the water. Promptly hiding under his black rubber seat cushion, Gay managed to avoid being seen by the Japanese ships surrounding him on all sides.

One of the most disheartening aspects of VT-8's destruction is that they might have unintentionally had direct fighter support had things gone a little differently. High above and behind them, hovering at 22,000 feet just over the eastern fringe of the Japanese formation, were ten Wildcat fighters of VF-6 under the command of Lt. James Gray. Upon being launched by *Enterprise*, he had found that her dive-bombers had already flown out of sight. He had thereupon mistaken Waldron's low-flying aircraft as his own VT-6.[16] Since Waldron's flight appeared to be alone, Gray had decided to fly top cover for them.

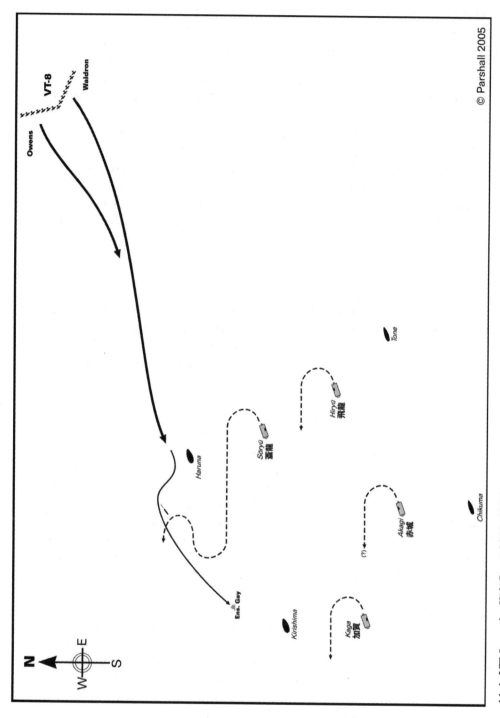

N
W — E
S

VT-8

Owens

Waldron

Ens. Gay

Haruna

Kirishima

Sōryū
蒼龍

Hiryū
飛龍

Tone

Kaga
加賀

Akagi
赤城

(?)

Chikuma

© Parshall 2005

11-1: VT-8 attacks *Kidō Butai*, 0920–0937.

Unbeknownst to Waldron, Gray had dutifully followed VT-8 down from the northeast. However, he wasn't flying terribly close escort, and he lost the TBDs below intermediate cloud cover just before Waldron began easing down to make his attack.[17] When Waldron's command disappeared, and subsequently did not reappear, Gray had no way of knowing that their attack had been unsuccessful. He had simply never seen them again, nor did he hear their calls for help. Not only that, but Gray and his command were subsequently to miss their own VT-6's call for assistance some twenty minutes later. The date of 4 June will forever remain as something less than a shining monument to American radio reception.

Like Waldron, Gray had sighted Japanese vessels at one o'clock at about 0910, and he had checked his forward progress. So far as he knew, *Enterprise*'s dive-bombers ought to be close at hand, and thus Gray had loitered on the edge of a battle he wasn't even aware of, in order to be available to support his dive-bombers when the moment came.[18] From where he circled, Gray was able to catch glimpses of *Kidō Butai* through the clouds. However, apparently at no time during the next forty-five minutes did he ever see more than two Japanese carriers—a clear indication that CarDiv 2 was operating at a goodly distance from CarDiv 1 during much of that time.

In fact, the evidence suggests that by about this time CarDiv 2 and CarDiv 1 had effected a de facto, if not an intentional, separation from one another. This makes a good deal of sense, in that the operational speed of CarDiv 2 was a good five to seven knots faster than CarDiv 1—if anyone was going to open up a gap, it would have been the speedier ships at the front of the formation. The Imperial Navy didn't mind having fairly loose spacing between their carrier divisions, and *Zuikaku*'s experience at Coral Sea, wherein she had been spared attack by fortuitously not being too close to *Shōkaku,* had been noted by the Japanese. Indeed, beyond mere reasons of defensive expediency, it is possible that a desire for operational separation may have entered into the last-minute adjustments of *Kidō Butai*'s formation this morning.

For his part, Gray continued loitering high above *Kidō Butai*'s eastern flank, making leisurely "S" turns to conserve fuel, and waiting for *Enterprise*'s dive-bombers to join him. He found it remarkable that there were no Zeros coming after him.[19] To Gray, it seemed that there must have been a breakdown in the Japanese CAP. The truth was that at 0910 the CAP was all at low level, and shortly would be pouncing on Waldron. However, the Japanese failure to discover and attempt to intercept Gray's command until much later does speak of the Japanese weakness at detecting and combating high-level threats, particularly in conditions of scattered cloud cover.

No one knew it at the time, but the truth was that *Kidō Butai* had just reached a crucial point of no return. If the Japanese were to launch aircraft against the Americans before their rendezvous with fate—now only an hour hence—they would have needed to start spotting them in the teeth of Waldron's attack. Yet, Nagumo still had no clear idea of exactly where the American carriers were, since *Tone* No. 4's spotting information was apparently not considered trustworthy. Not only that, but *Sōryū*'s Type 2 bomber had not radioed in any new information, either.

This was, in fact, VT-8's true contribution to the battle, and the meaning of its sacrifice—not (as commonly asserted) that it had drawn the CAP Zeros down to sea level. Rather, Waldron's head-on attack caused Nagumo to reverse course out of the wind. It also delayed his spotting by tying down the Japanese flight decks with yet more CAP operations. CruDiv 8's laying smoke in reaction to Waldron's appearance, as well as the force's antiaircraft fire thereafter, may also have attracted the unwanted attentions of yet another American torpedo squadron that was shortly to make its appearance.

It is probable that at this point (or perhaps even sooner) the *kanbaku* on CarDiv 2 had begun to be armed while still in the hangars.[20] Realizing that the flight decks were in constant operation, the armorers were going ahead and attaching bombs to their charges. If nothing else, it would shave five or ten minutes off the spotting process, whenever that was ordered. But as long as the Americans kept attacking, and new CAP fighters were needed, no one knew when that might be.

Far to the southwest of *Kidō Butai,* destroyer *Arashi* was still prowling fretfully in search of the elusive *Nautilus.* Starting at 0918, Lt. Cdr. William Brockman had dived to 200 feet, trying to shake the Japanese destroyer, but *Arashi* remained on the scent. At 0933 she made a final depth-charge attack. At that point, Commander Watanabe decided that even if he had not nailed the Yankee submarine, he had held it down long enough for the carriers to have made it safely through the danger zone. He thereafter set course north-northeast to rejoin *Kidō Butai.* Ironically, according to Brockman, *Arashi's* final pair of depth charges were the closest to the mark of any dropped thus far.[21] But as the sweating Americans listened below, the attacks died down, and *Arashi's* screws drew away. By 0955 even her echo ranging had ceased. *Nautilus* began heading back up to periscope depth.

Meanwhile, Petty Officer Amari and *Tone* No. 4 were still on the air. In fact, Amari was begging to break off his mission, reporting at 0930 that his fuel was running low and that he needed to return. He was told by Admiral Abe at 0935 to wait until 1000 to do so. Amari, probably nearly frantic by this time, replied at 0938 with a terse "I can't do it." In the meantime, *Chikuma* was launching its No. 5 aircraft, a Type 0 floatplane commanded by PO1c Takezaki Masatake, to contact the American fleet.

Depending on the ship concerned, the Japanese logged Waldron's gallant attack as petering out between 0930 to 0935. By that time, all of the American aircraft were in the drink. *Kidō Butai* was still on a course westward for the moment. Though the carriers remained in a roughly boxlike formation, their positions had shifted, with *Kaga* now leading *Akagi* in the southern column.[22] Before the Japanese could consider shifting course back to the northeast, even as *Arashi* was dropping her last charges and *Chikuma* was sending up her No. 5 plane, another attack developed.

At 0938 the Japanese sighted a low line of Devastators coming in from the south. This was VT-8's sister squadron, VT-6, from the *Enterprise,* commanded by Lt. Cdr. Eugene "Gene" E. Lindsey. Again, their low altitude approach meant that they were sighted while still a good distance from the fleet. *Akagi's* log avers that she saw the attackers fifty kilometers out. With *Kidō Butai* still heading west, the Americans were attacking from the port beam.[23]

From behind the windscreens of VT-6, the Japanese fleet was in "a very loose formation and appeared to have three carriers in the center. The outer screen was on a 15 mile circle and was composed of light cruisers [*sic*]. The inner screen was on an 8 mile circle and was composed of heavy cruisers and a few battleships. Destroyers accompanied each carrier and were present at other points in the screen. The carriers and accompanying destroyers maneuvered independently at high speed while the screening ships maintained their relative positions and were not making such high speeds."[24] This remarkably accurate description corresponds very closely with the facts. The four carriers were indeed in a box formation, albeit one that shifted at times into a ragged diamond. The two outer circles of screening vessels tended to turn in formation and tried to maintain their relative positions.

Immediately upon sighting *Kidō Butai,* Lindsey split his squadron into two divisions of seven planes apiece, hoping to gain a position to deliver a hammer and anvil attack against one of the carriers.[25] His target was *Kaga.* This was because VT-8's attack twenty minutes prior had disrupted any semblance of order in *Kidō Butai*'s formation. Whatever evasive pirouettes *Akagi* had performed during Waldron's assault—and the indications are that they were both extensive and swift[26]—had not been matched by her dowdier twenty-eight-knot cousin. This, in combination with the fleet's reverse turn meant that *Kaga* was now the southwestern-most carrier in the formation, and hence the one most likely to be singled out for VT-6's unwanted attentions.[27]

At 0938 *Kidō Butai* predictably commenced wide turns to starboard and course 300 degrees so as to put the American planes directly astern. Once again, the TBDs had to first overhaul their prey and then come around the bow for an attack. *Kaga*'s turn away also had the effect of leaving Lindsey's division hanging out in left field.[28] The American commander therefore led his men around to the north, while Lt. Arthur Ely, his exec, took his division more directly toward Okada's towering flight deck.

The one thing VT-6 had going for it, at least initially, was that there were no Zeros to be seen. In truth, *Kaga* was in something of a pickle. The CAP was up to thirty fighters, but most of the Zeros had been pulled off to the northeast to deal with Waldron's attack. As a result, this new assault from another quarter found *Kaga*'s own fighters out of position, and with few others nearby. *Kaga*'s turn away thus served a twofold need. It bought time for *Kaga* to complete warming up another set of six fighters. And it gave Captain Okada the chance to put out the word that a little assistance was in order.

Thus, for a time the Americans came in relatively unopposed. In fact, both American divisions made it past the outlying Japanese destroyers and were headed in toward *Kaga* before the Japanese CAP began to reassert its presence. Ely's division, being closest to the bulk of the Japanese fighters racing in from the east and northeast, not surprisingly came under fire first. Once again, the same general progression of destruction played itself out, with the Zeros slicing the American formation apart and spraying the Devastators with well-aimed bursts of fire. The Americans, unable to do much more than huddle up into smaller and smaller groups, fired back with their twin free machine guns. But the end result for Ely's division, though it took somewhat longer to unfold, could not help but be grimly similar to that of VT-8.

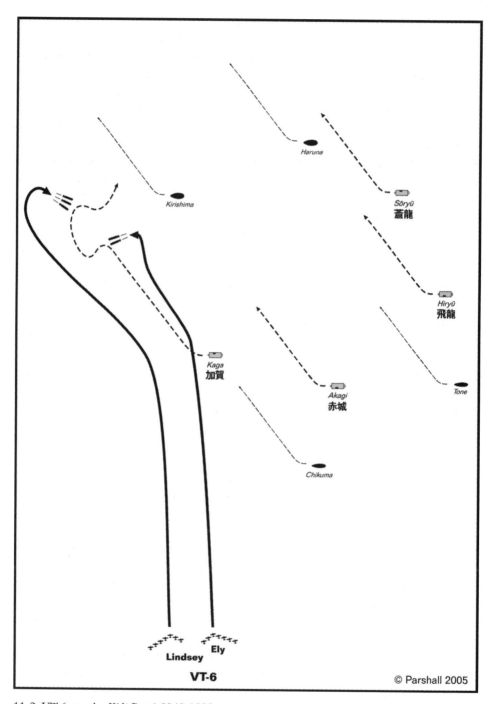

11-2: VT-6 attacks *Kidō Butai*, 0940-1000.

Overhauling *Kaga,* poky as she was, proved almost impossible as soon as the Zeros finally made their appearance. Ely's formation came apart under the increasingly heavy deluge of fire. One by one, the Devastators lost their battles and went flaming into the drink. However, Okada also did his best to maximize *Kaga's* own chances, staging a veritable seminar on how to handle a carrier against torpedo aircraft. Realizing that he was being pinned between two divisions, Okada continued boring away to the northwest as long as possible. Finally, two aircraft of Ely's division reached their drop points and released. Okada saw at once that the American drop angles were lousy. *Kaga* dodged them with ease, turning away to port and reversing course. This had the effect of bringing *Kaga* into the teeth of Lindsey's group, but Okada reversed course yet again and continued heading to the north-northwest, with the Americans now back on his port quarter.

For his part, Lindsey had thus far enjoyed remarkably good success. While Ely's men were being shot to pieces, the Japanese CAP hadn't been able to get a grip on him. True, there were Zeros around, and they were shooting, but they seemed to be out of cannon ammunition. Consequently, his group had yet to take any casualties, and he had managed to attain a position on *Kaga's* port beam that held out some hope of making a good attack. If they had been equipped with the newer, faster TBFs, they might have made it. But it was at this precise moment that everything fell apart. *Akagi* had launched a fresh *shōtai* of fighters under Lt. Ibusuki Masanobu (his second flight of the morning) at 0945. *Kaga,* for her part, finally hurled aloft six of her own Zeros at 1000, into the very teeth of Lindsey's final attack run. These *Kaga* fighters collectively were a somewhat ragtag group of ensigns and noncoms, but this group contained several seasoned veterans. It was these nine fresh Zeros that set upon Lindsey in the last minutes before he was able to gain a favorable attack position.

Lindsey, by this time, was desperately calling for support from his own fighters but was receiving no answer from Lieutenant Gray's Wildcats. They were still loitering high overhead, some twenty miles to the northeast. As with VT-8, because of the scattered cloud cover in the area and their high altitude, Gray had not observed VT-6's attack materializing on the opposite side of the enemy formation. Nor did he or his men hear Lindsey's radio calls for help. Thus, two opportunities for direct fighter support of the American torpedo aircraft had been lost.

Indeed, by about 0950, the fuel tanks in Gray's Wildcats had pushed well past half empty. If he didn't leave soon, he and his command weren't going to make it back. Reluctantly, he turned for home, but not before sending a sighting report back to *Enterprise* at 0952, followed by an elaboration at 1000.[29] This report, which explicitly mentioned the presence of only two Japanese carriers, was the first concrete sighting information that Task Force 16 had received since it had overheard Howard Ady and William Chase's PBY spotting reports during the morning.[30] It was only as Gray departed that the Japanese belatedly noticed the American fighters that had been circling ahead of their force for the better part of an hour. *Sōryū* quickly launched a *shōtai* of Zeros under PO1c Harada Kaname to go after Gray's group, which was thought to be a "horizontal bombing unit." By the time Harada and his men began to climb, though, Gray had departed the area.

Meanwhile, Lindsey's entire division was in terrible trouble. The commander was apparently the first to be shot down as this last-second opposition materialized almost out of nowhere. Lindsey's men kept shooting back and managed to send Sea1c Sano Shinpei's *Akagi* Zero down.[31] But four of the Americans were splashed in short order, and much as they tried, the remaining three found it impossible to attain a favorable drop angle. Finally, in desperation, the Americans let fly with their torpedoes at extreme range at about 1000. It was a valiant attempt, but Okada immediately treated them to an evasive turn back to the south, spoiling the chances of their fish.

The CAP thereupon sent the American survivors packing. Unfortunately for Lindsey's remaining men, they were now deep inside the Japanese formation, making getting out almost as problematic as getting in had been. Indeed, several VT-6 aircraft were still being attacked as late as 1010 as they were clearing the area to the east and southeast. Fortunately for the Americans, the wide spacing between the screening ships created large gaps to fly through. By the time it was all over, though, only five aircraft from VT-6's two divisions (three from Lindsey's, two from Ely's) remained aloft, all damaged to some degree, and one of these would not make it back home.[32] Neither Ely nor the dogged Lindsey was among the survivors.

Despite VT-6's gallant determination, both U.S. and Japanese analysts ironically later found fault with the attack. In his own comments on the squadron's after-action report, RADM Thomas C. Kinkaid concluded that "it is essential that the attack be pressed home *without delay* when the objective has been sighted."[33] For his part, Genda was inclined to agree with Kinkaid's basic assessment. He had watched VT-6 laboriously close on *Kaga,* with the American planes being shot down one by one. His professional interest piqued, Genda remarked that some of the Americans had "apparently hesitated to make a daring dash [toward us] in the face of attacks from both the air and sea."[34] In this respect, both Kinkaid and Genda were being critical of what they did not fully understand. When carrying a one-ton torpedo, "dashing" did not well describe the Devastator's handling characteristics.

Given the wretched stern chase it had been forced to make, by all rights VT-6 should have been annihilated in exactly the same manner as VT-8. But three factors had spared the lives of at least some of its aviators. First, the attack had developed along an axis the Japanese CAP was initially ill prepared to defend. As a result, fighter opposition was spotty at first, especially for Lindsey's division. The Americans had made it well into the heart of the Japanese formation before things began coming unglued.

Second, it was clear that the ability of the Zero to kill American aircraft was proportional to the amount of 20-mm cannon ammunition available. American carrier planes, even obsolete ones like the TBD, were quite sturdy. A good hit from an explosive cannon shell could potentially take one down, but it was much more difficult to do the same with just 7.7-mm machine gun fire. The Americans were lucky, in that having hunted Waldron's men to destruction just twenty minutes earlier, many of the Japanese fighters had "shot their bolt" and were low on 20-mm ammo. This undoubtedly spelled salvation for some of VT-6's aircraft.

Third, we know that at least some of the American aircraft were spared by Japanese fighters once they had dropped their torpedoes.[35] This hardly reflected an altruistic spirit on the part of *Kidō Butai*'s aviators. Like fighter pilots on both sides of this bitter Pacific struggle, they bore no great love for their counterparts and had already demonstrated this day that they would gladly machine gun American fliers, even in their parachutes, if the opportunity afforded itself.[36] Yet a TBD that had released its torpedo was no longer an immediate danger to the fleet, and some of the Japanese pilots at least were apparently being driven to conserve their ammunition for more worthy targets.

This last point is important, in that it gives a better sense for what the mood in the fleet probably was at around 1000. It would be tempting at this point in the proceedings to portray the Japanese attitude toward their enemies as being one of contempt. After all, aside from the B-17s, they had crushed every American attack thrown their way. Complacency would certainly appear to have been the prevalent attitude in the upper command ranks. While there may have been vexation at the delays imposed in launching the counterstrike, there is no sense from the accounts of the senior officers that there was any real fear about the ultimate outcome of the fight. Genda noted that his initial concerns over the force's ability to defend itself against American air attacks had now been swept away by the successful repulsion of Waldron's and Lindsey's attacks.[37] The picture one gets is that everyone on Nagumo's staff felt that they could absorb whatever attacks the Americans could mete out. True, there may have been irritation, and even concern at the delay, but a sense of real urgency about the matter seems to have been lacking. If this was truly their attitude, then it was founded on a lack of understanding of the capabilities of their opponents, as well as a failure to comprehend the frailties of an already overstretched air defense system.

The fact that at this juncture in the battle some of the Japanese CAP pilots would deliberately let American aircraft escape once they had dropped their weapons reveals a much different picture. There had to have been some sense among *Kidō Butai*'s fighter pilots that things were balanced on a bit of a knife's edge. The American attacks were incessant and were now beginning to arrive from different directions. The CAP had little in the way of long-range detection or guidance from their ships, so they couldn't simply guard a single "threat vector" along which the attacks would develop. Instead, the Zero pilots had to remain vigilant to the possibility of danger developing from almost any quarter. The CAP was therefore dispersed—roaming around in small elements near their home vessels, trying to stay alert to the visual cues of the pickets, and then pouncing on targets that came into their sector.

Further, the CAP had demonstrated that it had a tendency to bunch up. In several instances, the *entire* CAP had responded to an incoming attack, leaving *nothing* in reserve over other sectors of the fleet. The CAP behaved almost organically—like white blood cells swarming a toxin. Once the enemy was engaged by a single *shōtai,* it tended to pull adjacent *shōtai* into the fray almost magnetically. But there was little calculation in the CAP's response. If multiple attacks developed in rapid succession, the CAP's ability to "snap back" and react quickly to new threats was limited. This was all symptomatic of the Japanese lack of adequate fighter direction.

If the launch activities of the morning are any indication, the ship's captains and *hikōchō* were keenly aware of these deficiencies. Captain Okada and his counterparts knew that the only way to react quickly was to keep a sharp lookout and a brace of fresh fighters on deck that could be launched as new threats developed. Ammunition depletion only accentuated this risk of overstretching. Taken together, this couldn't have been a comfortable position to be in, especially immediately after repulsing an assault. The result was that the Japanese pilots (and their *hikōchō*) probably had a better appreciation of the dangers *Kidō Butai* was facing than anyone in Nagumo's staff.

Furthermore, it should have been of concern to both Nagumo and his staff that the fleet was being shoved around by these attacks. The attack by VT-8 had been equivalent to a stone thrown into a group of pigeons, blowing apart *Kidō Butai*'s formation and forcing it west. The attack by VT-6 had been a longer, more grinding affair. Nagumo and his carriers had had little choice but to run northwest for a full twenty minutes. Thus, a perceptive observer would have noticed that Japanese control over the flow of events was almost nonexistent. They were trying to recapture the initiative, but in truth they were still in "reaction mode." This was no way to win a battle.

Nevertheless, at 1000, with his ships now turning onto their new heading of 030, Nagumo sent an upbeat report of the battle to Yamamoto, Kondō, submarine commander Komatsu, and Tanaka's Invasion Force. "Carried out air attack of AF at 0630. Many enemy shore-based planes attacked us subsequent to 0715. We have suffered no damages. At 0728, enemy composed of 1 carrier, 7 cruisers and 5 destroyers sighted in (grid) position TO SHI RI 34, on course southwest, speed 20 knots. After destroying this [force], we plan to resume our AF attack. Our position at 1000 is (grid) HE E A 00, course 30 degrees, speed 24 knots."

This message captures both Nagumo's spirit and his intentions less than twenty minutes before total disaster overtook him. *Kidō Butai* was closing with the enemy. In the hangars of all four carriers, the arming process was surely complete, and they were waiting only for the go-ahead to start spotting the flight decks. Forty-five minutes after that, launch would be possible. It was true that the tempo of CAP operations had forestalled this action longer than Nagumo had wished. Still, in Nagumo's mind, the picture seemed to be improving now that *Kaga* had shaken off the last of her attackers.

Unbeknownst to Admiral Nagumo, just as VT-6 was in the final minutes of its ordeal, *Kidō Butai* had been sighted by two new, and entirely separate, American aircraft formations. The first was *Enterprise*'s entire dive-bomber group, under CV-6's air group commander, Lt. Cdr. Clarence Wade McClusky Jr. He was currently leading two squadrons: Scouting Six (under Lt. Wilmer Earl Gallaher) and Bombing Six, (under Lt. Richard Halsey Best). McClusky's group was approaching *Kidō Butai* from the southwest at an altitude of 19,000 feet.[38] This had come about in a completely unanticipated fashion. McClusky had set out from *Enterprise* at 0752, on course 231 degrees, expecting Nagumo to have continued on toward Midway. As such, he ought to have intercepted the Japanese about 142 miles out. Because of the delays in *Enterprise*'s flight operations, however, his thirty-three SBDs were on their own, with no fighter escort once Lieutenant Gray followed after Waldron's VT-8. Contact was swiftly lost with VT-6's fourteen TBDs following behind, as Lindsey apparently split the distance between McClusky's flight and Waldron's, opting for a course of about 240 degrees, which turned out to be a more or less direct line to the enemy.

As it developed, Nagumo's movement east at 0832 had the effect of leaving *Enterprise*'s dive-bombers too far south on their outbound route. This was further complicated by *Kidō Butai*'s turn to east-northeast at 0917, although VT-8's attack soon shoved the fleet back westward. McClusky had hoped to sight the Japanese at about 0920. But by then, *Kidō Butai* was, in fact, nearly due west of his group, at approximately his two o'clock position, and was currently running west itself. Cruising along at 20,000 feet, the cloud cover never allowed the Americans so much as a peep of the Japanese.

By 0930 McClusky knew he was directly over where Nagumo's projected course track ought to have taken his fleet. He saw nothing. Therefore, per his plan, at 0935 he turned to 315 degrees to fly up the approach course of the enemy. He intended to follow this reciprocal route for some fifty miles, until 1000. At that point, he would alter course northeast, fly a short distance, and then reluctantly head for home. Fuel was already getting low, and he didn't have all day. McClusky was banking that this rather basic search pattern would bring him at least a glimpse of the Japanese fleet. He eventually caught the glimpse he was hoping for, but it so happened that it was of only a tiny portion of Nagumo's fleet.

At 0955 McClusky spied the wake of a lone ship, northeast of him and headed over the horizon in the same direction. It was kicking up a very pronounced bow wave and moving fast.[39] He identified it as a cruiser. In fact, it was *Arashi*, which had been keeping *Nautilus*'s head down. Having broken off her attack fifteen minutes earlier, she was scrambling to return to the task force. Reasoning that this ship would lead him to the Japanese carriers, McClusky made to overhaul her from the southwest. At 1000 he was rewarded with the sight of many wakes dead ahead through the scattered clouds, some thirty-five miles ahead. At 1002 he radioed Raymond Spruance the electrifying news: "This is McClusky. Have sighted the enemy."[40]

Meanwhile, to the east of McClusky, a group of aircraft from *Yorktown* was also entering the battlefield. This formation consisted of VT-3 (under Lt. Cdr. Lance E. "Lem" Massey), VB-3 (led by Lt. Cdr. Maxwell F. Leslie), and VF-3 (under Lt. Cdr. John Smith "Jimmy" Thach). It will be recalled that the other American carrier aircraft formations had traveled outward in small groups and then been separated. Not so those of *Yorktown*, the most experienced of the American carriers. Because of careful planning, her group had remained closely coordinated, with each of the tactical elements remaining in sight of each other up until the time they initiated their attack. All three groups had been droning along on 240 degrees. At 1003 one of VT-3's crewmen spied smoke off to the northwest. VT-3, VB-3, and Thach's six accompanying fighters all turned right to approach the enemy. Thus, for the first time in the battle, an American carrier air group had the very real possibility of delivering a coordinated high-low assault against the enemy.

The effect of these totally unrelated sightings was to place *Kidō Butai* in grave danger. By dint of a healthy dollop of bad luck, the Japanese were now effectively placed between an enormous hammer and anvil. Previously, lone American

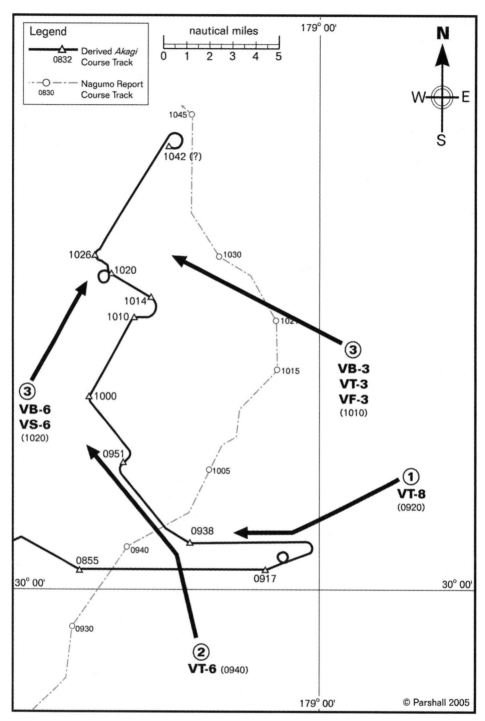

11-3: American air attacks on *Kidō Butai*, 0920–1020. This illustration shows how the Japanese carrier formation was shoved in new directions as a result of the ongoing American air attacks.

squadrons—attacking without support or the benefit of combined arms—had divided into two elements so as to try and catch single Japanese carriers between their attacking groups. This time the Americans were bringing four attack squadrons to the fight—three dive-bomber units and a torpedo squadron. More important, the American air groups were approaching along two separate axes, and yet were fortuitously arriving over the target at roughly the same time. Three of the American squadrons were coming in at high altitude, another fairly low, and there were even some fighters thrown in for good measure. This was far and away the most challenging threat the Japanese had faced all morning. And it was against this attack that Japanese air defenses would finally and catastrophically fail.

It's worth taking a moment to comment on the shape of the Japanese carrier formation at about 1000. With *Kaga* out of immediate danger, Nagumo ordered *Kidō Butai* to resume a northeast course of 030. Once again, the four carriers turned in their tracks to comply with their new orders. Out on the eastern edge of the carrier group, CarDiv 2 had effectively been isolated from VT-6's attack. *Hiryū* and *Sōryū* had loped northwest, roughly abreast, paralleling CarDiv 1's movements as the American attack had developed. Now, with another turn to the northeast, CarDiv 2 was placed in the van of the carrier group once more. *Sōryū,* as the easternmost carrier during the run northwest, was now in the front of the carrier formation, with *Hiryū* trailing her. Behind, the two carriers of CarDiv 1 brought up the rear, with *Akagi* off of *Kaga*'s starboard bow, but on roughly the same east-west line.

All semblance of a box formation had by now disappeared. Instead, Nagumo's carriers were strung out in a rough line ahead to the northeast. The distance between the two carrier divisions was almost certainly greater than 7,000 meters, and that between the lead ship (*Sōryū*) and *Kaga* (the most westerly) was probably more than 15,000 meters. Eyewitness accounts on board *Sōryū* at this time mention CarDiv 1 as being little more than vague blocky smudges on the horizon. Likewise, a diagram drawn by a *Sōryū* survivor shows *Sōryū* at the apex of a triangle, with *Kaga* on its left bottom corner and *Akagi* on its right bottom, which broadly fits the same picture.[41]

This positioning of *Sōryū* at the fore of the formation at 1000 stands in contrast with every preceding history of the battle, which universally have *Hiryū* in the lead. Indeed, it has always been supposed that the only reason *Hiryū* escaped the coming attack was because she was far enough in front of the rest of the carriers that she avoided the attention of *Yorktown*'s dive-bombers, which presumably came in from the southeast. However, a careful reading of the Nagumo Report and other evidence from both the American and Japanese side leads to a much different picture.[42] These matters are intriguing and important, for the exact shape and heading of Nagumo's carriers in this time frame has been the source of considerable disagreement down through the years. For the moment, we ask the reader to simply hold these thoughts, as the subsequent ten minutes, and the developing attacks of the Americans, will shed additional light on why this configuration for *Kidō Butai* makes better sense than previous renditions.

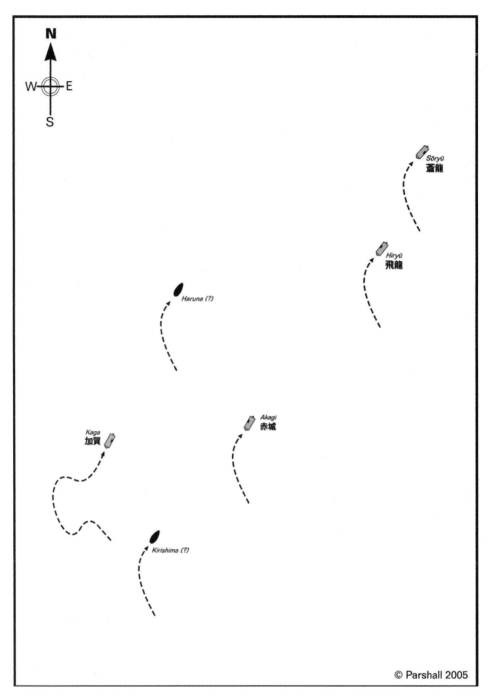

11-4: *Kidō Butai* formation at 1000, after change to course 030. The fleet at this time had been so distorted as to no longer really resemble a box formation at all, but rather a ragged line ahead, with *Kaga* trailing on the port quarter.

VT-6's survivors were still desperately struggling to escape the battlefield as VT-3's attack began materializing. At 1006 flagship *Akagi* spotted torpedo bombers some forty-five km distant at a heading of 118 degrees True, off the starboard beam. Whether her lookouts also glimpsed the American fighters and dive-bombers that were almost directly over VT-3 at this same time is open to speculation, but it is likely they did not. Captain Aoki apparently judged VT-3's threat to be distant enough that he could afford to make a brief digression to the east to land some fighters. *Akagi* turned to course 090 at 1010 and brought down three Zeros from her fifth and sixth watches. However, as the American torpedo planes continued boring in, *Akagi* turned her stern to them and headed northwest. As soon as the fighters were stowed, Aoki ordered another *shōtai* of Zeros spotted on deck and warmed up.[43] If this new American attack was of similar magnitude to the ones just before, *Akagi* might need to defend herself shortly. On *Akagi*'s air-control platform, *hikōchō* Masuda was having, in his own words, "One hell of a long day!"[44]

It has been commonly supposed that VT-3's attack preceded that of the *Yorktown* dive-bombers by a good bit. However, more recent scholarship on the American side of the battle has confirmed that VT-3's assault lasted longer than previously thought and culminated *after* the dive-bomber attack.[45] Like all the American torpedo attacks this morning, the fact that the TBDs were so slow meant that the attack took a while to develop. Not only that, but VT-3 would subsequently switch targets during its run in, lengthening the overall engagement. Indeed, some of the American dive-bomber pilots stated that after bombing *Kaga* and *Akagi,* they witnessed aircraft from VT-3 still heading northward to attack their target. For their part, the Japanese also saw the torpedo aircraft as part of a nearly simultaneous, continuous attack.

The Japanese CAP at 1010 consisted of thirty-six fighters, though shortly it would be up to forty-two. Many of these aircraft were undoubtedly still clustered near *Kaga* or engaged southeast of the fleet chasing VT-6's remnants. And as mentioned previously, *Sōryū*'s fifth patrol, under PO1c Harada, was heading east and climbing to chase after Gray's recently departed Wildcats. Shortly, however, Harada would bring his men about to confront the new threat developing to the southeast. Thus, the bulk of *Kidō Butai*'s fighters were likely distributed in a belt stretching roughly northwest to southeast across the force.

The appearance of VT-3 undoubtedly attracted the CAP's attention, as the Zeros then chasing VT-6 out ran headlong into the new attackers.[46] Heavy cruiser *Chikuma* thereupon began banging away with her main battery to attract the attention of the rest of the CAP. If the accounts of the American aviators in VT-3 and VF-3 are to be believed, thereafter the southeast axis very quickly filled up with Zeros.

By 1011 *Akagi* was running northwest. There is every reason to believe the other three carriers of *Kidō Butai* were following suit, or would shortly do so.[47] In truth, though, Massey had apparently never intended to attack CarDiv 1, but instead sent his squadron more to the north after *Sōryū*. At 1015, seeing the attack developing, *Sōryū* sent up PO1c Sugiyama Takeo's sixth watch of three fighters. *Hiryū* had launched PO1c Hino Masato's CAP *shōtai* (watch number 5C) two minutes earlier, at 1013. Thereupon, both carriers of CarDiv 2 had turned away from the American attackers as well.[48]

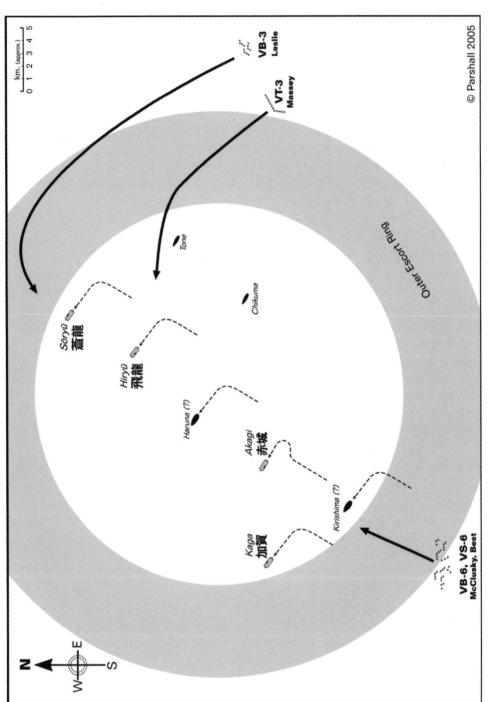

11-5: *Kidō Butai* immediately before attack. The carriers are in a loose line abreast, with the two carrier divisions widely separated. Positions of the other vessels are approximate (at best) and not necessarily to scale.

By 1015 or so, all four of Nagumo's flattops were running to the northwest. *Akagi* and *Kaga* were chugging along at twenty-two knots. *Hiryū* and *Sōryū*, however, being on the receiving end of VT-3's attack, were running flat out at thirty-four knots.[49] *Kidō Butai*'s formation was still a ragged line, but now it was a line abreast, stretched from southwest to northeast—a formation that was remarked upon by several American aviators. VB-6 observed the carriers running in a rough row from southwest to northeast, while VB-3 saw a row running more east to west.[50] From VB-6's point of view, the line stretched away to the north, with each carrier showing its port side to the incoming pilots. VB-3, however, saw the sterns of all the carriers as they were spread out in line abreast from left to right across their windscreens.

Sōryū was at the far right-hand end of the line, the most northerly of the carriers, and possibly the most easterly as well. *Akagi* and *Kaga* were the southernmost pair, separated from CarDiv 2 by a good stretch of water. The two ships of CarDiv 1 were arrayed on a rough parallel east-west, with *Kaga* the most westerly. From the vantage point of *Akagi*'s bridge, CarDiv 2 was off the starboard beam, and perhaps slightly astern. *Kaga* was plowing ahead off of *Akagi*'s port bow.[51] This jibes exactly with the diagram drawn by a civilian cameraman on board *Akagi*, which showed *Kaga* ahead of *Akagi* and to port. It also corresponds with the recollections of *Sōryū*'s crewmen, who would see *Kaga* off to port when she was attacked.[52] The two battleships, probably in reaction to VT-6's attack, had shifted formation such that they were off either beam of *Akagi*.[53] Meanwhile, destroyer *Arashi*, unaware of the enemy interlopers following her from above, was finally closing on the flagship, bearing 234 from *Akagi* at 1011.[54]

Kidō Butai's turning away from VT-3 also signaled the arrival of the first serious opposition to Massey's torpedo attack, in the form of numerous Zeros. VT-3 was eventually to be subjected to the same brutal handling that had been meted out to every American torpedo attack this morning. But for the first time in the battle, *Kidō Butai*'s CAP was confronted by American fighters. These were six Wildcats under the command of Jimmy Thach. Two of his fighters were flying 500 feet above and directly behind Massey's command, which was itself cruising at 2,500 feet. Thach's own foursome trailed further behind, and some 2,000 feet higher.[55]

It was against the American fighter escorts that the Zeros first committed themselves. In short order, Thach found himself confronted by an estimated fifteen to twenty.[56] So many Japanese fighters lined up against him that they had to take turns in order to attack efficiently. Thach quickly lost one of his planes to an attack delivered from below. Initially, he tried leading his group down to support Massey, but the faster Zeros never gave him a chance, penning the American Wildcats in before they could make a move. It looked like another quick, routine victory for *Kidō Butai*'s *kansen* pilots was shaping up.

At this juncture, faced with a truly desperate situation, Jimmy Thach boldly bet his life, and those of his men, on a new defensive tactic that he had been mulling over for several months. Despite not having had a chance to brief both of his remaining compatriots on his defensive formation, he managed to implement it anyway—the first combat usage of what was to become famously known as the "Thach Weave."

For the next twenty-five minutes, Thach's two-element division was under constant attack by a bevy of Zeros. The three Wildcats used his weaving tactic almost constantly to shoo them away from each other's tails and to take snapshots at their assailants as they closed briefly on head-on bearings.

The results of this prolonged encounter were nothing short of shocking to the Japanese. Not only was Thach able to save his own life and his two remaining aviators, but he personally succeeded in shooting down three Zeros in the process. One of his wingmen took down another.[57] To this point in the war, aerial combat had been pretty much a one-way street for Zero pilots—they dished it out, and the enemy died. Not so this time, as the Japanese grappled in increasing frustration with how to get an edge over the constantly maneuvering Grummans. This was perhaps the first concrete instance in the war in which American fighters demonstrated that they were taking the measure of their Japanese opposite numbers. It was a sensation that Nagumo's *kansen* pilots cannot have relished.

Meanwhile, VT-3 was proceeding northwest away from Thach, and the Japanese CAP was having similar, though less-protracted difficulties with the pair of Wildcats still flying close cover for the torpedo planes. One of the two American fighters, flown by Mach. Thomas F. Cheek, nailed *Sōryū*'s PO3c Kawamata Teruo almost immediately as he made a run on Massey's Devastators. Thereafter, though, the sheer number of Zeros first pried Cheek and his wingman, Ens. Daniel C. Sheedy, away from VT-3, and then eventually away from each other as well. The two American fighters were badly shot up in the process, but both had managed to escape by alternately ducking into clouds and diving down to hug the waves. In the process, Sheedy got into a wave-top tangle with another Zero and managed to kill it by getting the Japanese pilot to lose control of his aircraft and dip his wing into the water, cartwheeling him to his death.

By about 1020, VT-3 was finally deprived of its fighter cover. However, Massey had some altitude to play with, and as soon as the Zeros had hit Cheek and Sheedy, he had taken his squadron into a shallow dive, trading altitude for some additional speed.[58] This, in combination with the undue attention being visited on the American Wildcats, meant that VT-3 lost only a single aircraft during this juncture, that of Ens. Wesley Frank Osmus. VT-3 was able to proceed in good order, subjected to only minimal harassment from a few Zeros. However, Massey could probably see fresh fighters being sent up by *Sōryū* and subsequently turned his aircraft to close on *Hiryū*, which was somewhat to the southwest and seemed to be a little more attainable.[59]

What makes this interesting is that VT-3 was flying slow-moving aircraft, at fairly low altitude, and with a limited field of view. In such circumstances, it is probable that they altered course to attack the closest target they could find. Yet at the same time, the common wisdom has always maintained that *Hiryū* was spared from the forthcoming dive-bombing because of her distance from VB-3, whose faster-moving aircraft were supposedly boring in right behind VT-3. Had *Hiryū* been in the van of the carrier formation, Massey's target selection would have made little sense, as he would have been opting for a ship that was allegedly far more distant. Clearly, something in the common wisdom doesn't hang together. Either the shape of the Japanese formation was different than has been supposed (and *Hiryū* was located somewhere other than in the lead of the pack), or the VT-3/VB-3 attack developed in a different manner than has been previously portrayed. In fact, the answer was a little bit of both. It was *Sōryū* that lay to the north, with *Hiryū* south of her. And, as we shall see shortly, the attack from *Yorktown*'s dive-bombers ultimately developed from a different quarter than that of her torpedo bombers.

It took a while for *Hiryū*'s and *Sōryū*'s recently launched fighters to make their presence felt against Massey. In fact, it was not until his formation had closed to within a couple of miles of *Hiryū* that things began coming unglued. At this juncture, though, *Kidō Butai*'s fighters smashed into VT-3 with enormous violence. Prominent among the Zeros again was *Sōryū*'s Lt. Fujita Iyozo, now flying his third sortie of the morning. Fujita had missed breakfast before the morning strike and hadn't had a chance to grab a bite of lunch the last time he'd been on board *Sōryū*, either.[60] He was exhausted and hungry, a state probably not unlike many of his companions at this moment. His wingmen had disappeared, perhaps having been drawn into Thach's flying circus, leaving Fujita to press his early attacks alone. His perseverance paid off, though, as he succeeded in downing four of the attackers.[61]

Within seconds of the arrival of the CAP, Japanese fighters were positively swarming over Massey's shrinking formation, raining destruction on their hapless opponents with murderously precise runs. Once again, the TBDs lumbered ahead, spitting back fire at their assailants, and occasionally scoring. However, Fujita and crew began running up the score on their victims in short order. Massey's plane went flaming into the water almost immediately, and the American formation blew apart into two sections. The first division was decimated, leaving just one plane in the air. The second division was luckier, if such a phrase can be used to describe a near massacre, with four of its members being left to attack *Hiryū*.

But what of VB-3, which had started the engagement within visual range of VT-3? Given their higher speed, if the American dive-bombers had come straight in behind the TBDs, they should by all rights have arrived over the Japanese almost simultaneously, and from out of the southeast. However, this did not happen. Lt. Cdr. Leslie had seen Massey turn to the north and had indeed followed the torpedo bombers for a time. However, he did not want to alert Massey's target until he was in a position to directly support the torpedo attack. Accordingly, Leslie led his force north, along the eastern flank of the Japanese formation, so as to achieve a favorable attack position upwind of the target. This had the effect of extending VB-3's transit time as they made their way around to their final pushover point.

Leslie also was under the impression that his might not be the only *Yorktown* dive-bombers in the area. As far as he knew, *Yorktown*'s scouting squadron (VS-5) had been launched shortly after his, and therefore ought to be trailing his unit. He did not know that VS-5 was currently cooling its heels on board *Yorktown*.[62] Doctrine said that when two squadrons arrived at a target, the lead squadron should take the further target, so that the trailing squadron could hit the nearer target at roughly the same time. This reinforced Leslie's belief that he should attack *Sōryū*, which was slightly more distant. He even radioed VS-5 at 1015 to the effect that they should attack the target on the left (*Hiryū*), while he attended to the target on the right (*Sōryū*).[63] Thus far, he had not seen more than three carriers in the Japanese formation.[64]

At 1020 Leslie radioed Massey, asking if he was ready to begin his torpedo attack. Massey responded affirmatively. However, just moments later Leslie heard Massey frantically calling for fighter support as the CAP plowed into him.[65] It no longer made sense for Leslie to delay his own attack. By now, VB-3 had arrived in a favorable position to the northeast of the target. *Sōryū*, oblivious to his approach, had turned briefly from running northwest and was coming around to starboard to face them. She seemed to be preparing to launch more fighters.[66] On this angle, VB-3 would be able to attack upwind of the target, which was preferred as it gave better control over the angle of dive.[67] Even better, as *Sōryū* began turning back to the east to launch, her turn brought her length parallel to the attacking warplanes—an ideal situation.[68] This also explains how *Hiryū* managed to avoid being dive-bombed herself. Though her position in the middle of the formation had ultimately made her more attractive to VT-3's attack, it also neatly exempted her from the dive-bombing attacks. Swinging down from the north, VB-3's planes now found *Sōryū* directly in their path, with *Hiryū* a more distant option ahead of them (i.e., to the south). Leslie split his aircraft into three divisions and began easing down into his final approach.

Meanwhile, still unnoticed by the Japanese, *Enterprise*'s two dive-bomber squadrons were approaching *Kidō Butai* from the southwest. They, too, wanted a good attack position, preferably somewhat upwind, as well as one that would allow them to dive with the sun at their backs. As a result, *Enterprise*'s SBDs moved a good way northeast, and well into the heart of the Japanese formation, before banking left and initiating their final short approach from out of the southeast.

In doing so, the Americans first had to penetrate overtop the Japanese destroyer screen. This they apparently did without eliciting much in the way of warning from the ships scattered below—all eyes in the task force were glued to VT-3's attack. *Kidō Butai* as a whole, and its air defense personnel in particular, were suffering from what is known in modern military parlance as "target fixation." That is, they were focusing to the point of myopia on a single, though admittedly very important piece of data, and were no longer keeping track of the environment around them. This time, there would be no warning salvos from *Tone* or *Chikuma,* no smokescreens laid down by the outlying destroyers to warn of the enemy's approach.

There's no question that both the Americans and the Japanese were hindered in this respect to a certain extent by the weather. The Americans had been able to use the scattered clouds to their advantage. At the same time, though, none of the American squadrons were able to get a sense for the larger tactical picture. In fact, they couldn't even see the complete extent of the Japanese task force. Both the *Enterprise* and *Yorktown* pilots were in essence fighting their own separate battles—they weren't aware of each other until after their attacks had been delivered.

The Japanese CAP pilots were in the same boat, only more so. The majority of the Zeros were now at low altitude and were either attacking the American TBDs or fighting with Thach. The view from a fighter cockpit at low altitude is restricted in any case, and it was hardly surprising that they lost track of the overall flow of the battle. However, one of the most prized attributes of any fighter pilot is his ability to maintain both mental control and a conceptual grasp of the larger combat occurring around him. This is commonly referred to as "situational awareness"—a state of mental acuity and calmness under fire that is the polar opposite of "target fixation." Instead, the Japanese fighters were concentrating on killing VT-3. In the noticeably understated words of *Sōryū*'s after-action report, "There is a marked tendency for our fighters to overconcentrate on enemy torpedo planes."[69] This is perhaps understandable, given that Imperial Japanese Navy doctrine viewed torpedo aircraft as the most dangerous carrier-borne weapon. Yet, it seems clear that in this regard the Japanese CAP, despite the undoubted experience of its pilots, suffered a collective breakdown.

However, this tendency toward overpursuit applied doubly to the amount of effort the Japanese expended on Thach's section. Shooting down these American interlopers—who admittedly had inflicted unprecedented casualties on the Zeros—became a goal in and of itself. If Thach's recollections are to be believed, his three-plane formation was absorbing the attention of a third or more of the Japanese CAP. This reaction was totally out of proportion to the actual threat posed by his Wildcats. A far more intelligent approach would have been to detach a *shōtai* to keep the Americans busy, while the remaining dozen or so fighters went back down to attend to VT-3 or (better yet) climbed back up to top cover positions.

However, the fact that the Japanese fighters were now at lower altitude has also been somewhat misunderstood. Altitude, per se, was not the CAP's real problem at this time. After all, Zeros could climb at more than 4,000 feet per minute. Given five minutes' warning, they could have been back up to the likely altitude of any dive-bomber attack. Rather, the fact that they were arrayed along a northwest-southeast axis, with most of them concentrated in the southeast quadrant, meant that it was doubly difficult to spot dive-bombers approaching from distant, and orthogonal quarters.

Indeed, the Japanese CAP's problem was not an inability to compensate vertically, so much as its inability to react to the lateral distortions that were now being thrust on it. It had simply been pulled in too many directions during the past hour—northeast (VT-8), south-southwest (VT-6), and now southeast (VT-3/VF-3). Not only that, but the combined attack by VT-3/VF-3 was in the process of shooting down larger numbers of Japanese CAP fighters than any previous enemy had ever managed. Given this, it is hardly surprising that *Kidō Butai*'s attention—pilots, lookouts, and *hikōchōs* all—was glued along the southeast axis.

Despite the utter lack of fighter opposition at high altitude, the American dive-bombers did not have everything their own way. VB-3, for instance, was going into its attack with only thirteen armed aircraft out of its nominal strength of seventeen. Four of the SBDs, including Leslie's, had suffered problems with their new electrical bomb arming devices, leading them to accidentally jettison their ordnance into the Pacific some minutes before.

In the case of VS-6 and VB-6, things became somewhat confused between the two squadrons during the final moments. McClusky was presented with two CVs as he approached, one (the closest) on his left, and the other, a bit farther, on his right. These were *Kaga* and *Akagi*, respectively, with *Kaga* the westernmost carrier, and *Akagi* off her starboard quarter.[70] Doctrine dictated that each squadron should attack one carrier, and McClusky radioed instructions to that effect.[71] However, as mentioned previously, doctrine also said that when two squadrons attacked together, the leading squadron should take the further target.

However, Wade McClusky, despite being an excellent group leader, was also a former fighter pilot and had only recently transferred to dive-bombers. Not surprisingly, he was not as studied in attack doctrine as were his subordinates and consequently overlooked this guiding principle, with spectacular results. Switching on his radio, he directed Lt. Gallaher (Scouting Six's commander) to hit the near carrier on the left-hand side (*Kaga*). At the same time, he ordered Lt. Richard Best's Bombing Six to take the more distant right-hand carrier (*Akagi*). Satisfied that everything was now in order, McClusky decided to add his three-plane command element to Gallaher's strike. Opening his dive flaps, he radioed to his wingman, "Earl, Follow me down!"[72] Unfortunately, by dint of these orders, McClusky had unwittingly reversed doctrine. He ought to have ordered Gallaher's leading squadron to attack *Akagi* instead. As McClusky prepared to push over, unbeknownst to him, Dick Best and Bombing Six were moving into position a short distance below him, planning to attack the same carrier!

As an experienced dive-bomber, Lieutenant Best never doubted for a moment that doctrine would be followed in the matter of doling out attacks between the two squadrons. As such, he continued leading his squadron toward *Kaga,* specifically advising McClusky of that fact by radioing, "Group Commander from Six Baker One. Am attacking according to doctrine."[73] It is probable that both men transmitted to each other simultaneously, thereby jamming the other's transmission. Whatever the reason, neither McClusky nor Best heard the other's message. The net result of all this, though, was that *Kaga* would shortly find herself on the receiving end of a jumbo-sized attack.

The Americans had now set themselves up to deliver a killing blow from above, while the immediate battle still raged far below. By 1020 VT-3's attack was moving toward CarDiv 2 and was beginning to be savaged by the Japanese CAP. However, Nagumo had ordered *Akagi* and *Kaga* to launch fighters as soon as they were readied in order to stave off this obvious danger and to rotate in as replacements for those CAP fighters that needed replenishment. On *Akagi*, a group of Zeros under the command of PO1c Kimura Koreo were warming up on the flight deck and preparing for takeoff. *Kaga* was preparing to do the same. As it turned out, Kimura's was to be the last aircraft *Akagi* ever launched. The stage was now set for the single most decisive aerial attack in naval history.

12

A Fallacious Five Minutes—1020–1025

We pardon our readers for having turned the previous page with the understandable expectation of finding Dauntlesses hurtling downward from the heavens, only to discover that a brief but necessary piece of business remains before we get to the "exciting part." Before relating the particulars of the American dive-bomber attack, a final, crucial question must be answered. Namely, what exactly was occurring on the Japanese flight decks at this moment? This is a matter that has been incorrectly reported for the past sixty years, and it is vital to set the record straight. Please rest assured, however, that the bombing will commence promptly thereafter.

The common wisdom on this matter, as reported by Fuchida and endlessly parroted by every Western chronicler of Midway, is that at the moment of the decisive attack at 1020–1025 the Japanese were on the brink of launching their own massive counterstrike. The Japanese flight decks were supposedly packed practically wingtip to wingtip with bombers and escort fighters waiting to take off. Fuchida's description of a "fateful five minutes" in his book *Midway: The Battle that Doomed Japan* is worth quoting at length, as it sets the tenor for all subsequent accounts:

> Preparations for a counter-strike against the enemy had continued on board our four carriers throughout the enemy torpedo attacks. One after another, planes were hoisted from the hangar and quickly arranged on the flight deck. There was no time to lose. At 1020 Admiral Nagumo gave the order to launch when ready. On *Akagi*'s flight deck all planes were in position with engines warming up. The big ship began turning into the wind. Within five minutes all her planes would be launched.
>
> Five minutes! Who would have dreamed that the tide of battle would shift completely in that interval of time?
>
> Visibility was good. Clouds were gathering at about 3,000 meters, however, and though there were occasional breaks, they afforded good concealment for approaching enemy planes. At 1024 the order to start launching came from the bridge by voice tube. The Air Officer flapped a white flag, and the first Zero fighter gathered speed and whizzed off the deck. At that instant a lookout screamed "Hell-divers!" I looked up to see three black enemy planes plummeting towards our ship.[1]

This is good stuff—dramatic, chock full of suspense and fickle fate; in short, tailor-made for a great screenplay. It is also utter nonsense, at least in one key respect. In reality, when the Americans struck their fatal blow, the Japanese counterstrike was nowhere near ready to be launched on *any* of their four carriers.

The reason Fuchida's account is nonsense is because of the laws of space and time that had inexorably dictated *Kidō Butai*'s operations this morning. As we have seen, spotting a strike for launch was a complex process that typically took a minimum of around forty-five minutes and often occupied upward of an hour. During this time, the ship's flight deck was closed to operations, because aircraft were being spotted aft. Landings were completely impossible. And while fighters could theoretically take off from the bow during spotting, in practice we know of no instances where this was done. If Nagumo was indeed ready to launch at 1020, then the Japanese carriers had to have spent at least the previous three-quarters of an hour spotting their strike force. Yet, a simple perusal of *Akagi*'s flight operations for the late morning reveals the truth:

0837–0900—recover Midway attack force
0910—recover combat air patrol (CAP)
0932—launch CAP
0951—recover CAP
1006—launch CAP
1010—recover CAP[2]

In other words, from roughly 0837 onward, *Akagi* was conducting some sort of takeoff or landing operations (most of them associated with CAP fighters) every twenty minutes or so. Indeed, she had recovered three CAP fighters as late as 1010, a mere fifteen minutes before she was fatally bombed.

The 1010 recovery—that of PO1c Tanaka Katsumi, PO2c Ōhara Hiroshi, and PO1c Iwashiro Yoshio—demolishes Fuchida's account at a stroke. There was no slightest possibility that *Akagi* could have gotten her strike planes on deck, spotted, and warmed up in the fifteen minutes after these Zeros had landed. Nagumo needed forty-five minutes, not fifteen. Under such conditions, with the carriers under near-constant attack, it is understandable that *Akagi*'s *hikōchō* had not completed the process by 1025. In fact, spotting probably had not even begun. The situation was much the same aboard the other carriers. Each of them had launched aircraft since 1000, with *Kaga* and *Sōryū* having sent up fighters at 1000, *Hiryū* at 1013, *Sōryū* yet again at 1015, and *Akagi* latest of all at 1025.

Another crucial piece of evidence in this matter is *Hiryū*'s behavior. If Fuchida's account is to be believed, *Hiryū*, which was to escape the coming attacks, by all rights ought to have been launching her own strike aircraft at the very time her compatriots were being bombed. Yet, as we know, she was under attack by VT-3 throughout this time, and in any event, would not mount her own counterstrike until around 1050. This, in turn, means that she was no closer to being ready to go at 1020 than anybody else was. The conclusion is inescapable—the American attack found the Japanese in roughly the same position they had been in all morning, that is, looking for an opening in which to begin spotting the flight decks. The relentless, if hapless, American attacks had essentially paralyzed Nagumo since roughly 0700. Fuchida's "fateful five minutes" was nothing more than a fairy tale meant to hide this essential truth. Five minutes either way wasn't going to spare the Japanese. Like blood from a wounded patient, *time*—the lifeblood of decision and action—had been oozing out of *Kidō Butai* all morning, slowly and inexorably. Now the patient was beyond recovery.

None of this is meant to imply that the coming attack was not decisive as far as the battle was concerned—it most certainly was. Nor should it be assumed that there were no aircraft whatsoever on the Japanese flight decks at 1020—there most certainly were. But these aircraft were mostly, if not entirely, Zeros waiting to be launched to relieve the CAP patrols that were already in the air. This view is supported by both American eyewitness accounts and Japanese sources. The official Japanese war history series (*Senshi Sōsho*) explicitly states that at the time of the attack, *all four* Japanese carriers still had their attack aircraft in the hangars. The only aircraft on deck were either CAP fighters or, in the case of *Sōryū*, strike force escort fighters that were being launched to augment the CAP.[3]

This viewpoint, of course, stands in apparent conflict with certain eyewitness accounts made by American pilots, which often painted lurid portraits of bombs exploding among packed enemy squadrons, and Japanese planes being catapulted around the flight decks or enveloped in sheets of flame. While such accounts must be given due consideration, they must also be weighed against the authoritative written evidence that is available. Certainly these American pilot accounts contain elements of truth. The American bombing attack *did* cause spectacular fireworks, and Japanese aircraft *were* undoubtedly destroyed in the process. But cooler, more senior heads among the American pilots also observed a lack of planes on the Japanese flight decks. Lt. Dick Best commented that he saw very few Japanese aircraft topside during his attack run against *Akagi*.[4] Lt. Cdr. Maxwell Leslie, commander of *Yorktown*'s dive-bomber squadron, also noted in a draft of his official report that he did not see any planes whatsoever on *Sōryū*'s deck,[5] although the pilot just behind him, Lt. Paul Holmberg, thought he saw a Zero being hurled over the side.[6] Aboard *Kaga,* the situation was much the same, with torpedo bomber pilot Morinaga remarking that *Kaga* had only two or three aircraft on deck near the stern when the attack developed.[7]

These sober observations, in conjunction with the cold, hard data recorded in the individual Japanese carrier action reports, must be given precedence over the fragmentary and often conflicting reports of American pilots. Like aviators everywhere, they were prone to seeing what they wanted to see.[8] If they embellished the appearance of the stunning damage they inflicted on the Japanese, they are to be forgiven. Dive-bombing a moving target is difficult under the best of circumstances. When these stresses were compounded by antiaircraft fire, explosions, and violent aerial maneuvers, it is hardly surprising that the aviator accounts tended to focus on the more visible elements of their attacks. Indeed, in many cases they were simply looking for a hit, any hit, that occurred at about the time that their own bomb should have hit the target—a method that was reliable for the lead plane in a formation but decidedly less so for the ones following him down. None of this, however, detracted from the overall impressiveness, or the sheer horror, of the calamity they were about to unleash on their enemies.

13

The Iron Fist—1020–1030

At 1019 an inkling of what was coming was finally revealed to the Japanese. *Hiryū*'s senior lookout, a sailor named Yoshida, shouted that he sighted dive-bombers to port approaching *Kaga* from high overhead, altitude some 4,000 meters.[1] "How is *Kaga* firing?" demanded Yamaguchi. "Are her arrows raised?" meaning the status of her five-inch battery. "Low-angle!" came the reply. Yamaguchi immediately ordered a warning flashed to *Kaga*—"Enemy dive-bombers over your ship!" To his relief, *Kaga* shortly confirmed that she had received it. As they watched through their binoculars, *Kaga*'s guns began cranking skyward and "opened up all together" on the enemy planes. But it was too late.

At the same moment, one of *Kaga*'s officers, Lt. Cdr. Mitoya Sesu, was standing just outside the island, watching the preparations for the next CAP launch. Nearby was WO Morinaga Takayoshi, standing with a group of pilots in the center of the flight deck, including Maeda Takeshi, just aft of the amidships elevator. WO Yoshino Haruo, the commander of the morning's reconnaissance flight, had just come up from the ready room and was loitering in the antiaircraft galleries at the rear of the ship. They were all slated to go on the coming strike, and while they waited for their planes to be spotted, they had orders from the bridge to stand by as extra lookouts. Now they were scanning the sky. No one can say who spotted the attackers first—the sharp-eyed pilots or the lookouts in the air defense command post atop the island. But suddenly, at around 1022, everyone started yelling to the bridge "enemy dive-bombers!" Both Yoshino and Maeda couldn't help but admire the Americans' technique. No glide-bombing attacks here. They were coming in like the pros did, at ridiculously steep angles.[2]

Kaga most likely had already been turning to port to begin a brief run into the wind to launch fighters.[3] The Dauntlesses were attacking from her port quarter, and Captain Okada immediately ordered a radical turn to starboard, looping back northward.[4] Against Lofton Henderson's green pilots, such a maneuver might have worked. Against pilots of this caliber, though, there was little that Okada could do. "Nimble" did not well describe *Kaga* in any case—her 42,000 tons turned about as gracefully as a draft horse before the plow. Lumbering into her circle at something around twenty-four knots, she labored to increase her speed. Worse, to her lookouts it was apparent that she was being attacked by a swarm of aircraft, many of which

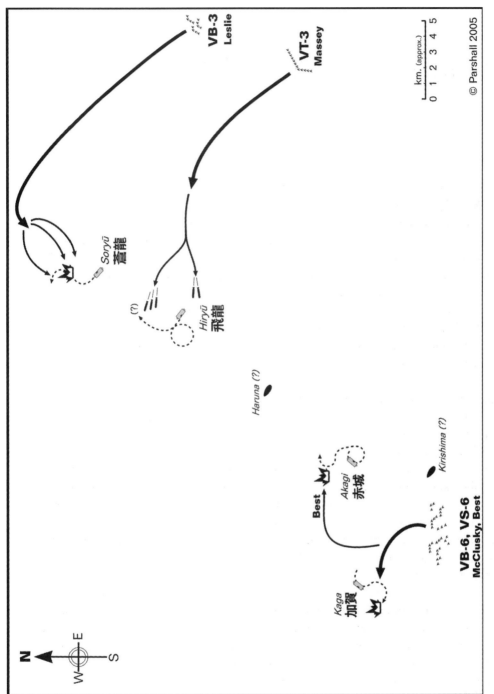

N
W — E
S

VB-3
Leslie

VT-3
Massey

Soryū
蒼龍

(?)

Hiryū
飛龍

Haruna (?)

Kirishima (?)

Best

Akagi
赤城

Kaga
加賀

VB-6, VS-6
McClusky, Best

km. (approx.)
0 1 2 3 4 5

© Parshall 2005

13-1: Decisive attacks against *Kidō Butai*. Dive-bombers mortally wound three of the Japanese carriers, while VT-3 attacks *Hiryū*.

hadn't even started their dives yet.[5] Once *Kaga* committed to her turn, it would be easier for the trailing aircraft to hit her.

The one thing *Kaga* still had going for her was her relatively large AA outfit. Her five-inch battery, sixteen barrels in all, trained skyward and began firing as rapidly as possible. Despite her antiquated fire-control system, the gunners did what they knew how to do best, throwing up a barrage of five-inch shells. The 25-mm automatics joined in as well, though they couldn't expect to hit much until the dive-bombers had already gotten low enough to release. This much credit must be given, though—*Kaga* was the only Japanese carrier that bagged a dive-bomber this day. She hit the sixth plane in line, that of Ens. J. Q. Roberts, and sent it slamming into the water close at hand. However, new attackers came charging down in rapid succession.

For a moment, *Kaga*'s evasive turn paid results. The first three planes missed, water columns from their 500-lb and smaller 100-lb bombs sprouting all around the big ship. Standing on the air-control station on the aft end of the island, *Kaga*'s *hikōchō*, Commander Amagai, watched as the bombs detached from the attacking aircraft and came floating down. You could actually *see* the damned things! They grew larger the closer they came, picking up speed all the while. Below and ahead of Amagai, Commander Mitoya beheld the same spectacle, and to him it seemed as if he could actually discern the individual coloring of the bombs. They seemed to be coming straight at him. In fact, he was pretty much correct in his assessment. While Amagai apparently remained standing, entranced by the scene, Mitoya had the good sense to hit the deck and cover his face. Further aft, Morinaga and his companions did likewise, as it was clear what was coming. For, despite Okada's valiant attempts, the end results were as inexorable as gravity—*Kaga* was simply crushed under an avalanche of explosives.

The fourth American plane to dive, that of Lieutenant Gallaher, was the first to draw blood, planting its 500-lb bomb on the flight deck aft, near the elevator. This bomb crashed into the crew spaces adjacent to the upper hangar deck and detonated, setting the berthing compartments afire. It also landed very near Morinaga and his companions, mowing down all but three of them (Yoshino Haruo being one of those spared), and probably doing the same to the gun crews in the starboard 25-mm AA galleries. Morinaga felt the searing heat on his upturned arm, but he dared not get up and run, for he could hear other bombs still coming down. From his perch on the air platform, Amagai saw the initial bomb disintegrate the ship's maintenance officer, Commander Yamazaki Torao, as he ran toward the island.[6]

Depending on where he was standing on the bridge, Captain Okada may not have even seen the first hit. He was still directing evasive maneuvers, and the Type 91 director tower behind the bridge blocked his view aft in any case. The next two planes missed, but then all hell broke loose. The seventh plane planted its bomb almost directly on the forward elevator, smashing it down into its well and then detonating in the fighter stowage spaces.[7] The frightful concussion blew out all the bridge windows. The helmsman remained at his post, as did Okada. But smoke and debris obscured all visibility from the bridge, and the helmsman could not control the carrier. Yelling into the voice tube, Okada quickly ordered that emergency steering be conducted from the engine spaces.

Rushing up to the bridge past Amagai, Mitoya found Okada looking somewhat stunned. Given that the ship was now unnavigable from the bridge, shouldn't the captain move below, he asked? But Okada replied vaguely that he would stay where he was, and Mitoya was told to check the damage aft and report back.[8] Perhaps Okada could get no response from the engineers below regarding taking over steering, and he wanted to alert them as to his desire to shift control of the ship.[9] Whatever the particulars, Mitoya was apparently dispatched on the errand. It was lucky for him that he was, because this would be Okada Jisaku's last order. Almost immediately thereafter, it seems clear that a bomb landed in front of, or more likely squarely on top of, *Kaga*'s command center.

Kaga's island, the first ever installed on a large Japanese carrier, had established the pattern for Japanese flattops. It was a diminutive affair. The air control post where Commander Amagai was stationed was a tiny platform located on the aft part of the structure. Situated a level above the flight deck, this post was overshadowed by the circular tower of the Type 91 director. From the air-control station, the bridge was entered by mounting a stairway that curved up around the right side of the director from the starboard rear. The bridge itself, perched some fifteen feet above the flight deck, was only about eleven feet on each side. It had windows on three sides, with open exits leading aft. Cramped and uncomfortable in any sort of bad weather, it more closely resembled a three-season porch than the nerve center of a 42,000-ton warship. It was utterly unprotected. The effects of a 500-lb bomb exploding anywhere in the vicinity can readily be imagined.

Across the water on *Akagi*, civilian cameraman Makishima Teiuchi had watched as *Kaga* had gone into her evasive turn. A few seconds later, large columns of water began erupting around her. He had been thinking that she might escape her tormentors, but then he witnessed orange flames suddenly blossoming around *Kaga*'s bridge. He groaned to himself, "She is beaten at last."[10] According to some reports, the bomb struck a fuel bowser parked directly in front of the island, causing it to explode and drenching the bridge in burning gasoline.[11] However, it is far more likely that a bomb hit the bridge itself. Indeed, the fuel cart may be entirely apocryphal—at least one *Kaga* aviator says that such devices were not even used,[12] and that he personally witnessed a bomb hitting the bridge.[13] Japan's official war history also specifically endorses the idea of a direct hit in this area.[14] Whatever the cause, the result was unarguable—*Kaga*'s command center was destroyed, the front half of the island shredded down to the bare steel skeleton and left blazing, and the ship's senior officers wiped out.[15] In fact, *Kaga* suffered more high-ranking officers killed than the other three carriers combined, and this early hit on the island was likely the reason for it.[16] Captain Okada Jisaku certainly died on the spot, and most likely his executive officer, Captain Kawaguchi Masao as well. With them went the ship's chief gunnery officer (Lt. Cdr. Miyano Toyosaburō), navigator (Cdr. Monden Ichiji), and communications officer (Lt. Cdr. Takahashi Hidekazu).[17]

Commander Amagai's position at the rear of *Kaga*'s island, shielded behind the bulk of the director, seems to explain his survival. Even so, he received wounds from the flying debris. Amagai shouted into the voice tube to the bridge but received no reply. Whether he made his way up to the bridge and discovered the scene of carnage, or simply put two and two together is unknown, but Amagai clearly realized that the command spaces were finished. He could see the flames licking the front of the structure.

In the interim, another bomb smacked home square amidships and a bit to port. Indeed, by now the situation was growing so confused that it was impossible to observe how many hits were occurring. The American planes were still coming down, perhaps more raggedly by this time, but still intent on taking pot shots at the now blazing carrier.[18] *Kaga* continued blundering around in a clockwise circle, beaten and blind, her dazed men waiting for the aerial pummeling to stop.

Maeda Takeshi had run off the flight deck almost as soon as the bombs began falling. The first hit had left him intact, along with Morinaga and Yoshino. He had what he thought was the good sense to duck below to the boat deck as the bombs kept coming down. Once there, he was sure, he would be under better cover. Unfortunately for him, one of the bombs plummeted into the ocean near at hand, just off the fantail to port.[19] The resulting explosion sent spray and bomb splinters blasting out across the boat deck. Maeda felt a searing heat in his leg and went down in a heap.

To the north, on *Hiryū*'s bridge, there were collective moans as *Kaga* burst into flames and began smoking heavily. *Hiryū* had tried to warn her, but it had all been for nothing. Her navigator, Commander Cho, later remarked, "It was like a horrible dream in slow motion; to see such a great carrier done in this easily." Almost immediately, though, the lookout started screaming in a loud voice that *Sōryū* and *Akagi* were under attack as well. Afraid that the man's near-hysterical demeanor would be bad for morale, Cho snapped at him to quiet down and use a lower voice. He could see, though, that the man was right. Cho tried to stay focused on driving *Hiryū* out of danger, as the torpedo plane attack was still coming in. But it was useless—everyone on the bridge was stunned into insensibility by the magnitude of the attack.[20]

At the time *Kaga* was attacked, *Sōryū* was still heading northwest. At 1024, though, she began a starboard turn to launch fighters.[21] Commmander Kanao Ryōichi, her gunnery officer, stood atop the carrier's island at the antiaircraft action station. He and his men were keeping an attentive lookout, especially toward the south, where VT-3's attack was unfolding. The sky was clouded with occasional patches of clear blue. Kanao could see no friendly CAP fighters; they had all been pulled away in other directions. Given that his ship was now, in effect, leading the carrier force, it was an uncomfortable feeling. In fact, there was something eerie in how calm the sky and sea looked.[22]

Below, on the bridge, *Sōryū*'s executive officer, Ōhara Hisashi, was watching the attack on *Kaga* unfold when the lookouts suddenly screamed from above "Enemy dive-bombers—hole in the clouds."[23] A lone aircraft broke into the sunlight. It was at an elevation of forty degrees, and was heading right to left to intercept *Sōryū*. A second plane quickly appeared 500 meters behind the first, which had already closed to within about 5,000 meters. On the air defense platform, Kanao shouted "Aim at the planes!" Quickly, the director and forward guns spun to face the attacker, as the director crew frantically tried to generate a solution.

Kanao yelled, "Commence firing!" even though the gun director was far from ready. But as he did so, he noticed that the starboard guns were about to reach their dead angles forward.[24] Grabbing the voice tube, he yelled down to the helmsman, "Give me left full rudder immediately!" Befitting her reputation as a responsive handler, *Sōryū* quickly began turning back to port to unmask her starboard batteries. The American dive-bombers—three or four of them—continued to close, still flying level. They were now at a 50-degree angle from the bow, approximately 4,000 meters away and turning toward the carrier. *Sōryū*'s 25-mm mounts were quicker to respond than her forward five-inch battery and began blazing away at the attackers. With their wings flashing in the sunlight, one after another, the American Dauntlesses finally pushed over into perfect dives.

What Kanao apparently didn't see was the other two elements of American aircraft, which were also attacking *Sōryū* from the port bow and astern. In other words, *Sōryū* apparently suffered a serious breakdown of her fire-control processes. Kanao was the gunnery officer—if he or the lookouts near him didn't see these planes, then the guns under his command as gunnery officer couldn't very well defend the ship against them, either. It is possible that *Sōryū*'s Type 94 director tower masked his view aft, or simply that the sky arcs for the two 12-cm spotting glasses facing aft (which were located a deck lower) were lousy. The net result, though, appears to have been that *Sōryū* continued to charge around in a left-hand circle, unaware that several more aircraft were attacking from different angles.

Kanao, however, was focused on the problem at hand. He was infuriated that the five-inch mounts had still not opened up on the American aircraft, and the 25-mm guns didn't seem to be hitting, either.[25] Angrily, he watched as the lead American plane began pulling out of its dive. And then he saw the bomb. Kanao ducked instinctively, looking for some sort of safety, but there was precious little to hide behind on the top of *Sōryū*'s tiny island.

The impact blew *Sōryū*'s exec across the bridge. Commander Ōhara didn't find the sensation particularly painful—it felt more like a steambath than anything else. Yet, as soon as he tried to regain his footing, the other men on the bridge immediately began applying towels to his face. He realized that he must have been burned more badly than he had supposed.[26] Still, Ōhara was lucky, because the bridge structure had at least protected the command staff somewhat—unlike their opposite numbers on board *Kaga,* they were all still alive. This could only have been the result of the distance from the impact point of the bomb, because *Sōryū*'s island was a near twin of *Kaga*'s.

In his exposed position, Commander Kanao's first sensation of the hit came from his hands, which felt like they had been skinned.[27] The nape of his neck stung as if an ice pick had been rammed into it. He realized that he had been flashburned. Luckily, Kanao's steel helmet had provided him with some measure of protection. His eyes were still shut, and when he tried opening them, something blazing red was floating hazily just in front of him. He closed them again. The burning sensation passed. Pulling himself off the glass-strewn deck and standing up, he discovered that he was alone. The other lookouts, the director crew, the communications talker—all of them were either dead at their posts or missing, blown overboard by the explosion. He vaguely remembered hearing moans. Had they been the last thin cries of his comrades as they died? The AA director at the rear of the bridge was crushed down against the deck. Kanao realized that it was only by sheer luck that he had survived.

Several decks almost directly below, Petty Officer Mori Jūzo was lounging in the pilot's ready room, which was located on the AA battery deck, a level below the island and on the starboard side. Mori was still waiting to be debriefed from the morning's mission and was passing the time eating rice balls.[28] Suddenly, the battle bugle had blown over the intercom, followed by a message that *Kaga* was under attack. Some of the other pilots ran out of the ready room up to the flight deck, but Mori stayed. He and about a dozen other men continued their conversation. Without warning, there came an enormous explosion, and the ship lurched to starboard. The first bomb landed very near the No. 1 AA gun (located at the starboard bow, forward of the island)[29] and demolished everything around it. The ready room lay not forty feet from the impact point—the forward bulkhead simply disintegrated, and flames poured into the compartment. Mori and his companions turned and ran for it, making their way aft toward what they hoped was safety.

Back atop the island, Commander Kanao marveled that he was still intact. As he looked down from his vantage, he saw that the rest of the ship was in pretty bad shape. A second bomb had landed in the middle of the flight deck and penetrated deeply into the lower hangar. Smoke was already pouring from the opening.[30] Just then, the third and last bomb landed on the flight deck aft with a flash like magnesium. Kanao flinched; the pain in his eyes was beyond imagination. Temporarily blinded, he thought he was going to die.

Below in *Sōryū*'s port engine room, Engineering First-Class Special Service Lieutenant Naganuma Michitarō felt and heard the tremendous initial explosion even above the roar of the ship's equipment. The whole ship trembled, and the vibrations caused a deep resonance in his body. Another explosion followed, and then a third. The engineers shouted out to each other. What had happened?

At that moment, *Sōryū*'s turbines went dead so abruptly that the men simply stared at the engines uncomprehendingly.[31] It was as if the ship had been stabbed through the heart. From further forward, someone yelled, "The boiler room was hit!" Another asked, "Was it a torpedo?" It was not an unreasonable question, given the ferocious nature of the initial explosions. In fact, the deep-penetrating second bomb had ruptured the steam pipes in the boiler spaces, scalding nearly all the crewmen there to death.[32] Topside, a huge cloud of white smoke was jetting from *Sōryū*'s midships.[33] Glancing down at his watch, Naganuma noticed it was 1030 right on the dot. He looked grimly around at his comrades. What would happen to them now?

Topside, the light in Commander Kanao's eyes slowly abated. He saw the entire flight deck from the island on back enveloped in a sheet of smoke. The fighters on deck were in pieces and burning. The explosions had also killed many sailors, including deck handlers and gun crews. Their bodies were strewn about in little white and tan piles. Kanao stood there, petrified, and wondered if he was the sole survivor in the sea of fire now engulfing *Sōryū*.

If the difference between victory and defeat was narrow at Midway, then nowhere was fate more poised on a razor's edge than the attack on *Akagi*. Unlike *Sōryū* and *Kaga*, which were both assaulted by a dozen or more bombers, *Akagi* was attacked by a grand total of three, and then only because of the quick thinking of Lt. Richard Best. Best had been about to dive *Kaga* with his entire squadron, but at the exact moment of pushover, he had witnessed McClusky's squadron heading in as well. Best managed to pull out of his dive, but almost the entirety of his squadron went with McClusky. Best, with Lt.(jg) Edwin J. Kroeger and Ens. Frederick T. Weber hanging off either wing, had maintained altitude and watched the outcome of the attack. Seeing that *Kaga* had obviously been smashed, Best decided to attack the other large carrier near at hand with his element. Such a meager force hardly constituted the sort of attack that would normally have been deemed necessary to destroy the flagship of *Kidō Butai*. But Best was determined to attack with what he had.

Best's group didn't have time to do things "by the book." Forming up for a sequential attack was standard doctrine, but instead Best's element attacked in the "V" formation they were already in.[34] He headed north briefly, then reefed his men into a right-hand turn to dive on the target. Best was in the center, his wingmen perhaps 75–100 feet on either side. The Japanese also noted that the Americans didn't appear to dive as steeply as *Kaga*'s assailants had.[35] It may well be that Best had lost some altitude during his abortive dive on that ship. As they swooped down, approaching *Akagi* from her port side, Best aimed for what he thought was *Akagi*'s island, but was actually her large, protruding stack on the starboard side. One of his wingmen aimed at the aircraft spotted on deck, the other chose the large, red *hinomaru* painted on *Akagi*'s flight deck near the bow. Best's men must have held their formation all the way down, for their bombs landed in the same rough "V" formation.

Incredible as it may seem, having just observed the attack on *Kaga*, *Akagi* was seemingly caught nearly unprepared by Best's sudden onset. It may be that Nagumo and his staff had judged that they were in the clear, at least for the moment. *Kaga*'s assailants were attacking roughly east to west, and away from them. But VT-3's attack was still developing to the northeast, and *Akagi* didn't want to get entangled with them, either. Thus, no one on board the flagship appears to have noticed Best until his trio was nearly atop *Akagi*. On the flight deck, PO1c Kimura had just been given the launch signal, and his Zero was heading down the deck and into the air. Suddenly, shouts rang out—enemy dive-bombers overhead! On the island, Commander Fuchida threw himself behind a bulkhead covered with a protective cloth mantelet.[36]

Like both *Kaga* and *Sōryū*, *Akagi*'s fate was in her own hands as far as AA fire was concerned. The only weapons that could be brought to bear in her defense were her own, and perhaps the tiny automatic battery of her plane guard destroyer, *Nowaki*. *Akagi*'s 25-mm guns began spitting out tracers at the three attackers. There was precious little opportunity to bring the portside trio of 4.7-inch mounts into action—there was no time to generate a good fire control solution.

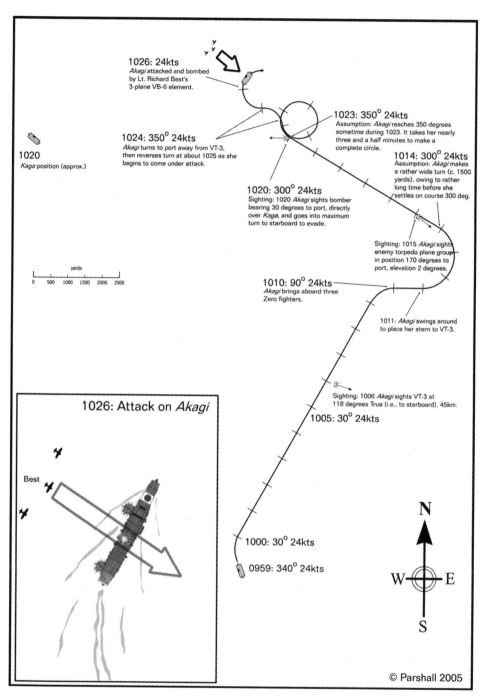

1026: 24kts
Akagi attacked and bombed by Lt. Richard Best's 3-plane VB-6 element.

1020
Kaga position (approx.)

1024: 350° 24kts
Akagi turns to port away from VT-3, then reverses turn at about 1025 as she begins to come under attack.

1023: 350° 24kts
Assumption: *Akagi* reaches 350 degrees sometime during 1023. It takes her nearly three and a half minutes to make a complete circle.

1014: 300° 24kts
Assumption: *Akagi* makes a rather wide turn (c. 1500 yards), owing to rather long time before she settles on course 300 deg.

1020: 300° 24kts
Sighting: 1020 *Akagi* sights bomber bearing 30 degrees to port, directly over *Kaga*, and goes into maximum turn to starboard to evade.

Sighting: 1015 *Akagi* sights enemy torpedo plane group in position 170 degrees to port, elevation 2 degrees.

yards
0   500   1000   1500   2000   2500

1010: 90° 24kts
Akagi brings aboard three Zero fighters.

1011: *Akagi* swings around to place her stern to VT-3.

Sighting: 1006 *Akagi* sights VT-3 at 118 degrees True (i.e., to starboard), 45km.

1005: 30° 24kts

1026: Attack on *Akagi*

Best

1000: 30° 24kts

0959: 340° 24kts

N
W — E
S

© Parshall 2005

13-2: The attack against *Akagi*. This figure shows the probable course track of *Akagi* from 0959 to when she was attacked at 1026 by Lt. Richard Best's three-plane element.

Like all Japanese captains, Aoki relied on the helm to save his ship. As Captain Okada had recently discovered, though, evading thirty-knot torpedoes was one thing—avoiding 250-knot dive-bombers piloted by professionals was quite another. Aoki put his ship into a maximum starboard turn, presenting his beam to the Americans—the most favorable attitude he could achieve under the circumstances. *Akagi* described a huge right-hand circle, heading first north and then back around to the east.

Nagumo's flagship very nearly escaped, and by all rights should have gotten away scot-free. If the element of surprise had been slightly less complete, her AA fire (or that of *Nowaki*) a little more effective, her maneuvers a little more violent, or the aim of her attackers a little less precise, *Akagi* might well have dodged the trio of bombs aimed at her, with incalculable consequences for the outcome of the battle. Had she emerged unscathed from this attack, her air group would have been added to *Hiryū*'s forthcoming strike, with potentially dire results for the Americans. Yet against all odds, *Akagi* received her mortal wound.

Most accounts credit the Americans with two hits and a near miss on the flagship, but on closer examination, this tally must be revised downward to a single direct hit. Almost all sources agree that the first of the three bombs slammed into the water about five to ten meters to port, and forward of the island (which on *Akagi* was on the port side of the vessel).[37] The resulting geyser towered high over the bridge (itself some eighty feet above the waterline), carrying away the radio antennae atop the island, and drenching everyone on the bridge with a flood of dirty seawater. Within the surreal forms of the deluge, Commander Sasabe thought he saw the apparition of his mother's face.[38]

The third bomb is widely credited with hitting the aft portion of the flight deck, but, in fact, it did not quite do so.[39] Civilian newsreel cameraman Makishima, who was on *Akagi*'s flight deck filming the attack on *Kaga* and the flagship, states explicitly that, while personnel located on her bridge might have deemed it a hit, in fact the bomb almost grazed the edge of the flight deck and plunged into the water alongside the stern.[40] The resulting geyser bent the edge of the flight deck upward, thus creating the illusion of a hit.

Numerous secondary sources describe huge fires breaking out as a result of the aft "hit," but this actually was very unlikely for several reasons. First, there were no planes currently in this area. *Akagi* had only CAP fighters on her deck at the time of the attack. While Dick Best noted during his dive that *Akagi*'s Zeros were taking off from fairly far aft,[41] they still would not have been spotted anywhere near the aft edge of the flight deck where the bomb came down. This is because the portion of *Akagi*'s flight deck in the vicinity of the "hit" was literally rounded down (to make landing easier) and wasn't used for spotting because of its relatively steep incline.

Even if a bomb *had* hit the flight deck in this area, it had absolutely no chance of carrying into the hangar deck and starting a fire there either, because in this portion of the ship there *wasn't* any hangar deck. The rearmost 125 feet of *Akagi*'s flight deck, from the aft edge of the rear elevator all the way to the stern, was held up by four enormous steel supports. Underneath the wooden flight deck itself there was nothing but steel girders, an overhead crane, and air space. Even if a bomb hit the flight deck squarely here, the deck would have initiated its fuse and the bomb would have detonated in midair above the boat deck and fantail. None of the primary Japanese sources mention any such thing. Furthermore, a bomb could not have carried down through the sixty-odd feet of air space, through the boat deck, and then through *Akagi*'s main armored deck to detonate in her engine and steering spaces—the fuse would have exploded the bomb long before. Indeed, the general-purpose high-explosive bombs used by the Americans in the attack, with their relatively light cases, would not have penetrated *Akagi*'s armored deck under any circumstances. In a nutshell, then, with no planes on the flight deck in the area, and no hangar deck below, there could not have been any fires of significance as a result of this hit. The Nagumo Report directly supports this view, describing the damage aft as not being fatal and further elaborates "damage: several holes to after deck, 1 emergency personnel killed."[42] This is hardly the sort of description one associates with the veritable holocaust on the flight deck often attributed to the hit aft. Nor does it match the very heavy and well-documented casualties suffered on *Sōryū* and *Kaga*'s hangar decks as the result of such blows.[43]

Thus, the first and third bombs were misses, with the third landing very close aboard indeed. It was the second bomb, landing at the aft edge of the middle elevator, which doomed *Akagi*. This weapon was almost unquestionably aimed by Best himself. He was a noted dive-bomber pilot and had a reputation for both boldness and consummate skill. In the words of his backseater, Aviation Chief Radioman James F. Murray, "Nobody pushed his dive steeper or held it longer than Dick."[44] Given the "V" formation Best's element dived in, it is almost inconceivable that the trajectories of the bombs could have crossed in midair. Furthermore, from what we know about how the bombs landed in relation to the ship and each other, that is, in a rough "V" pattern themselves, it is likewise almost a certainty that the center plane in the "V" dropped the bomb that hit dead center on *Akagi*. That plane was piloted by Lieutenant Best.

His 1,000-lb payload sliced through the flight deck and exploded in the upper hangar in the midst of the *kankō* parked there. To Commander Sasabe, *Akagi*'s navigator, the hit felt deceptively gentle. Fuchida, who was also near the bridge, remembered the bomb landing with a crash and a blinding flash. A blast of warm air washed over him. Yet the explosion was apparently also powerful enough to hurl aircraft over the side of the flight deck.[45]

Finally, just after 1035, VT-3's torpedo aircraft reached a position where they could begin a series of runs against Yamaguchi's flagship that would last until 1040.[46] Thus, VT-3's attack, although it was initiated well before the American dive-bomber attack, did not actually reach its conclusion until slightly after the dive-bombers had struck their respective targets. *Hiryū,* far from being immune by virtue of geographic distance, was now suddenly in the thick of things.

As before, Lt. Nagayasu's batteries began blazing away with everything they had, sending streams of tracers zipping out to greet the incoming American aircraft.[47] Only five American aircraft were left to make drops on *Hiryū,* doing so from between

600 and 800 yards out.[48] Not surprisingly, though, the TBD's drop angles were lousy. One of the fish, as the result of a faulty release mechanism, simply cartwheeled into the ocean, while another broached and ran along the surface like a small speedboat.[49] *Hiryū* apparently had no problem evading any of them. As they dropped, several of the American torpedo planes flashed by *Hiryū*'s bow, where they were taken under heavy AA and CAP fire again. Several were splashed shortly thereafter. In all, Zeros and perhaps antiaircraft fire ultimately accounted for ten of Massey's twelve aircraft.

Whether *Hiryū*'s AA contributed to the final demise of some of VT-3's remnants is unknown. However, it contributed to the demise of one Zero at least—that of Lieutenant Fujita. Hit by friendly fire while pursuing the Americans into the heart of the formation, his Zero had quickly caught fire. From *Hiryū*'s bridge, Lieutenant Nagayasu saw Fujita's plane hit and careen toward the water. Nagayasu was sure that the pilot had been killed. Fujita, however, was extraordinarily lucky. He was already at very low altitude—200 meters—but he climbed out of the cockpit and popped his chute, which fortuitously opened just before he hit the water.[50]

And then, just as quickly as they had come, the Americans were gone, roaring off toward the east, hugging the waves to escape retribution from both guns and fighters. The CAP fighters, many of whom had been engaged with VT-3 and who were now chasing the attackers away from the fleet, could only catch peripheral glimpses of the horror unfolding behind them. And under mounting pillars of smoke, the bewildered crews of three great ships turned to face the implacable foe that all sailors dread—fire.

14

Fire and Death—1030–1100

WW II–era warships were marvelously flammable. Anyone who has been on board a ship of that vintage will have noticed that one of the prevalent odors present is that of petroleum distillates, in the form of lubricants, solvents, gasoline, and thousands of tons of fuel oil. Added to this, of course, was ammunition for the ship's guns, which was stored primarily in the magazines, but smaller quantities of which were kept in ready storage lockers near the guns for quick access during an attack. In contrast to today's warships, oil-based paints were used extensively. Wiring ways were filled with insulation that could ignite at high temperature, as could piping insulation (which in Japanese warships was often made of wood). Damage-control lockers themselves contained wood beams for shoring, and additional shoring material was usually stowed in the overheads of companionways and anywhere else sufficient space could be found.

Warships were (and still are) full of paper—reports, forms, charts, manuals, and blueprints. Belowdecks, there was cotton bedding for the crew (which numbered between 1,100 and 1,700 men for each of the four carriers), as well as their clothing and personal effects. For the comfort of the men, Japanese berthing spaces often had false wooden flooring over the steel decks, with floor mats and wooden messing tables stored underneath. The galleys contained cooking oil, grains, and combustible foodstuffs. Grease deposits could be found in the stoves and ventilator ducts leading from these spaces. The sick bay stored ether and other volatile liquids. The ship's laundry contained uniforms and rags, as well as lint deposits in the dryers and ventilators. All Japanese shipboard furniture was wooden, including chairs, tables, workbenches and so on.[1] Wooden furniture made perfect sense for a country that had to import practically all its iron ore, and hence reserved steel for truly essential items. The net result is that warships of the day burned easily and well.

Aircraft carriers compounded these basic problems with specialized ones of their own. For one thing, their flight decks alone represented anywhere from 50 to 125 tons of combustible wood.[2] Far and away the worst fire hazard for carriers, though, was their aircraft fueling system. Carriers typically could refuel aircraft on both the hangar decks and the flight deck. A typical Japanese carrier had a dozen fueling points for both high-octane and normal-octane aviation gasoline on the flight deck, ten more on the upper hangar deck, and eight on the lower hangar deck.[3] A series of vertical fuel mains cross-connected the forward and aft aviation gasoline tanks to horizontal petrol lines (one apiece level for high- and normal-octane fuels) that ran around the circumference of each hangar deck.[4] Vertical risers fed the fueling stations located in the tubs along the edge of the flight deck. Thus, each carrier was crisscrossed by a web of fuel lines, each of which was filled during flight operations with highly flammable liquids. Furthermore, the nature of the cross-connections in the system made it likely that problems in one area of the ship would be carried to unaffected areas via the fuel lines themselves, and potentially all the way to the main avgas storage tanks.

The storage tanks were isolated from the ship's other spaces by cofferdam compartments filled with CO_2 gas, so as to insulate them from sparks and other hazards. However, the tanks and cofferdams on Japanese carriers were notable for being integrated into the actual structure of the ship. This meant that shock stresses applied to the outside of the hull were directly communicated inward to the avgas tanks, making them particularly vulnerable to cracking and leaking as a result of combat damage. In later years, the Japanese would fill these voids with concrete to try and minimize this hazard, but at the time of Midway, these structural deficiencies were evidently not appreciated.[5]

The second major complication with carrier design and operation was that of moving and stowing aircraft ordnance. Unlike a battleship or cruiser, whose ammunition-handling arrangements were flash tight and protected behind the heavy armor of the barbette and turret, carriers (particularly Japanese ones) were not provided with anywhere near the same degree of protection. Yet, the weapons being trundled about were in some senses more lethal than a battleship shell. General-purpose and semi armor-piercing bombs contain a much higher relative percentage of explosive than an armor-piercing shell, most of whose weight is comprised by the heavy metal casing necessary to pierce armor. A GP bomb can be nearly 50 percent explosive by weight. Against a lightly armored target, bombs cause much more damage proportionately than a shell. Unfortunately, this is equally true of the interior of one's own carrier, should such a bomb detonate there. As a result, carriers must take every possible precaution to prevent such events from occurring.

Japanese carriers typically stowed their aircraft ordnance in two bomb rooms fore and aft, as well as a torpedo magazine located adjacent to one of the bomb rooms (the location varied from ship to ship). Armor protection over the magazines for most Japanese carriers was minimal. There was always one, and sometimes several hoists leading upward from each bomb room. However, flashtight doors were apparently not fitted over the upper apertures of the hoists.[6] It can be seen that these arrangements would be barely adequate under normal peacetime operating conditions. If a large fire were present on the hangar deck, they might well be disastrous. With such flimsy precautions, it was imperative to follow proper ordnance-handling techniques, promptly stowing bombs and torpedoes back below when not in use.

All the navies of the time recognized the potentially lethal nature of fires and explosions on their carriers and took precautions to prevent them. The primary Japanese method of fighting fires hinged on isolating the conflagration and then actively extinguishing the blaze. All Japanese hangar decks were capable of being subdivided across their width by track-mounted, rolling fireproof screens. These were placed on either side of each of the elevator wells. Larger compartments were also divided in the middle. Thus, several subcompartments could be created at need to isolate a damaged or burning section of the hangar. If the screens were damaged, however, there were few physical obstacles to prevent fires from sweeping the length of the hangar.

Both upper and lower hangar decks were equipped with foam systems, which sprayed a mixture of seawater and soap bubbles onto the deck. The nozzles for these systems were placed at 1.5 and 2 meters above the deck, and were fed by fire mains that girdled the deck, much the same way as the fuel lines. Fire hoses, fed from ring mains powered by pump rooms deep below in the ship's machinery spaces, were also available on the hangar decks and flight decks. However, unlike American carriers, which could divide their mains into numerous segments, Japanese mains were simply divided port and starboard.[7] This meant that a single hit could knock out half the water supply on the ship. Furthermore, older vessels often used cast-iron water pipes, which were much more vulnerable to shattering than steel pipes.[8] As a result, Japanese carriers were much less likely to emerge with firefighting water pressure still available after taking a large bomb hit.

On the lower hangar deck, where explosive fuel vapors were most likely to accumulate, an additional CO_2 "flooding" system was deployed. A perforated metal pipe running the length of the overhead of each lower hangar deck section could be used to discharge CO_2 and extinguish flames. The CO_2 tanks for this system were stored at the bottom of the elevator wells. Sufficient tankage was provided to displace 18 percent of the total volume of the lower hangar space. This system depended on a tight seal of the fireproof partitions; a significant leak in the curtains or the bulkheads would admit enough oxygen to cause the system to fail. Even if successful, it was essentially a "one-shot" deal; once the CO_2 tanks were discharged, they could not be readily replenished. What the CO_2 system did was buy time for the firefighting teams. With the fire temporarily abated, the men could rush into a space and begin applying water to cool the debris, thus potentially bringing the fire to a halt in a large section of the hangar all at once.

All of these mechanisms were to some degree hampered by the construction of Japanese hangars.[9] Fundamentally, the two variables that affect hangar deck design are whether it is enclosed or unenclosed (in other words, whether it can be opened readily to the outside air), and whether the flight deck above it is armored or unarmored. Each of the three major carrier forces in the Second World War adopted different philosophies on this topic. The Royal Navy enclosed their hangars on all sides with storerooms, ready rooms, and other compartments, and placed a heavy armored deck over the top that composed a significant portion of the ship's longitudinal strength (a "strength deck" in the parlance). This had the advantage of directly protecting the hangar from bomb hits, but it also carried with it serious penalties. First, the addition of a heavy armored deck high in the ship's structure made limiting the size of the deck itself crucial as well as limiting the overall height of the ship. Dual hangar deck arrangements (i.e., two hangars stacked one atop the other) were impossible in such designs, because they would have raised topweight unacceptably (and thereby destabilized the ship). The fact that elevator openings also had to penetrate the strength deck meant that these openings had to be kept to a minimum in both number and size. This had a negative effect on aircraft handling and on how quickly the carrier could spot a strike for launch. As a result, Royal Navy carriers carried relatively small air wings. British fleet carriers deployed around 48 aircraft, in comparison to the 60–100 that the U.S. and Japanese Navies operated from their big flattops.

The U.S. Navy had opted for an unarmored flight deck on its carriers, and designed its ships so that the hangar deck was the strength deck. The lighter flight deck structure and lack of compartments surrounding the hangar allowed the hangar itself to be relatively large. Furthermore, the hangar was open on the sides in several locations, although it could be closed off from the elements by means of rolling metal screens. While these screens were not completely light tight (and therefore presented a hazard to a ship in blacked-out steaming conditions) or vapor tight, they could also be rolled up to expose the hangar completely. Thus, American carriers had the advantage of being able to refuel and warm up aircraft on the hangar deck if need be. Dangerous items in the hangar, such as explosive ordnance, could be expeditiously disposed of by simply shoving them out the openings and over the side. These same openings allowed escort ships to contribute directly to firefighting by letting them spray water directly into the hangar deck. It was recognized that the unarmored flight deck (though relatively easy to repair) exposed the hangar below to bomb damage, and there is no question that the Americans in some cases paid heavily for this design philosophy (particularly against the late-war *kamikaze* threat). The relative merits of armored vs. unarmored can be argued ad nauseam, but the bottom line is that the Americans were firmly committed to the proposition that an aircraft carrier was a power projection asset and that power projection was impossible without an adequately sized air group. Given these imperatives, the USN was apparently willing to accept the risks attendant in their designs. And it must be admitted, whatever their failings, that American carriers as a whole were highly successful during the course of the Pacific war.

The Japanese chose a design direction that in retrospect clearly afforded the worst of both the U.S. Navy's and Royal Navy's philosophies. However, this was not readily apparent before the war started. Japanese carrier designers favored enclosed hangars à la the Royal Navy. However, to facilitate the operation of an adequately sized air wing, most Japanese fleet carriers had at least two hangar levels; upper and lower. The hangars were not open to the elements beyond the provision of portholes in some locations and used forced air ventilation systems. For this reason, aircraft were not warmed up in the hangars, although refueling was performed there.[10] The practical effect of these arrangements in terms of damage control were potentially dire. Just like putting a firecracker in a tin pot, any detonation in an enclosed space tends to magnify the explosion. Japanese hangars were prone to the same phenomenon.

Japanese warships of this era often suffered from overweight and stability problems. Moreover, with their dual hangar configurations, some Japanese carriers had fairly tall profiles as well.[11] The dual hangar deck design meant that the Japanese had to reduce topside weight by any means possible. An armored flight deck à la British carrier designs was simply out of the question. Gun tubs were supported by braces and struts that would have looked flimsy to a Western observer, and protruding platforms in some cases carried perforated decks—all in an attempt to reduce weight. In sum, Japanese carriers were suspect from a structural standpoint, and were ill prepared to absorb damage and continue functioning. This was particularly true of *Sōryū* and *Hiryū,* which did not benefit from being constructed atop a relatively sturdy capital ship hull, as *Akagi* and *Kaga* were.

The Japanese suspected some of these weaknesses. In the design of the newer *Shōkaku*-class ships, for instance, the hangars contained bulkheads that were designed to be blown outward to vent the blast overpressures, albeit the design did not perform as advertised.[12] Yet at its root, the Japanese Navy was wedded to the primacy of the offense. They believed in power projection no less fervently than the American Navy did. But because of their design philosophies, Imperial Naval vessels were notably less damage resistant than those of their opponents. Now, after having suffered a shattering attack at the hands of the enemy, these weaknesses were about to be exposed in the most graphic manner imaginable.

Kaga was the first, and in many ways the worst hit of the three. At the time of the bombing attack, Lt. Kunisada Yoshio, *Kaga*'s assistant damage-control officer, had been belowdecks near the hangar, discussing the AA action with some other crewmen.[13] When the bombs came in, the noise was like battleship guns firing. The ship trembled hard. Soon after, the loudspeaker barked that two bombs had hit near the rear and there was a fire. Immediately, the lieutenant ordered all the men near him to grab fire extinguishers and begin to combat the blaze and sent messengers to roust further men to do the same. The men ran off to the hangar deck to carry out his orders. Kunisada himself left to gather more sailors, rounding up about twenty men in short order. He then started making his way back toward the hangar deck.

The conditions in *Kaga*'s hangars immediately after the bombing were horrific beyond description. Bodies and pieces of bodies of *Kaga*'s armorers and mechanics lay strewn everywhere among the wreckage of her aircraft. In the open air, a 1,000-pound general-purpose bomb has a 50 percent chance of killing anyone standing within a thirty-foot radius of the blast center.[14] Inside the confines of the hangar deck, these lethal effects were greatly magnified. *Kaga* lost 269 mechanics on 4 June, most of whom undoubtedly died on the upper hangar deck in the first few minutes of her ordeal.[15] Mechanics, plane handlers, and armorers alike were slaughtered by the score—blown apart, immolated, crushed under the aircraft they had been servicing, or mown down by shrapnel as they crouched on the bare metal deck, seeking shelter where there was none. In the swelter of the hangar, laboring heavily while pushing planes and ordnance around, many of the men had stripped down to shorts and short-sleeved cotton shirts. These men, even if they lived through the bombing, were likely to have received flash burns. Taken together, the initial hits on *Kaga* probably killed or badly wounded almost every man in the upper hangar.

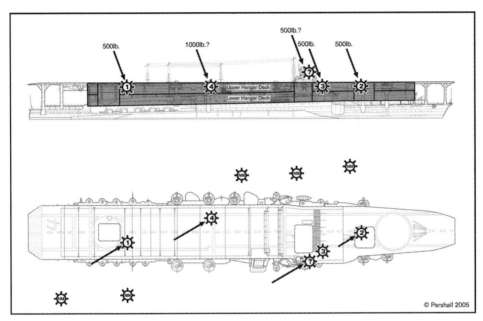

14-1: Known hit locations on *Kaga*.

The few men who survived there were undoubtedly shocked into near insensibility. The incredible noise of the explosions had been stunning even to men standing on the bridge—the noise level in the hangars had been literally deafening. The general cacophony, in combination with the explosions, fire, and rapid spread of smoke, meant that many of the men were incapable of action, either to save the ship or themselves. They would have wandered aimlessly, unsure of whether or how to escape the conflagration. Many were crawling. Others, perhaps many of the wounded, would have been unable to move far in any case. Even for those still mobile, the difference between life and death would have hinged on the slightest of happenstances. With the fires blazing up in all directions, running into the wrong burning corridor, or finding a hatch or companionway blocked in front of you meant death. Shutting oneself into a smaller compartment, even if it seemed to offer temporary sanctuary from the blaze in the hangars, brought death as well. Having the good fortune to have left the hangar for a quick trip to the head or to run an errand belowdecks, might have meant life.

Though Lieutenant Kunisada may not have realized it, with at least four hits placed along the length of *Kaga*'s upper hangar, any realistic hope of containing the ship's damage had been destroyed.[16] Japanese damage-control practice was to isolate the damaged area and fight the fire locally. Now isolation of a single problem area was no longer possible. Instead, *Kaga*'s hangar had been transformed into a time bomb. The concussions of the initial hits destroyed both her port and starboard fire mains, because three of the bombs hit within feet of the hangar bulkheads along which the mains ran. To make matters worse, the emergency generator for *Kaga*'s fire pumps was located, rather incredibly, on the upper hangar deck on the port forward five-inch gun sponson. This placed the generator some thirty feet away from the impact of the second bomb, almost certainly ensuring its outright destruction by fragments.[17] The first explosions likely killed or wounded many of the men in the damage-control stations scattered about the hangar deck. The fireproof roller curtains were probably open to facilitate easier movement of aircraft and ordnance. Even if the curtains were being used, several of them would have been destroyed immediately by the hits near the forward and aft elevators. Her CO_2 suppression system could not be employed.[18] Thus, *Kaga*'s firefighting capabilities were rendered null and void from the outset.

Aft of Kunisada, Warrant Officer Morinaga had discovered this already.[19] Hearing shouts that the hangar was on fire, he left the flight deck and headed below. When he arrived, though, the situation was already totally out of control. None of the fire mains were working, so he and some other men organized a bucket brigade from the ship's latrines, which surely must have been one of the most pathetic images in a day replete with grim irony and empty gestures. Next, he tried throwing inflammables overboard, but that proved futile as well—everything was on fire already.

Worse yet, *Kaga*'s hangar was littered with an incredible array of munitions. Between the arming of the first and second strike waves and the inability to stow the land-attack weapons, Kunisada would later estimate that *Kaga*'s hangars probably contained twenty torpedoes (240-kilogram warhead), twenty-eight 800-kilogram bombs, and forty 250-kilogram bombs.[20] This appalling total of nearly 80,000 pounds of explosives lay scattered everywhere, on aircraft, on bomb carts, or simply shoved against the hangar bulkheads to get them out of the way. The forward bomb hits both landed within spitting distance of the ordnance lift, which was abreast the midships aircraft elevator. The area around this lift was piled with 800-kilogram bombs waiting to be sent back below to the magazines. With the hangars fully enclosed, none of these weapons could now be jettisoned. The bombs were heavy enough, but the torpedoes were absolutely impossible to move. They weighed roughly 1,800 pounds apiece and were most likely affixed to an airplane to boot. With the elevators destroyed or inaccessible, there was no possibility of carrying them topside and heaving them overboard. And there was no way to move them out of harm's way on the hangar deck, since there were fires burning literally everywhere.

Far worse, though, was the fact that the American attack had caught *Kaga* with her fueling system unsecured. Her fuel mains had almost certainly been ruptured in one or more places by the hits. Even if only the Type 97s and Zeros were fully gassed, there were still almost 10,000 gallons of fuel sloshing about in the aircraft, in addition to what was now pouring from the fuel lines.[21] Freely flowing aviation fuel being dumped from many sources meant that the fuel was being distributed in large slicks all over the hangar deck. Not all of it was on fire yet. But in the presence of high ambient temperatures, aviation gasoline was now vaporizing at a prodigious rate. Though no one probably knew it, a catastrophic explosion on board *Kaga* could not be long in coming.

Much like *Kaga,* the situation on board *Sōryū* was beyond redemption in a matter of moments. The American bombs had landed almost perfectly so as to cause the

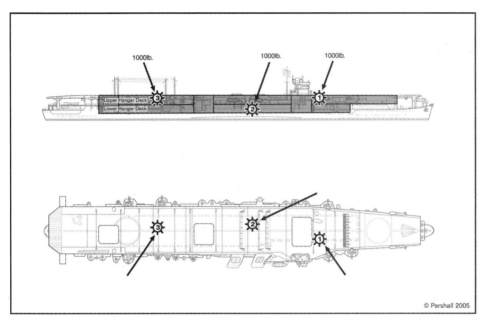

14-2: Known hit locations on *Sōryū*.

maximum destruction possible. *Sōryū*'s hangars were divided into three fireproof bays, but *Yorktown*'s bombers had neatly deposited a 1,000-pound bomb into each of them, destroying any possibility of localizing the blazes. The first hit had demolished the starboard side of the hangar, undoubtedly starting fires in the five-inch ammo ready room for mounts No. 1 and No. 3. For some reason, the second hit had penetrated very deeply, slicing through the upper hangar to slam into the lower hangar, into the midst of *Sōryū*'s *kanbaku* squadron. In the process, it had demolished the officers quarters on the port side of the hangar and blown fragments through the starboard bulkhead protecting the boiler uptakes, destroying them and taking the boilers off line.[22] The third bomb landed almost directly on the No. 4 arrestor wire, detonating in the upper hangar amidst the Type 97 *kankō* rearming from the Midway strike. This hit destroyed numerous aircraft and engulfed the rear of the hangar in fire. Thus, at the end of the attack, *Sōryū* found herself in a similar but worse state (if such were possible) than *Kaga*—not only afire from stem to stern, but also having suffered damage to both levels of the hangar. With fires already blazing on the lower hangar deck, and with no real way of fighting them in the boiler uptakes, workshops, and electrical trunks located just below the area of the hit, the overheads of boiler rooms Nos. 3, 5, and 6 would soon be directly exposed to the blaze. Equally as bad, *Sōryū*'s lighter construction meant that the hits did immediate, and probably irreparable, structural damage.

The decimation of *Sōryū*'s hangar crews was part and parcel with the terrible physical damage meted out to the ship. The horrific butchery inflicted in *Kaga*'s hangars was replicated here in full measure. Being the smallest of the Midway carriers, the slaughter was probably even worse. A total of 419 of *Sōryū*'s mechanics, maintenance personnel, and seamen died this day, and the immolation of the hangar decks in the first minutes undoubtedly accounted for the bulk of these casualties. Indeed, a third of *Sōryū*'s crew may well have been dead by the time the last of the American dive-bombers completed its attack.

None of *Sōryū*'s command staff, of course, could know the particulars of the disaster that had befallen their ship, but atop the island, Gunnery Officer Kanao could tell that the situation was grave. The ship was already smoking from stem to stern, thick vapors pouring forth from the bombs' wounds and spreading in black sheets across the casualties lying on the flight deck. As he cast his gaze southward, he could see *Akagi*. She was still moving at a good speed, but she too was afire.

There was nothing left for Kanao to do at the air defense post.[23] Everyone there was dead, and the director was out of action. Already he could hear heavy internal explosions beginning; some were sharp and jarring.[24] Others held the muffled thunder that betrayed deep damage to the ship's innards. He had no communication with any area in the ship, but he could imagine the horrible destruction being wrought below. Intense heat and smoke had already driven him back from the forward end of the air defense station in any case. He began climbing down the vertical steel ladder to the bridge. Peeking in, he was surprised to find that the command staff was still there. Captain Yanagimoto, Executive Officer Ōhara, *hikōchō* Kusumoto, and the navigator, Lieutenant Commander Asanoumi. Several of them were burned, but Yanagimoto was still determined to fight the ship. Shamed by abandoning his post while the bridge staff was still alive, Kanao determined to regain the top of the bridge and carry on with his duties. He turned, and began mounting the metal ladder once again. Yet, as he did so, another explosion rocked *Sōryū* and knocked Kanao from his perch. Instinctively, he grabbed for a line near to hand. But instead of checking his fall, it merely dropped him—albeit somewhat more softly than if he had fallen—down into the ocean below! There he stayed, clinging to the line, which still hung suspended from somewhere above.

Belowdecks in the engine spaces, Lieutenant Naganuma listened to the evil thunder of the explosions just above their heads. Suddenly, a violent crash bulged the deck down toward them, and red fire charged out of the ventilation ducts. Immediately, the order was given to shut them, but the explosions had warped the openings to such an extent that the smoke could not be stopped completely. The men began to cluster around those ducts that still brought in fresh air, sucking in each clean breath as if it were ambrosia.[25] Naganuma was suddenly struck by the image of dying carp, desperately gasping for air. The temperature was already beginning to rise alarmingly.

On board *Hiryū*, Yamaguchi and the staff of CarDiv 2 greeted the panoply of destruction that had befallen the Mobile Force with somber disbelief. The magnitude of the disaster lent an almost surreal quality to the situation—it was impossible for the men to truly comprehend what had just happened. Belowdecks, the men had to use their imaginations to picture the disaster unfolding, but given the tones of the

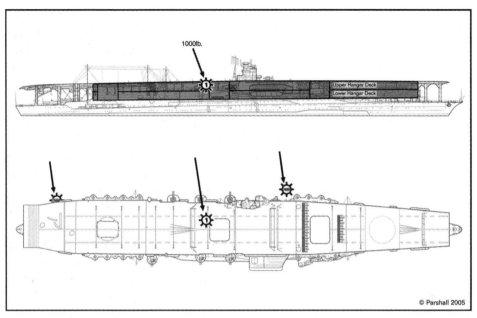

14-3: Known hit locations on *Akagi*.

voices over the loudspeakers or men running down from above with news, it was not hard to realize. In *Hiryū*'s main engine control room, Chief Engineer Aimune Kunize listened grimly as a voice from the bridge, probably Yamaguchi's or Kaku's, reported that all of the other carriers were hit, and that their teammate *Sōryū*, in particular, was burning very badly. It was up to the *Hiryū* to carry on the fight.[26]

Down in *Hiryū*'s ready room, one of her flight leaders, Lt. Shigematsu Yasuhiro, burst in amidst the lounging pilots. There he found Lieutenants Tomonaga and Hashimoto relaxing. "Hey!" he shouted to the assembled, "The *Akagi*'s damaged, the *Kaga* and *Sōryū* are burning—we're the only ship that hasn't been hit!" Rushing back topside, they joined the other crewmen on *Hiryū*'s flight deck gazing mutely on the terrible scene. Near at hand, *Sōryū* was heavily afire. Further aft, the other two carriers were clearly hit as well, with *Kaga* burning furiously. Yamaguchi tried to make out the situation on *Akagi*. She was still steaming northward. To the bridge watch, he announced that the flagship was still proceeding at good speed, and her damage appeared to be slight.[27]

Appearances were deceptive. In reality, Dick Best's bomb had landed in a position to do terrible damage to *Akagi,* although she did not "brew up" as quickly as her two stricken comrades. The hit undoubtedly destroyed the fireproof curtain between the hangar and the midships elevator well just forward, most likely blowing flaming debris downward into the lower hangar deck. The bomb also smashed the 4.7-inch ready ammunition lockers for the port-side AA guns, which were located adjacent to the impact area. Far worse, of course, was its effect on the torpedo aircraft just about to be spotted for the upcoming strike. These aircraft, eighteen in all, were fully fueled and armed with torpedoes. The bomb would have landed right on top of the aircraft parked nearest the elevator.

It appears that the hit took some time to initiate a large blaze on the hangar deck. Certainly, fire was not observed on the flight deck for several minutes afterward. This indicates that *Akagi*'s damage was initially fairly localized. Had her damage-control teams been able to react swiftly and appropriately to the situation, the fire might have been brought under control before it transformed itself into a more widespread conflagration. However, several factors conspired against this. The first, of course, was the condition of the hangar decks, which were packed with combat-loaded aircraft. A fire on so much as one of these, unless promptly extinguished, spelled disaster. Yet, getting to the blaze through the wreckage surrounding the hit would have been difficult. The second factor was the condition of the midships elevator. It is possible that when the elevator was dumped into its well, fire may have caught hold and smoldered underneath it in the machinery pit. With the elevator lying overtop, reaching the flames would have posed serious problems to any damage-control team. Whatever the situation, within about three minutes, things began to get out of hand, as the first of an interminable series of induced explosions took hold.

At 1029 Captain Aoki, keenly aware that the ordnance hoists gave direct access to the bomb and torpedo rooms below, gave the order to flood the ship's magazines. The forward storage areas complied at once, but the situation aft was more complex. According to Nagumo's report, the rear magazines could not be immediately flooded "because of valve damages."[28] This further supports the supposition that the rear portion of *Akagi* had suffered extensive shock damage from a near miss aft.

At 1032 *Akagi* attempted to use the CO_2 fire-suppression system located on the *lower* hangar deck to extinguish the blaze.[29] This indicates that the fire was already well established there within minutes of the initial attack. However, if the CO_2 system could be brought into play successfully, the fire would be confined to the upper hangar deck only, which presumably could then be brought under control. In such a fashion Captain Aoki's men would have been able to establish a firebreak of sorts and given themselves time and room to maneuver against the blaze above. It would also protect the ship's engines, and thereby *Akagi*'s pumping capacity, from further damage.

But it was not to be. With the fireproof screens around the central elevator well gone, it was impossible to seal off the damaged areas. It is probable, too, that the CO_2 flasks had been destroyed by the bomb, because they were typically housed at the bottom of the elevator well. If *Akagi*'s elevator had been dumped into its shaft, they were unlikely to have survived. As a result, *Akagi*'s efforts may have been foredoomed, although the damage-control personnel may not have been able to get close enough to the center elevator to realize that the system was nonfunctional.

Less likely is the possibility that the system worked, at least initially, or at least in some areas of the lower hangar. However, fires extinguished by CO_2-based systems have a nasty tendency of reigniting unless the inert gas can be constantly replenished or the area in question can then be consistently doused with enough water to keep smoldering combustibles below their ignition point.[30] Either way, the line of the lower hangar deck apparently could not be held. One can only imagine the gloom that must have pervaded *Akagi*'s crew when this attempt to prevent the fires from creeping lower into the ship was seen to be unsuccessful.

In the scant minutes wherein all this had transpired, the air battle continued largely unabated. As was previously related, the remnants of VT-3 were just now, at 1035, beginning their final runs against *Hiryū*. American dive-bombers, their ordnance expended, were trying to exit the scene. The Zeros, not surprisingly, were doing their level best to exact some measure of retribution for the calamity that had just befallen their carriers. Having shed their altitude in the course of their attacks, the SBDs were on the deck, usually alone or in small groups. Like any attack plane, their only real protection against a Zero was to stick in a tight formation of several aircraft and use the grouped firepower of their machine guns to fend off attacks. By themselves, Dauntlesses were normally rather vulnerable. However, now relieved of their bombs, and already short of fuel, they were at least fairly nimble. By racing away on the deck, they were also protected from attacks from below. Nevertheless, enraged by the success of the attack, the Japanese fighters went after them. Several SBDs were badly shot up and were lucky to be able to land on their carriers later in the day. Yet in a group, SBDs were much more difficult targets than TBDs. Indeed, the Japanese probably lost almost as many fighters in the immediate aftermath of the attack than they had in the half hour preceding it.

At about the same time on board *Kaga,* the bill for a full morning's worth of sloppy ammunition stowage procedures came due with cataclysmic interest. Within a few minutes after the initial hits, as aviation fuel continued pouring from the mains onto the deck, the combination of heated vapor and live flame triggered a fuel-air explosion. The initial blast was so massive that battleship *Haruna*'s executive officer was certain that no one on *Kaga* could have survived.[31] An enormous orange-black fireball mushroomed skyward and was rapidly followed by at least six more devastating blasts.[32] Not surprisingly, the retiring American aviators could not help but notice the explosions as well.[33]

Lieutenant Kunisada, with his hastily assembled damage-control team, had just been in the process of making his way into *Kaga*'s hangar when he and his men were blown to the deck by the enormous explosion.[34] Instantly, all light was lost, and they were plunged into darkness. Reaching into his pocket, Kunisada took out a flashlight and shone it around. Suddenly someone grabbed his leg. Aiming the light down, he saw a chief machinist, who groaned "I'm hit." Kunisada was able to make out that the man's leg was broken and his ankle twisted the wrong way. He leaned down to lift him up and try and help him to a side room away from the hangar, when a second terrible explosion knocked both men to the deck. Kunisada landed hard, and knew no more.

Crouching on the flight deck near the bridge, Amagai was stunned to watch the blasts literally blow out the hangar sides and hurl flame, equipment, and the bodies of crewmen into the water. As the explosions continued, the flames began moving toward the air station. All communications were severed with the rest of the ship—none of the voice tubes were operating. Amagai was momentarily consumed by sorrow for the men caught in the hangars and turned his eyes briefly toward the heavens. Looking away from the fires, he then noticed that *Akagi* and *Sōryū* were both ablaze as well. *Sōryū* was already dead in the water. Amagai's heart was seared by these images, and he felt unendurable mortification at the disaster that had overtaken the force. It was too much to be borne.[35]

With communications out and fires advancing toward him, the bridge was no place to stay, and Amagai scrambled down to the boat deck two levels below. Whether he knew it or not, he was *Kaga*'s senior surviving officer now, and, as such, command of the carrier fell to him. Yet, his exercise of command was largely directionless and did little to avail *Kaga*'s plight. Beyond the outright damage to the ship and loss of communications, three less-apparent factors were working against Amagai's ability to fight the ship. The first was that Amagai apparently did not know that he was in charge of the situation.[36] Even if he had, though, his ability to control the damage-control operations would have been hampered by a second failing—Japanese overreliance on its officer corps.

The Imperial fleet depended much more heavily on its officers of all ranks to perform complex technical operations than either the U.S. or Royal British Navies. Japanese officers, since they were committed to the force for an extended period of time, were given much more technical training than the enlisted men. Accordingly, Japanese officers in many cases fulfilled the role that in Western navies was accomplished by senior enlisted men. The importance of the officer corps in this respect is reflected by the fact that the Japanese Navy had a higher percentage of officers in its ship crews than its Western counterparts did. With *Kaga*'s senior officer corps decapitated by the initial attack, she was in an inherently inferior position with regard to damage control.

The third factor was Commander Amagai himself. As an aviator, he had little or no direct experience with fighting fires, coordinating communications, directing work parties, or any of the other myriad imperatives entailed in commanding a ship in *extremis*.[37] Damage control, at least as far as the Imperial Japanese Navy was concerned, was the preserve of specialists. Whereas by the end of the war, the U.S. Navy would push damage-control training and technique down through the ranks until everyone on board was familiar with the topic, the Japanese had no such conception. Damage control was a supernumerary function, handled strictly by engineering personnel. As a result, the death of her two senior engineering commanders meant that none of the senior officers left on board *Kaga* really had any idea of how to contain her damage, least of all the man nominally in charge of her.[38] Engineering personnel like Lieutenant Kunisada, who had the most knowledge of the survivors, were so far down the command chain that they, too, didn't realize that they were the last hope of the ship. None of these things boded well for *Kaga*'s odds of survival, and they help explain why *Kaga* was fated to suffer the highest casualties of any of the four carriers this day.

At 1040, though heavily damaged, *Akagi* was still proceeding north at battle speed 3. Suddenly, an American plane was spotted 20 degrees off the starboard bow.[39]

Captain Aoki immediately ordered the helm put hard over to starboard to present the interloper with a more difficult target angle. The starboard AA guns opened up as well, although their fire was less intense than it had been. The American plane passed to port without incident. But when Aoki ordered the rudder amidships, nothing happened. *Akagi* continued in a clockwise circle, her rudder jammed at 30 degrees to starboard. Aoki repeated the order, then immediately ordered engineering to check out the problem.[40]

Akagi's steering failure at this juncture is the final, conclusive piece of evidence supporting the aft bomb "hit" actually being a very near miss off the fantail. Nagumo's staff officer for navigation, Sasabe Toshisaburō, flatly stated that the aft hit "destroyed *Akagi*'s rudder."[41] The Nagumo Report also mentions that *Akagi*'s steering was damaged at 1042. This timing strongly indicates that the rudder failed as a result of some sort of previous damage, because no direct damage was being done to *Akagi*'s engineering spaces at this time, and the deaths of the engineering staff in the area by smoke inhalation (if indeed there were casualties there yet) would not have resulted in a steering casualty.

It is difficult to construct a damage scenario wherein the effects of a bomb hit on the flight deck aft would have affected the rudder in this fashion. A hit in this region would have vented the bomb's blast down into the atmosphere above the boat deck, rather than being transmitted directly to the ship's structure. By contrast, a near miss would have placed the 1,000-pound bomb in the water very near the ship's rudder. Water is an excellent conductor of shock waves—much better than steel. It must be recalled, too, that older warships such as *Akagi* were very prone to shock-related damage, as the physical principles underlying such damage were not well understood at the time of her construction.[42] A hit in the water close aboard would have transmitted a massive hammer blow to the hull structure and rudder that *Akagi*'s structure would have been ill prepared to handle.

A hit close aboard the aft section of the vessel also makes sense in the context of the American attack profile. Best's three-plane element had attacked from 80 degrees off *Akagi*'s port bow, whereupon she apparently began an evasive turn to starboard. As such, the American bombs would have been coming down port to starboard across her beam. On impact, a 1,000-pound bomb would be traveling at about 450 feet/second at an angle of perhaps 15–25 degrees from the vertical.[43] A bomb just missing the overhang on the port edge of the flight deck aft would continue downward and *inward* toward the ship, smacking into the water close aboard, and very near the rudder. *Akagi*'s rudders included heavy lateral bracing connecting the steering post assembly to the ship's side hull, thus providing a direct mechanism for transmitting shock stresses. The mining effect and subsequent whiplash from a 1,000-pound bomb detonating nearby would almost certainly have damaged the port rudder, causing it to jam later. Likewise, the mention of sprung watertight doors in the magazine, and the inability of flooding mechanisms to function, is indicative of the same sort of damage.

A crew would almost certainly have been dispatched immediately to diagnose the steering problem.[44] The engine spaces were already feeling the effects of the fire

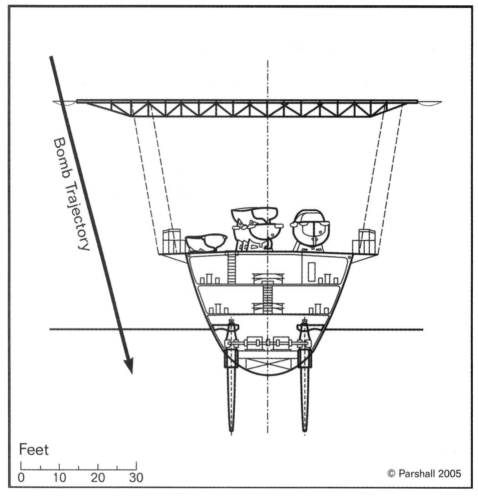

14-4: Cross section of *Akagi* at frame 220 in the area of the rudders, showing the likely trajectory of a near-miss bomb hitting the plane guard netting on the edges of the flight deck.

above, of course, with smoke being sucked down the ventilator intakes and pouring into the engineering compartments despite the best efforts to seal up the vents. Aoki's inquiry regarding the loss of steering must have been met with a groan—as if they didn't have enough troubles already. The most likely culprits for the steering failure would have been the steering telemotor controls. Given the proximity of Best's bomb hit to the bridge, it wouldn't have been unlikely for the wires there to have been cut. But apparently that wasn't the problem, nor were the stern steering motors at fault. The problem therefore lay with the steering mechanism itself.[45] About this time, Captain Aoki ordered the engines stopped. Then, at 1042 the chief engineer ordered the evacuation of the engine spaces, telling the men to report to damage-control stations topside.[46] It is likely, though, that a damage-control team would have continued trying to fix the rudder.

With the steering motors apparently in good condition, the men would have proceeded aft into the rudder room itself. The twin rudder posts, each taller than a man, were jammed into this tiny space where the ship's hull tapered sharply back to the stern. The aft end of the rudder room terminated in a six-foot-deep pit, where the posts descended to their watertight seals, and then out through the bottom of the hull. It wouldn't have taken long for the men to realize that the port rudder was damaged and would no longer turn.

Next, the emergency oil pump would have been tried, at which point the engineers would doubtless have traded fatalistic glances among themselves. They knew the chances of this hand-operated device working were slim indeed. It was common knowledge among the engineering staff that emergency steering arrangements on board their warships were unsatisfactory—the manual oil pump simply didn't have the torque necessary to turn the rudder post and its enormous counterbalance.[47]

Finally, in mounting desperation, some of the men would have groped their way back forward to fetch heavy screw jacks. There were lugs welded onto the sides of the tillers for this very purpose, and they would have rigged them in haste. But these efforts must have failed too; the port rudder simply would not move. *Akagi* was no longer navigable, and the prospects of her being able to steer any time soon seemed remote. Whether the engineers then abandoned this compartment or stayed, gagging and losing strength, to continue their efforts is unknown.[48] Equally unknown is whether they were able to apprise Aoki or Chief Engineer Tampo Yoshibumi of this situation before the command spaces topside were abandoned.

As it happened, shortly after *Akagi*'s steering failed, the situation on the bridge had deteriorated from merely bad to overtly life threatening. The fire, which had been confined to the hangar deck initially, had now broken through the flight deck, probably via the elevator well. At 1043 one of the two Zeros in Kimura's *shōtai* that hadn't made it off the deck caught fire directly abreast the bridge.[49] Immediately, a plume of heavy smoke began choking the men in the command area. It was clearly time to leave before Nagumo and his staff were roasted.

On the bridge, a singularly unpleasant debate had already been occurring for the past several minutes.[50] Perhaps numbed by fatigue, or a simple stunned incomprehension of the state of the ship, Nagumo was resisting shifting his flag to another vessel. Muttering "It is not time yet," the admiral stubbornly refused to face the facts and stood rooted to the deck near the ship's compass. Kusaka was getting nowhere in his efforts to persuade the admiral, when Captain Aoki finally spoke, saying to Kusaka, "Chief of Staff, as the ship's Captain, I am going to take care of this ship with all responsibility, so I urge you, the Commander in Chief, and all other staff officers to leave this vessel as soon as possible, so that the command of the force may be continued."[51] Thus fortified, Kusaka lost no time in applying his own pressure— the ship was afire and dead in the water, he pointed out. The radios were out, and it was clear that they simply could not longer direct the battle from her. Nagumo had his duty to do, Kusaka reminded him, and he owed it to the fleet to carry on the battle. Finally, Nagumo relented.

Unfortunately, leaving *Akagi*'s bridge wasn't as easy now as it would have been even five minutes before. The starboard side of the island was threatened by the flames; the door from the briefing room at the base of the island now opened directly onto the fire, and the air-control platform at the rear of the island was also being scorched.[52] The port side of the island was a sheer cliff, dropping eighty-odd feet straight down to the ocean below—a killing fall. Running down the ladder to look for a way out below, the staff flag secretary, Commander Nishibayashi, reported back that there was no escape that way, either. Thus, the only way down now was through the windows at the front of the bridge. Someone found a line, secured it to one of the window frames, and out they went.

Or almost. The distance was some fourteen feet down to the small fire-control platform at the front of the island, and then another six to the flight deck itself. In the event, it seemed rather more. Not only that, but *Akagi*'s bridge windows were only about twenty inches on a side. The diminutive Nagumo could scramble through without issue; the burlier Kusaka found it a rather tight fit. A few shoves from the staff, though, and he was expelled from the bridge. Whether from his rather corklike exit, or because rappelling down sheer metal structures was apparently not a normal part of a staff officer's duties, Kusaka proceeded mostly to fall to the platform below, badly spraining both his ankles, and burning himself for good measure.[53]

The weakened Fuchida found himself in worse straits yet. The last officer out of the bridge, he started shinnying down the line and had almost made it to the fire-control platform when an explosion knocked him roughly all the way to the flight deck. Where Kusaka had gotten away with mere sprains, Fuchida found himself with two badly broken legs, his ankles and arches crushed. Landing on the deck like a sack of grain, he simply lay there. Limping, even crawling away was out of the question. And the flames were advancing all the while. Thinking that this was the end, Fuchida considered his fate calmly, realizing that all he felt was an utter weariness at the whole affair. His clothing began to smolder from the heat. Then, miraculously, two enlisted men arrived on the scene in the nick of time. They picked him up and carried him forward to the anchor deck on the bow, where he rejoined Nagumo and the staff of First Air Fleet.[54]

Before leaving the bridge, Kusaka had directed *Nowaki* to come alongside to receive the admiral. However, light cruiser *Nagara* had drawn near as well. *Nowaki*'s launch, instead of ferrying the admiral to the destroyer, was ordered to take him and his staff to the cruiser. Not only was *Nagara* a larger vessel, but also she and all her sisters were designed to operate as destroyer squadron flagships, and as such had better communications facilities than their charges. Fuchida, although not part of the admiral's staff, was taken along as well.[55]

Nagumo boarded the launch, followed by the rest of the evacuees. As Genda was waiting to embark, a petty officer on *Akagi*'s bow noticed that his hand had been burned.[56] Pulling off one of his own white gloves, the man handed it to Genda, urging him to put it on. Turning to go, Genda was halted again by his young orderly, who had braved the darkness belowdecks to retrieve Genda's bank deposit book and personal seal (*han*) from his cabin. Genda was deeply moved by the kindness of the two sailors, both of whom he was now leaving behind to whatever fate awaited them. But Nagumo's staff were waiting, and Genda boarded the launch. The crew began pulling on the oars. On board *Akagi,* the survivors watched them go, then turned back to the desperate business at hand.

At the same time Nagumo was departing *Akagi,* a singularly less dignified and more massive debarkation was already under way on *Sōryū.* Her damage had been so rapid and severe, and the slaughter of her crew so wholesale, that only cursory efforts were made to save her. She had lost power almost immediately and by 1040 had slewed to a dead stop in the water, afire from stem to stern. Emergency steering arrangements were tried at 1043, but in the absence of propulsion they were superfluous in any case.[57] Clouds of whitish smoke poured from her port side, and the hangars were already completely consumed with fire.[58]

Executive Officer Ōhara, despite his severe burns, had left the bridge to try and take over the firefighting efforts. Moving down a deck to the air-control platform, he tried to assess the situation, but all communications were out. It was clear, though, that the ship's fire mains were destroyed. Leaving the air station for the flight deck, he finally fainted from his wounds and fell to the deck. There, another explosion must have blown him over the side without his even being aware. The gods smiled on the injured man, for his trajectory cast him clear of the lifeboat davits and other impaling obstacles and into the water beyond. He survived the long trip down to the ocean none the worse for wear. When Ōhara came to, he found another sailor, a pharmacist's mate, swimming next to him and slapping him to keep him from fainting again and drowning.[59] Ōhara would spend the next several hours in the water before being rescued.

On the bridge, Captain Yanagimoto quickly drew the obvious conclusion—*Sōryū* was doomed. At 1045 he gave the order to abandon ship.[60] Whether or not the order reached all the men, though, was questionable, as communications with the rest of the ship were undoubtedly disrupted. Whatever the reason, either the captain's order, or simply wishing to preserve their lives, men had already begun jumping into the water around the ship. Others were deposited there rather more bodily, as explosions continued wracking the ship. *Sōryū* had remained under command a mere twenty minutes from the time the first bomb struck. The ordeal of her men, though, was far from over.

With Admiral Nagumo in the process of transferring his flag, command over *Kidō Butai* briefly devolved on the screen's commander, RADM Abe Hiroaki, commander of CruDiv 8. Abe wasted little time in assessing the situation and initiating action. He had received a message at 1045 from *Chikuma,* informing him that her No. 5 plane had sighted "5 additional cruisers and 5 destroyers" some 130 miles from Midway. Dutifully forwarding that message to Yamamoto at 1047, he followed up three minutes later with a grim communiqué: "Fires are raging aboard the *Kaga, Sōryū,* and *Akagi* resulting from attacks carried out by enemy land-based and carrier-based attack planes. We plan to have the *Hiryū* engage the enemy carriers. In the meantime, we are temporarily retiring

14-5: Lt. Kobayashi Michio, commander of *Hiryū*'s 1054 strike force. The consummate skill of Kobayashi's unit was vividly demonstrated during the afternoon of 4 June. (Photo courtesy Michael Wenger)

to the north, and assembling our forces."[61] Immediately thereafter, Abe sent a terse message to Admiral Yamaguchi, "Attack the enemy carriers."

Six hundred miles to the west, Yamamoto's Main Body was plowing along in an allegorically apropos fog. The dense mists that had bedeviled *Kidō Butai* several days before now surrounded the commander in chief's formation. Several ships, including battleship *Nagato,* had gotten lost in the soup, slowing their progress and fraying nerves. Admiral Yamamoto sat silently, peering out of the windows at the white mantle. Suddenly, *Yamato*'s chief signal officer burst onto the bridge, his face grim, and handed Yamamoto a message form. Yamamoto read it, stunned. He let out a groan, then still staring out at the mists beyond, handed it back wordlessly to the signalman. To another sailor on the bridge, it seemed that the commander in chief had been turned to stone—not so much as an eyelid twitched on his countenance.[62]

On board *Hiryū,* Yamaguchi Tamon had needed no prompting to undertake offensive action. When Admiral Abe's message ordering him to attack was received at 1050, he was, in fact, just minutes away from launching. Not surprisingly, frantic preparations had been under way on *Hiryū* to get a counterstrike in the air since the American attack. The job fell to *Hiryū*'s dive-bomber unit, under the command of Lt. Kobayashi Michio, *buntaichō.* Kobayashi and his unit were widely regarded as among the best in the fleet.[63] He would personally lead the first *chūtai* of nine aircraft, while his deputy, Lt. Yamashita Michiji, would lead the second *chūtai.* Accompanying Kobayashi's eighteen Type 99 aircraft would be six Zeros under the command of Lieutenant Shigematsu, junior fighter *buntaichō.* He and the other pilots in the *chūtai* had already participated in the morning strike. Now Shigematsu led a grab bag collection of aircraft on this vital mission. There was no time to wait to rearm Tomonaga's remaining Type 97s, so this would have to be a one-dimensional strike.[64]

Kobayashi's aircraft were equipped with a standard antiship loadout wherein two-thirds of the aircraft carried 250-kilogram semi armor-piercing bombs, while the remaining third (one plane in each *shōtai*) carried a 242-kilogram high-explosive land bomb fused for instantaneous detonation. The high-explosive weapons were

14-6: *Hiryū* launching aircraft during the Battle of Midway.[65] This photograph, heretofore seen only rarely in the West, shows one Type 99 dive-bomber taking off and a second already in the air off *Hiryū*'s port bow. Previously labeled as having been taken sometime between 1 and 3 June, this photograph more likely shows Kobayashi's force departing the carrier at 1057 on 4 June. If so, it is one of the few photos we have of the Japanese carriers during the battle, and perhaps the only one taken from another Japanese vessel. Note the escort destroyer visible almost on the horizon just aft of *Hiryū*'s flight deck. A second is barely visible on the horizon just forward of the 25-mm antiaircaft tubs on *Hiryū*'s bow. (Photo courtesy KK Bestsellers)

intended to destroy AA guns and their crews, thereby hopefully suppressing the target's antiaircraft fire and making the task of the other aircraft that much easier.[66]

It was Captain Kaku who gave the final preflight briefing to the assembled pilots. In contrast to this morning's optimistic atmosphere, there was none of the usual banter and kidding among the pilots; the mood was now one of deadly seriousness. The men stood silent as Kaku laid out the objectives for the strike. *Hiryū*'s commander reminded them that theirs was the last intact aircraft unit in the fleet. Not only did they need to find the enemy and attack effectively, they also needed to return as large a percentage of their aircraft to *Hiryū*'s decks as possible for use in future operations. Therefore, Kaku urged caution; they must attack judiciously, not rashly. Grimly determined to do their best, the men ran to their planes and mounted.

At 1054, with the funeral pyres of CarDiv 1 still clearly visible on the southern horizon and her sister a raging bonfire nearby, *Hiryū* turned back east into the wind and began launching. All the aircraft were airborne by about 1058. Standing in the crew pits next to the flight deck, the deck crews wished them a silent farewell—all the hopes of the fleet now hung on the slender thread of *Hiryū*'s air group. To the force, Yamaguchi sent the following message: "All our planes are taking off now for the purpose of destroying the enemy carriers."[67]

15

Up the Steel Steps—1100–1200

After Kobayashi was launched, *Hiryū* apparently remained headed northeast on course 30 degrees and immediately brought down seven of *Akagi's* combat air patrol fighters. As it developed, the combination of *Hiryū's* earlier evasive maneuvers against VT-3 and her recent move into the wind to launch aircraft had brought her back into the vicinity of *Sōryū*. The condition of her wounded sister ship was positively dreadful. Flames were licking all along the flight deck, and dense clouds of black smoke were boiling from her innards. One crewman on board *Hiryū* remarked that "She looked like a giant *daikon* radish that had been sliced in two. Now [in places] it was possible to see right through her to the other side."[1] On the bridge, Yamaguchi turned to one of *Hiryū's* officers. "Can we contact her?" he asked. "I will try," the man replied and began to snap the shutters of a small signal lamp. "Try to save your carrier!" Yamaguchi signaled. The message was sent two or three times toward the fire-wracked flattop, but there was no reply.

Saddened, Yamaguchi turned away from the horrible spectacle. There was little anyone could do. However, one of *Hiryū's* consorts, cruiser *Chikuma*, had also been drawn like a moth to *Sōryū's* fiery agony and was even now slowing to a stop. At 1112 she sent over her No. 2 cutter to the stricken carrier's forecastle, where a damage-control party could be seen. Embarked on the cutter was a pharmacist's mate and seven sailors, clearly more to help with tending the wounded than with any firefighting. *Hiryū* herself could not linger. After their brief intersection, *Sōryū* was rapidly left behind to join the other two forlorn smoke columns further astern. It was the last time the men on board *Hiryū* would see their sister ship.

Having sent off the counterstrike, Yamaguchi shortly received a signal from *Chikuma's* No. 5 plane, which had relieved *Tone* No. 4. He radioed at 1110: "The enemy is in position bearing 70 degrees, distance 90 miles from our fleet's position." The enemy was indeed very close at hand. In fact, unbeknownst to Nagumo or Yamaguchi, *Chikuma* No. 5 was in contact with an entirely different American carrier force than Amari had originally detected. This was TF 17, centered around *Yorktown*. Amari had encountered it on his way back to *Kidō Butai*. Proceeding to the spot of Amari's latest sighting report, *Chikuma* No. 5 had duly stumbled across *Yorktown* as well.

What Yamaguchi thought of the enemy's proximity has not been recorded. Indeed, for the first forty-five minutes or so after *Kidō Butai's* catastrophic bombing,

Yamaguchi's actions were largely preprogrammed in any case. His last orders from Nagumo had been to assume a course of 030 degrees and close the enemy preparatory to launching a counterstrike. Strictly speaking, the attack on *Kaga, Sōryū,* and *Akagi* did not alter these orders a whit. Yamaguchi's launching his strike against *Yorktown* was not a response to the American attack at all, but simply the continuation of Nagumo's prior intentions. *Hiryū's* behavior confirms this. She dodged VT-3's attack in the 1030–1035 time frame, then apparently resumed 030 and went ahead with her launch. Furthermore, for a time at least, *Akagi* had followed her, until dropping back at 1042. At 1120, having left *Sōryū* astern, Yamaguchi blinkered all ships an update: "Second wave composed of 18 bombers and 5 fighters has taken off. Plan to have an additional 9 ship-based attack planes and 3 fighters take off in one hour. *Hiryū* plans to proceed towards the enemy on present course."[2]

If *Hiryū* was proceeding toward the enemy, she was doing so largely alone. Apart from a pair of destroyers, the other ships of *Kidō Butai* appear to have been busy elsewhere. *Nagara* was alongside *Akagi,* collecting Admiral Nagumo. Cruiser *Tone* and BatDiv 3 were apparently somewhere between *Hiryū* and *Nagara,* still within blinker distance of both parties, and thereby forming a "signal bridge" of sorts that linked the two.[3] Thus, Yamaguchi was operating without the benefit of any heavy cover.

After Kobayashi's departure, *Hiryū* began arming what remained of her *kankō* squadron for launch, hopefully before noon. Of the torpedo attack aircraft, seven were clearly serviceable, and another pair (including Tomonaga's) apparently had been patched up sufficiently to make the trip. Providentially, at 1130 another *kankō* deposited itself on *Hiryū's* deck. This was an *Akagi* aircraft flown by WO Suzuki Shigeru. Suzuki had taken off at 1015 from the flagship for a scouting mission, but had turned back (for reasons unknown) shortly thereafter. Finding his ship in flames, he had landed on *Hiryū* instead.[4] Under normal circumstances, the addition of a single torpedo plane to the roster would hardly have been cause for celebration, but in this case every plane counted. Suzuki's bird was promptly refueled and armed.

It was clear, too, that in order to make maximum usage of the meager assets at hand, it was imperative that good intelligence on the enemy's movements continue to be gathered. A happy thought, indeed, it was about six hours late in occurring to the Japanese. However, Yamaguchi relayed a message to CruDiv 8 at 1130, ordering additional aircraft to maintain contact with the enemy. Unfortunately, Japan's woes in the scouting department were ongoing. Amari's No. 4 plane had been replaced by *Chikuma's* No. 5 aircraft. However, the pilot of this new arrival, PO1c Takezaki Masatake, had thus far only observed TF 17 and *Yorktown.* As it developed, at the same time that *Chikuma* No. 5 was sending her sighting report at 1110, *Sōryū's* Type 2 aircraft was sending back a similar report detailing the position of TF 16. Unfortunately, it was later discovered that the radio in Iida's new bomber wasn't working. No one received his transmissions. It would not be until Iida returned to *Hiryū* in the early afternoon that Yamaguchi would finally have confirmation that the American order of battle included two separate task forces, with perhaps as many as three carriers.

Nagumo's launch pulled alongside *Nagara* at 1127. The admiral scrambled up a Jacob's ladder dropped over the side of the cruiser and onto her linoleum-covered decks. RADM Kimura Susumu, commander of Destroyer Squadron 10, received the admiral and his staff on the quarterdeck. Upon boarding the cruiser, Nagumo's first thought was to use *Nagara* to tow *Akagi* clear of the battle. Kimura, gazing on the panorama of the enormous blazing ship, greeted the suggestion with scant enthusiasm. He politely pointed out to his superior that given *Akagi*'s current circumstances such an operation would prove "difficult"—an understatement indeed.[5]

Meanwhile, on *Nagara*'s bridge, Kusaka was hunting around for a flag for *Kidō Butai*'s commander. *Nagara* wasn't accustomed to hosting such visitors, and Kimura's flag locker was devoid of the proper pennant for a vice admiral—a rising sun flag with a broad red stripe bordering the top edge. Kusaka resorted to the expedient of taking Kimura's rear admiral pennant, which had red stripes on both top and bottom, and simply tearing the bottom stripe off. In the words of one historian, "The effect was tattered, but certainly no worse than the fleet."[6]

Nagumo probably could not have cared less, as his mind was already on bigger game. In the midst of receiving Kimura's deferential disinclination to tow *Akagi* clear, Nagumo had been handed a message that caused him to focus on other matters. It was *Chikuma* No. 5's 1110 sighting report. Whereas a ninety-mile separation from the enemy might have given Yamaguchi pause, it was the best news Nagumo had received in hours. It apparently meant that the enemy had continued to close with his position, and along the same bearing. If this was true, with a bit of luck it might be possible to engage the Americans in a daylight surface action. To a man like Nagumo, this was an enticing prospect. A former torpedo officer, he knew what his surface forces could do to the enemy given the chance. Thus, far from moping about on *Nagara*, Nagumo shortly thereafter decisively reassumed command of the battle and tried to take the fight to the enemy.

For his part, since assuming a brevet command at 1050, Admiral Abe had been casting about for the best response to the situation. He had already notified Yamamoto and Kondō of the tragedy that had befallen *Kidō Butai*. But what best to do with the forces remaining? He had heard nothing from Nagumo and was probably beginning to fear the worst. At 1127 Abe tried to raise Nagumo directly, asking *Akagi* "Is your radio working?"[7] The lack of reply was its own answer. Abe—with *Chikuma* No. 5's recent sighting report in his hands as well—decided there was only one thing he could do, and that was attack the approaching enemy. At 1130 his flagship blinkered *Chikuma*: "Prepare for Torpedo Action." However, scarcely had he signaled *Chikuma* than the radio crackled with a hail from Admiral Kimura on *Nagara*, informing him that Nagumo had transferred his flag.[8]

To Abe's unspoken question of whether Nagumo was injured or capable of command came an immediate answer, as Nagumo shortly fired off a full update to Yamamoto, Kondō, and all commands: "*Akagi, Kaga,* and *Sōryū* sustained considerable damage as a result of enemy bombing attack at about 1030. Fires have broken out aboard them, and they are unable to participate in any operations. I (CinC First Air Fleet) have transferred to the *Nagara*. After attacking the enemy, I plan to lead my forces to the north. Grid position: HE I A 00."

Thereafter, the Mobile Fleet's new flagship began drawing away from the blazing *Akagi*. It was a poignant and symbolic moment. Proud *Akagi* had been Nagumo's home for fourteen months, since the formation of First Air Fleet. Those months had been heady ones for *Kidō Butai*. Now Nagumo would have to win or lose without her, with just a single carrier, two battleships, three cruisers, and five destroyers.

Despite this daunting prospect, Nagumo's reaction was aggressive. He was clearly focused on returning at least some of the punishment he had just taken. *Hiryū*'s counterattack should soon reach the enemy, with a second to follow. All that remained was for the surface ships to find an opening to contribute as well. *Nagara* continued accelerating, her bow cutting the water purposefully as Nagumo closed to rejoin the remainder of his fleet. Within ten minutes of leaving *Akagi* behind, he was back in blinker range of Abe on *Tone*. Having heard Nagumo's report to Combined Fleet at 1130, Abe anticipated matters and blinkered Nagumo at 1143: "[I] have a part of CruDiv 8, BatDiv 3, and DesRon 10 prepared to go to the attack of the enemy." Nagumo shortly blinkered back to Abe, "Hold up."[9] Eager as he was to close the enemy, he didn't want *Nagara* bringing up the rear. He would lead this counterattack in person. First, though, he needed to reform his scattered ships into some sort of battle formation.

As *Nagara* closed with the main gaggle of the Mobile Fleet, Yamaguchi also became involved. Hearing the radioed plans for attack, at 1147 CarDiv 2's commander countermanded his previous instruction regarding the screen for the damaged carriers. He radioed *Tone, Akagi, Kaga,* and *Sōryū,* instructing them to "Leave one destroyer with the damaged carriers, and have the others proceed on the course of attack." If there was to be a surface battle, Yamaguchi wanted all the offensive power that could be mustered. In the event, though, it appears that this message may have been garbled or simply ignored, as *two* destroyers were with each burning carrier from this time forward. *Isokaze* and *Hamakaze* stood by *Sōryū, Nowaki* and *Arashi* stuck close to *Akagi,* and *Hagikaze* and *Maikaze* sadly circled *Kaga*.[10]

If he had any objections to Yamaguchi's interjection, Nagumo gave no sign. Over the following minutes, he sent out orders informing his units that they should assemble, as he planned to "take to the attack now."[11] Just before noon, he amplified his instructions, ordering his formation to "form in order of DesRon 10, CruDiv 8, and BatDiv 3. Course 170 degrees, speed 12 knots." Shortly thereafter, *Nagara* came bounding up from the south, as the two battlewagons and Abe's sleek cruisers turned to meet her. The sense of excitement within the Mobile Fleet was palpable. Nagumo's strategy was a simple one: he would head nearly straight for the enemy on a reciprocal bearing. Under the cover of *Hiryū*'s strike waves, he would close to within gun and torpedo range. As if to further spur such hopes, word from Vice Admiral Kondō's 2nd Fleet arrived at noon: "[We are] in position YU MI KU 00 at 1200. Course 50 degrees, speed 28 knots. We are heading for the Mobile Force." With reinforcements on the way, Nagumo set off on his quest.

Thus, the common interpretation that Yamaguchi was essentially running the battle from *Hiryū*, with Nagumo in *Nagara* tagging along behind his subordinate, is not true. In fact, Yamaguchi and *Hiryū* trailed in Nagumo's wake, while his superior led his remaining heavy forces east, seeking battle. And while Yamaguchi essentially operated independently as far as air operations were concerned, his general course took its lead from Nagumo's own movements and were no more aggressive than those of his commander.

Knowing what we know today, the very notion of Nagumo's charging an enemy who had just devastated the mightiest carrier force in the world seems laughable. For his part, Nagumo certainly knew that he was engaged in a long shot. But his actions show that at midday on 4 June, making some kind of retaliation that would allow Kondō and Yamamoto time to enter the battle was absolutely foremost in his mind. Nagumo was acting promptly to seize what he felt was his only remaining chance in the battle. Escape was not part of his agenda, at least not yet. It cannot be ruled out, of course, that he was subconsciously seeking death in battle to atone for the debacle. But whatever the motivation, the picture that emerges is not one of a broken admiral, but rather a man desperately striving to make good on a decidedly grim situation.

His decision to attack in this manner was also supported by the "facts" that he had at hand, which suggested that the enemy lay only ninety miles distant. He first had to assemble his dispersed vessels. But as soon as he had done so, he shaped a course designed to bring him straight at the American's supposed position. If they could bridge the gap, an hour's gunnery from the battlewagons would be all it took to settle accounts. Not only that, but nightfall was coming, and with it the promise of reinforcement by Kondō's forces. Even if *Kidō Butai* could just locate the enemy in the coming darkness, Kondō might be able to finish the job.

It was true that Nagumo was down to just one carrier. But *Hiryū*'s own planes were even then counterattacking, which might even the odds a bit. And what is also often overlooked is that the Japanese were well aware of the brutal losses they had inflicted on the American's torpedo squadrons. Without torpedo planes, the enemy would have a much harder time sinking Nagumo's battleships, which could more easily shrug off hits from the Dauntlesses. Given that, it was not unreasonable to suppose that *Haruna* and *Kirishima,* as well as CruDiv 8—with their high speed and deadly torpedoes—might survive air attack long enough to close the range. This was especially true if *Hiryū*'s aircraft managed to cripple one of the enemy carriers.

Nagumo's naval culture surely exerted an influence on his behavior in this regard. Nagumo was conscious of the fact that Admiral Inoue had suffered considerable censure in the aftermath of the Battle of Coral Sea in the eyes of Combined Fleet's staff for allowing the loss of carrier *Shōhō,* and the crippling of *Shōkaku,* to lead him to "prematurely" abandon his enterprise. Nagumo's eagerness to launch a surface attack perhaps derived from a desire to not repeat such a "hasty" cessation of maximum effort. It must be recalled, too, that at this time only *Sōryū* had been definitively written off. It was not yet clear that *Kaga* and *Akagi* would not be saved and brought back into the battle.

Finally, it must be admitted that in behaving as he did, Nagumo was conforming to Japanese societal norms as well, which value the integrity of an act more than its likely results. In Japanese culture, there is a readier acceptance of the "nobility of failure" while giving it one's best effort. One of the most popular Japanese exhortations is *"ganbatte,"* which translates roughly to "Please continue trying to do your best." This principle applies equally when the task in question is difficult, odious, or even doomed. Winning is optional; trying your best is not. Likewise, performing in an honorable fashion today is more important than the long-term implications for tomorrow. This attitude is part of the enduring fascination of Japan's Navy, because it is so alien to Western modes of thinking. Taken together, it's somewhat easier to see why Nagumo believed at midday that, while the battle was desperate, it was not yet hopeless.

However, despite his understandable desire to take the battle to the enemy, both Nagumo and Yamaguchi would have done well to ponder the dangers *Hiryū* found herself in, especially given that the American carrier force was as yet undamaged. While the apparent proximity of the Americans was good news for Nagumo, it was quite the opposite for Yamaguchi's lone remaining carrier. Both Nagumo and Yamaguchi should have been concerned with keeping some distance between her and the more powerful American carriers. Instead, *Hiryū,* almost by default, continued closing with the enemy. There was no need to do this—even had *Hiryū* moved northwest, her aircraft had all the range they needed to strike back, and then some. Hitting back at the enemy made good sense. Needlessly exposing *Hiryū* to long odds did not. At this juncture in the battle, the principle of calculated risk that informed Chester Nimitz's strategy of "strong attritional tactics" was eminently suited to the Japanese position as well.

Indeed, a careful assessment of the odds against *Hiryū* would have revealed two things. First, immediately before Kobayashi's launching, Yamaguchi had exactly thirty-seven aircraft of all types left on board her—ten Zeros, eighteen dive-bombers, and nine carrier attack planes. Another twenty-seven CAP fighters were still aloft, most of them refugees from the other three carriers, for a total of sixty-four Japanese carrier aircraft of all types left in operation.[12] In other words, *Kidō Butai*'s airpower was down to about a quarter of what it had been at 0430. In terms of strike aircraft, the tally was even worse. *Hiryū*'s torpedo squadron had, for all intents and purposes, been wrecked already. This notched down the number of strike planes available to *Kidō Butai* to under a *fifth* of the morning's total.

Second, the nature of the morning's battle should have given Yamaguchi and Nagumo fair warning that they were most likely now badly outnumbered. The incessant American attacks had involved large numbers of aircraft, many of which were carrier types. It should have been apparent that the dive-bomber attack at 1020–1025 could not have been launched by a single American flight deck.[13] Japanese aerial attack doctrine was the same as that of the Americans on this point—committing a full attack squadron per enemy carrier in order to assure its destruction. The mere fact that three Japanese flattops had been attacked simultaneously argued strongly that the Americans had at least two carriers in the fight. Attacking such a powerful force was dangerous in the extreme, especially given the state of Japanese reconnaissance and their generally depleted airpower.

Notwithstanding the advisability of attempting a surface attack against the Americans, there was no reason to drag *Hiryū* into such a brawl if it could be helped. Both Nagumo and Yamaguchi knew that Kondō's Invasion Support Force was the nearest substantial Japanese formation to them. But they also knew that Kondō offered little in the way of immediate succor to the First Carrier Strike Force, having no airpower of its own. The other major force in the neighborhood, of course, was the Main Body. Bringing up the rear some 300 miles behind Nagumo, Yamamoto and his big guns could not hope to be in the battle for another day at least. Plus, there was little in the way of organic airpower in Yamamoto's force, either. Light carrier *Hōshō* provided a bare minimum of air cover over the Main Body, but was in no way a power-projection asset. Without aircraft to defend the battleship force, even the mighty *Yamato* would find herself in peril. The truth was that while the Main Body could potentially destroy an enemy surface force already brought to bay, it had neither the speed to overhaul the swift American carriers should they wish to avoid battle, nor the means to defend itself against the Americans if they retained air superiority. The same was true of Kondō's force as well.

If new airpower was to be scraped together, it would have to come from the Second Carrier Striking Force, centered on *Junyō* and *Ryūjō*. While neither of these carriers was the cream of the fleet, between them they could at least field about sixty aircraft, which was a credible number at this point in the battle. Yet, while the First Carrier Strike Force was burning off of Midway, *Dai-Ni Kidō Butai* was more than 1,600 miles to the north, involved in reducing Dutch Harbor's defenses. They wouldn't be able to rendezvous with Nagumo for several days at least. Even if they could do so, it would still be vital to preserve *Hiryū* and her polyglot air group. If nothing else, having the ability to put her thirty-seven Zeros over the Main Body would increase the odds of Yamamoto being able to bring the fleet's big guns to bear.

Given all this, Yamaguchi, and Nagumo in particular, needed to judge the situation very carefully. Since *Hiryū* was almost certainly outnumbered by her opponents, it was unlikely that she would be able to alter the tide of battle by herself. There would come a time, probably not far in the future, when CarDiv 2's flagship would no longer be capable of projecting a meaningful amount of firepower against the enemy. When that time came, the logical course of action would be to preserve her for future operations. As a result, the Japanese needed to fight smart. If they were to extricate *Hiryū* from this mess, she needed to be positioned at the limits of the enemy's range, so she could withdraw promptly when the time came.

This course of action, if it even occurred to Nagumo or Yamaguchi, apparently did not recommend itself. Their natural inclination was to fight, and fighting meant attacking. However, their manner of assault meant that they were essentially driving a wasting asset right into the enemy's maw. In truth, both admirals were somewhat to blame in this matter. Nagumo certainly seems to have neglected issuing any direct orders regarding *Hiryū*'s disposition, letting Yamaguchi handle her affairs directly. It's easy to believe that during this time of supreme crisis, Nagumo had largely reverted to his torpedo commander ways. He was focusing almost solely on the surface battle he was trying to create, rather on overseeing the fate of what was arguably still the single most important vessel in the Japanese force.

There is no indication that Yamaguchi gave any heed to this matter, either. Granted, in the absence of direct orders to the contrary, Yamaguchi was essentially constrained to follow Nagumo's general lead. But there is no evidence to suggest that he went down this path unwillingly. We know enough about Yamaguchi's character to believe that if the commander of CarDiv 2 had had reservations, he would have voiced them. We know, too, that Yamaguchi had been encouraged by Ugaki in times past to take such license if he felt he needed to. Ugaki had worried before the battle that First Air Fleet, under Nagumo's tepid leadership might not be able to "accomplish its mission in future sea operations in which every kind of change must be expected to happen."[14] And yet here, at a point in time in which Ugaki's favorite commander might have improvised a little, Yamaguchi stuck rigidly to a heroic script. In so doing, he would lead his remaining carrier to ruin precisely because of his unwillingness to adapt to changing circumstances, a failing that Ugaki had ironically pinned on Nagumo.

Much as with Nagumo's decision to close the enemy and fight on the surface, one can argue that Yamaguchi, too, was simply fighting according to his societal norms. But this is still unsatisfying. Later in the war, when Japan's defeat was both assured and readily apparent to all parties concerned, acts of folly and despair on the part of the Japanese would be more understandable. But this was June 4, 1942, and less than an hour ago Japan was doing well in both the battle and the war. Even now, with the situation in tatters, there were still things worth fighting for besides mere honor. Yamaguchi's attitudes and behaviors ought to have reflected these current realities.

Both Nagumo and Yamaguchi needed to take a broader view on their role in the war, and that of *Kidō Butai*. If Japan was to fight effectively, aggressiveness had to be tempered with savvy. Great risks would have to be taken, but the preservation of precious war-fighting capital—ships, people, initiative, and time—needed to be at least as important as simple belligerence. In Yamaguchi's hands were entrusted irreplaceable assets. His position carried with it a moral responsibility to the Japanese nation to fight in such a way as to make the best use of those assets. To this day, Yamaguchi, much more than Nagumo, receives the admiration of the Japanese people, because he fought with his heart. But against this must be set the ultimate condemnation of military performance: he didn't use his head. Nor did Nagumo.

This is not to say that either admiral was unintelligent—that clearly wasn't the problem. Yet, it is equally clear that their approach to warfare was mono-dimensional and limited to a sphere of combat that was primarily tactical, personal, and visual. Neither man was capable of placing his tactical decisions within the larger context of the nation's war-waging. Yet even now, with the odds against them, they still had the very real possibility of extracting some measure of revenge while simultaneously preserving *Hiryū* for future battles. And no matter whose societal math you used— Oriental or Occidental—bringing at least one of *Kidō Butai*'s carriers home was a damned sight better than losing all four. Given all this, as soon as Kobayashi's attack was in the air, *Hiryū* ought to have "poured on the coal" and headed northwest at her best speed. Instead, both Nagumo and Yamaguchi failed to recast their current plans in the face of the enemy's new advantage. In so doing, they jointly signed the warrant for the complete annihilation of *Kidō Butai*'s carriers.

If the remnants of *Kidō Butai* were now sailing straight for disaster, the Americans, for their part, were not in the best shape to take advantage of Japanese misfortunes. The U.S. Navy had landed a crushing blow on its enemy, but the cost had been high. The saga of *Hornet*'s air group is particularly pitiable in this respect, because almost all of its woes were self-inflicted. The exact tale of what happened to *Hornet*'s strike remains shrouded in mystery to this day, but the outlines of the situation were apparently as follows.[15] Once John Waldron and VT-8 had left the formation at 0825, Commander

Stanhope Ring continued leading his group west. However, as the minutes ticked by, no sign of the Japanese fleet had been forthcoming, because *Kidō Butai* was well south of the Americans. By around 0900, the situation was getting serious; many of the aircraft were beginning to run low on fuel. The Wildcats, having been up the longest, were the first to reach the point of literally no return, and at 0915 (without communicating to Ring) they turned for home. However, the fighter pilots had no clear idea of where home was. Worse yet, while they had radio homing devices (known as "Zed Baker") to detect signals from *Hornet,* they were notoriously cranky to use. The fighters were deliberately shedding altitude at a gradual rate, trading height for a bit of enhanced speed without having to burn any more gas. The downside of this tradeoff was that the lower they got, the harder it would be to stay above the visual horizon line to *Hornet* (wherever she was). The Zed Bakers required a clear line to the mother ship in order to work. Worse was the fact that even though some of the pilots did receive the signal, many of them didn't understand how to use their equipment well enough to home on it.[16]

The result was that none of VF-8's pilots were able to get a good lock on their ship. They continued blindly southeastward, searching the horizon in increasing desperation. At around 1000, one pilot sighted ship wakes far to the north, but they were deemed to be those of *Kidō Butai.*[17] None of the men wanted to risk ditching next to the Japanese fleet and being captured. As it developed, the wakes were those of TF 16. And instead of heading for home, VF-8's aviators were now proceeding into the trackless wastes of the Pacific. After missing TF 16, the outcome was inevitable. One by one, starting at around 1015, they began running out of fuel and ditching individually or in small groups. By 1050 the last of them had gone in the drink. Most of the men were destined to be picked up by ships or PBYs, but one was killed while ditching, and another crawled into his rubber life raft and disappeared, never to be seen again.

Meanwhile, Ring and *Hornet*'s SBDs had held course westward. Just five minutes after the fighters peeled off, at 0920, the SBDs received Waldron's announcement that he was under attack by enemy fighters.[18] VB-8's commander, Lt. Cdr. Robert R. Johnson, realized now that Waldron had been right all along. Pulling out his plotting board, he drew a 135-degree radial out from Midway and calculated where the Japanese fleet should be along that line. Accordingly, he shortly thereafter turned his seventeen SBDs left to a southeast heading to find the enemy carriers. However, he knew nothing of Nagumo's eastward movements during its recovery operations. As a result, Johnson was too far west in his reckonings. During his fifty-mile jog southeast, he spotted nothing. Things were now getting critical in the fuel department, and Johnson accordingly began taking his flight back to a northeast heading to close on where he hoped *Hornet* would be.

It was at this juncture that VB-8 encountered an American PBY, which blinkered them a course heading to Midway. Meanwhile, though, Johnson's highly respected executive officer, Lt. Alfred B. Tucker III, had just started picking up the Zed Baker signal from *Hornet.* It was now crunch time. Tucker decided to follow the Zed Baker signal, and his two wingmen followed him. Johnson, either not trusting the equipment or unsure that he could make the ship, opted for Midway with his fourteen remaining

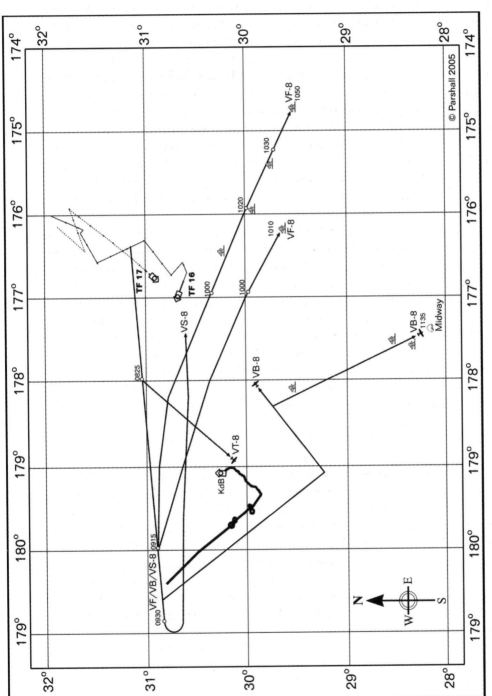

15-1: The travails of *Hornet*'s morning strike. Adapted from Lundstrom.

aircraft. Turning back to the southeast, they left Tucker to make his way back to the ship. Along the way, one of Johnson's planes suffered a catastrophic engine failure, leaving him to ditch 150 miles out. Two more ran out of gas just short of the island. The remaining eleven planes were greeted with antiaircraft fire from the island's Marine defenders, which damaged three aircraft. However, they managed to make their identities known and landed on Eastern Island at around 1135.

Johnson's departure at 0920 had left Stanhope Ring alone with *Hornet*'s scouting squadron. Ring immediately sent his wingman over to VS-8 to inform its commander, Lt. Cdr. Walter F. Rodee, that he was to continue following Ring. Rodee did as he was told until about 0940, but by then his fuel situation had reached the point where he had to break off for home. Rodee turned back to the east, and Ring's wingman went with him, leaving the air group commander on his own. He proceeded a bit farther and then turned around for the ship at high speed, overhauling VS-8 and arriving at *Hornet* at around 1118. Rodee and VS-8 set down shortly thereafter, followed by Tucker's detachment of three VS-8 aircraft at 1145.[19]

The net result was that *Hornet*'s air group had been gutted for absolutely no gain. Though no one on the American carriers realized it yet, VT-8 had been completely destroyed. Over a third of *Hornet*'s fighters were gone as well. A further third of the dive-bombers had ended up at Midway, where they were at least safe, but where they could not be used for carrier operations until they made it back to their ship. The remainder were on *Hornet*. But for the initiative of Waldron, none of Ring's group would have so much as *sighted* an enemy ship, let alone attacked one. And while Waldron had at least succeeded in bringing his force to battle, the truth was that he and his men had been slaughtered to little purpose. Ring's mission had been an outright disaster: he had compiled a 50 percent attrition rate and delivered zero in the way of combat results.

Enterprise fared better, though her losses were serious as well. VT-6 had been decimated. Only five of its aircraft survived their encounter with the Japanese CAP, and one of these didn't make it home. Another was so shot up that, after landing, it was judged to be useless. This left just three serviceable torpedo planes on board *Enterprise*. The dive-bombers fared poorly as well. Many had been damaged during their attack on *Kidō Butai,* and several ditched almost immediately afterward as a result. Having detoured far to the southwest before successfully locating the Japanese fleet, they had all been low on fuel even before the attack. After attacking, many of the SBD pilots correctly judged that they couldn't make the climb back up to altitude. This meant that their Zed Bakers had more difficulty in picking up their signals, although in many cases the problem was simply one of not having sufficient gas to make it back even if a homing signal *had* been detected. Damaged aircraft, wounded crewmen, and a rapidly worsening fuel situation compounded their navigational challenges still further. Not only that, but after the departure of the strike groups, *Enterprise* had been forced to unexpectedly maneuver to the southeast to put up additional CAP fighters. As a result, she couldn't possibly reach the location where the strike fliers thought she ought to be before they had to ditch.[20]

The result was something of a repeat of *Hornet*'s tragic VF-8 fiasco. Many of *Enterprise*'s dive-bombers returned to what they thought would be Point Option, only to find the open ocean. One by one, they went into the drink. Many were subsequently picked up by American PBYs or naval vessels, some after having drifted for days. Inevitably, however, a grim percentage of these men—including the crews of a group of four aircraft under Lt. Charles R. Ware of VS-6—were simply swallowed up by the impersonal vastness of the Pacific and never seen again.[21] When all was said and done, between combat losses, ditchings, and aircraft damaged beyond repair, *Enterprise* lost twenty-one dive-bombers, although the final tally did not become clear until the early afternoon.

Yorktown had perhaps been rewarded for her superior deck operations, or simply had been a little luckier. VT-3 had suffered cruelly and finished the morning down a dozen aircraft, including those that were too badly damaged to make it back home after their attack. But Max Leslie's Bombing Three returned to *Yorktown* without incident, though Leslie and another pilot would be forced to ditch because of fuel exhaustion before being recovered.[22]

Thus, the total tally of American aircraft lost on the morning strike was seventy—twelve fighters, twenty-one dive-bombers, and thirty-seven torpedo aircraft.[23] This represented about a 40 percent casualty rate in terms of the aircraft launched. The final tally of aviators lost was (thankfully) lower than this, as many were eventually rescued. But until the remaining aircraft were recovered and reorganized, the only readily available reserve force that could be considered a cohesive unit were the seventeen operational SBDs of *Yorktown*'s VS-5.[24] In total, the three American carriers between them scarcely mounted a single full air group (excluding fighters—whose casualties had been somewhat lighter) at this point.

Ten of VS-5's aircraft were currently spotted on *Yorktown*'s flight deck, along with a dozen CAP fighters. The SBDs were awaiting word to take off on a new scouting mission. Frank Jack Fletcher's knowledge of the Japanese fleet was still thin at this point. His latest information had been forwarded to him by Raymond Spruance at 1115—the 1000 sighting report from Gray's fighters.[25] Fletcher had also received a communication from one of Max Leslie's pilots at 1115 as VB-3 began landing, indicating that VB-3 had sunk an enemy carrier. This was splendid news, as far as it went. But Fletcher had been warned that the Japanese could be operating in two groups. If Gray had sighted only two enemy flattops, and Leslie's group had sunk one, that could mean that another pair lurked somewhere nearby. Accordingly, Fletcher judged that prudence dictated launching another reconnaissance mission to search the sea to his northwest out to a distance of 200 miles. He began launching these aircraft at 1133, and by 1150 both the SBDs and the new CAP Wildcats were aloft.

Even had Yamaguchi known of the terrible losses that the Americans had suffered, it should not have given him much comfort. For as bad as American casualties were, they retained two important advantages. First, once they reorganized their air groups, they would still have more than sixty dive-bombers.[26] In terms of raw ship-killing firepower, this represented more than quadruple what the Japanese could muster. Second, the Americans had three flight decks from which to operate. While this had created problems in coordination (and would do so again this afternoon), it also provided the Americans with a precious measure of redundancy. Having spare decks meant that they could suffer one of their ships rendered inoperable and still be able to find homes for any aircraft still aloft. On the Japanese side, of course, losing *Hiryū* meant losing the battle, period. These crucial advantages would become telling later in the afternoon.

Meanwhile, another battle was taking place on board the carriers Nagumo had left behind. This, too, was going badly for the Japanese. After Nagumo's launch had left *Akagi*, Captain Aoki had returned to the task at hand. Having been driven from the bridge, he and his officers congregated on the forward end of the flight deck for some time. At 1130 he ordered the ship's air personnel, along with *Akagi*'s wounded, to be transferred to *Nowaki* and *Arashi*. Then, at 1135 *Akagi* suffered a very large explosion in her hangar. This caused flames to worsen on the flight deck, which drove Aoki below to the anchor deck from which Nagumo had so recently departed. It was here that he would exercise command for the remainder of the day and much of the coming night.

In many of the accounts of the battle, the situations on board the carriers at this time are described as being remarkably similar. Yet, in fact, *Akagi* was to wage a very different struggle than *Kaga* or *Sōryū*. By 1140 *Sōryū* had been written off for the better part of an hour, with most of her crew already having gone into the water. *Kaga*'s fires were utterly out of control, although many men were still on board her. In contrast, the struggle to contain the blaze on *Akagi* developed into a grudging battle of attrition that lasted more than nine hours.

Her anchor deck was the heart of the resistance to the fires. The senior officers were all here, including her damage-control chief, Commander Dobashi. Perhaps to summon up the proper *samurai* spirit, Dobashi had girded himself for the tasks ahead by strapping on his officer's sword.[27] The medical staff, too, set up shop as best they could. However, with the bulk of their supplies left behind in the bowels of the ship, there was little they could do to treat the walking wounded who were now making their way forward.

The curving forward bulkhead of the hangar decks loomed over the bow like a cliff, ascending until it met the underside of the flight deck, some thirty-five feet overhead. Up this bulkhead mounted a stairway. Two flights of fifteen steps apiece led to hatches that gave access to the lower and upper hangars. Up these steel steps now trudged groups of men, members of the damage-control parties. One by one, they disappeared through the blackened doors into the canyons of fire beyond. Many of them would never return.

Dobashi and Chief Engineer Tampo had several daunting tasks confronting them. One was to fight the fires. The second was to ensure that the aft magazines had been successfully flooded. The third was to get crews back into the engineering spaces to assess whether *Akagi* could be made operational again. If they could at least get her moving, she might have a chance. Of the three Japanese carriers damaged thus far, she alone had at least some marginal hope of being saved. Saved, that is, if her wounds could be tended promptly, and if the right equipment was available. Indeed, had she been one of the newer American carriers, it's likely that she *would* have been saved, even if rendered hors de combat for months afterward. Unfortunately, Japanese damage-control practice was not equal to the task set before it this morning.

While a detailed comparative study of Japanese and American damage-control practices is beyond the scope of this work, some pertinent points can quickly be made. First, the total number of damage-control personnel on board a Japanese vessel was drastically lower than on a comparable U.S. warship. Whereas in 1942 a U.S. carrier could effectively number almost every one of its nonaviation staff as being able to contribute to damage-control efforts in some capacity, a Japanese carrier might only have between 350 and 400 men trained out of a crew of 1,500–2,000.[28]

Second, the Japanese Navy took far fewer precautions to preserve the damage-control capacity of its ships—both physical and human—than was prudent. The Japanese recognized the worth of distributing damage-control capability within a warship to prevent a single hit from destroying a significant percentage of that capability. However, they did not apparently copy the Americans' obsession with creating redundant backup systems. For example, they did not design their fire mains such that they could be divided into independent segments. Nor did they bother dispersing and protecting the damage-control parties throughout the ship. Official 1944 USN doctrine went so far as to direct damage-control personnel to lie flat on the deck during a surface action so as to avoid taking unnecessary fragmentation casualties from gun hits. One can scarcely see the Japanese, with such a fatalistic approach to the expenditure of their own human capital, even conceiving of such measures.

Third, the Japanese had nowhere near the specialized equipment the U.S. Navy used for fighting fires. Their emergency breathing gear was crude, and they had nothing like the ubiquitous "handy billy" portable gasoline-powered pumps, or portable generators, of the U.S. Navy. While portable pumps could not replace the ship's main pumps, they could buy time for damage-control teams to repair those primary systems and get them back into action. The Japanese did not introduce a similar device until 1944, and even then produced only a limited number per ship. Such emergency capacity as was available on their ships came from large, fixed emergency generators, or from manual pumps.

The final factor was Japanese damage-control practice appeared not to have nearly the same degree of systemization as that of the Americans.[29] This is graphically demonstrated by the topic of flooding control. The Japanese were very concerned with flooding and installed elaborate pumping and counterflooding mechanisms on their larger warships. Japanese damage-control centers contained pegboards showing pipelines, valves, and pumps, as well as the major tanks and voids, in order to control flooding. Yet even in this, the Imperial Navy's proficiency paled in comparison to its American rival. For instance, the Japanese apparently had no standardized closure conditions such as the USN's "X-Ray," "Yoke," and "Zebra" (which described a hierarchy of how pipe valves, hatch covers, and other openings within the ship should be secured depending on the steaming condition and battle readiness of the vessel). The Americans prepared extensive catalogs ("bills") of all valves, hatches, ventilators, drains, and other equipment that might factor into the equation. They also mapped the quickest routes to potential damage points while taking into account those hatches that would be closed under battle conditions. In sum, the impression one gets is that the Japanese did not approach the problem in the sense of a warship being a collection of interrelated systems, each of which could affect the others.[30] As an American commentator scathingly remarked about Japanese techniques, "damage control, as it is understood in the U.S. Navy, did not exist."[31]

Kidō Butai's shortcomings in firefighting technique were already apparent to the men struggling to contain the spreading blaze. By 1100 the fire on *Akagi* had become an inferno—making its way forward and consuming every scrap of inflammable material on the hangar decks in the process. Unfortunately for Commander Dobashi and his men, large gasoline-powered fires like these were essentially beyond the ability of World War II firefighting practices to extinguish. Even the U.S. Navy had concluded grimly that once an avgas fire "develops into one of major proportions, involving . . . ten or more planes, it will continue to burn until all fuel is consumed despite application of water, where water alone is employed."[32] The best one could really hope for was to ride the fires out, contain them, cut them off from their fuel, and hope they didn't destroy the ship before they burned out.

With an aviation gasoline fire, applying water has only a limited effect, because the gasoline simply floats on top of the water and continues to burn. Streams of water can, in some cases, prevent the fire from spreading, but they won't extinguish it. And if the crews are not careful, the water can actually slosh around and spread the burning gasoline over a wider area. Firefighting foam is much more effective, in that it smothers the blaze by separating it from its oxygen. But the temptation after foam has been applied is to hose it and the fuel away as soon as possible with water. This often has unforeseen and evil consequences. If the ambient temperature of the air or metal decks is still above the ignition point of the fuel, the application of water and subsequent dissolution of the foam simply reexposes the fuel to oxygen and can actually cause the fire to reignite. In *Akagi*'s case, this problem was probably moot—her foam system had been rendered ineffective from the outset. All the men had was water, and precious little of that. It is known that *Akagi*'s crew managed to rig a large hand pump on the anchor deck.[33] This made her efforts somewhat more effective than *Kaga*'s. But without automated pumping capacity, Commander Dobashi was bound to continue losing ground.

While *Akagi*'s situation took several hours to deteriorate beyond hope, *Kaga*'s situation was already grim. Trapped on the starboard boat deck, her *hikōchō*, Commander Amagai, was doing what he could. His selection of command location was more expedient than well thought-out. Smoke was pouring out of the ship and sweeping down from the flight deck above, making exercising control next to impossible. Warrant Officer Morinaga found the *hikōchō* here, after having had a little adventure of his own in making it to the boat deck.[34] Immediately following the large explosion in the hangar, he had found himself on the AA gallery level just above Amagai's position. Above him, the flight deck was completely engulfed in flames. Worse yet, the ladder leading down was red hot, leaving him trapped. Just below him, though, he could see the ship's cutter, still hanging from its davits. Seizing his opportunity, he jumped down on top of the boat, landing on the canvas cover. From there he was able to lower himself gingerly to the deck below.

Knocked unconscious by the earlier blasts, aviator Akamatsu Yūji finally awoke in the deserted ready room, head bleeding, and made his way up to the flight deck.

The steel plates rimming the wooden flight deck were already so hot that the rubber soles of his shoes melted. From where he was, he could see no way down except over the edge and straight into the ocean—a frighteningly long drop. Yet, the fires were coming up behind, and eventually Akamatsu had no choice. He plunged into the ocean, but his life jacket pulled him back up to the surface. All around him men were swimming, clutching whatever debris they could find. Eventually, he joined a group of other pilots supporting their injured squadron leader, Lieutenant Kitajima. After an hour, Akamatsu and his group were finally picked up by the destroyer *Hagikaze*.[35]

Kaga was actually still moving, crawling north at two to three knots. We know this to be true, because she was being followed by an American submarine. The long-suffering *Nautilus* had caught up to what was left of *Kidō Butai*. After the dive-bomber attack, her skipper, Lt. Cdr. William Brockman, had seen smoke columns on the horizon and selected the nearest one. *Akagi* avoided Brockman's attentions by virtue of remaining under power for some time before her rudder failed. Thus, *Kaga* found herself in a familiar position—"tail-end Charlie"—but this time in a formation of cripples, and with Brockman trying to close in. Trouble was, even after an hour's submerged movement, Brockman wasn't gaining. The conclusion was obvious—the big Japanese flattop was still limping along, even though she was wreathed in flames.[36]

On the face of it, this seems somewhat incredible, particularly given how quickly *Sōryū* had been rendered immobile. However, there were a number of factors that explain her ability to remain underway. First, *Kaga* had a larger number of decks between her hangars and the engine spaces, meaning that her engine room crews were protected for longer before the heat became intolerable. The fact that she had an armored deck above her vitals helped as well.[37] Finally, she had not taken a freak hit that detonated deep in the ship, as *Sōryū* apparently had. The net result was that at least one of *Kaga*'s engine rooms must have remained operative for some time. In the end, of course, it was a feat that would cost the lives of dozens of her engineers, who stayed at their posts and performed their duties until the end.

On *Sōryū*, the situation had been judged hopeless almost from the get-go. Captain Yanagimoto's "Abandon ship" at 1045 had found pilot Mori and the survivors from the ready room already clustered on the boat deck, one deck below the bridge.[38] The narrow walkway was packed so tight with men that they had to raise their arms above their heads. Yet, more kept pushing in to escape the fires on the hangar decks, which were steadily drawing nearer. The sailors finally resorted to standing on each other's shoulders in spots.

The cutter on the boat deck seemed an obvious gambit, so somebody made to lower it, but it stuck in the davits with one end still hanging from above. Realizing that the cutter was now useless, the men simply started jumping. Mori was scared—the distance looked too far. It was, in fact, some thirty-five feet—a comfortable enough sounding leap sitting in the safety of one's armchair, decidedly less so when clinging to a steel railing poised above the brink. But as he watched, Mori began to discern a rhythm to the waves, the long swells periodically bringing themselves closer to him. Timing his jump carefully, he jumped clear of the deck and grabbed for one of the lifeboat's ropes. Unfortunately for him, the line was no longer attached to anything, and he and the useless lanyard plummeted into the sea.

Bobbing to the surface, he swam clear of *Sōryū*'s hull. At that very moment, the cutter above him decided to come hurtling down, fortunately landing nearby, rather than on top of him. Because of its bizarre entry angle, it hit the sea upside down. But Mori and some of the other swimmers righted it and began bailing it out with their footwear. They then began the laborious task of paddling away from the ship.

On board *Akagi,* despite the steadily worsening conditions, men were still fighting the blaze in an organized fashion. But once the fires crept below the hangars, the situation became much more complex. The sheer number of spaces in the ship's innards meant that the fire had that many more places to fester in, dissipating the efforts of the crew still further. Despite the ever-present danger of unexploded munitions, it was probably easier to bring hoses into play in the relatively large space of the hangar decks. Even there, in fact, there probably wasn't enough room for more than a score of men to work at any given time.[39] But as the fire burned deeper, men would have been forced to battle it in the twisting, darkened corridors. Deck heights on most Japanese warships were very cramped by Western standards—no more than six or seven feet. In some cases, the clearance under the ductwork and other overhead hamper was as little as five. Firefighting would have to be done in smaller groups, cut off from each other, with little coordination between them.

The working conditions were nothing short of horrific. The crew hauled firefighting equipment into the ship's bowels, eyes watering and throats retching on the fumes suppurating from the smoldering bulkheads. Their mouths would in many cases have been covered by a wet rag, sometimes soaked with their own urine, to filter the worst of the fumes. Despite that, crawling along the decks would have been obligatory just to be able to breathe. Likewise, they would have dragged their comrades—shredded by bomb blasts, hideously burned, or choked by smoke—back out again to the anchor deck. As men in the bowels were overcome, the survivors on the anchor deck, in many cases already wounded themselves, would have had to rouse themselves and take their places on the fire line.

The plight of the engineering crews on all three ships, trapped in the engine spaces below the waterline, was bleaker still. Engine rooms are hot, unpleasant places to begin with, and the encroaching fires quickly rendered all of them nearly uninhabitable. It is hardly surprising that according to the common wisdom, the engine room crews of *Akagi, Kaga,* and *Sōryū* died to a man, with only a few escaping from *Hiryū*. However, on closer examination, it appears that such universal pronouncements are untrue.[40] *Kaga* and *Sōryū*'s engineers, it is true, died in droves. Two-thirds of *Kaga*'s were killed, and only a handful would ultimately survive from *Sōryū*'s. *Sōryū*'s black gang was simply trapped—given the fewer number of decks between the engine spaces and the hangars, the fire was on top of them almost immediately, blocking their escape paths. *Kaga*'s casualties appear to have been caused by her continued efforts to try and limp out of the area, which necessarily kept the engineers at their posts even as conditions deteriorated. *Akagi*'s engineers, however, fared somewhat better.

Akagi's official casualty list—267 men—is surprisingly low when compared to *Kaga*'s and *Sōryū*'s, especially given the length of her ordeal. Notwithstanding the loss of mechanics and armorers that must have occurred from the initial bomb, and the subsequent casualties among the firefighting crews, such a low loss rate hardly seems believable. Her relative good fortune was the result of two factors. First, she suffered only a single hit. This meant that fewer men were killed outright by the initial attack, unlike *Kaga* and *Sōryū*. This also ensured that *Akagi*'s fires were more localized and slower to develop into a general blaze, giving her crew more time to get out of the way. The second factor, of course, was that Captain Aoki had ordered the engineering spaces abandoned as soon as *Akagi*'s steering had failed at 1043. Better still, the internal communications on board ship were still in good enough shape, at least initially, that his orders were acted on promptly. This meant that while a portion of her 303-strong engineering staff eventually did perish, either belowdecks or in damage-control efforts, nearly two-thirds ultimately survived. This represented a far better survival rate among *Akagi*'s engineers than any of the other carriers would boast this day.

Back on *Kaga,* Amagai and Morinaga were now crowded with many aviators and other survivors into a steadily shrinking space that clung like an aerie to the side of the ship. Behind and above them the fires advanced steadily. Far below was the sea. Finally, on his own initiative, Amagai told the men to jump for it. Morinaga peeled off his flight suit and boots. Around them, some of the newer recruits were protesting that they didn't know how to swim. Amagai was adamant—they were dead for sure if they stayed where they were. Morinaga didn't wait, but jumped as far out as he could. It was a long way down. Others followed suit.

One man was going to perish regardless—Lt. Ogawa Shōichi, *Kaga*'s *kanbaku buntaichō,* and a famous veteran of the attack on Pearl Harbor, as well as the fighting in China. Ogawa had been badly wounded in the initial attack on *Kaga.* The long fall to the water would have killed him outright, and his wounds, he knew, were mortal in any case. Smiling complacently, he urged Amagai to abandon ship with the other pilots. Finally, Amagai bade him farewell and jumped into the sea with the last of the aviators. From below in the water, the men could see Ogawa still. He had crawled to the ship's railing and was waving and yelling encouragement to them. Then he lost his final strength and died in front of their eyes.

Hanging on to his line dangling below *Sōryū*'s bridge, Gunnery Officer Kanao was unaware of the fact that the ship had been largely abandoned above him. All he knew was that he couldn't swim worth a damn and that the lanyard was literally his lifeline. Grimly, he hung on for what seemed like hours.[41] After a while, one of the sailors swimming nearby noticed his plight and swam up to him. It turned out to be one of Kanao's subordinates, a midshipman. He tied the line around Kanao's waist.

At first Kanao was grateful, but being secured to a line was something of a two-edged sword. It assured Kanao's security, but also tied his motions to those of the ship. Though the water was calm and shiny (perhaps because of the oil being spread on it), *Sōryū* still rolled appreciably. When she did so, the line hauled Kanao bodily out of the water and slammed him against her flank. He quickly became adept at using his legs to cushion the blows, though it hurt. Still, it was better than drowning.

After a time, Kanao heard someone shouting his name. It was Lieutenant Commander Asanoumi, *Sōryū*'s navigator, who he had last seen on the bridge.

"Hi, Gunnery Officer!" Asanoumi shouted, "Abandon ship has been ordered. You must swim away from the ship."

"I cannot swim," Kanao called back. "Please go ahead."

"I'll swim then," Asanoumi said. "Try to fight back, don't give up!" The navigator swam on.[42]

Kanao wondered if perhaps the navigation officer was the last person he would see in this lifetime.[43] Despite the rope, he felt marooned in the middle of the ocean. He had no control over his fate—he could neither swim away nor climb back on board the ship. The only thing he could do was to cling to the line and try to survive the relentless buffeting against *Sōryū*'s hull.

Kanao suddenly saw someone on the bridge, looking out the window. It was Captain Yanagimoto. His face was scarlet red, and it reminded Kanao of the fairy-tale monsters of his childhood. It had a totally calm and relaxed expression, "like a Buddha," Kanao remembered later. "Skipper!" he tried to yell, but no sound came out. The next time he looked up, the face was gone. Other men apparently saw Yanagimoto as well, standing on the starboard side of the bridge, exhorting the men in the water. Soon afterward, though, the captain disappeared into the fires surrounding *Sōryū*'s island. So ended one of Japan's most beloved commanders.[44]

The ship was silent now. Kanao was overwhelmed with sorrow, both at his own likely fate and that of *Sōryū*'s skipper. Just then, he noticed a ladder floating closer to him from the direction of the carrier's stern. Desperate to have done with the line and his demoralizing suspension, he untied himself, let go, and splashed toward the ladder. Grabbing it, he simply held on for dear life.

16

Japanese Counterstrikes—1200–1400

On board *Hiryū,* Yamaguchi and his staff were beginning to get edgy. If *Chikuma* No. 5's previous report was correct, the enemy ought to have been close by. Not only that, but the scout had gone on the air at 1132 so that the *kanbaku buntaichō* could home in on its signal. Yet, it was now noon, Kobayashi had been in the air an hour, and no one had as yet received any report from him.

In fact, unbeknownst to Yamaguchi or his staff, Kobayashi had already sent two signals back to *Hiryū,* but neither of them was received (or perhaps decoded) until almost an hour later. As a result, the first intimation that Yamaguchi received that his force had, in fact, found the enemy did not occur until 1210. This signal, though, didn't come from Kobayashi, but from another anonymous aircraft in the dive-bomber *hikōtai.* It said simply: "Am bombing enemy carrier." After that, silence.

Yamaguchi was in the dark. However, he knew that at least some of his dive-bombers were now attacking an enemy carrier. That was good news, as far as it went. Furthermore, the fact that Kobayashi had managed to reach the enemy within an hour and ten minutes flight time meant that the Americans were indeed relatively close. This broadly confirmed *Chikuma* No. 5's spotting report. Yamaguchi took this opportunity to order the fleet's remaining scout planes put in readiness. Unfortunately, *Chikuma's* No. 4 plane was now the only long-range scout ready to go. *Chikuma* No. 1 had been recovered earlier with some sort of problem, and was down.[1] Neither *Tone's* No. 1 aircraft, nor Amari's No. 4 were ready, either. *Kidō Butai* was beginning to run short of quality scouts. For the time being, Yamaguchi was simply pressing ahead—preparing Tomonaga's follow-up strike (which would be ready within another hour or so) and hoping he would receive further information from Kobayashi in the meantime.

It would be right to wonder why prepping and spotting Tomonaga's sixteen-plane strike was taking so long, given that Yamaguchi originally wanted to launch at around 1220. After all, Tomonaga's group had returned to the ship almost three hours earlier. This delay couldn't be readily attributed to CAP operations. Kobayashi had taken off at 1057. Since then, *Hiryū* had landed six Zeros at 1134, and that was it. The rest of the force's fighters were staying aloft for the time being. *Hiryū's* flight deck was wide open for spotting. On the face of it, it would seem that Tomonaga should have been able to follow Kobayashi's group within about an hour and a half of the latter's launch. Yet apparently this wasn't possible.

There are two plausible explanations for what would develop into a two and a half hour separation between *Hiryū*'s two counterstrikes. Either the aircraft and hangar crews were exhausted by the day's operations, or Yamaguchi was hoping to locate and confirm a second target and then hit it as well. Either way, *Hiryū*'s operational tempo was slowing to a crawl. Like a drowning man, *Kidō Butai*'s efforts were becoming feebler and less well coordinated. The crisp synchronization of the morning's operations were gone at the very moment that decisive action was required. Instead, *Hiryū* was fighting raggedly, with an air of desperation.

A quarter past noon found Nagumo back in control of his fleet, and in effective communication with all units, including *Hiryū*. His flagship, *Nagara,* was leading the surface units of *Kidō Butai* toward the enemy along course 060 degrees. Kondō had sent word that his Second Fleet was rushing to reinforce Nagumo. Though Kondō could not arrive till early morning, Nagumo likely believed that if he could just survive till sunset after engaging the enemy, his battleships and cruisers could likely take good care of themselves in the darkness until help arrived to turn the tide.

It was at this juncture, after an hour and a half of silence since receiving Abe's 1050 communiqué, that Yamamoto finally made his presence felt. He and his staff had recovered from their earlier shock and formulated a plan to recover the situation. Removed from the battlefield, they, even more than Nagumo, retained an unwarranted optimism that the situation could yet be retrieved. As Combined Fleet's staff saw it, the biggest immediate worry was Nagumo's deficit in flight decks. When Kondō joined Nagumo, he would add light carrier *Zuihō* to the mix, but that was slender support at best. In a pinch, the ancient *Hōshō* might be committed as well. Finally, there was a slim possibility that either *Akagi* or *Kaga* could be restored to action—no reports of their abandonment had yet been received by Yamamoto, and he knew that they had been ordered to withdraw northwest. However, it did not take a tactical genius to see that the most potent resource for turning the tide of battle unfortunately lay with the two carriers tied up in the Aleutians Operation. The sooner Kakuta could bring CarDiv 4 south into the battle, the better. The obvious thing to do was to find a quick way to reorganize and concentrate as much of this strength as possible, while simultaneously calling on Kakuta's carrier force.

The American carriers were not the only problem that would have to be dealt with if the battle was to be turned around—there was still the question of Midway's airpower. The staff believed this threat could be neutralized by gun power. Kondō could detach Kurita's cruiser squadron to dash ahead and bombard Midway before dawn. If all went well, the Japanese would only have to contend with the American carriers come the morning of the 5th, and there was reason to hope that these would be whittled down in the meantime.

Accordingly, at 1220 Yamamoto sent out a general dispatch to his forces. First, as expected, the tanker force would withdraw from the Main Body, whereupon Yamamoto would move south to Nagumo's aid. The Midway Invasion Force was to withdraw temporarily to the northwest, while Kondō was to charge northeast toward *Kidō Butai.* Finally, the Second Mobile Striking Force was to come south. About an hour later, at 1310, he elaborated that Kondō should dispatch a portion of his force to "shell and destroy" the enemy air base on Midway. At the same time, he "temporarily postponed" the invasion of both Midway and Kiska.[2]

Spurred into action, *Kidō Butai* continued preparations for a surface battle. Nagumo shortly informed his entire force he planned "to destroy the enemy by daylight action" and that they should "expect to encounter the enemy momentarily." This last remark is puzzling, until it is recalled that Nagumo had assumed that the U.S. forces were presumably still closing his own, and the gap had supposedly been narrowing for the last two hours. If that was true, then Nagumo was within his rights to assume that contact would soon be made. *Chikuma* and *Tone* dutifully reported at 1225 and 1229, respectively, that they had completed preparations for torpedo action.[3]

It is true that at this point in the battle neither Yamaguchi nor Nagumo had much concrete information. Yet, despite the earlier fragmentary reports that the enemy lay within a hundred miles or so, the idea that either the enemy or Nagumo's force could somehow magically bridge the physical gap between them was folly. This could only have occurred if the enemy was interested in a surface brawl himself. The thought ought to have occurred to the commander of *Kidō Butai* that his opponents were unlikely to desire this.

The most likely explanation for Nagumo's reasoning is that he was reverse projecting his own preferred tactics on those of the enemy. That is to say, the overall Japanese plan at Midway was built on the concept of the Japanese carriers whittling down the Americans so that the Main Body could land the killing blow. Finding himself in a dramatically weakened position, he might have imagined that the Americans were going to come gunning for *him* with their own surface forces. Indeed, his earlier belief that the American forces were primarily surface oriented may have been coming back to haunt him. Of course, neither Fletcher nor Spruance had the slightest interest in participating in a surface battle, either during broad daylight or at night.

Nagumo may also have imagined that Kobayashi's strike would disable what he still hoped was just a single American carrier and thus transform the battle into a pure surface affair. But any staff officer worth his salt could have told him that the 1020 dive-bomber attack *had* to have been the work of more than one enemy carrier. Given that, and in the complete absence of any hard information regarding the results of Kobayashi's attack, Nagumo was clearly guilty of grasping at straws.

At 1240, however, came an update from *Chikuma*'s No. 5 search plane that finally put paid to these illusions. "Sight what appears to be two large enemy cruisers in position bearing 15 degrees, distance 130 miles from my point of origin. In addition, I see what appears to be 1 carrier and 1 destroyer. Course north, speed 20 knots."[4]

Nagumo's face surely fell upon receiving this news, and his subsequent actions revealed his realization of the full import of the message. The enemy force appeared to be shearing away north and opening the range. This killed any immediate hopes of bringing about a surface action. As Nagumo himself put it later, with a trace of unintentional irony: "From this it became evident that the enemy was trying to put distance between himself and us."[5] Nagumo thereafter chose to parallel the enemy's course and try to remain to the northwest of him. He would await the developments from *Hiryū*'s air strikes, the arrival of reinforcements, and new search reports before taking further action. Accordingly, at 1245 Nagumo changed course from 060 to due north, speed 20 knots.

At the same moment Nagumo was turning north, an additional snippet regarding Kobayashi's attack was finally received by *Hiryū*. One of the dive-bombers signaled: "Enemy carrier is burning. I see no friendly planes in range of visibility. I am homing." The interesting part of this message was not so much what it said, but who it came from. Neither Lieutenant Kobayashi, nor his second in command, Lieutenant Kondō, had transmitted it. Instead, it seems most likely that the message was sent from Ens. Nakayama Shimematsu, who commanded the lead plane in the 2nd *shōtai* of Kondō's 2nd *chūtai*.[6]

The fact that the 1245 transmission came from the middle of the 2nd *chūtai*'s batting order had to have caused some anxious looks on *Hiryū*'s bridge. Nakayama would have let his superiors report first if they had been able to. The fact that he had transmitted meant that he considered himself the senior survivor of the squadron. There was only one conclusion that could be reached: Kobayashi's attack had been very costly. However, until the dive-bombers landed, it would be impossible to gauge what impact they had made.[7]

Meanwhile, on board *Akagi,* a rather strange turn of events was taking place. At 1203 the flagship's engines had suddenly come to life. Slowly, the stricken giant began moving in a great circle to starboard, her rudder still jammed. To Captain Aoki, this was all rather mysterious—ships typically don't just "turn on" of their own accord. The fact that the engineering spaces had been deliberately abandoned at 1043 should have meant that the machinery had been secured in good order as well, making it less believable that *Akagi* had spontaneously reengaged her own engines. Thus, despite the Nagumo Report's characterization of *Akagi*'s movement as being "automatic," it is almost impossible to contrive a set of circumstances whereby she resumed her circling without human intervention.

Oddly enough, Commander Tampo had been in the engineering spaces just fifteen minutes before and was convinced that no one remained alive there. But in truth, his recent inspection was unlikely to have encompassed the entirety of the engine rooms, which were vast, dark, and exceedingly hot and smoky. The riddle needed solving, though, so an engineering ensign named Akiyama was dispatched forthwith back below.

Making his way down from the anchor deck, Akiyama would have passed through the officers berthing spaces in the bow, down through the ship's machine shops, and finally down another long vertical ladder that led to the electrical control rooms just forward of Boiler Room No. 1. He now stood on the lowest deck in the ship, some twenty-five feet below the waterline. Making his way aft through the pitch black, he might have peered into the boiler control room located at Frame 94, and then the one located further aft at Frame 108. Shining his light briefly on the dials and gauges within, Akiyama would have discovered that *Akagi* still had some level of steam in her boilers. Even in the midst of evacuation, there would have been no reason to have bled her steam off, particularly if it was hoped that power could be restored later.

The engine room controls themselves were located in both the forward and aft engine rooms. With the fumes growing worse and worse, Akiyama would have been lucky to have made it into the forward engine room at all. This compartment was cavernous, with choking vapors adding to the stygian blackness. Akiyama wouldn't have been able to see much more than what was directly in front of his flashlight's narrow blade of light—silent machinery and hurried glimpses of his fallen shipmates. But the aft engines were another 150 feet further astern, and the only way to get there was through cramped passageways that ran under the outboard shaft alleys. Given the horrendous atmospheric conditions, and finding nothing but corpses in the spaces he ventured into, it would not have been surprising if Akiyama concluded that conditions were untenable in the aft engine rooms as well. He couldn't really linger. His mission, after all, was to bring information back to Aoki and Tampo, and he couldn't very well do that if he was dead. Akiyama returned in short order to the anchor deck. Everyone in the engine rooms had succumbed, he reported.

Yet, Akiyama was almost certainly wrong in his estimation. Instead, it seems likely that there *were* men in *Akagi*'s aft engine room about noon, but that no one on her bow was aware of their actions. At this point, the two extremities of the ship were completely cut off from each other. Survivors were almost certainly gathered on the ship's fantail, many of which would have come up from the engine spaces via a hatch in the steering room spaces. It is quite possible that some of these men, perhaps led by some anonymous engineering lieutenant, went below again in an effort to flood the magazines and perhaps restore power to the ship.

This speculation is substantiated by the Nagumo Report itself. We know that *Akagi*'s aft magazines were not flooded until about 1300. Given the likely shock damage in the stern, which had evidently damaged the piping, the only way these spaces were going to be flooded was manually. If so, then somebody *had* to have ventured into the aft machinery spaces to do the deed. Not coincidentally, this would have put a damage-control party (almost certainly composed of engineering personnel) directly adjacent to the aft engine rooms. It would not have been surprising if they somehow managed to get the ship underway again. Whatever the explanation, *Akagi* was now moving, although her stately, blazing procession was ultimately doomed to lead nowhere.

However, her circling wasn't necessarily all bad. One of the beneficiaries was Fujita Iyozo, *Sōryū*'s fighter ace. Having been shot down over *Kidō Butai* during the torpedo attack on *Hiryū*, he had been drifting in his inflatable life vest with no way to attract anyone's attention. All the ships that he could see were on the horizon. He was still starving hungry, and all in all, things did not look good. However, to his amazement, he now saw *Akagi* moving again, and she seemed to be coming his way. Fujita started swimming.[8]

As *Akagi* moved, so too moved her escorts. Before long, Fujita found that destroyer *Nowaki* was heading in his general direction as well. Fujita began waving frantically. For a minute, it appears that *Nowaki* mistook him for an enemy aviator, as she cranked one of her 25-mm machine guns around toward him. However, at this point fate intervened yet again as both *Nowaki*'s navigator and her executive officer recognized the man in the water—all three of them had been Etajima classmates.[9]

Within minutes, strong hands helped Fujita climb to the destroyer's deck. In the distance, he could see other boats from *Nowaki* rescuing sailors from the burning carrier beyond, but he was too tired to really take in all the details. Then, after being given food and a dry uniform, the exhausted flier simply fell asleep where he sat, on *Nowaki*'s main deck.

At 1300 Yamaguchi finally received more definitive word about what he was up against, conveyed by Rear Admiral Kimura in *Nagara*. An American pilot from *Yorktown*'s VT-3 had been plucked from the water by *Arashi* and interrogated, and from him the Japanese had learned that there was not just one American carrier present, but three—*Yorktown, Enterprise,* and *Hornet!*[10] During his interrogation, the unfortunate prisoner—Ens. Wesley Osmus—divulged that *Yorktown* was operating separately from the other two flattops. He also related the details of the American sortie from Pearl Harbor, when they had reached Midway, and the composition of the American task forces.

Osmus's information wasn't perfect, but it confirmed two important points. First, the Japanese now knew that they were up against a powerful adversary. Second, since the American carriers were apparently operating separately, it was now unclear whether both American task forces had been found yet by the Japanese. This was shortly confirmed by *Sōryū*'s D4Y scout. Returning to the task force and finding *Hiryū*'s deck already spotted with torpedo planes, Iida dropped a message tube, which confirmed that the enemy was operating in two task forces, containing three carriers, with the second enemy task force located to the south of the formation Kobayashi had attacked.[11]

Here, from the mouth of the enemy, and from their own scouts, was confirmation of the grim odds facing the Japanese. Even presuming that Kobayashi's force had inflicted severe damage on one of the American flattops, *Hiryū* simply didn't have the strength to face another two. In fact, even attempting to construct a strategic calculus by means of simplistic math like "one of our carriers versus two of theirs" was facile, as it didn't plumb the depths to which *Hiryū*'s airpower had sunk. At this juncture, both sides were hurt—nobody was operating full air groups any longer. Combat strength was now measured by having both residual airpower *and* redundant flight decks. However, *Hiryū*'s air group was but a shadow of its former self, and Yamaguchi had only a single flight deck from which to attack. Had *Akagi* escaped her doom at the hands of Dick Best, Yamaguchi's approach to the battle might have made more sense. But now, more than ever, the intelligent course of action was for *Hiryū* to break off the action. Not opening the range to the enemy, even for the forty-five minutes remaining before Tomonaga would be able to take off, was simply the wrong thing to do, because it needlessly compounded *Hiryū*'s risks of detection and subsequent attack. Yet, the only discernible immediate response to the reports from the *Sōryū*'s scout plane and Ens. Osmus's interrogation was Nagumo signaling to *Tone* and *Haruna* at 1310 that they should launch reconnaissance aircraft to search between 0 and 90 degrees True to localize the second American task force.

Figuring out exactly where each of *Kidō Butai*'s constituent components was at this moment is a complex undertaking, because the Japanese force was scattered. The heavy units—CruDiv 8 and BatDiv 3—were sticking close to *Nagara,* while closing the Americans. As mentioned, though, Nagumo had subsequently changed course to 0 degrees (at 1245) and would shortly change course again to 070 degrees at 1322. He was to stay on this heading until he was finally rejoined by *Hiryū*, which was overhauling him from the south, at 1440.

Hiryū's whereabouts are more difficult to determine, as we have no surviving course chart for her. The evidence indicates that after moving away from the vicinity of *Sōryū* at around 1130, she had operated on a roughly back and forth course a bit east of the morning's disaster. Thus, when the likely courses of the *Nagara* and *Hiryū* groups are plotted, *Hiryū* ends up to the east and south of Nagumo's position after the latter started his noon counterthrust toward the Americans. Yet, while *Hiryū* was detached from Nagumo, the evidence suggests that she was still within blinker distance of him, probably using CruDiv 8 as an intermediary.[12] Hence, Yamaguchi was not really out of touch with Nagumo from the standpoint of command and control. Again, what all this points to is a rather different picture of Japanese command arrangements during the hours immediately after the 1020 catastrophe. Instead of tagging along behind Yamaguchi, Nagumo was attempting to lead from the fore. Likewise, Yamaguchi, despite his aggressive reputation, was far from closing the enemy, or even steering northeast, at anything like thirty knots. Instead, we see hints of a different picture, wherein *Hiryū* was essentially stalking the enemy, using Nagumo's forces as something of a shield while conducting her launches and recoveries. Then, when Nagumo eventually gave up the attempt to close with the enemy, he chose a course whereby *Hiryū* could rejoin him relatively quickly.

One imperative the Japanese did have at this juncture was maintaining contact with the one American carrier they *had* found. Unfortunately, Petty Officer Takezaki and *Chikuma* No. 5 were having a difficult time with this. As a result, they had been on and off the air during their mission. At 1217 Takezaki, who had lingered in the area of Kobayashi's attack, came on the air to report that he had been pursued by enemy aircraft and had lost contact with the task force. Three minutes later, though, he signaled that they had reestablished contact with the Americans. Thereafter, Takezaki's pilot, PO3c Hara Hisashi,[13] had played a cat and mouse game with the American fighters in the area, ducking into clouds when threatened. At 1314 Takezaki transmitted that he had sighted an enemy carrier task force on course 020, making twenty-four knots. Interestingly, he made no mention of whether the carrier he saw was burning, as Kobayashi's squadron had last reported it to be. *Yorktown* was still dead in the water at this point in time, so it seems likely that Takezaki was seeing TF 16 instead, although he didn't apparently realize it.

Hopefully, the forthcoming scouting launch would help remedy some of these deficiencies. One benefit of the enemy's proximity was that it allowed the Japanese to more usefully employ their shorter-ranged Type 95 spotting planes. At 1315 Abe had *Tone* signal his vessels to launch a total of five aircraft. Each plane was to search to 150 miles, then turn left for an additional thirty miles. The search lines would be as follows:

Search line No. 1, 90 degrees, *Tone.*
Search line No. 2, 70 degrees, *Tone.*

Search line No. 3, 50 degrees, *Chikuma.*
Search line No. 4, 30 degrees, *Haruna.*
Search line No. 5, 10 degrees, *Kirishima.*

However, five minutes later, *Haruna* blinkered back to report that she had already launched all three of her aircraft at 1300. Their orders were to fan out across an arc stretching from 40 degrees westward to 340 degrees. What Abe thought of his overeager subordinate's initiative remains a mystery, but as it transpired one of *Haruna*'s scout planes was destined to make a later contact with the Americans. This is odd in itself, in that at this point in the battle, the Americans were almost due east of *Kidō Butai,* meaning that *Haruna*'s northward-aimed fan of aircraft should have encountered nothing but open ocean. By the same token, whether *Kirishima,* in fact, ever sent off her own plane down the 10 degree search line, which should have overlapped one of *Haruna*'s birds, remains a mystery.

On board *Hiryū,* preparations for launching the next strike were finally being completed. By about 1300, ten Type 97 *kankō* were on deck and beginning to warm up. Since Yamaguchi's earlier communiqué to Yamamoto, it had apparently been decided to send along not three, but six more Zeros for the mission, led by Lt. Mori Shigeru. Mori, dividing his force into three two-plane *shōtai,* would lead a grab bag of fighters. One of these was flown by WO Minegishi Yoshijirō, who had actually been one of Kobayashi's fighter escorts earlier in the afternoon. He had come limping back to the ship not long after Kobayashi's departure, his plane shot up in a fracas with some American dive-bombers. Whatever damage he had suffered must have been fairly minor, as he was going back up just an hour and a half later.[14] He would lead the 2nd *shōtai.* The 3rd *shōtai* would be headed up by *Kaga*'s highly experienced PO1c Yamamoto Akira, flying with another survivor from *Kaga*'s fighter unit, PO3c Bandō Makoto.

Lieutenant Tomonaga would once again lead the Type 97 *hikōtai,* such as it was. He opted to split his tiny command into two five-plane *chūtai,* placing himself at the head of the first. The second would be headed up by Lt. Hashimoto Toshio, who was normally Tomonaga's observer/navigator. However, Tomonaga thought it best to split the two most-senior officers in the *hikōtai* between the two *chūtai.* As such, Hashimoto would be flying in PO1c Takahashi Toshio's plane.

Just then, it was discovered that the repairs made to Tomonaga's left wing fuel tank, which had been holed during the morning strike, had been ineffective. The tank still leaked.[15] When lugging a heavy torpedo, a Type 97's 225-liter outboard tanks couldn't be filled in any case, meaning that only Tomonaga's starboard 350-liter inboard tank could be fueled.[16] He probably wouldn't have enough gas to make it home from the mission. Several of the pilots requested that they take the damaged bird instead. But Tomonaga cheerfully declined, joking that the Yankees were only ninety miles away and that he could make it there and back again on just a single tank.[17]

The pilot briefing was delivered personally by Admiral Yamaguchi. He encouraged his men to do their utmost—they were truly the last hope for the force. Knowing that there were three American carriers out there, and that one had been hit already, it was absolutely imperative that they attack one of the undamaged American vessels. The

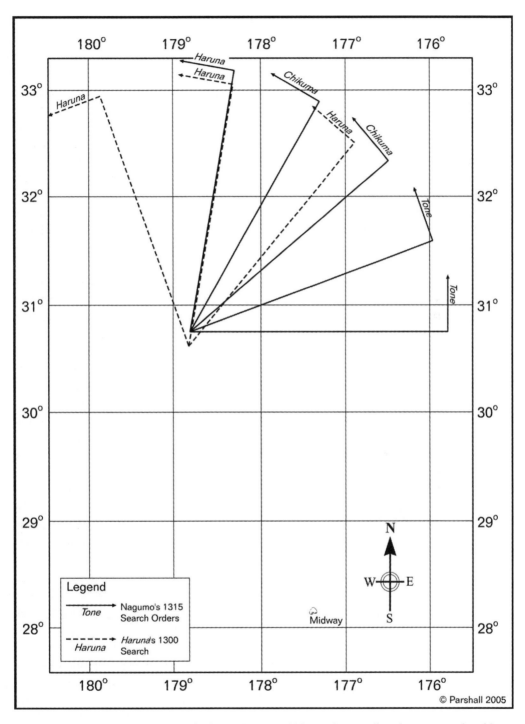

16-1: Japanese early afternoon search plans. *Haruna*'s 1300 search, as well as the routes ordered by Nagumo at 1315, are both indicated. Which of these individual search lines were actually flown, and by whom, remains a mystery.

men nodded grimly and started making their way to their waiting aircraft. Yamaguchi was clearly moved by the sacrifice of *Hiryū*'s *hikōtaichō*. As Tomonaga turned to mount his aircraft, Yamaguchi moved to shake his hand. Solemnly, he told the lieutenant, "I will gladly follow you." To the men standing nearby, it seemed clear that the admiral had no intention of returning alive from this battle if men like Tomonaga were already making the ultimate sacrifice for their country.[18]

At around 1315, while Tomonaga's unit was still being briefed, the first of Kobayashi's dive-bombers began returning. Finding the flight deck already spotted, one of them buzzed the ship and dropped a message, which Cdr. Kawaguchi Susumu, *Hiryū*'s *hikōchō*, retrieved. According to the note, the attack force had left the enemy force at a bearing of 080 degrees and ninety miles distant. It was composed of five heavy cruisers and a carrier, the latter burning heavily. Kawaguchi entrusted this information to Lieutenant Hashimoto, not knowing that Tomonaga's backseater would not be with him on this flight. Thus, Tomonaga was not in possession of the most current information on *Yorktown*'s location as he started his mission.[19]

At last all was in readiness. *Hiryū* began launching at 1330, watched intently by every man fortunate enough to be topside. None was more attentive than Admiral Yamaguchi, who stood gazing solemnly as the aircraft went up one by one. *Hiryū*'s final strike force assembled, wheeled, and made their way toward the eastern horizon. Win or lose, it was all down to this. Near at hand, Captain Kaku was already giving orders to begin landing Kobayashi's aircraft. After recovering them, *Hiryū* would swing out of the wind and take up a northerly course, intending to converge with *Nagara* and Nagumo.

When Tomonaga was on his way, Commander Kawaguchi cleared the deck and recovered aircraft. First to come down was *Sōryū*'s Type 2 recon bird, followed by the remnants of the dive-bomber strike force. Of the twenty-four aircraft *Hiryū* had sent aloft with Kobayashi at 1057, just six were landing now—five *kanbaku* and a Zero. The fighter and one of the *kanbaku* were both shot up to such a degree as to be unserviceable. Lieutenants Kobayashi and Kondō were not among the returning aircraft. The details of the mission were difficult to discern from the survivors—their accounts didn't jibe terribly well. As such, *Hiryū*'s officers found it difficult to piece together a cohesive account from the men until long after the battle was actually over.

Kobayashi's mission seemed to have started out well enough. After launching, the strike force had proceeded at relatively low altitude, because the visibility seemed better, though they climbed as they got closer to the suspected location of the American fleet.[20] Then at 1132 had come the welcome signal from *Chikuma* No. 5 that would guide the attack birds to the target, followed by *Hiryū*'s own message ten minutes later rebroadcasting the location of the Americans.

However, at about the same time, Kobayashi's bombers had lost their fighter cover. Lieutenant Shigematsu's Zeros spotted what appeared to be enemy torpedo aircraft below and ahead of them. He asked for, and received permission to engage them.[21] In retrospect, this was clearly a mistake. Indulging in a taste for combat against enemy aircraft that were of no immediate threat to *Hiryū* was a poor reason to forgo close support of Kobayashi's precious bombers. Yet this was typical for Japanese fighters, who had not yet begun to internalize the fundamental truth that close support was the *only* kind of support that really mattered.

Diving down with his six Zeros, Shigematsu had encountered not enemy TBDs, but Lt. Charles Ware's doomed flight of *Enterprise* SBDs. The ensuing affray had been sharp. The Japanese made numerous passes at the Dauntlesses but discovered for themselves what many of their CAP compatriots had already learned earlier in the morning—American dive-bombers were formidable opponents when they flew in close formation. The Zeros were rudely surprised by the hot reception they got. In fact, they succeeded in shooting down none of the SBDs. However, two *kansen* (WO Minegishi Yoshijirō and PO1c Sasaki Hitoshi) were damaged severely enough in return that they had to break off the fight and limp back to *Hiryū*.[22] In the end, only Minegishi's Zero managed to make it back, just in time to be turned around for Tomonaga's outbound strike mission. Sasaki was forced to ditch near one of *Hiryū*'s escorts at about 1230. It was thus a rather chastened Shigematsu who led his surviving quartet of Zeros back in pursuit of Kobayashi's force, which had gone on ahead. As it developed, Shigematsu's fighters were not available to Kobayashi when it counted most.

At 1152 *Yorktown*'s radar had detected an unknown flight of aircraft coming in.[23] Her radar operator was one of the best in the business, and he managed to coax from his rather primitive equipment the fact that these aircraft were in the process of climbing—something friendly aircraft looking to land would never have done.[24] The American CAP had just been in the process of rotating. However, *Yorktown* had twenty fighters up, and radar gave them time enough, barely, to send the majority to intercept Kobayashi. Even so, the Wildcats didn't have time to gain sufficient altitude, nor were they properly formed up, forcing them to attack singly or in small groups.

Kobayashi's formation was arrayed in a right echelon of two *chūtai,* each formed into its own "V" of three *shōtai.*[25] Kobayashi sighted the enemy carrier at noon and promptly sent a message to *Hiryū* announcing that he was attacking. Almost immediately thereafter, though, the *kanbaku* unit had been set upon by American fighters coming in from below and ahead. The Americans had pressed their attacks boldly. One Wildcat, piloted by Lt. (jg) Elbert S. McCuskey, took one run against the formation, came around for a second pass, and found itself facing Yamashita's 2nd *chūtai* almost head-on. Like a hawk hitting a flock of pigeons, McCuskey blew Yamashita's formation apart. Several Japanese pilots were forced to break ranks to avoid being rammed by his Wildcat. Meanwhile, Kobayashi's lead *chūtai* had been similarly thrown into confusion.

As soon as the Japanese formation had broken, a fresh group of American fighters had charged into their heart, firing with great precision. Several *kanbaku* had gone down in flames almost immediately, including the leader of the 2nd *chūtai,* Lieutenant Kondō. Lt. Arthur J. Brassfield single-handedly annihilated a *shōtai* of bombers that made it out of the melee and attempted to break toward *Yorktown.* Another pair was forced to jettison their bombs. In several cases, the nimble Type 99s tried maneuvering onto the tails of the American Wildcats, although this tactic had met with little success.

It was around this time that Shigematsu's Zeros finally rejoined the battle. It was a good thing, too, as new elements of Grummans were continually appearing on the

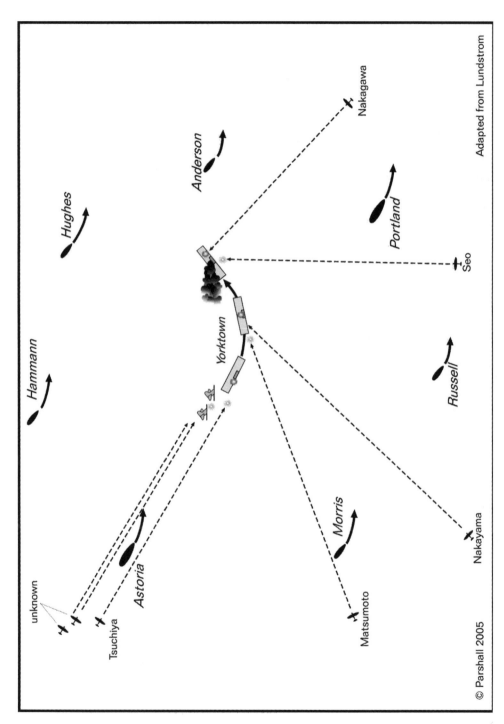

Hughes

Hammann

Anderson

Nakagawa

Portland

Seo

Yorktown

Russell

unknown

Tsuchiya

Astoria

Morris

Matsumoto

Nakayama

© Parshall 2005

Adapted from Lundstrom

16-2: *Hiryū* dive-bomber attack, 1211–1214.

scene. Thereupon, Shigematsu's quartet had a furious exchange with the American Wildcats, whose pilots were more than willing to mix it up with their opposite numbers. The results were again sharply unpleasant for the Japanese, with three of Shigematsu's men shot down for only a single Grumman bagged in return. The doughty Shigematsu was the only survivor.[26] Finally, at about 1210, the remaining seven armed *kanbaku* had begun their attack runs on *Yorktown*—a fact that one of their number, perhaps Lieutenant Nakayama, had thereupon signaled to *Hiryū*. The coherence of their original formation long since destroyed, the Japanese bombers were forced to attack singly or in small groups.

Before them lay the American task force. The enemy flattop had been closely guarded by a tight ring of cruisers and destroyers, each of which could contribute to the defense of the carrier in the center. The Japanese had come in from directions ranging across half the compass, peeling into sharp, precise dives. Just as the men of *Kidō Butai* had been forced to give grudging admiration to the technique of *Enterprise*'s and *Yorktown*'s dive-bombers two hours earlier, so too the men on *Yorktown* were aware that they were watching seasoned professionals in action. The Japanese pilots attacked coolly and deliberately, holding their dives to the absolute limit while displaying an utter disdain for the ferocious antiaircraft fire being directed back at them. These men were all part of Nagumo's "A-team" that had been held in reserve from the morning strike against Midway. The results of their attack on *Yorktown* proved that their admiral's faith in them had been well deserved.

The first Type 99 had attacked from directly astern, holding his dive to the last possible second. In fact, to several observers it appeared that this particular pilot had no intention of pulling out at all. However, contemptuous as Japanese *kanbaku* pilots were of antiaircraft fire, the immutable truth was that American flak was intense and accurate. The 1.1-inch machine guns located aft of *Yorktown*'s island summarily chopped this particular bomber into pieces just as it released its weapon—a 242-kilogram high-explosive bomb intended for flak suppression. The smashed *kanbaku* fell in three sections into the carrier's wake. Nevertheless, this pilot had aimed his weapon with great skill.[27] Tumbling end over end, the bomb hit *Yorktown* just abaft her midships elevator, detonating in a bright flash. It was almost as if the unknown pilot was exacting a posthumous retribution, as his bomb slaughtered the 1.1-inch crews who had just shot him down.

Despite the ship's temporarily lessened firepower, *Hiryū*'s second dive-bomber was given exactly the same treatment. Diving along a similar line from astern, his *kanbaku* was blown into pieces by flak and fell headlong into the ship's wake. The detonation of his high-explosive bomb peppered *Yorktown*'s stern with fragments and started some incidental fires on the fantail.

The third attacker, the last man from the 1st *chūtai* was PO2c Tsuchiya Takayoshi. Approaching from astern as well, Tsuchiya held a steep 75-degree dive down to low level and secured what appeared to be a hit with his semi armor-piercing bomb. In fact, though, he planted it close alongside the carrier's stern. Tsuchiya avoided the fate of his two comrades and managed to scoot away at wave-top height.

16-3: Japanese dive-bomber holding its dive down to the limit during Kobayashi's attack. Judging by the splash of another *kanbaku* off *Yorktown*'s bow, this aircraft is probably that of PO2c Tsuchiya Takayoshi. He has pressed his attack to within about 1600 feet of *Yorktown*, at an angle of around 65 degrees, and is just nearing his release point.[28]

Next came four aircraft from the 2nd *chūtai*. They attacked in an arc across *Yorktown*'s starboard beam. *Yorktown*, though, was a difficult target to hit, maneuvering as she was at thirty knots. Almost as soon as the 2nd *chūtai* started coming in, she began executing a turn to port to throw off their aim. The next attacker was PO1c Matsumoto Sadao, who began angling in almost immediately after Tsuchiya's run. Coming in slightly less steeply than Tsuchiya, he thought he secured a hit on the elusive carrier's stern. Yet he, too, had actually dropped his high-explosive bomb in *Yorktown*'s wake.

However, *Yorktown*'s luck had finally run out as the next *kanbaku* headed in. This bird was piloted by WO Nakazawa Iwao, in whose backseat rode Special Service Ens. Nakayama Shimematsu, leader of the 2nd *shōtai*. Nakazawa dove steeply from about 8,000 feet. His aim was true, and despite the heavy fire being thrown up by *Yorktown* and her escorts, he planted his 250-kilogram semi armor-piercing bomb directly amidships. Immediately, *Yorktown* began belching enormous clouds of thick black smoke.[29] Heavily damaged, her speed began dropping noticeably, which decreased her ability to fend off the next attack.

This was delivered by WO Nakagawa Shizuo, the leader of the 2nd *chūtai*'s 3rd *shōtai*. Taking a new tack, he came in on *Yorktown*'s starboard bow from about 7,500 feet. Whether the enemy carrier was distracted by Nakazawa's hit or her gunners were just less observant in this particular direction, his aircraft benefited from much-reduced antiaircraft fire. Nakagawa also eschewed normal dive-bombing technique in favor of glide bombing. He could have taught Lofton Henderson's men a thing or two about this overlooked attack method, as he slung his 250-kg bomb almost directly on top of the carrier's forward elevator.

Yorktown took a heavy hit, with the several fires resulting from this bomb threatening both the ship's magazine and its forward aviation gasoline stores. However, unlike Japanese carriers, the American flattop had protected herself better from her own avgas system. A fueling bowser that was on the flight deck before the attack had been unceremoniously consigned to the drink to remove its flammable contents from any possibility of harming the ship. More important, *Yorktown*'s personnel had earlier drained her fuel lines and flooded them with inert CO_2 gas. This was the first usage of this recent damage-control innovation. *Yorktown*'s experience in earlier battles was showing, and it paid handsome dividends. Had *Yorktown* been forced to fight a major avgas fire at this juncture, with six of her nine boilers already knocked off line, Nakagawa's hit could well have been fatal. As it was, however, her damage was manageable.

The seventh and last aircraft to dive was that of PO1c Seo Tetsuo, Nakazawa's wingman. Pushing over from about 8,000 feet, Seo aimed at the carrier's starboard beam. His dive was somewhat shallower than many of those that had preceded it. Whether the clouds of smoke billowing from *Yorktown* threw off his aim, or his dive simply needed a little steepening, Seo suffered a near miss close aboard *Yorktown*'s side.

All in all, *Hiryū*'s pilots had executed a superlative attack. Seven aircraft had secured three direct hits and two very near misses—an enviable rate of accuracy in anyone's book. Not only that, but judging by the smoke emanating from the target, and her rapidly decreasing headway, the carrier appeared to be heavily, perhaps fatally hit. Lieutenant Kobayashi would have been proud of his men.

The commander of *Hiryū*'s *kanbaku* unit, however, did not survive the attack. None of his aviators had seen what happened to him, despite the fact that he had lived through the initial fracas with the American Grummans. Indeed, it is clear that Kobayashi himself had witnessed Tsuchiya's initial hit on the target, because it was he who had broadcast at 1211—"[Message] Number Two. Fires break out on carrier. 0901 [*sic*]"[30] Yet when the attack was over, Kobayashi had simply disappeared.[31] The five survivors from *Hiryū*'s decimated group had thereafter made their way home without any of their senior leaders. Ensign Nakayama was now the sole surviving officer of what had once been one of the finest dive-bomber squadrons in the Imperial Navy. They had truly given their all. But would it be enough?

The outcome of Kobayashi's attack, in conjunction with the sighting reports from *Sōryū*'s speedy D4Y, should have given Yamaguchi (and Nagumo shortly thereafter) final, conclusive evidence that it was now time to break off the day's action and begin falling back on the Main Body. Both sides could do grade-school arithmetic. After debriefing Kobayashi's aviators, Yamaguchi would have known that he had hit an enemy carrier, but only one. That carrier was out of action, but whether it was in danger of sinking was unknown. Kobayashi's squadron had been gutted in the process, yet two other American carriers remained unfought. If closing the range with the Americans had been questionable after Kobayashi's launch, even with Nagumo's surface group pushed ahead in the van, it was doubly so now.

Indeed, Yamaguchi should have been able to divine at least *three* good reasons for advising Nagumo to break off offensive air activities immediately. First, even if Tomonaga's outbound group did achieve some results, it would likely be at the expense of most or all of his remaining aircraft. The relationship between the application of marginal force and taking disproportionate casualties was well known. If *Hiryū*'s eighteen dive-bombers had been chopped to pieces attacking a single enemy carrier, ten of the more vulnerable torpedo planes were likely to fare much worse in any subsequent strike against a pair of them.

Second, even if Tomonaga did achieve results against another enemy carrier, *Hiryū* would likely be in no position to exploit his success in any event. With her airpower caught in a downward spiral, *Hiryū*'s subsequent strikes could only be weaker. The truth was that at this point in the battle, *Hiryū* was really no longer in a position to tackle anything more formidable than a target barge. With the remnants of *Kidō Butai*'s CAP still overhead, she might have the ability to defend herself for a time. But she really had no offensive firepower left.

This leads directly to the third good reason for disengaging. In the absence of any real offensive capability, the preservation of an extremely valuable carrier for use in future operations should have taken precedence over trying to pull off a miracle. It certainly should have taken precedence over anyone's sense of personal honor. Given these same odds, an American commander's reaction would most likely have been to cut his losses and run for it, forthrightly and without embarrassment. Even granting that the ultimate power of decision lay with Nagumo, Yamaguchi had every reason to advise his superior that now looked like a good time to get out while the getting was good. He had certainly never been shy in making suggestions to his superior before this supremely important moment—now would have been a good time to reinforce his reputation for outspokenness.

However, Japanese admirals operated according to an entirely different martial calculus. Even before the cataclysmic 1020 attack, Nagumo had clearly wanted to engage the Americans in a surface battle. Now that the battle had turned against them, Yamaguchi saw no reason to modify that stance. Instead of being the centerpiece of his fleet, *Hiryū* was now just a disposable component. Yamaguchi would continue closing with his commander's flagship, which had the effect of trailing his own coattails in front of the enemy and increasing *Hiryū*'s danger measurably every minute.

The Americans, meanwhile, were trying their best to recover from Kobayashi's attack. *Yorktown* was crippled, drifting, with thick clouds of black smoke trailing from her innards. Her fires were serious, with damage-control parties busy in several places belowdecks. Down in her engine spaces, workmen were trying their best to bring at least some of her boilers back on line, despite the damage to her uptakes. *Yorktown*'s flight deck was also holed from bomb hits, and crews were scurrying to jury-rig patches using wooden beams and steel plates to cover her wounds. All in all, she was a mess. With her radar disabled and her command spaces bathed in smoke, Admiral

Fletcher rightly decided to transfer his flag to heavy cruiser *Astoria*. A whaleboat was brought alongside, and Fletcher made the trip over to the cruiser, arriving at 1324.[32]

Hornet and *Enterprise* were thus left with the task of recovering their own attack aircraft and those of *Yorktown*, many of which were still dribbling back from the morning's operations. Not only that, but they would have to put CAP assets not only over TF 16, but over *Yorktown* as well. *Enterprise* sent up additional fighters at 1235. But by 1258 *Yorktown*'s fighters were showing up at her sister's doorstep, looking for a place to land. For her part, *Hornet* had completed landing her own SBDs at 1209, while Kobayashi was attacking. She, too, had found *Yorktown* Wildcats needing to land and duly brought them down. In the process, though, one of Thach's morning strike escorts, carrying a wounded pilot, had landed hard enough to trigger its machine guns. The resulting spray of .50-caliber fire riddled the deck park forward and killed five men, including the son of a prominent U.S. admiral. As soon as she had cleared her decks from the latest fiasco of her miserable day, the last of her own CAP fighters needed to be brought on board. Thus, *Hornet* was occupied with recovery and launch operations from around noon until 1329.

On board *Enterprise*, Admiral Spruance was, for all intents and purposes, on his own. Seeing a towering column of smoke rising on the horizon as the result of the attack on *Yorktown*, he had promptly dispatched the heavy cruisers *Pensacola* and *Vincennes* and destroyers *Balch* and *Benham* to assist Fletcher's flagship. Yet, with Fletcher currently bobbing around in *Astoria*'s whaleboat, the senior American admiral was unable to assert any control over the battle. His subordinate, Spruance, was in the dark. He still had no clear idea where the remaining enemy carrier or carriers were located, and until he did, he couldn't order further strikes.

As *Hiryū* continued charging to the east, her three stricken compatriots were entering new stages of extremis. The fires had been blazing on *Akagi*, *Kaga*, and *Sōryū* for several hours now, and the ships were beginning to suffer permanent structural damage as a result. On board *Akagi* and *Kaga*, which each had an elevator that had been dropped into its well, the situation would have been aggravated, because the elevator shafts began acting like chimneys, venting smoke at the top and sucking air in through the bottom. The effect was to create a blast furnace. Steel structural members, having been heated too hot and for too long, were now glowing red and beginning to come apart under the strain. Even the incredibly sturdy riveted construction of the carriers' hulls and hangar decks could not withstand the combination of weakening frames being hammered by induced explosions. Under such circumstances, large chunks of the carriers, some weighing dozens of tons, were simply being blown overboard.[33]

Inside, the bulkheads in the vicinity of the fires were now mostly bare, red-hot metal, the chalky, sodium-silicate fireproof paint having been either flaked off in handfuls by the explosions or scorched away by the flames. The aircraft in the hangars had long since been melted down to aluminum slag, leaving only the glowing steel engine blocks deposited on the hangar decks. Not surprisingly, almost the entirety of the hangars on board both *Kaga* and *Sōryū* had long since been abandoned to the fires.

On *Akagi*, though, the struggle continued. The fact that she had managed to rig a pump on the bow helped matters, but it really only delayed the inevitable. Without the possibility of restoring power, and thereby vastly increasing her pumping capacity, she couldn't make any headway against the fires. Aoki essentially acknowledged this when, at 1338, he ordered the emperor's portrait transferred to *Nowaki*.[34] The imperial visage was sent over the side and into a waiting launch to make its way to *Nowaki*. It was doubtless clutched to the chest of some unknown officer, who would have perforce accompanied it to the bottom if an accident or misstep had cast him into the sea. Thus was Aoki's primary responsibility to the emperor absolved. It remained now only for the captain to share the fate of his ship, whatever that might be. *Akagi* continued her grim circling.

Even as *Akagi*'s engines persisted in their mysterious activities, *Kaga*'s machinery was finally closing down for good. Though she had been crawling northwest for some time now, between 1250 and 1300 she ground to a halt.[35] This final loss of power, and with it any hope of real damage control, led to the conclusion that it was time to transfer his majesty's portrait to a safer venue. At 1325 it was transferred to one of *Hagikaze*'s boats standing by the anchor deck.

Meanwhile, at about the same time, *Kaga*'s commanding officer—Commander Amagai—had apparently gotten himself back on board his blazing ship, most likely on the anchor deck as well. Despite the common wisdom on the matter, there is, in fact, considerable ambiguity concerning whether or not Amagai was, or even believed himself to be, in command of the burning carrier. He had jumped from *Kaga*'s boat deck earlier, yet *Kaga* had remained underway, and apparently nominally under command, during his time in the water or on *Hagikaze*. Someone, and it wasn't Amagai, must have made the decision to remove the emperor's portrait, and possibly ordered her engines shut down as well. Lieutenant Kunisada mentions in his account that the chief damage-control officer, the head of the First Damage Control Section, was apparently directing matters from the *Kaga*'s forecastle. If this is true, then he, and not Amagai, was most likely the acting commanding officer of *Kaga* in the period from 1300 to her final abandonment. Indeed, Amagai himself made the rather curious statement regarding his ordering the men over the side and then joining them. He said that he made the decision "believing that the skilled fliers, who could not be replaced, should be saved so that they could have another chance of fighting. . . . At the same time, I thought that the fate of the ship would be better left to her skipper or the second command officer in case he was killed."[36] The implication is that Amagai did not believe he was in command, nor was he certain that Captain Okada had even been killed. That Amagai subsequently filed the report on her loss only indicates that by then it had finally been ascertained that he was, in fact, her senior surviving officer. But there's no evidence to show that Amagai actually knew this at the time.

With *Kaga* now dead in the water, though, whoever was in charge decided that it was time to get the engineers out of the lower spaces. A messenger was sent below to the engine rooms to tell them to evacuate and come topside. However, he could not get through.[37] Some of them must have abandoned their posts, though, for the black gang was not entirely wiped out. However, 213 of her nominal complement of 323 engineers ultimately perished, including her chief engineer, Cdr. Utsumi Hachirō.[38] It's reasonable to imagine that many of them were either already dead by the time they were ordered to evacuate or were trapped below with no hope of escape. Their terrible fates can only be imagined as the fires finally worked their way down into the great ship's innards.

At about the same time, Lieutenant Kunisada was in a bind. After the enormous explosions in the hangar, he had finally come to his senses to find himself lying on the hangar deck.[39] Standing up in the smoky darkness, he had realized that he was near the midships elevator and could see some light coming down the well. He made for the command spaces. Whether by chance or design, though, he never reached the command spaces at all, and instead found himself fighting the fires on the lower hangar deck level, near amidships.[40]

Eventually, Kunisada found himself in the petty officers quarters. Inside, he found two engineering personnel taking shelter from the fire. Kunisada ordered one of them to open the porthole in the space, and the compartment immediately became bright with sunlight. He then shouted "Maintenance Officer is here! All section men come here to me! Gather in this light!"[41] Eventually, a total of eight men then showed up, half of whom were injured. Several were streaming blood, and all were already weary and darkened with smoke. One of them was the chief of the 3rd emergency section of damage-control personnel. This man (erroneously) told Kunisada that their mutual commander, the chief damage-control officer, and all his subordinates had been killed or wounded. He himself was the only man remaining from the third section. Kunisada thus believed himself *Kaga*'s senior damage-control officer.

The third section man was despondent and urged Kunisada to give in to the inevitable. "Come," he said, "let's go share the commander's fate!" He then turned to make his way back to the hangar so as to seek death in battle. Kunisada restrained him. Suddenly, the fire flared up near the entrance to the compartment, surprising the men inside. They slammed the porthole shut and tried to put out the fire, but the air quality worsened precipitously and breathing became difficult. There was no longer any way out, and Kunisada wondered if their fates were now sealed. As a last resort, he ordered all the men to clamber out of the porthole. As it happened, the antitorpedo bulge on *Kaga*'s hull formed a sort of shelf in this section of the vessel. It was wide enough for them to stand on.

Their perch was none too safe. Hanging above them and somewhat astern were the large gun tubs for the five-inch AA mounts. Unfortunately, the shell hoists for the guns were burning, and the shells in the hoists were detonating periodically. Ammunition for the machine guns was also cooking off farther astern, sending bullets whizzing about every so often. Visibility was rotten. They couldn't see the bow because of the bulk of the ship's funnel, and the stern was out of sight behind the fires.

One of Kunisada's party slipped off the bulge and plunged into the water. Someone threw him a line, and they all grabbed hold. But the man, injured or simply exhausted, failed to hold on and sank vertically into the sea. The water was so clear that they could see his white uniform shimmering below the surface as he slowly sank into the depths. It was a most depressing moment and brought home their isolation. Still, their precarious ledge was better than what lay waiting for them on board the ship. So there they huddled, waiting for whatever came next.

Kunisada's men were not the only ones to have exited the blazing ship via her portholes. In the ship's sick bay, the senior medical man present was an ensign.[42] There was no sign of the ship's surgeon. Knowing that the sick bay was cut off from the rest of the ship by the fires, the ensign sent a runner named Okamoto out to look for an escape route. However, none could be found. When Okamoto reported this to his superior, the officer simply said, "Many thanks for your good efforts," and sat back resignedly to face death. The decks around were getting hot, and the paint on the overheads was beginning to smolder and burn.

However, at this juncture another one of the men—a senior petty officer— noticed the portholes.[43] Hurriedly, he, Okamoto, and the other orderlies moved everyone they could, including all of the wounded strong enough to make it, out through the portholes. Unlike Kunisada's party, though, there was no torpedo bulge immediately below their perch—from the sick bay it was a straight jump into the ocean. In they went—all except the petty officer who had discerned the escape route. He himself was too stout to fit through. Thus, he stayed behind, along with those too badly injured to move, to await the fate that would not be long in coming.

Kaga's final demise might well have come at about this time, had it not been for a rather incredible stroke of luck. With the carrier having now ground to a stop, the *Nautilus* was finally given the rewards of her dogged pursuit. *Kaga* now lay motionless in front of Lt. Cdr. William Brockman's boat. He noted "two cruisers" escorting what he tentatively identified as a *Sōryū*-class carrier.[44] To the U.S. skipper, the stricken carrier appeared to be "on an even keel and the hull appeared to be undamaged. There were no flames and the fire seemed to be under control," although her topsides were already clearly demolished. Brockman also noted that the men on her bow seemed to be trying to rig her for towing.[45]

Brockman chose an approach course to attack her starboard side. Finally, at 1359, he let fly with four torpedoes at his helpless target, firing from somewhat astern at a track angle of 125 degrees. The range to the target was 2,700 yards. Brockman kept his scope up and noted the somewhat disconcerting fact that "the wakes of the torpedoes were observed through the periscope until the torpedoes struck the target."[46] Not surprisingly, the fact that Brockman could see the wakes meant that the Japanese could see them as well. It wouldn't take much guessing for *Kaga*'s escorts to determine from which direction the attack had come.

Lieutenant Kunisada saw the fish coming in.[47] From his perch on *Kaga*'s flank, the torpedo tracks stretched toward him like accusatory fingers. Yelling to the men around him to jump and swim for their lives, Kunisada leaped into the water. The others belatedly followed suit, and everyone swam madly away from *Kaga*. Lieutenant Commander Mitoya, likewise, saw the torpedoes heading for him and could do nothing but hold his breath.[48] Anyone in the water anywhere near the thunderous impact was as good as dead in any case.

In a war that would be replete with examples of faulty U.S. torpedoes, Brockman's attack was destined to be one of the crown jewels. The first of his four fish malfunctioned and never left the tube. Two others ran errantly, one missing *Kaga* astern, the other missing ahead. The fourth and final torpedo ran hot and true, aimed dead amidships. But when it struck *Kaga*'s heavy hull, its contact exploder was either faulty or was crushed by the impact—a common failing of U.S. submarine torpedoes at the time. There was no explosion. Instead, the fish broke in half, sending the warhead to the bottom and leaving the air flask and tail assembly bobbing in the water.[49] The men already swimming nearby greeted the scene with a mixture of rage and incredulous relief. Some of the sailors quickly seized on the unexpected life raft in their midst, but no one was happy with it. Several shouted curses and pounded it with their fists. It was just the latest abuse heaped on them in a morning already filled with more than their share of terror.

Oddly enough, *Nautilus*'s skipper came away with a much different impression of the attack's results. Brockman reported that "red flames appeared along the length of the ship from the bow to midships. The fire which had first attracted us . . . and was nearly extinguished . . . broke out. Boats drew away from the bow and many men were seen going over the side. Cruisers began reversing course at high speed and started to echo range."[50] This is a vivid description, and more than a little puzzling. It is no wonder that some have found *Nautilus*'s sinking claim hard to dismiss,[51] although it is incontrovertible that *Kaga* remained afloat.

Brockman was also correct that the "cruisers" were now gunning for his submarine. Destroyer *Hagikaze*, which had been off *Kaga*'s starboard quarter at the time of the attack, swung to starboard and went to high speed to close.[52] Commander Iwagami Jūichi immediately began laying down depth charges. Captain Brockman's report confirms the ferocity and speed of the first attack. At 1410 *Hagikaze* went thrashing directly overhead, and Brockman quickly reversed course and crash-dived to 300 feet. Eleven depth charges splashed into the water at 1422 and detonated with unpleasant results. Brockman noted that "This entire barrage was close and well placed except that the charges were set too shallow and exploded above the ship. A few small leaks were sprung [in the submarine]." Iwagami's first run had been good, and he lost no time in making another at 1431, which came even closer. *Nautilus*'s sound operator reported the noise of propellers "all around the dial," making it likely that *Maikaze* had also joined in the counterattack.[53]

Kaga's destroyers subjected *Nautilus* to a brutal ordeal for the next two hours and came within an ace of sinking the American submarine when two of its depth charges evidently clanged against the sub at 340 feet but did not explode. Despite this close call, after enduring forty-two depth charges, Brockman was eventually able to sneak away from his attacker, though he judged it unsafe to return to periscope depth till 1610.[54] Though Brockman opined that the Japanese broke off their attack too soon, he was understandably thankful that they had, as his battery was nearly exhausted. The actual damage to his old boat, however, proved negligible. All in all, though, *Nautilus* had made a well-earned escape after a day of aggressive attacks against the enemy. If the final prize of her efforts eluded her, it certainly was not for lack of trying.

Lieutenant Kunisada could observe little of the hunt for *Nautilus* from his current position. Now that he was in the water, he had no choice but to continue swimming. Many men were drifting about with him. Looking back at the ship towering high above him, he could see that her damage was severe but localized. Her upperworks were ablaze, with dull red fires visible through the many rents in her side. Heat shimmered off the metal. But the worst of the fires seemed to be dying down for the moment—the smoke coming from the ship was no longer oily black, but a lighter brown color. Kunisada could see, too, that the bridge had been crushed by the explosion that had killed Captain Okada. There were deep rents in *Kaga*'s side, particularly on the starboard side aft of the funnel, and on the port side forward. Some of these gashes ran nearly all the way to the waterline. Yet *Kaga*'s lower hull was remarkably intact. Despite her wounds, she still impressed the damage-control officer with her bulk, and seeming stability. On both the bow and stern he could see sailors clustered and firefighting efforts continued.[55]

While in the water, Kunisada encountered a communications man named Oda, who was still clutching a sheaf of *Kaga*'s messages in one hand while trying to swim. Oda was wounded in the leg and was bleeding. Kunisada, though impressed by the man's devotion to duty, nevertheless told him to throw the damned messages away and concentrate on saving himself. Oda responded to this direct order with relief, throwing the papers into the sea. Finding a piece of lumber, the two men hung on. They tried swimming toward the ship's stern, but either currents or wave action made this impossible, and they eventually gave up. They would not be picked up for several more hours, finally crawling on board *Hagikaze* at about 1600.[56]

WO Yoshino Haruo, *Kaga*'s reconnaissance flight leader, was in the water by now as well. Having made his escape from the flight deck shortly after the carrier was bombed, he had managed to pick his way down to the stern. He had found *Kaga*'s boat deck packed with survivors. As soon as *Kaga* lost power, he noticed a destroyer (probably *Hagikaze*) edging up to her stern and decided to swim out to her. Into the water he went, along with many other men. However, all of a sudden the destroyer turned about and disappeared—most likely in response to *Nautilus*'s attack. Now Yoshino's case was worse, and he didn't know if he could survive. In the end, though, *Hagikaze* returned, and he managed to make it on board about the same time Kunisada did. As he came dripping out of the water and onto the deck, he unexpectedly met a relative who served on the tin can. Deeply shamed by his appearance and at having been defeated in battle, Yoshino nevertheless accepted dry clothes from the man. He hoped that his relation would not tell everybody at home about his pitiable condition.[57]

Wounded torpedo bomber pilot Maeda Takeshi also made it on board. Like Yoshino, he had gone into the water as soon as *Hagikaze* had started to edge in. In fact, he had been bodily thrown into the water by other men on the fantail.[58] Seeing *Hagikaze* putting out her boats, they had assumed that any of the less severely wounded would be better off being picked up and taken to safety on the destroyer than waiting around on *Kaga*, where no medical attention could be provided. Upon *Hagikaze*'s abrupt exit from the scene, however, Maeda's hoped-for rescue evaporated, and his shipmates' intended kindness now placed him in grave danger. He had a life jacket, but he kept swallowing seawater in the long swells. Occasionally, as he surged to the tops of the waves, he could see *Sōryū* burning in the distance.

Finally *Hagikaze* returned, this time with knotted ropes lowered along both her flanks. Pulled out of the cold water, Maeda was in deep shock from both exposure and the bomb splinter still lodged in his leg. He wasn't feeling any pain. In fact, he found that he could walk on his wounded limb, despite having a smashed femur. When the shock wore off later, such a thing would have been unthinkable. His flight boots were long gone, and the hot cartridges from the destroyer's 25-mm mounts were everywhere underfoot. They made sizzling sounds when his wet socks struck them, burning his feet.[59] The young ship's doctor was too busy to attend to him properly—there was no anesthetic, and he'd already run out of bandages. He merely splashed iodine solution on Maeda's open wound. The pain was absolutely excruciating, but Maeda managed to keep his composure. Later, he would credit the cooler seawater and the iodine for saving his limb from gangrene. His abbreviated treatment at an end, the aviator slumped down on the deck to stare at *Kaga*.

To Maeda, the situation was beyond caring about, beyond any sort of reflection. He was just twenty-one years old, and his life as an aviator had been dangerous enough in peacetime. In wartime, it was more dangerous than almost anything. He knew that he was expendable. He'd been treated as such, treated "like a rag."[60] He didn't resent it—it was what he expected. So Maeda couldn't really comprehend "the Big Picture" of what losing this battle might mean to Japan, or its ability to win the war. He couldn't even consider what the future might bring. There was no future; there wasn't even a tomorrow. There was only the present moment. He was safe enough for the time being, but he was exhausted, he was famished, and his leg hurt like hell. *Kaga* continued burning.

In the sea next to the blazing *Sōryū*, Gunnery Officer Kanao had now been drifting on his ladder for some time, but his movement relative to the ship was almost imperceptible.[61] However, without his being aware of it, he had gradually begun to pull abreast of the anchor deck. Suddenly, somebody yelled down to him from above, "Look! There's the gunnery officer!" Looking up from his piece of flotsam, Kanao saw a sailor fasten a rope to the guardrail and rappel down. Grabbing the gunnery officer, the sailor and Kanao were soon hauled back up on deck. As they reached the top, many hands pulled them back over the railing. Kanao felt like a zombie; half-dead and half-alive. The sailors on the deck embraced him, cheering, "Gunnery Officer is alive! *Banzai* to our gunnery officer!"

Huddled on the anchor deck, Kanao found some forty or fifty men who had either not heard the order to abandon ship, or who preferred to take their chances here rather than in the water. Kanao slumped exhausted onto one of the anchor chains, utterly unable to move. Nearby, two or three sailors hauled out a box and broke it open. Inside were canned peaches. One of the sailors opened a can with his knife and handed it to Kanao, saying, "Help yourself, Gunnery Officer!" Kanao thanked him, but hesitated to take it. "There is enough for all of us," the sailor assured him, and continued passing out the cans to the others on the bow. Famished, Kanao consumed everything in the tin. The taste of the sweet fruit and nectar was indescribably delicious—Kanao couldn't remember ever having eaten anything tastier. Aft of their sanctuary on the bow, *Sōryū* continued burning and fuming.

17

Last Gasp—1400–1800

It was 1400, and cruiser *Tone* wasn't doing anything to improve her reputation for untimely floatplane launches. Now, some forty-five minutes after Admiral Abe had ordered the second set of recon birds aloft, *Tone* finally managed to send up her No. 3 and No. 4 planes. The reason for the delay is unclear. Her No. 3 aircraft, a Type 95, should have been ready to take off at short notice. It is possible that her No. 4 plane was still being turned around from the morning's flight. Whether Petty Officer Amari was in command again is unclear, but it seems likely that he was.

Just as with Kobayashi's earlier attack, Yamaguchi hadn't yet heard back from Tomonaga's flight. This wasn't really a cause for concern yet, as the *hikōtaichō* had only been gone for half an hour and would likely need another half hour to find the enemy. Sure enough, at 1426, Lieutenant Tomonaga came on the air to order his strike planes into attack formation. A few minutes later, *Hiryū* intercepted a simple, suggestive order from the flight leader: *"Zengun totsugeki!* (All forces attack!)" Clearly, Tomonaga's flight was about to go into battle.

Almost at the same time, *Haruna*'s No. 1 aircraft announced that he was under attack by American fighters and that he suspected American carriers were in the area. Yamaguchi might have thought that this transmission marked the end of his scout plane, but, in fact, this particular aircraft would eventually make it back to *Haruna*. Superb airmanship allowed the pilot to escape repeated attacks. However, his observer was killed, and the Type 95 would never fly again.

Had he known it, Yamaguchi had already lost another of his scout planes. Fate had finally caught up to *Chikuma* No. 5, which had been poking around the edges of the American formations all morning. PO1c Takezaki's bird had worked itself all the way around to the south of TF 16, scooting in and out of cloud cover when threatened by American fighters. At 1409, however, Takezaki had been caught dead to rights by a pair of Wildcats. A single pass was all it took to shoot the E13A1 to pieces; as the American fighters turned for a second run, the floatplane exploded. One of the crew members was seen to bail out just before the detonation, but there would be no survivors from this encounter.

Back on the home front, Yamaguchi was having his own problems with scout aircraft, both his own, and those of the American variety. First, at 1355 Nagumo received a

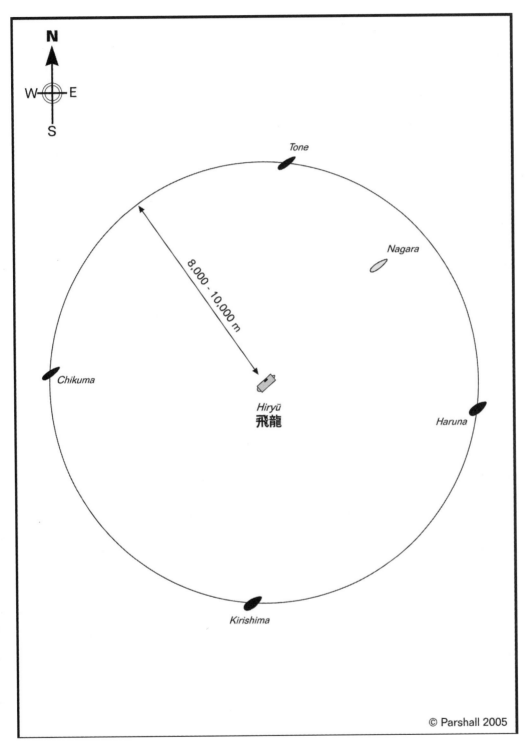

17-1: *Kidō Butai* formation, circa 1500, course 045 degrees.

transmission from one of *Haruna*'s planes (which one, we do not know), stating, "At 1240 the enemy was in position bearing about 90 degrees to port. It is composed of 5 large cruisers and 5 carriers; the latter were burning." However, Nagumo apparently retained some skepticism about the report, placing a question mark alongside the number "5" in his war diary. His next sighting of the enemy, however, was more concrete.

At 1420 *Chikuma* suddenly laid smoke and began blazing away at what it thought was a pair of American aircraft. Her sister ship *Tone* followed suit ten minutes later, and *Hiryū*'s CAP fighters quickly made tracks toward the intruders. The enemy interlopers beat a hasty retreat shortly thereafter. As it developed, the intruders were from *Yorktown*. It will be recalled that several hours earlier, at 1130, she had sent up ten SBD scouts from VS-5.[1] Their mission was to follow up on the success of the morning's dive-bomber attacks and determine if any other Japanese carriers were still lurking in the area. One of these sections, led by Lt. Sam Adams, had pushed its flight to the limit, further even than his original orders had called for. At 1430, on the return leg, Lieutenant Adams's persistence was rewarded when he spotted wakes.

Thus, even as Tomonaga was preparing to attack *Yorktown,* the curtain on *Hiryū*'s temporary immunity was being rung down. Lieutenant Adams had promptly gotten off a plain-language spotting report that placed the lone Japanese carrier bearing 279 degrees and some 110 miles from his point of origin (i.e., *Yorktown*'s 1130 launch position), at 31-15'N, 179-05'W.[2] His navigation was a little off—he placed *Hiryū* 38 miles northwest of where she actually was[3]—but his was one of the better American spotting reports of the day. Adams correctly noted that the Japanese were operating in two groups, with the carrier in one, and a surface group in advance of it.[4] As it happened, Adams spied *Kidō Butai* when Nagumo's force was still in the lead of Yamaguchi's carrier. With Adams's sighting, the fruits of Yamaguchi's decision to press northeast were beginning to be harvested. Had *Kidō Butai* turned northwest immediately after launching Tomonaga at 1330, *Hiryū* would have been almost 35 miles further west by 1430. This would have made Adams's detection almost impossible—the American SBDs had been at the limits of their range as it was.

Shortly after Adams's retreat, the two Japanese forces were reintegrated.[5] Nagumo promptly reorganized his formation with *Hiryū* at the heart of a box pattern of the force's heavy ships, still heading 045. BatDiv 3 took up the port flank in column, at a distance of ten kilometers from the carrier. CruDiv 8's *Tone* and *Chikuma* guarded the starboard flank of *Hiryū* at a similar distance.[6] Flagship *Nagara* took the van ahead of *Hiryū,* as usual, while the five remaining destroyers moved into picket positions in a loose circle around the formation as a whole.

In the midst of Nagumo's reorganization, Tomonaga's attack group came back on the air. It was Lieutenant Hashimoto, the 2nd *chūtai* leader, announcing "I carried out torpedo attacks against an enemy carrier and saw two certain hits." Yamaguchi and his staff were elated—two hits were almost certainly enough to put any carrier out of commission. Yet, even before Hashimoto made his report, Yamaguchi was already thinking ahead to future operations. Seeing that *Hiryū* was already scraping the bottom of the barrel in terms of airpower, CarDiv 2's commander was casting about for any additional airpower he could find. At 1430 he had radioed destroyer *Nowaki*, ordering her to relay to *Akagi* that if the flagship had any aircraft on deck, they should take off at once and transfer to *Hiryū*. It may be that Yamaguchi was aware that *Akagi* had once again managed to get underway and was hopeful that she might yet be made operational. It was a fool's hope. By 1430 *Akagi* no longer had any intact aircraft on board, let alone a flight deck worthy of the name.

Kidō Butai's former flagship was, in fact, lying motionless once again beneath an enormous column of oily smoke. Her engines, which had propelled her in a stately clockwise circle for nearly two hours, had finally shut down again at 1350. It may well have been that whatever damage-control personnel who had flooded her aft magazines, and presumably restarted her engines as well, had either withdrawn again or been overwhelmed. Alternately, the flagship's boilers, apparently long since untended, may have finally lost steam pressure. Whatever the reason, *Akagi* was once again stationary except for the long, slow rhythm of the swells lapping against her sides.

The grim struggle against her fires, though, ground on relentlessly. To use damage-control parlance, both hangar decks and the decks immediately beneath them were still "fully involved," meaning they were completely afire. *Akagi's* crew, though, was not giving up and continued putting firefighting parties into the fray, trying to make their way aft. It would appear that in some areas, at least, progress was being made. At 1450 contact was temporarily reestablished with the survivors clustered on the stern and would be again, intermittently, over the next few hours.

On both *Akagi* and *Kaga,* the medical staffs, or what was left of them, were faced with a horrendous task.[7] Gathered on the weather decks fore and aft with the other survivors, they were plying their trade with whatever was at hand. The results can only have been pitiable. The survivors were suffering from a variety of injuries, the most prevalent being burns and shrapnel injuries. There was no way to treat these wounds beyond the most basic bandaging and splints. Deep-penetration wounds would have likely killed their recipients relatively quickly through loss of blood. The burn victims, however, lingered in agony. In some cases, the badly injured intentionally made their way back into the hangar fires to die there, rather than suffer further.

As the day wore on, the initial patient load was steadily augmented by wounded firefighters bearing similar wounds. However, there were new types of cases as well—smoke inhalation, heat exhaustion, and heat stroke. Smoke inhalation would have been very common within the closed spaces of the carrier as men battled the blazes. Combustion of plastics, wool, silk, nylon, rubber, and paper can all lead to the production of cyanide gas, and all of these materials were certainly present. Damage-control officer Kunisada noted that on board *Kaga* the oil-based paints on the bulkheads had burned, releasing thick toxic fumes.[8] Such conditions were ubiquitous. In many cases, men would have simply passed out, never to awaken again.

For those men who staggered or were dragged to safety, there was little relief. Effective treatments for smoke inhalation include administering humidified oxygen as well as the introduction of fluids, either orally or intravenously. For heat exhaustion and heat stroke, administering fluids, and in extreme cases wrapping the patient in wet towels to reduce body temperature, were both required. None of these remedies, of course, were feasible on the anchor deck of a burning warship.

For the rest of the crews, fatigue and thirst were taking their toll. Spirit of *Bushidō* or no, the men were exhausted. The deck crews had been awake since about 0230, in combat from 0600 on, and fighting fires since 1030. There was no ready access to food or drinking water on the burning warships. The firefighting was being done with seawater, of course. As a result, by the midafternoon, the men were beginning to fail physically, making them torpid. Firefighting crews would have become increasingly inefficient and liable to make mistakes. Physical exhaustion, coupled with the knowledge that for all intents and purposes they had already lost the fight against the fires, can only have led to a gradual flagging of effort as men resigned themselves to the inevitability of losing their ships.

As if to punctuate this knowledge, at 1500 an enormous explosion occurred in the forward area of *Akagi*'s hangars, probably near the bomb lifts. The blast blew open the curved forward bulkhead that overhung the anchor deck. Smoke and flame poured forth. Whether this blast put the hand-operated pump on *Akagi*'s forecastle out of business is unknown, but at the very least it brought home to the men clustered there the reality of the situation. The fires were in charge.

While Yamaguchi had been handling the air operations on *Hiryū*, Admiral Nagumo was busily considering how to continue the battle beyond 4 June. At 1420, just before Tomonaga had announced he was attacking the American carrier, the commander of *Dai-ichi Kidō Butai* had transmitted a signal advising Admiral Kakuta and *Dai-ni Kidō Butai* of his position and intentions. After destroying the enemy task force to the east, he said, he planned to proceed northward. He instructed Kakuta to rendezvous with him "as soon as possible."

It would be easy to believe that Kakuta was already moving south at this very moment. Indeed, Yamamoto's earlier orders would seemingly have had the effect of making that force stop in its tracks, come about, and move speedily to Nagumo's rescue. In fact, though, Kakuta was at this very moment heading *north,* toward Dutch Harbor.

The previous day had seen this force execute a desultory attack on the American island that had been characterized mostly by foul weather, bad luck, and poor results. Today, however, Admiral Kakuta had been determined to renew his efforts starting at around noon. For whatever reason, Yamamoto's 1220 order to Kakuta was not received until shortly after 1500, meaning that Kakuta was already committed to his attack on Dutch Harbor when the news arrived that things were not going well to the south. Kakuta duly sent his reply at 1530 that he would turn his force around as soon as his strike was recovered.[9] But before making any sort of a high-speed run, Kakuta would need to refuel his ships.[10] Accordingly, he shaped a course for a meeting with the force's oilers some twelve hours hence. Once refueled on the morning of the 5th, he would begin his long voyage south.

Meanwhile, having gotten his initial report from Lieutenant Hashimoto regarding the most recent strike against the Americans, Admiral Yamaguchi in *Hiryū* had no choice but to wait for his torpedo bombers to return. Thereafter, he already knew what he was going to do, and at 1531 he radioed Nagumo that, "After definitely establishing contact with our Model 13 experimental ship based bomber, we plan to direct our entire remaining power (5 bombers, 5 torpedo planes, and 10 fighters) to attack and destroy the remaining enemy forces in a dusk engagement."[11] Yamaguchi went on to elaborate a minute later on the earlier results of Kobayashi's earlier strike, which he claimed were "five direct hits [against] an *Enterprise*-class [carrier] with #25 [semi armor-piercing] bombs, causing her to break out with big fires. The above carrier and 5 large cruisers were the only ships sighted at the time of the attack, but according to reports from [our] Type 13 experimental ship based bomber, there are two additional carriers about 10 miles away. . . . The second attack wave took off at 1320, and the third (6 ship-based bombers and 9 ship-based fighters) are at present preparing to take off."[12] Thus, Yamaguchi was committing himself and *Hiryū* to yet another strike without understanding the real results of Tomonaga's effort.

At 1520 *Tone*'s No. 4 plane reported on the enemy force he was scouting, describing it as having six cruisers as its nucleus, accompanied by six destroyers, and preceded at a distance of twenty miles (!) by a single carrier.[13] Again, it is difficult to explain what *Tone* No. 4 and Amari thought they were seeing at this juncture, given that carriers do not typically sail unescorted by themselves. The only possible explanation is that *Tone* No. 4 (ducking in and out of clouds) was not seeing the entire picture.[14]

Admiral Abe came on the air himself at 1535 to inform Admiral Nagumo that his No. 5 aircraft had also sighted the enemy force earlier in a position "bearing 114 degrees, distance 110 miles from us at 1530." Shortly thereafter, *Chikuma*'s No. 4 plane announced that he had come up empty on his search line and was therefore returning home. Having now a fairly good sense as to where the enemy lay, this wasn't particularly shocking news. With the Americans pinned down, Abe was determined to maintain contact with them. At 1537 he radioed *Chikuma* to send up a replacement to relieve her No. 5 plane, which had been aloft since 0938.[15] *Chikuma* No. 5 had not reported in some time, and the cruiser radioed it at 1540. No reply was heard, of course; *Chikuma* No. 5 and its crew were already dead.

Nagumo was concerned by these sighting reports. The range to the Americans was still apparently opening, and his goal of bringing them to bay in a surface fight was looking more and more unlikely.[16] As a result, Nagumo decided to change his tactics. *Kidō Butai* would withdraw temporarily to the northwest as soon as Tomonaga's strike was recovered. He would then attempt a final air strike at dusk, followed by a return movement to the east with his surface forces after darkness had finally fallen.

At 1540 *Hiryū* began landing Lieutenant Tomonaga's survivors. Nagumo and Yamaguchi must have observed the proceedings with a definite air of grimness. As expected, Tomonaga was not among the returning aircraft—that was no surprise. Worse, only nine of Tomonaga's sixteen aircraft were returning—four Zeros and five Type 97s. Of these, two *kankō* and three Zeros were shot up beyond repair.[17]

The details of the mission were soon known to Yamaguchi and his staff. Tomonaga's strike, like Kobayashi's, had started out uneventfully enough.[18] After forming up, Tomonaga's formation had climbed to 13,500 feet (4,000 meters) and set out eastward. Finding the Americans had been surprisingly easy. Lieutenant Hashimoto, at the lead of the 2nd *chūtai,* had simply scanned the sea ahead with his binoculars. At 1430, he was able to discern wakes thirty-five miles ahead and 10 degrees to the right.[19] Hashimoto instructed his pilot, PO1c Takahashi Toshio, to fly up to the 1st *chūtai* and Tomonaga. There, the two lieutenants had quickly conferred via hand signals and decided to head toward the enemy.

As they drew closer, the collection of distant wakes began resolving themselves into an enemy task force with a carrier at its center. From what Tomonaga and Hashimoto could tell, the enemy carrier was uninjured. It certainly wasn't burning, and both she and her consorts were making what appeared to them to be twenty-four knots on a heading of roughly 90 degrees. Hashimoto and Tomonaga justifiably assumed that this was indeed an undamaged enemy worthy of their attentions.

What the two flight leaders could not know was that this carrier was, in reality, Kobayashi's earlier victim—*Yorktown.* Though *Hiryū's kanbaku* had left her burning and largely without power, American damage control had been superb. Her radar had been repaired, and by 1400 her fires were out. More important, by 1430 she had brought enough of her boilers back on line to work back up to nineteen knots—not exactly speedy, but hardly a sitting duck, either.

It was a good thing *Yorktown* was able to move, because at 1355 her radar picked up Tomonaga's incoming flight. Even before the raid warning had come in, her deck crewmen were already readying her Wildcats, led by the redoubtable Jimmy Thach, to reinforce the CAP. Her low speed was going to make taking off a bit trickier, but nobody doubted that they had any real choice except to try. Now, upon receiving word that another enemy attack was developing, *Yorktown's* fueling system was immediately shut down, and the pilots rushed to their aircraft. None of the Wildcats had more than twenty-three gallons of fuel, and two of the ten fighters spotted on the deck were actually judged structurally incapable of flying. Six more Grummans were already overhead, and four of these were vectored toward the attack. The remaining pair was held overhead to cover Thach's takeoff, which would not be completed before Tomonaga made his appearance. Meanwhile, *Yorktown* called for help from TF 16 and was informed that eight more Wildcats were being sent over.

As it stood, the Japanese overtook *Yorktown* from the carrier's port quarter. Tomonaga began letting down from 4,000 meters in a shallow glide to gain speed. He then split his formation, ordering Hashimoto's 2nd *chūtai* to sweep around the north edge of the enemy fleet so as to attack from the carrier's starboard bow. Meanwhile, Tomonaga would lead the 1st *chūtai* against her port beam. The escort fighters also split, with Lieutenant Mori's two-plane *shōtai* sticking with Hashimoto, while WO Minegishi's pair went with Tomonaga. Yamamoto Akira's *Kaga shōtai* split the difference between the two *kankō* groups. At 1434 Tomonaga radioed his force to attack.

The Japanese began shedding altitude rapidly. Thus far they hadn't encountered any enemy fighters, but at 1438, just as Tomonaga was passing through 4,000 feet, his *chūtai* was jumped by a pair of Grummans. They singled out one of the trailing *kankō* (probably either WO Ōbayashi Yukio or Sea1c Suzuki Takeshi's aircraft) and sent it spinning into the water.[20] Fortunately, Minegishi's pair of Zeros interceded before

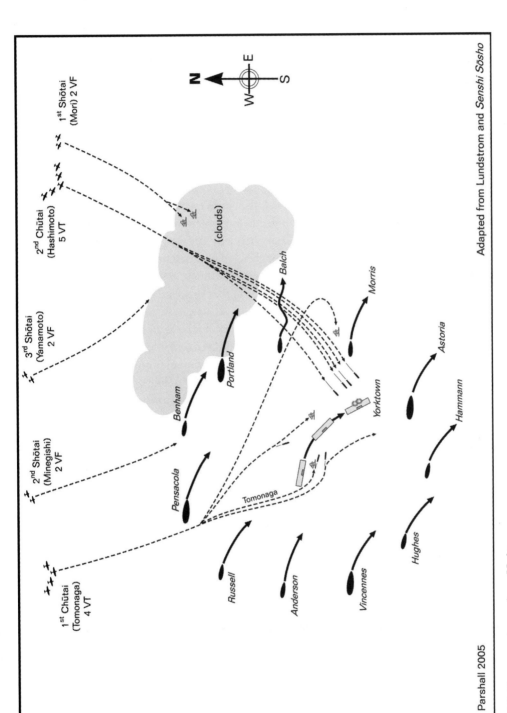

1st Shōtai (Mori) 2 VF

2nd Chūtai (Hashimoto) 5 VT

3rd Shōtai (Yamamoto) 2 VF

2nd Shōtai (Minegishi) 2 VF

1st Chūtai (Tomonaga) 4 VT

(clouds)

N
W · E
S

Balch

Morris

Benham

Portland

Astoria

Pensacola

Yorktown

Hammann

Russell

Tomonaga

Anderson

Vincennes

Hughes

Parshall 2005

Adapted from Lundstrom and *Senshi Sōsho*

17-2: Tomonaga's attack on *Yorktown*.

the Wildcats could inflict any further damage. A brief, violent combat ensued, during which both American fighters were picked off.[21]

Breaking out of a cloud bank, Tomonaga and his men could clearly see the American carrier ahead of them, still some ten miles away. She was turning away from them and onto a southeast heading, not only to avoid her onrushing attackers, but also to launch the fighters that could be seen on her deck. Around her, the American cruisers and destroyers were closed up in a tight ring about 3,000 meters across. At 1440 Tomonaga repeated his earlier message to Hashimoto, telling the 2nd *chūtai* to attack from the left as he took his four remaining planes in.[22]

The 1st *chūtai* closed quickly on the target. They were now at a very low level—200 feet or less—and racing in at nearly 200 knots, a speed that would have made any Devastator pilot green with envy.[23] However, as the 1st *chūtai* came within six miles of the formation, the American escorts cut loose with everything at their disposal. Flashing strings of tracers reached out their deadly fingers to meet the Japanese pilots, while all around them mushroomed the black puffs of exploding heavy shells.

Resolutely, Tomonaga drove his men through a gap between heavy cruiser *Pensacola* and the destroyer *Russell*. Bursting into the inner ring, though, he discovered *Yorktown* had presented her stern to him. Tomonaga, realizing that this would present him with an unfavorable target angle, split his forces again. He sent two aircraft to the left so as to work their way around the carrier's port side and gain her bow, while he led his own wingman around the carrier's starboard quarter to attempt to come up her other flank. If successful, they would catch *Yorktown* between the hammer and tongs.[24]

It was at this juncture, though, that things began rapidly falling apart for *Hiryū's hikōtaichō*, as the newly launched American fighters quickly made their presence known. Tomonaga was their first target, the victim of the most famous American fighter pilot of 4 June—Jimmy Thach. Appearing out of nowhere, the American ace made a flat run on the *hikōtaichō's* right side, holing his plane badly and setting it afire. In a stunning display of airmanship, though, Tomonaga was able to keep his blazing *kankō* straight and level and delivered a textbook torpedo drop on *Yorktown's* starboard quarter.[25] As soon as the fish was away, Tomonaga's left wing buckled, sending *Hiryū's* leader slamming into the water close astern. His torpedo missed.

Tomonaga's wingman managed to escape his leader's fate, at least for the time being. Dropping his torpedo near Tomonaga's, he turned to fly up *Yorktown's* starboard side. His fish, too, missed the target. Flying low, the *kankō* continued on through the American formation, broke back out through the screen, and headed away to the south. Shortly thereafter, though, he ran into a trio of Grummans coming up from TF 16 to the south and was quickly shot down.[26]

Meanwhile, the pair of *kankō* that Tomonaga had sent around *Yorktown's* port side had also run into trouble. The first of these had made a beeline up *Yorktown's* flank, intending to round on her port bow and make his drop then. In the process, the pilot flew almost entirely through the formation and back to the ring of destroyers in front of *Yorktown*. Here, though, he had found another Grumman coming at him head-on, firing. Damaged, the *kankō* jettisoned its fish and turned for a suicide run against the carrier. But the Wildcat, piloted by Lt. Bill Leonard, stuck to his tail, firing from below and setting the torpedo plane on fire. In the end, Leonard brought the *kankō* down, crashing it off *Yorktown*'s port bow.

His companion met a similar fate. Another of *Yorktown*'s Wildcats[27] had braved the storm of antiaircraft fire from his own ships and attacked the Nakajima from directly behind. It wasn't enough to prevent the Japanese aviator from dropping his fish, nor passing close enough to the American ship that her startled sailors were able to see the plane's rear gunner stand up and shake his fist at them.[28] It was a last gesture of defiance, though, as the *kankō* exploded almost instantly thereafter—its fuel tanks detonated by either the Grumman's bullets or *Yorktown*'s own flak. Its fish, too, missed. Thus, Tomonaga's 1st *chūtai* had been wiped out without inflicting any damage on the American carrier.

Hashimoto's 2nd *chūtai,* though, fared differently. They were headed in a "V" toward the gap between heavy cruiser *Portland* and the destroyer *Balch*. Hashimoto took his men down to the deck and roared into the American formation. The antiaircraft fire that came back at him was stunning in its magnitude and variety. Everything from machine guns to five-inch flak was hurtling past him. To Hashimoto, the shrapnel rattling off his wings and fuselage reminded him of the sound hail made hitting a metal roof back home.[29] It was terrifying, but it didn't deter him.

Most of the enemy Grummans had been pulled away in pursuit of Tomonaga's flight, but not all of them. Fortunately, Hashimoto still had Lieutenants Mori's and Yamamoto Tōru's Zeros along with him. When one of the enemy Wildcats suddenly appeared ahead of them, the two *kansen* wasted no time in jumping all over him, leaving Hashimoto's *chūtai* to continue speeding ahead. However, in the process, two more Grummans joined the fight and shortly flamed both the *Hiryū* Zeros before they even knew they were there, killing both Mori and his wingman.[30]

Hashimoto, observing all this from his plane, was sure that he was next. He banked his formation slightly to the left to take advantage of some cloud cover, hoping to throw the American fighters off the trail. It was at this moment, however, that *Kaga*'s two Zeros, flown by PO1c Yamamoto Akira and PO3c Bandō Makoto, showed up. They initiated an intense low-level engagement with the Wildcats, which removed the immediate threat from Hashimoto's *chūtai*.[31]

Emerging from his cloud bank, Hashimoto found that his formation had become jumbled. He was now on the left side of his group instead of leading the formation. There was little time left to correct these problems, though, as American flak began thundering at them again as soon as they left the protection of the clouds. More American fighters shortly appeared, one of them making a beam run directly at Hashimoto's plane. But at this point he was close enough to the target that the Grummans had little chance. Not only that, but he still had fighter cover. Indeed, just as Hashimoto's forthcoming attack climaxed, the last Wildcat off of *Yorktown*'s flight deck, that of Ens. George Hopper, was set upon by either Kitani or Minegishi's Zero and shot down almost as soon as he took off.[32]

Pilot Takahashi was now taking Hashimoto's plane down to within 100 feet of the water, the flak continuing to explode all around them. The Japanese had a phrase that crystallized their philosophy regarding torpedo attacks—*Nikuhaku-hitchū*

17-3: Hashimoto Toshio, postwar, in the uniform of the Japanese Self-Defense Forces. (Photo courtesy Michael Wenger)

("press closely, strike home"). Hashimoto intended to do precisely that. He knew his torpedoes were deadly, fast, and accurate. All he needed was a good drop to take this carrier out of the battle. At 600 meters, the lieutenant released his fish, aiming for the carrier's midships. Three of his squadron mates did the same, hoping to concentrate their damage. However, at this critical juncture, when every piece of ordnance counted, the lone *Akagi kankō* (that of Warrant Officer Nishimori) suffered a failure in its torpedo release gear! Despite its crew's efforts, the fish remained attached to the plane.[33]

Having made their drop, there was nothing left to do but run for it. Hashimoto led his flight across *Yorktown*'s bow and away to the southeast. Looking back, he strained for any sign that his torpedoes had found their mark. Suddenly, one after the other, two enormous geysers lifted their ponderous white heads over the enemy flight deck. Hashimoto felt a surge of elation—they had indeed struck home!

By the time he reached the squadron's rendezvous point, though, it was clear that the price *Hiryū* had paid for this latest success had once again been steep. Lieutenant Tomonaga was nowhere to be found, nor was Lieutenant Mori. Just five *kankō* were left—all from the 2nd *chūtai*—and four Zeros. Three of the torpedo planes were so badly shot up it seemed unlikely they would make it home, let alone be of further use in the battle. If this was victory, it was the sort of victory *Hiryū* could ill afford. Hashimoto dutifully radioed his assessment of the attack back to the flagship at 1445.[34]

The 2nd *chūtai*'s torpedoes did tremendous damage to *Yorktown*.[35] The first slammed home at Frame 90, knocking three boilers off line at once. Steam pressure immediately fell and the carrier listed 6 degrees to port, but *Yorktown* had continued swerving to port and remained underway. For about thirty seconds there was some chance of minimizing the damage, and orders were being given to the forward generator room to shift oil to starboard tanks so as to correct the list. However, just as these orders were being given, the second torpedo struck a bit forward of the first, at Frame 75. This second hit was a real haymaker, instantly flooding the forward generator room and killing power throughout the entire ship. Though the ship's emergency generator did kick in, an unlucky short circuit took it off line immediately. Since *Yorktown* was already turning, this loss of power jammed her helm 15 degrees to port. The big carrier rapidly coasted to a stop and began heeling further to port as water poured into her hull.[36]

17-4: Decisive damage to *Yorktown*. Despite the heavy flak surrounding the carrier, the second of the Hashimoto *chūtai*'s torpedoes strikes home against *Yorktown*'s port side. This hit knocked out the ship's power plant, preventing the rapid counterflooding needed to correct the sharp list resulting from the two hits on the port side. Flooding and loss of power contributed greatly to the decision subsequently to abandon ship. (Naval Historical Center)

The second hit had damaged her forward pumps as well, making counterflooding impossible. As a result, *Yorktown*'s list grew worse, to the point where just standing on the flight deck became difficult. Within seventeen minutes, her list reached 23 degrees. *Yorktown*'s skipper, Captain Elliott Buckmaster, was rightly concerned that she would capsize, which would inevitably lead to a heavy loss of life among his crew, particularly those still belowdecks at their battle stations. To prevent such a catastrophe, Buckmaster reluctantly began ordering his crew over the side at about 1500.[37] Hashimoto's group, in a brilliantly executed attack, had precisely accomplished their intent to concentrate torpedo damage amidships. Though it had taken two strikes to do it, *Yorktown* was now finally, definitively, out of the battle.

Once Hashimoto had been debriefed, at 1600, Yamaguchi dutifully reported the results of the strike up to Nagumo, stating, "Two certain torpedo hits on an *Enterprise*-class carrier (not the same one as reported bombed)."[38] CarDiv 2's leader followed up half an hour later with another message to Nagumo that *Hiryū*'s third attack wave would "take off at 1800 to engage the enemy at dusk" and went on to request that the force's float recon planes maintain contact with the enemy.[39] Though Yamaguchi still sought to attack, Nagumo was now finally inclined to start getting *Hiryū* out of the danger zone. At 1550 he had received word from *Tone*'s No. 4 plane of two enemy carriers with two escorts. It appeared that despite Hashimoto's best efforts, at least two enemy flattops remained operational. With the odds not getting perceptibly better, and *Hiryū*'s second strike home, it was time to start opening the range. Thus, as soon as *Hiryū* had recovered her aircraft, she began her belated retreat to the northwest, turning to course 315 and ringing up twenty-eight knots.[40]

At the same time, Nagumo was still trying to assess if there was any hope of retrieving at least some of the burning carriers and shepherd them from the battlefield. To that effect, he sent a message to the commander of Destroyer Division (DesDiv) 4 at 1600 that he should make every effort to escort the damaged vessels and retire to the northwest.[41] However, by this time, neither *Akagi, Kaga,* nor *Sōryū* had been mobile for the better part of three hours, *Kaga* having been the last to lose power. For its part, DesDiv 4 remained silent, perhaps unwilling to dispel the admiral's hopes in the matter. The three towering smoke columns still visible on the horizon behind *Nagara* ought to have been testament enough as to the reality of the situation.

A half hour later, with Hashimoto's strike now recovered, Nagumo felt even more strongly that *Hiryū* needed to be opening the range and hightailing it west toward Yamamoto and Kondō. At 1630, even as Yamaguchi announced plans for a third attack and asked for increased scouting, Nagumo ordered Mobile Fleet to come hard left to a due west course.[42]

Unbeknownst to Yamaguchi and Nagumo, even as Hashimoto had landed, American retribution for *Yorktown*'s crippling was already forming up and heading for *Hiryū*. As soon as Lieutenant Adams's sighting report had come in at 1445, TF 16 had begun readying for a strike. *Enterprise* immediately began spotting a composite dive-bomber group composed of both her own aircraft and those of *Yorktown*. All told, there were fifteen aircraft from *Yorktown*'s Bombing Three, joined by seven aircraft from Scouting Six and four from Bombing Six. All were under the command of Lieutenant Gallaher.[43] At 1525 "The Big 'E'" turned into the wind and began launching.[44]

Meanwhile, the disjointed nature of *Hornet*'s flight operations continued. She, too, had monitored Lieutenant Adams's transmission and had dutifully spotted her own strike force at 1456.[45] However, not having received any orders from *Enterprise* (TF 16's flagship) with regards to an impending strike, *Hornet* had broken her spot at about 1510 to recover her VB-8 SBDs that had previously landed on Midway, as well as seven CAP fighters. The result was that when *Enterprise* signaled at 1517 that she would begin launching at 1530, *Hornet*'s Captain Marc Mitscher was caught flat-footed.[46]

Hurriedly respotting the deck, *Hornet* managed to put up sixteen SBDs under the command of Lt. Edgar E. Stebbins by 1600.[47] At that point, though, *Enterprise*'s aircraft were already heading out to the target. *Hornet* therefore cut her launch short, sending Stebbins chasing after the *Enterprise* strike.[48] Several of *Hornet*'s SBDs, despite being warmed up and ready to go, were left sitting in the hangar, much to the disgust of their aviators. Thus, once again the Americans had squandered an opportunity to put together a coordinated multicarrier strike. In the end, though, none of the confusion on board *Hornet* detracted from the material point—that at this stage of the battle both of TF 16's carriers individually possessed sufficient force to overwhelm *Hiryū*'s feeble remaining defenses.

This phase of the battle was also a busy one for the Japanese scouting planes, which were continuing to send back information on American fleet movements. At 1545, *Tone* No. 3 sighted "what appears to be 6 enemy cruisers in position bearing 94 degrees, distance 117 miles from my take off point. Enemy is on course 120 degrees, speed 24 knots."[49] This was followed just five minutes later by a new report from *Tone* No. 4, advising that the enemy fleet contained "two carriers" accompanied by destroyers—clearly a reference to TF 16. CruDiv 8's two ships were busily supporting these efforts. *Chikuma* was in the process of getting ready to launch yet another follow-up scouting mission with her No. 2 aircraft (a Type 95),[50] which went up at 1606.[51]

For their part, the American CAP fighters were putting the heat on the Japanese recon birds, aided by their carriers' radars. At 1610 the hard-worked *Tone* No. 4 had reported that he was being pursued by American fighters and was homeward bound.[52] Indeed, a section of *Yorktown*'s Grummans attacked both of *Tone*'s Nos. 3 and 4 planes at this time. *Tone* No. 4 managed to scoot into cloud cover and make her way out of the area, partly because the Wildcats chasing Amari suffered from jamming guns and low ammunition.[53] *Tone* No. 3, however, was not so lucky, being downed at 1633.[54] Once again, there were no survivors.

In the meantime, *Kidō Butai*'s reconnaissance efforts were again being augmented by yet more captured American aviators. A little after 1630, after having turned west, *Nagara* spotted a mysterious red object in the water and apparently jogged northward to investigate it.[55] It turned out to be a life raft, from which destroyer *Makigumo* shortly rescued two fliers from Scouting Six—Ens. Frank W. O'Flaherty and his gunner, AMM2c Bruno P. Gaido. After bombing *Kaga* earlier in the morning, Flaherty had exited the battle area to the northeast with Ware's section, but had run out of gas on the return home. It was their misfortune to be spotted after *Hiryū's* westward turn. Though initially treated well, they were predictably subjected to a threatening interrogation. The two yielded accurate details concerning Midway, but nothing of value on the American carriers. Like Ensign Osmus before them, these prisoners were eventually executed.[56]

By 1655 Admiral Abe in *Tone* felt that he had a good enough sense of the enemy's composition to send Nagumo a surprisingly accurate appraisal of the latest spotting intelligence. He reported that by "Coordinating various reports, the large enemy force is apparently composed of 2 carriers and 6 large cruisers accompanied by about 8 destroyers. Two float recco planes have been sent to obtain more intelligence."[57]

Simultaneously, Combined Fleet flagship *Yamato* made her helpful presence known once again, as Admiral Ugaki sent a message to his counterpart on Nagumo's staff, Admiral Kusaka, as well as Admirals Yamaguchi and Abe, asking them to "report progress of attacks on Midway (particularly whether or not friendly units will be able to use shore bases on Midway tomorrow . . .)."[58] At the moment, Yamamoto and his staff still allowed themselves a guarded optimism. Though roughly handled, Nagumo's force was apparently still in the fight. *Hiryū* was even now probably in the midst of launching a third strike against the enemy carriers. Though its chances for success seemed slim, Yamaguchi had apparently already crippled at least two of the enemy's carriers. Come nightfall, *Hiryū* with the rest of Nagumo's force would shape course to rendezvous with Kondō's onrushing fleet, which in turn would be joined the following morning by the massed force of the Main Body itself. If all went well, a reasonable semblance of a Combined Fleet would be deployed to cover the renewal of the landing operations. Whatever American carriers remained could be brought to bay by the fleet's powerful battleships and cruisers, while *Hiryū's* remaining aircraft provided the necessary combat air patrol cover.

The fantastical nature of the 1655 message demonstrated just how out of touch Yamamoto and his staff were. Just as at Coral Sea, where Combined Fleet headquarters had soundly rebuked Admiral Takagi for a perceived lack of offensive spirit (despite the fact that both his carriers had been effectively knocked out of action), so now the dull displeasure of Combined Fleet's staff could be detected from afar. Blissfully ignorant, or simply unwilling to admit the true nature of the combat conditions then pertaining, and physically located so as to be of no use whatsoever to the ongoing operation, Yamamoto's staff was clearly having difficulty coming to grips with reality. This trend would only get worse as the evening continued.

By 1640 the situation on board *Kaga* finally reached the point where further firefighting was useless. The truth was that there was very little left of the ship to save by this time—eight hours of fire and explosions had left her a gutted shell. Commander Amagai correctly realized that staying on board simply meant condemning more of *Kaga's* crew to a pointless death. He ordered *Kaga* abandoned and the remainder of the crew to be taken on board the destroyers.[59]

On board *Hagikaze*'s sister *Maikaze,* her skipper, Cdr. Nagasuki Seiji, continued watching *Kaga* burn with awed dismay. "She was a huge bonfire. There, surrounded among the flames, stood the bridge looking like a volcano that had melted down; a lava slag."[60] Given this, it was understandable that Commander Nagasuki looked with incredulity on a message from Yamamoto himself, asking him "to determine if *Kaga* can be towed, and to advise" his . . . superiors of her condition. Nagasuki replied with blunt clarity, saying it was "simply impossible." It's not clear if Yamamoto received this, but apparently Nagumo did, for he subsequently radioed *Yamato* at 1700, "*Kaga* is inoperational in position HE EA 55. Survivors transferred to DDs."[61]

Sōryū's condition at this point was much the same as *Kaga*'s, with many men already in the water. Still, survivors clustered on both extremities of the ship. As the afternoon wore on, the decision was evidently made to remove these men as well. *Sōryū*'s destroyers, which had apparently been hanging off a good distance from the stricken vessel during this phase of the battle, now began their recovery operations in earnest again.[62]

On *Sōryū*'s anchor deck, Commander Kanao noticed a ship approaching at high speed. Incredibly, for a moment, Kanao wondered if it were an enemy. Given the condition of *Sōryū,* should he kill himself to escape the shame of capture? But he carried no pistol, the way the pilots did, so there was no way to do the deed. Suddenly, he remembered that the forward AA guns were still in order. If it was an enemy warship, they could at least fight back and die like warriors. He immediately ordered, "Gunners, man your battle stations!" As the other vessel closed, though, he and the men were relieved to see that she flew the Imperial Navy's ensign. It was *Hamakaze*. With tears in their eyes, the men on the foredeck waved their caps at the destroyer.[63]

Hamakaze stopped several hundred meters away and started to signal them. Not having a signalman in their ranks made deciphering the message difficult, but Kanao finally made out that the tin can was ordering them to abandon ship. Simultaneously, the destroyer lowered one of her cutters.

Kanao managed to flag back: "Our ship is disabled. We want to remain on board."

Hamakaze answered quickly, "Enemy carriers are approaching. Abandon ship immediately!"

Kanao thought that *Hamakaze* must be mistaken, or that he had read the signals wrong. Nevertheless, in short order the cutter was alongside and the destroyermen began urging the crew on the bow to abandon ship. Kanao was torn. He was not convinced that the enemy was approaching. Yet, Yanagimoto had ordered the ship abandoned as well, and if they remained there, they might well be hindering *Hamakaze* in continuing the fight. Some of the other sailors opined that if the situation on board *Sōryū* improved, perhaps they could reboard the carrier. Finally, seeing no other way out, Kanao and the men cheered "*Sōryū—Banzai!*" three times and started to load their wounded onto the boat.

At the same time *Hamakaze* was sending over her boat, *Chikuma*'s cutter (which had been left behind to render assistance to the stricken carrier), was still trolling about and plucking survivors out of the water. *Hamakaze* eventually picked them up after they had finished their work, and at 1802 the boat was cut loose and abandoned.[64]

As far as the destroyers could tell, they had now gotten everybody off the ship that could be rescued.

Yet even now, there were apparently still men on board *Sōryū*. Deep in her hull, the final fate of the engine room crews had been grimly unfolding for some time.[65] The temperature had by now soared well beyond the point where humans could stay alive for any length of time. Engineering Lieutenant Naganuma was dizzy, and several of the sailors around him were squatting on the deck plates. As one such man crouched at Naganuma's feet, he shouted at him, "Hey, come on, we are in a battle!" He kicked at the man's legs to rouse him back to his post. But the sailor no longer moved.

Naganuma was streaming with sweat. He tried to keep drinking, but almost instantly he would be thirsty again. Soon, the drinking water was exhausted. The men were sweating rivers. One of them said, "Well, it's unavoidable. We must drink the water from the *fukusuiki* (the water recovery plant for the boilers)." Desperately, they began pouring the distilled boiler feedwater into cups for the men, who greedily lapped it up. To Naganuma, the water made him feel uneasy in his gut.

An engineer that he knew, who was usually quite diligent, stepped up to Naganuma. In the dim battle lighting, he looked half-mad.

"*Kikaichō* (head of machinery), I have a favor to ask."

"What is it?" Naganuma replied.

"I borrowed 2 *yen* 50 *sen* from a petty officer in the starboard engine room, but I haven't returned it," the sailor said. "I don't know how he is now, but the money is in my private box, so could you please give it back to him, sir?"

Naganuma was taken aback by the enlisted man's request. "What are you talking about?" he snapped. "We are in battle now! Do it after it's finished."

"No, *Kikaichō*; I am no longer all right." And without another word, the man fell to the deck to lie beside Naganuma's feet. The lieutenant simply stood there, paralyzed. It was clear that, distilled water or not, the conditions in the engine rooms were going to kill them all, as the temperature literally headed for the boiling point. Many of the men were already dead or dying from the appalling heat and smoke. But what was there to do? The passages topside were all aflame, with the hangar deck above them a mass of fire.

Finally, someone spoke up, "Hey, let's go through the double hull!" Naganuma followed three or four men to a service manhole that led down below the engine deck plates to a crawl space in the bilges. There was already seawater down there, and as the men crawled in the water came up to their heads. For a while they simply crouched there, not knowing what to do. At least it was cooler.

After a time, Naganuma became perplexed. "Hey, something is odd," he remarked.

His senior engineman, Ensign Iizuka, who had yet to enter the pool below the floorplates, was writing down the names of those who had fallen and their last words in a notebook. He looked up from his scribing. "What is it, sir?" "Well, look at this depth meter," Naganuma said.

He pointed out the graduation, which showed by how many feet below the waterline the bottom of the double hull was located. "It looks like the level has deepened." There was no question; *Sōryū* appeared to be taking on water. It wasn't a lot yet, since the crawl space was still not completely full. But it seemed impossible to exit that way by crawling forward through the bilges, since who knew if the space would fill further while they were exiting?

Iizuka said, "Well, it cannot be helped. Shall we try topside again?" Naganuma had no response. Communications with the bridge had been totally terminated long before. If there had been an order to abandon ship, Naganuma had never heard it. Even the emergency lights had now gone dark. Despairing of progressing further into the water-filled crawl way, Naganuma's party now crept dripping out of the ship's bilges and made their way back into the infernal heat of the engine spaces. With the help of a hand light, they tried to evacuate upward through another waterproof hatch. However, try as they might, it would not budge. Naganuma cursed the door's design. Then, one of the men noticed a dim light coming down from abovedecks. The enginemen moved forward to see what it might be. Coming nearer, they could see that an explosion or bomb had blown a hole through the top of their prison. Just beyond, a companionway ran upward toward freedom. But the exit at the top was ringed with fire. For the moment at least, there seemed no way out.

On *Hiryū,* preparations for Yamaguchi's dusk strike were already under way. Convinced (with reason) that his aircraft had badly damaged two of the American carriers, Yamaguchi was determined to attack the third. Unfortunately, he now had practically nothing left with which to do it. He was down to just four serviceable dive-bombers and five torpedo planes, plus *Sōryū*'s D4Y, which was intended for scouting. Nevertheless, he was planning on getting in one last blow at dusk, when the Americans would hopefully be less wary, and with a smaller CAP overhead. Lieutenant Hashimoto would be in charge of the effort.[66]

The planes were not yet on deck, though, and would not be spotted for another half hour or so.[67] Yamaguchi had hoped to launch earlier, at 1630, and Captain Kaku had apparently begun the briefing process, only to have it all called off as the result of an intriguing episode. Kaku could see that many of the aviators were on their last legs as a result of the day's constant flight operations. As a result, he ordered stimulants distributed to them. There had been a mix-up in getting the pills, mysteriously labeled "Aviation Tablet A," up from the sick bay. The aviation mechanic who had been sent below to fetch them brought back a bottle of tablets, which *hikōchō* Kawaguchi thought looked suspiciously like sleeping tablets. Captain Kaku thereupon flew into a towering rage at the unlucky mechanic. A quick call down to the infirmary confirmed that "Aviation Tablet A" was indeed correct. But the incident demonstrated that everyone's nerves were frayed, not least the captain's. Yamaguchi thereupon decided to push things back ninety minutes and use the lull to feed *Hiryū*'s crew. None of the aviators had even had lunch yet. The strike leader, Lieutenant Hashimoto, was too tired to eat—he simply went back down to the ready room and fell asleep on one of the brown leather couches.[68]

Overhead circled thirteen Zeros, the majority having just been launched at 1627—a composite group of seven *Sōryū* and *Kaga* planes, led by *Kaga*'s Lt. Iizuka Masao. They joined four *Akagi* fighters under Lt. Shirane Ayao, and a pair of *Kaga* birds as well. The disposition of these fighters is unknown, although judging by the composition of the group as a whole, they were likely roaming about in two- and three-plane *shōtai,* covering different quadrants of the formation. It seems clear, too, that some of the aircraft at least were stacked at different altitudes—somebody on *Hiryū* (likely Captain Kaku or *hikōchō* Kawaguchi) had learned their lesson with regards to American dive-bombers. By this time, the force's cruisers and battleships had all joined up with *Hiryū.* The heavy units were in their accustomed positions, with BatDiv 3 in the starboard column, and CruDiv 8 to the port, all spread widely around *Hiryū.*[69] *Nagara*'s position was in the van.

Hiryū's final test was not long in coming, as *Enterprise*'s composite air group was now close by. *Enterprise*'s Lieutenant Gallaher had spotted *Hiryū* at 1645, after first flying north of the burning hulks of the carriers he had helped destroy in the morning. With *Hiryū*'s formation discernible ahead at a range of forty miles, Gallaher had begun gradually letting down from 19,000 feet in preparation for initiating his attack run.[70] As he did so, passing the formation's port side, he circled to the west, so as to attack out of the sun. He ordered Bombing Six's aircraft to follow his Scouting Six aircraft in attacking the enemy carrier. *Yorktown*'s Bombing Three (under Lt. DeWitt Wood Shumway) was slated to attack "the nearer battleship"—*Haruna*—which was ahead and to starboard of the CV.

Despite the better CAP arrangements, the Japanese apparently did not receive adequate warning of this incoming attack, either. The position of the sun certainly had something to do with this, but so, too, did the fact that the remaining CAP pilots were undoubtedly just as exhausted as the deckhands on board *Hiryū.* So it was that Admiral Yamaguchi's flagship did not notice the enemy aircraft over her until 1701, three minutes after Gallaher had begun a shallow descent to his pushover point.[71]

As it happened, just before at 1656, Nagumo had signaled his force, ordering "Turn to course 120 degrees, speed 24 knots." Nagumo's order was not intended as an evasive maneuver, but rather an intentional change in base course, confirmed by radio from *Tone* to CruDiv 8 and the battleship's planes at 1700.[72] It may have been related to the seaplane recovery operations that were soon to follow, or (less likely) to the planned launch of *Sōryū*'s recon plane, but this is not clear.[73] Regardless of why it occurred, Nagumo's last-minute maneuver had the effect of bringing *Kidō Butai* into a sharp turn just as the *Enterprise*'s SBDs began their dives. This may have further amplified *Hiryū*'s already well-documented evasive skills.

Some 5,000 meters off *Hiryū*'s starboard bow, *Chikuma* had just completed her turn to the east at 1701 when she spotted Gallaher's bombers as they were about to push over.[74] Behind her, *Tone* saw Shumway's group three minutes later and cranked her guns around to port as fast as she could to engage the enemy. But once again, the heavy units that might have been able to contribute some volume of fire to *Hiryū*'s defense were too far away to really do anything meaningful.

For her part, as soon as the Dauntlesses were sighted, *Hiryū* immediately began putting up antiaircraft fire. Simultaneously, Captain Kaku ordered his speedy carrier to continue her hard port turn, bringing her bow around into his assailants.[75] This forced the Americans into steeper dives to compensate for *Hiryū* scooting out of

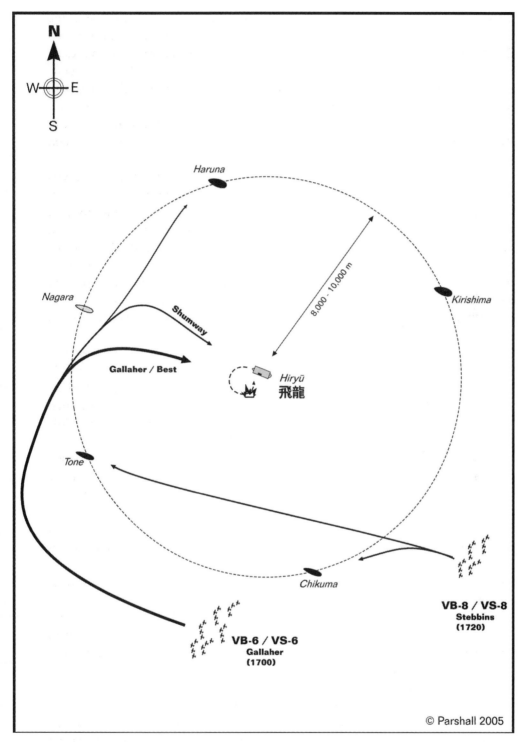

17-5: Decisive attack on *Hiryū* at 1701–1710 by VB-6/VS-6.

sight beneath their engine cowlings. The combination of heavy antiaircraft fire and a very speedy ship made this the toughest target the Americans had faced all day. The fact, too, that *Hiryū*'s CAP was at altitude meant that they could also make their presence known. The Zeros slashed frantically at the attacking SBDs, knowing full well that it was now do or die—if *Hiryū* was taken down, they would have no place to land and no hope left in the battle. The American pilots were amazed to see Zeros following them all the way down, performing acrobatic maneuvers worthy of an air show in their attempts to deflect this final attack. Two SBDs were hit in their dives and slanted into the water.[76]

It would seem that Captain Kaku's radical turn, as well as the efforts of fighter leaders Shirane and Iizuka, did at least some good.[77] The first few bombs from Gallaher's section missed their target. Not surprisingly for a composite air group composed of aviators from two carriers, the American attack suffered from a lack of coordination. To the westward, *Yorktown*'s aircraft were already on their way toward *Haruna,* but the pilots could clearly see the large white columns of misses erupting around the elusive *Hiryū.* Upon seeing this, Lieutenant Shumway's section, followed by all but the last of the *Yorktown* sections designated for *Haruna,* made a snap decision to attack *Hiryū* instead.[78] Or at least that is what Shumway subsequently claimed in his report. However, the near-simultaneous timing of his section's attack suggests that he had made the bold, if somewhat subversive decision to disregard Gallaher's earlier assignments well before observing the results of his superior's attack. In the process, however, Shumway's group passed directly in front of Lt. Dick Best's VB-6 aircraft, who were just beginning their own dives. For the second time this day, Best was left with no choice but to reef his men back upward again. Unfortunately, not only did this spoil their initial attack run, but it had the effect of stringing them out in the face of *Hiryū*'s Zeros. In an instant, Best's wingman, Ens. Fred Weber, was shot out of the air and killed. As soon as *Yorktown*'s aircraft were out of the way, Best lost no time pushing over again with his remaining three aircraft.[79]

Hiryū was now on the receiving end of an attack much like *Kaga*'s. She was committed to her left-hand evasive turn and had too many enemies overhead and too little antiaircraft fire to deal with them. Her Zeros, though valiant, were outnumbered by the SBDs. And with deadeyes like Dick Best interspersed throughout the three distinct packs now hurtling downward on her, the final results were likewise all but inevitable. The first hit was probably delivered by Shumway himself and was followed in quick succession by three more. All of them were 1,000 pounders, and all landed on the forward third of the flight deck.[80] This is particularly intriguing in light of the fact that several of the American aviators commented afterward that they had used *Hiryū*'s *hinomaru* as a convenient aiming point.

The results could hardly have been more appalling for the Japanese. *Hiryū*'s flight deck was blown upward by the detonations, then collapsed down upon itself as the hammer blows continued. Heavy fires broke out at once. Anyone in the forward hangar, where nineteen Zeros were currently stowed, would have been killed instantly. Even more spectacular, one of the bombs also smashed into *Hiryū*'s forward elevator, chopping the lift into pieces and hurling one large portion against the front of her

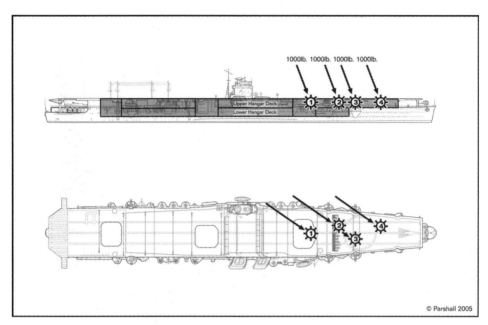

17-6: Hit locations on *Hiryū*.

island.[81] The bridge windows were smashed, flinging Captain Kaku and everyone else to the deck. Astern and one deck below, Commander Kawaguchi was blown completely off the air-control platform at the back of the island and onto the flight deck.[82] Standing nearby was his assistant, WO Arimura Yoshikazu, *Hiryū*'s bomber maintenance chief. Arimura was badly wounded on his left side by the blast, suffering a broken jaw, punctured lung, and multiple fractures in his left leg. He collapsed in a heap on the air platform.[83] Kawaguchi himself was amazingly unhurt, and was just picking himself back up from the flight deck when another bomb landed.[84]

Down in the ship's port after engine room, an ensign named Mandai had heard the bugles sound over the intercom, meaning an air action was underway. Then he heard the first bomb land. This was no near miss alongside, as the force of the detonation pushed down directly on the ship, rather than shoving it laterally. Then more hits. The lights went out, and the battle lighting came on. Almost immediately, though, smoke began pouring through the engine room ventilators. A pair of ratings who had just gone above to get food for the engine room crews hurriedly scurried back below— the spaces above were already afire.[85] Nevertheless, in the main engineering control room, Chief Engineer Aimune Kunize maintained the ship under way. Although the hatchways to the other machinery spaces were blocked, he soon had a minor blaze in No. 4 engine room extinguished and had reestablished communications with the other engineers.[86] Aimune had no intention of bringing *Hiryū* to a halt before he was told to. Indeed, Captain Kaku urged him to give him everything he had, so as to drive *Hiryū* out of the battle area as quickly as possible.

In the ready room below the island, torpedo aviator Hashimoto was still catnapping when he was thrown off of his couch by the first detonation, then was knocked to the deck again as the bombing continued. The ready room quickly began filling with smoke. Hashimoto ran toward a patch of light, which turned out to be an opening made by one of the explosions. The reason for the light now became evident—the space beyond was already catching fire. He crawled on his hands and knees through the compartment, grateful for the gloves on his hands. Sparks and burning ashes were falling on him. His hair began to smolder. Groping his way through the rapidly gathering smoke, he encountered another sailor, who offered him a gas mask. Even half-burned as it was, it was still better protection than nothing.[87]

Finally making his way up to the flight deck, Hashimoto gazed in amazement at the wreck of the elevator, standing almost at attention as it leaned against the island.[88] To the wounded Arimura, also lying nearby, the now-vertical lift reminded him of the sails of a sailing ship.[89] Hashimoto was immediately pressed into service by *Hiryū*'s executive officer, who ordered everyone in the vicinity to begin cutting loose the hammock mantelets from around the bridge.[90] They served no more use now and were sure to catch on fire.

This much must be said for *Hiryū*—her damage-control parties were prompt and fairly efficient. By some miracle she still had one of her fire mains working[91] and parties began making their way forward at once, reeling the hoses out from the crew pockets along the sides of the flight deck. Lying where he was amidst the wreckage and dead and injured crewmen, Arimura could do nothing to assist the crewmen. He couldn't even move. And all the while the flames were getting closer. Suddenly, a sailor came along and picked him up from amid the carnage and began carrying him up the companionway onto the bridge. Thinking better of this, though, the rating instead turned around and made for the flight deck, where they were both knocked over by overeager sailors plying their hoses. Arimura was intensely irritated, but could do little about it. He was dumped on the flight deck farther aft.

Those few American dive-bombers who had not yet committed to their dives were now picking out new targets. From where they sat, *Hiryū* was obviously finished. As a result, several bombers scooted over to attack battleship *Haruna* instead. The fast battlewagon, however, remained as wily as ever and avoided anything more serious than a pair of near misses.

Hiryū continued racing blindly forward at thirty knots, smoke streaming from her bow down the length of her flight deck. Captain Kaku had no real choice in the matter—as long as the dive-bomber attack was ongoing, he needed to keep *Hiryū* moving at her best speed. However, a thirty-knot wind over the bow had the effect of fanning the flames toward the stern and making firefighting efforts even more difficult. Worse yet, almost as soon as the first group of American dive-bombers finished with *Hiryū,* at 1720 another group showed up.

This was *Hornet*'s late-launching SBD contingent. Fortunately for *Hiryū*, they, too, could see that diving on her was a waste of time—the carrier was aflame practically stem to stern. As a result, they focused their efforts on *Tone* and *Chikuma* instead.[92] Apparently, Japanese battleships and heavy cruisers were immune to damage this day, though given that they were hardly smaller or speedier than ships like *Hiryū*, the futility of the American attacks appears to make little sense. Nevertheless, *Tone* and *Chikuma* garnered little more than a bucket of near misses from their encounter with *Hornet*'s fourteen aviators. Thus, *Hornet*'s misery for this day was complete—her torpedo squadron wiped out, her dive-bomber and fighter squadrons badly depleted, and not so much as a single hit on an enemy vessel to show for it. It had indeed been a dismal combat debut for the most recent American carrier to join the Pacific Fleet.

Ten minutes after *Hornet*'s planes departed, the final U.S. air attacks of this long and costly day began rolling in. *Chikuma* sighted them first, at 1742—large, four-engined shapes. Lt. Col. Sweeney's B-17s were back, for the second time this day. He had only six aircraft with him this time, but propitiously he approached the battlefield at the same time as a separate flight of six Flying Fortresses from Barking Sands airfield in Hawaii showed up, under the command of Major George A. Blakey.[93] Blakey had been sent up to reinforce Midway's depleted air group, only to be told just before landing on the island that he should instead fly to the northwest and attack the fourth Japanese carrier. His group had been low on fuel, but he had complied. They also didn't have the gas necessary to make it up to a proper altitude, so they stuck to a comparatively low altitude of 3,600 feet.[94] Despite being the first to attack, two of Sweeney's planes failed to drop during their initial runs and, coming around to make a second pass, were actually the last to release their weapons this evening. Thus, Sweeney and Blakey didn't exactly attack in concert, but the Japanese could hardly tell the difference.

The results were the same as the earlier B-17 attacks; namely, nothing. The bombers droned overhead, the Japanese barked back at them, and the bombs all fell in the water. *Chikuma* reported bombs dropped astern of her at 1745, and more landing off her port side at 1749.[95] However, Blakey's element gave *Hiryū* a scare. *Hikōchō* Kawaguchi, standing on the blazing carrier's flight deck, stared back goggle-eyed as they thundered in at low altitude at 1815—the big Boeings were quite a sight! Once again their bombs went into the drink, this time about 500 meters away from the ship.[96] But these particular B-17s were low enough to strafe, and their intense .50-caliber machine gun fire managed to knock out one of *Hiryū*'s antiaircraft batteries, killing several gunners in the process. Thereupon, Sweeney and Blakey swung their bombers for home, although not in any organized fashion.[97] *Chikuma* did not log the last of them as departing until 1832.[98]

As the American aircraft began retreating, some of them being chased out of the area by the remaining Zeros, the Japanese fighter pilots' moods were grim. They knew that they would be facing a water landing sometime in the reasonably proximate future. *Hiryū* would never handle another airplane. One by one, the Japanese fighters returned, continuing to fly their sad patrols above their burning carrier. *Hiryū* raced northwest, wreathed in smoke and flames.

18

Scuttlings—1800–Dawn, 5 June

iryū's bombing did not spell the end of combat operations this day, but it did mark a watershed moment for the Americans, wherein they could switch their focus from gaining victory to consolidating their gains. As the reports of the successful attack came back to TF 16 and 17, Admirals Frank Jack Fletcher and Raymond Spruance began considering what actions were needed to conclude the day's activities. For Fletcher, the immediate priority was what to do with the crippled *Yorktown*. By 1639 all her survivors had been removed—a remarkably fast evacuation. She now lay dark and silent. Evening was coming, and the prospect of the Japanese attempting to force a night action was not lost on the commander of TF 17. *Yorktown* was a sitting duck. Given that Japanese search aircraft were in the area, it seemed reasonable to suppose that their warships would come gunning for her if given the chance. Six of his destroyers were packed with survivors, making their participation in any surface action problematic at best. Wisely, Fletcher chose to vacate the area with all of his warships and move closer to Spruance's formation. At 1732 *Astoria* led the rest of *Yorktown's* escorts away from her, though at 1800 he ordered destroyer *Hughes* to return once more to the derelict.[1] *Hughes* mission was to stand by *Yorktown* throughout the night and sink her if need be to prevent her being captured or boarded.[2] If all went well, Fletcher would return for her in the morning. He had radioed Hawaii to send a fleet tug to her assistance. But the sight of *Yorktown*, forlorn and listing, dwindling against the horizon, was one that saddened many of the men crowded on board TF 17's decks. *Yorktown* had fought bravely, and she didn't deserve to end up this way; abandoned, a castoff. Leaving her to her fate was a bitter pill to swallow.

Beyond *Yorktown's* disposition, Fletcher also had to decide how best to prosecute the battle. TF 17's power projection capability was now nil, and his ability to exercise tactical command over TF 16 was severely hampered. Therefore, when Spruance dutifully asked his superior for further instructions, Fletcher graciously replied that he had none, and that he would conform to Spruance's movements.[3] Fletcher had, in effect, told his subordinate to fight the battle as he saw fit—a profoundly selfless and practical act on the part of the senior American admiral.

Spruance, for his part, wisely wanted no part of a night battle with the Japanese. The day's events had turned out remarkably well for the Americans, but Spruance was also cognizant of the heavy cost that victory had extracted. *Yorktown* was crippled, the air groups badly depleted, and the torpedo squadrons practically wiped out. Spruance knew that the Japanese probably outgunned him in surface forces and would be itching to even the score. He knew that at last report, the Japanese invasion forces to the west were still bearing down on the island. Furthermore, he had no idea whether he had accounted for all the Japanese carriers in the neighborhood. While none of his sighting reports thus far had betrayed the presence of any more than four carriers, intelligence reports prior to the battle had indicated the Japanese might use as many as five flight decks.[4] Indeed, the fact that some of Sweeney's B-17s had been set upon by Zeros well after *Hiryū* had been bombed might indicate that the enemy had another carrier.[5]

Furthermore, no one knew what tomorrow might bring and whether or not they would have to fend off yet more Japanese attacks on the island. To do that, he needed to preserve his remaining strength at all costs. This was no time for rashness. Charging west after the enemy, despite the fact that the Japanese had been badly beaten, could offer Spruance nothing that was worth the risk of jeopardizing either of his remaining carriers. Accordingly, he determined that after recovering aircraft (which would be completed by about 1915), he would move east until midnight. Thereafter, he would turn north for an hour, and then return west as the night waned. According to his logic, he would thereby preserve his standoff distance to the Japanese but also be in a position to support Midway by daybreak.

Spruance was subsequently criticized for his perceived lack of aggression in following up his victory as promptly as possible. In so doing, the logic goes, he missed opportunities for attacking Yamamoto's Main Body or Kondō's support forces, both of which he might have been engaged had they been closer the following day. Such criticisms not only ignore the fact that the information Spruance had at his disposal was far from perfect, but they also ignore the primary aim of Chester Nimitz's battle plan—to destroy the Japanese carrier fleet. This Fletcher and Spruance had achieved. At this juncture, the only way Yamamoto or Kondō's forces could reverse the verdict of the day was if Spruance allowed them to, by blundering under their guns. Spruance had won air supremacy for the U.S. Navy and thereby owned the initiative. No Japanese force in the vicinity, no matter how powerfully armed, had the ability to force the issue, so long as Spruance kept them at arm's length. His movement east guaranteed that he would retain his current advantages. By so doing, he wisely sealed his victory over the Japanese.

Much like Admiral Fletcher, around 1800 Admiral Nagumo was faced with a very difficult decision: what should be done with the burning carriers? The conventional wisdom has always claimed that *Sōryū* and *Kaga* sank shortly thereafter of their own accord. However, a careful reading of the evidence reveals that Nagumo had both carriers deliberately scuttled.

The reasons for this are manifold. However, at the core lay Nagumo's desperate desire to try and find a way to move actively against the Americans, which by late afternoon meant precipitating a nighttime engagement. Kondō was clearly of like mind as he continued charging eastward to Nagumo's aid. At 1750, doubtless thinking that his ships would be called on to join with Nagumo's in their sweep eastward,

Kondō radioed the units of his subordinate commands, detailing the manner in which they would engage the enemy. As was to be expected, they would rely mainly on torpedoes.[6] Kondō ordered the torpedoes in his force set to a relatively shallow running depth of four meters—an implicit indication that Kondō expected to be fighting cruisers and destroyers this evening, and not heavier carriers and battleships.[7] The problem was that at that very moment, when the Japanese forces needed to be most active, the majority of Nagumo's remaining destroyers were essentially immobile, tied to their burning charges.

Near at hand, *Kazagumo, Makigumo, Yūgumo* and one other unnamed destroyer were actively assisting Yamaguchi's burning flagship.[8] Some sixty miles to the south, *Isokaze* and *Hamakaze* bore witness to *Sōryū*'s agony, while not far to the southeast from them, *Nowaki* and *Arashi* were keeping watch over Nagumo's former flagship. Still further west and south, *Hagikaze* and *Maikaze* attended to *Kaga*. Thus, ten of Nagumo's tin cans were currently unavailable for night operations, and some were quite far away. *Kaga*'s two consorts were nearly eighty nautical miles from Nagumo's flag—a good three hours' steaming, and the guards around *Akagi* and *Sōryū* weren't much closer. Clearly, if the force was to mass in time to fight a surface battle to the east, it was essential to deal intelligently and expeditiously with the stricken carriers. Therefore, despite Nagumo's obvious desire to continue trying to save them for as long as possible, as dusk came on other factors began taking precedence.

Nagumo needed destroyers for two reasons. First was their firepower. Unlike the Americans, who believed in the primacy of gunfire during night combat, the cornerstone of Japanese night tactics was the devastating Type 93 torpedo (more popularly known in postwar American parlance as the "Long Lance").[9] Between Nagumo's eleven destroyers and three cruisers, his diminished fleet mounted 120 torpedo tubes. Eighty-eight of them were carried by the destroyers, making their participation indispensable.

The second reason was that of scouting. Before the advent of radar, the only way to locate an enemy at night was to find him either with spotting aircraft or with one's own warships. *Nagara* had the only night-capable recon plane in the force, and it was unlikely that her E11A1 would be able to sniff out the Americans by itself, although the moonlight might be a factor in its favor.[10] Realistically, though, Nagumo's only hope was to spread his vessels out and search optically. Standard night-search doctrine prescribed a number of linear formations that were all designed to cover as much territory as possible while still maintaining central control over the formation. Once the enemy was found, the detecting ship would maintain contact, while the rest of the formation was pulled together preparatory to initiating a concentrated attack. The relationship between numbers of ships and searching was straightforward—the more ships available, the more area that could be searched. The converse was also true— every destroyer absent this night would cost Nagumo as much as fifteen kilometers of search frontage and a commensurately lessened chance of detecting the enemy. Consequently, the destroyers had to be freed up somehow.

Simply rescuing the crews of the stricken carriers and leaving their hulks to founder was not an option. Nagumo and his staff knew that fire in and of itself does not normally cause ships to sink. While a fire may gut a vessel and utterly ruin it, without a mechanism for admitting water into the hull, a ship may float almost indefinitely even after the blaze is out. Such indeed was the case for all the Japanese carriers at Midway. None of them—with the possible exception of *Akagi,* as the result of her near miss astern—had received any underwater damage. And despite what Lieutenant Naganuma may have been witnessing in *Sōryū*'s engine rooms, none of the carriers seems to have suffered much damage to their watertight integrity. Therefore, none of them was likely to go down by herself any time soon.

The destroyers themselves were also in danger. At 1830, having received a sighting report indicating (erroneously, as it turned out) that significant enemy forces were approaching, the commander of DesDiv 4, Captain Ariga Kosaku, issued a startling order to *Nowaki, Hagikaze, Hamakaze,* and *Isokaze*: "Each ship will stand by the carrier assigned to her and screen her from enemy submarines and task forces. Should the enemy task force approach, engage him in hit-and-run tactics and destroy him."[11] Not only that, but American submarines were apparently still skulking about—at 1800 *Akagi* was advised to be on the lookout for one in her vicinity.[12] The ongoing risk to the escorts—loitering almost stationary around their charges, whose giant pillars of smoke could not help but attract unwanted attention—was increasingly difficult to justify. The only intelligent thing to do was to scuttle any carrier that couldn't make it back home under her own power.

Of the four flattops, *Hiryū*'s condition was the most obvious to Nagumo. She was still capable of making twenty-eight knots and appeared as if she might be salvageable. *Akagi*'s situation was less clear. Indeed, her own crew was still trying to determine what the final outcome of their nine-hour ordeal was going to be. By now, they knew that their firefighting efforts had availed them nothing; the flagship was largely burned out and wrecked. But there remained the possibility that her engines might yet be made operational. At 1820 an engineering party again attempted to descend into her machinery spaces to assess their state but was turned back by conditions below. Finally, at 1915 her chief engineer announced to Captain Aoki that there was no longer any possibility of her operating under her own power.[13] Aoki knew that the jig was up and wasted no more time giving the order at 1920 that all hands should prepare to abandon ship. He signaled *Nowaki* and *Arashi* that they should come alongside to begin transferring her personnel.

Kaga and *Sōryū*'s status, though, was ascertained—and acted upon—rather more quickly. Starting at 1732, Captain Ariga began sending out feelers to the other escorts to assess their status. He radioed *Isokaze,* ordering her to continue standing by her charge, but also inquiring whether *Sōryū* might be "operational if her fires were brought under control?"[14] The reaction of *Isokaze*'s skipper, Cdr. Toyoshima Shunichi, to the question of whether *Sōryū*'s smoldering, motionless hulk could be made operational is unrecorded. In the event, *Isokaze* took her time in answering, finally responding at 1802 that *Sōryū* had no chance of navigating under her own power and that her survivors had already been taken on board.

At 1800, just before *Isokaze* replied, Ariga sent another message to both *Sōryū* and *Kaga*'s escorts, asking whether either carrier was in danger of sinking. *Kaga*'s escorts had previously signaled at 1700 and 1715 that she was inoperational, that the emperor's portrait had been taken on board *Hagikaze,* and that *Kaga*'s crew had been recovered. *Maikaze* reiterated this same message again at 1750. Consequently, neither *Maikaze* nor *Hagikaze* bothered to reply to Captain Ariga's 1800 query—the implication of their silence was clear enough.[15]

By around 1805, then, Ariga knew that *Kaga* and *Sōryū* were clearly beyond hope. As a result, the only possible course of action open to the Japanese was to call a halt to the desultory firefighting efforts. Any parties still on board the two vessels needed to be recovered, any men left in the water picked up, and the carriers disposed of so that their destroyers could go about their business. This is exactly what transpired.

It must be noted that no explicit order to scuttle *Sōryū* or *Kaga* is preserved in the primary signal record of the day—the Nagumo Report. Instead, the previous accounts of the battle would have us believe that *Sōryū* and *Kaga* sank strictly of their own accord.[16] *Senshi Sōsho* also supports this notion, at least with regards to *Kaga*.[17] Yet, it is fascinating to note that in *Kaga*'s case *Senshi Sōsho* admits that it draws primarily from the remembrances of Commander Amagai for its account of her sinking, and Amagai maintained that *Kaga* had not been scuttled.[18] Yet, it has already been established that Amagai was not always the most reliable witness to the day's events.[19] Furthermore, there is no question that he, as senior surviving officer, had more personal embarrassment to suffer from her scuttling than any of her other survivors. Taken together, his rather strange, unsolicited denial of *Kaga*'s scuttling to his American interrogators shortly after the war begins to take on the character of a man who "doth protest too much." And there are numerous pieces of evidence that suggest a rather different picture.

At the top of the list are the particulars surrounding the demise of the two carriers. Both sank within twelve minutes of each other at around 1915, ostensibly as the result of large explosions on each. But both carriers had now been burning for nearly nine hours, with no indication that they were prepared to sink any time soon. Indeed, the fires on both were apparently subsiding to some degree. For that reason, *Sōryū*'s *hikōchō,* Commander Kusamoto, was assembling a firefighting party to return to the ship at around 1900. However, as he was about to do so, he was obliged to refrain from his actions because *Sōryū,* in the words of *Senshi Sōsho,* "began to sink."[20] This is an interesting turn of phrase to use in conjunction with what was supposed to have been a sudden, cataclysmic explosion.

Likewise, there was apparently a small firefighting party still on board *Kaga* at this time as well.[21] A cutter had been sent over from the *Hagikaze* to bring them off, but the men had merely asked that a hand pump be sent over instead. Shortly thereafter, the cutter returned, this time with a *written order* that the men abandon the ship. The presence of a written order suggests a rather premeditative quality to her forthcoming demise. Finally, it is interesting to note that at almost this same time, 1920, Captain Aoki finally ordered *Akagi* abandoned. As he did so, he specifically requested that she be scuttled by torpedo—though that order was subsequently countermanded.[22] In sum, the spontaneous presence of large explosions on both *Kaga* and *Sōryū* within twelve minutes of each other at about this time is clearly a little too convenient to be believable.

Another interesting piece of circumstantial evidence is a gap in the recorded communications of DesDiv 4. Captain Ariga's orders to his units were all dutifully recorded in the Nagumo Report. But there is a gap of three numbered messages from Ariga between 1830 and 2100. This omission in his recorded conversations, coming just after his earlier pointed inquiries as to the status of the carriers, is intriguing to say the least, especially since any messages ordering the disposal of the carriers would logically have been issued during this time period. Although it is impossible to say for certain that such messages were transmitted by Ariga, it must also be noted that the Japanese were not shy about destroying the operational records associated with this particular battle, particularly those that contained unpleasant facts. This is apparently what happened for the logs of *Tone* and *Chikuma* after the battle, logs that might have helped explain the failure of *Tone*'s No. 4 aircraft to launch on time during the morning. It is perhaps not surprising that the recorded messages for DesDiv 4 met the same fate.

Taken together, it is clear that the reason that *Sōryū*'s *hikōchō* was not allowed to reboard *Sōryū* at about 1900 was that her fate had been determined even as Kusamoto was assembling his damage-control party. One can well imagine his shock at being informed that his ship was about to be scuttled. While we can only speculate on Kusamoto's reaction, we know how at least one of *Sōryū*'s senior officers felt about the matter. On board *Isokaze*, *Sōryū*'s gunnery officer, Commander Kanao, greeted the news that she was shortly to be scuttled with rank incredulity. He argued bitterly with *Isokaze*'s Commander Toyoshima, saying that the order should not be carried out. Japan, Kanao asserted, had already won the war, and that instead of sinking *Sōryū*, the destroyer ought to be towing her home instead! Toyoshima, apparently divining that Kanao was unwilling or unable to drop the matter, finally instructed a nearby sailor to accompany the overwrought officer to Toyoshima's own cabin, so that he might get some much-needed rest. Grudgingly, Kanao left the destroyer's bridge and went below. Once in Toyoshima's cabin, his exhaustion finally overcame him, and he passed out.[23] With Kanao out of the way, Toyoshima was able to begin preparations for the grim business at hand.

Sōryū, however, was not yet completely abandoned. Lieutenant Naganuma and his small party of men had finally made their way out of the engine spaces. The vessel was empty of life and burning all around them, and they were not yet outside the ship's structure.[24] To Naganuma, it appeared that she had also taken on something of a list. From where they stood, it looked like the only way out was up another companionway and through a hole made by a bomb hit. Yet all around them were flames and hot metal; the railing on the stairway was a light peach color from the heat. Looking around, Naganuma and a few of the men found some water in buckets. Pouring it on themselves, they charged up the stairway, only to be driven back by the intense heat. Naganuma determined to try again. Pouring another bucketful over himself, he clenched his eyes shut and ran for it. Somehow he managed to make it up to the deck. Another engineer, Horita Kazuaki, was right behind him, but that was it. The others were either unable or unwilling to try their chances. From below, Naganuma heard them singing a military song. The sound was enough to make Naganuma weep.

Now on deck, Naganuma and Horita debated what to do. The ship was noticeably deeper in the water, but they did not know whether or not it was safe to start swimming. Suddenly, there was a large jolt, which (as we shall see) was likely one of *Isokaze*'s torpedoes striking the ship, probably at around 1912. Naganuma's decision was made for him as he and his companion were thrown into the ocean. Naganuma suddenly was concerned lest the ship sink too close to them and they be dragged under by the suction. They simply swam for it. After about 200 meters, he looked back over his shoulder.

Sōryū's bow hung above them almost vertically. To the two men in the water, their eyes stinging from fuel oil, the hull of the carrier seemed enormous. As they watched, fascinated, *Sōryū* plunged rapidly backward into the sea. The water, which had been calm up to this point, was suddenly choppy. Enormous bubbles and spouts of water were still leaping up from the ship's grave. The two survivors realized with horror that they were being dragged back in toward the ship. Naganuma and Horita struck out again with a will, trying desperately to escape the vortex. Soon, though, the terrifying moment was passed, and they were left to make their way unmolested. They also found that they were not alone—other small clumps of men still remained in the water.

Naganuma wondered what was to become of him. At a conscious level, he felt ashamed that he had survived and remorseful for his lost companions. He heard their doomed singing in his head yet again. He was not a strong swimmer and could only manage to keep himself afloat with the breaststroke. No floating wreckage presented itself, so he had no choice but to make do the best he could. He realized that he was very hungry, and wondered if he was going to live. He found, though, that he no longer feared death. Living or dying—either seemed acceptable. His body, though, ignored his internal musings and simply kept swimming.

Finally, a destroyer hove into view. Naganuma recognized it for a *tokugata* ("special type"—the Japanese name given to the world's first modern destroyer, the *Fubuki*, and all her numerous descendants). The ship was closing to within a few hundred meters in the rapidly gathering darkness, and Naganuma realized that it was now or never. His ambivalence to the prospect of death suddenly vanished—he waved his arms and shouted himself hoarse. Gratifyingly, a sailor on board the destroyer waved back. Not knowing what else to do, Naganuma simply floated, waiting. Finally, a canvas bucket was cast down to him, and he grabbed hold. Strong hands pulled him upward effortlessly, along with Horita. Naganuma fainted as soon as he hit the deck.

Down in the captain's cabin on board *Isokaze*, Kanao had heard and felt two large explosions. Lurching back to consciousness, he was at first sure that *Isokaze* had been hit. But the ship was moving, and nothing seemed amiss. Still too exhausted to move, he had not been able to determine the nature of the explosions and soon passed out again. It was not until the next morning that his shipmates told him *Isokaze* had scuttled *Sōryū* with three torpedoes. She had begun listing soon after the hits and had then upended and sank stern first with an eerie gurgling at 1913.[25] Five minutes later, a large underwater explosion occurred in her grave. Out of her nominal complement of 1,103 officers and men, 711 had perished—the highest mortality percentage of any of the Midway carriers.[26]

At 1915 *Hamakaze* radioed a single terse message to Nagumo: "*Sōryū* has sunk."

Somewhere to the west, a similar scene was playing out around *Kaga*. Belowdecks on *Hagikaze,* Yoshino Haruo heard the intercom hiss and then announce, "Regrettably, since we cannot tow *Kaga* back home, with remorse we will now sink her. All those who are able . . . should go topside immediately to . . . say farewell."[27] Yoshino made his way topside, already teeming with *Kaga*'s men. Akamatsu Yūji was there as well.[28] Over 700 of the carrier's survivors now crammed the two diminutive tin cans, and it was literally standing room only for the unwounded. The casualties littered the deckplates everywhere. *Hagikaze* was lying off *Kaga*'s starboard side, with both ships' bows pointing generally northward.[29] The sun had gone down some twenty minutes before, at 1856, leaving *Kaga* lit by the sunset. To Yoshino, the scene had the appearance of a shadow painting. The aviator could detect no signs of *Akagi* anywhere—she must have been out of sight over the horizon. Then he took a last long look at his ship.

It was clear that even if she could have been towed all the way back to Japan, *Kaga* would never sail again. Here, at the end of her terrible trial, everyone could see that she was fit for nothing more than the scrapyard. Her lower hull appeared to still be in good shape. But everything above was wrecked. Her midsection, from the bridge all the way aft to the rear elevator, had been utterly destroyed. Induced explosions had remorselessly demolished the hangars, chewing their way down all the way to the level of the lower main deck and the eight-inch casemate mounts.[30] Where the hangars used to be, only a hellish pit of smoking, blackened metal remained. It was filled with charred structural members, melted and deformed aircraft pieces, and sundry equipment from the decks above—a hideous, tumbled graveyard lying over the hundreds of men who lay entombed in the engine rooms. The pit still smoked and spat. Yoshino could see all the way through the abyss to the sea beyond. It was as if the heart had been ripped out of the vessel. Only at the extreme rear, where the flight deck was supported by four massive pillars (and there had been nothing to burn) did a stump of intact decking remain. It stood there, suspended fifty feet above the ghastly charnel house of the hangars, almost in mockery of the countless sorties that had emanated from what had once been one of the largest flight decks in the Japanese Navy.

The damage to the forward hangars was similar, although somewhat less severe. However, the port side of the forward hangars was blown asunder, doubtless because the ordnance lift had been located here. Flames, though much diminished now, still greedily licked at the openings. *Kaga*'s island was smashed, almost as if a giant's hand had slapped the bridge, crushing it forward and down.[31] The whole of it was charred and black, the paint having been consumed in the blaze, leaving only the scorched metal. Inside, the bodies of Captain Okada and his senior officers still lay where they had fallen. In all, 811 of her crew now lay dead within the shattered wreck.[32] To Yoshino and the other men who had served on board her, *Kaga*'s current state was cause for the bitterest sorrow. He now tasted the full dregs of defeat for the first time.[33]

Hagikaze's skipper, Commander Iwagami Jūichi, could waste no more time observing nautical niceties. He had already brought his destroyer into an optimal firing position, a couple thousand meters off *Kaga*'s starboard side. He could hardly have missed so massive a target. The survivors heard the hiss of compressed air as both of the destroyer's quadruple torpedo tubes were slewed around to port.[35] On

18-1: Artist's rendition of *Kaga*'s condition immediately before being scuttled.[34]

command from the captain, a single fish was fired from each and slapped into the water. Japanese torpedoes were wakeless, and there was no telltale trail of bubbles to mark their progress. The refugees simply waited—Japanese destroyer men knew their business, and no one doubted the outcome. Just over a minute later, two enormous waterspouts announced the hammering arrival of the torpedoes' 1,000-pound warheads, striking *Kaga* slightly aft of midships. The power of the hits heaved seawater several hundred feet into the air, whereupon it cascaded back down in white clouds to smother the smoking wreck beneath. There were no other explosions.[36] Kunisada arrived on deck only just in time. He had been sleeping in a corner below but had been roused by communications man, Oda, his companion of many hours together in the water, who informed him that *Kaga* was soon to be sunk.[37] Painfully, he had made his way topside to the foredeck, where he found *hikōchō* Amagai standing beside the forward five-inch gun mount, staring off at the hulk. Maeda Takeshi stood watching as well, tears streaming freely down his face, like many of his shipmates around him.[38]

Slowly, and still on an even keel, *Kaga* began swooning stern first into the waiting arms of the sea. On *Maikaze*, one of the carrier's aviators, Lt. (jg.) Morinaga Takayoshi watched in silence.[39] *Maikaze*'s skipper, Cdr. Nakasugi Seiji, remembered later that "it was a horrendous sight to see a huge warship like this vanish. But she went nobly."[40] It took several minutes, so dignified was her sinking. Finally, at 1925 the water closed over the forward flight deck, and she was gone. Only massive bubbles and some floating debris remained. The men simply stared. The sun, too, had now fully departed, and darkness descended.

Next to Kunisada, Amagai mumbled to himself "I should have died with her," and his head fell. The *hikōchō* was dejected in the extreme, and regretted leaving the ship. Amagai blurted out to the damage-control officer that of the fourteen senior officers on board, only he and the chief surgeon had survived the ship's ordeal. Many of them had been lost in the initial moments of the attack. One of the few to survive the blaze, the ship's chief paymaster, Lt. Cdr. Matsukawa Takeshi, had at least made it into the water with a group of other survivors, but Amagai had seen his strength finally give out. Matsukawa had simply said to the men bobbing around him, "I'm dying now," and had sunk out of sight. Amagai particularly lamented the losses among the engineering staff. Scarcely a stoker or engineer was to be seen among the survivors.[41] Kunisada consoled Amagai as best he could. The lieutenant, too, felt that he should have shared the carrier's fate, but there was no helping it now. Wrapped in these somber thoughts, both men felt *Hagikaze's* deck plates begin vibrating as the destroyer worked up speed. She and *Maikaze* were clearing the area, heading toward *Akagi. Kaga* was left alone to drift down into her watery grave, some 17,000 feet below.

Meanwhile, to the north around *Hiryū,* the last of the Zeros was finally down by about 1910.[42] Nine aircraft in all ditched, and ironically not a single pilot from *Hiryū* was among them—they had all been refugees from either *Sōryū* or *Kaga.* One by one, they plopped into the water close aboard the Japanese escorts. *Nagara* and the destroyers swung into action picking up the pilots. *Kidō Butai* was now completely devoid of air cover. This wouldn't matter much in the coming darkness, but all the men of the task force knew what it would mean come the morrow. To one sailor on board *Yūgumo,* the fleet's fate now was "a matter of time. We resolved to do our utmost and await the orders of God."[43]

Hiryū remained underway at twenty-eight knots. But despite her ability to steam, she was in desperate peril. The fires were eating away at her remorselessly, moving aft along the hangar decks. Down in the engine spaces, Ensign Mandai and Chief Engineer Aimune were still stuck. Mandai began noticing that the white overhead paint was blackening as the deck above heated. Soon, burning flecks of paint were drifting down onto the grease-covered engines, starting little fires wherever they touched.[44] The air was stifling, and the ventilators were beginning to admit smoke and fumes into the compartments. Once the paint was off the overheads, the engineers could only watch in horror as they slowly turned red and began to glow.

Nagumo, like Spruance, had no idea what this night would bring. Indeed, he still had no very clear idea of what he was up against. Between 1320 and 1832, *Tone* No. 4 and No. 3, and *Chikuma* No. 2 and No. 3 had all been on the air at one point or another, having spotted portions of the American forces.[45] But these reports did little to enlighten Nagumo as to the true strength or intentions of the enemy. It was apparent that the American carrier formations were operating separately and that his aircraft were consequently catching only fragmented glimpses of their total strength. However, as the day wore on, and the magnitude of the defeat grew, so too did the scale of the enemy in the eyes of Nagumo. By the time the last of his aircraft broke off contact, around 1830, Nagumo was convinced that he was still up against a large number of American carriers, despite his having (so far as he knew) already knocked out two flattops.

Furthermore, it appears that CruDiv 8 did Nagumo a disservice in terms of accurately transmitting what its floatplanes were observing. Crucially, the matter of the Americans' course was bungled. At 1728 *Chikuma*'s No. 2 aircraft stated that the Americans were retiring to the east on a course of 070 degrees, modifying this at 1732 to a course of 110 degrees. Subsequently, at 1810 *Chikuma* No. 2 reported the Americans on a heading of 170 degrees, that is, due south. Neither of these courses would bring the American carriers near *Kidō Butai*, which was then almost due west of TF 16. Yet at 1830, when CruDiv 8 offered up its own staff assessment, it reported the Americans were heading *westward*. Worse, it overestimated the size of the American fleet, pegging them at four carriers, six cruisers, and fifteen destroyers.[46] CruDiv 8's air staff was apparently certain that *Chikuma* No. 2's previous reconnaissance reports had been of separate forces—indeed, that *Chikuma* had simultaneously sighted two task forces containing two carriers apiece while flying near a cloud bank at low altitude.[47] However, the reasoning behind CruDiv 8's staff reversing the direction of the American advance remains largely unfathomable. At this point in the battle, Nagumo was in no position to argue with what his remaining air assets were allegedly telling him, nor to quibble over the size of the enemy force that had smashed the four finest carriers in the Imperial Navy.

Though he had now disposed of two of his cripples, Nagumo found himself in no better position to prosecute a night battle than he had been before. Not only were the enemy forces arrayed against him apparently far more powerful than originally thought, but he also still had very few destroyers close at hand. By 2100 the weary Mobile Fleet was in position 32°-10'N, 178°-50'E on course 320, making twenty knots.[48] Thus far, the burning *Hiryū* was still managing to maintain good speed. For the time being, therefore, Nagumo's priority was clearly to continue shepherding the stricken carrier, while waiting for his other destroyers to rejoin him.

However, it does not appear that the destroyers were making good progress in this regard. At 2100 Captain Ariga of DesDiv 4 signaled Sixth Fleet's submarines and Kondō that six of his ships were still maintaining patrols quite near *Akagi*.[49] Not only that, but *Isokaze, Hamakaze,, Hagikaze,* and *Maikaze* were all loaded to the gills with survivors. If and when *Akagi* was finally scuttled, *Nowaki* and *Arashi* would be similarly burdened, because the flagship's refugees were even now being brought on board.

Nowaki duly reported completing her mission of mercy at 2200. Only one man remained on board *Akagi* now—Captain Aoki. He had informed his staff that such was his attachment to the carrier that her fate would be his own as well.[50] They were disinclined to allow him to stay, but the captain furiously insisted on it. He ordered them to tie him to the anchor capstan, and there they left him. However, *Akagi*'s final fate was to be long in coming, as Yamamoto personally ordered at 2225 that the scuttling be delayed.[51]

As events would prove, though, no orders would be forthcoming from Yamamoto regarding her final disposition for seven more hours. By 0030, having left Aoki aboard *Akagi* more than two hours earlier, her *hikōchō*, Masuda Shōgo, apparently decided that enough was enough.[52] Organizing a party, he piled into one of *Arashi*'s cutters, taking Commander Miura, *Akagi*'s navigator, and Captain Ariga with him. Rowing back over to *Akagi*, they found Captain Aoki still lashed to the ship. Over his protests, Commander Miura pointed out that since *Akagi* would (eventually) be scuttled by their own torpedoes, he didn't have to sacrifice himself in this way. Aoki was still unwilling to depart. Finally, Captain Ariga, who was senior to Aoki, gave him a direct order.[53] Aoki had no choice now but to follow his staff back to *Arashi*. In retrospect, it might have been kinder for Aoki had his men left him be. Destined to be the only Japanese carrier commander to survive Midway, he would be haunted by *Akagi*'s loss the rest of his life.[54]

Meanwhile, *Hiryū* had finally ground to a halt at 2123.[55] Up until this point, *Hiryū* still had both a working fire system and engine power. Her crew had been fighting the fires with every hose at their disposal. But with power gone, their efforts were flagging. Now, the flagship of DesDiv 10, destroyer *Kazagumo* undertook the dangerous task of moving close alongside the carrier. Her sisters, *Makigumo* and *Tanikaze,* also played hoses across *Hiryū*'s wounds, pouring water into her. Even these efforts were not enough, though, and at 2130 *Yūgumo* headed over toward cruiser *Chikuma,* so that the latter could pass across more lengths of hose to her.[56] The result of all these efforts was that *Hiryū* had now taken a 15-degree list to port as her hangar decks filled with firefighting water.[57]

This list made things very difficult for *Kazagumo* as she worked alongside the convulsing carrier. Commander Yoshida Masayoshi brought her as near as he could; too near, in fact, for the galleries of *Hiryū* broke the destroyer's mast. The other destroyers played continuous streams of water onto the fires as best they could, while the heavier units continued circling the wounded ship at a respectful distance.

At this point, *Kidō Butai* was no longer really capable of bringing the fight to an outsized enemy, and as the evening wore on, Nagumo had begun to realize it. Accordingly, at 2130 he transmitted a fateful status report to Yamamoto, basically repeating CruDiv 8's earlier erroneous assessment of five enemy carriers (later revised downward to four), six cruisers, and fifteen destroyers, all heading westward.[58] He also informed Yamamoto that his own forces were protecting *Hiryū* and were retiring to the northwest at eighteen knots.

For Yamamoto, the last hour had been stressful in the extreme. At 1800 he had received a report from Nagumo confirming that *Kaga* was done for,[59] followed shortly by news of *Hiryū*'s bombing.[60] By now, Yamamoto and Ugaki were both becoming increasingly concerned about Nagumo's handling of the battle. Subsequently, the *Yamato* had transmitted orders to all units of Combined Fleet at 1915 that were intended to set the night's priorities. Yamamoto signaled:

1. The enemy fleet, which has practically been destroyed, is retiring to the east.

2. Combined Fleet units in the vicinity are preparing to pursue the remnants and at the same time, to occupy AF (Midway).

3. The Main Unit [i.e., Yamamoto's Main Body] is scheduled to reached position (grid) FU ME RI 32 on course 90 degrees, speed 20 knots, by 0000, 6th [i.e., June 5th, local time].

4. The Mobile Force, Occupation Force (less CruDiv 7), and Advance Force will immediately contact and attack the enemy.[61]

Five minutes later, Yamamoto sent additional amplifying instructions. Submarine *I-168*, which had been loitering off of Midway, was to shell the enemy airfield. Meanwhile, Kurita's CruDiv 7 was to approach Midway and deliver another shellacking as soon as was practicable.[62] In layman's terms, the effects of these two sets of orders was to goad both Kondō and Nagumo into initiating a surface action ASAP, while the Main Body continued coming up in support. The invasion of Midway was still officially on, and in preparation for that, the airfield conclusively had to be put out of commission.

To say that these transmissions were somewhat divorced from reality is a gross understatement. Yamamoto was trying to run his ruined battle by remote control, while completely unaware of the tactical conditions pertaining. In the words of Ugaki, though, Combined Fleet's staff believed that "The fate of this operation entirely depended upon the night engagement." Yet, at this critical juncture, it was Ugaki's opinion that Nagumo's command had become "entirely passive."[63] This was an ironic statement, in that it was partly the aggressiveness of Ugaki's favorite, Admiral Yamaguchi, that had led *Kidō Butai* to the point where it could no longer realistically take the offensive.

However, it is important to note that at this point in time Yamamoto and Ugaki had different information in hand than Nagumo. The only report the commander in chief had received from CruDiv 8 was *Chikuma* No. 2's 1733 transmission indicating the enemy carriers were retiring to the *east*. This had arrived on the bridge of *Yamato* at 1836.[64] Combined Fleet's staff had apparently not received any of CruDiv 8's subsequent flawed analyses regarding the likely strength of the enemy, or his latest movements. Thus, Nagumo's 2130 transmission opining that the enemy consisted of five carriers heading *west* appeared to Ugaki and Yamamoto to be totally without basis. Nagumo's corollary decision to withdraw to the northwest was the final straw. In Ugaki's opinion, "a strong lashing order by the supreme command" was the only way to remedy the prevailing situation.[65]

Ugaki, as we know, had never been shy of applying the lash when it came to the commander of *Kidō Butai*. It came, at 2255, in the form of an order relieving Nagumo of command and ordering Kondō to take control of the Mobile Force, except for *Hiryū, Akagi,* and their respective escorts. Nagumo Chūichi was stripped of command and left to preside over the fates of two burning derelicts, while the aggressive Kondō was put in charge of the coming night battle. Twenty-five minutes later, Yamamoto radioed Kondō, asking him to elaborate on the movements of CruDiv 8 and the second section of BatDiv 3. In other words, he no longer trusted Nagumo to give him credible information regarding the movements of *Kidō Butai*'s heavy forces.

Nagumo's reaction to his relief is not recorded, but it cannot have been a happy one. Stuck as he still was on the cramped bridge of *Nagara,* he had watched as his command over the day's events had constricted into a smaller and smaller sphere. Now, he was completely out of the loop. Ironically, just five minutes before Yamamoto relieved him, he had transmitted a message to the commander in chief amplifying his earlier assessment and repeating that the Americans were heading west with four carriers. He also clarified that none of his own carriers was operational.[66] At 2330, half an hour after being relieved of command, and probably imagining that Yamamoto simply didn't have adequate information in hand when he made his decision, he rebroadcast to Yamamoto that two *Hornet*-class carriers, and two others of unidentified class, were in the enemy fleet. It was as much as if to say, "Perhaps you didn't comprehend what was communicated earlier." Yamamoto and Ugaki, though, weren't in a mood to quibble over the facts.

For his part, Kondō was quick to implement his superior's bidding. At midnight, he sent out orders to his subordinate commands—DesRon 2, CruDiv 5, CruDiv 4, and DesRon 4—informing them that they should expect to encounter the enemy some time after 0100. The cruiser squadrons were to be distributed in line abreast, with the second section of BatDiv 3 (*Hiei* and *Kongō*) trailing them by some ten kilometers. The destroyer squadrons would take up either flank of the search line, with a six-kilometer separation between all ships.[67] He instructed *Kidō Butai* to participate from the north. Nagumo, however, apparently did not comply with either Yamamoto or Kondō's orders. It is difficult to escape the impression that "strong lashing orders" notwithstanding, *Kidō Butai* was solely focused on saving *Hiryū,* if at all possible, and rescuing survivors.[68]

Nagumo's noncompliance raised some eyebrows in his force. The skipper of battleship *Kirishima,* Captain Iwabuchi Sanji, sent a message over to Admiral Abe in CruDiv 8, politely opining that, as a supporting force, they perhaps ought to be supporting the night action currently getting under way. Speaking up in such a fashion was bold enough, but it was rather unprecedented that Iwabuchi also bypassed his own divisional commander to send the message directly to the screen commander. The implication was clear: Iwabuchi felt that the screen should be pressing eastward without waiting for Kondō. Abe declined to answer his subordinate, and the screen stayed where it was. Nagumo would be fully occupied with *Hiryū* until 0112, when he finally came about and began moving not east, but west toward the Main Body.[69]

The reason for Nagumo's final retirement is clear—around midnight, it became apparent that *Hiryū* was done for. Although she had wallowed to a stop some two and a half hours earlier, it seemed for a while as if her fires were being tamed. However, two minutes before midnight, *Hiryū* was hit by another tremendous induced explosion, and the fires on the hangar deck once again blazed up fiercely.[70] Although Captain Kaku would hang on for another few hours, Nagumo apparently felt that the ship's doom was sealed.

At about the same time, judging that he had moved eastward long enough to forestall any Japanese attempt to engage him, Admiral Spruance was considering his next course of action. Heading directly up the enemy's line of retreat to the northwest would place his own forces in potential jeopardy, he concluded. Therefore, he came about to shape a course due west, at a leisurely fifteen knots. Thereafter, Spruance decided to get some rest. If ever the phrase "ice water in the veins" applied to a man, it was to Raymond Spruance. But as he explained to an interviewer years later, "I had good officers with me; they knew their jobs; they would carry on. Why should I not sleep soundly?" Furthermore, he knew that tomorrow's actions would be potentially just as dangerous, and he needed to be fresh to face them.[71]

Back on board *Yamato,* Spruance's opposite numbers were suffering from the same stress-induced fatigue and poor judgment that the American admiral sought so assiduously to avoid. As Spruance was turning in, Yamamoto and Ugaki were beginning to have doubts about the wisdom of their earlier orders. It was now 2330, and the enemy had yet to be encountered. Ugaki concluded that there was "little prospect of challenging the enemy with a night engagement before dawn" and warned the operations room not to let the night engagement force go too far, "thus bringing the situation after dawn beyond control."[72] Some quick usage of the calipers on the map also revealed another fact—Kurita's CruDiv 7 would never reach Midway before they were hopelessly exposed to American airpower. Accordingly, at 0015, Yamamoto issued orders ordering Kondō and Nagumo (less *Akagi, Hiryū,* and their escorts) to all fall back on Yamamoto's Main Body.[73] Five minutes later, he signaled Kurita's CruDiv 7 to abort its bombardment.

These orders were clearly precursors to the inevitable. Still, there were men in Combined Fleet's staff who could not, or would not, let go of the notion that victory could somehow still be wrested from the enemy. Kuroshima and Watanabe, the two staff officers with perhaps the greatest emotional investment in its planning, came up with the idea that the Main Body's battleships should continue advancing on Midway the following morning and pulverize it with their heavy guns. Carrying what he later termed his "crazy explanation" up to the bridge in a frenzy of excitement, Watanabe laid out his plan. Yamamoto listened to his staff officers politely, then said, "I am sure you have studied in the Naval Staff College that Navy history teaches us not to fight against land forces with naval vessels."[74]

A suddenly chastened Watanabe responded that he had.

"Your proposal is against fundamental naval doctrine," Yamamoto ground on, "And it is too late now for such an operation. This battle is almost coming to an end."[75] He ended by criticizing his staff's willingness to take unfounded risks. "You've been playing too much *shogi!*"[76] Ugaki lost no time in piling on his own disapproval. "You ought to know very well the absurdity of attacking a fortress with a fleet!" he said, continuing, "It is the plan of a fool without a brain to challenge a hopeless game of *go* again and again out of desperation!"[77]

Watanabe and Kuroshima retreated back to *Yamato*'s operation room. To Watanabe, it was clear that Yamamoto had already given up on the operation, and now he had little choice but to cut new orders of the most dreadful kind. When next he returned to *Yamato*'s bridge, he was carrying a draft order to reassemble the fleet and fall back toward Japan. Yamamoto dutifully approved them, and at 0255, *Yamato* began transmitting:[78]

> Combined Fleet DesOpOrd #161:
> 1. Occupation of AF (Midway) is canceled.
> 2. The Main Unit will assemble the Occupation Force and the First Mobile Force (less the *Hiryū* and her escorts), and will carry out refueling operations during the morning of 7 June.
> 3. The Screening Force, *Hiryū,* and her escorts, and the *Nisshin* will proceed to the same position.
> 4. The Landing Force will proceed westward, out of Midway's air range.[79]

The Japanese had been defeated, and it was time to cut their losses. Yamamoto continued hurrying east with the Main Body to meet up with the shattered remnants of Nagumo's force.

Of all the Japanese formations now in the vicinity of Midway, Admiral Kurita's four cruisers were by far the most exposed. They had been racing east, led by *Kumano,* with her sisters *Suzuya, Mikuma,* and *Mogami* in train. Destroyers *Asashio* and *Arashio,* as well as the oiler that had been accompanying them, had long since been left behind.[80] CruDiv 7 contained four of the swiftest ships in the Japanese inventory, capable of knocking down thirty-five knots. They were using a healthy dose of that speed now. Each was heavily armed as well, sporting ten eight-inch guns and a lethal battery of twelve twenty-four-inch torpedo tubes. They could inflict enormous harm on Midway's airfield, if they could get within range.

By 2245 Midway was tantalizingly close. Unfortunately for Kurita, Yamamoto's orders canceling the bombardment mission, had mistakenly been first sent to CruDiv 8, not CruDiv 7, resulting in a delay of more than two hours before he finally received them about 0230.[81] By this time, Midway was less than fifty nautical miles away.[82] To the men on *Kumano*'s bridge, the order was a bitter disappointment. They had come so far, only to have to turn about at the last moment. Having no choice, however, Kurita ordered his force to a new course to the northwest, to close on the Main Body.

At 0215 Kurita's force was sighted by the American submarine *Tambor,* which was surfaced in her patrol area. *Tambor* noted an unidentified force to the south of its position, composed of "four large ships" bearing 279 True from Midway, course about 50 degrees. Having been warned that U.S. ships might be in the area, Lt. Cdr. John W. Murphy came south, paralleling and shadowing them, but hesitating to radio a notice while still trying to identify the ships. Shortly after, *Tambor* temporarily lost contact in the gloom. At 0238, though, the submarine found her quarry again, noting with surprise that the ships now appeared headed north toward her.

It was true. Just before this Kurita had finally received the mistransmitted recall order, and at 0230 commenced to change course to break off to the north. This sent his four swift cruisers heading directly toward the skulking *Tambor*. However, almost immediately a sharp-eyed lookout on board *Kumano* sighted the American submarine ahead and to port of the Japanese column. The flagship immediately flashed the warning "*Aka! Aka!* (Red! Red!)" down the line, ordering an evasive turn in echelon to port. Moving at high speed, Kurita's squadron was thrown into confusion. *Kumano* cut very sharply to port, heading almost due west before rounding back to a northwest course. Behind her, *Suzuya* only turned about 45 degrees and quickly found herself closing on the flagship. She swerved to starboard, cutting across *Kumano*'s wake, and barely missing her astern.[83]

Next in line astern, *Mikuma* conformed to *Suzuya*'s movements, finding herself off *Suzuya*'s port beam. Seeing *Suzuya* veering away to starboard to avoid ramming *Kumano*, *Mikuma* likewise adjusted her own course more to the west to avoid becoming entangled with the flagship. In doing so, though, she brought herself directly into the path of the southernmost cruiser, *Mogami*. *Mogami* had sheered out of line very sharply to port, then watched as the rest of the formation appeared to be making off to the northwest, leaving her behind. Her skipper, Captain Soji Akira, thereupon corrected her course yet again, turning back to starboard to head more to the northwest in pursuit of the flagship.

It was at this moment that *Mikuma* suddenly hove into sight, crossing *Mogami*'s bow right to left. At the last second, Soji attempted to turn back to port, but it was too late. *Mikuma*'s captain, Sakiyama Shakao, did not see his sister ship coming up from the south and held course due west until almost the last second. So it was that *Mogami*, still desperately turning to port to avoid the unavoidable, rammed *Mikuma* almost directly under her bridge.[84]

The blow was glancing, as such things go. Captain Soji's last second maneuvering at least resulted in *Mogami*'s hitting her sister fairly obliquely. Nevertheless, the impact of a 13,000-ton cruiser traveling at twenty-eight knots could not help but be calamitous. Amid the cacophonous shrieking of tearing steel, *Mogami*'s thin, graceful bow ground itself to destruction on *Mikuma*'s heavy armor belt. By the time her forward momentum was fully checked, *Mogami*'s prow had been spectacularly crumpled all the way back to the No. 1 main turret. What remained was forty feet shorter and wrenched almost perpendicularly to port. *Mogami* lay dead in the water, drifting backward from *Mikuma*. *Mikuma*'s damage was fairly minor. Her plating was stove in around the wound, but the majority of the damage was above the waterline. However, a fuel tank next to boiler room No. 4 was leaking oil from a gash twenty meters long and six meters wide. Other smaller gashes could be seen below the No. 2 five-inch gun mount and the mainmast.

There was no other option except for both ships to get back up to speed as best they could and make their way out of the area. Admiral Kurita reluctantly ordered *Kumano* and *Suzuya* ahead at high speed. *Mikuma* was detached to escort *Mogami* out of the battlefield. Kurita radioed for DesDiv 8 to come east and meet the lagging pair. The best speed *Mogami* could do was twelve knots,[85] and even at this slow pace she handled like a barge. Limping away, less than a hundred miles away from an enemy base, the odds were not good for her survival.

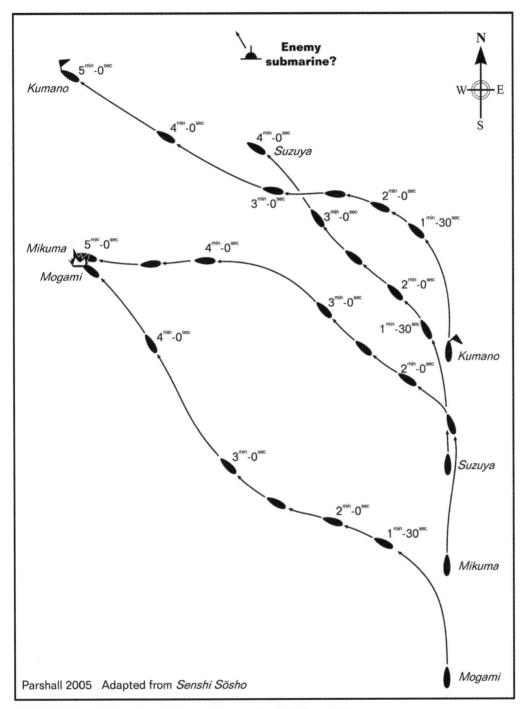

Enemy submarine?

Kumano — 5^{min}-0^{sec}

4^{min}-0^{sec}

4^{min}-0^{sec}
Suzuya

2^{min}-0^{sec}

3^{min}-0^{sec}

1^{min}-30^{sec}

3^{min}-0^{sec}

Mikuma — 5^{min}-0^{sec}

4^{min}-0^{sec}

Mogami

2^{min}-0^{sec}

3^{min}-0^{sec}

1^{min}-30^{sec}

Kumano

4^{min}-0^{sec}

3^{min}-0^{sec}

2^{min}-0^{sec}

Suzuya

3^{min}-0^{sec}

2^{min}-0^{sec}

1^{min}-30^{sec}

Mikuma

Parshall 2005   Adapted from *Senshi Sōsho*

Mogami

18-2: Collision of *Mogami* and *Mikuma*. (Source: *Senshi Sōsho*, p. 476)

Japanese damage control, as we have seen, was often far from exemplary. Yet on this occasion *Mogami*'s damage-control officer, Lt. Cdr. Saruwatari Masayushi, displayed an acumen that would have made any navy proud. He rallied the disoriented repair parties in the bow area and oversaw the shoring up of the watertight compartments in the area. If his ship was going to be rammed bent-prowed into a seaway, she would need all the stiffening she could get. Next, he ordered the jettisoning of every piece of inflammable material that could be found.[86] Almost heretically, in a navy that exalted firepower above all other things, this included the cruiser's torpedoes.

Mogami carried twenty-four Type 93s. Each of these thirty-foot monsters was equipped with a 1080-pound explosive charge—the largest, most lethal torpedo warhead in the world. Being powered by pure oxygen, every one was filled with enough oxidant and kerosene fuel to escalate almost any fire into a catastrophic inferno. If they were attacked by aircraft—and any fool could tell that they were likely to be on the receiving end of such unwanted attentions once the sun rose—a bomb hitting amidships would have the potential of igniting a total of twelve tons of high explosives, twenty-four *thousand* liters of compressed oxygen, and a couple tons of kerosene to boot. Accordingly, Saruwatari summarily consigned the Type 93s to the deep. *Mikuma*'s damage-control officer, however, judged that since her own damage was slight, she would be best served by retaining her Type 93s. The comparative wisdom of these two decisions would be graphically demonstrated over the following days.

Meanwhile, out in the gloom, *Tambor* remained blissfully ignorant of the havoc she had caused, and even the identity of the prey she had stalked. At 0251 *Tambor* noted the strange ships had changed course even farther to the west from their northerly heading, after which she lost contact. It was not until 0300 that Lt. Cdr. Murphy finally got off a contact report to Pearl Harbor and Midway. Worse yet, his report was incredibly vague—since the unidentified vessels had been moving at high speed and changing direction several times, Murphy was reluctant to give a course for them, and reported only "many ships." Nor did he even suggest that they might have been enemy vessels. It was not until 0437 that Murphy finally confirmed that the "many ships" in question were, in fact, enemy cruisers.[87] This tardiness was soon to cause great frustration for Admiral Spruance.

In the meantime, another submarine, this one Japanese, was also at work off Midway. Unlike CruDiv 7, no one had bothered getting word to *I-168* that the bombardment mission was now off.[88] Lieutenant Commander Tanabe duly surfaced his vessel off the east side of the lagoon at 0120 and let fly with a few rounds. It wasn't long, however, before the marine gunners made out the low silhouette of the Japanese sub and began answering back.[89] When the searchlights flipped on, pinning Tanabe's sub in their beams, he decided that that was enough for one night and submerged again. His eight rounds landed mostly in the lagoon and caused no damage to the American base.[90] However, his shelling certainly rattled the American defenders. They had no way of knowing what the next day would bring and whether they might have Japanese battlewagons parked on their doorstep in the morning.

Even before Tanabe's visit, Midway had already been a hive of activity. The island was in a shambles, with bombed installations and the destruction from Tomonaga's morning attack still in evidence everywhere. The fuel tanks on Sand Island had continued to blaze well into the night, meaning that refueling the base's B-17s was proceeding laboriously by hand.[91] Indeed, even as Tanabe was shelling the island, Midway still had combat aircraft in the air. These were not patrol aircraft, but rather a squadron of dive-bombers.

Some eight hours earlier, at 1700, a patrolling PBY had reported three burning carriers to the northwest of the island. Though it had been drawing close to sundown, Captain Cyril Simard ordered his base's remaining attack aircraft into action. He designated Major Benjamin Norris, who had taken command of Lofton Henderson's VMSB-241, to lead out his aircraft—six SBDs and six of the older SB2Us.[92] However, Norris, mindful of the toll Zeros had extracted previously, opted for a night attack, with he and his men taking off at 1915. Two hours later, Simard ordered Midway's eight-strong PT boat squadron to proceed to the same area.

Neither mission was successful. Norris and his squadron found the sea empty, *Kaga* having sunk just ten minutes after they had taken off from Midway. The weather had closed down in the interim, and the Marine aviators found themselves battling squalls and a low overcast in pitch darkness on the way home. Major Norris now paid the price for requesting a night mission, as he apparently became disoriented in the gloom. His squadron members suddenly noticed that their commander had banked into a sharp descent. His squadron followed him from 10,000 feet down to a mere 500, then broke off when they saw what was coming. Norris and his plane were never seen again.[93] Some of Norris's men became lost on the way back to base, and the last of them didn't land until 0145. The PT boats, too, spent a long, fruitless evening chasing around in search of Japanese vessels that had already sunk.

At 0230, even as he was wondering what to do about *Hiryū*, Admiral Nagumo sent out a comprehensive "battle summary" to Yamamoto.[94] In it, he described the day's happenings in more detail, noted the damage to his ships, but still opined that *Hiryū* might yet be able to be saved. However, even as his superior was informing Yamamoto of these matters, Yamaguchi was preparing to play out his final act. In contrast to Nagumo, Yamaguchi had concluded the carrier was beyond salvation. At 0230 he ordered the crew assembled in preparation of abandoning ship.[95] By 0250 the remaining crew—nearly 800 men—were gathered on the flight deck near the bridge. The bridge was smoldering, and fires still burned in the hangar deck forward, casting a weird light on the proceedings.

As soon as all were assembled, Captain Kaku and the admiral addressed the men.[96] Kaku spoke first, exhorting them to carry on the fight. They would, he was sure, become the core of an increasingly powerful Japanese Navy.[97] Yamaguchi then went on to say that he was proud of *Hiryū*'s crew. He placed the loss of *Hiryū* and *Sōryū* solely on his own head, and as atonement for those failings, he intended to stay on board to the end. The rest of the men, he commanded, were to abandon ship and "carry on their loyal service to the emperor."[98] Next, Yamaguchi ordered the men to face west toward Tokyo and three *banzais* were issued. Last of all, *Hiryū*'s battle ensign and the admiral's flag were lowered. There was an ominous braying of bugles—the ship's crew were playing *Kimigayo,* Japan's national anthem, as the flags were taken down for the last time.[99]

It has been noted by another historian that your average Western admiral would surely have forgone the necessity of keeping "800 crewmen standing around for over half an hour on a flaming, badly listing carrier, while he indulged his taste for melodrama."[100] But in Japan it's important to observe the niceties, regardless of the immediate circumstances surrounding them. Even the wounded were in attendance. Bomber maintenance chief Arimura, despite his serious injuries, remembered watching the flags come down from where he lay on the flight deck.[101] Now, with the ceremonies concluded at 0315, Captain Kaku finally gave the order for the exodus to get under way. There was no panic. Arimura was carried to the aft end of the flight deck with the other injured men. He was terribly thirsty and called out for water. His punctured lung was turning every breath into a bloody froth, and one of the men nearby said that if he drank any water, he would die. Another sailor demurred, saying "*Yosh!* (It'll be all right!)," and instead handed Arimura a beer. If the maintenance chief were destined shortly for the hereafter, far better to meet it on terms of equanimity. Arimura, however, had no intention of giving up the ghost just yet, and to him the beer was the very nectar of the gods.

Makigumo was waiting alongside the carrier's port side. Like *Kazagumo* before her, *Hiryū*'s overhanging flight deck demolished her mainmast in the process.[102] First over the side was a lieutenant, clutching the emperor's portrait. Next came the wounded. Arimura was tied to a board and lowered to the destroyer's deck. The wounded were soon packed into every available spot. They were being attended to as best *Makigumo*'s crew might, but the conditions for providing decent care were far from ideal. Flight Lt. Kadano Hiroshi, *Hiryū*'s third-section attack aircraft *buntaichō,* was a typical case. His *kankō* had been damaged in the morning strike on Midway, and his leg had been badly shot up by American fighters.[103] Now, the corpsmen told him the limb had to come off. The only available space for the amputation was the deck in one of *Makigumo*'s heads.[104]

With the crew in the process of debarking, Yamaguchi said good-bye to his staff. It was at this point that Captain Kaku announced that he, too, was going to share *Hiryū*'s fate.[105] Yamaguchi understood his sentiments. "Let us enjoy the beauty of the moon," the admiral intoned. "How brightly it shines," agreed *Hiryū*'s skipper, "It must be in its twenty-first day."[106]

Lt. Cdr. Kyūma Takeo, CarDiv 2's engineering staff officer, took this opportunity to intercede with Captain Ito, Yamaguchi's chief of staff. Surely, Kyūma said, the admiral's staff ought to try to rescue him, even if they had to do it by force. Itō demurred, saying that even if the staff physically carried him off the ship, the strong-willed admiral would surely kill himself later. Yamaguchi having declared his intention to stay on board, Itō felt that the "thoughtful way would be to let him do as he wishes." Thereupon, Itō approached Yamaguchi directly, declaring that the admiral's staff had decided that they wished to stay with him to the end. Yamaguchi would have none of it. "I am very pleased and touched by the staff's desire to remain with me, but you young men must leave the ship. This is my order."[107] The same stern reply was given to *Hiryū*'s executive officer, Commander Kanoe Takashi, when he suggested that the carrier's senior officers should stay with Captain Kaku.[108] Failing mass suicide, Kyūma suggested to chief of staff Itō that they ask the admiral for a souvenir to remember him by. Yamaguchi swept off his cap, handing it to Ito. The admiral and his staff then drank a final toast of farewell.[109]

The ship's paymaster noted that there was still a lot of money in the ship's safe and wondered what ought to be done with it. "Leave it where it is," Captain Kaku said, "we'll need it to cross the River Styx!" To which Yamaguchi piped in, "That's right; we'll need it for a square meal in hell!"[110] Itō asked if the admiral had any final messages before they departed. "Yes," responded Yamaguchi, he had two. "Tell Admiral Nagumo that I have no words to apologize for what has happened. I only wish for a stronger Japanese Navy, and revenge." The second message was for Captain Abe Toshio, the commander of DesDiv 10, in *Kazagumo*. "Scuttle *Hiryū* with your torpedoes."[111]

The speech making was now at an end, and Itō and the others departed. But it was not until 0430 that all of *Hiryū*'s crew finally left the ship, with Itō and Kyūma being the last off. As Kyūma climbed down a rope into a small boat, he lost his composure at the prospect of losing "the greatest man he had ever met in [his] whole life." He had been on the admiral's staff since December 1940 and was the longest-serving staff member in Yamaguchi's entourage.[112] Looking back at the still-burning *Hiryū*, he could see Kaku and Yamaguchi standing on the bridge, waving.[113] What happened to the captain and admiral after that is anyone's guess. They certainly could not have made their way below to their cabins, as these were in the bow of the ship, which was wrecked by the fires. Where Kaku and Yamaguchi met their end will remain forever unknown.

At 0510, with the sun already rising in the east, *Makigumo* prepared to carry out Yamaguchi's final wish.[114] *Kazagumo* was already departing, leaving just *Hiryū*'s plane guard destroyer to do the deed. As a precaution, *Makigumo*'s navigator, Lieutenant Commander Tamura, was sent back to the carrier to ensure that everyone was off the vessel. Climbing back on board, he made his way to the bridge, but found no one there. Tamura returned to *Makigumo*. The loudspeakers suddenly blared out on the destroyers, "We are right now going to torpedo and sink *Hiryū*. Battle stations torpedo port side, target *Hiryū* bearing 90 degrees. Prepare to fire." Everywhere on board men were weeping, her survivors clutching the railings. *Makigumo* fired a single Type 93 torpedo. It ran too deep and missed her. Circling to starboard to double the range, her skipper, Commander Fujita Isamu, fired a second. This one hit fairly far forward, near the ship's starboard bow gangway. The explosion was spectacular, shoving the carrier's prow out of the water and bouncing it to port.[115] Unusually, there was no huge water column, as was the case with most Type 93 hits. Most likely the fish had struck far enough forward that it had simply blown through the relatively narrow hull structure there, venting much of its force laterally into the water beyond.[116] Whatever the nature of the hit, Commander Fujita apparently judged that *Hiryū* would not survive it. He turned *Makigumo* for home.

It was at this very juncture that a group of men suddenly appeared on *Hiryū*'s flight deck, waving their deck caps at the departing destroyer. But she did not come about. Fearing air attack as day broke, Commander Fujita apparently judged it better to simply leave the newfound survivors behind.[117] Rather callously, he blinkered back to the men—a signal whose meaning is now lost, as none of the survivors on *Hiryū's* flight deck had the ability to decipher his message.[118] Then he cleared the area. This is all rather strange, because Fujita apparently had every opportunity to promptly come about and rescue these hapless survivors in a timely fashion, thus saving destroyer *Tanikaze* from the rather long, dangerous, and ultimately futile mission of mercy that she would be ordered to perform on the morrow.

On board *Nagara,* Nagumo and his staff were grappling with how to atone for their failures in battle. Chief of staff Kusaka was finally having his burns and other wounds attended to in *Nagara's* sick bay when his second in command, Captain Ōishi, approached him. The other staff members had made up their minds to commit suicide, Ōishi said, and he urged Kusaka to convince Nagumo to do the same.[119]

In response, Kusaka ordered Ōishi to assemble the staff in the sick bay. Then he laid into them. "I am against suicide," he told them firmly. His voice rising, he continued, "You are just like hysterical women; first you get excited over easy victories and now you are worked up to commit suicide because of a defeat! This is no time for Japan for you to say such a thing. Why not think of turning a misfortune into a blessing through your efforts?" He ended by saying that he was going to tell Nagumo of his opinion.[120]

Kusaka was as good as his word and went to find Nagumo in his cabin. The commander of First Air Fleet, to Kusaka, appeared very downcast. Kusaka wasted no time in strongly voicing his opinions that suicide would solve nothing and that Japan needed them to continue their efforts. Nagumo didn't perk up noticeably, replying to Kusaka that he appreciated his advice, but adding, "you must understand that everything a Commander in Chief does cannot be by reason."[121]

To Kusaka, this clearly indicated that Nagumo was still contemplating suicide. "Come on," he continued, "What can you accomplish with a defeatist attitude?"

Nagumo at this point relented. "Very well. I will never commit a rash act."

In fact, there is every indication that Nagumo never rallied completely from this stunning defeat. His son recalled afterward that the admiral said nothing of Midway until 1944, when he was about to depart for the island of Saipan to take command of its garrison. After swearing them to secrecy, he conveyed the news of the terrible calamity to his two sons. Breaking into tears as he relayed his story, he described the destruction of his force and the slaughter of his men.[122] Nagumo left shortly thereafter, and would never return to Japan, eventually committing suicide as the final defense of Saipan collapsed around him.

Nagumo's former flagship was about to meet her demise. Much like her fires, the debate over what to do with *Akagi* had sputtered fitfully all night on board *Yamato*. Now, as dawn approached, the argument blazed up again. Had the Americans been defeated by Kondō's eastward rush, it was conceivable that they could have towed *Akagi* back to Japan.[123] Indeed, even as late as 0220, Kondō had radioed Captain Ariga of DesDiv 4 asking Ariga to "Inform condition of *Akagi* immediately."[124] However, with daylight coming on, American airpower would clearly prevent *Akagi*'s being saved.

To Captain Kuroshima, *Akagi*'s impending demise was symbolic of the ruination of the operation as a whole.[125] It was simply unthinkable that the flagship should be scuttled. Weeping in frustration, he shouted, "We cannot sink the Emperor's warships with the Emperor's own torpedoes!"[126] Staff officer Watanabe remembered that with Kuroshima's anguished outburst, "Virtually all the members of Yamamoto's staff choked and stopped breathing."[127] It had been a long night, and Combined Fleet's staff was at the point of emotional collapse.

To Chief of Staff Ugaki, *Akagi*'s miserable fate was, of course, a cause for great regret. He couldn't help shedding a few tears for his commander in chief, guessing Yamamoto's feelings for his old ship. Yet, in the end, as Ugaki realized, "sentiment is sentiment, and reason is reason."[128] Yamamoto concluded the same thing. To do otherwise was to unnecessarily risk the other units still around her, or worse yet, to potentially allow her to fall into enemy hands. When he finally spoke, it was in grave, deliberate tones. "I was once the captain of *Akagi*," he said, "and it is with heartfelt regret that I must now order that she be sunk." Answering Kuroshima's concerns over the manner of her disposal, he added, "I will apologize to the Emperor for the sinking of *Akagi* by our own torpedoes."[129]

At 0450 the word finally came down to Captain Ariga that *Akagi* was to be scuttled, some seventeen and a half hours after the beginning of her ordeal. Each ship of DesDiv 4 was to fire a Type 93 torpedo from a distance of between 1,000 and 1,500 meters.[130] Ariga's flagship *Arashi* formed *Nowaki, Hagikaze,* and *Maikaze* into line behind her, and they passed up *Akagi*'s starboard side from astern at twelve knots. Not unlike soldiers in a firing squad, each destroyer launched a single torpedo as they swept by. Then Ariga's formation cut in front of *Akagi*'s bow, heading north to rejoin Nagumo.[131] Two or three torpedoes slammed into the carrier's starboard side, heaving enormous waterspouts into the air. When the mist subsided, the men crowded along the railings could see *Akagi* quietly bowing her proud head in surrender to the sea. As she nosed under, everyone on board the destroyers broke into shouts of *"Banzai! Akagi banzai!"* By 0520 Japan's most famous carrier lifted her stern into the air, briefly exposing her mighty propellers. Then she was gone "as if pulled down by a huge hand" as *Maikaze*'s commanding officer described it, carrying 267 crewmen with her into the abyss.[132] Nothing but enormous bubbles remained on the surface to mark her grave.

19

Retreat

The morning sun rising over *Nagara*'s stern mocked the limp national standard hanging there. Even as *Akagi* was sliding down into oblivion, *Nagara*'s bow was pointed west, carrying Nagumo ever closer to the Main Body. Around the diminutive flagship clustered a sadly shrunken formation. *Kirishima* and *Haruna*, now the largest ships in Nagumo's fleet, plodded stolidly along on either side. All around *Nagara*, their decks carpeted with survivors, paced the force's destroyers. The carrier men, still in shock from the previous day's ordeal, had spent the night sleeping exposed on the tan linoleum decks of their former escorts. Now, with light creeping over the horizon, they continued to lie where they had fallen, too exhausted or injured to move.

Nagumo's flight operations commenced at dawn, but they were a pale shadow of yesterday's undertakings. On board the cruisers and battleships, solitary engines coughed to life, echoing hollowly over the water. It was nothing like the dull roar of entire squadrons that had thrummed with life the day before. At 0441, *Chikuma* sent up her No. 1 and No. 4 aircraft to make sure the Americans weren't following their retreat.[1] It wasn't much in the way of airpower, but it would have to do, for far from going "into his shell," Nagumo was actually looking for openings to renew the battle with what meager assets were left to him.

No fighters would be overhead this day, and the weather was clear. Men that had cursed the fog a few days earlier now prayed for its return. Defeated, Nagumo and his men knew they had no choice now but to steel themselves for whatever dreadful consequences might accrue from their current state. If American carrier aircraft found them now, they would be almost powerless to repel their attacks. These same men remembered running rampant through their beaten foes just a few months before. Allied warships in the waters around Java; merchant ships and pleasure craft packed with civilians trying to flee the impending falls of Singapore and Surabaja—they had cut them all down like wolves among the sheep. Now the tables were turned, and it was the worst feeling in the world. They could expect no mercy.

On board *Yamato*, Admiral Yamamoto had also rallied somewhat. Though he knew that the odds were distinctly against him, he had decided to try to salvage what he could from the situation. However, he had precious little to work with. His forces were essentially devoid of air cover, whereas the Americans now possessed total air supremacy. Even when Kondō and Nagumo rejoined his fleet, he would have to contend with a dwindling fuel supply. Nagumo's ships would be packed with survivors, many of them wounded. And he had no clear idea of the enemy's intentions.

Nevertheless, he retained enough of a sense of opportunism to recognize that since the American carriers were near at hand, operations in the Aleutians could proceed unmolested. Kakuta's carriers would continue steaming south, of course. But Hosogaya's Northern Force could invade Kiska and Attu, albeit this couldn't occur until the 7th. Hosogaya's force already had the same idea and asked permission to carry out their invasion despite its being canceled the previous day.[2] After conferring with his staff, Yamamoto cut orders authorizing what Ugaki termed the "devil-may-care" landing operations, which resulted in Hosogaya heading northeast once again at 1000.[3]

Yamamoto's immediate problem, however, was that sunrise had found his Main Body all alone on the high seas, despite the fact that Nagumo's forces were to have joined up with him about this time. Yet even from high atop *Yamato*'s mighty fire-control director, there was still no sign of *Kidō Butai*. Kondō, at least, was on schedule, with his Second Fleet closing with the Main Body by 0815.[4] Yet Yamamoto was irritated that the rendezvous with Nagumo had failed. *Hōshō* was ordered to launch a few of her old torpedo planes to search for *Kidō Butai*. Yamamoto had little time to waste this morning. He needed to know Mobile Fleet's course and position ASAP if he didn't want confusion to reign over his forces. Dutifully, the ancient little carrier huffed and puffed into the wind, struggling against a rather heavy swell. Her skipper, Captain Umetani Kaoru, would later earn a moment's commendation from Ugaki for "completing her duty with a small number of planes in the face of bad weather."[5] One by one, the old torpedo planes rolled down her pitching deck, as *Hōshō* sent forth her small but tangible contribution to the battle's history.

One of *Hōshō*'s planes discovered Nagumo in short order, steaming a bit to the north and east of Yamamoto's course. After a brisk exchange of messages, Nagumo was able to set a converging course. *Chikuma* would subsequently sight the reassuring pagoda superstructures of the Main Body thirty-seven kilometers distant at 1205. By 1300 CruDiv 8 was taking station within the Main Body, though the last of the destroyers would not close with Yamamoto till 1700.[6]

However, far more interesting than the discovery of Nagumo's truant force would be a startling encounter had by another of *Hōshō*'s planes just a short time later. At around 0700, not long after takeoff, one of these aircraft unexpectedly stumbled across Admiral Yamaguchi's flagship, drifting on the blue Pacific. *Hiryū* was still visibly burning but seemed in no immediate danger of sinking. The pilot passed right down her length from bow to stern, then banked back over her starboard beam, with the aircraft's observer taking photographs as they went. His snapshots froze *Hiryū* near the end of her dreadful ordeal and remain among the most dramatic photographs of the war in the Pacific. Perhaps most amazing of all, the aviators could clearly see men standing on the flight deck, waving their caps! *Hōshō*'s plane began tapping out a sighting report at 0720.[7]

The men in question were the same crewmen who had unsuccessfully tried to flag down Commander Fujita and *Makigumo* about two hours earlier. They had been understandably heartened to see *Hōshō*'s plane. After its departure, these crewmen

19-1: *Hiryū* burning on the morning of June 5, 1942, as photographed by one of *Hōshō*'s Type 96 carrier attack planes, piloted by Warrant Officer Nakamura Shigeo. This photo, taken by the aircraft's commander, Special Service Ensign Ōniwa Kiyoshi, clearly shows the enormous hole in the forward flight deck, the result of four bomb hits. A portion of the forward elevator has been blown against the forward end of the island. The ship is still afire amidships. Note, too, the apparent absence of any list.[8] (Naval Historical Center)

retreated to the boat deck to await a rescue. However, at around 0830, they were surprised to discover that they were not alone. Hearing voices, they went back topside, where they unexpectedly encountered a party of over thirty men crouched down on the flight deck.

These newcomers were the survivors of Cdr. Aimune Kunize's engine room gang. Long ago, heat and smoke had driven them from the engine control room containing the voice tube that was their communications lifeline to the bridge. Having lost touch with Staff Engineering Officer Kyūma, the latter had presumed them dead hours before abandoning the ship. Thus, Aimune and his men, though far from dead, had been completely unaware of the order to abandon ship.[9] At 0510, they heard and felt the "whump" of *Makigumo*'s torpedo striking home. Having not heard a peep from the bridge in hours, Aimune judged that it was time to get out of the bowels of the ship.[10] Most of the exits were still blocked, but they had found a way up to the next deck, where a fire was smoldering in the ship's rice storage area.

Unfortunately, there was apparently no way out from the long corridor they were trapped in—the hatches at either end were blocked. Finally, one of the men spotted light coming from one of the welds, where fire or shrapnel had punched a small hole in the bulkhead. They were peeping into the ship's lower hangar deck, lit by dim sunlight.[11] Aimune wasted no time in sending someone back below to fetch a hammer and chisel—if they couldn't find an exit, they'd make one instead. Eventually, they managed to chisel a narrow opening large enough for a man to climb through.

Making their way into the hangar after 0800, they found everything deserted and strangely quiet. Fires were still burning here and there, but more unnerving was the sunlight streaming into the hangar through the enormous hole that had been blown in the flight deck. Finally making their way topside and looking about, they could see that the ship had been abandoned hours before. Commander Aimune, Ensign Mandai, and the men were understandably furious and dejected.[12] Worse, the men could see water slowly swirling on to the hangar deck forward. Ineffective as *Makigumo*'s hit had been, *Hiryū* clearly wasn't going to float forever.

To Commander Aimune, the situation appeared hopeless. Dropping onto the flight deck, he thanked the men for their good efforts and prepared for the end. Ens. Mandai, utterly spent by the long night's action, dozed off, only to be awakened by the small band of survivors from *Hiryū*'s fantail. They quickly reported the exciting news of a Japanese plane having flown overhead earlier. It was clear from their description that it had been a carrier aircraft—it even had fixed landing gear.[13] This unexpected news gave Aimune's party renewed hope. If there had been a Japanese carrier aircraft overhead, they might be rescued yet.[14] The problem was that *Hiryū* was beginning to sink noticeably by the bow—they didn't have much time left to escape.

Leading the party down to the ship's fantail, Aimune found two launches still lashed to the deck, and a thirty-foot cutter already in the water immediately astern the ship. They set to work freeing the launches, but *Hiryū* began pitching down to take her final plunge. Aimune told the men to jump in and swim for the cutter.[15] Over the side they went. Ensign Mandai hit the water and dove deep. When he made it back to the surface, he looked over his shoulder in awe. There were *Hiryū*'s giant propellers, coming up out of the water over his head, flashing wetly in the sun. He turned and swam like the devil,

19-2: The other classic shot of *Hiryū* on the morning of 5 June. *Hiryū*'s deck-edge radio aerials have been raised into the vertical position, undoubtedly to avoid fouling the destroyers that were near her fighting the fires. The ship is still afire and appears to be somewhat down by the bow. (Naval Historical Center)

not wanting to be sucked under as *Hiryū* went to her grave. The next time he looked back, she was gone, carrying 389 of her crew with her. Shortly thereafter, an enormous undersea rumble announced her final demise. Aimune and thirty-eight of the men made it into the cutter. Their watches had all stopped working between 0907 and 0915, putting a reasonable time box around the moment of *Hiryū*'s final sinking.[16]

The men found the cutter stocked with hardtack, water, tallow, and beer.[17] They were confident that Yamamoto would return for them soon. But, in fact, they would be adrift for the next fourteen days, until being spotted by an American PBY and recovered by the seaplane tender *Ballard* on 19 June. Along the way, they were to suffer many hardships. Four of the men died of their wounds or exposure before being rescued; a fifth died the night after being brought on board *Ballard*. Commander Aimune, for all his wiliness in getting his men out of *Hiryū*'s bowels, demonstrated less concern for them once they were in the boat together. Despite their dire collective circumstances, he insisted on consuming more than his fair share of the food and beer.[18] While he didn't know it at the time, he very nearly ended up as shark chum as a result of his insensitivity. A thirty-foot open boat drifting on the Pacific was rather a misguided place to pull rank over an extra bottle or two of Asahi *biiru*![19]

As it happened, the Americans were having their own problems this morning, and many of them stemmed from submarine *Tambor*. For one thing, she had not managed to launch a torpedo attack against the cripples of CruDiv 7. *Mogami*'s twelve-knot speed of advance had proved enough, barely, for the Japanese ships to stay ahead of the submerged American submarine.[20] More critically, as mentioned previously, *Tambor*'s skipper, Lt. Cdr. John Murphy, had failed to describe the enemy's course or speed of advance adequately, leaving Raymond Spruance (who didn't receive Murphy's message until 0400) in the dark concerning the Japanese force's intentions.

The time from midnight to dawn was critical in positioning Spruance's forces for the following day's operations. He had kept what they felt to be a safe distance throughout the night, intending to avoid entanglements with any Japanese forces in the area. Spruance personally didn't believe that the Japanese force *Tambor* had spotted would still be intent on attacking the island after the pummeling they had taken on the 4th. But the potential downside of being wrong wasn't worth the risk.[21] As such, he didn't come westward until he knew the Japanese were retreating, which *Tambor* did not relay until after 0600. Had Spruance had this information in hand sooner, it would have measurably increased his odds of inflicting greater harm on the enemy than was to be the case. Nimitz, an ex-submariner, was understandably furious with Murphy's performance, subsequently relieving him of command.[22] In fact, the American submarines as a whole had performed poorly. Of twelve boats, only *Nautilus* (the oldest of the lot) had actually managed to attack the enemy.[23]

Beyond not being optimally positioned for launching follow-up operations, American airpower was also badly depleted. Midway's various squadrons, except for the PBYs, had been savaged. The Marines were down to just four fighters and about twelve dive-bombers.[24] Many of the other aircraft left on the atoll were either unflyable junk or too badly shot up to participate in combat. Midway had, in fact, been flying damaged aircraft back to Hawaii during the night—a flight of four B-17s

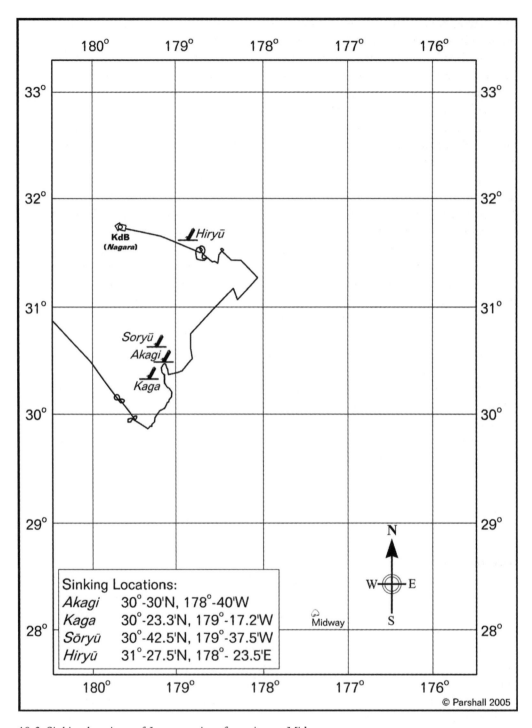

19-3: Sinking locations of Japanese aircraft carriers at Midway.

was waiting to take off even as Tanabe's *I-168* had been shelling the lagoon.[25] Dawn on the 5th therefore found the atoll's airpower nearly crippled.

Based on *Tambor*'s initial reports, though, the first item of business for Midway was to attempt to localize the Japanese units Murphy had sighted. Midway's Catalinas began taking off at 0415, fanning out in an arc to the west from 020 degrees to 250 degrees.[26] Today, though, the PBYs would only search out to 250 miles. Capt. Cyril Simard's primary concern was ensuring that the atoll was not about to be invaded. If an invasion fleet materialized, the PBYs in the air needed the endurance to return all the way to Pearl Harbor without refueling. This had serious repercussions for Spruance, though, as it essentially deprived his carriers of longer-ranged scouting assets. In so doing, Simard also lessened the odds of Spruance's locating Nagumo and Yamamoto.

Spruance's own air formations were scarcely in better shape than Midway's. Split between *Hornet* and *Enterprise* were a total of around sixty attack aircraft, plus fighters—about a full carrier's worth. The Japanese would surely have traded places with him this morning, but Spruance's hand was not strong enough for him to want to push his luck. While he had sufficient Dauntlesses in hand to project meaningful firepower, many of them would need to be devoted to scouting activities.

Beyond locating and attacking the Japanese, the other major task was trying to save *Yorktown*. Under the *Hughes*'s watchful presence, she had survived the night and by morning appeared to be in no worse shape than she had been twelve hours earlier. Her commanding officer, Captain Elliott Buckmaster, had meanwhile succeeded in convincing Admiral Frank Jack Fletcher that the carrier could still be saved.[27] He wanted to put a handpicked party of salvagers on board the carrier, try and restore power, and get her out of the area. Fletcher assented. In fact, on the night of the 4th, Chester Nimitz had already ordered minesweeper *Vireo* and the fleet tug *Navajo*, which were at Pearl and Hermes Reef, and French Frigate Shoals, respectively, to begin moving toward *Yorktown*. Unfortunately, the men Buckmaster felt he needed were scattered across all the various vessels of TF 17, which had rescued the carrier's crew. Transferring them onto the destroyer *Hammann* took until 1127, at which point she began heading back toward *Yorktown*.

Back on board *Yamato*, *Hōshō*'s sighting report of *Hiryū* reached a flabbergasted Yamamoto and Ugaki at around 0730. *Yamato* flashed a message to Nagumo: "Has the *Hiryū* sunk? Advise of developments and position."[28] For his part, Nagumo was just as confused by the news as his superiors. At 0820 the word flashed out to *Tanikaze*: "According to reconnaissance by *Hōshō* plane at 0720, the *Hiryū* was burning in position FU RO RI 43 (32°-10'N, 178°-50'E). A number of survivors were on deck. Investigate condition and take off survivors."[29] Commander Katsumi Motoi duly swung his ship out of formation and raced eastward back toward *Hiryū* and the enemy. As events would prove, she was to have a long, dangerous day atoning unfairly for her sisters' earlier mistakes.

Scarcely had word about *Hiryū*'s mysterious nonsinking been received than news reached Nagumo concerning another derelict. At 0652 a garbled message from *Chikuma*'s No. 4 search plane had been intercepted by *Nagara*. It seemed to mention an enemy carrier. At 0800 *Chikuma* blinkered a full rebroadcast to *Nagara*: No. 4

had sighted an "enemy *Yorktown*-class carrier listing to starboard [*sic*] and drifting in position bearing 111 degrees, distance 240 miles from my take-off point. One destroyer is in the vicinity."[30] In due course, word went out to Tanabe's *I-168,* which was still loitering near Midway.[31] He shortly set a new course to the northeast. It would take him a day to reach his new target, but from all reports, it didn't look as if this particular American carrier was going anyplace soon.

The Americans were beginning to get back their own scouting reports by now. At 0630 a PBY picked up *Mogami*'s and *Mikuma*'s trails. In *Mikuma*'s case, there literally was a trail, as she was streaming a ribbon of bunker oil from her damaged fuel tanks. This PBY transmitted that it had detected "two battleships," bearing 264, 125 miles from Midway, on a course of 265 at a speed of fifteen knots.[32] A second PBY amplified this report, describing two large capital ships, both damaged, and one leaking oil.[33]

Captain Sakiyama of *Mikuma* was well aware they had been sighted, sending word to his superiors at 0623 that his position was 28°-10'N, 179°-30'W, speed twelve knots.[34] Though *Mikuma* was capable of nearly full speed, Sakiyama was loath to abandon sister *Mogami.* Whatever attacks came, Sakiyama resolved that he and Soji would face them together. They both knew that the main Japanese forces were well to the north and west at this time, but Captain Sakiyama had wisely opted to steer due west, so as to put as much ocean between them and their enemies as possible. There would be time enough later to figure out how to rejoin the Main Body. The sight of an American PBY at 0630, though, meant that the jig was up far sooner than either ship would have wished.

Midway lost no time in attacking the cripples, ordering the remnants of VMSB-241 to take off immediately. At 0700 Capt. Marshall "Zack" Tyler, the squadron's third commander in two days, led out a flight of a dozen dive-bombers—six Dauntlesses and a like number of SB2Us, divided into two sections.[35] About forty miles away from the target, the Marine aviators easily picked up *Mikuma*'s glistening exudation, and turned to follow it. Shortly thereafter, the two Japanese ships hove into view.

Capt. Tyler's Dauntless squadron attacked from out of the sun at 10,000 feet. The older Vindicators, led by Capt. Richard Fleming, opted for a glide-bombing attacking from 4,000 feet.[36] *Mikuma* and *Mogami,* despite their damage and very low speed, proceeded to throw up a veritable torrent of antiaircraft fire. Tyler's men went first, but *Mogami*'s heavy fire meant all they could manage was to sequentially deposit their bombs in the water alongside the cruiser.

Next came Fleming's men. They focused their attack on *Mikuma,* which was on *Mogami*'s port bow, and were subjected to a similarly withering barrage. This time, though, the Japanese drew blood, as Capt. Fleming's aircraft was struck almost at the outset of his dive. He attempted to control his aircraft but went flaming into the ocean.[37] Accounts vary as to whether pilot or gunner attempted to get out of their aircraft—neither survived. One thing that is clear, though, is that despite popular folklore to the contrary, Capt. Fleming did not crash his aircraft onto *Mikuma*'s No. 4 turret. The most reliable witnesses on the American side attest that his plane crashed into the sea, and the only Japanese source to ever state that Fleming hit the ship was in no position to witness the event.[38] The rest of Fleming's section all missed the cruiser

RETREAT 363

with their bombs. The net result was that both Japanese cruisers emerged unscathed from their first ordeal.[39]

However, more trouble was not long in coming. Almost as soon as the American dive-bombers had been seen off, a pack of eight B-17s showed up. Under the command of Lt. Col. Brooke E. Allen, these came in at 20,000 feet in two elements of four aircraft each. Once again, the big four-engined bombers merely deposited a total of thirty-nine 500-pound bombs harmlessly in the drink, mostly around *Mogami.* *Mikuma* triumphantly signaled "although attacked by eight B-17s at 0834, we drove them off without damage." So far, at least, their luck had held out. If this was the best that twenty American bombers could manage against twelve-knot targets, they might make it out yet. Indeed, as if buoyed by her good fortune, *Mogami* at 1130 cranked up to fourteen knots.[40]

Task Force 16 had the same information in hand as Simard and might have attacked *Mogami* and *Mikuma* as well. But Spruance was far more interested in knowing if there were any remaining Japanese carriers to the northwest of the island. While waiting for a clearer picture to emerge, he turned due west at 0930, passing only fifty miles north of Midway.[41] He was now in a perfect position to foil any renewed landing attempt while evaluating the morning's reports. However, instead of a clearer picture emerging, things began to get more confusing as the morning wore on. At 0700 Midway radioed that a PBY had detected "Two enemy cruisers bearing 286, distance 174, course 310, speed 20 knots." Though Spruance didn't know it, this was Kurita's *Kumano* and *Suzuya* steaming to rejoin Kondō. At 0800, another report was received, detailing "Two enemy battleships, 3 or 4 cruisers, 1 aircraft carrier on fire bearing 324 distance 240 [miles from Midway] course 310 speed 12." In retrospect, the carrier was plainly *Hiryū,* although it is less apparent what other vessels were in her vicinity that could have been sighted. But that wasn't all. At 0853 another PBY sighted a carrier "bearing 335 distance 250 from Midway course 245 at 2020 GCT [0820 local]."[42] Finally, at 0907, Midway rebroadcast the following, "05200 [0800] enemy cruisers, auxiliaries and some destroyers screening burning carrier 2 battleships well ahead of group."[43]

To Spruance and his staff the overall impression was that there was indeed an enemy carrier still out there. On the basis of the reports they already had in hand, they were convinced that *Akagi, Kaga,* and *Sōryū* had been dispatched. But so far as they knew, *Hiryū* had only been crippled, and no one would discount the possibility that an undiscovered fifth Japanese carrier still lurked nearby.[44] Accordingly, Spruance decided to leave Midway to the business of dealing with the two "battleships" while he sought bigger prey to the northwest.

In the event, though, Spruance didn't end up getting a strike off until around 1512.[45] It would have been launched an hour sooner had not a rather bizarre incident occurred on *Enterprise*'s bridge. Captain Miles Browning, Spruance's chief of staff, drafted an attack plan that called for launching the force's SBDs at 1400. During the briefing, *Enterprise*'s aviators were informed that they would be launching at a range of 240 miles from the contact—extreme range for the Dauntless.[46] Worse yet, upon closer examination, Browning's plan failed to account for the distance that the Japanese warships would most likely have moved in the interval from launch, meaning that the actual range was closer to 275 miles.[47] Browning had also specified that the planes were to be armed with 1,000-pound weapons—decreasing their effective range still further. Lieutenant Shumway, slated to lead *Enterprise*'s attack, was concerned enough about the outlines of the plan that he took them to *Enterprise*'s air group commander, Wade McClusky, who was lying in the ship's sick bay. McClusky promptly went ballistic. Though wounded, he made his way up to the flag bridge, dragging Earl Gallaher and *Enterprise*'s skipper, Capt. George Murray, along with him. He confronted Browning in front of Spruance, contending that the mission could not be carried out as planned. Browning, without explanation, brusquely ordered the aviators to carry out their orders. McClusky thereupon inquired if Browning had ever flown an SBD. Browning answered that he had. McClusky then pressed him on whether he had ever flown a late-model SBD, equipped with self-sealing tanks (which carried less fuel), armored seats, a 1,000-pound bomb, and a full load of avgas? Browning admitted he hadn't. The argument quickly turned openly hostile, whereupon Spruance sided with McClusky, saying simply, "I will do what you pilots want."[48] Clearly, Spruance had discerned from the previous day's events that his senior aviators knew their business. Browning stormed off the flag bridge in a rage, sulking in his cabin until another staff member persuaded him to return to his duties.[49]

The upshot of this almost farcical episode was that *Enterprise*'s aircraft, and *Hornet*'s too, had to be rearmed with 500-pound weapons before the strike went up. By the time the switch out had occurred, middle afternoon was wasting away. *Enterprise* launched thirty-two SBDs at 1512. *Hornet* sent up eleven aircraft at 1530, followed by twenty-one shortly thereafter at 1543. Incredibly, despite the new arming orders, seven of *Hornet*'s scouts still carried 1,000-pound bombs. Commander Stanhope Ring, leader of *Hornet*'s ignominious combat debut the day before, once again led her attack and commanded the lead element. Lt. Cdr. Walter F. Rodee was in charge of *Hornet*'s second group, including the overloaded planes of VS-8.[50] All three strikes targeted the same burning carrier—the *Hiryū*. Of course, *Hiryū* had already sunk.

However, there was a Japanese ship entering Ring's bull's-eye: destroyer *Tanikaze*. She was still retracing Nagumo's earlier retreat, searching vainly for Yamaguchi and his flagship. In fact, *Tanikaze* had already been swiped at by some planes from Midway. At 1636 a quintet of B-17s had dropped bombs on her. All of them landed clear on either side of the bows, and *Tanikaze* suffered only a drenching of her superstructure. Undeterred, Commander Katsumi continued on his way. But seventy-odd minutes later, Ring's twelve SBDs appeared in the skies above the destroyer.

Ring had spotted *Tanikaze* at 1715, identifying her as a "light cruiser." As it developed, both *Hornet*'s and *Enterprise*'s planes were to consistently identify *Tanikaze* as a light cruiser this day. It is likely that dusk conditions, as well as the fact *Kagerō*-class destroyers sported an oversized forward stack, may have compounded this impression. But Ring's assigned target was much bigger—a carrier and her escorts—so for the moment he pressed on, leaving *Tanikaze* behind.

However, after having droned through the sky for 315 miles—well beyond the estimated contact point—Ring had had enough.[51] It was getting close to return time, and he decided to swing around and go after the one definite enemy sighted. After the past two days, Ring was understandably loath to let this opponent go. At about 1808, he attacked.

It was a hectic few moments for *Tanikaze,* as the SBDs dove on her. Her report shows twenty-six aircraft, dropping "very near misses" that bracketed both bows and the starboard quarter.[52] One miss off the stern was close enough to draw blood: bomb fragments slashed through the aft No. 3 5-inch turret, inducing an explosion that killed the entire six-man turret crew.

The reason *Tanikaze* rather dramatically overcounted the number of planes attacking her is that she was, in fact, shortly assaulted by an additional pack of dive-bombers. *Enterprise*'s composite squadron had been flying steadily west-northwest toward the reported position of the damaged Japanese carrier, strung out in a scouting line formed by nine planes of VS-6 and seven planes of VS-5. About 100 miles away from the presumed position of the enemy carrier, they had begun climbing. The ceiling was 13,000 feet, and visibility was hazy.[53]

By 1800, the expected carrier was nowhere in sight. Having overheard Ring's contact report, though, *Enterprise*'s planes began searching to the southwest. At 1820, "a lone enemy vessel was sighted, believed to be a light cruiser of the *Katori*-class, on course west, speed 20 knots."[54] Lt. Shumway logically decided to attack this target. It was growing dark, his planes were running low on gas, and as near as he could tell, there were no other enemy ships in the area. The end result was more trouble for the hard-pressed *Tanikaze*.

Commander Katsumi must have shaken his head in frustration as he barked out orders for yet more evasive maneuvers. The search for *Hiryū* was proving a distinctly hazardous undertaking, and seemed likely to cost him his own ship before sunset. One by one, the enemy dive-bombers pushed over on him like kingfishers. VB-3 attacked first, beginning at 1834, followed in succession by VB-6, VS-6, and finally VS-5.

Yet once again luck was with the *Tanikaze*. In this, she was aided by the growing darkness, which made it more difficult to see the fleeing ship against the dark waters. Katsumi's skill as a ship handler, too, was undoubted—*Tanikaze* went to high speed and lurched into a series of violent "S" turns. The U.S. Navy's report affirms this, saying, "Because of the cruiser's high speed, maneuverability, and the heavy weather conditions, a very elusive dive bombing target was presented." As a result, most of the bombs landed fairly wide.

The other thing the Americans noticed was the large volume of antiaircraft fire, as *Tanikaze*'s crew threw everything they had at the attackers. Their prodigious efforts were rewarded. Near the end of the last attack, one stricken SBD was seen by both sides crashing directly into *Tanikaze*'s wake. With tragic irony, this SBD was piloted by none other than Lieutenant Adams of Scouting Five, who had produced the decisive sighting of *Hiryū* the preceding afternoon.

More than a bit frustrated, TF 16's aviators turned and began the long, dangerous flight home. They would eventually be recovered well after nightfall, and only after Admiral Spruance elected to take the rather bold step of turning on the carriers' deck lights to guide his men home. Spruance later explained that "If planes are to be flown so late in the day that a night recovery is likely, and if the tactical situation is such that the commander is unwilling to do what is required to get the planes back safely, then he has no business launching the attack in the first place." His men, in turn, demonstrated their own worth by completing a near-perfect recovery sequence on board the carriers. Only one aircraft was lost, running out of fuel just before landing. Both crewmen were recovered.[55]

Tanikaze, for her part, still wasn't quite done. At 1845 five B-17s commenced dropping fifteen 600- and eight 300-pound bombs on her from 11,000 feet. She understandably counted eleven planes, as several of them made more than one run. *Tanikaze* was not hit and, incredibly, seems to have contributed in knocking down at least one B-17. This plane, apparently hit by AA fire, subsequently had to jettison its belly fuel tank and was never heard from again. A second ran out of fuel on the way home and ditched. These two were the only B-17s lost in the battle.[56] Finally sunset came, and *Tanikaze,* finding nothing in the area, was understandably happy to quit the field and quickly sped westward to rejoin Nagumo. Undiscovered somewhere nearby, Chief Engineer Aimune's cutter drifted morosely toward its eventual rescue at the hands of the enemy.

As it happened, two other Japanese destroyers had scuttled through the waters west of Midway this afternoon, but had been lucky enough to avoid detection. These were *Arashio* and *Asashio,* hastening to join the screen of the *Mikuma* and *Mogami.* At 1800 they had signaled that after finishing refueling they expected to rejoin *Mogami* and her sister at 0500 the following morning.[57]

Even if this duo had been detected, it is unlikely that they could have been attacked. TF 16 was through with launches for the day. It was too dark, and *Asashio* and her sister too far away to justify a further attempt. But Spruance knew that there would be good targets waiting in the morning. Indeed, the latest sighting reports received from Midway via Nimitz at 1941 actually said that one of Midway's patrol planes had been attacked by Japanese carrier fighters. It was true—at 1812, as the sun dipped toward the horizon, Lt. (jg) Dale S. Newell of VP-44 had had the dubious honor of finally sighting the Japanese Main Body. *Zuihō's* CAP thereupon received their own baptism of fire by chasing off the American interloper.[58]

Lieutenant Newell had come upon Combined Fleet at an interesting moment. Only an hour before, the last straggling destroyers of Nagumo's fleet had rejoined the Main Body. The Japanese were busy receiving short action reports, and cross-decking personnel. Destroyer *Isokaze* had pulled alongside *Chikuma* and was conscientiously sending over the fire and rescue party the cruiser had left behind with *Sōryū* the previous morning.[59] The Japanese listened nervously to the chatter indicating enemy planes overhead, but they felt that the approaching sunset would soon offer cover.[60] Apparently it did, for other than an unknown aircraft bombing *Haruna* at 1700 and scoring a near miss,[61] no other Japanese ships were attacked today.

With Yamamoto, Kondō, and Nagumo now all merged into one formation, Combined Fleet shifted from its northwest course and headed due west as dusk drew on.[62] They proceeded slowly, while that evening the destroyers transferred *Kidō Butai's* survivors to *Nagato* and *Mutsu.* They were heading away from Midway, but not necessarily away from battle. Mindful that the enemy's pursuit might offer renewed opportunities, Yamamoto was not quite ready to give up yet. He would hold the Midway invasion forces on standby at a safe distance and see what developments the next day might bring.

20

And Death to the Cripples . . .

A s dawn's early light broke on 6 June, the battered Second Section of CruDiv 7 was still struggling to clear the battle zone. *Mikuma* remained more or less intact, but her speed—and thus her fate—was tied to that of her wounded sister. Shoving aside a cataract of water from her crushed prow, *Mogami* was still making fourteen knots and had the possibility of doing even better.[1] The sea was moderate, and the welcome arrival of DesDiv 8 soon after dawn bolstered the men's spirits still further.[2]

Yet even now Admiral Raymond Spruance was maneuvering to abort their escape. TF 16 now lay 350 miles northwest of Midway. At 0500 Spruance had put up a fan of eighteen searching SBDs from *Enterprise* to cover his western flank out to a distance of 200 miles. It didn't take long for one of the Dauntlesses to flush out the Japanese cruisers, radioing at 0645 that he had spotted one battleship, one cruiser, and three destroyers steaming west at ten knots. Besides an unaccountably slow speed estimate, though, a further distortion resulted when a garble in deciphering turned the message into a report of "one carrier and five destroyers."[3] Needless to say, this latter report—particularly its unintentional mention of a carrier—elicited immediate interest on *Enterprise*'s bridge. The reported position of the Japanese was only 128 miles southwest of TF 16.[4]

However, recalling the goose chase after the "damaged carrier" just the day before, Spruance was determined to take no chances. He ordered cruisers *Minneapolis* and *New Orleans* to launch their floatplanes to maintain contact with this new "carrier." However, even as these scouts were warming up, one of *Hornet*'s SBDs returned at 0730 and dropped a message clarifying that it was, in fact, two cruisers and two destroyers that had been sighted. Thus, when the cruisers started catapulting their floatplanes at 0745, Spruance now thought he might be dealing with *two* separate enemy formations, one of which included a carrier.[5] Spruance ordered speed increased to twenty-five knots on a southwest course and instructed *Hornet* to launch her attack group. *Enterprise* would follow suit as quickly as possible.

Hornet already had a force of SBDs spotted on deck for just such a contingency. Shortly before 0800, she began launching the first of eleven aircraft of VB-8. Another fourteen SBDs, drawn mostly from VS-8 but including one apiece from VS-5 and VS-6, went up right after. Eight carried 500-lb bombs; the remainder lugged 1,000-

pounders. Eight Wildcat fighters accompanied them. Considering the opponent, this was a strong strike. Leading it again was *Hornet*'s Stanhope Ring, trying for one last shot at redemption.

However, the hoped-for carrier was soon to prove a chimera. After Ring's aircraft had departed, more of the morning's search aircraft began landing, and the error in transmission was quickly discovered and corrected. There was no carrier, but there was apparently big ship game out there nonetheless. Indeed, Spruance still believed that there might be two separate formations in proximity to one another. At 0850 the *Enterprise* radioed to Ring: "Target may be a battleship instead of a carrier. Attack!"[6]

By now the Japanese were fully aware of the way the morning was shaping up. Captain Sakiyama of *Mikuma* had spotted two of *New Orleans*'s floatplanes and opened fire on them. The Americans kept a healthy distance, maintaining contact and guiding Ring's strike force right to their targets, which he sighted at 0930. As far as he could tell, though, neither of the two larger ships was a battleship.[7] Remembering that two enemy forces had been reported, he prudently withheld his attack, instead heading west to ensure that he didn't miss any bigger game. However, the minutes ticked by, and he saw nothing. Below, the *Mikuma* and *Mogami* were passing by his left side. His flight had already missed the optimum push-over point. Still seeing nothing ahead, Ring decided that one contact in the hand was worth two in the bush. He now commenced a wide circle around to begin a second approach from ahead and out of the sun. As the attack began unfolding, the *Mikuma* flashed word at 0945 "attacked by a large number of enemy planes and one seaplane in sight."[8] At 0950 Ring led his men into their dives.[9]

The Japanese ships increased speed and began spitting out AA. As it happened, their fire proved as effective, if not more so, than that of *Kidō Butai*'s carriers two days before. Despite having no air cover, the Japanese gunners shot down two SBDs, with the loss of both of their crews.[10] Ring was once again destined for disappointment, as his section managed no better than a "paint-scraper" near miss alongside *Mikuma*. Scouting Eight had a bit more success with *Mogami,* connecting with two bombs. One landed atop No. 5 turret, killing the entire turret crew.[11] The second smashed through the aircraft deck and started fires in the torpedo room beneath it. Now Lieutenant Commander Saruwatari's earlier precaution of dumping *Mogami*'s Type 93 torpedoes paid off. While the bomb hit was destructive, there were no secondary explosions, and the fire was extinguished within an hour. As for DesDiv 8, both destroyers were strafed but emerged otherwise unscathed.[12]

Surveying the results after reforming his aircraft, Ring answered a query from *Enterprise* by radioing: "No CV sighted. Attacked CA supported by 3 DD. One hit. Enemy course 270, speed 25. No Air Opposition."[13] The last part was significant, as it confirmed that there was no Japanese carrier in the area. This was a disappointment, but it seemed possible that the reported "battleship" was still lurking out there somewhere.

Watching Ring's aviators depart, *Mikuma*'s skipper surely wished for a Japanese carrier near at hand as well, albeit for entirely different reasons. But the fact was that Captain Sakiyama's small squadron was alone on the sea, far distant from Kurita's other two cruisers, and even farther from any help the Main Body might provide.

A quick tally of the damage was compiled, and then a situation report flashed to Yamamoto and Kondō at 1045. The news still wasn't all bad. *Mogami* had only received "light damage," and "three" enemy aircraft had been shot down.[14]

However, at exactly the same moment Sakiyama was sending his report, further trouble was being sent his way. One by one, thirty-one SBDs began rolling down *Enterprise*'s flight deck as she followed up *Hornet*'s strike with one of her own. Like *Hornet*'s morning strike, this was a polyglot unit—SBDs from VB-3, VS-5, VB-6, and VS-6 were all participating. Sixteen planes of VS-5 and VS-6 combined to form one squadron, with planes from VB-6 forming a third division. With them went twelve Wildcat fighters. Overall command of the formation fell on Lt. Wallace "Wally" Short of *Yorktown*.[15]

At 1057, while Short was still orbiting TF 16 awaiting departure of the last of his aircraft, he received an additional message indicating that the Japanese battleship was apparently somewhat farther ahead of the assigned target.[16] Not surprisingly, he was ordered to seek it out first. A few minutes later came yet another change. Given the importance of the target, the last three torpedo planes remaining from VT-6 would be coming up to join him as well. At 1115 the SBDs formed up and departed, boring away westward in lazy "S" turns to let the slower TBDs puff along behind. The dive-bombers climbed to 22,500 feet, leaving the torpedo planes at low altitude.[17]

Captains Sakiyama and Soji had changed their own plans in the meantime. The implication of the continued presence of *New Orleans*'s floatplanes was obvious and mandated a response. At 1100 the *Mikuma* radioed that they were under pursuit by enemy aircraft and surface ships. They were consequently shifting course to the southwest to make a run for Wake's air cover, the island being 710 miles distant.[18] Yamamoto's staff on board *Yamato* could only listen with growing consternation and fear for the safety of the two cruisers. Their fears were well founded, because the time had finally come for CruDiv 7 to pay the check.

At noon *Mikuma* was still leading *Mogami* west-southwest. Both ships were making close to twenty knots, with the two destroyers in screen. Great waves were being raised by *Mogami*'s shattered bow as she bulled her way through the water at the best speed she could manage. This last-gasp effort was putting a severe strain on the forward bulkheads, but Captain Soji dared not slow down now. It had been two hours since the last American attack, and they were creeping ever closer to Wake. However, they were still at least a day's steaming from friendly fighter cover. And now, the instrument of their final ruin came into view.

Wally Short's strike group had sighted the fleeing Japanese at 1211. However, for the moment he did not alter course. The Japanese watched as the Americans flew by, heading west in search of the nonexistent battleship. But even though the SBDs were headed out of the area, coming up from astern were the American Wildcats and the three TBDs of VT-6. The fighter leader, Lt. Jim Gray, feared the TBDs might attack the cruisers solo, so he led his fighters down for a closer look at the targets Short had just bypassed. The Japanese responded with another blistering AA barrage, spitting defiance back at the Wildcats.

It may well be that because of her damaged bow *Mogami* appeared fore-shortened and smaller than her sister. For whatever reason, though, Gray and other American pilots consistently mistook the pair for one battleship and one heavy cruiser, even though *Mikuma* and *Mogami* were identical. This had an effect on the postbattle reports the Americans would file regarding this attack. However, Gray was impressed by the robust defense and large size of Japanese cruisers. He was convinced that an oversight had been made, and that at least one of the two was the "battleship" that everyone was seeking this morning. He promptly radioed Short, advising him to reverse course.

Over the radio, Gray's pilots were remarking on the warm reception they were receiving, while Short and his men listened with growing concern. Behind them was a perfectly valid target. Ahead of their windscreens, despite excellent visibility, was . . . nothing. All they could see was sun and empty ocean. They had already flown thirty miles west of the Japanese ships when Gray anxiously radioed that one of the passed targets appeared to be a battleship. That was the last straw. With a curt signal, Short brought his entire squadron around to the east, commencing a long, high-speed approach from about 21,000 feet. His SBDs were descending from out of the sun and downwind, converging rapidly with the Japanese ships on their opposing course of about 240 degrees.[19] *Mikuma* was still in the lead, and it was this ship that Short and most of his aviators targeted.

However, as they began their approach, the Japanese formation abruptly slowed and changed course. The rearmost ship (*Mogami*) was coming under attack and looping out to starboard. As it developed, not all of Wally Short's squadron had, in fact, followed him on his abortive westward search. The last section in the long string of American aircraft, that of VB-3, had "departed from the search ahead and attacked the rear CA."[20] Almost immediately, two bombs slammed into *Mogami,* one amidships on the aircraft deck and the other forward of the bridge, inflicting medium damage.[21]

However, as a result of her sister's evasive maneuvers, *Mikuma* in the fore began circling to starboard to conform to *Mogami*. This had the effect of reversing *Mikuma*'s relative positioning, making her now tail-end Charlie in the formation. Thus, *Mikuma* had her attention distracted, and as a result, the Americans caught her flat-footed. Short pushed over at 14,000 feet and was in a 70-degree dive on her when she suddenly spotted the new menace and opened "a heavy stream of automatic gun fire."[22] She would keep this up until the first bomb hit.

As *Mikuma* came out of her starboard turn, the first hit was delivered against the roof of the No. 3 main turret, directly in front of the bridge. The explosion shattered the turret, blowing a sheet of lethal fragments across the front of the ship's superstructure.[23] Several officers, including the commander of the starboard AA guns, were killed outright. Worse, this initial hit coincided precisely with Captain Sakiyama's sticking his head out a manhole cover on the top of the bridge. Severely wounded, he lost consciousness immediately and slumped backward into the bridge.

Commander Takashima Hideo, *Mikuma*'s executive officer, leapt to take charge. But two more bombs slammed home, blasting through the decks to shatter the starboard forward engine spaces.[24] Great blasts of smoke and fire boiled up, and

Mikuma was staggered. Bombs were still coming down, crashing into the sea and drenching the ship with towering columns of water.

Takashima tried to increase speed and evade, but his efforts were cut short abruptly. Even before the last of Short's SBDs had dropped, two more bombs blasted the aircraft deck and tore down into the port aft engine room, exploding with devastating force.[25] Immediately, a huge fire broke out in the vicinity of the torpedo tubes. *Mikuma* quickly slobbered to a halt. She had been crushed by at least five direct hits and two close near misses (and possibly more). On board *Mogami,* her officers and men watched with sinking hearts as their would-be rescuer now became substitute victim. With angry spears of fire and dark black smoke pouring from her superstructure, from *Mogami*'s bridge *Mikuma* appeared so obviously finished that at 1420 *Mogami* radioed as much back to Yamamoto.[26] Though sorely damaged herself, *Mogami* began closing her sister to render assistance.

High above, Wally Short collected his planes and found to his delight that he had suffered no losses. Arguably, this was true only because the three TBDs from VT-6 prudently declined to attack when they observed the accurate AA fire the Japanese ships were throwing up. The American torpedo plane squadrons had lost too much already, and Spruance had made it crystal clear to their pilots that they were not to risk themselves if the Japanese had so much as a single AA gun in operation.[27] As a result, the American fliers began their journey back to *Enterprise* at full strength, having almost certainly wrecked one of their targets.

"Almost certainly," because even in the immediate aftermath of the American attack, there remained still some slight doubt as to *Mikuma*'s fate. True, she was dead in the water, but two of her four engine rooms remained operable, and it might be possible to get her underway again if her fires were put out. There seemed to be some hope of the latter, at least initially. Though fires were raging amidships, she appeared to be on an even keel and was not settling visibly. Her executive officer semaphored *Mogami*: "I am taking command of the ship," and it seemed that order might be returning.[28] Captain Soji did not rule out the prospect of his *Mogami,* or the destroyers, towing *Mikuma* to safety—if they could avoid further attacks. But within an hour of the attack, the matter was rendered moot.

Just before 1358, the fires around *Mikuma*'s torpedo storage racks finally precipitated the calamity that was almost inevitable from the moment the first bomb landed amidships. With an appalling eruption, a number of *Mikuma*'s torpedoes exploded. The entire aircraft deck was reduced to a blackened tangle of junk, and even the mainmast came crashing down on top of the wreckage. The ship's superstructure was left almost unrecognizable from the funnel back to No. 4 turret. Far worse than the damage topside, though, was the damage belowdecks. Although not obvious at first, the explosion and earlier bomb hits in the port machinery spaces had ruptured the bottom of the cruiser.[29] *Mikuma* started sagging to port and settling deeper into the water. The men on board *Mogami* were under no illusions regarding the inevitable outcome of this misfortune. At 1358 she morosely radioed word of *Mikuma*'s explosion and opined that there was "little prospect of her being recovered."[30]

Mikuma might be doomed, but Combined Fleet was convinced there was still an opportunity to avenge her, and they were determined to exploit it. Just before Wally Short's attack struck home, the main Japanese fleet had broken formation and detached a fast striking element to lunge south in support of Sakiyama. From the Japanese perspective, 6 June offered the possibility of a renewed carrier battle, this time supported by their full surface strength. At 1340 Kondō sent orders to his Occupation Force and CruDiv 8, the barest details of which convey something of the Japanese renewed excitement and hope of snatching victory from defeat:

> 1. Main Force of Occupation Force, less BatDiv 3 and DesRon 2, with CruDiv 8 destroy enemy carrier force and assist *Mogami* and *Mikuma*. Course west.
> 2. Supply Force is waiting at position FU KO N 39 (30°-10'N, 167°-50'E).
> 3. *Zuihō* prepare to attack enemy CV.
> 4. Prepare to utilize full strength of all available seaplanes. Three-seaters to search, two-seaters to attack enemy carrier with two ordinary [SAP] bombs each.[31]

One of the most incredible things about this order is *Zuihō* being ordered to prepare her aircraft for an attack. In fact, Kondō had already ordered her at 0015 to move with a single destroyer to a position to deliver air attacks to cover CruDiv 7's retreat.[32] *Zuihō* would later turn in an illustrious battle record, and her captain, Ōbayashi Sueo, was destined to become a respected carrier skipper. Yet the fact was that *Zuihō* just had nine torpedo bombers to throw into the fray, along with six Zeros and six older A5M fighters. It is stunning that the Japanese were even considering offering battle under these terms, particularly given the fact that Yamamoto was even now receiving signals that *Mikuma* and *Mogami* were undergoing a heavy air attack. At this point, the Americans had at least three times as much firepower as *Zuihō*, *Hōshō*, and all the floatplanes the Japanese could scrape together. To say that Yamamoto was grasping at straws was putting it mildly, and it's lucky for the Japanese that they didn't come within range of Spruance's warbirds this day. Had they done so, the misfortunes they had suffered on 4 June would almost certainly have been sharply augmented.

Yamamoto didn't know it, but his forces had just scored their biggest success of the entire battle. Throughout the morning, Captain Elliott Buckmaster's efforts to save the wounded *Yorktown* had slowly been yielding fruit. Destroyer *Hammann* had nuzzled up to her starboard side and put the captain's salvage party on board her just before dawn. The destroyer still lay alongside, providing power and support as *Yorktown*'s crew busied themselves with remedying her various maladies. Five other destroyers circled the carrier in ceaseless patrol.

Yorktown's fires were now out, and her port list had already been considerably abated by both portable pumps and counterflooding her starboard tanks. Topside, men were cutting away many of her portside guns so as to reduce the weight on her threatened flank. In the hangar, other sailors were lowering spare aircraft from the overheads and shoving them over the side.[33] Most important of all, minesweeper *Vireo* had secured a towline to *Yorktown* at 1308 on the 5th and was dragging her clear at three knots.[34] If things kept up, Captain Buckmaster might yet pull off one of the war's more masterful demonstrations of damage control.

However, even as the Americans were laboring with a will, Lieutenant Commander Tanabe and *I-168* were moving in to put an end to this particular feel-good story. This was precisely the sort of mission that Japanese submarines were built and trained to perform—hunting and sinking enemy capital ships. Japanese fleet boats were neither nimble nor terribly quiet, but there was no denying the lethality of their torpedoes, if they could be put to use. And as luck would have it, Tanabe would benefit from an unexpectedly promising set of circumstances in which to set up his attack.

Having crept north toward his quarry all during the 5th, he had welcomed the opportunity to travel on the surface once nightfall came. Throughout the night he cruised ahead at sixteen knots, trusting in the sharp eyes and superb night optics of his lookouts to sight his quarry before he was sighted in turn.[35] Belowdecks, the crew had completed preparations for an attack. Many of the men were too keyed up to sleep, and instead waited anxiously, chattering among themselves as the night wore away.[36]

At 0410 Tanabe's confidence in his lookouts had been rewarded, as one of them shouted out that he had a contact off the starboard bow. The skipper scanned the eastern horizon himself in the growing light of dawn. Finally, there could be no doubt of it—the wounded American carrier gradually resolved itself, almost precisely where Tanabe had expected to find her. Even with his submarine still concealed in the westward gloom, and his target silhouetted by the rising sun, Tanabe reacted cautiously, chopping his speed to twelve knots to cut his wake. He submerged at 0600 as increasing visibility made his approach ever more perilous.[37]

Tanabe had been determined to close as near as possible to the enemy carrier before launching his attack. Yet, it would be tricky. Six destroyers guarded her, and he had a healthy respect for American sonar. As luck would have it, though, acoustic conditions were miserable. One of the American destroyermen afterward lamented that "propeller noises could not be heard at any range."[38] This was probably an exaggeration, but there was no denying that the Americans were completely unaware of *I-168*'s stealthy approach.

Tanabe was concerned as well by the telltale wake his periscope might make on the smooth waters and resolved to use it only sparingly during the middle portion of his approach—once every half hour, and then only for a single five-second exposure.[39] Instead of the scope, he would navigate using his sound gear and by dead reckoning. This was a bold move, but in his estimation of the relative risks, Tanabe was probably right again—his greatest danger under the acoustic conditions then pertaining was really from the hundreds of eyes on board the various American warships guarding the crippled carrier.

Getting *I-168* inside the ring of pickets to set up his attack was far from easy. Tanabe took a visual fix on the target at 15,000 meters, and then started moving in. Over the next four hours, he risked only occasional glances with his periscope as he picked his way inward. But the fleeting visual sightings he did make revealed something odd—he was not closing on the target in the fashion he had expected. *Vireo*'s low-speed towing of *Yorktown* was apparently fouling up his calculations ever so slightly.

Finally, it was time to risk penetrating the inner picket line, which was about 2,000 meters from the carrier.[40] Tanabe knew that no further periscope sightings would be possible until the final attack.

The American escorts were pinging away with their sonar, and Tanabe and his men could hear them clearly.[41] Tanabe rigged the vessel for depth charging just in case, but again their luck held. *I-168* apparently benefited from a strong thermal layer, because none of the American destroyers got so much as a whisper of an echo back from her hull. Finally, Tanabe decided it was time to chance a sighting and raised his scope for a quick look. He was stunned to discover *Yorktown* practically atop him, a mere 500 meters away.[42] He could clearly discern the faces of the American sailors on board her. Hurriedly retracting his scope, he realized he was now too close to the target—the torpedoes wouldn't arm before striking home. He had to come about and open the range a bit. This he did, finally reaching a position 1,500 meters from the carrier's starboard side. Tanabe noticed that during this critical juncture, the American destroyers seemed to have ceased sonar operations entirely.[43]

Tanabe knew that *I-168* would get only one attack, and he was determined to make it count. The captain decided to forgo firing a spread wider than 2 degrees.[44] This was an all or nothing attack—he would fire his fish in a very tight pattern and hope that a number of them struck home.[45] At about 1331, Tanabe let fly with his first pair of Type 89 torpedoes, followed seconds later by the second pair.[46] He immediately dove to *I-168*'s maximum depth of 100 meters and headed toward the target, figuring that it would be safer if he were in direct proximity to a sinking carrier than if he were out in the open where the American destroyers could get at him.[47] In the sub's cramped, sweaty control room, the men counted out the seconds since the torpedoes' launch. About forty seconds later, they were rewarded with the sound of three powerful detonations.

Tanabe's attack was devastating. The Americans had sighted the torpedoes inbound, but there was nothing they could do about it. With no engine power of her own, and still being towed by *Vireo*, the men on board *Yorktown* had little choice but to watch the fish come in. *Hammann*, still nestled as she was against *Yorktown*'s starboard quarter, was in exactly the same position. Tanabe's first fish hit *Hammann* dead amidships in the No. 2 fire room, blowing her in two. Ripping away her mooring lines from *Yorktown*, the destroyer drifted astern and started sinking immediately. Her crew began jumping into the water as fast as they could. Unfortunately, *Hammann*'s own depth charges detonated shortly after her stern left the surface.[48] The resulting underwater explosions crushed many of her survivors. *Hammann* lost 81 of her crew of 228.

Two other torpedoes rushed underneath *Hammann* and slammed into *Yorktown* at Frames 84 and 95 on her starboard side, while the fourth missed astern.[49] These two hits finished *Yorktown*. Externally, her condition didn't change all that noticeably— Tanabe's fish had struck on the opposite side of Hashimoto's, which had the effect of counterflooding the ship still further and bringing her list down. But *Yorktown*'s flooding could no longer be contained. Captain Buckmaster had his salvage party shut every watertight door they could, but they couldn't reach them all. The men could hear the sea pounding against the ship's centerline bulkhead in the spaces the latest torpedo hits had flooded.[50] At 1550 Buckmaster decided that it was best to remove the salvage party to the safety of the *Vireo*. He would wait out the evening in hopes that when the larger fleet tug *Navajo* arrived, he would be able to put the salvage party on board again and complete the repairs necessary to get her home. It was to be a forlorn hope.

Tanabe, for his part, had expected the real battle to begin after he had launched his torpedoes. Destroyers *Gwin, Monaghan,* and *Hughes* did not disappoint him, subjecting *I-168* to a series of violent depth-charging attacks over the next two hours. By the end of it, *I-168*'s batteries were practically dead, some of the battery casings having cracked and spilled sulphuric acid into the seawater of the bilge, thereby releasing chlorine gas into the sub's hull.[51] The fumes grew so bad that even the rats crawled out from the bilges to escape.[52] Her compressed air supply had been reduced to the barest margins necessary to blow the tanks, and her diving planes weren't working properly. One of the forward torpedo tube seals had leaked, partially flooding the torpedo room and trimming the sub by the bow.[53] Her lights—and then even her emergency lights—had failed, leaving the bridge crew operating by hand lamps in the increasingly foul air.[54] By the time the Americans were through, *I-168* had essentially been reduced to a wreck.

Yet just at the moment when Tanabe had no choice but to surface, the Americans broke off their attack. Tanabe came up at 1640, prepared for a last-ditch fight on the surface with his deck gun. But when he emerged from the conning tower hatch, the American destroyers were retreating, about 10,000 meters away.[55] The *Yorktown* was nowhere in sight, leading Tanabe to believe that he had sunk her. Not wishing to stay in the neighborhood, he ordered *I-168* to start her diesels so that she could move away on the surface.

This was perhaps Tanabe's one order this day that was less than inspired, for the cloud of diesel smoke as the engines were fired up brought the American destroyers down on *I-168* again. Tanabe had no choice but to run for it. The Americans bracketed his weaving boat with gunfire. However, the light was fading, and the heavy engine exhaust created a small smoke screen for *I-168* to hide behind. Though the range was closing inexorably, none of the Americans' shots hit. Finally, having had bare time to vent the sub's atmosphere and recharge her air flasks somewhat, Tanabe took her down again, reversing course in his smoke cloud as he did so.[56] This time the Americans seemed to have lost her—their depth charging was desultory and ill aimed. Eventually, Tanabe was able to sneak away for good. He would make it home to Kure, his fuel tanks nearly dry, having pulled off one of the most impressive submarine victories of the entire war.

Meanwhile, *Mikuma*'s executive officer, Takashima, was beginning to come to the same conclusions regarding his ship's likely fortunes that *Mogami* had already conveyed to Yamamoto. *Mikuma* was visibly settling. Her midships were a raging inferno, and there didn't appear to be any means of bringing her fires under control. After hearing some anxious-sounding damage-control reports on the smoke-filled bridge, Takashima gave the order to prepare to abandon ship. He instructed the ship's

20-1: *Mikuma* under attack at 1500. An enormous explosion from a recent bomb hit, or continuing explosions in her torpedo storage area, can be seen rising overhead. *Mogami* is visible to the right. One destroyer is dimly visible between the two; a second is barely visible to the left underneath the plume of the explosion. (Naval Historical Center)

repair parties to suspend their work aft and instead begin dragging shoring timbers to the ship's foredeck to construct life rafts. *Mogami* and *Arashio* were close at hand, while *Asashio* circled to provide air defense.

For the moment, no enemy aircraft were in sight, and after a few more minutes, Takashima gave the order to evacuate. Since *Mikuma* was still burning and exploding, it was too dangerous for *Arashio* to approach.[57] *Mikuma*'s men would have to make their way over to the rescue ships either by swimming or on board rafts. The sailors started throwing timbers, vests, and anything else that might float over the side. Then they began jumping into the sea. On the ship's foredeck, the gravely injured Captain Sakiyama and others of the wounded were the first to be lowered onto the first raft. With the second raft went *Mikuma*'s paymaster and her air officer, taking important documents and materials. Splashing into the calm sea, the rafts shoved off for *Arashio*.

Commander Takashima watched all this stoically from *Mikuma*'s ruined bridge. The reason he had sent the important materials with the second raft was that he would not be accompanying them himself. Though Captain Sakiyama yet lived and technically remained in command, the actual responsibility for *Mikuma* had fallen to Takashima. It was he who had directed the ship's final efforts. As such, he saw it as his duty to share *Mikuma*'s fate.

So he would, and unfortunately for the Japanese, so would many hundreds of others. In fact, the bulk of *Mikuma*'s crew would be lost, for hardly had Captain Sakiyama's raft been hauled on board *Arashio* when a third wave of enemy aircraft came roaring in at 1445 to attack the hapless little force. These were twenty-three SBDs sent up from *Hornet* at 1345. With TF 16 having now closed the range to the Japanese considerably, each plane could carry the heavier 1,000-lb. bomb. This last strike didn't have fighter cover, but by then it was clear that none was needed.

Blazing *Mikuma* was a sitting duck. *Mogami* and *Arashio,* currently hove to near her, would be in nearly as much trouble if they didn't clear out immediately. Frantically, the rescue ships began moving away from the stricken cruiser. Left behind in the water were hundreds of men, cheated at the chance for life just when it appeared they would be rescued. Hundreds of others still remained on board the shattered *Mikuma,* some of them by their own preference.

One of the latter was the commander of the main battery fire-control center, Lt. Koyama Masao. When Takashima ordered Abandon Ship, Koyama had refused to go and instead asked his senior petty officer to be his second as he committed *hara-kiri* (ritual suicide) atop a forward gun turret.[58] Having not been able to see his guns smash the enemy, he could at least perform this final service. Against the tragic backdrop of *Mikuma*'s loss, many Japanese subsequently found some comfort in the telling of Lieutenant Koyama's heroic dedication to his duty. If the indications are correct, Koyama was already dead by the time the third attack wave struck the vessel.

The American bombers dove at around 1500. *Mogami* and *Arashio* did not have a chance to move too far from *Mikuma* before the enemy was upon them, the ocean churning into froth around all three ships from exploding bombs and bullets. The Americans pressed their attack with the same ferocity as before, but not so accurately. Even so, both cruisers were hit again, and one of the destroyers as well.

Destroyer *Arashio* took a bomb hit near her No. 3 turret aft. Tragically, it exploded among the massed survivors of *Mikuma,* who had just been pulled from the water. Thirty-seven men were killed outright, and the commander of DesDiv 8, Cdr. Ogawa Nobuki, was wounded.[59] This same hit started a fire and knocked out *Arashio*'s steering. Fortunately for the destroyer, no further damage was forthcoming, and the fire was soon extinguished. Though forced to resort to manual steering, *Arashio* was subsequently able to escape, following *Mogami* and *Asashio* west. Her sister *Asashio* had not been struck directly, but had lost twenty-two men to strafing.

Mogami took a bomb on the seaplane deck, which started a horrendous fire near the ship's sick bay.[60] All the doctors and orderlies were either killed outright or wounded, leaving the wounded men unable to save themselves as the fires roared in. Worse yet, this was at least the third hit near the aircraft deck in the same day and the bulkheads had been badly warped by the blasts. As a result, many of the escape hatches in the vicinity had been damaged. The conflagration was spreading, and Lieutenant Commander Saruwatari once again made the tough call of taking the "apparently unmerciful step" and ordering the entire compartment sealed off by closing all the undamaged hatches around it.[61]

This wrenching decision gave damage control the crucial edge they needed. At length, the raging fire was checked and gradually brought under control. Saruwatari later recalled that when the compartments were reopened, it was found that several men had indeed been trapped and perished there. Their bodies were found contorted in their last throes next to the dogged hatches. One sublieutenant had clearly committed *hara-kiri* to end his life before the fires burned him alive. Saruwatari "trembled with great sorrow" to see the bodies of his shipmates thus, but *Mogami*'s damage-control officer had once again made the critical decision that saved his ship.

Fortunately, despite the bomb hit and fire, *Mogami*'s engines remained operable. After a series of quick inquiries with the two destroyers, Captain Soji took stock of the situation and decided his course of action. At 1500 *Mogami* radioed the word of the third attack and reported that she, *Mikuma,* and *Arashio* had sustained bomb hits.[62] *Mikuma* was done for, and the same would hold true for *Mogami* if she didn't vacate the area immediately. More than three hours of daylight remained, meaning that further attacks might be forthcoming. Thus, with heavy hearts among the men, at 1525 *Mogami* set a course due west with both destroyers, leaving *Mikuma* and her crew to their fates. Between them, the three ships had only managed to pull her dying skipper and 239 other officers and men on board.[63]

By some miracle, *Mogami*'s speed mounted steadily until she was making around twenty knots. Given her damaged state, this was rather incredible, a fact that was remarked on by Ugaki, who wryly noted, "At 1525 *Mogami* reported that she was heading due west at 20 knots to lure the enemy toward our Main Force. That *Mogami* with her bow damaged managed to put up such a high speed . . . is partly because her damage control has progressed and also partly because she made a desperate effort to get out of a trap."[64] *Mogami* would make good her escape, rejoining Kondō's Second Fleet the next day. Though her fire amidships had been contained, it wasn't totally extinguished until several hours after sunset.[65] Later, dockyard workers found "800 large or small holes in portside," the effect of which was to turn the ship's flank into "something like a honeycomb." Surprisingly, *Mogami*'s casualties totaled only 9 officers and 81 petty officers and men killed, with another 101 wounded.[66] She was fortunate indeed to have survived at all, and at the top of the list of reasons why must stand the courageous actions of her damage-control officer, Lieutenant Commander Saruwatari.

Left behind by her consorts, *Mikuma* continued burning and slowly settling. She lingered on for at least four hours or more, increasingly heeled over to port, but not trimmed noticeably by either the bow or stern. No Japanese warship would ever see her again, but her last hours would achieve graphic immortality, thanks to the U.S. Navy. This latter fame came about because the American pilots returning to TF 16 could not agree on what it was that they had attacked. Many of the aviators were convinced *Mikuma* was a battleship, while others thought she was a cruiser of some kind. There was even less agreement on *Mogami*'s identity, and given her smashed

20-2: *Mikuma* after attacks, 6 June. Nos. 1 and 2 main turrets have been trained hard abaft to port. No. 3 turret, blasted by a bomb hit, is skewed to starboard, with its right barrel elevated. The roof of No. 2 turret has been blown off by an internal explosion. The rear half of the stack has been destroyed, and the ship is noticeably settling. Amidships, where the torpedoes have exploded, the ship's upper works have been completely destroyed, along with the mainmast. The ship is still afire throughout her superstructure area. (Naval Historical Center)

bow, this is perhaps not surprising. Spruance listened to these conflicting reports with growing impatience, for if his men had missed the "battleship" previously reported, he wanted to know about it while there was yet time for a final strike. Finally, at 1553 *Enterprise* launched two SBDs to photo recon the targets and settle the argument.[67] The Japanese ships were by now little more than ninety miles away, but there wasn't much time to get the job done—dusk was approaching.

However, there was still plenty of light at 1715 when the pair of SBDs arrived above the stricken Japanese cruiser. She was floating forlornly in the hauntingly beautiful glow of the coming sunset. They marked *Mikuma*'s position as 29°-28'N, 173°-11'E. The planes circled slowly at about 100 feet as the camera shutters snapped, freezing *Mikuma* in all her dreadful agony. Though *Mogami* was now long gone, the photo planes did see her far on the western horizon, in position 29°-24'N, 172°-20'E on a westerly course. They also noted two destroyers with her, apparently trying to screen the damaged cruiser with smoke.[68]

20-3: *Mikuma* after attacks, 6 June. One of the most famous photographs of the war, the magnitude of the destruction on board can clearly be seen. Both portside torpedo tube mounts have been trained outboard, either by the explosions themselves or more likely during a last-ditch attempt to jettison the torpedoes. Her aircraft deck is a smoldering ruin. The wreckage atop No. 4 eight-inch turret, erroneously labeled in many accounts as the remains of Captain Fleming's dive-bomber, is, in fact, most likely debris from either the aft superstructure or perhaps the mainmast itself. Human touches can also be seen. A sailor is visible astern climbing down a rope ladder, with others in a small raft by her stern. Aft, men in white uniforms can be seen near the fantail. The heads of swimmers in the water are also visible. The knowledge that almost none of the men seen in this evocative image survived their ordeal makes it all the more poignant. (Naval Historical Center)

Shortly thereafter, the Americans left *Mikuma* to her fate. One of her few survivors would later recall that it was about dusk when her list to port began to increase more rapidly. Finally, with a great billow of smoke and steam, she turned onto her port side and sank, the first Japanese cruiser to be lost in the war.[69] The approximate time and position was 1930 at 29°-28'N, 173°-11'E.[70] Partly because of the ferocity of the fires and explosion, but mostly because of the curtailment of the rescue operation, the loss of life upon *Mikuma*'s sinking was extremely heavy. A full 700 officers and men of her nominal crew of 888 perished.[71] Included among them was her captain. As if his spirit was seeking to hasten to rejoin his fallen warriors, Captain Sakiyama Shakao would later succumb to his wounds and die on board *Suzuya* on 13 June.[72]

20-4: *Mikuma* after attacks, 6 June. Although blurry, this shot shows the immense devastation wrought on *Mikuma*'s superstructure, midships, and funnel. Also apparent is the hull damage suffered from her ramming by *Mogami*—her hull plates are heavily dished in just forward of No. 2 five-inch antiaircraft mount, near the bridge. (Naval Historical Center)

Further west, Captain Soji, on board *Mogami*, did make one last attempt to avert the loss of life he knew would accrue from *Mikuma*'s sinking. After sunset, he ordered *Asashio* to return and "make every effort to rescue *Mikuma*'s survivors and later rejoin us." *Asashio* apparently did so, but found nothing in the darkness apart from dark waters covered with even darker oil. According to her log, "not even one survivor could be rescued."[73]

Yet two men ultimately escaped the fate of their ship and were eventually rescued by the submarine *Trout* on 9 June. One was chief radioman Yoshida Katsuichi; the other was a third-class fireman named Ishikawa Kenichi. When rescued, Yoshida was suffering from crushed ribs and required hospitalization, and could provide few details of *Mikuma*'s final hours.[74] Ishikawa, however, was only twenty-one years old and in good health. After *Mikuma* went down, he and Yoshida found themselves with seventeen other sailors on a raft. They drifted through that night and all the next day. One by one, all but these two had succumbed to their wounds or the lack of food and water.

The Japanese did not know it, but by the evening of the 6th, the Battle of Midway was all but over from the victor's point of view. Admiral Spruance had decided he had pushed his luck far enough. His carrier forces had now reached a point over 400 miles west of Midway. The risk of submarines and air attack was growing with each mile. He was also determined not to be drawn into range of Wake Island's bombers, nor to blunder into Yamamoto's powerful surface guns—both of which aims the Japanese were energetically trying to bring about. More concretely, the majority of his destroyers were getting critically low on fuel. Accordingly, he gave the order at 1907 for TF 16 to reverse course, suspend any further chase, and head for Pearl.[75] All that remained for the Americans now was to continue their anxious search for survivors on the vast ocean. The Japanese, however, were as yet unaware of their opponent's decision to withdraw, and for them it would take one more day for the curtain to fall.

Dusk on the 6th on board *Yamato* found Yamamoto and his staff in a state of growing unease. From where they sat, the American carrier fleet appeared to be in pursuit, and there was now a concern that the Invasion Force itself might soon be endangered. Preliminary estimates had concluded that the American force harrying the *Mikuma* group contained one or two carriers with accompanying cruisers. But this was only part of the enemy force, at least when the available intelligence was collated. The Japanese now believed that no less than five or six (!) American carriers had been concentrated in the Midway area during the battle, out of which "only two [had] been destroyed so far." The Japanese considered it reasonable to assume that even counting their battle losses, the enemy "still [had] three or four carriers, including converted ones on hand." Of these, it was further assumed that "at least one regular carrier, two converted carriers, several destroyers and cruisers" were in immediate pursuit of the Japanese forces.[76] It was guessed that these American carriers would first finish off *Mogami* and the two DesDiv 8 destroyers. Then after temporarily withdrawing east, it was expected that they would turn again and attack the Invasion Force on the morning of the 7th.

This would never do. Accordingly, at 1550 Yamamoto decided he would take the Main Body south after Kondō to guard against this worst-case scenario.[77] Simultaneously, he hoped to lure the enemy carriers within range of Wake Island's bombers. With any luck, a close night engagement could be forced in this way, too. The alternative was to risk waiting until the morning of 7 June, braving a hail of enemy air attacks, and then hoping to charge into the enemy's midst. If all the available planes from *Zuihō* and *Hōshō* could somehow destroy the enemy's flight decks, the Main Body might make it into gun range.

Doing so, however, would require rescheduling the fleet's appointed refueling rendezvous a second time.[78] This had originally been scheduled for morning of the 6th but had been moved back twenty-four hours to the morning of the 7th. Now it was shifted again and the tankers told to proceed to a different locale by the next afternoon, with fueling most likely to occur on the 8th.[79] It was likewise decided to shift the tanker train further south, as Ugaki feared that while Kondō was rushing south through fog at twenty knots, he was "not paying attention to anything other than rescuing the second half of the Seventh Cruiser Division."[80] In other words, in his zest to rescue *Mogami*, Kondō might well run out of fuel.

In fact, Kondō's wasn't the only formation in such danger. Yamamoto's own destroyers were running low as well, making the refueling DesRon 3 and DesRon 10 absolutely essential. The only way to do so was from the fleet's battleships, and shortly after 1700 the Main Body swung around to course 040 and began refueling its escorts. During the same period, the opportunity was taken to shift more of *Kidō Butai*'s survivors from the crowded destroyers to *Nagato* and *Mutsu*. Finally, after each destroyer had taken on an average of 150 tons of fuel, refueling was suspended at 2330.[81] Fifteen minutes after midnight, *Yamato* came about and resumed her dash southward at eighteen knots.

In these early morning hours of 7 June, Yamamoto tried to grab whatever rest he could. But it was difficult, for he was suffering from an acute stomachache (later discovered to be an infestation of roundworms).[82] Under the circumstances, the chief's condition concerned Ugaki and his staff almost as much as the possibility of contact with the enemy. There was one bit of good news, though. From the north came word that Hosogaya's Aleutians Force had made a successful surprise landing on Kiska Island at 0120. Not long after, word came that Attu Island had been taken as well.[83] A long, uncertain night followed, with nerves taut and tensions high, as Kondō's force might report engaging the enemy at any moment.

However, the morning brought neither enemy attacks, nor even snooping planes. At length, Kondō reported that he had sent out search aircraft far and wide, but had found only empty sea. Even longer-ranged searches from Wake Island came back with the same negative answer. It gradually dawned on the Japanese that the U.S. carrier force had withdrawn from the scene. Ugaki remarked at this point that "We had no choice but to give up our intention of launching an all-out counterattack with the whole Combined Fleet."[84]

These words signaled the abolition of the final Japanese hopes of somehow reversing the verdict of what more than one called "The Tragic Battle." Spruance's prudence had paid off. For the Japanese, it meant that saving *Mogami* and DesDiv 8 "despite their being considered doomed for a while,"[85] was the only apparent consolation prize of the battle, along with securing two miserable, mist-shrouded islands in the Aleutians.

Unbeknownst to Yamamoto, though, the dawn of the 7th brought the final, and clearly the most important, Japanese accomplishment of this otherwise disastrous campaign. At 0501 *Yorktown* finally sank. It had been apparent during the dawn hours that her end was near. Finally, at 0443 she had turned completely onto her port beam ends, revealing the deep wounds left by Tanabe's strike. For some time she just lay there, like an exhausted, harpooned whale. Then the stern began to lower, until at last gallant *Yorktown* lifted her bow ever so slightly and slid stern first beneath the waves, descending gracefully three miles to the seabed.[86] There she would lie in sepulchral darkness for nearly fifty-six years, until rediscovered in 1998 by an undersea expedition led by Dr. Robert Ballard.

Even now, with the end of the battle clearly in sight, certain loose ends vexed the harried and tired Combined Fleet staff. Since *Tanikaze*'s run back toward *Hiryū* had been interrupted, the carrier's final fate remained unclear. It was felt that if she had actually been boarded by the enemy, then they would have intercepted some indication of this in the American's radio traffic.[87] However, submarines dispatched to confirm her sinking found nothing.

As a final, and as it developed, futile ruse, the heavy cruisers *Myōkō* and *Haguro,* one destroyer division, and a tanker were ordered on the evening of the 7th to try and lure the enemy westward with false messages.[88] This effort, like all the others before them, came to nothing, though they kept at it till 13 June.[89]

However, with sunset and the descent of darkness on the 7th, at long last it was time for most of Combined Fleet to begin its weary, disconsolate voyage back to the Inland Sea. Apart from some designated reinforcements to the Aleutians covering forces, the rest of the fleet was now going home. Yet, as the fleet's course was adjusted at midnight, there came a final ignominy. During the turn to starboard, destroyer *Isonami* slammed her starboard bow into destroyer *Uranami*'s port side amidships. *Uranami* received damage to her funnel uptakes, cutting her speed to twenty-four knots, but *Isonami* got the worst of the encounter. A meter of her bow was chopped off, and she could consequently make only eleven knots.[90] Once again, a collision had dangerously cut the speed of two vessels. Though the fate of *Mikuma* and *Mogami* was still fresh in everyone's mind, DesRon 3's flagship, the light cruiser *Sendai,* stayed behind with her wounded charges. But by now the enemy was far behind, and *Sendai* would shepherd her little ones home without incident. The accident only stretched already-worn nerves, and now even the fiery Ugaki was truly ready to be quit of the whole debacle. Yamamoto had long since decided likewise. The Battle of Midway was over.

21

A Bitter Homecoming

Emperor Hirohito had not learned of how the Battle of Midway was going till nearly the end of the day on 5 June, Tokyo time, when an official of the Naval General Staff found the courage to inform the emperor of the disaster then unfolding. Stunned into silence, Hirohito had withdrawn and had held audiences only with Naval Staff officers, after which he largely kept his own counsel on the matter. Even Lord Privy Seal Kido Kōichi, one of the most-trusted members of Hirohito's inner circle, was not informed of the disaster until 8 June. Kido's diary of that fateful meeting shows that Hirohito chose to put a brave face on the matter, despite Kido's assumption that the news of the Navy's losses would cause him "untold anguish." However, the emperor's countenance "showed no trace of change."[1] Hirohito went on to declare that though the loss was regrettable, the Navy should "not lose its fighting spirit." He told Kido that he had ordered Admiral Nagano "to ensure that future operations continue [to be] bold and aggressive." For his part, Kido was suitably moved: "I was very much impressed by the courage displayed by His Majesty today and I was thankful that our country is blessed with such a good sovereign." There is some question, though, whether or not the cloistered emperor truly understood the full import of the calamity.

What *is* clear, however, is that Hirohito assumed an active role in covering up the matter. On 10 June, at a joint command liaison meeting, the Navy made a presentation on the battle that concealed the true magnitude of the losses from the Army representatives present.[2] Thus, the Army was left in the dark for some time afterward regarding the Navy's ability to carry out further operations. Moreover, Hirohito took steps to ensure that news of the disaster was tightly controlled, both within the military and Japanese society. Outside of the emperor and top members of court, almost no civilian in Japan knew what had happened. Even the knowledge disseminated among the ranks of the military was carefully controlled. On 9 June, Hirohito designated General Andō Kisaburō, a devotee of Tōjō, to serve as minister without portfolio in coordinating this task.[3]

It was a shattered, somber fleet that reentered Hashirajima on the afternoon of 14 June. The final run in toward Japan had been tense, jittery, and full of submarine alerts. Dense fog hung over the Inland Sea; so much so that the Main Body had had to be guided through the narrow Bungo Suidō by aircraft sent out from the Saeki Naval Air Group. *Yamato* dropped anchor at 1900.[4] As she did so, she was met by a launch from *Nagara,* which had made port the day before. Though he had been asked to report on the 15th, with a commendable sense of duty Admiral Nagumo chose to face Yamamoto without delay.[5] The following morning, *Nagara* drew near battleship *Kirishima.*[6] A file of boats then ferried the exhausted and frustrated officers of First Air Fleet over to her, as she had been designated the temporary headquarters of the Mobile Fleet.

Once on board, Lt. Cdr. Yoshioka Chūichi, First Air Fleet's assistant staff air officer and Commander Genda's right-hand man, began working on completing Nagumo's official report. It was already overdue, and Yoshioka had significant obstacles to surmount in compiling it. Not only did the excessive secrecy interfere with his fact checking, but only two major sources of documentation had been rescued from the destroyed ships: *Akagi*'s logbook, and the detailed action reports of the four carrier air groups. From these, Yoshioka was charged with compiling a chronicle of the action. Given the lack of available materials from the carriers, he was understandably obliged to fall back on the reports of BatDiv 3, CruDiv 8, and DesRon 10. He interviewed Nagumo and appended the admiral's written battle summary. Despite time pressures, Yoshioka ultimately completed his task with commendable skill. The result was the famous "Nagumo Report," which described the actions of First Air Fleet from 27 May to 9 June 1942.[7] The report is dated 15 June 1942, although reports were filtering in as late as 21 June.

While Yoshioka and First Air Fleet staff were thus cloistered, the rest of the fleet was recuperating, reprovisioning, and caring for the wounded. Sadly, for many of the men, making it back to port was only the beginning of their ordeal, rather than the end. On 11 June Hirohito issued a directive to the Naval General Staff that might have caused many of the sailors to doubt His Majesty's benevolence, namely, that the Midway wounded were to return to Japan under tight security and be forbidden contacts, "until they could be healed, heartened, hushed, and reassigned."[8]

This policy was put into effect as soon as the fleet reached Hashirajima. The wounded were transferred to the hospital ships *Hikawa Maru* and *Takasago Maru,* which in turn transported 280 and 338 cases, respectively, to naval hospitals at Kure, Sasebo, and Yokosuka.[9] Many of the men were classified as "secret patients" and quarantined in special wards, cut off from both other sailors and family alike, in order that no word escaped regarding *Kidō Butai*'s destruction. Both Fuchida and maintenance man Arimura suffered these indignities, as did *Sōryū*'s badly burned executive officer, Cdr. Ōhara Hisashi. Only specially cleared nurses and doctors were allowed into the wards, and there were fewer of those than need wanted. No communications in or out, not even letters from home, were permitted. Some of the men weren't allowed to leave for a year or more and were shamed by the medical staffs at having been defeated.[10]

Those left uninjured were also deemed second-class citizens. Many of the surviving officers were dispersed to outlying commands. The bulk of the enlisted men were designated as replacements for units in the South Pacific and were sent there as expeditiously as possible. No home leaves were allowed. The survivors thus were denied a final chance to say good-bye to family and loved ones before being shipped to the southern theater, where many of them would ultimately meet their deaths.[11] Thus, the Imperial Navy compounded its own errors by treating its own men shamefully.

Civilian cameraman Makishima Teiuchi, who had filmed the attacks on both *Akagi* and *Kaga,* only to lose his priceless footage in the subsequent fire, found himself in an internment camp of sorts for several weeks. Even when released, he was warned not to go to Tokyo or he would be arrested by the *kempeitai,* the dreaded military police.[12] He, too, was shortly shipped back out to the South Seas, far away from anyone to whom he could spill the beans.

To the Japanese public, the battle was portrayed as a great victory. On 11 June, for instance, the *Japan Times and Advertiser* trumpeted "Navy Scores Another Epochal Victory!" and claimed two American carriers sunk.[13] Within days, another American heavy cruiser and submarine were added for good measure. Japanese losses were left curiously vague, although an 11 June broadcast with prominent civilian naval commentator Itō Masanori noted that Japan had lost two carriers in return. Nevertheless, this was a small price to pay, Itō said, considering the "brilliant war results" obtained off Midway, which were "beyond all imagination." The latter statement was certainly true, but not in the way Itō intended.[14]

This marked a rather radical departure in the history of Japanese wartime propaganda. Up until then, it had been customary to provide filtered views of the fighting in China that avoided unpleasant details. However, the Japanese news had not previously resorted to telling blatantly fabricated lies. Hirohito, though, was pleased with the public's response and the next day floated the idea of issuing an Imperial Rescript to the commanders at Midway commemorating Midway.[15] Hirohito's advisers, however, persuaded him otherwise, pointing out that things were not so desperate as to lower His Majesty's heretofore sacred pronouncements to the level of propaganda.

From the Midway wounded, however, there was no way that the disaster could be concealed entirely. Maeda Takeshi, recovering from his leg wound, found out about the Navy's cover-up when one of the nurses snuck a copy of *Asahi Shimbun,* Japan's leading daily newspaper, into his ward. There, large as life, were the headlines that Maeda knew were all a "big lie."[16] To Maeda's way of thinking, if Japan had to resort to such outrageous deceits, it couldn't win the war.

On 10 June, the Navy Ministry had sent a message to its commands, declaring, "it was decided to quote our damage in the Midway Sea Battle as one carrier lost, one carrier heavily damaged, one cruiser heavily damaged, and 35 planes failing to return."[17] Officially, Ugaki announced on the 15th that, "except for those made public by the General Staff, nothing should be revealed about Midway and the Aleutian operation inside of as well as outside the Navy. In the Navy it would be announced that *Kaga* was lost, while *Sōryū* and *Mikuma* were seriously damaged, but their names would not be announced in public."[18] The final policy on how the Battle of Midway was to be "understood" or reported, even in official communications, was fixed and issued on 21 June. A bulletin by the chief of staff for the Sixth Fleet spelled out the new orthodoxy:

As for the ships lost and heavily damaged [at Midway], the policy about announcing is [that] secrecy will be maintained . . . and discretion manfully exerted.

Kaga, Sōryū, and *Mikuma* will be taken off the ship's register when there is suitable opportunity.

Akagi and *Hiryū* will remain on the ship's register for the time being, but will not be manned.

The transfer [reassignment] of crews will be ordered gradually.

Concerning those KIA, the personnel bureau and personnel section will gradually notify the families of the deceased, but the name of the ship sunk will not be mentioned. The policy is to handle the killed merely as individuals. . . .

Concerning damages: *Akagi* and *Hiryū* both caught fire and were heavily damaged. *Tanikaze, Isokaze,* and *Arashi*: each slightly damaged. *Mogami, Isonami,* and *Uranami* were hit. *Mogami* moderately damaged, and others, slightly damaged.[19]

Thus, the need for secrecy trumped all other considerations. This gives an indication about how the aftermath of the battle was discussed, even into the postwar years. In an immediate sense, the admission that *Akagi* and *Hiryū* were so heavily damaged as to be unmanned may have been just a face-saving move. Reading between the lines, it still meant that all four carriers had been knocked out. What is equally intriguing is the point-blank obfuscation regarding *Akagi* and *Hiryū*'s scuttlings, despite literally thousands of witnesses. Similarly, one wonders why there was a difference between the details of *Sōryū* and *Kaga*'s fabricated fates and those of *Akagi* and *Hiryū*. It suggests that the scuttling of *Sōryū* and *Kaga* may even have been concealed from the Naval General Staff after the battle. Given such an atmosphere, it is not surprising that many of the records of the battle (ship's logs, war diaries, etc.) were destroyed after the war.

No such indignities as were heaped on the Navy's wounded were inflicted on Combined Fleet's leadership or staff, despite their bearing most of the immediate responsibility for the catastrophe. In fact, to outward appearances, nothing happened that would indicate a great battle had just been lost. No announcements were made. No heads rolled, nor were there any major changes made to staff appointments. Admiral Yamamoto was still in charge of Combined Fleet. Admiral Nagumo was put back in charge of the new carrier force centered on *Shōkaku* and *Zuikaku.*

To the Western observer, this all seems rather incredible. After all, Yamamoto and Nagumo had just presided over a naval disaster rivaling Salamis or Trafalgar. Without delving too deeply into the reasons and responsibility for the disaster (we'll deal with that shortly), the fact remains that in a Western navy, a failure of this magnitude would most likely have resulted in the swift punishment of any responsible parties. At the very least, careers would have been ruined. Yet, Nagumo continued in his current role until October 1942, and Yamamoto would remain head of Combined Fleet until his death in April 1943. How did this occur?

The short answer is that even in the wake of his greatest defeat, Yamamoto was still in a position of strength. First, at least in the eyes of the Japanese public, which had been fed a steady diet of victory since the outbreak, Yamamoto was the "genius" behind the Navy's triumphs. Having just proclaimed Japan's most recent "victory," cashiering a man who spent a significant portion of his time answering adulatory fan mail from the nation's schoolchildren would raise ugly questions as to why he was being replaced.

Indeed, even in the dark days of late 1944, when any fool could tell that the war wasn't going well, Japan's military *never* had the moral fortitude to admit that it had lost so much as a single battle to date. With the Navy already in cover-up mode after Midway, how could anyone, even within the Navy, come out and say what needed to be said? This speaks volumes about the larger needs of the Navy as an organization— that the assessment of responsibility (and the ability to truly learn from the battle) was secondary to preserving internal solidarity and organizational loyalty while maintaining outward appearances.[20]

It must be remembered that the defeat at Midway had an impact on interservice relationships with the Army. The underlying tensions between the two services remained fixed, and it is almost certain that the Navy would have wanted to prevent the Army from making any hay as a result of the defeat. Indeed, the Navy initially concealed the full extent of its losses even from Tōjō, despite the fact that he was the head of the government.[21] As such, it is perhaps not surprising that the Navy was reluctant to undertake dramatic shake-ups in Combined Fleet's command structure.

The same motivation was true for Naval GHQ. Admitting failure at Midway also meant admitting that the Navy's strategy-making procedures had been hijacked by a subordinate command. Throughout the 1920s and 1930s, numerous incidents of such insubordination had occurred within both branches of the services. The truth was that superior commanders within the Japanese military hardly ever brought their subordinates to heel, and Admiral Nagano wasn't about to start with Yamamoto.

While the Japanese utterly failed to come to terms with their defeat at the level of high command, the Navy itself *did* make adjustments. In the area of carrier design and operation, for instance, the Japanese reacted in several ways. First and foremost, a higher proportion of refueling and rearming activities were now to be performed on the flight deck. It was recognized that the enclosed space of the hangar, while better sheltered, also held the potential for disaster should a hit be taken. Japan's carrier designs also morphed to meet the perceived threat. Carrier *Taihō*, then building, would sport a heavily armored flight deck, as would supercarrier *Shinano*—converted from the hull of a *Yamato*-class battleship. Both of these carriers were intended to operate in the fore of any new battle, serving as armored refueling points for the air groups of the more vulnerable fleet carriers coming up behind. These latter vessels—the carriers of the *Unryū* class that would emerge in 1944—were almost carbon copies of the basic *Hiryū* design. Yet, they would incorporate important improvements. Each had only two elevators, augmenting the strength of the flight deck (albeit at the cost of slowing deck operations). Increased use of foam firefighting equipment was incorporated, and the Navy also began to employ the American technique of draining fuel lines when not in use. Portable damage-control equipment, such as gas-powered pumps, would begin making its appearance later in the war as well.

Not surprisingly, the whole topic of damage-control procedures was reappraised, particularly with respect to firefighting technique. Accordingly, new courses for damage control were established.[22] Specially selected enlisted men from the ship construction and engineering branches were given one-week courses at the Workshop and Repair School in the fundamentals of damage-control technique.[23] Likewise, all line officers were given at least some training, amounting to about two weeks during wartime. However, the Navy was churning out officers and enlisted men at a prodigious rate. Training for line officers had fallen from three years to just eighteen months, and that of enlisted men had dropped from six months to four. A few week's worth of training was hardly sufficient to transform raw recruits into seasoned practitioners, especially when it appears that much of the training was less hands-on than simply watching demonstrations in firefighting given by "the experts."[24] This was compensated, to a degree, by regular exercises aboard ship.[25] However, *Shōkaku*'s, *Hiyō*'s, and *Taihō*'s subsequent losses because of faulty damage control, particularly with regard to firefighting technique, leaves open the question as to whether or not the Japanese actually made significant strides in these areas after Midway.

Pilot training also had to be accelerated in the wake of such a serious defeat, and the Japanese took steps in this direction as well. The numbers of cadet pilots graduating had already increased in 1941, although they would not swell dramatically until 1943. In this way, the Japanese managed somehow to continue fielding air units throughout the theater.[26] However, the way in which the Japanese went about fulfilling their needs was far from optimal.[27] Given their numerical inferiority, it was inevitable that the length of training would decline as the war went on. Yet the Japanese made no effort to ensure that the training that *was* provided was of the best possible quality. This, in turn, was linked directly to the uncaring attitude with which the Japanese military treated its human capital. Unlike the United States, which rotated experienced aviators home and then either promoted them to squadron commands or put them into training billets, Japanese aviators were rarely furloughed. Often, this was simply the result of vast difficulties encountered by Japan's overworked merchant marine in moving men and matériel around such an enormous battlefield. But the common lament in the forward squadrons became *Shinanakute wa kaeshite moraenai*—"They won't let you go home unless you die."[28]

The outcomes of Japan's belated expansion of her pilot training program were twofold. First, the vital knowledge and techniques of the veteran airmen were not passed along in turn to the newer Japanese aviators being rushed into service. As a result, these youngsters were fed raw into combat against increasingly well-trained American pilots. The quality of Japanese air groups, as a result, became increasingly uneven, with diminished cohesiveness in comparison to the elite early-war squadrons. Often, too, these replacement pilots made crucial mistakes early in their combat careers that led to their simply being killed off, when a similar error in training might have been caught and corrected had more experienced instructors been present. Japan's combat aircraft, which lacked adequate protection for their pilots, only compounded this trend. Thus, by the end of 1942, Allied intelligence had already noticed the beginnings of a sharp decline in the effectiveness of Japanese air units.

This was negatively reinforced by the second major outcome of Japan's misguided pilot rotation policy—the deterioration of the veteran aviators themselves. Caught in the horrendous physical conditions of the South Pacific, where heat, humidity, disease, and poor food and water were the norm, and subjected to the unremitting strain of combat, many of the early-war veterans inevitably fell apart physically and emotionally. Despite their fearsome early-war reputations, Japanese aviators weren't supermen, and no one could reasonably be expected to continue functioning under such conditions indefinitely. As a result, even men with hundreds of hours of combat under their belts became increasingly sloppy and uncaring. In a military that already took the word "fatalism" to new extremes, the results were inevitably much higher casualties among senior aviators than real need demanded. As 1943 opened, therefore, airmen from the prewar cadres were more and more difficult to find—they had almost all been killed.

Intriguingly, one of the most immediate effects from the Battle of Midway was a change to Japanese carrier doctrine. In this area, at least, the Japanese made an honest effort to diagnose and correct what had gone wrong. In fact, this process actually began before the fleet anchored at Hashirajima. At 0800 on 10 June,[29] as the Main Body was still steaming back to Japan, *Yamato* had requested *Nagara* to come alongside. One by one, the members of First Air Fleet staff were winched over to the battleship via breeches buoy. They were then shown below to meet with Yamamoto in the admiral's cabin.

It was an emotional moment. Ugaki remarked later that Nagumo's staff were still in their heavy winter uniforms and looked "considerably exhausted" by their ordeal.[30] The atmosphere was uncomfortable. Kusaka, ashamed, started the briefing by saying, "Admittedly, we are not in a position to come back alive after having made such a blunder, but we have come back only to pay off the scores some day." He had concluded by asking Yamamoto to give them another chance. Yamamoto, obviously deeply moved, replied that he would.

Kusaka had then proceeded to report on the reasons for the disaster. Among other things, he noted that the searches on the flanks of the Carrier Force were not sufficient and opined that it would have been better to have launched some aircraft earlier in the morning, before daylight, with others launched closer to dawn. Here, indeed, was the genesis for the more sophisticated two-phased searches that would later be formalized within the Imperial Navy's scouting doctrine. Kusaka, rather presciently, also anticipated the need for functionalizing the carrier divisions within a task force, including using one group for attacking, and another for maintaining the readiness of a reserve force. He further advocated the usage of a dedicated carrier for interceptors. Crucially, Kusaka also acknowledged that there were situations when speed of reaction was more important than an escorted strike.[31] It's clear that a number of these elements were carried forward into Combined Fleet's reassessment of its doctrine.

This process continued rapidly after the fleet made port in Kure. The first, most visible change was the disbanding of First Air Fleet, which was renamed Third Fleet. The Fifth Carrier Division (*Shōkaku* and *Zuikaku*) was officially recognized as the core of this new carrier force and was renumbered the First Carrier Division. CarDiv

4 (*Junyō, Hiyō,* and *Ryūjō*) was renumbered CarDiv 2. Battleships *Hiei* and *Kirishima* (now designated the 11th Battleship Division) were attached directly to Third Fleet, thereby formally removing them from the battle line and First Fleet. Likewise, the two operational survivors of CruDiv 7 (*Kumano* and *Suzaya*), and the veterans of CruDiv 8 (*Tone* and *Chikuma*) were directly attached to Third Fleet as well.[32]

Third Fleet's core unit was to remain the carrier division, but it would be a three-ship unit composed of two heavy and one light carriers. The light carrier was charged with fleet defense and would carry primarily fighters. The heavy carriers would retain a mixed air wing, but the mixture of aircraft was adjusted. Fewer torpedo aircraft were to be carried, in preference for more fighters and dive-bombers. *Shōkaku* and *Zuikaku*'s fighter and dive-bomber complements were increased from twenty-one to twenty-seven apiece, while the torpedo planes were reduced from twenty-one to eighteen. The roles of the aircraft were modified as well, with faster, more agile dive-bombers designated as the main attack weapon for holing flight decks and rendering the enemy carriers inoperative. Torpedo planes would then be used to attack and sink damaged carriers.[33]

The battle plan for the carrier fleet was changed drastically as well. Much like the agonizing reappraisal that the U.S. Navy had undergone in the aftermath of Pearl Harbor, the Imperial Navy now grappled with the doctrinal consequences of its own calamity. Combined Fleet for the first time now explicitly recognized that the aircraft carrier was "the center, the main objective, of the Decisive Air Battle; surface forces will cooperate with them."[34] The battle squadrons of the Navy were subordinated to the purposes of the carriers—a radical shift in attitude. Given its earlier triumphs, of course, it is ironic that the Imperial Navy had taken six months longer than its opponent to come to this conclusion. But from now on, battleships and other screening units were to be directly incorporated in the carrier fleet, and would steam with them to the anticipated scene of battle.[35] Direct visual contact would be maintained with all units, so that the force as a whole could operate under conditions of strict radio silence. The carrier fleet would also rely more heavily on the reconnaissance assets of other vessels and land-based air groups.

However, upon reaching the battle area, the screening forces were to be split off. A novel formation was worked out that was designed to provide the maximal amount of warning time to the carriers of incoming enemy air attacks, even at the expense of the fleet's battleships. The carrier division was to be preceded by a scouting line of battleships, cruisers, and destroyers that would be placed anywhere from 100 to 200 nautical miles in front of the carriers. These vessels were to be arranged in line abreast, spaced apart roughly at the limits of visual range. In addition to giving earlier warning of enemy aircraft, the scouting line also placed the eyes of the fleet (the cruiser and battleship scout planes) in the van, where they could find the enemy more easily. In addition, it was felt that a widely distributed van formation would aid search aircraft attempting to return to the fleet when all ships were operating under conditions of radio silence. A friendly plane had a good chance of running across at least one of the vessels in the van, which could in turn direct it to its mother ship. Finally, the heavy units in the van itself could be used to attack enemy units with gunfire that had already been damaged by dive-bomber attacks, thus augmenting the ship-killing power of the fleet as a whole.[36]

The proposed formation was not without its share of critics. It was recognized that the ships in the van were likely to absorb damage for the carriers. While this was not an "official" function of the van, it was apparent enough to the officers who would command the vessels located there, eliciting criticism that they were "nothing but sacrifices for the carriers."[37] Furthermore, it was felt by some that the detachment of the van units left the carriers less well screened than they ought to have been. Conversely, the lack of screening units might be compensated for by a lessened chance of being attacked in the first place. Given that the carriers were almost solely responsible for providing their own flak in any case, this rationalization may not have been as far-fetched as it appears. It was also hoped that the installation of radar would aid the fleet's air defenses still further.[38] However, the very shape of the screening dispositions betrayed a lack of understanding of radar's potential in antiair warfare.[39]

As it happened, these new plans had just been agreed upon in principle by Third Fleet's staff when the campaign at Guadalcanal burst forth unexpectedly. News had come in on Friday, 7 August, that the islands of Tulagi and Guadalcanal had been heavily attacked and that American carriers were operating off the islands. *Shōkaku, Zuikaku,* and *Ryūjō* all sortied for Truk, with the intent of battling the Americans immediately thereafter. Third Fleet staff's plans were so new that their doctrinal concepts hadn't been distributed to Admiral Nagumo's ships before they left. It was hoped that the fleet's staff would have time to go over them at Truk. However, as events transpired, CarDiv 1 didn't even call at Truk before heading to what would later be called the Battle of the Eastern Solomons. To get the plans to Nagumo, a naval aircraft flew them out to the carriers and delivered them by hand. No time was available for any training exercises. As a result, Third Fleet's new doctrine had little impact on the battle itself.

The tale of Third Fleet's doctrinal developments is a fitting place to end our narrative, because it is a parable for how the Imperial Navy would fight the remainder of the Pacific war—a day late, and a dollar short. Third Fleet's efforts at self-appraisal were honest, and their resulting doctrine contained some useful elements. If nothing else, the Navy's new battle plan finally placed the aircraft carrier at the apex of its naval hierarchy and sought meaningful ways for the fleet's heavy units to contribute to the success of the carriers, rather than the other way around. But these efforts were completely eclipsed by the speed with which the Americans had gone over from the defense to the offense. Their ability to launch a counteroffensive in a theater of operations as far flung as the Solomon Islands was truly stunning and caught the Japanese completely by surprise. From now on, it was the Americans who would hold the initiative. The Japanese would still win tactical victories, but for all their efforts they would never be able to reassert any meaningful influence over the flow of strategic events. In the end, Third Fleet's efforts would not be remembered as being a key element in the resurrection of Japan's carrier force. Rather, it would be nothing more than a footnote in the coming tale of the total ruination of the Japanese Navy.

PART III
Reckonings

22

Why Did Japan Lose?

ven sixty years on, correctly identifying the reasons for Japan's defeat at Midway is not a simple task, because the battle defies simple answers. Indeed, the scale and complexity of the struggle result in a host of possible reasons for the catastrophe. Unfortunately, many of these reasons turn out to be proximate, rather than root causes. Yet, if any lessons are to be gained from history, the true sources of failure must be uncovered. It is to a careful consideration of these issues that we now turn.

This quest will necessarily set aside the more prominent reasons on the American side for their having *won* the battle. Code breaking, of course, stands at the top of the list, and Admiral Chester Nimitz's bold leadership, as well as strong performances by Admirals Frank Jack Fletcher and Raymond Spruance played important roles. Finally, the individual skill and bravery of the American soldiers, sailors, and airmen involved in many cases provided the difference between victory and defeat. But all of these were factors beyond Japan's control. And it is safe to say that even despite these virtues, the Americans could not have won the battle without the unwitting assistance of their foes. Given the disparity in the naval forces then available in the Pacific, Midway was truly the Imperial Navy's to lose. Why did they do so?

An appropriate place to begin the search is with the contemporary Japanese perspectives on the matter. Before Admiral Kusaka ever set foot on board *Yamato* on 10 June, he had clearly been doing a great deal of thinking on the reasons for the defeat. Inevitably, given his proximity to the battle and his ignorance of American code-breaking activities, some of his conclusions were valid, some less so. In Kusaka's opinion, the Nagumo Force's fogbound radio transmission on the 2nd might well have led to their detection. Kusaka also noted that the aerial searches on the eastern flank of the force were not commenced early enough and should perhaps have been launched before dawn. The fact that all four of Nagumo's carriers were slated to carry out attacks on Midway, as well as holding forces in reserve, Kusaka felt, led to confusion when the initial sightings of American carriers were reported.[1] He also bemoaned the lack of fighters for the second attack wave (although we know in retrospect that this is questionable), and that concentrating the force's carriers meant they were caught in a group.[2]

Admiral Ugaki, in his own personal diary, endorsed some aspects of Kusaka's analysis, such as the disadvantages associated with tactical concentration of the force's carriers. He noted, too, the lack of adequate reconnaissance. However, Ugaki was less concerned with Nagumo's scouting at the tactical level than he was with the failure of Operation K (which left the departure of the American carriers from Pearl Harbor undetected) and the fact that the heightened state of alert on Midway itself had not been adequately understood. He noted that the sheer size of the operation, and the distribution of the forces, was such that Nagumo could not be rapidly reinforced when needed. Ugaki also rightly harbored doubts concerning the security of Japanese plans. Whether the Americans had detected Japanese forces as they sortied from bases like Saipan, or the Northern forces had been sighted by a Russian merchant ship, or Japanese radio security had simply been inadequate, Ugaki did not know, but his "suspicion about these questions [was] not lacking."[3] Finally, Ugaki conceded that the main cause for the defeat might have been "that we had become conceited because of past success" and thereby failed to anticipate the steps that might need to be taken if an "enemy air force should appear on [Nagumo's] flank."[4] As we shall see, the Imperial Navy's hubris before the battle is a theme that has resonated with historians down to the present day, and for good reason.

Fuchida Mitsuo, writing shortly after the war, expanded on the theme of overconfidence, ascribing it to what he referred to as "Victory Disease" (shōribyō)—a fatal conceit and sloppiness born of contempt for the enemy. Beyond such moral failings, Fuchida also expounded a litany of faults in other aspects of the operation, including a lack of strategic intelligence on American actions and faulty scouting arrangements both before and on the day of the battle.[5] To these were added the dispersion of Japanese forces, caused by a failure to maintain focus on the primary objective of the operation—the destruction of the enemy fleet. Instead of keeping this goal "unequivocally fixed as the foremost aim of the operation," Combined Fleet allowed its plans to be driven by an "undue emphasis on securing the best possible meteorological conditions for the Midway landing operations."[6] Fuchida also commented on the technological backwardness of the Imperial Navy (as manifested by its lack of radar) and its continuing reliance on the battleship as the arm of decision.[7]

At the level of command, Fuchida also rightly contended that Admiral Yamamoto's insistence on directing the operation from on board Yamato had hampered his control of the battle. Admiral Nagumo, in turn, was faulted for failing to "enforce adequate search dispositions on the morning of the Midway strike."[8] More questionably, though, Fuchida cited the admiral for failing to use a two-phase search, as well as failing to dispatch a replacement for Tone's No. 4 plane instantly when it became apparent that its launch would be delayed. In this, Fuchida overlooked the fact that two-phase search techniques had yet to be incorporated into doctrine. Likewise, he ignored the fact that even had Tone's sole remaining long-range search aircraft been ready, the time required to get it on the catapult, warmed up, and into the air would hardly have been less than it actually took to launch Amari. The same criticism, of course, applies to any notion of replacing the cruiser scout with an additional Type 97 from either Akagi or Kaga.

Thus, the Japanese were fairly perceptive in identifying many of the proximate causes of the defeat, though obviously both Ugaki and Fuchida were totally unaware of the code-breaking activities that had played such a critical part in the American victory. Fuchida had also identified perhaps the strongest recurring emotional theme of the battle—the conceit of the Japanese. Not surprisingly, though, neither Ugaki nor Fuchida was able or willing to take their analysis further to look at *organizational* failings within the Navy. Admiral Ugaki did apparently offer Kusaka and First Air Fleet staff apologies on behalf of Combined Fleet headquarters for its faults in the battle.[9] However, this was little more than a polite nothing that reflected no real contrition or reflection on his part. Instead, the sense that one gets from Ugaki's diary is that things were very much business as usual in Combined Fleet after the defeat. There were no wrenching reassessments regarding how strategic command was exercised within the Navy.

Turning to the Americans, and their perceived reasons for Japan's defeat, the very technical postwar study conducted at the American Naval War College rightly cited the overconfidence of Japanese forces.[10] Likewise, Yamamoto's excessive reliance on the element of surprise in developing his plans was carefully noted. In the war college's opinion, though, a truly cardinal sin was Yamamoto's designing his plan around America's *perceived intentions* rather than their *capabilities*.[11] In so doing, Yamamoto blinded himself to the possibility that the Americans might actually wish to fight and might therefore intentionally place themselves in a position to do so.

Other American commentators have mirrored this tendency to ascribe the Japanese defeat to errors of analysis, while also picking up on the Victory Disease theme. For instance, Gordon Prange, in his widely read *Miracle at Midway,* mirrored Fuchida's opinion that the Japanese had forgotten the principle of the objective and had focused on capturing the island rather than on destroying U.S. ships.[12] Likewise, he echoed Fuchida's opinion that Yamamoto's commanding the battle from on board *Yamato* had been a mistake.[13] Prange also correctly noted that Japan had lost the element of surprise, had dispersed its forces over too great an area, and therefore lacked superiority at the point of contact.[14]

More questionably, however, he criticized the Japanese for having failed to carry on the fight even after *Hiryū*'s demise, asserting:

> Yamamoto's forces still far outnumbered and outweighed Fletcher's in surface units. Even in carriers, from his own, Kondō's, and the Aleutian Force he could have summoned one carrier and three light carriers, with a total air strength of about fifty Zeros and sixty bombers. This was air power not to be shrugged off, especially as the Japanese believed they had sunk two out of three U.S. flattops. Instead, following the loss of Nagumo's carriers, Yamamoto . . . scurried homeward with his massive force like a lumbering Saint Bernard . . . pursued by a scrappy terrier.[15]

This is folly, of course, as his analysis totally discounts the primary role of airpower in the battle, as well as the fatally dispersed nature of the air assets left to the Japanese, none of which were true fleet carriers. It likewise fails to acknowledge Nagumo's aggressiveness in the afternoon of the 4th, or Yamamoto's unsuccessful attempts to lure Spruance's forces into another engagement on the 6th and 7th. Prange concluded his analysis with a rather strange admonition of Nagumo for having made Tomonaga's morning attack against Midway *overlarge* for its intended purpose. Prange's notion that the initial attack should have been conducted on a scale more on par with Kakuta's much smaller attack on Dutch Harbor is clearly misguided, as it violates the cardinal military principle of using the maximum practical force available so as to simultaneously increase the enemy's casualties, while minimizing one's own.[16]

Walter Lord, author of the other seminal American account of the battle, *Incredible Victory,* placed *Tone* No. 4's delayed departure, as well as Nagumo's decision to rearm his aircraft for a second attack against Midway, at the top of his list of failures for the battle. Without fully understanding the dynamics of Japanese carrier operations, he understandably also blames Nagumo for not having attacked the American carriers as soon as they were detected. Lord correctly noted the rigidity of Japanese planning—in that the Americans were expected to react in a scripted fashion—as well as the fatal dispersion of Japanese forces.[17] Not surprisingly, too, he also commented on the "dangerous contempt" for the enemy, as manifested in Victory Disease.

As can be seen, the majority of the reasons uncovered by both Japanese and American observers were proximate causes, with one exception—Victory Disease. Thus, the first task requisite with the completion of this survey of the reasons for defeat is to examine more closely this important recurring theme. It is demonstrable, though, that Victory Disease was only one among a considerable number of key factors in the defeat.

The term "Victory Disease" is commonly used to designate the casual, overconfident mental attitude that took hold in the Japanese Navy after an uninterrupted string of victories in the first six months of the conflict. The resulting loss of operational sharpness, and the rash of sloppy mistakes that followed, are held up by many as being a fundamental cause for the defeat. The man who first popularized the phrase, Fuchida Mitsuo, noted that the chief symptom of the disease was simple conceit. It was the Navy's "arrogant underestimation of the enemy," as well as its "blithe assumption that [the enemy] would be taken by surprise" that led to the catastrophe. Fuchida chalked up the dispersal of forces under Yamamoto's battle plan to similar arrogance. Yet, in his opinion, the malady was more dire than many other observers noted. Victory Disease, Fuchida asserted, was responsible not just for the defeat at Midway, but was "the root cause of Japan's defeat . . . in the entire war" as well. Further, he felt that Victory Disease's root causes lay not just in six months of victories, but rather in the Japanese national character. Fuchida wrote that, "there is an irrationality and impulsiveness about our people which results in actions that are haphazard and often contradictory. A tradition of provincialism makes us narrow-minded and dogmatic, reluctant to discard prejudices and slow to adopt even necessary improvements if they require a new concept." He concluded that these weaknesses "rendered fruitless all the valiant deeds and precious sacrifices of the men who fought [at Midway]."[18]

Other Japanese veterans have commented on this phenomenon as well. For his part, Cdr. Chihaya Masatake acidly remarked that Midway was "the most splendid defeat the Japanese Navy had scored in its history up to that date," though many defeats even "more splendid were yet to come." In his opinion, the cause of that defeat "was nothing to wonder about. We as good as planned for it. If we had escaped that terrible disaster on that occasion, we should have met the same fate somewhere else in the Pacific theater, perhaps in the course of 1942. . . . [It was] something pre-ordained. Why? Because it was visited on the Japanese navy to penalize its absurd self-conceit."[19]

It must be admitted that the concept of Victory Disease has a certain appeal to it. The Japanese *were* overconfident going into the battle. They *were* guilty of ignoring the various warning signs that manifested themselves from the time of Coral Sea onward. They *did* underestimate the resolve and the fighting abilities of the Americans. Yet, to suggest that six months of easy victories, or even years of hubris before the war, had proven fatally corrosive to the rational faculties of Japanese commanders from Yamamoto on down seems too simplistic. After all, humble militaries don't typically win. Indeed, before Midway, self-confidence to the point of arrogance was a crucial ingredient in Japan's *victories*. Thus, while the symptoms of this mental malady certainly played a significant part in the outcome, Victory Disease alone does not explain the breadth or the enormity of Japan's defeat at Midway.[20] It was an important factor, but only one of several.

Likewise, arbitrarily selecting a group of command decisions (and the individuals to go with them) to blame for the defeat is also too simplistic. This cuts against the grain of many military histories, since books on great battles customarily end by pointing the finger of blame at *somebody,* to establish responsibility for the defeat. This is not to say that there isn't ample personal blame to be apportioned regarding Midway—there is. Indeed, at a superficial level, it would be fairly easy to pick out three crucial personal failures, a cursory accounting of which (albeit with a slightly revisionist twist) might go something as follows.

Personal failure number one was the inability of *Chikuma*'s No. 1 search plane to detect the American carriers on search line No. 5 between about 0615 and 0630. This stands in contrast to the conventional wisdom, which holds that it was *Tone* No. 4's late launch, combined with Nagumo's decision to rearm his reserve aircraft with land attack weapons, that ultimately doomed the Japanese forces. But a careful examination of the facts shows that *Tone* No. 4's failings, while serious, were also somewhat immaterial to the larger issue. Likewise, Nagumo's decision to rearm, while ultimately costing his force some amount of time, was also immaterial to this same problem; namely, that by 0630 the Japanese could no longer forestall the launch of the American aircraft that would crush *Kidō Butai*. Neither *Tone* No. 4's late launch nor Nagumo's rearmament orders had any bearing on this fatal loss of initiative. And once lost, it is almost certain that no admiral—not Nagumo, not Yamaguchi, perhaps not even Horatio Nelson himself—would be able to get it back.

The issue of *Chikuma* No. 1's oversight leads to the second critical failure—Commander Genda's search plan. The lack of a two-phase search—even if it had been incorporated into Japanese doctrine at the time—had nothing to do with the case. The basic problem was simply too few airplanes and too much ocean to cover. Had more aircraft been aloft, and their search sectors been overlapping, *Chikuma* No. 1's failure might not have been irretrievable. As it was, the breaking of a single link of the reconnaissance plan led to the complete unraveling of the plan as a whole.[21]

The final failure, of course, lies in Admiral Yamamoto's battle plan. There is no question that his operational scheme featured an overly rigid timetable and a counterproductive dispersal of forces. By making the assumption that the Americans were beaten, and therefore had to be baited into fighting, Yamamoto made the crucial mistake of letting perceived intentions on the part of the Americans drive his force structure and dispositions.[22] The plan that emerged from this flawed belief was a crazy quilt of formations and objectives, none of which were mutually supporting. When one of the legs of the table was kicked out, the entire article promptly collapsed under the weight of its own foolishness. The result was a catastrophe worthy of Xerxes at Salamis, or Czar Alexander I at Austerlitz.

However, while assigning blame to particular individuals may be emotionally satisfying, in many cases it only identifies proximate causes and fails to probe the roots of the defeat. *Why* was Genda's search plan so scanty? *Why* was Yamamoto's battle plan flawed? Would a different air officer have created a better search plan for *Kidō Butai*? And by the same token, would another Japanese admiral have created a sounder operational plan for Combined Fleet? As will be seen, the answer to both of these questions is "Probably not." Or at least not in early 1942. Why is *that*? To resolve these issues, a closer examination of the whole nature of failure within military institutions is required, as well as a deeper understanding of the Imperial Navy's culture.

To this end, important insights can be gleaned from the cogent study by Eliot Cohen and John Gooch entitled *Military Misfortunes: The Anatomy of Failure in War*, which lays out a useful framework for analyzing why militaries fail in battle.[23] As *Military Misfortunes* points out, there has been a natural tendency on the part of both the public and historians to assign blame mostly to individuals, "criminalizing" military failure by indicting one or more commanders. While such an approach is superficially appealing, it often ignores deeper layers of organizational failure. Cohen and Gooch make an important point, since modern military commanders rarely exercise absolute power over their forces and are unable to survey the entire battlefield over which they exercise command. In addition, as militaries have grown more complex to tackle larger, more demanding missions, their internal systems—doctrine, training, staff operations, even how a group of aircraft is spotted and launched from a flight deck—have grown more complex as well, and thereby more prone to failure. This is certainly true of the Japanese at Midway. This is not to say that individuals did not make mistakes. But by the same token, upon closer examination, it is clear that it wasn't just Yamamoto or Genda who failed at Midway—in several important ways, the entire institution of the Japanese Navy was to blame as well.

Cohen and Gooch propose that all military failures fall into three basic categories: failure to learn from the past, failure to anticipate what the future may bring, and failure to adapt to the immediate circumstances on the battlefield. They further note that when one of these three basic failures occurs in isolation (known as a *simple failure*), the results, while unpleasant, can often also be overcome. *Aggregate failures* occur when two of the basic failure types, usually learning and anticipation, take place simultaneously, and these are more difficult to surmount. Finally, at the apex of failure stand those rare events when all three basic failures occur simultaneously—an event known as *catastrophic failure*. In such an occurrence, the result is usually a disaster of such scope that recovery is impossible. Sadly for the Japanese, Midway must join the ignominious ranks of this level of calamitous compound failure.

The first of these deadly military sins—failure to learn—indicates that a military has been either unable or unwilling to adequately address the lessons of the past. This may stem from a frank inability to understand or adequately analyze what actually went wrong (or right) in earlier campaigns. Alternately, a military organization may be forced, by tradition, politics, or other impediments, to "put the blinders on," thereby hampering its self-analysis and performance in future operations.

Examined in this light, it is clear that the Imperial Navy's failure to draw correct conclusions from the past stemmed in large part from its crowning naval triumph at Tsushima in 1905. From that decisive victory, the Japanese drew three fundamental conclusions that would ultimately lead them to decisive defeat. First, Tsushima seemed to confirm the notion that naval power could be used to shape and control conflicts so that they remained localized and were fought for limited objectives. The Japanese Navy's role in the Russo-Japanese War was to isolate the Korean peninsula, thwart the activities of the Russian squadrons at Port Arthur and Vladivostok, and fight a decisive battle with the main Russian battle fleet when it finally appeared near the Home Islands. In this role, it was eminently successful, and the war was largely fought on ground chosen by the Japanese.

Second, Tsushima (falsely) taught the lesson that victory at sea devolved solely from winning climactic fleet engagements. This lesson seemed inescapable, since Tsushima was one of the most decisive naval battles in history, resulting in the utter annihilation of the Russian fleet. At the negligible cost of three torpedo boats sunk, moderate damage to three capital ships and some other smaller combatants, and the deaths of 110 sailors, Japan had caused thirty-four of the thirty-eight Russian vessels that entered the Straits of Tsushima to be either sunk, scuttled, captured, or interned. Over ten thousand Russian sailors were either killed or captured.[24] Very shortly thereafter, Russia had been forced to initiate peace negotiations. If Tsushima seemed to prove anything, it was that a single battle *could* determine the fate of two antagonists. Indeed, in the Japanese view, a single battle was *likely* to determine the outcome of the war as a whole.

Third, Tsushima implanted in the Imperial Navy the unfailing belief in the primacy of offensive factors, as compared to defensive considerations. In that battle, the superior speed of the Japanese battle line had allowed it to maneuver freely and had been critical in dictating the gunnery range to the Russians. By the same token, Japan's unorthodox adoption of relatively lightweight main battery ammunition (whose armor penetration characteristics were inferior, but whose weight of explosive charge was much greater) had inflicted enormous damage to the upperworks and control centers of the Russian battleships, thereby throwing the enemy line into confusion. Thus, the Japanese believed that by bringing greater firepower to bear at decisive ranges, they would be able to defeat more numerous opponents. The seeds of this dogma had already been planted during the Navy's formative years, as the Japanese naturally adopted the policies of their mentor, the Royal Navy, which advocated an aggressive attitude toward naval engagements. But Tsushima cemented the notion that big guns were the final arbiter of any naval encounter,[25] a belief further reinforced by the clash of heavily armed battle lines at Jutland.[26]

These three lessons were later fused unhealthily with Japan's growing fixation after the First World War on the possibility of war with the United States. The Japanese understood that any such conflict would pit them against a foe whose numerical superiority was ultimately ensured by overwhelming industrial might. Seeing no way to fight numbers with numbers, the Imperial Navy fell back on the unswerving belief that quality—if wielded with superior skill and Japanese fighting spirit (*Yamato damashii*)—must be able to defeat quantity. From this fundamental belief flowed every doctrinal and warship design tenet in the Imperial Navy. As a result, the other traditional roles that great navies throughout history have embraced—protecting one's commerce, destroying the commerce of the enemy, and conducting amphibious landings—were strictly subjugated to the Imperial Navy's overriding need to augment the fleet's raw offensive strength. Speed, range, and firepower were everything.

The problem was that none of these dictums was appropriate in the context of a global war in the Pacific, particularly a protracted one. In the matter of using naval power to limit the scope of a conflict, it is ironic that Japan's opening moves in the Pacific war had exactly the opposite effect. By attacking Pearl Harbor, the Imperial Navy unilaterally ensured that the scope of the war it unleashed would be unlimited. Now, instead of having to control a limited number of seaways that led to a single geographic center of gravity (such as Korea had been in 1904–05), Japan had elected to wage war across the entire expanse of the Pacific. Under these circumstances, any geographical proscription of the conflict was impossible.

As for the cherished notion of creating a single decisive battle that would decide the course of the war, the Imperial Navy searched in vain throughout the conflict for such an engagement—first at Midway, and then elsewhere. The Japanese completely failed to understand that a power like the United States could never be brought to ruin—or even to the bargaining table—as the result of a single engagement, no matter how successful it was. The industrialized, massively mobilized nature of World War II ensured that protracted warfare was practically inevitable. In such a setting, nations could be defeated only after the application of levels of cumulative force and destruction that beggared the imagination.

The third lesson from Tsushima manifested itself in the Imperial Navy's continuing overemphasis on offensive factors. At the strategic level this meant that its naval force structure, while formidable in frontline strength, did not possess the characteristics needed for the protracted war it had unwittingly purchased for itself. And operationally, it meant that Japan came to Midway armed with a doctrinal outlook rigidly inclined toward the offensive. This is evidenced by Genda's eschewal of "wasting" air assets on scouting operations,[27] Nagumo's obvious preference for a coordinated counterstrike against the Americans (even at the expense of speed), and the fact that Japan's warships were ill prepared to accept battle damage and survive. All of these factors had deleterious effects at Midway.

However, perhaps the most important learning failure of the Imperial Navy concerned lessons not from prior wars, but rather from the first five months of the Pacific war itself. At the top of this list must stand the Navy's inability to correctly perceive the underlying reasons for its success up until April 1942. Granted the Japanese had never fought a carrier vs. carrier battle prior to Coral Sea. Yet, operational mass was clearly the key to its two most successful campaigns of the initial war period—Pearl Harbor and the Indian Ocean foray. On both of these occasions, Japan had equipped *Kidō Butai* with every available fleet carrier in the inventory and, in the process, had presented its opponents with an insuperable tactical problem. Japan had won not because of its racial superiority, or *Yamato damashii,* but because the Imperial Navy brought *more* flight decks and *more* aircraft to the point of contact than its enemies could muster in return.

By the same token, when the Japanese had attacked with marginal forces—most notably at the Battle of Coral Sea, but also in such land operations as the protracted siege of Bataan and the initial abortive invasion of Wake Island—they had found the going much tougher. One might argue that at Coral Sea, the Japanese did not actually believe their forces were going to be marginal to the task, given the anticipated level of opposition. But this merely betrays the Japanese failure to appreciate the capacity of modern carrier forces to move across vast distances and launch powerful raids deep behind the nominal "front line." As was pointed out earlier, the only way for the Japanese to avoid being outnumbered and ambushed by a suddenly appearing enemy carrier task force that "wasn't supposed to be there" was to bring the entirety of their own carrier force to every major operation. There really was no middle ground in terms of force allocation. Thus, without realizing it, the Japanese had ironically disproved their own cherished notion of quality triumphing over quantity. Instead, *quantity had arguably been the critical factor in Japan's seminal victories to date.* Given that fact, bringing the entire carrier force to an operation such as Midway was absolutely imperative.

An astute naval leadership would have noticed this correlation, but the Imperial Navy did not. Whether the cause was Victory Disease, or a simple disinterest in learning lessons at this stage of the conflict, the result was a lessening of intellectual rigor in the Navy during the first part of 1942. An accurate perception of the strengths of massing many carrier decks together should have inclined the Japanese toward a policy of fighting fewer battles but carrying a bigger stick to each. Instead, the Imperial Navy exhibited a penchant for doing precisely the opposite. The battles of Coral Sea and Midway make it clear that the Japanese Navy was going after too many objectives at once. It was dispersing its carrier assets, thereby casting aside its proven formula for victory. In the process, it was unnecessarily elevating the Navy's risk by placing irreplaceable combat assets in situations where its weaker opponent could temporarily concentrate superior numbers against them.

The fault in this respect can rightly be laid primarily at the feet of Admiral Yamamoto, for it was he who had the dominant hand in crafting the Navy's strategy. Yet, it is apparent that Naval GHQ played a role as well, because it was they who persuaded Yamamoto to take on operations like Coral Sea and Operation AL, both of which would detract from the overall strength that the Navy could wield against primary objectives. Not only did Yamamoto accept these extra burdens with minimal protest, but when he *did* argue against them, it was never because they dispersed his available carrier power, but because they did not figure into his overall conception for how a decisive battle was to be contrived. Had he been wise, he would have vigorously contested all such secondary operations as being truly dangerous to Japan's overall strategic calculus. For this reason alone, Yamamoto should never have countenanced independent operations by CarDiv 5. By the same token, Naval GHQ should not have pushed the matter. For the fundamental truth remains that had CarDiv 5 been present in its entirety at Midway, it is difficult to see how the Americans could have won, despite their superior intelligence and demonstrable luck. But neither Yamamoto nor Naval GHQ apparently realized that preservation of Japan's critical offensive mass was essential to its ability to conduct decisive battles.

There is a further irony, however, in that Yamamoto and Naval GHQ's failure to appreciate the virtues of mass at the *operational* level was matched by an *overemphasis* on conservation of mass by Nagumo and his staff at the *tactical* level. In fact, *both* of these tendencies had a dire impact on the outcome of the battle. On the face of it, this seems contradictory—*mass* should be either "good" or "bad." But this points out the difficulty of meting out simple prescriptions for victory or defeat in this very complex battle. Had Yamamoto supplied his subordinate with true superiority of naval airpower at the point of contact, it could have widened Nagumo's tactical options immensely. Likewise, had Nagumo been less concerned with launching a massed counterstrike from his four decks during the battle, his options would have been commensurately widened.

Other opportunities for learning during the early part of the war had also presented themselves, although more fleetingly. The outcome of Coral Sea, for instance, could have been such an occasion, but for various reasons it wasn't. For one thing, after recovering from its initial fury at Admiral Takagi for supposedly failing to prosecute the battle aggressively enough, Combined Fleet's staff had then swung around in fairly short order to believing that the operation had actually been another Japanese victory. In so doing, it blinded itself to its own shortcomings, particularly with regard to having adequate forces on hand. This opportunity was complicated, of course, by the fact that the time interval between Coral Sea and Midway was so short. As such, there was scant time for the fleet to fully absorb the two most important tactical implications of the engagement, namely, that American carrier aviators should not be discounted and that lone carrier divisions were not a replacement for a fully constituted *Kidō Butai*.

Yet, while it is true that the Japanese Navy was operating on an impossibly tight schedule and that there was little time to absorb and process battle lessons, it is also interesting to note that the time period between the Indian Ocean operations and

Midway hints at the start of a "learning gap" appearing between the two navies. This was a phenomenon that would become increasingly evident as the war progressed—the U.S. Navy as an organization often (although not always) had a superior capacity for absorbing battle lessons and translating them into doctrinal and technical modifications that would aid it in future battles.

For instance, the incident in the Indian Ocean, wherein a handful of British bombers succeeded in surprising *Kidō Butai* and nearly bombing *Akagi,* should have been a wake-up call to the Japanese fleet that their air defense arrangements were inadequate. It is clear that the Japanese took notice of this incident—*Hiryū's* after-action report emphasized the need for better long-range detection capabilities against enemy aircraft. Yet, it doesn't appear that any concerted effort was made to enhance the capabilities of the fleet's primary defense mechanism—its combat air patrol—the failure of which would doom Nagumo just two months later at Midway.

It is true that two months didn't offer much time for the organizations within the Japanese Navy responsible for producing doctrine (such as the Yokosuka Air Group) to absorb the problem and produce a response. Furthermore, before the advent of radar, and in the absence of adequate ship to plane communications because of substandard radios in the Zero, there was only so much that could be done to improve CAP performance. Thus, complex changes in the carrier air defense arrangements certainly couldn't be expected within this time frame. By the same token, though, even some relatively simple changes at the tactical level—insisting that the fighter *shōtai* observe an iron discipline in maintaining their sectors and requiring them to remain stacked at prescribed altitudes—could have produced positive results at Midway. In the absence of such discipline, though, the Japanese CAP operated organically and tended to overreact, thereby affording the enemy open avenues of approach.

In contrast, it is striking that in the immediate aftermath of Coral Sea, *Yorktown's* crew was able to devise and implement a significant innovation in the area of damage control that would go on to have a major impact for the Americans. Machinist Oscar W. Myers, *Yorktown's* air department fuel officer, had observed that the demise of *Lexington* was the result (among other things) of an aviation gasoline fire on her hangar deck. He therefore contrived the notion of draining the fuel system after usage and filling the pipes with inert CO_2 gas.[28] *Yorktown's* skipper, Capt. Elliott Buckmaster, was quick to give his permission to this innovation, which almost certainly prevented *Yorktown's* suffering a calamitous fire during Kobayashi's dive-bomber attack on 4 June.

Similarly, American fighter pilots were finally beginning to come to grips with the Japanese Zero. Though the genesis of Jimmy Thach's famous "Thach Weave" maneuver dated from as early as November 1941, his implementation of it (albeit on a very limited scale) at Midway was symbolic of the U.S. Navy's efforts to learn and innovate in the face of Japan's early-war superiority. This is not to imply that the Japanese Navy was incapable of learning; that was certainly not the case. But it is equally clear that at this point in the war, the accumulated pressures of six months of defeats were forcing the U.S. Navy to adapt frantically, and often successfully. In contrast, six months of victories were not creating the same imperatives within the Imperial Navy.

The overall conclusion is inescapable—the Japanese Navy had a learning problem. The cherished precepts that it had carried down from Tsushima—the value of geographically limited wars, the primacy of offensive over defensive factors, and the supremacy of big-gun navies—were largely inapplicable to World War II. Furthermore, at its highest levels of command, the Navy had also failed to grasp the lessons of the war they had launched. Not the least important of these principles was the overriding importance in carrier warfare of numerical superiority, despite having emphatically driven that very point home for all the world to see at Pearl Harbor.

After failures of learning come those of anticipation. As Cohen and Gooch point out, "The essence of a failure to anticipate is *not* mere ignorance of the future, for that is inherently unknowable. It is, rather, the failure to take reasonable precautions against a known hazard."[29] Along with its failures in learning, it is clear that the Imperial Navy failed to anticipate as it went into the battle of Midway.

At the level of operational planning, Genda was clearly guilty of failing to foresee that a larger number of scouting aircraft would be required to implement a thorough search. Furthermore, his plans should have accommodated the possibility of variable weather conditions around the objective. Not only that, but as has been previously pointed out, Genda—bright and generally competent as he was—was the product of a military culture that emphasized the preservation of offensive mass at almost all costs. Carrier attack planes could be used as scouts during transits to the battlefield. But once battle was joined, scouting with attack aircraft was to be avoided. If there weren't enough floatplanes to do the job, it just didn't get done. In short, if Genda's plan was flawed, it had failed along institutionally predictable lines.

More puzzling, though, is Nagumo's failure—on the basis of the intelligence he had in hand before the battle—to anticipate that the American carriers might be present off of Midway. It is clear that Nagumo probably ought to have been suspicious of the level of American activity in the area, if nothing else. But he chose not to act on this intelligence. In retrospect, Nagumo's indecision was probably partly the result of his own personality, which (by this point in his career) was rigid, uninspired, and unfamiliar with the technical intricacies of the force he commanded. These tendencies were further reinforced by the military culture prevailing in the Imperial Navy, which valued conformity and obedience over creativity or personal initiative.

However, as Admiral Ugaki, the U.S. Naval War College, and Walter Lord all noted, the most crucial oversight in this respect was Yamamoto's failure to take precautions against the possibility that the Americans might, in fact, be present off Midway in advance of their scripted arrival time in his battle plan. This was driven by his personal belief that the Americans were all but beaten and would need to be lured out to battle. As such, it was apparently inconceivable that they would be lying in wait. As was mentioned previously, Yamamoto was clearly guilty of the sin of planning operations around perceived enemy intentions, rather than on the basis of the enemy's likely capabilities.

The corollary failure that flowed from this assumption was Yamamoto's decision to disperse his forces in the face of the enemy. By subdividing his superior mass into a welter of smaller formations that were not mutually supportive, the overall battle plan was unnecessarily weakened. Despite the plan's details having been created by his operations officer, Captain Kuroshima Kameto, as commander in chief, Yamamoto must shoulder ultimate responsibility for this action. Yet it is interesting to note that throughout the war, even as their strength weakened relative to the Americans, the Japanese never lost their fondness for complex dispersed operations. For instance, one of Yamamoto's eventual successors, Admiral Toyoda Soemu, created a similar monstrosity in 1944. Toyoda's "*Sho Go 1*" plan, conceived for the defense of the Philippines, featured multiple widely separated formations. Two separate battle squadrons were designed to converge on the American invasion beaches at Leyte, while Ozawa's carrier force acted as bait to lure the American fleet northward and open the way for the battleships. Japanese operations in the early battles around Java and at Coral Sea, as well as later operations in the Eastern Solomons and Santa Cruz, also featured multiple Japanese formations maneuvering without the ability to mutually reinforce one another.

The conclusion from this is apparent. Had Yamamoto not been in charge of Combined Fleet in April–May 1942, whoever was commanding *Rengō Kantai* would likely have introduced a comparable level of complication into what ought to have been a relatively straightforward exercise. Complex operations were endemic to the Imperial Navy, not just Yamamoto. This love of intricacy can be clearly detected in the 1920s and 1930s, when Japanese doctrine and fleet exercises envisioned elaborate encircling maneuvers—often taking place at night—unfolding like clockwork to trap the unwitting Americans.[30]

It is clear in this regard that Japanese naval strategy was influenced from its very inception by Oriental philosophies on the conduct of war, which emphasized the value of deception and indirect approaches. Akiyama Saneyuki, the most brilliant thinker at the Imperial Navy's Staff College at the turn of the twentieth century, drew heavily not only on contemporary Western naval practices, but also on ancient Oriental military masters such as Sun Tzu as he began hammering out Japanese naval strategic thought at that time. Akiyama's principles, in particular his love of indirect approaches so as to conceal the true objective of an operation, were seen by the Japanese as laying the strategic foundation for the victory at Tsushima. From there, they were carried forward into the interwar period and obviously still exerted a powerful influence at Midway.[31]

Unfortunately, at Midway the Japanese encountered a strategic problem where subtlety was a dangerous luxury. If ever a situation called for using brute force, this was it. But Yamamoto, shaped by his institutional training, adopted an elegant strategic approach that suited his service's martial sensibilities, and it is likely that any other graduate of the Imperial Naval Staff College would have done likewise. In a nutshell, Japanese naval strategy was warped and was likely to produce unworkable solutions no matter who was in charge of the planning. In this sense, Chihaya's complaint that the Japanese Navy had as "good as planned for" its defeat at Midway is true—but the reasons for that defeat reached back well before six months of overweening pride brought them into focus. Instead, they had been built into the Navy's strategic outlook over the course of decades.

One failure of anticipation, though, cannot be traced to institutional roots. This was Yamamoto's and Ugaki's high-handed behavior during the May war games on board *Yamato*. War gaming, when used objectively, is one of the most important tools at the disposal of a professional military, revealing unforeseen dangers and developing contingency plans to guard against them. In this vein, the May games were ostensibly intended to prepare the fleet's tactical commanders for the coming operation. Yet from the very outset, Combined Fleet's Midway games were a farce. Rather than being approached honestly and openly, the entire exercise was subordinated to the overriding political agendas of Admiral Yamamoto. The games were merely a tool for pushing Combined Fleet's operational concepts through, no matter what objections might be raised. Late-issued operational plans and blatantly rigged officiating not only led to the sullen resignation of Admiral Nagumo from the proceedings, but also to a sense that the remainder of the participants were merely "going through the motions." Thus, Combined Fleet's commander in chief willfully mishandled one of his most useful analytical tools on the eve of his most important battle.

Only a single insight worthy of the name emerged from this entire exercise—the awareness that if an American carrier force appeared unexpectedly on Nagumo's flank, it could produce very unpleasant consequences for the operation as a whole. But that realization merely resulted in the issuance of a slapdash verbal instruction, namely, that Nagumo should keep half of his aircraft armed for a naval strike at all times. During the actual battle, this same instruction did little except needlessly restrict the force commander's options. Thus, Yamamoto's sole attempt to rise to the challenge of anticipating the enemy's actions was counterproductive.

In sum, the Japanese Navy was clearly guilty of several crucial errors of anticipation. Genda's anemic reconnaissance scheme, Yamamoto's obtuse battle plan, even *Kaga*'s unlikely resurrection at the hand of Ugaki during the May war games—all were indicative of a Navy that had failed miserably to foresee what the future might bring. Instead, they habitually assumed that a "best case" rather than a "worst case" scenario would unfold in their favor—a bad idea in military planning.

Thus, the Japanese came to Midway with a flawed doctrine, having drawn the wrong conclusions from the past, and having failed to absorb the most critical lesson from the current conflict (failure one). Moreover, their battle plan was similarly flawed and did not consider contingencies such as the American fleet being present off of Midway (failure two). Nevertheless, despite these glaring problems, Nagumo still might have won the battle, or at least have made the outcome more even, *if* the Japanese had been able to adapt to the challenge of their changed circumstances. After all, even without *Shōkaku* and *Zuikaku,* the four carriers of *Kidō Butai* were still the most powerful, proficient naval air force on the planet. But here, too, the Imperial Navy failed on several levels, both strategically immediately before the battle, and operationally during its course.

By far the most important reason for these adaptive failures was an unhealthy rigidity on the part of the Japanese regarding the sanctity of battle plans. Indeed, this is a common theme for the imperial military that can be seen not only at Midway, but throughout the Pacific war as well. "Plan inertia," for wont of a better term, was endemic to the mind-set of the Imperial Navy and was the result of many factors. First, while characterizing a culture in general terms is always suspect, it is probably safe to say that Japanese society prizes order above most things. Furthermore, it is demonstrable that the Japanese as a people, from the youngest to the oldest, intensely dislike making mistakes, particularly in public. Plans—like social rituals—are a natural way of establishing and codifying order and minimizing mistakes. This keenness on planning still manifests itself today in Japan, with many large Japanese corporations creating business plans that in some cases attempt to look into the future for decades—far longer than the five-year horizons considered typical for large Western businesses. Likewise, while the degree of actual control Japan's postwar Ministry of International Trade and Industry (MITI) had during the decades of Japan's "economic miracle" may be arguable, the fact that Japan was one of the few capitalist industrialized nations to engage in a systematic exercise in national economic planning is not.

Not surprisingly, these central cultural tendencies manifested themselves from the very beginnings of the Imperial Navy. Furthermore, the Navy's plans had been seen as paying substantial benefits throughout that time. It was good planning that had allowed the Japanese to beat the Russians, particularly at Tsushima, but more generally through the creation of the highly cohesive, tactically homogeneous battle force that fought that war. In the same vein, the interwar Navy had put great store in policies such as the "Eight-Eight Fleet," which sought during the years between 1907 and 1922 to create a powerful fleet of eight new dreadnoughts and eight battlecruisers with which to counterweigh American naval power in the Pacific. The notion of the Eight-Eight fleet, the underlying rationale for which was actually fairly abstract (and questionable), had become "an unquestioned article of faith" in the Navy up until the time the Washington Naval Treaty did away with it.[32] This same tendency resurrected itself during the 1930s in the form of increasingly ambitious naval replenishment plans, known informally as Circle Plans (*Maru Keikaku*), which greatly expanded the power of the fleet immediately before the war.[33]

On a more day-to-day basis, the Navy's annual operational plan (*nendo sakusen keikaku*), which was in force from 1 April to the following 31 March of each year, defined in great detail the Navy's activities for the following year.[34] Drawn up by the Navy General Staff, the plan detailed the training to be carried out, maneuvers to be held, and the tactical problems to be solved thereby. Included in each were also detailed prescribed orders for first mobilizing the fleet (*suishi jumbi*—"preparatory fleet mobilization") and then shifting it over to wartime hostilities (*nendo teikoku kaigun senji hensen*—"annual Imperial Navy plan for wartime organization"). During any given year, of course, the Navy was expected to be devoting itself to attaining the tactical proficiency necessary to win the Decisive Battle, many of whose tactical precepts had become increasingly scripted and choreographed as the 1930s went on.[35]

This love of planning had paid handsome results during the opening moves of the Pacific war for both Japanese service branches. The proficiency demonstrated during the attack on Pearl Harbor is the most famous example of this. Admiral Yamamoto, and more particularly Capt. Kuroshima Kameto, had taken a bold operational vision and hammered it into a sound operational plan in very short order. Pearl Harbor introduced the revolutionary use of massed carrier airpower, as well as tactical innovations like the famous use of wooden fins that enabled air-dropped torpedoes to operate in the shallow waters of the harbor. No less inspired was the Imperial Army's routing of the British in Malaya—an invasion force on bicycles harrying a professional army twice its size to utter destruction in just nine weeks—which was built around a core of solid staff work completed before the war. In the course of these planning exercises, the Japanese Army had identified key overland attack routes, as well as the degree of combat engineering (particularly bridge-building) capabilities that would be required to win the campaign.[36] All of these efforts had resulted in brilliant, and well-deserved, victories.

Yet, too much of any good thing can have its drawbacks, and it is clear that the Japanese held their plans in such high regard that, once in place, they were loath to alter them. This manifested itself in Yamamoto's failure to adapt to the setback at Coral Sea. By not allowing Operation MI's timetable to slip, he lost the chance to include either member of CarDiv 5 in the starting lineup, and thus condemned Nagumo to fight on even terms at Midway, rather than from a position of strength. By the same token, Yamamoto's failure to adjust to Nagumo's one-day delay in sailing meant that Tanaka's Invasion Force was prematurely exposed to detection, which confirmed the Americans in their suspicions that Japanese carriers could shortly be expected off Midway. Neither did he adjust his plans when it became evident Operation K would fail to produce timely information on the disposition of the American fleet.

At an operational level, plan inertia manifested itself in a stubborn unwillingness to adapt immediately before and during battle. Karl von Clausewitz's famous maxim that "No battle plan survives first contact with the enemy," probably never met with a less enthusiastic audience than the Imperial Navy. Obviously, Vice Admiral Nagumo had his share of difficulties in this respect. Besides his unwillingness to act on his latest intelligence estimates, Nagumo also failed in two other critical respects. First, he didn't launch a quick counterstrike against the Americans when the occasion demanded. Second, by closing directly on the Americans once they were discovered, he maneuvered his force in such a way as to expose it to greater danger than was prudent. In both of these instances, of course, he was influenced by prevailing Japanese doctrine, which favored closing aggressively with the enemy and delivering a coordinated, annihilating blow.

Yamaguchi, of course, did not adapt successfully to his circumstances, either. By failing to carefully gauge the strength of *Hiryū* and her air group, he placed his force in an increasingly dangerous position with little chance of commensurate reward. Yamaguchi stands as the archetypal Japanese warrior in this respect—aggressive, unwilling or unable to back down, and more concerned with preserving his own personal honor than preserving the combat assets of the nation. And as has been shown, contrary to the prevailing view of the battle, Nagumo was his coequal in this aggressiveness, even when the long odds against his success militated strongly for an expeditious withdrawal.

British Field Marshal William Slim, who had been defeated in Burma by the Japanese in early 1942, but who would later return the favor by crushing them in the same theater in 1944, beautifully captured the spirit of his enemies in an excerpt written about the Japanese Army. He remarked:

> The Japanese were ruthless and bold as ants while their designs went well, but if their plans were disturbed or thrown out—ant-like again—they fell into confusion, were slow to re-adjust themselves, and invariably clung too long to their original schemes. This, to commanders with their unquenchable military optimism, which rarely allowed in their narrow administrative margins for any setback or delay, was particularly dangerous. The fundamental fault of their generalship was a lack of moral, as distinct from physical, courage. They were not prepared to admit that they had made a mistake, that their plans had misfired and needed recasting. . . . Rather than confess that, they passed on to their subordinates, unchanged, the order that they themselves had received, well knowing that with the resources available the tasks demanded were impossible. Time and again, this blind passing of responsibility ran down a chain of disaster. . . . They scored highly by determination; they paid heavily for lack of flexibility.[37]

This passage might just as easily have been written about Midway, as it perfectly encapsulates the problems the Japanese had when it came to altering their battle plans. In the matter of lack of moral courage, Yamamoto, Nagumo, and Yamaguchi were all quite clearly guilty as charged. Equally perceptive is Slim's insight that sticking with a plan, even a bad plan, was a mechanism whereby the Japanese individual could personally absolve himself of responsibility for a defeat. Too often, though, the price for doing so was needless casualties, or even the outright destruction of one's force, typically followed by the atoning suicide of the commander in question. All in all, this was not an effective model for winning a war against a numerically superior opponent.

By the same token, it is clear from many of the failures of learning and adaptation just discussed that the Japanese entered the Battle of Midway wearing doctrinal handcuffs, the effect of which was to retard still further their ability to innovate. Whereas American doctrine is generally presented to a commander as a codification of guidelines concerning the effective conduct of combat, the very nature of the Japanese military culture made its own doctrine far more rigid with regards to interpretation. This manifested itself in Nagumo and Genda's disinclination to augment their tactical scouting assets with carrier strike assets, even in the face of accumulating evidence that the Americans were more alert than they ought to have been.

In the same way, the apparent unwillingness of First Air Fleet staff to even consider splitting the attacking power of *Kidō Butai* after discovering the Americans later in the morning originated in doctrinal imperatives. Launching a quick attack against the Americans with CarDiv 2's *kanbaku* before Tomonaga's recovery, difficult though this would have been to implement, might have given the Japanese their best possibility to inflict more harm on their opponent than they actually managed. Yet,

Japanese doctrine prescribed massed airpower as the correct answer to any tactical problem that arose, and Nagumo and his staff dogmatically stuck to that formula.

Likewise, Nagumo's doctrinaire decision to close directly on the Americans had the effect of leaving his fleet positioned between two hostile forces (Midway and the American carriers). A decision to maneuver more freely, either to the north or northwest, could have mitigated some of the advantages that the Americans had accrued by virtue of the superior (and wholly intentional) initial positioning. Despite the Japanese love of indirect approaches at a *strategic* level, their love of closing directly to knife-fighting range at the *tactical* level was never better demonstrated than at Midway.

Some of these problems stemmed from the simple fact that in early 1942 the aircraft carrier was still a brand-new weapon system. As such, the body of doctrinal thinking in all the carrier navies was relatively small and still maturing. Other navies might have viewed an immature doctrine as being a tacit admission that some degree of interpretation by unit commanders would be required during the course of battle. The Japanese apparently did not see things this way—they stuck to the playbook, small as it might be. When improvisation *was* called for, they answered with the most expedient, and transparent tactic available—charging the enemy. Thus, in the critical matter of adaptation, the Japanese likewise failed abysmally.

Taken as a whole, the inescapable conclusion that emerges from a careful examination of the battle is the fact that the Japanese defeat was not the result of some solitary, crucial breakdown in Japanese designs. It was not the result of Victory Disease, nor of a few crucial personal mistakes. Rather, what appears is a complex, comprehensive web of failures stretching across every level of the battle—strategic, operational, and tactical. Every aspect of the enterprise was tainted in some way. The surface manifestations of these deeper failures may ultimately have been a host of mistakes committed by individuals. And some of those mistakes were clearly more important that others. But the vast majority of them were in some way symptomatic of larger failures within the Japanese military and within the Navy's cultural fabric, its doctrine, and its preferred modes of combat. They were the end products of an organization that failed to learn correctly from its past, failed to plan correctly for its future, and then failed to adapt correctly to circumstances once those plans were shown to be flawed.

Intriguingly, the seeds of many of these errors had been planted some forty years before, through the initial teachings of the Japanese Naval Staff College, and from the flower of Japan's greatest victory—the Battle of Tsushima. They had lain unnoticed all that time, growing unchecked, waiting for the right time, place, and individuals to give them expression. Instead of culling these warped seedlings, the Japanese Navy had fostered their growth in the 1930s. The twin pressures of a violent nationalism, combined with the sure knowledge that they would be the underdog in any war with America, had conspired to skew Japan's naval policies and doctrine still further during that time period. As a result, by the time the Pacific war began, and despite its undoubted *tactical* prowess, the Navy's ability to mentally fight the war at a strategic and operational level was already fatally damaged. It was at Midway that the breadth of these shortcomings finally revealed themselves, with catastrophic results for both the Imperial Navy and the Japanese nation. Of course, in the larger context of the war, the Battle of Midway was just one of the first of a much greater harvest of bitter fruit that would fall from the poisoned tree of Japanese militarism.

The military defeats that began with the Battle of Midway stem from the harsh reality that, far from being the truly modern, progressive institution that it fondly imagined itself to be, the Imperial Navy was in fact possessed of the most parochial of outlooks. Instead of the quick, limited war Japan's military leadership envisioned, the Pacific war soon revealed itself to be all encompassing and all consuming. In a shockingly short time, America had begun waging war against Japan across every strategic dimension available to a great industrial power—military, political, economic, and scientific. Japan was assaulted on the ground, through the air, and on and under the sea. Ultimately, it was beaten decisively in every one of these arenas. In this sense, Midway was merely symptomatic of the Imperial military's larger failings. Most obvious was their fatally misguided decision to launch a war of aggression against the most powerful nation on earth. Having done so, moreover, they found themselves engaged in a conflict whose scope and complexity forced its participants to evolve at a frenetic pace. As it developed, for the Japanese this was a particularly daunting challenge. Despite the amazing speed with which they had modernized their fighting forces after 1848, they were still bound by thought patterns linked to an earlier military and cultural era, as well as the warped legacy of Tsushima. In the final analysis, it is no exaggeration to say that the conflict the Japanese military instigated in 1941 was not only beyond its resources, but also beyond its understanding.

23

Assessing the Battle's Importance

Having examined why the Japanese lost, the next step is to consider the impact of that loss. Much like identifying the true reasons for failure, evaluating the importance of the Battle of Midway is a slippery proposition. For an engagement often labeled the "decisive" battle of the Pacific war, this is inevitable—great battles by definition spawn a wealth of downstream consequences, each of which can be looked at independently. Accordingly, answers to the question "what did Midway really mean?" typically come in three varieties—material, strategic, and counterfactual. The first focuses on the importance of such things as aircraft losses, the loss of skilled aircraft mechanics, and the size of Japan's pilot training programs. The second analyzes what effect the defeat at Midway had on Japan's strategy for the remainder of the war. The third seeks to illustrate the importance of Midway by creating "what if" scenarios (some well thought out, some verging on the delusional) that change the outcome of the Second World War in some way, depending on the outcome of this one battle. All of these will be considered in turn. Yet, within the scope of an operational-based study such as this one, the first imperative is to consider what it meant to Japan to lose the services of four aircraft carriers.

The question might better be phrased in terms of what it meant to lose two carrier divisions, in particular Carrier Divisions 1 and 2. Stated this way, the question acknowledges that the Japanese Navy had brought the concept of multicarrier operations to a higher level of practice than any other navy. It also emphasizes that what was lost was not just "X number" of ships, planes, or men, but rather a well-functioning assemblage of the three. CarDivs 1 and 2 were incredibly complex weapons systems, forged through years of training and experimentation. All the material elements composing these systems need to be considered when assessing the damage suffered on 4 June, 1942.

There has been a tendency when analyzing the battle to both under- and overestimate the importance of these material factors. For instance, most early accounts of the battle casually assumed that the sinking of the Japanese carriers ipso facto destroyed the cream of Japan's carrier aviators and therefore put a stop to Japanese expansion. The truth is more complex. Works such as John Prados's *Combined Fleet Decoded* have corrected the record by noting that the battle itself did not signal the end of the Japanese naval aviator corps. This view is directly supported by the carriers' operational records. *Kaga* suffered twenty-one aircrew deaths (both in the air and on board ship), *Sōryū* ten, and *Akagi* a mere seven. *Hiryū*'s air group was the exception, suffering casualties in excess of 50 percent, with seventy-two fatalities, including her air group leader and many officers.[1] Included with these must also be the eleven floatplane crewmen who perished. However, the deaths of 110 airmen, though painful, did not constitute a disaster in itself. In fact, Japan would lose the same number of aviators (110) at the Battle of the Eastern Solomons in August 1942,[2] and thirty-five more than that (145) at the Battle of Santa Cruz in October 1942.[3] The losses at Midway certainly did not radically degrade the fighting capabilities of Japanese naval aviation as a whole, which probably boasted around two thousand carrier qualified aircrew at the beginning of the war.[4] Rather, it would take the hellish attrition of the Solomons campaign to initiate a fatal downward spiral in Japanese carrier aircrew proficiency, with the Battle of Santa Cruz marking the effective end of the elite prewar cadres.

Prados also notes the negative effects that losing hundreds of highly skilled aircraft mechanics and technicians had on the Imperial Navy. The Midway carriers between them counted 721 aircraft technicians killed, or more than 40 percent of the total number embarked. These men were difficult to replace, given Japan's less-mechanized society than that of its foe, the United States. Their loss (in conjunction with the large number of skilled technicians who were later to be isolated and effectively lost at Rabaul during the Solomons campaign) would have a direct impact on Japan's ability to field a modern carrier aviation force during the battles of 1944. To the toll of mechanics might also be added the deaths of other essential crewmen, such as flight deck crew, armorers, and other personnel involved in supporting flight operations. These men had trained together for years to reach the highest level of operational proficiency the Japanese Navy would ever attain.

This attrition in personnel points to a more abstract loss, namely, that of organizational knowledge. It is not possible simply to conjure up three thousand men, a hundred fifty aircraft, and two carriers and expect them to operate smoothly. *Shōkaku* and *Zuikaku* discovered this during the early phases of the war. Their tardy rearming operations in the Indian Ocean had certainly caused Nagumo considerable distress. Likewise, while recovering the final strike of 8 May at the Battle of the Coral Sea, a lack of deck-handling speed on board *Zuikaku* had forced the jettisoning of a dozen precious aircraft over the side in order to recover the remainder of the planes still aloft. Thus, even several months after being commissioned, it is clear that CarDiv 5 was still not operating at the same level as CarDiv 1 and 2, despite having spent much of its time in company with the veteran carriers. Eventually, *Shōkaku* and *Zuikaku* would both exhibit a very high level of operational ability, but reaching that level took a long time. At a point in the war when Japan needed to be fighting as audaciously and efficiently as possible, the void left by the loss of two senior carrier divisions could not be filled by more junior practitioners.

All of these points have merit. Aircraft were certainly precious to Japan at this point in 1942. And the collective worth of human, organizational, and tactical capital must certainly be borne in mind, particularly in a war in which the Japanese so frequently squandered these important commodities. But the point that gets lost in all this is the critical significance of the flight decks themselves. It's almost as if the rush to acknowledge the importance of pilots and airplanes to the new mode of warfare has blinded modern observers to the overwhelming importance of the *aircraft carrier* as a strategic naval asset. Without flight decks to deliver planes and pilots into combat, the naval aviation revolution was negated, because at a fundamental level, "power projection" absolutely requires a base from which to project it. And it was this mobile base that was by far the most expensive and least expendable component in the overall system.

Japan began the war with nine carriers. Six of them—*Akagi, Kaga, Sōryū, Hiryū, Shōkaku,* and *Zuikaku*—were fleet carriers, large and fast enough to operate a credibly sized air group. The other three were light carriers *Hōshō, Ryūjō,* and *Zuihō*. Of these three, *Hōshō* was old, tiny and slow. *Ryūjō* was scarcely better, being cramped, structurally suspect, and possessed of but a single suitable elevator. Of the three, only *Zuihō* was truly capable of being integrated into the main carrier fleet. By the time of Midway, Japan had already commissioned and then lost *Zuihō*'s equally useful sister, *Shōhō*, at the Battle of the Coral Sea. Japan had also commissioned *Junyō* and *Hiyō*. Converted ocean liners, they were larger than the light carriers and could actually mount a decent-sized air group. However, they were possessed of cranky hybrid power plants (composed of military boilers mated with commercial-type turbines) that produced suboptimal speeds. As a result, while they were used in the role for wont of anything better, they were hardly adequate replacements for true fleet carriers.

The reality was that the smaller Japanese carriers could only play bit parts in the Pacific war. This is not to say that they weren't useful—they were certainly welcome additions for supporting amphibious landing operations, and they could provide a limited local air presence. But they came with many drawbacks, the most fundamental being the small size of their air groups. Carrier air groups are subject to economies of scale. They need to be large enough to scout and to supply defensive fighters to protect the mother ship and still be able to deliver a large offensive punch. Delivering a single attack with, say, thirty-two attack aircraft is almost always superior to sending in two separate sixteen-plane attacks, because larger strike forces have a better chance of saturating the enemy's defenses. Having a single carrier large enough to launch a decisive strike on its own was an important advantage in this respect. With an air group of twenty to thirty aircraft, light carriers simply did not have enough planes to go around. They could barely screen themselves, let alone deliver an attack of credible size.

Furthermore, the shipboard infrastructure necessary to support the air group—repair shops, command and control facilities, fueling stations, magazines, and bomb storage rooms—was also more efficiently delivered via a larger ship. Not only that, but it was easier to provide adequate escorts for a single large warship than for two smaller ones mounting the same number of aircraft—a critical factor in a navy as short of destroyers as Japan's. For all these reasons, deploying two light carriers did not produce the effectiveness or efficiency of a single fleet carrier with an air group of more than sixty aircraft. Light carriers could only complement, not replace, the functions of the fleet carriers. And with the exception of *Zuihō,* none of them were really worth the extra effort of slowing the fleet carriers down in order to have them around.

Viewed in this light, it is apparent that the coin of naval power in the Pacific war must be measured by the number of *fleet* carriers available to the opposing navies. Reckoned this way, Japan started the war at something like parity with the U.S. Navy. The USN fielded five large carriers—*Lexington, Saratoga, Yorktown, Enterprise,* and *Wasp*—to Japan's six. By the time of Midway, the addition of *Hornet* had been negated by the loss of *Lexington,* as well as heavy damage to *Saratoga,* leaving the score six to four in favor of Japan. The number of naval aircraft carried by these respective forces only slightly favored the Japanese, though, because of the larger American air groups. After Midway, however, the ratio was three to two in favor of the United States, a significant shift.

The importance of these vessels is even more obvious, considering that each of them represented a phenomenal expenditure of national resources. At the time of their completion, *Akagi* and *Kaga* were by far the most expensive warships ever built for the Japanese Navy to that date, costing roughly ¥53 million apiece to complete. In terms of specific cost (i.e., cost/ton of displacement), they were twice as expensive as a battleship of the same era. This was a result of the intricate nature of carrier design, including the provision of complex pumping and aviation gasoline systems, elaborate damage-control equipment, and the emplacement of defensive guns and their associated fire-control systems. In *Akagi*'s and *Kaga*'s cases, these costs were driven even higher by the redesign efforts necessary to convert existing capital ship hulls into functional carriers. Each had also undergone comprehensive, multiyear refits in the 1930s, consuming millions more. *Sōryū* and *Hiryū,* with their relatively modest price tags of ¥40.2 million, must have seemed like bargains when they were completed in 1937 and 1939. To these basic procurement costs, of course, must also be added the price of their air groups, and the annual costs of operation.[5] Accordingly, any analysis of the Midway battle that fails to accord the proper gravity to losing the core component of a national defense capability that was fourteen years in the making (i.e., *Kidō Butai*) utterly misjudges the nature of the Pacific war. Big carriers didn't just grow on trees—losing four of them in an afternoon was tantamount to a national disaster. Particularly within the time frame of the short conflict Japan hoped to fight, these losses were crushing and utterly irredeemable.

One might contend that the losses in aircrew and/or aircraft were of similar magnitude, but neither of these arguments is supportable. Of the two, the case for human capital perhaps has more merit, in that Japanese carrier aircrewmen were, at the time, among the most highly trained aviators in the world. The airmen lost at Midway would certainly have been useful in forthcoming carrier battles in the Solomons. However, it is worth remembering that seventy-four of these men were killed in the air, doing what carrier airmen are supposed to do, that is, attacking the enemy or defending the fleet. Even if Japan had won the Battle of Midway with their carriers unscathed, these men would still have been dead. Only the remaining thirty-six were shipboard fatalities.

It must also be recalled that the relatively small size of Japan's naval air corps was largely a self-imposed limitation. As a nation of over eighty million people, Japan certainly had the population necessary to develop a much larger cadre of pilots had it decided to do so. The reasons Japan chose to create an artificially small group of elite pilots, instead of a larger corps of aviators who were merely very good, lies outside the scope of this study.[6] So, too, does Japan's failure to recognize and correct its deficiencies in this area while there was still time to do so in early 1942. However, the fact that she was eventually able to find pilots, however poorly trained, for the 50,000 aircraft she would lose during the war establishes beyond doubt that the necessary manpower was available.

Any assessment of the scale of Midway's human losses must also be measured against the backdrop of the grim combat in the South Pacific that unfolded beginning in August 1942. It was here, in the daily patrols, skirmishes, and raids that lasted until 1944 that the crème of Japan's naval air forces would be destroyed—some 2,817 naval aircraft alone between April 1942 and April 1943.[7] Callous as it may seem, the existence or nonexistence of roughly one hundred carrier aircrew meant relatively little when set against this aerial meat grinder. People and planes were merely fuel for the vast furnaces of attritional combat that would soon be blazing on the southern borders of the empire.

For a reader in this century, living in a wealthy country where the loss of a single multimillion-dollar fighter is front-page news, it is difficult to internalize the scale and intensity of the violence that occurred during the Second World War. Aircraft were cheap. A typical fighter cost between $50,000 and $100,000; a medium bomber roughly double that.[8] They were produced in huge numbers. The United States built in excess of 306,000 combat aircraft during the war; Japan more than 67,000.[9] Planes were a commodity, like trucks or artillery tubes, and were treated as such. They were consumed at frightening rates. The United States lost somewhere between 9,000 and 27,000 aircraft to all causes in the Pacific theater alone, depending on the sources consulted. Japan lost 38,000 to 50,000 during the same period. Even accepting the more conservative figures, Japan was producing a weekly average of around 350 planes, and was losing over 200 of them. Granted that in 1942 the Japanese aircraft industry was not yet producing at nearly the rate it would in 1944, but these figures make it clear that even the loss of 257 carrier planes and floatplanes over three days could be made good in a few weeks. Conversely, the carrier losses themselves were not made good on a one-for-one basis until the commissioning of *Shinano* on 19 November, 1944, 127 weeks after the debacle of Midway, and at a point when the war was already all but lost.

A corollary to the loss of these four ships was the permanent loss of tactical homogeneity in the Japanese carrier force. Uniformity of operational characteristics was a central principle that had guided the Japanese Navy's shipbuilding policies since its inception and that had served the Navy well from Tsushima onward.[10] The six heavy carriers that attacked Pearl Harbor composed an exceptionally well-balanced formation—the stolid warhorses of Carrier Division 1, the dashing cavaliers of Carrier Division 2, and the promising yearlings of Carrier Division 5. The pairs of ships that made up these three carrier divisions were well matched in terms of their speed, range, and aircraft complements. The reason for employing ships of roughly similar capabilities is simple—in the heat of battle, compensating for ships possessing widely differing capabilities introduces an unnecessary element of complexity into an already-chaotic situation. Uniformity lessens command and control friction. Losing CarDivs 1 and 2 permanently destroyed the admirable balance and integration that had existed in the Japanese carrier force.

After the battle, *Shōkaku* and *Zuikaku* were a solid core around which to rebuild, but Japan's inadequacies in shipbuilding meant that its two remaining fleet carriers would have a supporting cast of bit players, most of whom were really not up to their parts. *Taihō,* commissioned in 1944, was the only new fleet carrier Japan built during the entire war that was worthy of keeping company with *Shōkaku* and *Zuikaku.* These three were the only carriers that Japan possessed during the war that were in any way comparable to the three American *Yorktown*-class carriers, let alone the dozen *Essex*-class carriers that followed them. The *Unryū*-class vessels, though worthy successors to *Hiryū* and *Sōryū,* were not nearly as capable as their American opponents. The remainder of Japan's flight decks were conversions and misfits. So, despite being able to field nominally similar numbers of carriers in 1942 and 1944, Japan's carrier force never remotely approached the balance, cohesiveness, and striking power of *Dai-Ichi Kidō Butai* at the beginning of the war. Men and planes could be replaced, but the four Midway carriers could not. Their loss permanently ruined what had been the most successful Japanese naval weapon system of the war, and hence must be ranked as far and away the most important material loss of the battle.

A second facet of any assessment of Midway must be the strategic consequences of having lost, which requires looking beyond mere tabulation of physical losses. The material forces of the United States and Japan were not static—they were always changing in relative strength depending on a variety of other factors—geography, weather, lines of communication, and who held the strategic initiative. Thus, H. P. Willmott noted in his analysis of the Battle of Coral Sea that the balance sheet for the engagement had to be assessed not materially, but rather "in terms of the demands made on resources by time and distance. The ability to concentrate mobile forces to dictate the direction and tempo of future operations was the all-important factor in the conduct of the Pacific war. The true cost of the battle was not to be found in calculations of ship losses but rather in contrasting the effect of the battle on the carrier forces."[11] This calculus applies equally well to Midway, and the true locus of that battle's downstream effects rightly lies in the waters off Guadalcanal.

Japan had entered the war with the intention of eventually moving to a barrier defense backed by mobile carrier and air forces. The real litmus test of Japanese strategy was therefore to capture what was needed while preserving its strategic mass for as long as possible. As was noted earlier, the best way to preserve mass is to use it en masse instead of doling it out in penny packets. Using overwhelming force tends to keep casualties to a minimum. For the Japanese, if an objective wasn't important enough to require sending all six carriers, it wasn't worth going after at all. Japan violated this principle by initiating the action in the Coral Sea. She paid the ultimate price for her violation a month later at Midway. One immediate consequence of the calamity was that Operation FS—the occupation of Fiji and Samoa to cut off Australia from her lines of communication with the United States—was canceled. Another consequence was the obviation of Japan's barrier strategy before it had truly begun. Without a powerful carrier striking force to transport aircraft to outposts under attack, the strategy was unworkable.

This was illustrated when the Americans unexpectedly counterattacked at Guadalcanal in August 1942. The occupations of both Guadalcanal and Tulagi by the Japanese was both an extension of their defensive perimeter outward from the main Japanese base in the region, Rabaul, and an offensive move to apply pressure against Australia's supply lines. As such, Guadalcanal was essentially an outpost of Japan's defensive barrier in the southwest Pacific.

Had the Japanese won the Battle of Midway, an American operation like Guadalcanal most likely could never have occurred, at least not when it did. However, the victory at Midway gave the Americans rough parity in fleet carriers and enough confidence in their abilities that they were willing to fight in a remote backwater like the Solomons. Likewise, the rough parity of carrier forces of the two sides contributed to the protracted nature of the bloody struggle for the island.

It is important to understand that the Japanese, while privately acknowledging the seriousness of the defeat at Midway, did not feel that they had been condemned ipso facto to fighting on unequal terms around Guadalcanal. It did not affect their strategic formulations, and it did not temper their aggressiveness. Indeed, in the short term, they were able to stay in the game in the waters off Guadalcanal. At this point in the conflict, even after the losses she had suffered, Japan still possessed the means to equip the air groups of several more fleet carriers, had the ships themselves been available. The truth of this statement is revealed in the prodigious scale of aerial resources the Japanese were ultimately able to commit to the Solomons contest, as well as the fact that Japan deployed credible air groups at various points in the struggle on board *Hiyō, Junyō,* and *Zuihō.*

With *Shōkaku* and *Zuikaku* forming the basis of their new mobile force, and the unexpected woes of the American carriers at the hands of Japanese submarines (*Saratoga* was torpedoed and put out of action again from September to November 1942, and *Wasp* was sunk by *I-19* on 15 September), the odds did not turn against Japan immediately. Of the two major carrier battles fought off Guadalcanal—Eastern Solomons and Santa Cruz—the Japanese lost the former but arguably won the latter. But even when they achieved what appeared to be temporary victories in the waters around Guadalcanal, they lacked the strength to capitalize on their triumphs. They could no longer "close out the deal" by inflicting a final, crushing defeat, driving off the American support vessels, and exterminating the U.S. forces on the island. Had even *Hiryū* or *Akagi* survived Midway, which was not inconceivable, the Japanese might have had the requisite strength to prevail four to six months later in these crucial waters.

Much worse lay in store after the Imperial Navy conceded defeat at Guadalcanal. By the end of 1942, the carrier forces of both sides were exhausted and depleted, leaving the remainder of the brutal fighting in the Solomons to be conducted by surface vessels and land-based airpower. The carrier fleets would not meet again in battle until 1944. But by the middle of 1943, the Americans were commissioning *Essex*-class fleet carriers at the rate of one every other month, a production rate that the Japanese in their wildest dreams could never equal. With nine very serviceable light carriers of the *Independence* class also having been commissioned in the same year, American naval aviation was now poised to transform the Pacific war.

At the same time, not only had the Americans fundamentally altered the raw numbers in the fleet carrier equation, they had also radically transformed the intrinsic power of the individual flight decks themselves. The addition of a new generation of carrier aircraft (in particular the excellent F6F Hellcat fighter), the improvement of air search and fire-control radar, the maturation of the Combat Information Center (CIC) in combination with more effective fighter-vectoring techniques, and the enormous increase in the number and effectiveness of shipboard antiaircraft batteries (including those armed with radar proximity-fused ammunition) all meant that ship-for-ship American carriers were now markedly superior to those of the Japanese. Almost as important was the U.S. Navy's development of a sophisticated mobile logistics capability—fast oilers and transports, repair ships, and floating dry docks—giving the Americans an unparalleled ability to forward deploy their fleet anchorages and then keep carriers operating in enemy waters for weeks at a time through underway replenishment. Not only was American naval aviation thus capable of threatening areas of the empire once thought to be off-limits, it could also maintain a much higher tempo of operations than the imperial fleet could. So impressive was this cumulative leap in technology and operational technique that, in effect, the Americans emerged in late 1943 with an entirely new navy.[12]

All of these factors came together during the American invasion of the Gilbert Islands in November 1943. To support Operation Galvanic, the U.S. Navy employed six fleet, five light fleet, and seven escort carriers. The Japanese Navy had no possibility of interdicting such a powerful armada. Several of their carrier air groups had recently been transferred to Rabaul for temporary duty in stemming the American tide then rising in the Solomons. They had been chewed to pieces in the process, ruining the ability of their carriers to offer battle. The best the Imperial Navy could manage was sending a few cruisers and a squadron of submarines to the Gilberts. Just three months later, the Americans used a similarly enormous carrier force to crush the heretofore unassailable Japanese base at Truk. In the process, they sank nearly 150,000 tons of merchant shipping and annihilated Japanese airpower on the atoll. The pattern was now set for subsequent American offensives through the Central Pacific, in which their powerful carrier task groups operated practically at will, bringing hundreds of aircraft to their objectives, and destroying whatever naval opposition stood in their way.

Here, then, is the crux of the matter as it relates to Midway and the larger strategic forces at play in the Pacific war. In an immediate sense, an American victory at Midway was vitally important in restoring the parity of forces in the Pacific, and thereby speeding up the tempo of the war. But viewed in the longer term, the battle's strategic importance is less profound. Whether or not *Kidō Butai* had survived intact at Midway, it is clear that the very best the Japanese could have hoped for by the end of 1943 was the ability to offer battle on terms that were merely disadvantageous, rather than utterly ruinous. Even had every carrier that attacked Pearl Harbor in December 1941 sallied forth intact in 1943 to face the Americans off the Gilberts, the outcome there would almost certainly have been disastrous. At most, the defeat at Midway cost the Japanese approximately eighteen months of strategic leverage that their four carriers might have bought them. But in the end, win or lose at Midway, the vast industrial resources of the United States gave its navy an absolutely irrevocable writ of strategic dominance in the Pacific war.

This leads to the third major topic to be considered—answering the hypothetical question of what it might have meant for the Japanese to *win* at Midway. Throughout the years, the various answers to this question—seen in both books and an endless stream of Internet bulletin board and listserve conversations—have spanned the gamut from measured to downright hysterical. Hawaii would have been captured; the West Coast of the United States would have been threatened or even invaded; Australia would have been captured; America would have abandoned the Pacific and focused on Germany; or, alternately, America would have poured yet more resources into the Pacific at the possible expense of the European theater of action, leaving Germany to triumph over Russia and the Allies to lose the war; Japan would have eventually have been conquered by the Russians instead of the Americans—the list goes on and on.

The authors (well, one of them, anyway) heartily dislike alternative history. Such exercises tend to be biased from the outset and are often used disingenuously to prove pet opinions, rather than to explore openly the downstream ramifications of a given scenario. Even used honestly, they are inherently dodgy propositions. One can think of an alternative history as being a flow of changed events radiating forward from a given point in time. The problem is, the further one goes beyond the immediate implications of the changed event, the less one can predict with accuracy what might happen. That, in turn, means that there is a time threshold before which one is (at best) engaged in educated speculation, but after which one is simply indulging in largely meaningless conjecture. Alternative history can't "prove" anything—all it can do is suggest possible outcomes. Likewise, when someone says that the effects of the Americans losing at Midway were "incalculable," they should be held to *exactly* that level of precision. The results of such a hypothetical loss, strictly speaking, are, by definition, incalculable, in that they cannot be pinned down with any exactness, pro or con. Not only that, but anyone with sufficiently deep knowledge of a given historical event can usually construct several plausible downstream scenarios from the same event that would lead to *opposite* ultimate outcomes.

For instance, had *Akagi* escaped her ultimately fatal attack at 1026, would this have turned the tide of the battle in favor of the Japanese? Perhaps, but perhaps not. One thread of argument might suggest that with one additional flight deck, and a bit of luck, the Japanese could have "won" the battle three carriers to two, forestalled or beaten the Americans at Guadalcanal, and thus held off defeat until 1946. Conversely, maybe *Nautilus* or some other U.S. submarine might have gotten lucky (they were certainly due) and sunk Nagumo's flagship sometime during the early afternoon, leading to exactly the same historical outcome. The answer is completely unknowable.

Nevertheless, it is impossible to write a book on Midway and not consider some of the more prominent of these hypotheses. At the very least, the question of what would have happened to Hawaii in the event of a Japanese victory needs to be addressed, as well as the likely strategic ramifications of a Japanese victory vis-à-vis the Pacific war as a whole. There's no question that the Japanese were interested in capturing Hawaii. John Stephan's superbly researched *Hawaii Under the Rising Sun* makes it clear that the Japanese were actively investigating such operations from the outset of hostilities and planning continued as late as September 1942. However, the pertinent question is not whether the intention was there or not—it clearly was—but whether the Japanese ever had the military means to achieve their aims.

Answering this question is relatively easy. Win or lose at Midway, the Japanese could never have taken the Hawaiian Islands under any foreseeable circumstances. The reasons are manifold and clear-cut. By April 1942, the Americans had 62,700 Army troops (two full infantry divisions, plus support troops) in Hawaii, and another 8,900 air personnel.[13] The U.S. Army expected this total to reach at least 115,000 ground and air personnel in the near future. This figure does not include the tens of thousands of U.S. Navy personnel located at Pearl Harbor. Thus, even had the Japanese followed up a victory at Midway in short order with an attack on Hawaii, they would have had to contend with a Hawaiian garrison of at least 100,000–150,000 U.S. servicemen. These American troops were primarily located on Oahu, which was small enough to defend in depth but big enough to maneuver on, making it an enormously difficult nut to crack.

The Japanese themselves thought that capturing such a stronghold would require at least three infantry divisions, or roughly 45,000 troops.[14] This was certainly a parsimonious number of troops to commit to such an undertaking, but, even so, it represented an invasion force ten times larger than the one they had planned to employ at Midway and three times larger than they had ever amphibiously landed at one time. It is doubtful that Japan had the sealift capacity to contemplate such an undertaking across nearly 4,000 miles of open water in any case. Nor is it likely that even if the Japanese had been so lucky as to have captured the islands, that they would subsequently have been able to keep their troops in supply, let alone the civilian population.

Even if sufficient transport could have been found, a Japanese assault force would have landed in the face of withering American fire, without much in the way of specialized equipment, and without an effective naval gunfire or air-support doctrine. In the unlikely event that Japanese troops managed to gain some kind of foothold, given the size of Oahu and the depth of the American defenses, there could be none of the bold flanking movements that the Imperial Army had used to such great effect in Malaya. Hawaii would most likely have to be taken frontally. Considering the heavy losses the Japanese had suffered attempting a similar landing on Wake at the beginning of the war, not to mention the appalling slaughter that American Marines would inflict on the Japanese in similar circumstances at Guadalcanal just two months later,[15] the conclusion seems inescapable that a Japanese landing on Oahu would have resulted in a bloodbath worthy of the Somme. Granted, the Japanese were hardly squeamish over taking such losses, but it is difficult to see how such an invasion could have succeeded.

Furthermore, the Japanese would have to secure air superiority over Hawaii with carrier assets alone—their land-based aircraft at Midway, over a thousand miles away, could play no real role in such an invasion. Yet, unlike the carrier task forces the Americans would go on to employ in 1944, even at the height of its powers *Kidō Butai* never had the ability to stand off an enemy's island bastion for weeks on end and beat it into submission. In the first place, *Kidō Butai* couldn't bring a sufficient number of aircraft to get the job done. By April 1942, Hawaii boasted 275 combat aircraft, a figure that had increased as the battle at Midway had loomed. In the event of an American defeat there, Hawaii's air force could have been augmented still further by naval aircraft shuttled in from *Saratoga* or *Wasp,* much as the Americans went on to do at Guadalcanal. This meant that *Kidō Butai,* even with all six carriers available, would have fought against Hawaii from a position of numerical parity at best. But more important, the logistics for a sustained Japanese carrier presence off the shores of Hawaii simply weren't there. *Kidō Butai* could mount raids, but it could not project sustained power ashore. This meant that Japanese ground forces, even if they managed to stay ashore, would probably lack consistent air cover while trying to conduct offensive operations—not a good recipe for ultimate success.

It is true that if the Hawaiian Islands couldn't be captured, the Japanese might have tried blockading them instead, using a combination of submarines and surface forces. But Japanese doctrine looked down on commerce raiding, and as a result, their subs never proved as effective in this role as they might have been. For their part, Japanese surface forces couldn't hope to operate in the face of American land-based airpower without *Kidō Butai* to support them. Yet, the presence of Japanese carriers in the area would have necessarily been sporadic. Even in the face of a concerted blockade, it is almost impossible to imagine the Americans being willing to sacrifice the garrison and the large civilian population there. If maintaining the logistical flow to the islands necessitated sustaining Murmansk-like losses in the supply convoys, so be it, but the convoys would still have been sent. America was engaged in a total war, and failure was not an option. Just as the British had risen to the London Blitz and defended Malta in the Mediterranean, and the Russians had endured the seemingly endless siege of Leningrad, so too would the Americans have been determined to hang on to Oahu—their last outpost in the Pacific. The only logical conclusion one can reach from all this is that Hawaii was largely impregnable. Its value as an American naval base might have been diminished in the short term. But the islands themselves most likely could never have been taken.

The wider ramifications of a Japanese victory at Midway are less easy to gauge. It is certainly true that the American counteroffensive at Guadalcanal would never have been launched under such circumstances. Australia and New Guinea would likewise have been in greater danger as a result of America's inability to forestall continued Japanese incursions. Barring the successful occupation of Hawaii, the Japanese certainly would have moved into the South Pacific largely unimpeded, occupying the New Hebrides, Fiji, Samoa, and Tonga. It is possible that they would have contemplated landings in Northern Australia as well. In the short term, then, the Allied position in this area of operations would have been made much more precarious. But it is unclear whether the Japanese really could have used the time that a victory at Midway would have purchased to good effect.

No amount of territory that Japan captured in the South Pacific could solve its basic strategic problems. Taking Tonga, or even Brisbane, couldn't bring the Americans to the negotiating table. It couldn't forestall the inexorable completion of the naval forces then building in America's shipyards. Nor could it help Japan build her own carriers any faster. One thing that the breathless proselytizers of Midway doomsday scenarios always fail to note is that in all the territory Japan had added to her empire since December 1941, there was not a single production center worthy of the name. Whereas the Germans had benefited significantly from capturing such complexes as the Skoda arms works in Czechoslovakia, the factories around Paris and in the Rhône-Alpes region, and the shipyards in Brest and St. Nazaire, no comparable facilities existed anywhere in Asia. Apart from Japan and the United States, there wasn't a single shipyard in the Pacific capable of launching a warship larger than a destroyer. The only decent dry dock anywhere south of Kyūshū was located 2,700 miles away, in Singapore. Thus, Japan's conquests contributed practically nil to her industrial capacity.

Likewise, the raw materials that Japan secured in the East Indies still had to be transported home and turned into finished products. Not only that, but Japan's own industrial base had already been largely "maxed out" during the heated military expansions of the 1930s.[16] In contrast to the American economy, which had been underutilized during much of the same time period, and thus had plenty of unused capacity, Japan had no such "headroom" for significant growth. Worse still, there is credible evidence to suggest that absorbing the lower per capita GDP regions like the East Indies represented a significant hindrance to efficiently mobilizing the Japanese economy.[17] Thus, both militarily and economically, territorial indulgences like taking the Solomons or Fiji were ultimately futile, in that they extended the Japanese defensive perimeter for little real gain. There was nothing in the South Pacific worth capturing from a resource standpoint, and those garrisons would have to be manned and supplied, thereby stretching Japan's already-fragile logistical resources even further. Taken as a whole, it is arguable that the Japanese sticking their necks out even further would merely have left them that much more exposed when the inevitable American hammer blows began in 1944.

Likewise, while invading northern Australia would have been a blow to Allied fortunes, and would have potentially deprived them of a useful base in the short term, in the long term it is difficult to see how such a move could have measurably improved Japanese fortunes. In the first place, the Australians had several superb infantry formations of their own. It is likely that they could have held their shores against the invader, or at least inflicted very serious casualties on them. After all, the Australians, unlike the British in Malaya, would have been fighting for hearth and home. Second, it seems equally unlikely that the Japanese could have occupied the entire subcontinent, meaning that Sydney, Perth, and probably even Brisbane couldn't have been brought effectively under Japanese control. Third, it has to be admitted that while Australia was a useful base for the Allied counteroffensive, it wasn't vital in the same way that holding Britain was for conducting operations against the continent of Europe. As the Americans were to demonstrate in 1944 in the Central Pacific, they had the means to punch directly through the heart of Japanese defenses and make their way toward the Home Islands. Nothing that happened at Midway in 1942 could change the overall parameters of that equation come 1944.

Overall, it seems clear that much of the wild speculation regarding the possible negative effects of an American loss at Midway is unwarranted. As we have seen, the American strategic position in the Pacific could be damaged, but not irretrievably so, for the simple reason that Hawaii could never have been taken away. In contrast, there's no question that in the short term, such a defeat would have carried heavy penalties, particularly with regard to the South Pacific and Australia. The war might have been lengthened somewhat. But in the long term, the Americans were in a truly unique position of strength. The U.S. economy was already more than six times larger than that of Japan at the outbreak, and would expand by 50 percent during the war.[18] More important, U.S. industry was essentially immune to Japanese attack. The American naval building program could not be forestalled, meaning that Admirals Ernest King and Chester Nimitz knew with absolute certainty that their naval power was going to be decisively superior to that of Japan in the relatively near future.

This raises the final conundrum surrounding the true meaning of winning or losing at Midway. Since the day the battle was fought, the American victory there has been labeled as being "decisive." But the foregoing analysis has shown that, win or lose at Midway, it was extremely unlikely that the Americans were going to lose the war in the Pacific, and it was equally unlikely that the Japanese were going to win. How, then, can such a battle be considered decisive? As H. P. Willmott pointed out, there is a basic contradiction in simultaneously thinking that the Americans were bound to win the war *and* that the Battle of Midway was decisive. To be decisive, Midway had to be a defeat from which the Japanese could not recover, of the sort, for example, that the Japanese inflicted on the Russians at Tsushima. But that was clearly not the case, Willmott notes, given the vigorous Japanese naval actions later in 1942 around the Solomons. Midway might also be termed "decisive" if it had completely altered the course of the war, but that also seems untrue. If the defeat of Japan "was assured because of the disparity of national resources, Midway was at best only a milestone on the road that led to defeat; it was not a signpost that marked a parting of the way, one track leading to American victory and the other in precisely the opposite direction." This leads back to the logical contradiction in asserting simultaneously that Midway was a decisive battle and that American victory was inevitable, because "the notion of an inevitable victory is irreconcilable with that of a decisive battle."[19] If Midway merely hastened by some months a foregone conclusion to the conflict that still lay some years in the future, as seems to be the case, then it cannot legitimately be termed decisive.

Arguing that the outcome of the war in the Pacific was inevitable is not suggesting that the defeat of the Axis Powers in WW II was likewise guaranteed. Richard Overy's superb *Why the Allies Won* vigorously refutes the economic determinist stance regarding WW II, showing just how many critical hinge points there were in that conflict. His study and others render highly dubious any assertion that an Allied victory over the Axis as a whole was inevitable.[20] This is because the real strategic locus of the war as a whole lay not in the Pacific, but rather in Europe generally and on the steppes of Russia in particular. Victory in the European theater was far chancier for the Allies, given the immense collective economic strength of Nazi Germany and her satellite assemblage of allied and conquered territories. It would not be until Russia's survival was assured, in late 1942, that the war in Europe began to veer away from the brink of disaster.

But paradoxically, within the more limited context of the Pacific war, it was absolutely certain that the Allies (chiefly represented by the United States) would ultimately defeat the sole Axis power in the region, Japan. The reasons for this are twofold. The first was one of simple geography. Germany was in no position to assist Japan militarily in any substantial sense, even if it had wanted to. Thus, a German victory in Europe was not necessarily a guarantor of Japan's ultimate security. The second, more important reason was America's enormous advantages in productive capacity relative to that of Japan. Indeed, this basic fact was well understood by both parties, as an exchange immediately prior to the war between the American chief of naval operations, Adm. Harold R. Stark, and Japan's special ambassador to the United States, Adm. Nomura Kichisaburō illustrates. With war clouds gathering, Stark remarked to Nomura,

> If you attack us we will break your empire before we are through with you. While you may have initial success . . . the time will come when you too will have your losses, but there will be this great difference. You will not only be unable to make up your losses but will grow weaker as time goes on: while on the other hand we will not only make up our losses but will grow stronger as time goes on. It is inevitable that we shall crush you before we are through with you.[21]

Stark's comments precisely foretold the long-term strategic dynamics that would play out in the war that Japan would shortly initiate. Indeed, if anything, he understated the case, as Japan's ruinous, almost preindustrialized postwar economic situation vividly demonstrated.

It is true that this "inevitable" victory might not have occurred if the American will to victory had flagged. In light of modern defeats in places like Vietnam, Beirut, and Mogadishu, it is fashionable these days to question whether the American populace in WW II would have had the determination to see the war through to a successful finish in the face of something like a Japanese victory at Midway. However, this notion is unsupportable, being based on a postwar mind-set that did not pertain during 1942. In the first place, drawing parallels between defeats in Lebanon, Somalia, and Vietnam is not germane. These were all "optional wars," for want of a better phrase. The American public knew that, win or lose, nothing that happened on those battlefields necessarily affected the global security of America, or would have a dramatic impact on their way of life. The same most certainly cannot be said of World War II. Once

France fell, Britain was attacked, and then the bombs fell on Pearl Harbor, the American public somberly grasped the fundamental magnitude and importance of the struggle before them. The knowledge that this was total war, fought against evils of an appalling and absolute nature, pervaded the country. It steeled the collective resolve of the nation and prepared it for massive sacrifices of blood and treasure in ways that are lost on generations raised during and after Vietnam. World War II was fought by a generation that had grown up in full knowledge of the horrendous sacrifices that had been made in World War I. People of that era understood the level of effort that would be required—no one was under any illusions that they were in for anything other than a long, bitter, and bloody war. And so indeed it proved.

In the end, Midway stands as the most important battle of the Pacific war, not because it was decisive in an absolute sense, and not because it won the war in a day, but because of its immediate practical effects on American military options in the Pacific. In the succinct words of the Naval War College study of the battle, Midway "put an end to Japanese offensive action . . . and . . . [restored] the balance of naval power in the Pacific."[22] In this modern era of unchallenged American naval supremacy, merely restoring parity may not seem like much of an accomplishment. But it must be recalled that Midway was fought "between one navy at the peak of its strength and another if not at its nadir then close to it."[23] In the dark months of 1942, being able to claw back to parity was an enormous achievement. Thus, Midway clearly delineated where and when the strategic momentum in the Pacific war shifted over to the Americans. The Battle of Coral Sea had provided the first hints that the Japanese high-water mark had been reached, but it was the Battle of Midway that put up the sign for all to see. Midway also marked the gateway to the attritional war that would be fought in the Solomons, a campaign that would irreparably ruin the Japanese Navy by destroying its elite naval aviation cadres and wrecking its surface forces beyond redemption. Midway didn't produce these consequences by itself, but it created the circumstances whereby the Japanese Navy would be fed into the shredder.

24

The Myths and Mythmakers of Midway

As was stated in the introduction, all great battles inevitably create their own mythos. That is, every battle of note is comprised of a series of significant moments that provide a framework for understanding the outcome of the battle as a whole. They are the crucial, causative events that people look at and say, "Oh, so this is why things turned out as they did." Such a mythos clarifies and simplifies actions that are invariably messy, complex, and almost incomprehensibly violent. The present account, it is true, is a revisionist one, in that it disputes many of the beliefs regarding the Battle of Midway that have been in print for the last sixty years or so. It's appropriate, then, to end by briefly reexamining some of the conventional wisdom, and then attacking the last, and greatest, of the misconceptions that is still attached to this battle. The issues addressed so far include the following:

"At the time of the decisive American dive-bomber attack at 1020–1025 on 4 June, the Japanese carriers were just minutes away from launching a decisive counterattack against the American carriers." *This is categorically not true and is one of the biggest fallacies in the conventional Japanese account. At the time of the decisive attack, the Japanese were at least a half hour away from being able to launch a strike, and few, if any, Japanese attack planes were on deck.*

"The Aleutians Operation was an elaborate feint designed to lure the American fleet out of Pearl Harbor." *Not true. The simultaneous launch of operations in the Aleutians was designed to capitalize on the Americans being busy elsewhere, so that objectives in the Aleutians could be seized without hindrance. Operation AL was an invasion in its own right, strategically timed, and not merely a diversion.*

"During the transit to Midway, Admiral Yamamoto withheld important intelligence from Admiral Nagumo that might have changed the course of the battle. As a result, Nagumo was in the dark concerning the nature of the threat facing him at Midway." *Not true. While Yamamoto did not communicate to Nagumo, there was no need to, as* Kidō Butai *was perfectly capable of independently receiving timely intelligence from the First Communications Unit in Tokyo. Akagi's intelligence estimate before the battle reveals that Nagumo had most of the important pieces of information already in hand. What is less clear is why he did not act on that intelligence.*

"Had the Japanese implemented a two-phase search plan on the morning of 4 June, they would have succeeded in locating the American fleet in time to win the battle." *Perhaps, but in 1942 the Japanese (and Americans) had yet to incorporate the notion of a two-phase search into their doctrine. Such a search plan was never an option, and it was disingenuous for Fuchida Mitsuo to imply that it was.*

"The late launch of cruiser *Tone*'s scout plane doomed Admiral Nagumo's efforts to win the battle." *Not true. If anything,* Tone No. 4*'s late launch and subsequent improvised search route led to the discovery of the Americans earlier than ought to have been expected. The true failures in scouting during the battle began with the failure of Japan's submarines to arrive on station on time, followed by the abandonment of Operation K, and culminated with* Chikuma No. 1*'s failure to locate the Americans in the 0615 time frame.*

"Had Nagumo not decided to rearm his aircraft with land attack weapons, he would have been in a position to attack the Americans as soon as they were discovered." *Not true. The reserve strike aircraft were not spotted on the flight deck when the Americans were detected. Given the time required to spot the decks, Nagumo's odds of launching an attack before Tomonaga's return were low at best. The ceaseless American air attacks had destroyed any reasonable possibility of spotting the decks before Tomonaga's return because of the constant launch and recovery of combat air patrol (CAP) fighters.*

"The sacrifice of Torpedo Eight was not in vain, since it pulled the Japanese CAP fighters down to sea level, thereby allowing the American dive-bombers to attack." *Not true. VT-8's demise happened a full hour before the decisive attack, giving plenty of time for the CAP Zeros to resume their correct stacking had they maintained discipline. Rather, VT-8's contribution was the same as VT-6's—disrupting the counteroffensive activities of the Japanese carriers.*

"The Japanese naval air corps was all but wiped out at the Battle of Midway." *Not true. Japanese casualties at Midway amounted to fewer than a quarter of the aviators embarked. Rather, it was the attritional campaign in the Solomons that destroyed the elite corps of Japanese naval aviators.*

However, the most pernicious myth concerning the Battle of Midway has never been seriously questioned even though evidence to the contrary was readily available. The continuance of this myth suggests that it fits conveniently into the glorification of this, possibly the greatest U.S. naval victory of all time. Appealing as the myth is to any historian who becomes involved in studying Midway, its attractiveness must not outweigh a careful cross-checking of sources and a dispassionate evaluation of the factual evidence. The myth in question is the persistent belief that in defeating the Japanese the Americans miraculously triumphed against "overwhelming odds." With no disrespect intended toward the late Walter Lord, who generously assisted the authors in the creation of this work, the foreword to his otherwise very laudable *Incredible Victory* nevertheless encapsulates this belief as eloquently as anything else in print:

By any ordinary standard, they were hopelessly outclassed. They had no battleships, the enemy eleven. They had eight cruisers, the enemy twenty-three. They had three carriers (one of them crippled); the enemy had eight. . . .

They had no right to win. Yet they did, and in doing so, they changed the course of a war. More than that, they added a new name—Midway—to that small list that inspires men by shining example. Like Marathon, the Armada, the Marne, a few others, Midway showed that every once in a while "what must be" need not be at all. Even against the greatest of odds, there is something in the human spirit—a magic blend of skill, faith and valor—that can lift men from certain defeat to incredible victory.[1]

Lord certainly didn't invent this notion. But he articulated a general postwar attitude that has been echoed endlessly in almost every American text on the battle until it has been accepted as holy writ. It is a conviction that has been subtly reinforced by the very titles of the two most important English-language histories of the battle—*Miracle at Midway* and *Incredible Victory*—and less subtly amplified by numerous TV documentaries, by every talk given at a WW II veteran's group, and by hundreds of Internet discussions that have self-referentially reinforced the notion. It has gotten so out of hand, in fact, that historian John Lundstrom has jokingly coined a phrase to describe it—"Incredible Victory Disease." However, the notion that Midway was somehow a miraculous triumph, fought in the face of crushing Japanese superiority, is a fallacy, and one greatly in need of dispelling.[2] Furthermore, it is a fallacy that can be easily refuted at two different levels of analysis—first, by examining the opposing forces and their operational plans during the battle, and second, by analyzing the command decisions of the two opposing supreme commanders—Yamamoto Isoroku and Chester Nimitz.

First, the numbers. It is quite true that in May of 1942, the Combined Fleet enjoyed an aggregate numerical advantage over the U.S. Navy in the Pacific and conceivably could have brought overwhelming firepower to bear anywhere in that theater of operations. It is further true that the bulk of Combined Fleet was indeed operating in support of Operations AL and MI on the morning of 4 June. But the Japanese battle plan ensured that the majority of this force could not have engaged any American units on that day. Claiming that the American defenders at Midway somehow fought against this impressive array of warships in toto—when the majority of the Japanese vessels participating never fired a shot in anger, never once raised their speed of advance (or retreat) in reaction to an impending American attack, were never even sighted by so much as an American scout plane—is to overstate the matter egregiously.

The forces that deserve to be tallied were those present at the point of tactical contact on the morning of 4 June and that were within a day's steaming distance of the island of Midway itself. By those qualifications, *Nihon Kaigun* had exactly two formations worth considering—Nagumo's First Mobile Striking Force and Tanaka's Invasion Force. The latter can be disregarded, as, by definition, it was incapable of offensive action. For his part, Nagumo brought twenty warships to face the U.S. Navy's twenty-five. He was operating a grand total of four aircraft carriers and 248 carrier aircraft. The Americans, between their three carriers (none of which can be honestly described as "crippled"), mounted a total of 233 carrier aircraft and could call upon another 120-odd aircraft from Midway. Like the Japanese, the Americans had four airstrips from which to operate, with the added benefit that one of theirs could not be sunk. In other words, where it really counted, it was the *Japanese* who were outnumbered in terms of both warships and aircraft, not the other way around.

Some may protest that Yamamoto's Main Body should be included in this equation, as well as Kurita and Kondō's support forces, since they were also driving on Midway. However, advocates of this line of reasoning ignore the obvious fact that as far as Nagumo and the outcome of the battle was concerned, those forces might as well have been on the moon. The outcome at Midway was determined in the space of about six hours, between 0430 and 1030. By the end of that period, the battle was fundamentally decided in favor of the Americans. The only thing left to be seen was whether *Hiryū* would exact some measure of retribution before she, too, was finally caught and smashed. Nothing that Yamamoto's Main Body or the other support formations could do was going to reverse that decision, because, in truth, they were in no position to support anything. Thus, the only forces that are relevant in a discussion of who outnumbered who were the ones in a position to have exchanged actual blows on 4 June, meaning Nagumo's and Fletcher's, period.

It is quite true that in comparison with Fletcher's command, Nagumo could muster superior gun power in the form of his two fast battleships, not to mention the combat capability provided by the torpedoes of his destroyers and cruisers, if it ever came to that. But of course it never really could have come to that, and neither of these measuring sticks was at all relevant to the outcome of the battle. Admirals Fletcher and Spruance had no interest in becoming embroiled in a surface fight and maneuvered their forces carefully so as to avoid any chance of such entanglements. Thus, Nagumo could never salvage victory from defeat by using his superiorities in, say, night fighting. A surface battle could only build on the success that his aircraft brought him—it could never replace them. It was aircraft and flight decks that were the true index of victory or defeat, and it is clear that the Japanese enjoyed no numerical advantage in this respect.

To be sure, it is also true that in several key qualitative areas such as aircraft performance (at least in terms of fighters and torpedo aircraft), pilot experience, and the ability to mass the offensive firepower of their carrier air groups, Nagumo possessed distinct advantages. Their importance should not be discounted, as shown by the effectiveness of *Hiryū*'s strikes against *Yorktown* with a relatively small number of planes and with no advantage of surprise. Thus, a real understanding of the battle requires weighing the strengths and weaknesses of both forces, and, hopefully, this study has indicated the intricate matrix of qualitative factors, doctrinal subtleties, planning shortcomings, and sheer good and bad fortune that played into the final outcome of the battle. Too often, however, the casual reader of popular history prefers to ignore such subtleties and to focus instead on simplistic numbers and catch phrases like "overwhelming odds." They paint for themselves a mental picture of veritable hordes of Japanese being fended off by a ragtag (but plucky) band of hideously outnumbered Americans. While serious studies of the battle have provided a more nuanced picture, they have not been as direct as they might in disparaging this chauvinistic, overly simplified view.

The myth of supposedly overwhelming Japanese force runs into further problems, because it contradicts other popularly held notions about Midway, such as the perceived incompetence of Admiral Yamamoto. Some Western observers have argued for Japan's stunning numerical advantages while simultaneously attacking Yamamoto's unwise dispersal of his assets. Yet, if Nagumo's defeat was truly as miraculous as these same writers would have us believe, then Yamamoto can hardly be faulted for dispersing his forces after first equipping his subordinate Nagumo with such a wealth of military force that, apparently, only an act of God was sufficient to defeat it. The inconsistency is obvious: either Yamamoto did *not* provide sufficient forces to Nagumo (and the odds were thereby considerably less in Japan's favor than the popular wisdom would have us believe) *or* Yamamoto's battle plan wasn't as deeply flawed as it has been made out to be. Both positions cannot be true. The view argued here has been that Yamamoto's battle plan was indeed badly flawed, in that it assumed that the Americans were mentally beaten, and that stealth and deception were therefore to be prized above sufficiency of force at the point of contact. In hindsight, Nagumo's force was clearly inadequate for the task at hand. It should never have left port without one, and preferably both, of CarDiv 5's carriers. To do otherwise was to cut the margin of sufficiency too fine, as was disastrously demonstrated. Indeed, the real miracle of Midway (from the American point of view) may well have been Yamamoto's failure to provide Nagumo with sufficient forces to guarantee victory in battle, given that he might readily have done so.

Even greater problems occur when those who hew to the myth evaluate the performance of Admiral Chester Nimitz. If one believes in the notion of overwhelming Japanese superiority, then Nimitz's decision to engage the enemy and accept the horrific odds against him must be judged reckless in the extreme. Nothing less can explain his willingness to walk clear-eyed into a fight, pitting his allegedly pathetic force against the Japanese juggernaut to contest a speck of land that was entirely disposable and that could be isolated and recaptured at any time. However, we take the view that Nimitz was an exceptional commander who had a finer appreciation of the odds facing him than many commentators do sixty years after the battle. Based on estimates of four to five Japanese carriers, he was within his rights to suppose that his forces, if positioned correctly, could carry the day. It is true that the actual day's events were a nearer run than Nimitz would have wished, but that is largely the result of poor decisions by American commanders further down the chain of command and to a lack of experience in conducting multicarrier operations. The critical American failing of the morning—the dissipation of their attacking air formations—was beyond Nimitz's control. Had the bulk of the American carrier aircraft, including *Hornet*'s, been able to arrive simultaneously in the area of *Kidō Butai* and delivered a coordinated attack, the entire Japanese force might well have been knocked out in a single blow. Indeed, any American carrier task force in 1944—when the U.S. Navy was at the top of its game—would probably have done so as a matter of course.

The unglamorous truth is that the U.S. Navy, at an operational level, fought much of the morning of 4 June suboptimally in terms of scouting, flight deck operations, and coordinated delivery of firepower. In the process, they dug themselves into such a hole that success could only be bought at the cost of many aviators' lives. Managing to prevail despite those mistakes was a testament to the skill and courage of the Americans. But in a wider view, it cannot be taken as some kind of miracle that three American carriers were able to prevail against four of Japan's. As far as Nimitz's reputation is concerned, his forces' *operational* performance should not reflect on his overall *strategic* calculus, which was fundamentally solid. Nimitz knew that the odds he faced were worth accepting. Even had he lost the contest, his initial decision to offer battle—on the basis of superior military intelligence, rough parity of airpower, and with the advantage of surprise—would have been no less sound.

On balance, it would be wisest to avoid entirely words like "miraculous" or "incredible" when describing this brilliantly conceived, hard-fought, but rather evenly matched American victory. "Glorious" it most certainly was; "miraculous" it clearly was not. The battle provides an ample amount of excitement, given the real power of the Japanese forces, the crucial American mistakes that might have cost them their triumph, and the heroism exhibited on both sides, with no need to exaggerate for chauvinistic satisfaction the odds the Americans faced.

It is ironic, of course, that one of the primary figures responsible for erecting the prevailing American mythos of the Battle of Midway is Japanese. It should be clear that the account put forward here differs radically from Fuchida Mitsuo's influential book *Midway: The Battle that Doomed Japan*. In fact, in many ways Fuchida's work was the catalyst for creating this one, as it became increasingly apparent that crucial details he supplied were contradicted by a variety of authoritative sources. At the same time, a sweeping critique of Fuchida was not to be undertaken lightly, given that he is arguably the single most important translated Japanese source on the battle. Likewise, calling his credibility into question also calls into question key elements in the accepted Western account. But the very fact that particulars drawn from Fuchida formed the core of the "Japanese side" of that account made it vital to check his operational details thoroughly, and it is clear in retrospect that previous Western historians failed to do so.

It is relatively easy to see why this appraisal never took place. In the first place, Fuchida's status as a premier carrier aviator bolstered his credibility from the first. Even during his initial interviews in 1946 for the United States Strategic Bombing Survey (which are an important touch point for any work dealing with Pacific war history), his American interrogators noted that Fuchida "answered questions frankly and carefully. He was considered one of the most lucrative sources of information and a reliable witness." There were many things to recommend Fuchida to a Western audience. He was charming, intelligent, and articulate. He also gained authority thanks to a gift for self-promotion. He subsequently became great friends with Gordon Prange, author of the phenomenally successful *Miracle at Midway,* and it is likely that this friendship precluded Prange's questioning Fuchida too closely. Not only that, but few Westerners in the 1960s and 1970s were in any position to critique Japanese carrier operations. Perhaps the only individuals capable of doing so were the U.S. naval officers charged with preparing the USSBS and ATIG reports immediately after the war,[3] particularly the latter, since they were tasked with probing Japanese carrier operational technique. Yet, their knowledge was apparently not applied to the study of any specific battle, and since that time the ATIG accounts have lain largely forgotten by historians.

Japan was similarly devoid of critics, at least initially. When Fuchida and Okumiya's book was first published in 1951, Japan was emerging from the initial phase of U.S. occupation, which was accompanied by strict censorship. The Japanese military had been utterly disgraced. Former officers were in no hurry to talk about their wartime experiences. When the first censorship bans were lifted, however, Fuchida moved quickly to get his version of the story out.

Roger Pineau, a former U.S. intelligence officer during the war, seized on Fuchida's manuscript in 1953 as a tremendous addition to the Western literature. Midway was rightly seen as the critical battle in the Pacific, and there was no question that a man of Fuchida's stature would have an important viewpoint on it. As one of Japan's foremost carrier aviators, the man who had led the attack on Pearl Harbor, and as Carrier Division 1's air group commander, Fuchida clearly had access to information from Nagumo's inner circle. In the absence of a detailed account from Genda at this time, and the deaths of Yamamoto, Nagumo, and Yamaguchi during the war, Fuchida (along with Admiral Kusaka) was one of only a handful of senior officers likely to be privy to the command decisions of the day. He would certainly seem to be the ideal chronicler of the attack on *Kidō Butai* on 4 June. Along with the USSBS interviews and the Nagumo Report, Fuchida's book became one of the three cornerstones of the Japanese-English account on the battle, and it was woven deeply into the major Western histories.

Unfortunately, it is clear in retrospect that Fuchida was not a faithful narrator. Indeed, our own work spends much of its time correcting the errors Fuchida introduced into the record. Given all this, one is left to ponder two things. First, was Fuchida merely a poor observer, or did he willingly alter the historic record? And if he did, why did he fabricate such a tale?

The first point is relatively easy to answer—Fuchida Mitsuo did not tell the truth. Unquestionably, it is harsh to use the blunt word "lie" to characterize the statements of an eyewitness, but his distortions of the events are so numerous and so critical to the overall understanding of what happened that the term is completely justified. For example, Fuchida claimed Nagumo lacked critical information on the eve of the battle, when, as was shown in chapter 6, *Kidō Butai*'s communication procedures were clearly giving Nagumo timely access to intelligence data and also informed him of the failure of Operation K to reconnoiter Pearl Harbor. In the same vein, Fuchida faulted Genda for not using a two-phase aerial search plan, even though such doctrine was not introduced until 1943. These incorrect details, in turn, alter the calculation of where blame should lie for any errors committed. Some of Fuchida's misstatements deal with seemingly minor things, like how quickly and easily the Japanese could land their air groups on carriers. Yet, it becomes apparent that such details, in turn, can cause a critical misevaluation of the timing of aircraft operations. And, of course, his most blatant untruth concerned the state of the Japanese flight decks immediately before the decisive American attack at 1020–1027 on 4 June. This last point is not trivial, as Fuchida's deliberate distortion of the details surrounding this crucial event led to the rapid obscuring of contrary evidence, such as postwar interviews with other Japanese officers who plainly stated that armed and fueled aircraft were in the hangars when *Akagi, Kaga,* and *Sōryū* were struck, not on deck. Furthermore, recent scholarship has shown that Fuchida lied not only about the Battle of Midway, but also about Nagumo's apparent unwillingness to launch a follow-up strike at Pearl Harbor.[4] Fuchida must be judged as any other participant in battle would be. An occasional error in observation is forgivable. But Fuchida's account reveals a pattern of distortions and outright falsehoods that alter the picture of the battle in critical ways. They also have the effect of making Fuchida look better at the expense of his colleagues. These aren't accidents—they are the marks of a man with an agenda.

There are several good reasons for his behavior. The first pertains to Combined Fleet and First Air Fleet staff immediately after Midway. Despite Admiral Yamamoto's statement that he alone was to blame for the catastrophe, it seems unavoidable that Admiral Nagumo and his staff would have had some explaining to do upon their return. Fuchida, though not directly in the chain of command, would certainly have been part of the group under scrutiny, along with Admiral Kusaka and Commander Genda. The mental anguish can only be imagined that these individuals must have experienced as the Main Body made its way back to Japan after the devastating defeat.

As Paul Dull noted in his study of the Japanese Navy, the phrase "*Ko narimashita*"—"It happened this way"—is more socially acceptable to the Japanese than "*Ko shimashita*"—"I (or some other man or men) did it this way." To say otherwise is to offend the Japanese sensibility and its sense of history.[5] Taken in this light, an explanation to Naval General Headquarters by *Kidō Butai*'s officers that went roughly along the lines of "We were within *minutes* of launching the strike that would destroy the enemy, but then the fates of war intervened" was probably a fairly palatable tale. Whether this rendition of events was concocted as a group, devised by Fuchida alone, or simply the result of some unspoken understanding between Nagumo and his senior officers is impossible to know. Whatever the case, it apparently played well enough at Naval GHQ that it served its purposes.

A "fates of war" account (for want of a better name) matched the generally known facts closely enough that no one at Naval GHQ was going to know anything different, at least in the short term.[6] Not only that, but it was certainly much more agreeable than the unalloyed truth of the matter, which was, "Because of the Navy's (i.e., Admiral Nagano's and Naval GHQ's) utter inability to conceive of a way to bring the war to closure, a badly flawed operational scheme was created by the chief of Combined Fleet (Admiral Yamamoto) that attempted to be a substitute for truly strategic-level thinking. As a result of this plan, the commander on the scene (Admiral Nagumo) was inevitably placed in a position where he and his men (Admiral Yamaguchi, Kusaka, and Genda) committed irretrievable operational blunders. This, in conjunction with an ill-conceived response to the sudden appearance of American forces, resulted in the needless loss of irreplaceable national assets." Indictments of the entire upper echelon of the Navy were evidently not welcome at this point in the war. Indeed, throughout the war the Japanese Navy (and Army as well) demonstrated a remarkable inability to ask tough questions and learn from its mistakes. This tendency was further reinforced by the strong sense of in-group loyalty displayed by members of the Navy's officer corps toward one another. In the face of unwelcome circumstances, this loyalty often took on the form of a code of silence among the ranks of Etajima graduates.[7] It is not surprising, therefore, that a "fates of war" explanation was generally acceptable within the Navy.

This organizational failing becomes more understandable when placed within the context of Japan's gothically dysfunctional wartime leadership. It must be recalled that even in the best of times, the Navy's relationship with the Imperial Army was strained. The Navy regarded those in the Army as uneducated bumpkins, whose understanding of strategy and international relations was abysmally plebian. The Army, for its part, regarded those in the Navy as arrogant elitists who had been lavished with a grossly disproportionate share of the nation's resources. Both parties were largely correct in their mutual assessments. By the time of Midway, far from having been improved by Japan's string of victories, relations between the two services had retreated into icy formality. Indeed, it has been recounted elsewhere that when Japan's prime minister, General Tōjō Hideki, finally learned of the calamity at Midway, far from being horrified at what the defeat portended for the nation's ability to prosecute the war, his initial reaction was one of "waspish self-satisfaction that the Navy had been defeated in an action that the army had opposed."[8]

Operating on such a twisted political landscape, where rational decision making was nearly absent from the scene, it is perhaps not surprising that the Navy's overriding goal was rallying itself internally and presenting a united front to the Imperial Army, rather than learning the hard lessons the battle had to offer. Under such pressures, it is all too easy to imagine a story being arrived at that played to institutionally and culturally acceptable themes, while deliberately playing down the fact that *Kidō Butai* was unprepared to launch a counterstrike at 1020.

After the battle, Fuchida was part of a Battle Lessons Research Committee chartered with compiling information and presenting strategic and tactical lessons learned from the Midway engagement. Fuchida claims that six copies of the final report of the committee were produced, all of which were lost in the general destruction of records that occurred after the war. Fuchida, however, apparently rediscovered a draft manuscript of the report in his footlocker after the armistice, and those notes formed the basis of his account.[9] It's likely that what he had was a surviving copy of the Nagumo Report, or some work derived from it, since a careful analysis of Fuchida's book reveals almost no factual details or maps not found in the Nagumo Report itself. Where he introduces distortions and sensationalism is in the narrative accounts of events like the 1020 attack.

The circumstances under which Fuchida produced his book in 1951 also help account for its distortions. He was writing for the Japanese lay public at a time when the civilian mood in Japan was (rightly) extremely critical of the military's performance during the war. Former military officers were not held in high esteem. In this context, it seems clear that Fuchida had an agenda, namely reestablishing the reputation of the Navy and portraying *Kidō Butai* in the most favorable light. Fuchida was well within his rights for wanting to paint a positive picture of the crack military unit he had served with, as *Kidō Butai* was legitimately the finest carrier force in the world at the outbreak of the Pacific war and had performed brilliantly up until Midway. His method of doing so, however, continued the military's tradition of not facing up to ugly truths, as well as preserving a code of silence around embarrassing matters. In a sense, Fuchida's book is a final testimony to the less-than-honest thinking that prevailed in the Navy during the war.

Fuchida went about his task shrewdly, creating an account that paid lip service to Japanese mistakes, while hiding key operational details. He also benefited from a sort of "first mover" advantage by being the first account published. In effect he dared people to call him a liar. None were willing to do so while he was alive. Fuchida also took the opportunity to direct clever criticism on his colleagues, while painting himself as having been more knowledgeable at the time of the battle than he actually was. The overall picture that emerges is of a man who wanted to be recognized as *the* authority on the battle, while still carefully distancing himself from any personal responsibility for the disaster.

These strategies were relatively successful in 1953. Fuchida's intended audience was not terribly sophisticated in military affairs, nor was it likely to probe the underlying details of his account. Japan's official war histories had yet to be written, and there was a dearth of solid material to either confirm or deny his version of events. Most Japanese naval officers weren't talking about the war, a trend which regrettably resulted in the vast majority of these men taking their accounts to the grave. Fuchida's story was a good one, and it played well to his intended audience. After all, Japan had just suffered an enormous national humiliation, one particularly devastating to a society that viewed itself as uniquely superior. Japan's defeat could not be denied, but some sense of national pride might be regained by revealing some moments of nobility within that defeat. Thus, if he took a few liberties with his interpretation of events, he probably was not outside the bounds of accepted artistic license, and he wasn't likely to be questioned closely about operational facts in any case.

The same was true in the West. Indeed, the very fact that Fuchida's account fit nicely with the prevailing American mythos surrounding the battle probably shielded it from closer scrutiny. Fuchida's rendition of the American dive-bombers hurtling downward at the last second to win the day is very much in keeping with the American view of the battle, wherein the "good guys," through courage, fortitude, and not a little luck, snatch victory from the very jaws of defeat. As such, Fuchida's story nicely bolstered the broader tenor of the winner's rendition of events. But it also still managed to acquit the Japanese force with some degree of honor. All in all, his account was "good stuff"—tailor-made for a blockbuster Hollywood movie. With such an account in place, there seemed little need to develop additional Japanese sources. As a result, the Western record regarding the Japanese side of the battle remained essentially unchanged for almost half a century.

The fact that Japanese carrier operations were so poorly understood in the West didn't help matters any. It was only with the publication of books by authors such as David Evans, Mark Peattie, and John Lundstrom that the technical and doctrinal details concerning the Imperial Navy's carriers began coming to light. Those records that had existed in English before the publication of these works were primarily technical in nature and had not been placed within the larger context of the Imperial Navy's development and doctrine. As a result, up until the 1990s, Western scholars—at least those who could not or would not consult the Japanese sources—were in no position to be able to analyze Japanese accounts with any accuracy.

In Japan, however, things had moved ahead. The publication of the official Japanese war histories (*Senshi Sōsho*) in the late 1970s inevitably called Fuchida's version of events into question. The Midway volume of *Senshi Sōsho* left no doubt that Nagumo's counterstrike was far from being ready when the fatal American dive-bomber attack occurred. This directly called into question the "fateful five minutes" rendition that Fuchida had put forth, and in the eyes of most knowledgeable observers in Japan, he was discredited. Apparently, however, no one bothered telling the Americans this.

This fact was brought home to the authors in 2000. The authors' suspicions about Fuchida's account were already taking form by then, because certain points in his book did not mesh with accepted descriptions of Japanese carrier deck operations. There were also discrepancies between his account and some of those found in the Strategic Bombing Survey interviews. However, it was a conversation between the authors and John Lundstrom that crystallized the matter. Lundstrom had noticed, in one of those rare epiphanies when the obvious suddenly reveals itself, that the photographs taken by American B-17s over *Kidō Butai* on 4 June showed completely empty flight decks on three of the Japanese carriers at around 0800. What did that *mean*? To be sure, the pictures were taken more than two hours before the American attack, but it caused Lundstrom to pose an interesting question. Had Nagumo's reserve strike force *ever* been on the deck at any time during the battle? That question, in turn, catalyzed the authors' efforts to develop a model that described carrier operations such as deck spotting and rearming. This, in conjunction with the surviving Japanese carrier action reports from the battle that detailed the launching and recovery of CAP fighters, began raising serious doubts about the accuracy of Fuchida's rendition of the 1020 attack.

In an effort to ascertain the validity of this approach, separate inquiries were sent to two knowledgeable Japanese sources, politely asking for their insights on the matter. This was done in an extremely circumspect fashion, on the assumption that Fuchida was still held in high regard in Japan and not wanting, as foreigners, to appear disrespectful toward a famous war hero. Given how cautiously those inquiries were posed, the responses that came back were startlingly blunt in their outright dismissal of Fuchida and were later echoed by other Japanese sources as well. One summarized the matter flavorfully:

To tell why Fuchida's book contains transparent lies, it's necessary to explain the background of the time it was written. Until around Showa 27 (1952), Japan's speech and writing was under . . . censorship . . . so they could not say what they wanted. However, since around Showa 28 (1953) . . . "Cheering up" memoirs by mainly former military personnel were rushed out. . . . Of course, the mental pressure of those who were truly incompetent and responsible, and who tried to conceal their own faults, gave strong effect as well [*sic*]. Fuchida's *Midway* or Kusaka's *Kidō Butai* that came out almost simultaneously, could be regarded as nonsense books which were meant to conceal failures and incompetencies of such kind, and to protect each other. If they are still among the few books available [on the Battle of Midway] that have been translated into English, it's a funny story.[10]

Very funny indeed, as well as a cutting indictment of Western scholarship. Fuchida's rendition of events had, in effect, distorted the West's study of the battle for fifty years. True, the language barrier had played a major part in this failure to access newer Japanese sources, but it must also be admitted that American complacency contributed to this scholarly lethargy. Indeed, this lethargy was such that crucial details from other sources were ignored, apparently as being "unreliable," because of Fuchida's greater standing in American historical circles. Fuchida may not have been telling the truth, but Western scholars had only themselves to blame for having failed to access the contemporary sources that were available in Japan and that had lain untouched for decades.

It is to be hoped that the common wisdom surrounding the Battle of Midway can now return to a more elastic state, wherein scholars can make new contributions to our understanding without being held hostage by a single account. It will be increasingly impossible for one survivor's account to have the same effect on the study of Midway in any case, as the veterans who fought the battle are, sadly, declining rapidly in number. Indeed, the real decision makers at Midway—Yamamoto, Nagumo, Genda, Kusaka, Yamaguchi—have all been dead for years. From now on, like it or not, the study of this enormously important battle will necessarily be based less on survivor accounts and more on the interpretation of operational data.

The increasing importance of such data was one reason this study placed considerable emphasis on technology and doctrine. It turned out that the placement of airplanes in a carrier hanger, the mounting systems that secured bombs and torpedoes to those planes, and the speed of elevator movements yielded important information on how strikes were prepared. Similarly, the doctrine of launching massed air strikes produced important benefits in some situations and caused fatal delays in others. Hopefully, our approach likewise has yielded important new perspectives and is not simply a convenient "angle" that rehashes well-known facts in an effort to make them appear fresh.

Similarly, the discrediting of many of the commonly held beliefs concerning the battle was the inevitable result of a careful reexamination of the previous accounts and a determined effort to probe new information that has become available. Our object was not to pick a fight with existing opinions in the hope of creating controversy. Rather, it was done in hopes of establishing a firmer foundation for future studies of the battle—a foundation robust enough not to be held hostage by any one account or source. By adding newer tools into the mix—computer-aided reconstructions, marine forensics, and naval architecture among others—this study seeks a broader, more fully integrated approach than prior histories of the battle.

Without question, elements of this account will be modified and reinterpreted in the future, perhaps drastically. This process will doubtless accelerate as optical scanning and computer-aided translation technologies begin eradicating the language barriers that have plagued the study of the Pacific war. Such revisions are only to be expected—indeed, they are to be welcomed. It is only by constantly endeavoring to dig more deeply that a closer approximation of the truth can be achieved. The Battle of Midway, and the legacy of the brave men of both countries who fought and died there, deserves no less.

Glossary of Terms

The following terminology is used with regards to carrier and naval aviation operations.

Barrier—Crash barrier; a wire barrier designed to catch aircraft that have missed normal arrest before they crash into any aircraft stowed forward on the flight deck

BatDiv—Battleship Division, typically a group of two to four ships

Buntaichō—Division leader

CAP—"Combat Air Patrol"; the standing patrol of fighter aircraft over a task force

CarDiv—Carrier Division, typically a group of two or three carriers

Chakkan shidōtō—carrier landing light array; a visual landing aid

Chūtai—Air group division; six or nine aircraft

CIC—Combat Information Center; central location for gathering and coordinating air search (radar) and CAP fighter vectoring operations

CruDiv—Cruiser Division, typically a group of two to four ships

Dai-ichi—Number One, First

Dai-ni—Number Two; Second

DesDiv—Destroyer Division, typically composed of four ships

DesRon—Destroyer Squadron, typically a group of several divisions

Hikōchō—Carrier air officer (responsible for deck activities and CAP direction)

Hikōkitai—Carrier air group

Hikōtaichō—Commander of the carrier air group

Hinomaru—Large rising sun symbol painted on the forward flight deck of the Japanese aircraft carriers at Midway

HYPO—American code-breaking radio intercept unit

Kanbaku—Abbreviation for *kanjō bakugekiki*, a carrier dive-bomber

Kanchō—Ship's captain

Kankō—Abbreviation for *kanjō kōgekiki*, a carrier attack bomber

Kansen—Abbreviation for *kanjō sentōki*, a carrier fighter

Kidō Butai—Mobile Force, sometimes rendered Strike Force; the operational designation for a Japanese carrier task force

Kikaichō—Head of machinery; engineering chief

Kōkū Sentai—Carrier Division

Kōshaki—Fire-control director

Mantelet—A protective covering composed of rolled hammocks, designed to keep splinters from vital command spaces, such as the island of an aircraft carrier

Nikuhaku-hitchū—"Press closely, strike home"; the motto of Japanese torpedo tactics

PBY—American amphibious patrol plane

Plane Guard—A destroyer stationed ahead of the carrier during takeoff and aft of the carrier during landings, charged with rescuing aircraft crews

Rengō Kantai—Combined Fleet; the entirety of Japan's operational wartime fleets.

Renzoku shūyō—Continuous stowage technique for carrier landings

SBD—American dive-bomber

Seibichō—Chief maintenance officer

Seibiin—Crew chief

Shō-hikōchō—Assistant to the air officer

Shōtai—Air group section; three aircraft

Shōtaichō—Section leader

TBD—American torpedo plane

TBF—American torpedo plane

Tōjōin—Ship's crew

Tokaki—Ordnance mounting bracket

Tokkogata—"Special type"; the name used for Japanese destroyers

Tonbo-tsuri—"Dragonfly-fishing"; the rescue of aircraft crewmen from an aircraft that suffered a mishap during takeoff. Usually accomplished by the carrier's plane guard destroyer.

Type 91 torpedo—Japanese standard aerial torpedo

Type 93 torpedo—Japanese standard shipborne torpedo

VB—Bombing Squadron. Usually referred to by its numerical squadron number, that is, either "VB-6" or "Bombing Six"

VF—Fighter Squadron. Usually referred to by its numerical squadron number, that is, either "VF-3" or "Fighting Three"

VS—Scouting Squadron. Usually referred to by its numerical squadron number, that is, either "VS-6" or "Scouting Six"

VT—Torpedo Squadron. Usually referred to by its numerical squadron number, that is, either "VT-8" or "Torpedo Eight"

Wire—landing wire; arresting wire. Hydraulically or electrically tensioned cable designed to rapidly decelerate a landing aircraft

"Zengun totsugeki!"—"All forces attack!"

Appendix 1: List of Personnel

The following list of personnel that appear in the narrative is provided as a quick reference guide to the many individuals involved in the battle.

Abe, RADM Hiroaki—commander, Cruiser Division 8
Abe, Capt. Toshio—commander, Destroyer Division 10
Abe, Lt. Zenji—*Junyō* dive-bomber group leader
Adams, Lt. Samuel—*Yorktown* SBD pilot, VB[S]-5
Ady, Lt. Howard P.—PBY pilot, VP-23
Aimune, Cdr. Kunize—*Hiryū* chief engineer
Akiyama, Ens.—*Akagi* engineering crewman
Amagai, Cdr. Takahisa—*Kaga* air officer
Amari, PO1c Hiroshi—commander, *Tone* No. 4 aircraft
Aoki, Capt. Taijirō—commander, carrier *Akagi*
Ariga, Capt. Kosaku—commander, DesDiv 4
Arima, Cdr. Takayasu—staff officer, submarines, Combined Fleet
Arimura, WO Yoshikazu—*Hiryū* bomber maintenance chief
Best, Lt. Richard H.—commander, VB-6
Blakey, Maj. George—USAAF B-17 unit commander
Brockman, Lt. Cdr. William H.—commander, submarine *Nautilus*
Browning, Capt. Miles R.—Admiral Spruance's chief of staff
Buckmaster, Capt. Elliott—commander, carrier *Yorktown*
Chase, Lt. William E.—PBY pilot, VP-23
Dobashi, Cdr. ?—*Akagi* damage-control officer
Egusa, Cdr. Takashige—*Sōryū* dive-bomber leader, *hikōtaichō*
Ely, Lt. Arthur—executive officer, VT-6
Fleming, Capt. Richard E.—Marine dive-bomber unit commander, VMSB-241
Fletcher, RADM Frank Jack—commander, Task Force 17, and of American carrier striking force.
Fuchida, Cdr. Mitsuo—*Akagi* torpedo bomber group leader, *hikōtaichō*
Fujita, Cdr. Isamu—commander, *Makigumo*
Fujita, Lt. Iyozo—*Sōryū* Zero pilot
Fujita, RADM Ryūtaro—commander, Seaplane Tender Group

Fukudome, RADM Shigeru—head of the Plans Division, Naval GHQ

Gallaher, Lt. Wilmer Earl—commander, VS-6

Genda, Cdr. Minoru—staff air officer, First Air Fleet

Gray, Lt. Richard—commander, VF-8

Halsey, VADM William F. Jr.—senior American carrier admiral, on medical leave during the Battle of Midway

Hara, RADM Chūichi—commander, CarDiv 5

Harada, PO1c Kaname—*Sōryū* Zero pilot

Hashimoto, Lt. Toshio—unit commander, *Hiryū* torpedo bomber group

Henderson, Maj. Lofton R.—commander, VMSB-241

Horita, Kazuaki—*Sōryū* engineering crewman

Hosogaya, VADM Moshirō—commander, Fifth Fleet

Ibusuki, Lt. Masanobu—*Akagi* Zero pilot

Ichiki, Col. Kiyonao—commander, Imperial Army's Midway Invasion Force

Iida, PO1c Masatada—*Sōryū* D4Y pilot

Inoue, VADM Shigeyoshi—commander, Fourth Fleet

Ishikawa, Kenichi—*Mikuma* sailor

Itō, Capt. Seiroku—CarDiv 2 chief of staff

Iura, Cdr. Shōjirō—staff officer, submarines, Naval GHQ

Kaku, Capt. Tomeo—commander, carrier *Hiryū*

Kakuta, RADM Kakuji—commander, Second Mobile Striking Force

Kami, Capt. Shigenori—staff officer, Plans Division, Naval GHQ

Kanao, Cdr. Ryōichi—*Sōryū* chief gunnery officer

Kaneko, Lt. Tadashi—6th *Kū* fighter group leader

Kanoe, Cdr. Takashi—*Hiryū* executive officer

Katsumi, Cdr. Motoi—commander, destroyer *Tanikaze*

Kawaguchi, Cdr. Susumu—*Hiryū* air officer (*hikōchō*)

Kimura, RADM Susumu—commander, Destroyer Squadron 10

King, Adm. Ernest J.—commander in chief, United States Navy

Kobayashi, Lt. Michio—*Hiryū* dive-bomber group leader

Koga, PO Tadayoshi—*Ryūjō* Zero pilot

Komatsu, VADM Marquis Teruhisa—commander, Sixth Fleet (submarines)

Komura, Capt. Keizō—commander, cruiser *Chikuma*

Kondō, VADM Nobutake—commander, Midway Invasion Force Main Body

Kondō, WO Isamu—*Sōryū* D4Y commander

Koyama, Lt. Masao—*Mikuma* gunnery officer

Kunisada, Lt. Yoshio—*Kaga* damage-control officer

Kurita, VADM Takeo—commander, Midway Close Support Group

Kuroda, Lt. Makoto—*Chikuma* air officer (*hikōchō*)

Kuroshima, Capt. Kameto—Combined Fleet staff officer, in charge of operations

Kusaka, RADM Ryūnosuke—chief of staff, First Air Fleet

Kusumoto, Cdr. Ikuto—*Sōryū* air officer (*hikōchō*)

Kyuma, Lt. Cdr. Takeo—CarDiv 2 staff engineering officer

Leslie, Lt. Cdr. Maxwell "Max" Franklin—commander, VB-3

Lindsey, Lt. Cdr. Eugene Elbert "Gene"—commander, VT-6

Maeda, WO Takeshi—*Kaga* torpedo bomber pilot

Makishima, Teiuchi—civilian cameraman on board *Akagi*

Mandai, Ens. Hisao—*Hiryū* engineering officer

Massey, Lt. Cdr. Lance Edward "Lem"—commander, VT-3

Masuda, Cdr. Shogo—*Akagi* air officer (*hikōchō*)

McClusky, Lt. Cdr. Clarence Wade, Jr.—commander, *Enterprise* Air Group (CEAG)

Mitoya, Lt. Cdr. Sesu—*Kaga* communications officer

Mitscher, Capt. Marc A.—commander, carrier *Hornet*

Miura, Cdr. Gishiro—*Akagi* navigator

Miwa, Capt. Yoshitake—staff officer, Combined Fleet

Miyo, Cdr. Tatsukichi—staff officer, Plans Division, Naval GHQ

Mori, PO2c Jūzo—*Sōryū* torpedo bomber pilot

Morinaga, WO Takayoshi—*Kaga* Type 97 pilot

Murata, Lt. Cdr. Shigeharu—commander, *Akagi* torpedo bomber group

Murphy, Lt. Cdr. John—commander, submarine *Tambor*

Murray, Capt. George—commander, carrier *Enterprise*

Nagano, Adm. Osami—commander, First Section (Planning) of the Naval General Staff

Naganuma, Lt. Michitarō—*Sōryū* engineering officer

Nagayasu, Lt. Yasukuni—*Hiryū* gunnery officer

Nagumo, VADM Chūichi—commander, First Mobile Striking Force (*Kidō Butai*)

Nakagawa, WO Shizuo—*Hiryū* dive-bomber pilot

Nimitz, Adm. Chester W.—commander in chief, U.S. Pacific Fleet

Nishibayashi, Lt. Cdr. ?—First Air Fleet flag secretary

Nishimura, RADM Shōji—screen commander, Invasion Force Main Body

Norris, Maj. Benjamin—Marine dive-bomber unit commander, briefly commander VMSB-241

Oda, ?—communications personnel, *Kaga*

Ogawa, Lt. Shōichi—commander, *Kaga* dive-bomber group

Ōhara, Cdr. Hisashi—*Sōryū* executive officer

Ōishi, Capt. Tomatsu—senior staff member, First Air Fleet

Okada, Capt. Jisaku—commander, carrier *Kaga*

Okumiya, Lt. Cdr. Masatake—staff officer, Second Mobile Striking Force

Ono, Lt. Cdr. Kenjiro—First Air Fleet staff intelligence officer

Ono, WO Zenji—*Akagi* Zero pilot

Osmus, Ens. Wesley F.—TBD pilot, VT-3

Ōta, Capt. Minoru—commander, Midway naval landing force

Ozawa, VADM Jisaburō—noted carrier aviation advocate, instrumental in establishing First Air Fleet

Ring, Cdr. Stanhope C.—commander, *Hornet* Air Group (CHAG)

Rodee, Cdr. Walter F.—commander, VS-8

Sakiyama, Capt. Shakao—commander, cruiser *Mikuma*

Saruwatari, Lt. Cdr. Masayushi—chief damage-control officer, *Mogami*

Sasaki, Cdr. Akira—Combined Fleet staff officer

Shiga, Lt. Yoshio—commander, *Junyō* fighter group, *hikōtaichō*

Shannon, Col. Harold D.—commander, Marine Sixth Defense Battalion

Shigematsu, Lt. Yasuhiro—*Hiryū* Zero pilot

Shirane, Lt. Ayao—*Akagi* Zero pilot

Short, Lt. Wallace "Wally"—commander, *Yorktown* VB[S]-5

Shumway, Lt. DeWitt Wood—Dive-bomber pilot, *Yorktown*, VB-3

Simard, Capt. Cyril T.—commander, NAS Midway

Soji, Capt. Akira—commander, cruiser *Mogami*

Spruance, RADM Raymond A.—commander, Task Force 16

Sugiyama, Gen. Gen—Head of the Imperial Army General Staff

Sweeney, Lt. Col. Walter C.—USAAF B-17 unit commander

Takagi, VADM Takeo—commander, carrier striking force at the Battle of Coral Sea

Takashima, Cdr. Hideo—executive officer, cruiser *Mikuma*

Takasu, VADM Shirō—commander, Aleutians Screening Force

Takezaki, PO1c Masatake—pilot, *Chikuma*'s No. 5 aircraft

Tampo, Cdr. Yoshibumi—chief engineer, *Akagi*

Tanabe, Lt. Cdr. Yahachi—commander, submarine *I-168*

Tanaka, RADM Raizo—commander, Midway Invasion Force

Tanaka, Lt. Gen. Shinichi—head of operations, Imperial Army General Staff

Thach, Lt. Cdr. John Smith "Jimmy"—commander, VF-3

Tōjō, Gen. Hideki—prime minister of Japan

Tomioka, Capt. Sadatoshi—staff officer, Plans Division, Naval GHQ

Tomonaga, Lt. Jōichi—commander, *Hiryū* torpedo bomber group, *hikōtaichō*

Toyoshima, Cdr. Shunichi—commander, destroyer *Isokaze*

Ugaki, RADM Matome—chief of staff, Combined Fleet

Waldron, Lt. Cdr. John—commander, VT-8

Ware, Lt. Charles R.—division leader, VS-6

Watanabe, Capt. Yasuji—staff officer, Combined Fleet

Yamada, Lt. Shōhei—commander, *Akagi* dive-bomber group

Yamagami, Lt. Masayuki—commander, *Ryūjō* torpedo bomber group

Yamaguchi, RADM Tamon—commander, Second Carrier Division

Yamamoto, Adm. Isoroku—commander in chief, Combined Fleet

Yamamoto, Cdr. Yūji—staff officer, Plans Division, Naval GHQ

Yamamoto, PO1c Akira—*Kaga* Zero pilot

Yamashita, Lt. Michiji—executive officer, *Hiryū* dive-bomber group

Yamazaki, RADM Shigeaki—commander, Aleutians submarine force

Yanagimoto, Capt. Ryūsaku—commander, carrier *Sōryū*

Yoshida, Katsuichi—*Mikuma* sailor

Yoshioka, Chūichi—First Air Fleet assistant air officer, compiler of the Nagumo Report

Yoshino, WO Haruo—*Kaga* torpedo plane commander

Appendix 2: Japanese Order of Battle

This appendix contains an updated order of battle that corrects many errors of naming found in previous accounts. It also details more precisely the number of aircraft involved in the battle.

THE MIDWAY OPERATION (MI)

First Carrier Striking Force

VADM Nagumo Chūichi
Chief of staff: RADM Kusaka Ryūnosuke

Carrier Division 1—VADM Nagumo
Akagi (flagship)
Personnel:
Captain Aoki Taijirō
Air officer: Cdr. Masuda Shōgo
Air unit commander: Cdr. Fuchida Mitsuo
Aircraft:
    18 A6M2 carrier fighters (Lt. Cdr. Itaya Shigeru)
    18 D3A1 carrier bombers (Lt. Cdr. Chihaya Takehiko)
    18 B5N2 carrier attack aircraft (Lt. Cdr. Murata Shigeharu)
    6 A6M2 fighters (6th Air Group)

Kaga
Personnel:
Captain Okada Jisaku† (posthumously promoted to rear admiral)
Air officer: Cdr. Amagai Takahisa
Air unit commander: Lt. Cdr. Kusumi Tadashi† (posthumously promoted to commander)
Aircraft:
    18 A6M2 carrier fighters (Lt. Satō Masao)
    18 D3A1 carrier bombers (Lt. Ogawa Shōichi†)

27 B5N2 carrier attack aircraft (Lt. Kitajima Ichirō)
9 A6M2 carrier fighters (6th Air Group)
2 D3A1 carrier bombers (cargo—*Sōryū*)[1]

Carrier Division 2—RADM Yamaguchi Tamon[†] (posthumously promoted to vice admiral)
Hiryū (flagship)
Personnel:
Capt. Kaku Tomeo[†] (posthumously promoted to rear admiral)
Air officer: Cdr. Kawaguchi Susumu
Air unit commander: Lt. Tomonaga Jōichi[†] (posthumously promoted to commander)
Aircraft:
    18 A6M2 carrier fighters (Lt. Mori Shigeru[†])
    18 D3A1 carrier bombers (Lt. Kobayashi Michio[†])
    18 B5N2 carrier attack aircraft (Lt. Kikuchi Rokurō[†])
    3 A6M2 carrier fighters (6th Air Group)

Sōryū
Personnel:
Capt. Yanagimoto Ryūsaku[†] (posthumously promoted to rear admiral)
Air Officer: Cdr. Kusumoto Ikuto
Air unit commander: Lt. Cdr. Egusa Takashige
Aircraft:
    18 A6M2 carrier fighters (Lt. Suganami Masaharu)
    16 D3A1 carrier bombers (Lt. Ikeda Masahiro)
    18 B5N2 carrier attack aircraft (Lt. Abe Heijirō)
    3 A6M2 carrier fighters (6th Air Group)
    2 D4Y1 carrier bomber (experimental reconnaissance aircraft—one aircraft possibly lost prior to fleet's departure from Hashirajima)

Support Group
RADM Abe Hiroaki

Cruiser Division 8—RADM Abe
Tone—Capt. Okada Tametsugu (flagship)
Aircraft:
    3 E13A1 Type 0 float reconnaissance (one likely inoperable)
    2 E8N2 Type 95 float reconnaissance
Chikuma—Capt. Komura Keizō
Aircraft:
    3 E13A1 Type 0 float reconnaissance
    2 E8N2 Type 95 float reconnaissance

Battleship Division 3 (Section 2)—RADM Takama Tamotsu
Haruna—RADM Takama (flagship)
Aircraft:
    3 E8N2 Type 95 float reconnaissance
Kirishima—Capt. Iwabuchi Sanji
Aircraft:
    3 E8N2 Type 95 float reconnaissance

Screen: Destroyer Squadron 10
RADM Kimura Susumu
Nagara—Capt. Naoi Toshio (flagship)
Aircraft:
    1 E11A1 night reconnaissance seaplane

Destroyer Division 4—Capt. Ariga Kosaku
Nowaki—Cdr. Koga Magatarō
Arashi—Cdr. Watanabe Yusumasa
Hagikaze—Cdr. Iwagami Jūichi
Maikaze—Cdr. Nakasugi Seiji

Destroyer Division 10—Capt. Abe Toshio
Kazagumo—Cdr. Yoshida Masayoshi
Yūgumo—Cdr. Semba Shigeo
Makigumo—Cdr. Fujita Isamu

Destroyer Division 17—Capt. Kitamura Masayuki
Urakaze—Cdr. Shiraishi Nagayoshi
Isokaze—Cdr. Toyoshima Shunichi
Tanikaze—Cdr. Katsumi Motoi
Hamakaze—Cdr. Orita Tsuneo

Supply Group
Capt. Ota Masanao
Oilers:
Kyokutō Maru—Capt. Oto
Shinkoku Maru
Tōhō Maru
Nippon Maru
Kokuyō Maru
Akigumo—Cdr. Sōma Shōhei

Main Body

Admiral Yamamoto Isoroku, commander in chief, Combined Fleet
Chief of staff: RADM Ugaki Matome

Battleship Division 1—RADM Takayanagi Gihachi
Yamato—RADM Takayanagi (flagship)
Nagato—Capt. Yano Hideo
Mutsu—RADM Kogure Gunji

Carrier Group

Hōshō—Capt. Umetani Kaoru
Aircraft:
     8 B4Y1 carrier attack aircraft—Lt. Irikiin Yoshiaki
Yūkaze—Lt. Cdr. Kajimoto Shizuka

Special Force

(carrying midget subs):
Chiyōda—Capt. Harada Kaku
Nisshin—Capt. Komazawa Katsumi

Screen: Destroyer Squadron 3

RADM Hashimoto Shintarō
Sendai—Capt. Morishita Nobue (flagship)

Destroyer Division 11—Capt. Shōji Kichirō
Fubuki—Lt. Cdr. Yamashita Shizuo
Shirayuki—Lt. Cdr. Sugawara Rokorō
Murakumo—Lt. Cdr. Higashi Hideo
Hatsuyuki—Lt. Cdr. Kamiura Junnari

Destroyer Division 19—Capt. Oe Ranji
Isonami—Cdr. Sugama Ryōkichi
Uranami—Lt. Cdr. Hagio Tsutomu
Shikinami—Lt. Cdr. Kawahashi Akifumi
Ayanami—Cdr. Sakuma Eiji

1st Supply Unit (oilers)
Capt. Nishioka Shigeyasu
Narutō—Capt. Nishioka
Tōei Maru

Guard Force (Aleutians screen)

VADM Takasu Shirō
Chief of staff: RADM Kobayashi Kengō)

Battleship Division 2
Hyūga—Capt. Matsuda Chiaki (flagship)
Ise—Capt. Takeda Isamu
Fusō—Capt. Obata Chozaemon
Yamashiro—Capt. Kogure Gunji

Screen
RADM Kishi Fukuji

Cruiser Division 9
Kitakami—Capt. Norimitsu Saiji (flagship)
Ōi—Capt. Narita Mōichi

Destroyer Division 20—Capt. Yamada Yūji
Asagiri—Lt. Cdr. Maekawa Nisaburō
Yūgiri—Cdr. Motokura Masayoshi
Shirakumo—Cdr. Hitomi Toyoji
Amagiri—Capt. Ashida Buichi

Destroyer Division 24—Capt. Hirai Yasuji
Umikaze—Cdr. Sugitani Nagahide
Yamakaze—Lt. Cdr. Hamanaka Shūichi
Kawakaze—Lt. Cdr. Wakabayashi Kazuo
Suzukaze—Lt. Cdr. Shibayama Kazuo

Destroyer Division 27—Capt. Yoshimura Matake
Ariake—Lt. Cdr. Yoshida Shōichi
Yūgure—Lt. Cdr. Kamo Kiyoshi
Shigure—Cdr. Seo Noboru
Shiratsuyu—Lt. Cdr. Hashimoto Kanematsu

2nd Supply Unit (oilers)
Capt. Eguchi Matsuo
San Clemente Maru—Capt. Eguchi
Tōa Maru

Midway Invasion Force

VADM Kondō Nobutake
Chief of staff: RADM Shiraishi Kazutaka

Main Body

Cruiser Division 4 (Section 1)
Atago—Capt. Baron Ijūin Matsuji (flagship)
Chōkai—Capt. Hayakawa Mikio

Cruiser Division 5—VADM Takagi Takeo
Myōkō—Capt. Miyoshi Teruhiko
Haguro—Capt. Mori Tomokazu

Battleship Division 3 (Section 1)—RADM Mikawa Gun`ichi
Kongō—Capt. Koyanagi Tomiji
Hiei—Capt. Nishida Masao

Screen: Destroyer Squadron 4

RADM Nishimura Shōji
Yura (CL flag), Capt. Satō Shirō

Destroyer Division 3—Capt. Oe Ranji
Murasame—Lt. Cdr. Suenaga Naoji
Samidare—Cdr. Matsubara Takisaburō
Harusame—Lt. Cdr. Kamiyama Masao
Yūdachi—Cdr. Kikkawa Kiyoshi

Destroyer Division 9—Capt. Satō Yasuo
Asagumo—Cdr. Iwahashi Tōru
Minegumo—Lt. Cdr. Suzuki Yasuatsu
Natsugumo—Lt. Cdr. Tsukamoto Moritarō

Carrier Group

Capt. Ōbayashi Sueo
Zuihō—Capt. Obayashi
Aircraft:[2]
      6 A6M2, 6 A5M4—Lt. Hidaka Moriyasu
      12 B5N2—Lt. Matsuo Kaji
Mikazuki—Lt. Cdr. Maeda Saneho

Supply Group

Capt. Murao Jirō

Oilers:

Sata—Capt. Murao

Tsurumi—Capt. Fujita Toshizō

Genyō Maru

Kenyō Maru

Akashi (repair ship)—Capt. Fukuzawa Tsunekichi

Close Support Group

VADM Kurita Takeo

Cruiser Division 7—Vice Admiral Kurita

Kumano—Capt. Tanaka Kikumatsu (flagship)

Suzuya—Capt. Kimura Masatomi

Mikuma—Capt. Sakiyama Shakao† (posthumously promoted to rear admiral)

Mogami—Capt. Soji Akira

Destroyer Division 8—Cdr. Ogawa Nobuki

Asashio—Lt. Cdr. Yoshii Gorō

Arashio—Cdr. Kuboki Hideo

Nichiei Maru (oiler)

Transport Group

RADM Tanaka Raizō

Transports (about 5,000 troops—Capt. Ōta Minoru (IJN) and Col. Ichiki Kiyonao
    (Army))

Kiyozumi Maru

Keiyō Maru

Zenyō Maru

Goshu Maru #2

Tōa Maru

Kano Maru

Argentina Maru

Hokuriku Maru

Brazil Maru

Kirishima Maru

Azuma Maru

Nankai Maru

Patrol boats #1, #2, #34 (carrying troops)

Akebono Maru (oiler)

Destroyer Squadron 2
Rear Admiral Tanaka Raizō
Jintsū—Capt. Kozai Torazō (flagship)

Destroyer Division 15—Capt. Satō Torajirō
Kuroshio—Cdr. Ugaki Tamaki
Oyashio—Cdr. Arima Tokiyoshi

Destroyer Division 16—Capt. Shibuya Shirō
Yukikaze—Cdr. Tobita Kenjirō
Amatsukaze—Cdr. Hara Tameichi
Tokitsukaze—Cdr. Nakahara Giichirō
Hatsukaze—Cdr. Takahashi Kameshirō

Destroyer Division 18—Capt. Miyasaka Yoshito
Shiranuhi—Cdr. Akazawa Shizuo
Kasumi—Cdr. Tomura Kiyoshi
Kagerō—Cdr. Yokoi Minoru
Arare—Cdr. Ogata Tomoe

Seaplane Tender Group

RADM Fujita Ryūtarō

Seaplane Tender Div 11
Chitose—Capt. Furukawa Tamotsu
Aircraft:
    16 F1M, 4 E13A
Kamikawa Maru—Capt. Shinoda Tarohachi
Aircraft:
    8 F1M, 4 E13A
Hayashio—Cdr. Kaneda Kiyoshi
Patrol Boat #35 (carrying troops)

Minesweeper Group

Capt. Miyamoto Sadatomo
Minesweepers:
Tama Maru #3
Tama Maru #5
Shōnan Maru #7
Shōnan Maru #8
Subchasers *#16, #17, #18*
Sōya (supply ship)—Cdr. Kubota Toshi

Meiyō Maru (cargo)
Yamafuku Maru (cargo)

Advance (Submarine) Force (6th Fleet)

VADM Komatsu Teruhishi
Chief of staff: RADM Mito Hisashi
Katori—Capt. Owada Noboru (flagship, at Kwajalein)

SubRon 3
RADM Kōno Chimaki
Rio De Janeiro Maru (flagship, at Kwajalein)

SubDiv 19—Capt. Ono Ryōjirō
I-156—Lt. Cdr. Ōhashi Katsuo
I-157—Lt. Cdr. Nakajima Sakae
I-158—Lt. Cdr. Kitamura Soshichi
I-159—Lt. Cdr. Yoshimatsu Tamori

SubDiv 30—Capt. Teraoka Masao
I-162—Lt. Cdr. Kinashi Takakazu
I-165—Lt. Cdr. Harada Hakue
I-166—Lt. Cdr. Tanaka Makio

SubDiv 13—Capt. Miyazaki Takeji
I-121—Lt. Cdr. Fujimori Yasuo
I-122—Lt. Cdr. Norita Sadatoshi
I-123—Lt. Cdr. Ueno Toshitake (all assigned to transporting gas and oil to French
    Frigate Shoals or Laysan Island)

Shore-Based Air Force, 11th Air Fleet

VADM Tsukahara Nishizō (at Tinian)
Chief of staff: RADM Sakamaki Munetaka

Midway Expeditionary Force
Capt. Morita Chisato
(transported by CV of 1st & 2nd CV strike force)
Aircraft:
    36 Zeros—Lt. Cdr. Kofukuda Mitsugu
    10 land-based bombers (at Wake), 6 flying boats (at Jaluit)

24th Air Flotilla
RADM Maeda Minoru

Chitose Air Group—Capt. Ōhashi Fujirō
Aircraft:
    36 Zeros, 36 torpedo planes (at Kwajalein)

1st Air Group—Capt. Inoue Samaji
Aircraft:
    36 Zeros, 36 torpedo planes (at Aur and Wotje)

14th Air Group—Capt. Nakajima Daizō
Aircraft:
    18 flying boats (at Jaluit and Wotje)

THE ALEUTIANS OPERATION (AL)
(Aleutians Force, 5th Fleet)
Second Carrier Striking Force

RADM Kakuta Kakuji

Carrier Group

CarDiv 4—Rear Admiral Kakuta
Ryūjō—Capt. Katō Tadao (flagship)
Air unit commander—Lt. Yamagami Masayuki
Aircraft:
    12 A6M2—Lt. Kobayashi Minoru
    18 B5N1 and B5N2—Lt. Yamagami
Note: 12 of the A6M2 pilots were members of 6th Air Group
Junyō—Capt. Ishii Shizue
Air unit commander—Lt. Shiga Yoshio
Aircraft:
    18 A6M2 (including 12 aircraft from 6th Air Group)—Lt. Shiga
    15 D3A1—Lt. Abe Zenji

Support Group

Cruiser Division 4 (Section 2)
Maya—Capt. Nabeshima Shunsaki
Takao—Capt. Asakura Bunji

Screen: Destroyer Division 7—Capt. Konishi Kaname
Akebono—Lt. Cdr. Nakagawa Minoru
Ushio—Lt. Cdr. Uesugi Yoshitake
Sazanami—Lt. Cdr. Uwai Hiroshi
Teiyō Maru (oiler)

Main Body

VADM Hosogaya Moshirō
Chief of staff: Capt. Nakazawa Tasuku
Nachi—Capt. Kiyota Takahiko (flagship)

Screen

Lt. Cdr. Takeuchi Hajime
Inazuma—Lt. Cdr. Takeuchi
Ikazuchi—Lt. Cdr. Kudō Shunsaku

Supply Group

Fujisan Maru (oiler)
Nissan Maru (oiler)
3 cargo ships

Attu-Adak Invasion Force

RADM Ōmori Sentarō
Abukuma—Capt. Murayama Seiroku

Destroyer Division 21—Capt. Shimizu Toshio
Wakaba—Lt. Cdr. Kuroki Masakichi
Nenohi—Lt. Cdr. Terauchi Saburō
Hatsuharu—Lt. Cdr. Makino Hiroshi
Hatsushimo—Lt. Cdr. Kohama Satoru
Magane Maru (minelayer)
Kinugasa Maru (transport, 1200 army troops under Maj. Hozumi Matsutoshi)

Kiska Invasion Force

Capt. Ono Takeji
Cruiser Division 21
Kiso—Capt. Ono
Tama—Capt. Kawabata Masaharu
Asaka Maru (aux. cruiser)—Capt. Ban Jirō
Awata Maru (aux. cruiser)

Destroyer Division 6—Capt. Yamada Yusuke
Hibiki—Lt. Cdr. Ishii Hagumu
Akatsuki—Lt. Cdr. Takasuka Osamu
Hokaze—Lt. Cdr. Tanaka Tomō
Hakusan Maru (transport, 550 troops under Lt. Cdr. Mukai Hifumi)
Kumagawa Maru (transport, 700 labor troops with const. equip.)

Minesweeper Division 13—Capt. Mitsuka Toshio
Hakuhō Maru
Kaihō Maru
Shinkotsu Maru

Submarine Detachment

SubRon 1
RADM Yamazaki Shigeaki
I-9—Cdr. Fujii Akiyoshi (flagship)

Submarine Division 2—Capt. Imazato Hiroshi
I-15—Cdr. Ishikawa Nobuo
I-17—Cdr. Nishino Kōzō
I-19—Cdr. Narahara Shōgo

Submarine Division 4—Capt. Nagai Mitsuru
I-25—Cdr. Tagami Meiji
I-26—Cdr. Yokota Minoru

Aleutian Seaplane Tender Force

Capt. Ujuku Keiichi
Kimikawa Maru (seaplane tender)—Capt. Ujuku
Aircraft:
     8 3-seat floatplanes
Destroyer *Shiokaze*—Lt. Tanegashima Yōji

† = Killed in Action

Appendix 3: The Carriers of *Kidō Butai*

AKAGI

Specifications

Builder:	Kure Naval Dockyard
Laid down:	Dec 6, 1920
Launched:	Apr 22, 1925
Commissioned:	Mar 25, 1927

As Built

Displacement:	26,900 tons (standard), 34,364 tons (normal)
Length:	857 ft 0 in (OA), 816 ft 7 in (WL), 764 ft 5 in (PP)
Beam:	95 ft 0 in
Draught:	26 ft 6 in
Machinery:	Gijitsu Honbu geared turbines, 19 Kampon boilers (19.3 kg/cm^2 generating saturated steam), 4 shafts (210 rpm)
Performance:	131,000 shp; 31 knots
Bunkerage:	3,900 tons fuel oil, 2,100 tons coal
Range:	8,000 nm at 14 knots
Flight-deck dimensions:	562 ft 0 in x 100 ft 0 in, plus 60 ft (approx) and 160 ft (approx) flying-off platforms at hangar-deck levels
Elevators:	2 (38 ft 6 in x 42 ft 8 in, 42 ft 0 in x 27 ft 6 in)
Arrester wires:	Longitudinal system initially, then 6 cross-deck wires (electrically controlled)
Hangar decks:	3 (upper, middle, and lower; lower used for disassembled aircraft stowage only)
Hangar dimensions:	upper 516 ft x 75 ft (approx), middle 557 ft x 75 ft (approx), lower 170 ft x 50 ft (approx); upper

and middle hangar area, 80,475 sq ft total (approx),
lower hangar 8,515 sq ft (approx)

Aircraft:	60
Armament:	10 x 8 in/50-cal LA, 12 x 4.7 in/45-cal HA, 22 MGs
Armor:	6 in belt, 3.1 in deck
Complement:	1,600
Cost:	¥53,000,000 (approx)

As Reconstructed (1935–38)

Displacement:	36,500 tons (standard), 41,300 tons (normal)
Length:	855 ft 3 in (OA), 821 ft 5 in (WL), 770 ft 0 in (PP)
Beam:	102 ft 9 in
Draught:	28 ft 7 in
Machinery:	Gijitsu Honbu geared turbines, 19 Kampon boilers (19.3 kg/cm^2 generating saturated steam), 4 shafts (210 rpm)
Performance:	133,000 shp; 31.25 knots
Bunkerage:	5,775 tons fuel oil, 225,000 gallons aviation fuel
Range:	8,200 nm at 16 knots
Flight-deck dimensions:	817 ft 6 in x 100 ft 0 in
Elevators:	3 (38 ft 6 in x 42 ft 6 in, 42 ft 0 in x 27 ft 6 in, 37 ft 6 in x 41 ft 3 in)
Arrester wires:	9 (hydraulic)
Hangar decks:	3 (upper, middle, and lower; lower used for disassembled aircraft stowage only)
Hangar dimensions:	upper and middle 620 ft x 75 ft (approx), lower 170 ft x 50 ft (approx); upper and middle hangar area 93,000 sq ft (approx), lower hangar 8,515 sq ft (approx)
Aircraft:	91 (total, when recommissioned); 63 operational (approx) in 1941
Armament:	6 x 8 in/50-cal LA, 12 x 4.7 in/45-cal HA, 28 x 25 mm AA
Fire-control equipment:	1 x Type 89 (8 in LA), 2 x Type 94 (4.7 in AA), 6 x Type 95 (25 mm AA)
Armor:	6 in belt, 3.1 in deck
Complement:	1,630

Notes

At the time of the Battle of Midway, *Akagi* was the flagship of First Carrier Division, the First Air Fleet, and the First Mobile Striking Force. Originally laid down as a battle cruiser in 1920, she had instead been completed as an aircraft carrier after

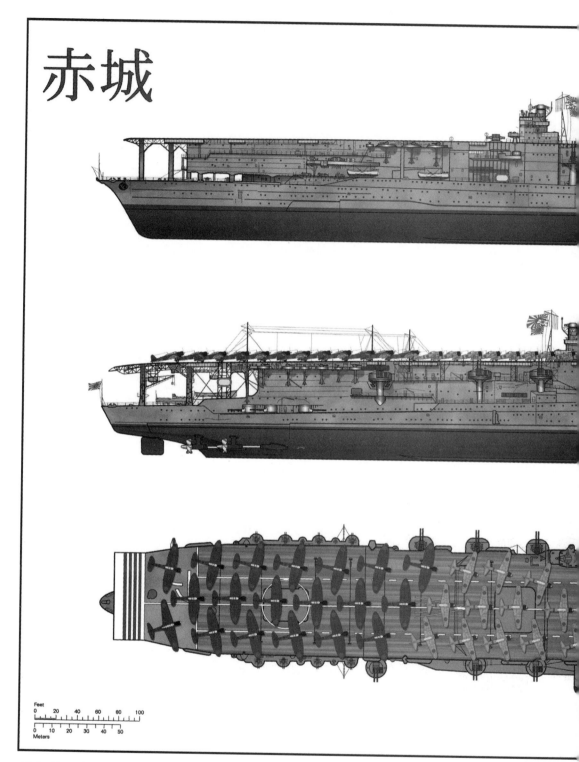

赤城

Feet
0　20　40　60　80　100

0　10　20　30　40　50
Meters

A3-1: Aircraft carrier *Akagi*.

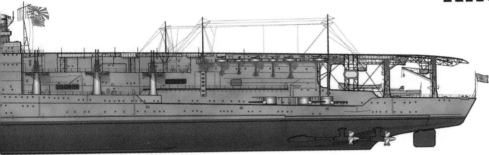

Akagi

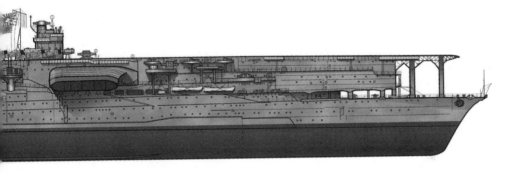

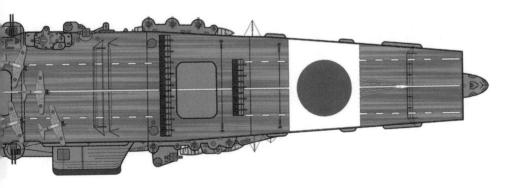

© Parshall 2005

Japan's ratification of the Washington Naval Treaty of 1922. *Akagi* was launched in 1925 and commissioned two years later.

As originally built, *Akagi* had three aircraft flight decks and no superstructure. Operational experience developed through her first years of service made it clear that she would need to be reconstructed. She was taken in hand for a complete refit beginning in October 1935. Financial difficulties slowed her conversion, and it was not until August 1938 that *Akagi* was returned to active service. As reconstructed, with a full length flight deck, enlarged hangars, a third elevator, and a true carrier island, she was one of the most capable carriers in the world, despite her relatively advanced years.

KAGA

Specifications

Builder:	Kawasaki Dockyard Co. and Yokosuka Naval Dockyard
Laid down:	Jul 19, 1920
Launched:	Nov 17, 1921
Commissioned:	Mar 31, 1928

As Built

Displacement:	26,000 tons (standard), 33,693 tons (normal)
Length:	782 ft 6 in (OA), 771 ft 0 in (WL), 715 ft 1 in (PP)
Beam:	97 ft 0 in
Draught:	26 ft 0 in
Machinery:	Brown-Curtiss geared turbines, 12 Kampon boilers (19.3 kg/cm^2 generating saturated steam), 4 shafts (210 rpm)
Performance:	91,000 shp; 28.5 knots
Bunkerage:	3,600 tons fuel oil, 1,700 tons coal
Range:	8,000 nm at 14 knots
Flight-deck dimensions:	560 ft 0 in x 100 ft 0 in, plus 60 ft (approx) and 160 ft (approx) flying-off platforms at hangar-deck levels
Elevators:	2 (37 ft 8 in x 39 ft 5 in, 35 ft 0 in x 52 ft 0 in)
Arrester wires:	6 (electrically controlled)
Hangar decks:	3 (upper, middle, and lower; lower used for disassembled aircraft stowage only)
Hangar dimensions:	upper 415 ft x 65 ft (approx), middle 470 ft x 75 ft (approx), lower 116 ft x 48 ft (approx); upper and middle hangar area 62,225 sq ft (approx), lower hangar 5,568 sq ft (approx)
Aircraft:	60

Armament:	10 x 8 in/50-cal LA, 12 x 4.7 in/45-cal HA, 2 MGs
Armor:	6 in belt, 1.5 in deck
Complement:	1,340
Cost:	¥53,000,000 (approx)

As Reconstructed (1934–35)

Displacement:	38,200 tons (standard), 42,541 tons (normal)
Length:	812 ft 6 in (OA), 788 ft 5 in (WL), 738 ft 2 in (PP)
Beam:	106 ft 8 in
Draught:	31 ft 1 in
Machinery:	Kampon geared turbines, 8 Kampon boilers (22 kg/cm^2 generating saturated steam), 4 shafts (2 x 210 rpm, 2 x 280 rpm), 4 shafts
Performance:	127,400 shp; 28.3 knots
Bunkerage:	8,208 tons fuel oil, 600 tons avgas
Range:	10,000 nm at 16 knots
Flight-deck dimensions:	815 ft 6 in x 100 ft 0 in
Elevators:	3 (37 ft 8 in x 39 ft 5 in, 35 ft 0 in x 52 ft 0 in, 42 ft 0 in x 31 ft 5 in)
Arrester wires:	9 (hydraulically controlled)
Hangar decks:	3 (upper, middle, and lower; lower used for disassembled aircraft stowage only)
Hangar dimensions:	upper and middle 615 ft x 88 ft (approx), lower 116 ft x 48 ft (approx); upper and middle hangar area 108,240 sq ft (approx), lower hangar 5,568 sq ft (approx)
Aircraft:	91 (total, when recommissioned); 72 operational (approx) in 1941
Armament:	10 x 8 in/50-cal LA, 16 x 5 in/40-cal DP, 22 x 25 mm AA
Fire-control equipment:	2 x Type 89 (8 in LA), 2 x Type 91 (5 in AA), 6 x Type 95 (25 mm AA)
Armor:	6 in belt, 1.5 in deck
Complement:	1,708

Notes

Perennial companion to *Akagi*, *Kaga* was laid down as a battleship in 1920. With Japan's acceptance of the Washington Naval Treaty, work on all capital ships was halted in 1922, leaving *Kaga* half-built. She would have been scrapped or expended, had not the Tokyo Earthquake of 1923 damaged *Akagi*'s sistership, *Amagi*, so badly on the building ways that she had to be written off as a total loss. In her place, *Kaga* was selected for completion as an aircraft carrier. She was launched in 1925 and

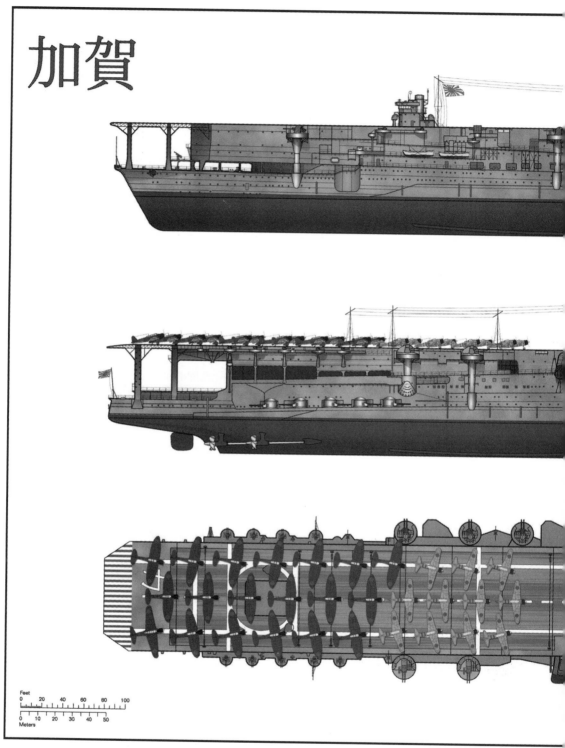

加賀

Feet
0 20 40 60 80 100

0 10 20 30 40 50
Meters

A3-2: Aircraft carrier *Kaga*.

Kaga

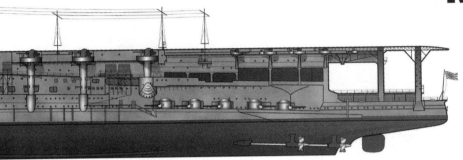

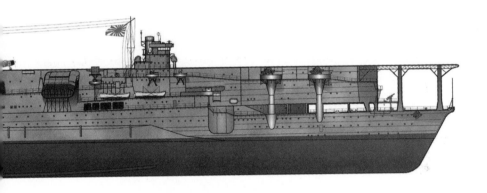

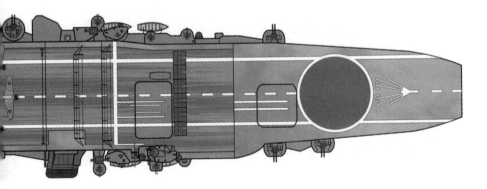

commissioned three years later after a lengthy fit out.

Like *Akagi, Kaga* was originally commissioned with three flight decks, none of them being full-length. Likewise, her early service showed the deficiency of her original design. Beginning in June 1934, she was taken in hand for a refit. *Kaga's* hull was lengthened (for greater speed), and a single, full-length flight deck erected. Her hangar spaces were enlarged, a third elevator added, and an island built. Her heavy and light antiaircraft armament was increased, and she was given new engines and boilers as well. When she emerged, she was one of the largest carriers in the world and possessed the biggest flight deck in the Japanese Navy until the commissioning of *Shōkaku* in 1941. While her lower speed meant that she was never quite as useful as *Akagi*, she remained a well-regarded vessel until the time of her sinking.

SŌRYŪ

Specifications

Builder:	Kure Naval Dockyard
Laid down:	Nov 20, 1934
Launched:	Dec 21, 1935
Commissioned:	Jan 29, 1937
Displacement:	15,900 tons (standard), 18,800 tons (normal)
Length:	746 ft 5 in (OA), 729 ft 9 in (WL), 677 ft 7 in (PP)
Beam:	69 ft 11 in
Draught:	25 ft 0 in
Machinery:	4 sets geared turbines, 8 Kampon boilers (22 kg/cm^2, 300°C), 4 shafts (340 rpm)
Performance:	152,000 shp; 34.5 knots
Bunkerage:	3,670 tons fuel oil, 150,000 gallons avgas
Range:	7,750 nm at 18 knots
Flight-deck dimensions:	711 ft 6 in x 85 ft 4 in
Elevators:	3 (37 ft 9 in x 52 ft 6 in, 37 ft 9 in x 39 ft 4 in, 38 ft 8 in x 32 ft 10 in)
Arrester wires:	9 (hydraulically controlled)
Hangar decks:	2
Hangar dimensions:	upper 562 ft x 60 ft x 15 ft (approx), lower 467 ft x 60 ft x 14 ft (approx); 61,740 sq ft (approx)
Aircraft:	68 (total, when commissioned); 57 operational (approx) in 1941
Armament:	12 x 5 in/40-cal DP, 28 x 25 mm AA
Fire-control equipment:	2 x Type 94 (5 in AA), 5 x Type 95 (25 mm AA)
Armor:	1.8 in belt, 1 in deck (2.2 in over the magazines)
Complement:	1,103
Cost:	¥40,200,000

Notes

Sōryū was Japan's first truly modern aircraft carrier and remained the archetype for all future Japanese carriers. Her sleek cruiser-type hull, combined with powerful machinery, gave her very high speed. Twin downswept stacks mounted to starboard vented exhaust gases away from the flight deck. She possessed dual hangar decks served by three elevators, making her capable of handling a comparatively large air wing for her size. However, she was lightly constructed, carried practically no armor, and was thus highly vulnerable to attack. Nevertheless, the Japanese Navy found her extremely useful, and she was well liked.

HIRYŪ

Specifications

Builder:	Yokosuka Naval Dockyard
Laid down:	Jul 8, 1936
Launched:	Nov 16, 1937
Commissioned:	Jul 5, 1939
Displacement:	17,300 tons (standard), 20,250 tons (normal)
Length:	745 ft 11 in (OA), 721 ft 9 in (WL), 687 ft 5 in (PP)
Beam:	73 ft 3 in
Draught:	25 ft 9 in
Machinery:	4 sets geared turbines, 8 Kampon boilers (22 kg/cm^2, 300°C), 4 shafts (340 rpm)
Performance:	153,000 shp; 34.5 knots
Bunkerage:	4,400 tons fuel oil (approx), 150,000 gallons avgas
Range:	10,330 nm at 18 knots
Flight-deck dimensions:	711 ft 6 in x 88 ft 6 in
Elevators:	3 (42 ft 8 in x 52 ft 6 in, 42 ft 8 in x 39 ft 4 in, 38 ft 8 in x 42 ft 8 in)
Arrester wires:	6 aft, 3 forward, all hydraulic
Hangar decks:	2
Hangar dimensions:	upper 562 ft x 60 ft x 15 ft (approx), lower 467 ft x 60 ft x 14 ft (approx); 61,740 sq ft (approx)
Aircraft:	73 (total, when commissioned); 59 operational (approx) in 1941
Armament:	12 x 5 in/40-cal DP, 31 x 25 mm AA
Fire-control equipment:	2 x Type 94 (5 in AA), 5 x Type 95 (25 mm AA)
Armor:	3.5 in belt (magazines 5.9 in), 1 in deck (2.2 in over the magazines)
Complement:	1,103
Cost:	¥40,200,000

蒼龍

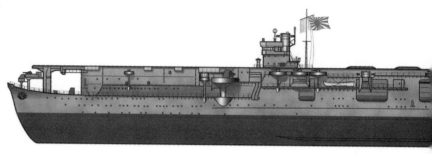

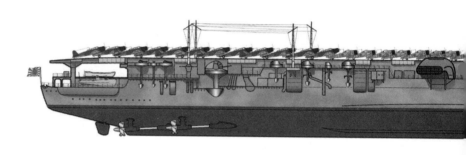

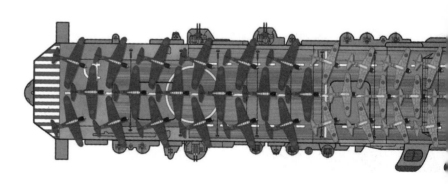

Feet
0   20   40   60   80   100

0   10   20   30   40   50
Meters

A3-3: Aircraft carrier *Sōryū*.

Sōryū

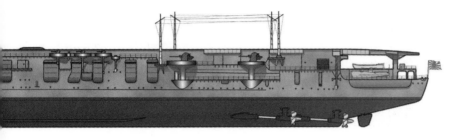

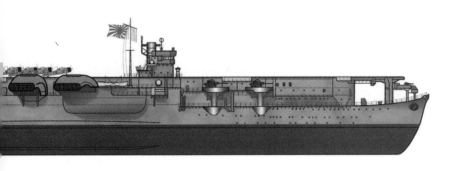

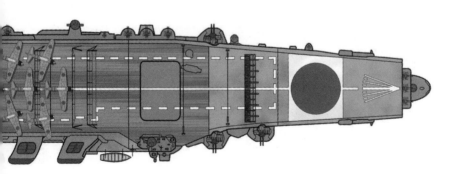

飛龍

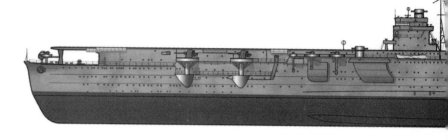

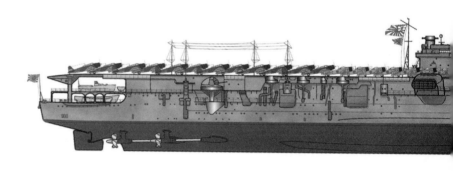

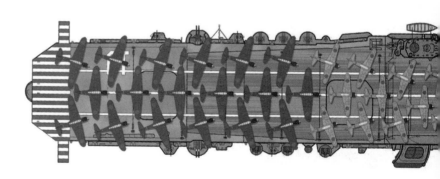

Feet
0 20 40 60 80 100

0 10 20 30 40 50
Meters

A3-4: Aircraft carrier *Hiryū*.

Hiryū

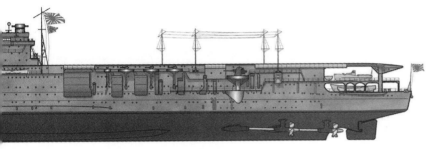

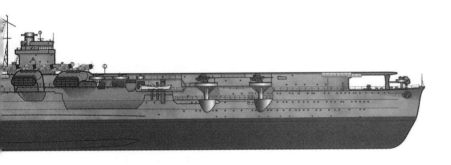

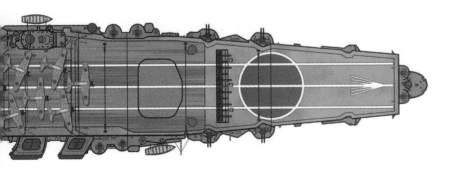

© Parshall 2005

Notes

Commissioned two and a half years after her slightly smaller sister, *Hiryū* improved on *Sōryū*'s design in a number of respects. Her slightly greater beam meant that her fuel capacity (and hence cruising range) were increased by about 20 percent. She was also somewhat better protected, although only marginally so, and remained profoundly vulnerable to attack. Nevertheless, with her long range, high speed, and relatively large air wing, she was well regarded by the Japanese. Even after the splendid *Shōkaku*-class carriers were commissioned in 1941, the *Hiryū*'s basic design was judged to be easier to produce, and as such served as the template for the late-war *Unryū*-class carriers.

Casualties

The following casualty figures are developed from Sawachi Hisae, *Midowei Kaisen: Kiroku,* which lists the name, province of birth, term of service, age, and rank of every Japanese fatality in the battle, grouped by the vessel they were serving aboard.

	Akagi	*Kaga*	*Sōryū*	*Hiryū*	*Total*
Seamen	72	261	113	78	524
Airmen	6	16	10	66	98
Mechanics	68	268	279	106	721
Engineers	115	212	242	121	690
Maintenance	1	18	27	6	52
Medical Officer	-	1	-	1	2
Medics	-	3	1	-	4
Clerks	5	32	38	14	89
Civilian	-	-	1	-	1
Total	**267**	**811**	**711**	**392**	**2181**

(Casualty figures developed from Sawachi Hisae, *Midowei Kaisen: Kiroku*)

Air Group Casualties

It should be noted that Hisae's loss figures for casualties among the carrier air crews are internally inconsistent. While her summary data lists a total of 98 carrier aircrew fatalities, a hand count of the individual ship returns indicates a larger figure. As a result, we are persuaded to accept James Sawruk's and Mark Horan's detailed casualty figures, which were developed directly from Japanese air group records. These show aircrew losses as follows:

Akagi:	7
Kaga:	21
Hiryū	72
Sōryū	10
Total	110

It is unclear whether these new totals impact the total crew casualties listed in Hisae or not.[1]

Notes on Carrier Data

Regarding the Illustrations

The illustrations show the carriers on 4 June, 1942. For all four ships we used the photographic record to amend and correct details found on other drawings. However, the photographic record for these four ships during the war, particularly *Sōryū* and *Kaga,* is sparse. This complicated the task of preparing illustrations of the flight deck marking schemes, because these were apparently changed aboard the four carriers just days before *Kidō Butai* sailed for Midway.

The most striking change to the flight deck markings was the painting of a large red rising sun emblem ("*hinomaru*") on the forward flight deck. This augmented the white *kana* symbols ("*a*" for *Akagi,* "*hi*" for *Hiryū,* "*sa*" for *Sōryū*[2] and "*ka*" for *Kaga*) that were already present on the port quarter of the flight deck for aircraft recognition purposes. The photographic record from Midway includes a number of overhead shots of the carriers taken by B-17 bombers (one picture of *Akagi,* two of *Sōryū,* and three of *Hiryū*[3]). The picture of *Akagi* clearly shows both the *hinomaru* and the *kana* symbol. In addition, her *hinomaru* is completely enclosed in a white rectangle spanning the width of the flight deck. The picture of *Sōryū* shows the *hinomaru* (enclosed like *Akagi*'s in a large white rectangle), but the *kana* symbol, if present, is indistinct. *Hiryū*'s photos show the *kana* symbol and *hinomaru* as well. Her *hinomaru* is not enclosed in a white rectangle, although it does have a white border. In addition, unlike *Akagi* and *Sōryū,* her white deck stripes are clearly visible trisecting the *hinomaru* itself. No photographs of *Kaga* from 4 June have survived, but is presumed that she had roughly the same configuration as *Hiryū,* that is, a freestanding *hinomaru* unenclosed by a white background.

Regarding Aviation Fuel

Finding accurate figures for aviation gasoline storage is a maddeningly difficult problem, because few reference books indicate their sources, and none of them indicate whether they are using English or U.S. gallons as a measure. As a result, we have used plans of the ships as a source to derive the tankage volume. Volume is given in U.S. gallons, which is .1336 cubic feet, or 3.7854 liters.

Kaga: 154,000 U.S. gallons (20,550 cubic feet of tankage (as derived from plans) x 7.48 gallons/cu ft.)

Akagi: 150,000 gallons (20,054 cubic feet, as derived from plans)

Hiryū: 134,000 gallons

Sōryū: 134,000 gallons

Regarding Spare Aircraft

Reference works on the Japanese Navy can leave the reader with a deceptive portrait of the number of aircraft aboard Japanese aircraft carriers. For instance, the figure of "91 aircraft" carried aboard the *Kaga* found in many naval reference books has to be used with some caution. *Kaga* may very well have carried 91 aircraft at some point in her career, but it is clear that she never carried 91 *active* aircraft, nor did she carry 91 aircraft around the time of the Battle of Midway.

There are three factors that explain this apparent discrepancy. The first is that Japanese carriers often carried spare aircraft that were counted in the total. These planes were stored in a semiassembled state near the hangars. In the case of *Akagi* and *Kaga,* these aircraft were carried in a third, lower hangar abreast the eight-inch casemate guns. On *Hiryū* and *Sōryū,* there were storage bays on the port side of the elevator wells on both the upper and lower hangar decks. Aircraft stored in such a fashion were not readily available, and thus cannot be included in the operational totals. However, since they were available as replacements to the air groups within a matter of days, and were organic to the air groups, they deserve to be included in the overall totals.

The second factor is that combat aircraft in 1942 were larger than their predecessors in the 1920s, and hence fewer of them could be carried into battle than before. Third and last is the fact that the nominal published aircraft totals did not account for the fact that not all aircraft stow with the same degree of efficiency. For instance, the Type 99 dive-bomber took up a great deal of space belowdecks, whereas the Type 97 torpedo bomber did not. This despite the fact that both aircraft were roughly the same size when their wings were unfolded. Carrier air group composition therefore played a role in determining aircraft totals aboard ship.

Appendix 4: The Aircraft of *Kidō Butai*

This appendix provides technical information on the major types of aircraft carried by the Japanese aircraft carriers, as well as the floatplanes carried by Battleship Division 3 (*Haruna* and *Kirishima*) and Cruiser Division 8 (*Tone* and *Chikuma*).[1]

Mitsubishi A6M2 Model 21

Official designation:	Navy Type 0 Carrier Fighter
Subsequent Allied code name:[2]	"Zeke"
Description:	Single-seat carrier-borne and land-based fighter
Crew:	1
Powerplant:	One Nakajima Sakae 12 fourteen-cylinder air-cooled radial, 940 hp at takeoff, driving a three-blade propeller
Armament:	Two 7.7 mm Type 97 machine guns, two 20 mm Type 99 cannon
Bomb load:	Two 60 kg (132 lb) bombs, one 330 liter (72.6 Imp gal) drop tank

Dimensions

Span:	39 ft 4 in
Length:	29 ft 8 in
Height:	11 ft 6 in
Weight	
Empty:	3,704 lb
Loaded:	5,313 lb

Performance

Maximum speed:	331 mph at 14,930 ft
Cruising speed:	207 mph
Climb:	19,685 ft in 7 min 27 sec
Service ceiling:	32,810 ft
Range:	1,010 nm (1,675 nm max)

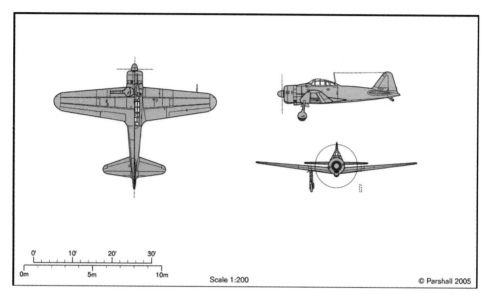

A4-1: Mitsubishi A6M2 Model 21 carrier fighter

Notes

The standard carrier and land-based naval fighter at the outbreak of the war, this airplane was carried by all four Japanese carriers at the Battle of Midway. One of the finest fighters in the world at the time, the Zero was fast, was extremely maneuverable, and carried good firepower. In the hands of a skilled pilot, it was an extremely dangerous opponent. However, light construction and lack of armor and self-sealing fuel tanks were critical defects that would begin to make themselves felt as the war progressed.

Nakajima B5N2

Official designation:	Navy Type 97 Carrier Attack Aircraft
Subsequent Allied code name:	"Kate"
Description:	Single-engine carrier-borne torpedo bomber
Crew:	3 (pilot, observer/navigator/bomb aimer, radio operator/gunner)
Powerplant:	One Nakajima NK1B Sakae 11 fourteen-cylinder air-cooled radial, 1,000 hp at takeoff, driving a three-blade propeller
Armament:	One flexible rear-firing 7.7 mm Type 92 machine gun
Bomb load:	One 800 kg (1,764 lb) torpedo, or 800 kg (1,764 lb) of bombs

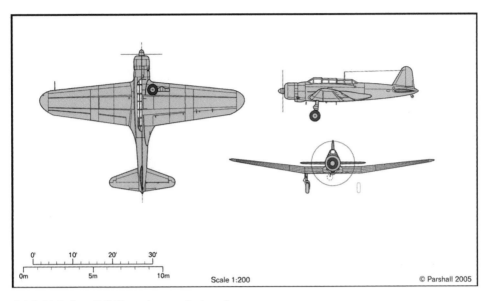

A4-2: Nakajima B5N2 carrier attack aircraft

Dimensions

Span:	50 ft 10 in
Length:	33 ft 9 in
Height:	12 ft 1 in
Weight	
Empty:	5,024 lb
Loaded:	8,378 lb

Performance

Maximum speed:	235 mph at 11,810 ft
Cruising speed:	161 mph at 11,810 ft
Climb:	9,845 in 7 min 40 sec
Service ceiling:	27,100 ft
Range:	528 nm (1,075 nm max)

Notes

Probably the finest torpedo bomber in the world at the outbreak of the Pacific war, the B5N was large, relatively fast, and capable of hauling a heavy bomb or torpedo load. It was used alternately in both reconnaissance, level-bombing, and torpedo-attack roles. At the time of the Battle of Midway, newer model B5N2s equipped all frontline carrier units. However, older B5N1s were still in service in second-line units.

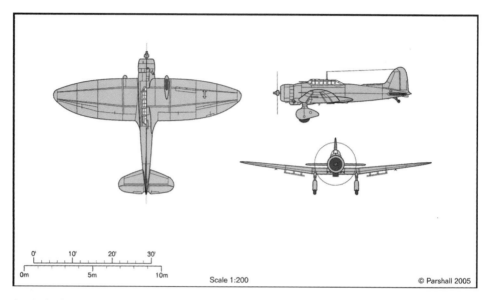

A4-3: Aichi D3A1 carrier bomber

Aichi D3A1

Official designation:	Navy Type 99 Carrier Bomber
Subsequent Allied code name:	"Val"
Description:	Single-engined carrier-borne and land-based dive-bomber
Crew:	2
Powerplant:	One Mitsubishi Kinsei 43 fourteen-cylinder air-cooled radial, 1,000 hp at takeoff, **or** Mitsubishi Kinsei 44 fourteen-cylinder air-cooled radial, 1,070 hp at takeoff, driving a three-blade propeller
Armament:	Two forward-firing 7.7 mm Type 97 machine guns, one flexible rear-firing 7.7 mm Type 92 machine gun
Bomb load:	One 250 kg (551 lb) bomb under the fuselage and two 60 kg (132 lb) bombs under the wings

Dimensions

Span:	47 ft 1 in
Length:	33 ft 5 in
Height:	12 ft 7 in
Weight	
Empty:	5,309 lb
Loaded:	8,047 lb

Performance

Maximum speed:	240 mph at 9,845 ft
Cruising speed:	184 mph at 9,845 ft
Climb:	9,845 ft in 6 min 0 sec
Service ceiling:	30,050 ft
Range:	795 nm

Notes

D3A1s equipped all frontline carrier dive-bomber formations at the time of the Battle of Midway. A nimble aircraft, the D3A was also a very stable dive-bomber. By the time of Midway, it was intended that the D3A should have been superseded by the newer D4Y. But slow production of the latter meant that the D3A eventually soldiered on well past its useful service life as the war progressed.

Yokosuka D4Y1

Official designation:	Experimental Model 13 Carrier Bomber[3]
Subsequent Allied code name:	"Judy"
Description:	Single-engined carrier-borne and land-based dive-bomber/reconnaissance aircraft
Crew:	2
Powerplant:	One Aichi AE1A Atsuta twelve-cylinder inverted-vee liquid-cooled engine, 1,200 hp at takeoff, driving a three-blade propeller
Armament:	Two fuselage-mounted 7.7 mm Type 97 machine guns, one flexible rear-firing 7.92 mm Type 1 machine gun
Bomb load:	One 250 kg (551 lb) bomb stowed internally, and two 60 kg (132 lb) bombs under the wings

Dimensions

Span:	37 ft 9 in
Length:	33 ft 6 in
Height:	12 ft 1 in
Weight	
Empty:	5,739 lb
Loaded:	8,047 lb

Performance

Maximum speed:	343 mph at 15,585 ft
Cruising speed:	265 mph at 9,845 ft
Climb:	9,845 ft in 5 min 14 sec
Service ceiling:	32,480 ft
Range:	850 nm

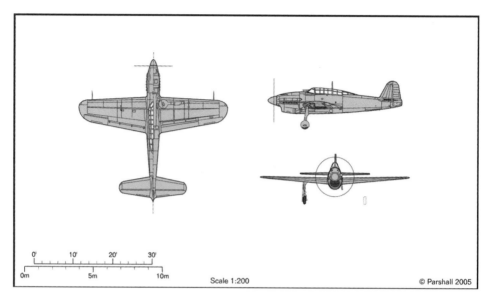

A4-4: Yokosuka D4Y1 carrier bomber

Notes

At the time of the Battle of Midway, a handful of prototype D4Y carrier bombers had been produced, and full-scale production was pending. At least one of these prototypes was shipped on board *Sōryū* and used as a reconnaissance plane during the battle, a role for which its high speed suited it eminently.

Aichi E13A

Official designation:	Navy Type 0 Reconnaissance Seaplane
Subsequent Allied code name:	"Jake"
Description:	Single-engined, twin float reconnaissance seaplane
Crew:	3
Powerplant:	One Mitsubishi Kinsei 43 fourteen-cylinder air-cooled radial, 1,000 hp at takeoff, driving a three-blade propeller
Armament:	One flexible rear-firing 7.7 mm Type 92 machine gun
Bomb load:	One 250 kg (551 lb) bomb under the fuselage, or four 60 kg (132 lb) bombs, or depth charges

Dimensions

Span:	47 ft 6 in
Length:	37 ft 0 in
Height:	24 ft 3 in

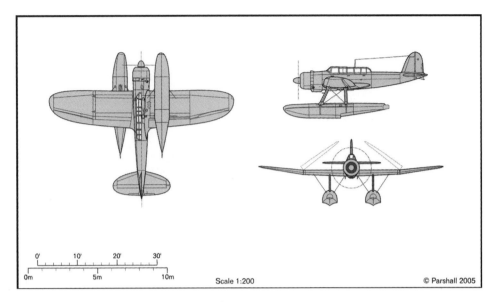

A4-5: Aichi E13A reconnaissance seaplane

Weight

Empty:	5,825 lb
Loaded:	8,025 lb

Performance

Maximum speed:	234 mph at 7,155 ft
Cruising speed:	138 mph at 6,560 ft
Climb:	9,845 ft in 6 min 5 sec
Service ceiling:	28,640 ft
Range:	1,128 nm

Notes

The standard long-range float scout plane carried by most Japanese heavy cruisers. A mixture of Type 0 and Type 95 float aircraft were carried by cruisers *Tone* and *Chikuma* (CruDiv 8) at Midway.

Nakajima E8N2

Official designation:	Navy Type 95 Reconnaissance Seaplane
Subsequent Allied code name:	"Dave"
Description:	Single-engined reconnaissance seaplane
Crew:	2
Powerplant:	One Nakajima 2 KAI 2 nine-cylinder air-cooled radial, 630 hp at takeoff, driving a two-blade propeller

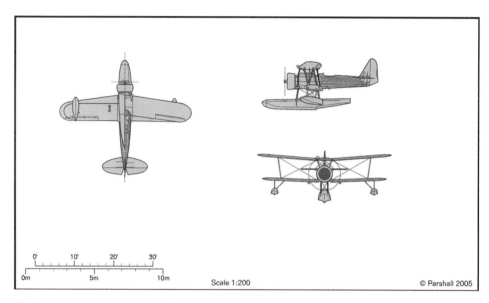

A4-6: Nakajima E8N2 reconnaissance seaplane

Armament:	One fixed forward firing 7.7 mm machine gun and one flexible rear-firing 7.7 mm machine gun
Bomb load:	Two 60 kg (132 lb) bombs

Dimensions

Span:	36 ft 0 in
Length:	28 ft 10 in
Height:	12 ft 7 in
Weight	
Empty:	2,910 lb
Loaded:	4,189 lb

Performance

Maximum speed:	186 mph at 9,845 ft
Climb:	9,845 ft in 6 min 31 sec
Service ceiling:	23,850 ft
Range:	485 nm

Notes

The older Type 95 was used for spotting and fleet support duties such as ASW patrol. By the time of Midway, it no longer possessed the necessary range to operate as a true reconnaissance plane. Type 95s were carried on board both the heavy cruisers *Tone* and *Chikuma,* as well as the battleships *Haruna* and *Kirishima.*

Appendix 5: Japanese Amphibious Operations against Midway—An Analysis

Had the Japanese triumphed against the U.S. Navy in the naval phase of the Battle of Midway, the stage would have been set for an amphibious landing against the atoll on the morning of 6 June. Down through the years it has commonly been supposed that the Japanese would have overwhelmed the American defenders with a combination of air and gun power, paving the way for a successful landing by Colonel Ichiki's detachment and Captain Itō's Naval Special Landing Force.[1] Perhaps this is simply a natural outgrowth of the mistaken belief surrounding the relative odds in the naval conflict, that the fallacious notion of overwhelming Japanese numerical superiority should have been extended by proxy to the relative odds facing the American ground defenders. But was a Japanese victory really the likely outcome of such an encounter?

In fact, a more dispassionate analysis reveals nearly as many flaws in the Japanese plans for the invasion as beset the battle at the strategic level. Instead, a careful examination almost inevitably leads to the conclusion that the Japanese faced formidable obstacles, not only of numbers and geography, but also of amphibious doctrine, training, and coordination. As a result, Midway's defenders would likely have held the atoll, at least in the short term.[2]

Even postulating a naval victory, in truth the Imperial Navy was miserably prepared to support a landing against Midway. The Japanese Navy had little in the way of either an established ground attack doctrine for its aircraft, or a tested naval gunfire support doctrine. Given the hostility between the two branches of the imperial services, this is not surprising. The Navy saw its mission as the destruction of enemy warships, not supporting the landing of Army troops. The practical effect of this, though, was to render distinctly less effective any air support the carriers of *Kidō Butai* might be able to provide. The positions of the U.S. Marines ashore were well sited and emplaced. In some cases, they were equipped with reinforced concrete shelters, which were nearly bombproof. Even the less well-protected troops were well dug in and protected by sandbags and natural fortifications. The attack by Tomonaga's strike force on the morning of 4 June, while destroying some of the more-visible facilities on the islands, such as oil tanks and barracks, had degraded the real defensive capacity of the Marine defenders hardly at all. Not a single heavy gun of any sort had been put out of commission, and total personnel losses were six KIA.[3] There is no reason to suppose that one or two additional strikes by Japanese carrier aircraft on 5 June and the morning of 6 June would have appreciably altered this basic equation before the landings occurred. In other words, the majority of the Marines' weaponry would likely have remained intact.

By the same token, the guns of CruDiv 7—the cruisers *Kumano, Suzuya, Mikuma,* and *Mogami*—were ill equipped to perform much better. Given the rigid operational timetable laid down by Yamamoto, and the stated intention to land the troops at first light,[4] their bombardment of the islands could not help but be desultory. Tarawa, Kwajalein, and a dozen other sites in the Central Pacific subsequently demonstrated to the Americans that dug-in island defenses were generally proof against heavy-caliber weapons, even when over extended periods of time. A quick bombardment from shipborne eight-inch guns with no practice in target identification or selection simply wasn't going to get the job done. The Marines might have been shaken by it, but odds were that they would have survived largely undamaged.

Admittedly, the Japanese also had the ability to direct gunfire against targets of opportunity on Midway once the landings were under way and the American weapons exposed themselves. But it was unlikely that any Japanese warships would want to close the range too closely until the four seven-inch guns emplaced on the southern shores of Sand and Eastern Islands were taken out. Even then, it is extremely doubtful that Japanese fire would have been terribly accurate, since such missions were not a part of their normal doctrine. Likewise, it is almost impossible to anticipate any of the landing troops having the ability to communicate with the warships directly—the necessary doctrine and portable radio equipment simply weren't there.

Beyond these hurdles, Midway's geography also presented a very difficult target. It is almost completely surrounded by an exposed coral reef. There are gaps on the western side, but they do not constitute a useful approach, leading as they do to wide shallows of unpredictable depth. To the south, a small gap had been blasted for the ship channel, but it lay directly under the heavy guns of both islands. The result is that most of the shoreline could not be directly approached by landing craft. The tidal range at Midway is quite small, with a mean range of only nine inches, and a diurnal range of fifteen inches, meaning that there is no high tide that can be counted on to whisk landing craft over the reef and allow them access to the beaches unhindered. This, in turn, meant that the *daihatsu* barges would have had to discharge their human cargo on the farther side of the reef. This was never less than 200 yards from shore, and sometimes as much as double that. After being "landed," the men would first have had to wade onto the reef itself, exposing them to fire. From there, they would have to slog back into the lagoon toward the beaches, through water that in many cases would have come up to their chests, all the while under heavy fire. It was precisely to defeat this sort of natural obstacle that the Americans went on to develop the famous Amtrac amphibious landing craft. In June 1942, the Japanese could only have dreamed of owning such a vehicle.

Ashore, the Americans were well entrenched and numerous. Depending on which sources are consulted, there were anywhere from 3,000 to 4,500 personnel on the islands.[5] The majority of them, being Marines, were infantrymen by original training whatever their current operational capacity. The Americans had laid antiboat obstacles in the water. Along the beaches, rows of electrically detonated mines had been planted along with seemingly endless strands of barbed wire. The Marines had even gone so far as to create more than 1,500 improvised explosive devices for use against tanks. A platoon of M3 Stuart light tanks was hidden in the heavy underbrush of Sand Island's interior. Even before the addition of "Carlson's Raiders," the Sixth Defense Battalion's order of battle included five five-inch guns, four three-inch antiboat guns, twelve three-inch AA guns, forty-eight .50-caliber machine guns, and thirty-six .30-caliber machine guns.[6] The total number of three-inch AA guns on both islands was twenty-four, and was further bolstered by the addition of 37-mm and 20-mm automatic guns in the hands of an antiaircraft defense unit. "Wreck 'em on the reef!" was the motto of Midway's commander, Colonel Harold Shannon, and we have no reason to doubt that every weapon at the colonel's disposal would have been unleashed as soon as the Japanese barges reached that unfortunate aquatic terminus.

Despite their successes in amphibious operations in the Pacific to date, the truth was that the Japanese had little experience against defended beachheads. Their doctrine called for landings against undefended locales, typically at night. On those occasions when they had been forced to make daylight assaults against dug-in positions—such as those on Wake Island, as well as some minor operations against the Bataan peninsula in the Philippines—the results had been singularly unpleasant. It certainly didn't auger well for the Midway operation that neither the Army nor the Navy landing forces had apparently rehearsed their respective parts in any detail, let alone exercised them *together,* before having sailed from their separate ports of embarkation.

The most likely outcome of such a haphazard and ill-supported operation being thrown against the heavily armed and entrenched defenders at Midway was outright disaster. While alternative history can never be absolutely predictive, we need only fast-forward two months to the subsequent destruction of Colonel Ichiki's detachment early in the Guadalcanal campaign to glimpse the likely outlines of such a landing at Midway. There, Ichiki had chosen to charge a much less well dug-in Marine position on the banks of Alligator Creek. The result was that he and more than 700 of his men were slaughtered by a combination of automatic weapons fire and canister shot from the American's 37-mm guns. At Midway, the presence of some 2,500 attackers didn't alter this basic equation a whit.[7] In fact, the Americans had vastly superior firepower to draw on, and much better fire lanes to boot. Their weapons could engage the enemy at range, while they were still well out on the reef. Even if any of the Japanese made it to the beach (in itself a dubious proposition), it is almost inconceivable that two shattered, geographically separated light infantry regiments equipped with nothing more than rifles, light mortars, and a smattering of medium machine guns would have been able to prevail against an entrenched American force backed by mobile armor. Rather, all signs indicate that the lagoon would have been full of Japanese corpses by about the middle of the afternoon, leaving the imperial warships witness to an unprecedented slaughter.

Once the initial wave of troops was expended, there was no reserve capable of mounting a second offensive. The Imperial Navy might have had the ability to bombard the place, but it certainly didn't have the means to bring it to heel once Ichiki and the naval landing troops were dead. The best they could have hoped for at that juncture was a violent standoff, wherein the Imperial Navy's warships took what retribution they could while their logistical tether allowed. In the end, though, it is likely that *Kidō Butai* and Japan's capital ships would have had no choice but to withdraw, leaving the smashed island still in the hands of the Americans—for the time being at any rate.

Appendix 6: Discovery of Carrier *Kaga*

Technological advancements in underwater exploration methods have begun opening the great naval battlefields of the past. The discovery of the Japanese battleship *Yamato* in 1985 was followed by the even more impressive location of the German battleship *Bismarck* in 1989. These events marked a watershed, in that they demonstrated that it is possible to locate and photograph vessels whose sinking positions were known only inexactly. Since the beginning of the 1990s to the present day, several important naval battle sites have been documented in this fashion. Along the way, the ranks of rediscovered great warships has swelled with the addition of such notables as the battle cruiser HMS *Hood*, battleship *Scharnhorst*, submarine *I-52*, and numerous wrecks around the island of Guadalcanal, including the cruisers *Atlanta* and *Canberra*, and battleship *Hiei*.

Not surprisingly, the Battle of Midway has earned its share of attention in this respect. Dr. Robert Ballard, who located both the liner *Titanic* and the *Bismarck*, in 1998 succeeded in finding the USS *Yorktown* in 16,650 feet of water. *Yorktown* was discovered to be in nearly perfect condition, having impacted on the bottom upright and intact, with very little subsequent damage to her hull and fittings. However, she still clearly bore the scars of her numerous torpedo hits. Extensively photographed, she is (ironically perhaps) the most visible physical relic of the battle still remaining. The island of Midway itself no longer is open to tourists, and much of the physical evidence of the great battle that was fought there has long since been removed.

During the same expedition, Dr. Ballard tried unsuccessfully to locate the carrier *Kaga* as well. This is perhaps not surprising, as *Kaga*'s recorded sinking positions were contradictory, and her movements after her fatal dive-bombing were not well understood at the time. However, just a year later, in September 1999, a joint expedition between the undersea exploration firm Nauticos and the Naval Oceanographic Office yielded an important discovery. Rather than simply searching around the recorded positions of *Kaga*'s sinking, Nauticos used the logs of the American submarine USS *Nautilus*, which had attacked *Kaga* during the middle hours of 4 June, as the basis of its search. Using sophisticated renavigation techniques, Nauticos and the Oceanographic Office decided on a different survey area—one that varied considerably from *Kaga*'s recorded sinking location. Sidescan sonar surveys of the target area yielded a hard contact, which was subsequently located and photographed by an ROV.

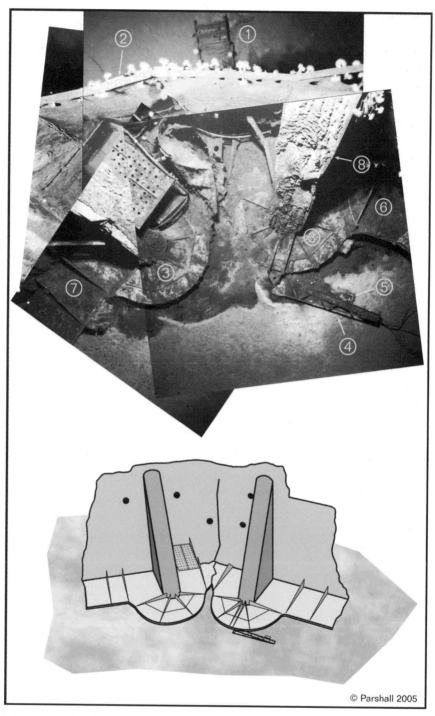

A6-1: Photo mosaic of *Kaga* wreckage discovered in September 1999. View is from the top, looking down at the ocean floor. Key: 1—companionway leading into berthing compartment; 2—bottom edge of exterior bulkhead; 3—25-mm twin gun tub; 4—landing light array (*chakkan shidōtō*) arm; 5—1-kw landing light; 6—gallery deck leading aft; 7—gallery deck leading forward; 8—support column for 25-mm gun tub. (Photo courtesy Nauticos)

The find was not the main wreck of *Kaga,* but rather a very large piece of her wreckage. There, nearly 17,000 feet down, was a 50-foot-long section of hangar bulkhead sticking upside down from the bottom. Attached to it, also inverted, were two tubs for 25-mm antiaircraft guns. And attached to one of the gun tubs was what turned out to be a landing light array (*chakkan shidōtō*) used by pilots to land their aircraft on the flight deck. As it happened, the authors were subsequently contacted by Nauticos and performed the necessary forensic analysis to definitively identify the wreckage as having come from *Kaga.*[1]

The significance of the find is threefold. First, it demonstrates that modern undersea search techniques have advanced far beyond the realm of simply opening up all the available reference books on a given ship's sinking position, drawing a box around the various reported sinking locations, and looking there. Now, sophisticated renavigation techniques can lead to considerably improved and refined search strategies. Second, the artifact solidifies the notion that *Kaga*'s main wreck must lie somewhere nearby. The artifact serves as the logical starting point for any future expedition.

Third, and most important, the wreckage discovered in 1999 gives mute testimony to the violence and fury of the calamity that overtook *Kaga.* This artifact—as big as a house, and weighing many tons—had been blown off the starboard side of *Kaga*'s hangar deck like a piece of wet cardboard. Crumpled and bent nearly in half, the weight of the twin 25-mm mounts in the gun tubs had caused it to fall upside down some three miles to the ocean floor. We know from Yoshino Haruo's description of *Kaga* immediately before she sank that this same process of explosive destruction had consumed the entire mid-portion of the ship, leaving her a burned-out hulk.

The authors hope that another opportunity will present itself to document this important battlefield. With the known position of *Kaga*'s artifact as a starting point, locating her main wreck should not be difficult. From there, on the basis of our better understanding of *Kidō Butai*'s formation and distribution at the time of the fatal attack, as well as *Akagi* and *Sōryū*'s subsequent movements, it may be possible to locate these latter two carriers as well. Finding *Hiryū* will be more difficult, as her sinking was not observed by any warship. However, even documenting the locations of three of *Kidō Butai*'s carriers would greatly increase our knowledge of this crucial battlefield. As a seafaring country with a long and glorious naval tradition, we owe it to ourselves, and our descendants, to discover as much as we can about *all* the great ships involved in our nation's battles before the implacable forces of time and the sea destroy their crucial evidence forever.

Appendix 7: Japanese Aircraft Tail Codes at the Battle of Midway

Japanese carrier aircraft were identified by means of alphanumeric codes painted on their tails. The first two or three characters indicated the carrier division and carrier to which the aircraft belonged. For example, Carrier Division 1 was designated by the prefix letter "A," with the flagship *Akagi*'s aircraft being "AI-" and *Kaga*'s being "AII-". The ships in Carrier Division 2 carried "BI-" and "BII-".

Following the divisional prefix on the tail was a three-digit suffix indicating the aircraft type. Planes with "-1xx" were fighters, "-2xx" were dive-bombers, and "-3xx" were carrier attack (torpedo) aircraft. Thus, "AI-121" would indicate a fighter from *Akagi*'s fighter group, and "AII-201" would indicate a *Kaga* dive-bomber.

Likewise, the rear fuselage of the aircraft was painted with vertical bands just in front of the tail to indicate the mother carrier and its place within the carrier division. A single red band around the fuselage meant the lead carrier in Carrier Division 1— *Akagi*, whereas two red bands meant the second carrier—*Kaga*. A single blue stripe meant the lead carrier in Carrier Division 2, whereas a single white stripe designated the lead carrier in Carrier Division 5, and so on.

Here's where things get complicated. At the time of the Pearl Harbor attack, *Sōryū* was the flagship of Carrier Division 2. As such, her aircraft were designated "BI-xxx," and *Hiryū*'s "BII-xxx". As would be expected, *Sōryū*'s aircraft carried a single blue fuselage band, and *Hiryū*'s two. However, in late April 1942, Admiral Yamaguchi, commander of Carrier Division 2, switched his flag to *Hiryū*. The reasons for doing so are obvious—*Hiryū* was newer and had a much larger island and better command facilities. According to the conventional wisdom, Carrier Division 2's aircraft designations should have been reversed as a result of this switch, with *Hiryū*'s aircraft marked "BI-xxx," and those of *Sōryū* "BII-xxx," along with corresponding changes in the fuselage bands. However, it is not entirely clear whether this was actually done.

Obviously, there were practical limitations to doing so. In the first place, the labor associated with having to repaint identification codes and markings on more than a hundred aircraft on two carriers cannot be underestimated. Particularly in the frantic few weeks of training between when CarDiv 2 returned from the Indian

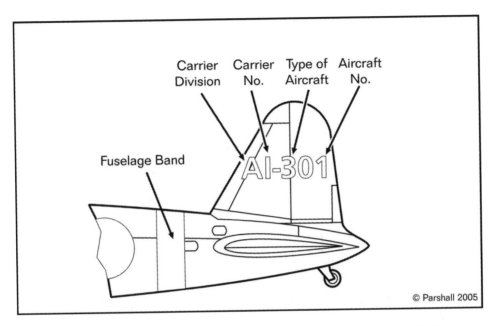

A7-1: Japanese aircraft tail code markings. The example shown is the tail of the lead aircraft of *Akagi*'s carrier attack aircraft unit, that of Commander Fuchida Mitsuo.

Ocean on April 22 and left again for Midway on May 25, this would have been a large undertaking, although certainly achievable.

More important, though, is the fact that the designations of warships, and their relative status within a division, were not supposed to be directly under the control of the fleet's operational commands. Instead, they were mandated by the Navy Ministry. According to a letter from Capt. (Ret.) Kitazawa Noritaka, of the history department for Japan's National Institute for Defense Studies, the codes were established by the minister of the navy in 1936 and were given to the individual ships themselves, and not to the division. This meant that a shift in the flag's location was nothing more than a convenience for the flag—it meant nothing in terms of the relative standing of the vessels themselves as far as the Navy Ministry was concerned. Furthermore, it meant that a carrier division was not formally empowered to change the designation of its vessels or aircraft. Regardless of where Yamaguchi flew his flag, *Sōryū* was still the senior vessel in the division in the eyes of the Navy Ministry.

This regulation was subsequently changed in November 1944, and thereafter the designation power was granted to the commander in chief, Combined Fleet. However, at the time of Midway the original 1936 regulation was still in force.[1] No official documentation has been discovered indicating that the Navy Ministry changed the designations of CarDiv 2's vessels as a result of Yamaguchi's change of flag. Given the apparently last-minute nature of the shift, the subsequent destruction of both vessels, and the death of Yamaguchi, this is hardly surprising. In sum, if the letter of the Navy's regulations was indeed being followed, *Sōryū*'s aircraft should have retained their original "BI-xxx" designations, and *Hiryū*'s her "BII-xxx" codes at the Battle of Midway.

However, it seems likely that the 1944 regulation was simply a belated de facto recognition of a condition that had already existed for several years before. Noted aviation historian Osamu Tagaya notes that tail codes for aircraft assigned to *Naisen Butai* (Zone of the Interior) air forces in China *before* war broke out were indeed designated by the Navy Ministry. However, once the war in China began, and *Gai-Sen Butai* (Outside or Overseas Forces) were committed, the evidence suggests that these aircraft designations were controlled directly by Combined Fleet. In other words, just because the 1944 regulation is the only one that has surfaced thus far pertaining to this matter, does not mean that this was the first time that actual jurisdiction of the codes had been ceded to Combined Fleet.[2]

Furthermore, there is credible direct evidence that asserts that *Hiryū*'s codes *were* changed. First off, the Nagumo Report states that after the temporary shift of the flag to *Sōryū* in early May 1942, *Hiryū* was subsequently "permanently assigned as Flagship."[3] This strongly indicates that, at least in the eyes of Combined Fleet, *Hiryū* was now to be treated as the new flagship.

In addition, several eyewitness accounts assert that the aircraft tail codes were, in fact, changed immediately prior to Midway. An account from Mr. Arimura Yoshikazu provides direct evidence to that effect. Arimura was in charge of carrier bomber maintenance aboard *Hiryū* at the time of Midway and was obviously in a position to comment on the status of her aircraft tail codes, since the men who would have had to do the repainting were under his command. Arimura, in response to written questions from Jon Parshall, stated that *Hiryū*'s codes had been changed to "BI-xxx." He further indicated that the codes had been changed at the time of Nagumo's departure from Hashirajima on 27 May. His statement was confirmed by another Midway veteran, Maeda Takeshi. While firsthand accounts, particularly at 60 years remove, must be treated with caution, the state of *Hiryū*'s codes at that time is an objective, binary piece of data. Mr. Arimura was clearly in a position to know about this matter, and he left no doubt about his belief that the codes had been changed. As a result of these pieces of evidence, the authors, and Osamu Tagaya, lean toward the opinion that *Hiryū*'s tail codes were indeed changed.[4] However, until concrete evidence, such as a photograph of either a *Sōryū* or *Hiryū* aircraft at the time of the battle, or an official memo from the Navy Ministry acknowledging the command change materializes, the truth of the matter will remain unknowable.

As to the tail codes assigned to individual pilots, they are not nearly as well known at Midway as they were during the Pearl Harbor operations. In fact, most of the "known" codes are simply extrapolated from the known codes used by Pearl Harbor pilots who were still present on the same carriers six months later, such as Egusa Takashige's famous *Sōryū* No. 231 dive-bomber. Even this carries with it an element of risk, in that it assumes that these pilots would not have been assigned to new aircraft or *shōtai* aboard their ships in the interim. This matter is further complicated by the fact that, in some cases, replacement aircraft were numbered identically with aircraft that had been lost previously.[5] As a result, in most cases, the Midway aircraft tail codes are simply not known. Inquiries to knowledgeable Japanese sources revealed that a comprehensive set of these tail codes does not appear to exist in Japanese.

Appendix 8: Japanese Radar at Midway

The possibility that the Japanese employed radar at Midway remains one of the tantalizing mysteries of the battle. Commander Amagai, *Kaga*'s air officer, stated in his postwar interrogations for the United States Strategic Bombing Survey that *Hiryū* was equipped with radar during the battle. He describes the unit as a prototype, characterized by a large, rotating bedspring antenna, and mentions further that it did not perform very well. The reason *Hiryū* was equipped with such a unit was supposedly because of the large size of her superstructure.

At the time, Amagai's statement was discounted because of the countervailing statements of *Hiryū*'s air officer, Commander Kawaguchi Susumu, and *Akagi*'s captain, Aoki Taijirō, both of whom stated categorically that no radar was in operation on any ship during the battle. Furthermore, most contemporary sources regarding the development of Japanese shipborne radar date its development as being too late to be installed aboard the Midway carriers. The initial unit, the prototype of the Type 21 surface search radar, used a mattress antenna like the one Amagai described. But it was only installed in May 1942 aboard the battleship *Ise,* and was tested thereafter in the Inland Sea.

However, additional evidence surfaced in the 1990s that resurrected the debate. The first was a little-known report published immediately after the war by the Army Air Force's Air Technical Intelligence Group. This report also interviewed Commander Amagai, and he again made the same statements regarding *Hiryū*'s radar. The second source was a statement in the *Hiryū* air unit's Midway action report, which contained a cryptic reference to "the radar plots of the combat air patrol."[1] However, the wording in the report left it unclear as to whether the alleged "radar plot" that the *Hiryū* report was referring to was that of *Hiryū* herself or that of the enemy carrier formation that was being described in the same paragraph.

The third clue was the publication of John Prados's *Combined Fleet Decoded.* In it, Prados made the statement that during the Indian Ocean raids, *Hiryū* was equipped with some sort of new detection gear that had a blind spot at the rear of the ship. The source of this statement was said to be *Hiryū*'s detailed action report from the sortie.[2]

To the authors of this work, this raised intriguing possibilities. It was known that Commander Amagai was *Hiryū*'s *hikōchō* during the Indian Ocean operations and was only transferred aboard *Kaga* after he returned to Kure in late April. He would have had a hand in writing the air combat portions of *Hiryū*'s action report from the Indian Ocean. The fact that such a piece of detection gear was supposedly mentioned in an *internal* Japanese action report shed a whole new light on things—Amagai may have lied to his American interrogators, but what motivation would an officer aboard *Hiryū* have had in lying in two separate action reports, which would (presumably) never have been read by the enemy? Furthermore, certain elements of the story made sense—*Hiryū did* have the largest superstructure of any of the Japanese carriers, and a large superstructure would be required in order to house the extra equipment and personnel needed to operate such a device. What better platform to try the new equipment out on than one of the units that had borne the lion's share of the action thus far? Clearly, having a primitive radar on *Hiryū,* and in action, would have garnered more practical information on this equipment's usages in combat than a similar unit aboard an older battleship whose operations thus far in the war had involved mostly swinging at anchor at Hashirajima. It became imperative, therefore, to locate this action report.

Easier said than done, as it turned out—the original copy had disappeared from the National Archives! Finally, though, through the efforts of John Lundstrom, a copy was turned up.[3] And here the trail quickly dead-ended. *Hiryū*'s Indian Ocean report, rather than describing a piece of radar equipment aboard her, simply commented on the glaring need for newer detection equipment:

> With the search installations at present on the HIRYŪ class [i.e., referring to the standard spotting glasses atop the island, as well as gun director optics used for such searches—*JP*], it is very difficult to sight targets at an altitude over 5000 meters. At present . . . an enemy bomber unit that breaks into the center of the cruising disposition from the rear . . . cannot be sighted. On the AKAGI there have been many times when the first warning was the splash of the bombs. . . . As a counter-measure, it is necessary to install AA search radar or sound equipment at once.[4]

While the report was fascinating in painting a picture of the very calamity that would befall Japan's carriers at Midway, it was clear that radar was not aboard *Hiryū* at the time of the Indian Ocean operations.

Other evidence further contradicts the notion that *Hiryū* carried radar at Midway. A careful examination of the two close-up pictures taken of *Hiryū* during the battle reveals no evidence of any radar antenna aboard the ship.[5] Furthermore, an examination of *Hiryū*'s movements during the war discloses that other than a brief time near Kure around Christmas 1941, *Hiryū* was never in a yard long enough to have been fitted with a prototype radar before the Indian Ocean operation. Such an installation would have required the services of a major shipyard and several weeks to accomplish—it certainly couldn't have been effected in Staring Bay or the other backwaters that *Kidō Butai* had frequented in the south.

Likewise, *Sōryū* and *Akagi* had adhered to roughly the same breakneck operational tempo. And *Kaga,* though in Kure yard for quite a while having her bottom repaired at around the same time that *Ise*'s prototype set was installed, had far too small a superstructure to accommodate such equipment even if it had been available. In the final analysis, then, it seems certain that no Japanese carrier had radar at Midway. Commander Amagai's statements must be categorized as either misrememberings or as deliberate misstatements intended to confuse his American interrogators.

Appendix 9: Chronology of Japanese Fighter Operations

The following tables provide information pertaining to the fighter operations occurring on board each Japanese carrier on June 4, 1942. Launch and recovery for each plane of the watch are usually known, as are the pilot's name and rank. The pilot's graduating class from flight school, as well as his fate (if known) is recorded. It should be noted that several aircraft were orphaned by the destruction of *Akagi, Kaga,* and *Sōryū* during the course of the day and subsequently operated off of the *Hiryū.* These aircraft are detailed under their parent ship.[1]

A note on pilot classes is worth mentioning. The standard pilot training course (*Sōren*) had been put in place in 1912 and included both officers and enlisted men. However, to further expand the pilot pool, the Flight Reserve Enlisted Trainee (*Yokaren*) program was established in 1930. This program was aimed at talented youngsters who were better educated than the enlisted men, yet would not require several years of general naval training. The pressures of the China Conflict exacerbated the need for recruits, and the *yokaren* program was expanded to include an accelerated training course for students with a better education. These *Kō* (A) category students spent twelve to fourteen months in general training, compared to the two and a half years required of the primary school graduates under the old system, which were now designated *Otsu* (B) course students. To further complicate the situation, in 1940 recruits brought into the naval air service from noncommissioned ranks under the old *Sōren* system were instead placed in what was now called the *Hei* (C) course category within the *Yokaren* program.[2] Each of these classes is so noted on the aviator's record.

Akagi

CAP Watch	Launched	Recovered	Duration	Rank[3]	Last	First	Class	Fate	Notes
Midway Strike	0426	0859	4:33						
A1	0426	0659	2:33	PO1c	Tanaka	Katsumi	ko1		
A1	0426	0659	2:33	PO2c	Ōhara	Hiroshi	sōren50		
A1	0426	0659	2:33	Sea1c	Sano	Shinpei	sōren49		
A2	0543	0726	1:43	WO	Ono	Zenji	otsu2		
A2	0543	0750	2:07	PO1c	Taniguchi	Masao	sōren51		
A2	0543	0750	2:07	PO3c	Takasuga	Mitsuyoshi	sōren51		
A3	0655	0859	2:04	Lt.	Ibusuki	Masanobu	sōren32		
A3	0655	0720	0:25	PO1c	Iwashiro	Yoshio	ko2		
A3	0655		?	PO3c	Hanyu	Toichirō	sōren51	KiA	Shot down, USAAC B-26s, 0705–0725
A4A	0710	0736	0:26	Lt.	Kaneko	Tadashi	sōren26		6th *Kōkūtai*, CO[4]
A4A	0710	0859	1:49	PO1c	Okazaki	Masayoshi	sōren38		6th *Kōkūtai*
A4A	0710	0859	1:49	PO3c	Kurauchi	Takashi	sōren45		6th *Kōkūtai*
A4B	0710	0736	0:26	PO1c	Tanaka	Katsumi	ko1		
A4B	0710	0736	0:26	PO2c	Ōhara	Hiroshi	sōren50		
A5	0808	0910	1:02	WO	Ono	Zenji	otsu2		
A5	0808	1010	2:02	PO1c	Tanaka	Katsumi	ko1		
A5	0808	1010	2:02	PO2c	Ōhara	Hiroshi	sōren50		
A6A	0832		?	PO1c	Taniguchi	Masao	sōren51	OK	Forced landing, rescued by a destroyer
A6A	0832	0951	1:19	PO3c	Takasuga	Mitsuyoshi	sōren51		
A6B	0832	1010	1:38	PO1c	Iwashiro	Yoshio	ko2		
A6B	0832		?	Sea1c	Sano	Shinpei	sōren49	KiA	Shot down by VT-6, 0940–1010
A7A	0932	1100	1:28	Lt.	Shirane	Ayao	sōren31		Recovered by *Hiryū*

Akagi (cont.)

CAP Watch	Launched	Recovered	Duration	Rank	Last	First	Class	Fate	Notes
A7A	0932	1100	1:28	PO1c	Kikuchi	Tetsuo	sōren39		Recovered by *Hiryū*
A7A	0932	0951	0:19	PO1c	Kimura	Tadao	ko1		
A7A	0932	1100	1:28	WO	Ono	Zenji	otsu2		Recovered by *Hiryū*
A7B	0932	1100	1:28	PO1c	Ōmori	Shigetaka	sōren33		Recovered by *Hiryū*
A8	0945	1700	7:15	Lt.	Ibusuki	Masanobu	sōren32	OK	Forced landing, fuel exhaustion, 1700, rescued by ?
A8	0945	1100	1:15	PO2c	Iishi	Seiji	sōren50		Recovered by *Hiryū*
A8	0945	1100	1:15	Sea1c	Ishida	Masashi	sōren55		Recovered by *Hiryū*
A9	1025	1100	0:35	PO1c	Kimura	Koreo	ko1		Recovered by *Hiryū*
A10	1200	1500	3:00	WO	Ono	Zenji	otsu2		Recovered by *Hiryū*
A10	1200	1500	3:00	PO1c	Kimura	Tadao	ko1		Recovered by *Hiryū*
A10	1200	1500	3:00	Sea1c	Ishida	Masashi	sōren55		Recovered by *Hiryū*
A11	1400	1900	5:00	PO1c	Ōmori	Shigetaka	sōren33	OK	Forced landing, fuel exhaustion, 1900, rescued by *Nagara*
A11	1400	1430	0:30	PO1c	Kikuchi	Tetsuo	sōren39		Recovered by *Hiryū*
A11	1400	1812	4:12	PO2c	Iishi	Seiji	sōren50	OK	Forced landing, fuel exhaustion, 1812, rescued by ?
A12	1534	1900	3:26	Lt.	Shirane	Ayao	sōren31	OK	Forced landing, fuel exhaustion, 1900, rescued by *Nagara*

Kaga (cont.)

CAP Watch	Launched	Recovered	Duration	Rank	Last	First	Class	Fate	Notes
Midway Strike	0430	0850	4:20						
K1	0430	0800	3:30	PO1c	Yamamoto	Akira	sōren24	OK	
K1	0430	0800	3:30	PO1c	Hirayama	Iwao	sōren38	OK	
K2A	0700	0730	0:30	Ens.	Yamaguchi	Hiroyuki	otsu1	OK	Engage USA B-26s
K2A	0700	0730	0:30	PO1c	Toyoda	Kazuyoshi	ko1	OK	Engage USA B-26s
K2A	0700	0730	0:30	PO3c	Bandō	Masahi	sōren48	OK	Engage USA B-26s
K2B	0700	0800	1:00	PO2c	Sawano	Shigerō	sōren46	OK	Engage PBY, VT-8 (detch)
K2B	0700	0800	1:00	PO2c	Kaneko	Ichirō	otsu8	OK	Engage PBY, VT-8 (detch)
K3A	0815	0910	0:55	Ens.	Yamaguchi	Hiroyuki	otsu1	OK	Engage USA B-17s
K3A	0815	0910	0:55	PO1c	Toyoda	Kazuyoshi	ko1	OK	Engage USA B-17s
K3A	0815	0910	0:55	PO3c	Bandō	Masahi	sōren48	OK	Engage USA B-17s
K3B	0815	0910	0:55	PO2c	Sawano	Shigerō	sōren46	OK	Did not see action
K3B	0815	0910	0:55	PO2c	Kaneko	Ichirō	otsu8	OK	Did not see action
K4	0830	1130	3:00	PO1c	Yamamoto	Akira	sōren24	OK	Recovered by Hiryū
K4	0830		?	PO1c	Hirayama	Iwao	sōren38	KiA	Shot down by American aircraft, 1006–1040
K4	0830	1130	3:00	Sea1c	Nakaue	Takahashi	sōren53	OK	Recovered by Hiryū
K5A	0920	1130	2:10	Lt.	Iizuka	Masao	sōren34	OK	Recovered by Hiryū
K5A	0920	1130	2:10	PO1c	Suzuki	Kiyonobu	sōren28	OK	Recovered by Hiryū
K5A	0920	1130	2:10	PO1c	Nagahama	Yoshikazu	ko2	OK	Recovered by Hiryū
K5B	0920		?	PO2c	Sawano	Shigeto	sōren46	KiA	Shot down by American aircraft, 1006–1040
K5B	0920	1130	2:10	Sea1c	Egawa	Yoshio	sōren53	OK	Recovered by Hiryū
K5B	0920		?	Sea1c	Takahashi	Ei-ichi	sōren53	KiA	Shot down by American aircraft, 1006–1040
K5C	1000	1130	1:30	PO1c	Ogiwara	Tsugio	sōren30	OK	Recovered by Hiryū

Kaga (cont.)

CAP Watch	Launched	Recovered	Duration	Rank	Last	First	Class	Fate	Notes
K5C	1000	1130	1:30	PO2c	Kaneko	Ichirō	otsu8	OK	Recovered by *Hiryū*
K5D	1000		?	Ens.	Yamaguchi	Hiroyuki	otsu1	KiA	Shot down by American aircraft, 1006–1040
K5D	1000	1130	1:30	PO3c	Bandō	Masahi	sōren48	OK	Recovered by *Hiryū*
K5E	1000		?	PO1c	Toyoda	Kazuyoshi	ko1	KiA	Shot down by American aircraft, 1006–1040
K5E	1000	1130	1:30	Sea1c	Takaoka	Matsutarō	sōren54	OK	Recovered by *Hiryū*
K6	1534	1900	3:26	PO1c	Nagahama	Yoshikazu	ko2	OK	Forced landing, fuel exhaustion, 1900, rescued by *Nagara*
K6	1534	1900	3:26	Sea1c	Egawa	Yoshio	sōren53	OK	Forced landing, fuel exhaustion, 1900, rescued by ?
K7	1627	1900	2:33	Lt.	Iizuka	Masao	sōren34	OK	Forced landing, fuel exhaustion, 1900, rescued by *Nagara*
K7	1627	1900	2:33	PO1c	Suzuki	Kiyonobu	sōren28	OK	Forced landing, fuel exhaustion, 1900, rescued by *Hagikaze*
K7	1627	1900	2:33	Sea1c	Nakaue	Takahashi	sōren53	OK	Forced landing, fuel exhaustion, 1900, rescued by *Hagikaze*

Hiryū

CAP Watch	Launched	Recovered	Duration	Rank	Last	First	Class	Fate	Notes
Midway Strike	0428	0910	4:42						
H1	0428	0700	2:32	Lt.	Mori	Shigeru	sōren31	OK	
H1	0428	0700	2:52	PO2c	Yamamoto	Tōru	sōren40	OK	
H1	0428		?	PO2c	Sakai	Ichirō	otsu8	KiA	Shot down by VT-8 (Det.), 0705–0725
H2	0525	0740	2:15	PO1c	Hino	Masato	sōren27	OK	
H2	0525	0700	1:35	PO1c	Sasaki	Hitoshi	ko3	OK	

Hiryū (cont.)

CAP Watch	Launched	Recovered	Duration	Rank	Last	First	Class	Fate	Notes
H2	0515	0740	2:25	Sea1c	Kotaka	Kenji	sōren54	OK	
H3	0612		?	WO	Kodama	Yoshimi	otsu2	KiA	Shot down by VMSB SBDs, 0755–0805
H3	0612	0840	2:28	PO2c	Todaka	Noboru	otsu8	OK	
H3	0612	0840	2:28	Sea1c	Yumoto	Sueyoshi	sōren54	OK	
H4	0825	1134	3:09	Lt.	Mori	Shigeru	sōren31	OK	
H4	0825	1134	3:09	PO2c	Yamamoto	Tōru	sōren40	OK	
H4	0825	1134	3:09	Sea1c	Kotaka	Kenji	sōren54	OK	
H5A	0937		?	PO1c	Tokuda	Michisuke	sōren40	KiA	Shot down, Great CAP, 1006–1040
H5A	0937		?	PO2c	Nitta	Haruo	sōren48	KiA	Shot down, Great CAP, 1006–1040
H5B	0937		?	PO1c	Muranaka	Kazuo	otsu6	OK	Forced landing, 1006-1040, rescued by *Nowaki*
H5B	0937	1134	1:57	Sea1c	Hayashi	Shigeru	sōren55	OK	
H5C	1013		?	PO1c	Hino	Masato	sōren27	KiA	Shot down by American aircraft, 1006–1040
H5C	1013	1134	1:21	PO1c	Satō	Taka-aki	sōren43	OK	
H5C	1013	1134	1:21	PO2c	Harada	Toshiaki	sōren41	OK	
Kobayashi Strike	1057	1320	2:23						
Tomonaga Strike	1330	1535	2:05						
H6	1212	1459	2:47	PO1c	Satō	Taka-aki	sōren43	OK	
H6	1212	1459	2:47	PO2c	Harada	Toshiaki	sōren41	OK	
H6	1212	1459	2:47	Sea1c	Hayashi	Shigeru	sōren55	OK	

Sōryū

CAP Watch	Launched	Recovered	Duration	Rank	Last	First	Class	Fate	Notes
Midway Strike									
S1	0430	0910	4:40	PO1c	Harada	Kaname	sōren35	OK	Engaged Midway VT
S1	0430	0730	3:00	PO1c	Okamoto	Takahashi	sōren43	OK	Engaged Midway VT
S1	0430	0730	3:00	PO3c	Nagasawa	Genzō	sōren50	OK	Engaged Midway VT
S2	0600	0730	1:30	PO1c	Oda	Harunobu	sōren29	OK	
S2	0600	0730	1:30	PO1c	Tanaka	Jirō	sōren39	OK	
S2	0600	0730	1:30	PO2c	Takashima	Takeo	sōren44	OK	
S3	0710	0930	2:20	Lt.	Fujita	Iyozō	sōren33	OK	Engaged Midway VT, VMSB SBD
S3	0710	0930	2:20	PO1c	Takahashi	MuneSaburō	sōren30	OK	Engaged Midway VT, VMSB SBD
S3	0710	0930	2:20	PO3c	Kawamata	Teruo	sōren54	OK	Engaged Midway VT, VMSB SBD
S4	0945	1025	0:40	Lt.	Fujita	Iyozō	sōren33	OK	Engaged VT-6, VF-3/VT-3; shot down by own AA, bailout at 1025, rescued by Nowaki
S4	0945	1310	3:25	PO1c	Takahashi	Munesaburō	sōren30	OK	Engaged VT-6, VF-3/VT-3; recovered by Hiryū
S4	0945		?	PO3c	Kawamata	Teruo	sōren54	KiA	Engaged VT-6, VF-3/VT-3; shot down, VF-3 (Cheek), 1010–1020
S5	1000	1320	3:20	PO1c	Harada	Kaname	sōren35	OK	Engaged VT-3, VSB-6; recovered by Hiryū
S5	1000	1320	3:20	PO1c	Okamoto	Takahashi	sōren43	OK	Engaged VT-3, VSB-6; recovered by Hiryū
S5	1000		?	PO3c	Nagasawa	Genzō	sōren50	KiA	Engaged VT-3, VSB-6; shot down by American aircraft, 1006–1040
S6	1015	1310	2:55	PO1c	Sugiyama	Takeo	sōren26	OK	Engaged VT-3; recovered by Hiryū
S6	1015	1310	2:55	PO1c	Noda	Mitsuomi	ko2	WiA	Engaged VT-3; recovered by Hiryū
S6	1015	1310	2:55	PO2c	Kaname	Yoshimatsu	sōren41	OK	Engaged VT-3; recovered by Hiryū
S7A	1627	1900	2:33	PO1c	Sugiyama	Takeo	sōren26	OK	Engaged VSB-63; forced landing, fuel exhaustion, 1900, rescued by ?
S7A	1627	1900	2:33	PO2c	Kaname	Yoshimatsu	sōren41	OK	Engaged VSB-63; forced landing, fuel exhaustion, 1900, rescued by ?
S7B	1627	1900	2:33	PO1c	Harada	Kaname	sōren35	OK	Engaged VSB-63; forced landing, fuel exhaustion, 1900, rescued by DD
S7B	1627	1900	2:33	PO1c	Takahashi	Munesaburō	sōren30	OK	Engaged VSB-63; forced landing, fuel exhaustion, 1900, rescued by ?

Akagi Fighter Pilot Roster (18)				
PO1c	Tanaka	Katsumi	kō1	OK
PO2c	Ōhara	Hiroshi	sōren50	OK
Sea1c	Sano	Shinpei	sōren49	KIA
WO	Ono	Zenji	otsu2	OK
PO1c	Taniguchi	Masao	sōren51	OK
PO3c	Takasuga	Mitsuyoshi	sōren51	OK
Lt.	Ibusuki	Masanobu	sōren32	OK
PO1c	Iwashiro	Yoshio	kō2	OK
PO3c	Hanyu	Toichirō	sōren51	KIA
Lt.	Shirane	Ayao	sōren31	OK
PO1c	Kikuchi	Tetsuo	sōren39	OK
PO1c	Kimura	Koreo	kō1	OK
PO1c	Ōmori	Shigetaka	sōren33	OK
PO2c	Ishii	Seiji	sōren50	OK
Sea1c	Ishida	Masashi	sōren55	OK
PO1c	Iwama	Shinaji	kō2	KIA
PO3c	Mori	Sakae	sōren50	OK
PO2c	Kawada	Yozo	kō4	OK

Kaga Fighter Pilot Roster (17)				
Lt.	Iizuka	Masao	sōren34	OK
PO1c	Tanaka	Yukuo	otsu6	KIA
Sea1c	Takaoka	Matsutaro	sōren54	OK
PO1c	Suzuki	Kiyonobu	sōren28	OK
PO1c	Nagahama	Yoshikazu	kō2	OK
Sea1c	Takahashi	Ei-ichi	sōren53	KIA
PO1c	Ogiwara	Tsugio	sōren30	OK
PO1c	Ito	Hiromi	sōren47	KIA
Sea1c	Egawa	Yoshio	sōren53	OK
PO1c	Yamamoto	Akira	sōren24	OK
PO1c	Hirayama	Iwao	sōren38	KIA
Ens.	Yamaguchi	Hiroyuki	otsu1	KIA
PO1c	Toyoda	Kazuyoshi	kō1	KIA
PO3c	Bandō	Masahi	sōren48	OK
PO2c	Sawano	Shigeto	sōren46	KIA
PO2c	Kaneko	Ichirō	otsu8	OK
Sea1c	Nakaue	Takahashi	sōren53	OK

Hiryū Fighter Pilot Roster (18)				
Lt.	Shigematsu	Yasuhiro	sōren34	OK
WO	Minegishi	Yoshijirō	otsu2	OK
PO3c	Chiyōshima	Yutaka	sōren50	OK
Lt.	Mori	Shigeru	sōren31	OK
PO2c	Yamamoto	Tōru	sōren40	OK
PO2c	Sakai	Ichirō	otsu8	KIA
PO1c	Hino	Masato	sōren27	KIA
PO1c	Sasaki	Hitoshi	kō3	OK
Sea1c	Kotaka	Kenji	sōren54	OK
WO	Kodama	Yoshimi	otsu2	KIA
PO2c	Todaka	Noboru	otsu8	OK
Sea1c	Yumoto	Sueyoshi	sōren54	OK
PO1c	Tokuda	Michisuke	sōren40	KIA
PO2c	Nitta	Haruo	sōren48	KIA
PO1c	Muranaka	Kazuo	otsu6	OK
Sea1c	Hayashi	Shigeru	sōren55	OK
PO1c	Satō	Taka-aki	sōren43	OK
PO2c	Harada	Toshiaki	sōren41	OK

Sōryū Fighter Pilot Roster (18)				
Lt.	Suganami	Masaji	sōren27	OK
PO1c	Mita	Iwao	kō2	OK
Sea1c	Iwabuchi	Yoshio	sōren56	OK
Ens.	Tanaka	Taira	sōren19	OK
PO2c	Ogino	Kyoichirō	sōren44	OK
PO3c	Furukawa	Nobutoshi	sōren45	OK
PO1c	Harada	Kaname	sōren35	OK
PO1c	Okamoto	Takahashi	sōren43	OK
PO3c	Nagasawa	Genzō	sōren50	KIA
PO1c	Oda	Harunobu	sōren29	OK
PO1c	Tanaka	Jiro	sōren39	OK
PO2c	Takashima	Takeo	sōren44	OK
Lt.	Fujita	Iyozō	sōren33	OK
PO1c	Takahashi	Munesaburō	sōren30	OK
PO3c	Kawamata	Teruo	sōren54	KIA
PO1c	Sugiyama	Takeo	sōren26	OK
PO1c	Noda	Mitsuomi	kō2	WIA
PO2c	Kaname	Yoshimatsu	sōren41	OK

Consolidated Operational Log

The following table shows the air operations aboard each carrier as a single chronology. The "Action" column denotes the aircraft launched in the following format: Carrier Name (Initial)/Watch Number (Number of Aircraft). Thus "A1(3)" indicates *Akagi*'s No. 1 watch, which consisted of three aircraft. By the same token, "KFS(1)" indicates a single strike-escort fighter from *Kaga*; "KBS(6)" indicates a six-plane *chūtai* of dive-bombers used as temporary emergency CAP by *Kaga*.

	Disposition of Fighters					Combat Air Patrol				
Time	*Akagi*	*Kaga*	*Hiryū*	*Sōryū*	Action	*A*	*K*	*H*	*S*	Total CAP
0428	3/9/13/0	2/9/16/0	3/9/9/0	3/9/9/0	launch CAP - A1(3), K1(2), H1(3), S1(3)	3	2	3	3	11
					*launch Midway Strike Force	0	0	0	0	11
					*launch carrier Type 97 recon	0	0	0	0	11
0445					*Midway Strike Force departs	0	0	0	0	11
0515	3/9/13/0	2/9/16/0	6/9/6/0	3/9/9/0	launch CAP - H2(3)	0	0	3	0	14
0542					engage PBY - A1(3)	0	0	0	0	14
0543	6/9/10/0	2/9/16/0	6/9/6/0	3/9/9/0	launch CAP - A2(3)	3	0	0	0	17
0600	6/9/10/0	2/9/16/0	6/9/6/0	6/9/6/0	launch CAP - S2(3)	0	0	0	3	20
0608					engage PBY - A2(3), S2(3)	0	0	0	0	20
0615	6/9/10/0	2/9/16/0	9/9/3/0	6/9/6/0	launch CAP - H3(3)	0	0	3	0	23
0620					*Strike Force Fighter Unit engages VMF	0	0	0	0	23
0634					*Strike Force Attack Unit bombs Midway	0	0	0	0	23
0640					*Strike Force Bomber Unit bombs Midway	0	0	0	0	23
0655	9/9/7/0	2/9/16/0	9/9/3/0	6/9/6/0	launch CAP - A3(3)	3	0	0	0	26
0659	6/9/10/0	2/9/16/0	6/9/6/0	6/9/6/0	recover CAP - A1(3), H1(2), H2(1)	-3	0	-3	0	20
0700	6/9/10/0	7/9/11/0	6/9/6/0	6/9/6/0	launch CAP - ^K2A(3), K2B(2)	0	5	0	0	25
0705	6/9/10/0	7/9/11/0	6/9/6/0	9/9/3/0	launch CAP - S3(3)	0	0	0	3	28
					engage NAS VT - A2(3), A3(3/*1), K2B(2), H1(1/*1), H2(2), H3(3), S1(3), S2(3), S3(3), joined A4A(3), A4B(2)	0	0	0	0	28

(cont.) Time	Disposition of Fighters				Action	Combat Air Patrol				Total CAP
	Akagi	Kaga	Hiryū	Sōryū		A	K	H	S	
0710	11/9/5/0	7/9/11/0	6/9/6/0	9/9/3/0	launch CAP - A4A(3), A4B(2)	5	0	0	0	33
0725	10/8/5/2	7/8/11/1	5/9/6/1	9/9/3/0	*Strike Force departs Midway [LOSSES]	-1	0	-1	0	31
0730	9/8/6/2	4/8/14/1	5/9/6/1	3/9/9/0	recover CAP - A3(1), K2A(3), S1(3), S2(3)	-1	-3	0	-6	21
0736	5/8/10/2	4/8/14/1	5/9/6/1	3/9/9/0	recover CAP - A2(1), A4A(1), A4B(2)	-4	0	0	0	17
0740	5/8/10/2	4/8/14/1	3/9/8/1	3/9/9/0	recover CAP - H2(2)	0	0	-2	0	15
0745					@ B-17s sighted	0	0	0	0	15
0750	3/8/12/2	4/8/14/1	3/9/8/1	3/9/9/0	recover CAP - A2(2)	-2	0	0	0	13
0755					@ engage VMSB-SBD - A3(1), A4A(2), H3(3/*1), S3(3), joined KFS(1), KBS(6), A5(3)	0	0	0	0	13
0800	3/8/12/2	0/8/18/1	3/9/8/1	3/9/9/0	recover CAP - K1(2), K2B(2)	0	-4	0	0	9
0805	3/8/9/2	0/8/18/1	3/9/8/1	3/9/9/0	*Strike Force returns - A	0	0	0	0	9
0808	6/8/9/2	0/8/18/1	3/9/8/1	3/9/9/0	launch CAP - A5(3)	3	0	0	0	12
0810	6/8/9/2	1/7/18/1	3/9/8/1	3/9/9/0	*Strike Force returns - K - KFS(1), KBS(6) join CAP	0	1	0	0	13
0815	6/8/9/2	6/7/13/1	2/9/8/2	3/9/9/0	launch CAP - K3A(3), ^K3B(2) [LOSSES]	0	5	-1	0	17
0820					@ engage VMSB-SB2U - A3(1), A4(2), A5(3), H3(2), S3(3), joined H4(3), K4(3), A6A(2), A6B(2)	0	0	0	0	17
					@ engage B-17s - K3A(3), joined SFS(9)	0	0	0	9	26
0825	6/7/13/1		5/9/5/2	3/9/9/0	launch CAP - H4(3)	0	0	3	0	29
					*Commence Strike Force recovery - A	0	0	0	0	29
0830	9/7/10/1		5/9/5/2	3/9/9/0	launch CAP - K4(3)	0	3	0	0	32
					*launch special recce plane - S	0	0	0	0	32
					*Strike Force returns - H	0	0	0	0	32
0832	10/8/5/2	9/7/10/1	5/9/5/2	12/0/9/0	launch CAP - A6A(2), A6B(2)	4	0	0	0	36
0835	10/8/5/2	9/7/10/1	5/9/5/2	12/0/9/0	*Strike Force returns - S - SFS(9) join CAP	0	0	0	0	36
0840	10/8/5/2	9/7/10/1	3/9/7/2	12/0/9/0	recover CAP - H3(2)	0	0	-2	0	34
					*Commence Strike Force recovery - K	0	0	0	0	34
					*Commence Strike Force recovery - S	0	0	0	0	34
0850	10/8/5/2	8/0/18/1	3/9/7/2	12/0/9/0	*Strike Force recovered - K - inc KFS(1), KBS(6)	0	-1	0	0	33

(cont.) Time	Disposition of Fighters				Action	Combat Air Patrol				Total CAP
	Akagi	Kaga	Hiryū	Sōryū		A	K	H	S	
0859	7/0/16/2	8/0/18/1	3/9/7/2	12/0/9/0	recover CAP - A3(1), A4A(2)	-3	0	0	0	30
0905	7/0/16/2	8/0/18/1	3/9/7/2	12/0/9/0	*Strike Force recovered - A	0	0	0	0	30
0905	6/0/17/2	3/0/23/1	3/0/16/2	6/0/15/0	*Commence Strike Force recovery - H	0	0	0	0	30
0910	6/0/17/2	9/0/17/1	3/0/16/2	6/0/15/0	recover CAP - A5(1), K3A(3), K3B(2)	-1	-5	0	0	24
0920	6/0/17/2	9/0/17/1	3/0/16/2	6/0/15/0	*Strike Force recovery complete - S, H - inc SFS(6)	0	0	0	-6	18
0920					launch CAP - K5A(3), K5B(3)	3	3	0	0	24
0922					engage VT8 - A5(2), A6A(2), A6B(2), K4(3), K5A(3), K5B(3), H4(3), SFS(3), joined A7A(3), A7B(2), H5A(2), H5B(2)	0	0	0	0	24
0930	6/0/17/2	9/0/17/1	3/0/16/2	3/0/18/0	recover CAP - S3(3)	0	0	0	-3	21
0933	11/0/12/2	9/0/17/1	3/0/16/2	3/0/18/0	launch CAP - A7A(3), A7B(2)	5	0	0	0	26
0937	11/0/12/2	9/0/17/1	7/0/12/2	3/0/18/0	launch CAP - H5A(2), H5B(2)	0	0	4	0	30
0940					engage VT6 - A5(2), A6A(2), A6B(2/*1), A7A(3), A7B(2), K4(3), K5A(3), K5B(3), H4(3), H5A(2), H5B(2), joined A8(3), S4(3), S5(3), K5C(2), K5D(2), K5E(2)	0	0	0	0	30
0945	14/0/9/2	9/0/17/1	7/0/12/2	3/0/18/0	launch CAP - A8(3), S4(3)	3	0	0	3	36
0945					recover CAP - SFS(3)	0	0	0	-3	33
0951	12/0/11/2	9/0/17/1	7/0/12/2	3/0/18/0	recover CAP - A6A(1), A7A(1)	-2	0	0	0	31
1000	12/0/11/2	15/0/11/1	7/0/12/2	6/0/15/0	launch CAP - K5C(2), K5D(2), K5E(2), S5(3) [LOSSES]	-1	6	0	3	39
1006					*Great CAP - A6A(1/*1), A6B(1), A7A(2), A7B(2), A8(3), K4(3/*1), K5A(3), K5B(3/*2), K5C(2), K5D(2/*1), K5E(2/*1), H4(3), H5A(2/*2), H5B(2/*1), S4(3/*2), S5(3/*1), joined H5C(3/*1), S6(3), A9(1)*	0	0	0	0	39
1010	9/0/14/2	15/0/11/1	7/0/12/2	6/0/18/0	recover CAP - A5(2), A6B(1)	-3	0	0	0	36
1013	9/0/14/2	15/0/11/1	10/0/9/2	6/0/18/0	launch CAP - H5C(3)	0	0	3	0	39
1015	9/0/14/2	15/0/11/1	10/0/9/2	9/0/12/0	launch CAP - S6(3)	0	0	0	3	42
1024	9/0/14/2	15/0/-/12	10/0/9/2	9/0/12/0	*Kaga bombed - lost 2+9K	0	0	0	0	42

(cont.)	Disposition of Fighters					Combat Air Patrol				
Time	*Akagi*	*Kaga*	*Hiryū*	*Sōryū*	Action	A	K	H	S	Total CAP
1025	10/0/13/2	15/0/-/12	10/0/9/2	9/0/-/12	launch CAP - A9(1)	1	0	0	0	43
	10/0/-/15	15/0/-/12	10/0/9/2	9/0/-/12	*Sōryū* bombed - lost 9+3S	0	0	0	0	43
1026	10/0/-/17	10/0/-/17	10/0/9/2	9/0/-/12	*Akagi* bombed - lost 7+6A	0	0	0	0	43
1040	8/0/-/17	10/0/0/17	6/0/9/6	6/0/-/15	Great CAP ends [LOSSES]	-1	-5	-4	-3	30
1057	8/0/0/17	10/0/0/17	6/6/3/6	6/0/0/15	*H-1st Strike - HS1(6)	0	0	0	0	30
1100	1/0/7/17	10/0/0/17	6/6/3/6	6/0/0/15	H-recover CAP - A7(4), A8(2), A9(1)	0	0	0	-7	23
1120					1st Strike engages Ware - HS1(6)	0	0	0	0	23
1130	1/0/7/17	0/0/10/17	6/6/3/6	6/0/0/15	H-recover CAP - K4(2), K5(8)	0	0	0	-10	13
1134	1/0/7/17	0/0/10/17	0/6/9/6	6/0/0/15	H-recover CAP - H4(3), H5(3)	0	0	0	-6	7
1158		0/0/10/17		6/0/0/15	1st Strike engages USN - HS1(4)	0	0	0	0	7
1200	4/0/4/17	0/0/10/17	0/6/9/6	6/0/0/15	H-launch CAP - A10(3)	0	0	0	3	10
1208		0/0/10/17		6/0/0/15	1st Strike bombs *Yorktown*	0	0	0	0	10
1212	4/0/4/17	0/0/10/17	3/6/6/6	6/0/0/15	H-launch CAP - H6(3)	0	0	0	3	13
1230	4/0/4/17	0/0/10/17	3/4/7/7	6/0/0/15	H-recover 1st Strike - HS1(1)	0	0	0	0	13
					ditch HS1(1)	0	0	0	0	13
1310	4/0/4/17	0/0/10/17	3/4/7/7	2/0/4/15	H-recover CAP - S6(3), ? S4(1)	0	0	0	-4	9
1320	4/0/4/17	0/0/10/17	3/1/7/10	0/0/6/15	H-recover CAP - S5(2)	0	0	0	-2	7
					*1st Strike returns [LOSSES]	0	0	0	0	7
1330	4/0/4/17	0/2/8/17	3/5/3/10	0/0/6/15	*H-2nd Strike - HS2(4), KS2(2)	0	0	0	0	7
	4/0/4/17	0/2/8/17	3/4/4/10	0/0/6/15	*H-recover search - S	0	0	0	0	7
1338	4/0/4/17	0/2/8/17	3/4/4/10	0/0/6/15	*H-recover 1st Strike - HS1(1)	0	0	0	0	7
1400	7/0/1/17	0/2/8/17	3/4/4/10	0/0/6/15	H-launch CAP - A11(3)	0	0	0	0	7
1430	6/0/2/17	0/2/8/17	3/4/4/10	0/0/6/15	H-recover CAP - A11(1)	0	0	0	3	10
1441		0/2/8/17		0/0/6/15	2nd Strike engages USN	0	0	0	-1	9
1459	3/0/5/17	0/2/8/17	0/4/7/10	0/0/6/15	H-recover CAP - A10(3), H6(3)	0	0	0	0	9
1534	4/0/4/17	2/2/6/17	0/4/7/10	0/0/6/15	H-launch CAP - A12(1), K6(2)	0	0	0	-6	3
1535	4/0/4/17	2/2/6/17	0/2/7/12	0/0/6/15	*2nd Strike returns [LOSSES]	0	0	0	3	6
1540	4/0/4/17	2/2/6/17	0/0/9/12	0/0/6/15	*H-recover 2nd Strike - HS2(2)	0	0	0	0	6

(cont.)	Disposition of Fighters				Action	Combat Air Patrol				
Time	Akagi	Kaga	Hiryū	Sōryū		A	K	H	S	Total CAP
1627	4/0/4/17	5/2/3/17	0/0/9/12	4/0/2/15	H-launch CAP - S7A(2), S7B(2), K7(3)	0	0	0	7	13
1640	4/0/4/17	5/1/4/17	0/0/9/12	4/0/2/15	H-recover 2nd Strike - KS2(1)	0	0	0	0	13
1655					engage VB & B-17 - A11(2), A12(1), K6(2), S7(4), K7(3)	0	0	0	0	13
1700	3/0/4/18	5/1/4/17	0/0/9/12	4/0/2/15	ditch A8(1)	0	0	0	-1	12
1703	3/0/-/22	5/1/-/21	0/0/-/21	4/0/-/17	*Hiryū bombed - lost A4, K4, H9, S2	0	0	0	0	12
1730	3/0/-/22	5/0/-/22	0/0/-/21	4/0/-/17	ditch KS2(1)	0	0	0	0	12
1812	2/0/-/23	5/0/-/22	0/0/-/21	4/0/-/17	ditch A11(1)	0	0	0	-1	11
1900	0/0/-/25	5/0/-/22	0/0/-/21	4/0/-/17	ditch A11(1), A12(1)	0	0	0	-2	9
1910	0/0/-/25	0/0/-/27	0/0/-/21	0/0/-/21	ditch K6(2), K7(3), S7A(2), S7B(2)	0	0	0	-9	0

Notes:

Individual carrier fighter totals are denoted as follows:

# of aircraft on CAP / # of aircraft on strike missions / # aboard ship / # lost thus far

Fighters carried (organic Hikōtai + 6th Kōkūtai): Akagi=18+6, Kaga=18+9, Hiryū=18+3, Sōryū=18+3

[LOSSES] - losses in recent actions are tabulated and added to total.

^ - signifies a CAP mission that participated in no actions.

Appendix 10: Japanese Strike Rosters, Operations MI and AL

The following tables show the organization and personnel involved in each major Japanese airstrike carried out during Operations MI and AL.

Operation MI Rosters

Midway Strike Force[1]
Launch time: 0430
Overall commander: Lt. Tomonaga Jōichi

Akagi Carrier Fighter Unit
Aircraft: 1 lost, 3 damaged but serviceable, 5 OK
Personnel: 1 MIA

Chūtai	Shōtai	Plane		Pilot	Observer	Radioman	Fate
1	1	1		Lt. Shirane Ayao			Recovered 0900–0910
1	1	2		PO1c Kikuchi Tetsuo			Recovered 0900–0910
1	1	3		PO2c Ishii Seiji			Recovered 0900–0910
1	2	1		PO1c Ōmori Shigetaka			Recovered 0900–0910
1	2	*2	*	PO1c Iwama Shinaji			Shot down by Eastern Island AA
1	2	3		PO3c Mori Sakae			Recovered 0900–0910
1	3	1		PO1c Kimura Koreo			Recovered 0900–0910
1	3	2		PO2c Kawada Yōzō			Recovered 0900–0910
1	3	3		Sea1c Ishida Masashi			Recovered 0900–0910

Akagi Carrier Bomber Unit
Aircraft: 1 out of commission, 4 damaged but serviceable, 13 OK
Personnel: no casualties

Chūtai	Shōtai	Plane	Pilot	Observer	Radioman	Fate
1	21	1	PO1c Yoshida Kiyoto		Lt. Chihaya Takehiko (B)	
1	21	2	PO1c Akimaru Tamotsu		PO1c Yamamoto Giichi (Yoshikazu)	
1	21	3	Sea1c Akutagawa Takeshi		PO3c Sasaki Mitsuo	
1	22	1	WO Ozeki Hei-ichi		Lt. (jg) Motoyama Yasuyuki	
1	22	2	PO1c Yamada Kōsaku		PO2c Tsuchiya Ryūroku	
1	22	3	Sea1c Ono Takeshi		PO2c Matsuo Tsutomu	
1	23	1	PO1c Takano Hideo		WO Shimizu Takeshi	
1	23	2	PO3c Mukaga Sakae		PO2c Kawai Yutaka	
1	23	3	PO2c Kato ?		PO3c Ōishi Kyōzaburō	
2	25	1	Lt. Yamada Shōhei (B)		WO Maekawa Kenji	
2	25	2	PO1c Kouno Takuji		PO1c Tsuchiya Mutsukuni (Mutsuo)	
2	25	3	PO3c Mochizuki Isaku		PO3c Hasegawa Kikunosuke	
2	26	1	PO1c Tanaka Yoshiharu		Ens. Saito Chi-aki	
2	26	2	PO3c Amamiya Isao		PO1c Yamashita Toshihei	
2	26	3	PO2c Ishii Shinichi		PO2c Horie Kasumi	
2	27	1	PO1c Suzuki Kaname		WO Nosaka Yoshimori	
2	27	2	PO3c Kikuchi Goichi		PO2c Iida Yoshihiro	
2	27	3	Sea1c Yamakawa Mitsuyoshi		PO2c Aioi Toyujirō	

Key: * = plane or pilot missing, destroyed, or killed; + = plane or pilot damaged or wounded, (H) = *hikōtaicho*, (B) = *buntaichō*, OOC = Out of commission. Note: *Akagi*'s records do not detail the fates of the bomber unit aircraft.

Kaga Carrier Fighter Unit
Aircraft: 1 lost, 1 out of commission, 7 OK
Personnel: 1 MIA, 1 died of wounds

Chūtai	Shōtai	Plane	Pilot	Observer	Radioman	Fate
1	1	1	Lt. Iizuka Masao			Recovered 0840–0850
1	1	+2	* PO1c Tanaka Yukio			Recovered 0840–0850, pilot died of wounds in the cockpit
1	1	3	Sea1c Takaoka Matsutaro			Recovered 0840–0850
1	2	1	PO1c Suzuki Kiyonobu			Recovered 0840–0850
1	2	2	PO1c Nagahama Yoshikazu			Recovered 0840–0850
1	2	3	Sea1c Takahashi Ei-ichi			Recovered 0840–0850
1	3	1	PO1c Ogiwara Tsugio			Recovered 0840–0850
1	3	*2	* PO1c Itō Hiromi			Shot down by fighters
1	3	3	Sea1c Egawa Yoshio			Recovered 0840–0850

Kaga Carrier Bomber Unit
Aircraft: 1 lost, 4 damaged but serviceable, 13 OK
Personnel: 2 MIA

Chūtai	Shōtai	Plane	Pilot	Observer	Radioman	Fate
1	21	1	Lt. Ogawa Shōichi (B)		WO Yoshikawa Katsumi	
1	21	2	PO1c Tanaka Takeo		PO1c Katsumi Hajime	
1	21	3	PO1c Miyanaga (Miyabara) Naga-ichi		PO3c Hirayama Shigeki	
1	22	1	Lt. (jg) Nakamura Gorō		PO1c Uchikawa Yuusuke	
1	22	2	PO2c Murakami Yoshiki		Sea1c Kuroki Yoshizou	
1	22	*3	* Sea1c Watanabe Ri-ichi (Toshikazu)		* PO3c Kimura Noboru	Shot down by AA during dive, crashed on Sand Island
1	23	1	PO1c Hikiune Yukio		WO Kawai Jirō	
1	23	2	PO2c Nishimori Toshio		PO1c Bekku Toshimitsu	
1	23	3	PO2c Kojima Tokuo		PO2c Kojima Takehiko	
2	24	1	WO Okewatari Rikichi		Lt. Watanabe Toshio (B)	
2	24	2	PO2c Ono Gen		PO2c Koretsune Go-ichi	

Kaga Carrier Bomber Unit (cont.)

Chutai	Shotai	Plane	Pilot	Observer	Radioman	Fate
2	24	3	PO3c Yamaguchi Rishichi		PO2c Iwamasa Masao	
2	25	1	PO1c Imamiya Sadamu (Tamotsu)		WO Nakajima Yonekichi	
2	25	2	PO2c Yoshimoto Tsunehide		PO3c Nagamine Yuki-o	
2	25	3	PO3c Towata Kimoyi		PO2c Kitamura Ichirō	
2	26	1	WO Fujimoto Takuma		PO1c Ichimachi Hiyakazu	
2	26	2	PO1c Suzuki Ki-ichi (Toshio)		PO2c Watanabe Masazō (Masanari)	
2	26	3	Sea1c Yaou Hajime		Sea1c Kawaguchi Toshimitsu	

Kaga's records do not indicate the precise fates of her bomber group.

Hiryū Carrier Fighter Unit
Aircraft: 2 out of commission, 7 OK
Personnnel: no casualties

Chutai	Shotai	Plane	Pilot	Observer	Radioman	Fate
1	1	1	Lt. Shigematsu Yasuhiro			Recovered 0905
1	1	2	PO1c Muranaka Kazuo			Recovered 0905
1	1	3	PO2c Nitta Haruo			Recovered 0905
1	2	1	WO Minegishi Yoshijirō			Recovered 0905
1	2	2	PO1c Satō Takaaki			Recovered 0905
1	2	3	PO3c Chiyōshima Yutaka			Recovered 0905
1	3	1	PO1c Tokuda Michisuke			Recovered 0905
1	3	2	PO2c Harada Toshiaki			Recovered 0905
1	3	3	Sea1c Hayashi Shigeru			Recovered 0905

Hiryū Carrier Attack Unit
Aircraft: 5 lost, 5 out of commission, 8 damaged but serviceable
Personnel: 12 MIA, 1 WIA

Chutai	Shotai	Plane	Pilot	Observer	Radioman	Fate
1	1	+1	Lt. Tomonaga Jōichi (H)	Lt. Hashimoto Toshio	PO1c Murai Sadamu	Recovered OOC, damaged by fighters
1	1	+2	PO1c ??? Yoshihiro	PO1c ??? Yukio	PO1c Nakano ???	Recovered OOC
1	2	1	PO1c Takahashi Toshio	Ens. Akamatsu Saku	PO3c Koyama Tomio	Aborted shortly after takeoff, recovered OK
1	2	2	PO1c Sugimoto Hachirō	PO1c Hijikuro Sadayashi	PO3c Yaguchi Kazumari	Recovered OK
1	3	*1	* PO2c Ohisa Haki	* PO1c Tobu Shigenobu	* PO1c Morita Hiroyashi	Shot down in sea by fighters
1	3	*2	* PO2c Miyauchi Masaji	* PO2c Yamada Teijiro	PO2c Miyagawa Tsugumune	Shot down in sea by fighters
2	1	*1	* Lt. Kikuchi Rokurō (B)	* WO Yumoto Noriyoshi	* PO1c Narasaki Hironori	Forced landing near Kure after being damaged by fighters
2	1	+2	PO1c Araya ???	PO1c Sakato Yukio	Sea1c Kurara ???	Recovered OOC
2	2	*1	* PO1c Sakamoto ???	* CPO Tatsu Rokurō	* PO2c Ninomiya Kazutoshi	Shot down in sea by Midway AA
2	2	2	Sea1c Nakao Harumi	PO1c Maruyama Taisuke	Sea1c Hamada Giichi	Recovered OK
2	3	1	WO Ōbayashi Yukio	PO1c Kudō Hiroyaki	PO1c Tamura Mitsuru	Recovered OK
2	3	+2	Sea1c Kimura Jinichi	PO2c Yoshimura ???	PO2c Moriguchi ???	Recovered OOC
3	1	+1	+ Lt. Kadano Hiroshi (B)	WO Yokota Masaharu	PO3c Omiya Tokazu	Recovered OOC, damaged by fighters
3	1	2	PO1c Ishii Yoshikichi	PO1c Kobayashi Masamatsu	PO3c Shimada Kiyokasu	Recovered OK
3	2	*1	WO Nonaka Satoru	PO1c Nakamoshi Masaharu	PO2c ??? Hidetoshi	Forced landing near *Kidō Butai*, crew rescued by a cruiser
3	2	2	Sea1c Suzuki Takeshi	PO1c Saitō Kiyoaki	PO2c Suzuki Mutsuo	Recovered OK
3	3	1	PO2c Yanagimoto Takurō	PO1c Etō Chikashi	PO2c Kasai Kiyoshi	Recovered OK
3	3	2	PO3c Nagayama Yoshimitsu	PO1c Nakamura Toyohiro	Sea1c Obama Haruo	Recovered OK

Sōryū Carrier Fighter Unit
Aircraft: 9 OK
Personnel: no casualties

Chūtai	Shōtai	Plane	Pilot	Observer	Radioman	Fate
1	1	1	Lt. Suganami Masaji			Recovered 0850–0910 (6) or 0945 (3)
1	1	2	PO1c Mita Iwao			Recovered 0850–0910 (6) or 0945 (3)
1	1	3	Sea1c Iwabuchi Yoshio			Recovered 0850–0910 (6) or 0945 (3)
1	1	1	Ens. Tanaka Hira			Recovered 0850–0910 (6) or 0945 (3)
1	2	2	PO2c Ogino Kyoichirō			Recovered 0850–0910 (6) or 0945 (3)
1	2	3	PO3c Furukawa Nobutoshi			Recovered 0850–0910 (6) or 0945 (3)
1	3	1	PO1c Sugiyama Takeo			Recovered 0850–0910 (6) or 0945 (3)
1	3	2	PO1c Noda Mitsuomi			Recovered 0850–0910 (6) or 0945 (3)
1	3	3	PO2c Yoshimatsu Kaname			Recovered 0850–0910 (6) or 0945 (3)

Sōryū Carrier Attack Unit
Aircraft: 3 lost, 5 out of commission (1 aboard *Hiryū*), 10 damaged but serviceable
Personnel: 3 MIA, 1 WIA

Chūtai	Shōtai	Plane	Pilot	Observer	Radioman	Fate
1	41	1	WO Kasahara Jisuke	Lt. Abe Heijiro (H)	PO1c Ono Toshi	
1	41	2	PO1c Ushio Minosuke	WO Fujinami Kanji	PO2c Wakamiya Hideo	
1	41	*3	PO3c Kayahara Yoshihiro	*PO1c Tanaka Keisuke	*PO2c Ogawa Masaji	Shot down by fighters
1	42	1	PO1c Satō Hisao	WO Nakamura Hiroto	PO1c Watanabe Yūzō	
1	42	2	PO3c Fujiwara Karoku	PO1c Iwai Ri-ichi	PO3c Nishida Takao	
1	42	3	PO2c Iwata Tada-aki	PO1c Kaguma Kumekichi	PO2c Doi Keiji	
2	43	1	Lt. Itō Tadao (B)	WO Kawamoto Yoeda	PO1c Ōta Goro	
2	43	2	WO Ōtawa Tatsuya	PO1c Muhatake Shōichi	PO2c Karatani Teishigeru	
2	43	+3	PO2c Tsurumi Shigeru	PO2c Konnō Kiyoshi	PO3c Ukigatani Hiroshi	
2	44	*1	PO1c Mori Jūzō	WO Kanai Takekatsu	PO2c Hosada Kiyohito	Damaged by fighters, forced landing near *Kidō Butai*, crew rescued by *Uranami*
2	44	2	PO2c Kimura Tadashi	PO1c Katō Toyonori	PO3c Akihama Tetsurō	

Sōryū Carrier Attack Unit (*cont.*)

Chūtai	Shōtai	Plane	Pilot	Observer	Radioman	Fate
1	41	1	WO Kasahara Jisuke	Lt. Abe Heijiro (H)	PO1c Ono Toshi	
1	41	2	PO1c Ushio Minosuke	WO Fujinami Kanji	PO2c Wakamiya Hideo	
1	41	*3	* PO3c Kayahara Yoshihiro	* PO1c Tanaka Keisuke	* PO2c Ogawa Masaji	Shot down by fighters
1	42	1	PO1c Satō Hisao	WO Nakamura Hiroto	PO1c Watanabe Yūzō	
1	42	2	PO3c Fujiwara Karoku	PO1c Iwai Ri-ichi	PO3c Nishida Takao	
1	42	3	PO2c Iwata Tada-aki	PO1c Kaguma Kumekichi	PO2c Doi Keiji	
2	43	1	Lt. Itō Tadao (B)	WO Kawamoto Yoeda	PO1c Ōta Goro	
2	43	2	WO Ōtawa Tatsuya	PO1c Muhatake Shōichi	PO2c Karatani Teishigeru	
2	43	+3	PO2c Tsurumi Shigeru	PO2c Konnō Kiyoshi	PO3c Ukigatani Hiroshi	
2	44	*1	PO1c Mori Jūzō	WO Kanai Takekatsu	PO2c Hosada Kiyohito	Damaged by fighters, forced landing near *Kidō Butai*, crew rescued by *Uranami*
2	44	2	PO2c Kimura Tadashi	PO1c Katō Toyonori	PO3c Akihama Tetsurō	
2	44	3	PO3c Satō Nagasaku	PO2c Andō Hyakutoshi	Sea1c Nagai Fukutarō	
3	45	1	PO1c Harada Tadasumi	Lt. Yamamoto Sadao (B)	PO2c Suzuki Shirō	
3	45	*2	PO1c Ochi Masatake	WO Yashiro Shichirō	PO1c Hayakawa Junichi	Damaged by fighters, forced landing near *Kidō Butai*, crew rescued by *Maikaze*
3	45	3	PO3c Miyazaki Tokusaburō	PO1c Sano Satori	PO2c Ezuka Hisashi	
3	46	1	PO2c Nejiki Tadanori	WO Ohasama Kaichi	PO1c Maruyama Tadao	
3	46	2	PO2c Kawajima Kōji	PO1c Sugiyama Hirotomo	PO2c Arai Tatsuo	
3	46	3	PO2c Tanabe Masanao	PO2c Satō Hisashi	PO2c Arai Tatsuo	Damaged by fighters, recovered OOC *Hiryū*

Note: *Sōryū's* returns are incomplete in terms of noting which individual aircraft were damaged or rendered OOC.

Kobayashi Strike Force

Launch time: 1057
Overall commander: Lt. Kobayashi Michio

Hiryū Carrier Fighter Unit
Aircraft: 4 lost, 1 out of commission, 1 damaged but serviceable
Personnel: 3 MIA

Chūtai	Shōtai	Plane	Pilot	Observer	Radioman	Fate
1	1	1	Lt. Shigematsu Yasuhiro			Recovered 1338
1	1	*2	* PO2c Todaka Noboru			Shot down by *Yorktown* fighters
1	1	*3	* Sea1c Yoshimoto Suekichi			Shot down by *Yorktown* fighters
2	1	1	WO Minegishi Yoshijirō			Damaged by fighters, recovered OOC 1230
2	1	*2	PO1c Sasaki Hitoshi			Damaged by fighters, ditched 1230, pilot rescued
2	1	*3	* PO3c Chiyōshima Yutaka			Shot down by *Yorktown* fighters

Hiryū Carrier Bomber Unit
Aircraft: 13 lost, 1 out of commission, 2 damaged but serviceable, 2 OK
Personnel: 26 MIA

Chūtai	Shōtai	Plane	Pilot	Observer	Radioman	Fate
1	1	*1	* Lt. Kobayashi Michio (B)		WO Ono Yoshinori	Shot down by *Yorktown* fighters
1	1	*2	* PO1c Yamada Kihichiro		* PO1c Fukunaga Yoshiteru	
1	1	*3	* PO3c Sakai Hideo		PO3c Yamaguchi Buichi	
1	2	*1	* Lt. Kondō Takemori (B)		* WO Maeda Takashi	
1	2	*2	* PO2c Nakao Nobumichi		* PO1c Okamura Hidemitsu	
1	2	*3	* Sea1c Seki Masao		* PO1c Tanaka Kunio	
1	3	*1	* PO1c Imaizumi Tamotsu		* PO1c Kazuma Rihei	
1	3	2	PO2c Tsuchiya Takayashi		PO2c Egami Hayata	3rd to dive, miss, HE
1	3	*3	* PO3c Koizumi Naoshi		* PO2c Hagiwara Yoshiaki	
2	1	*1	* WO Nishihara Toshikatsu		* Lt. Yamashita Michiji (B)	
2	1	2	PO1c Matsumoto Sadao		PO1c Yasuda Nobuhiko	4th to dive, miss, SAP

Hiryū Carrier Bomber Unit (*cont.*)

Chūtai	Shōtai	Plane	Pilot	Observer	Radioman	Fate
2	1	*3	* PO3c Kuroki Junichi		* Sea1c Mizuno Yasuhiko	5th to dive, hit, SAP
2	2	1	WO Nakazawa Iwao		Ens. Nakayama Shimematsu	
2	2	2	PO1c Seo Tetsuo		PO3c Murakami Chikayoshi	7th to dive, miss, unknown bomb type
2	2	*3	* PO1c Kondō Sumio		* PO3c Iwabuchi Yoshiaki	
2	3	1	WO Nakagawa Shizuo		PO1c Ōtomo Ryuji	6th to dive, hit, SAP
2	3	*2	* PO2c Ikeda Kōzō		* PO3c Shimizu Takumi	
2	3	*3	* Sea1c Fuchigami Issei		* Sea1c Nakaoka Yoshinaru	

Note: a number of these aircraft were destroyed by antiaircraft fire from *Yorktown* and her escorts.

Tomonaga Strike Force

Launch time: 1330

Overall commander: Lt. Tomonaga Jōichi

Hiryū Carrier Fighter Unit
Aircraft: 3 lost, 1 damaged but serviceable
Personnel: 3 MIA

Chūtai	Shōtai	Plane	Pilot	Observer	Radioman	Fate
1	1	*1	* Lt. Mori Shigeru			Shot down by fighters
1	1	*2	* PO2c Yamamoto Tōru			Shot down by fighters
1	2	1	WO Minegishi Yoshijirō			Recovered 1540
1	2	2	Sea1c Kotaka Kenji			Recovered 1540
1	3	*1	* PO1c Yamamoto Akira			*Kaga* fighter; ditched, fuel exhaustion, 1730, rescued by *Hagikaze*
1	3	2	PO3c Bandō Masahi			*Kaga* fighter; recovered 1640

Hiryū Carrier Attack Unit
Aircraft: 5 lost, 4 out of commission, 2 damaged but serviceable
Personnel: 15 MIA, 1 WIA

Chūtai	Shōtai	Plane	Pilot	Observer	Radioman	Fate
1	1	*1	* Lt. Tomonaga Jōichi (H)	* Ens. Akamatsu Saku	* PO1c Murai Sadamu	Shot down by fighters
1	1	*2	* PO1c Ishii Yashikichi	* PO1c Kobayashi Masamatsu	* PO3c Shimada Kiyokasu	Shot down
1	1	*3	* PO1c Sugimoto Hachirō	* PO1c Hijikuro Sadayoshi	* PO3c Yaguchi kazunari	Shot down
1	2	*1	* WO Obayashi Yukio	* PO1c Kudō Hiroyuki	* PO1c Tamura Mitsuru	Shot down
1	2	*2	* Sea1c Suzuki Takeshi	* PO1c Saitō Kiyoaki	PO2c Suzuki Mutsuo	Shot down
2	1	1	PO1c Takahashi Toshio	Lt. Hashimoto Toshio	PO3c Koyama Tomio	Recovered
2	1	2	PO2c Yanagimoto Takurō	PO1c Etō Chikashi	* PO2c Kasai Kiyoshi	Recovered
2	1	3	PO3c Nagayama Yoshimitsu	PO1c Nakamura Toyohiro	Sea1c Obama Haruo	Recovered
2	2	1	WO Suzuki Shigero	WO Nishimori Susumu	PO1c Horii Takayuki	*Akagi* bomber; recovered OOC
2	2	2	Sea1c Nakao Harumi	PO1c Maruyama Taisuke	Sea1c Hamada Giichi	Recovered OOC

Reconnaissance Flights

Phase 1 Search:

Air Group	Type	Plane #	Pilot	Observer	Radioman	Fate
Kaga	B5N2			WO Yoshino Haruo		Search line #1. Recovered by Kaga
Akagi	B5N2		WO Suzuki Shigero	WO Nishimori Susumu	PO1c Horii Takayuki	Search line #2. Recovered by Hiryū
Tone	E13A	1				Search line #3. Recovered by Tone
Tone	E13A	4		PO1c Amari Hiroshi (Yoji?)		Search line #4. Recovered by Tone
Chikuma	E13A	1				Search line #5. Recovered by Chikuma
Chikuma	E13A	4				Search line #6. Recovered by Chikuma
Haruna	E8N2	7				Search line #7. Recovered by Haruna

Follow-up Contact Planes:

Air Group	Type	Plane #	Pilot	Observer	Radioman	Fate
Sōryū	D4Y1	201	PO1c Iida Masatada		WO Kondō Isamu	Recovered by Hiryū
Chikuma	E13A	5	* PO3c Hara Hisashi (Iwai)	* PO1c Takezaki Masatake	* Sea1c Taguchi Hiroya	Shot down by fighters
Chikuma	E13A	4				
Tone	E13A	4				
Tone	E8N2	3	* Lt. (jg) Hasegawa Tadayuki		* PO1c Ōtake Akira	Shot down at 1633, VF-6 (Sumrall, Achten)
Kirishima	E8N2	?				
Haruna	E8N2	7				
Haruna	E8N2	8				
Haruna	E8N2	9				

Tabulation of Japanese Aircraft Losses During the Battle of Midway, June 4, 1942

	Akagi			Kaga			Hiryū			Sōryū				Cruisers
	VF	VB	VT	VF	VB	VT	VF	VB	VT	VF	VB	VT	VSO	VSO
Midway Strike	1+1	0+0	-	1+2	1+2	-	0+0	-	5+12	0+0	-	3+3	-	-
CAP actions	3+2	-	-	5+4	0+0	-	6+5	-	-	3+2	-	-	-	-
Searches		-	-	0+0	-	-	0+0	-	-	-	-	0+0	-	2+5
Lost aboard ship	7+1	18+1	17+2	2+0	17+4	27+9	-	-	-	9+1	18+1	14+2	-	6+6
Cargo with ship	6+0	-	-	9+0	-	-	3+1	-	-	3+1	-	-	-	-
Kobayashi Strike	-	-	-	1+0	-	-	4+3	13+26	-	-	-	-	-	-
Tomonaga Strike	-	-	1+0	-	-	-	2+2	-	5+16	-	-	-	-	-
Aboard Hiryū	4+0	-	-	4+0	-	-	6+0	5+1	8+6	2+0	-	1+0	1+0	-
Forced landings	4+0	-	-	5+0	-	-	-	-	-	4+0	-	-	-	-
AIRCRAFT LOST (248 carrier +8 cruiser)	25	18	18	27	18	27	21	18	18	21	18	18	1	8
TOTAL CARRIER AIRCREW (480+)	18+6	36	54	18+9	36	81	18+3	36	54	18+3	36	54	0	?
AIRMEN LOST (110 carrier +11 cruiser)	4	1	2	6	6	9	11	27	34	4	1	5	0	11
AIRMEN SURVIVED (370+ carrier)	21	35	52	21	30	72	10	9	20	17	35	49	0	?

Note: X+Y means X aircraft and Y aircrew. Two Sōryū Type 99 carrier bombers carried as cargo on Kaga are counted against Sōryū's total.

Operation AL Rosters

Dutch Harbor Strike Force[2]

Launch time: 0240, 3 June[3]
Overall commander: Lt. Shiga Yoshio

Ryūjō Carrier Fighter Unit
Aircraft: 3 OK
Personnel: no casualties

Chūtai	Shōtai	Plane	Pilot	Observer	Radioman	Notes
1	1	1	PO1 Endō Makoto			Recovered 0645
1	1	2	PO1 Koga Tadayoshi			Recovered 0645
1	1	3	PO1 Shikada Tsuguo			Recovered 0645

Ryūjō Carrier Attack Unit
Aircraft: 1 lost, crew names not recorded
Personnel: 15 MIA, 1 WIA

Chūtai	Shōtai	Plane	Pilot	Observer	Radioman	Notes
1	1	1	PO1 Nishimura Hiroshi	Lt. Yamagami Masayuki	PO2 Endō Shōji	Recovered 0650
1	1	2	Sea1 Shimada Kazue	PO2 Satō Yoshitomi	PO2 Hoshino Seiichi	Recovered 0650
1	3	1	PO2c Horiuchi Tsutomu	WO Uchimura Kahei	PO3c Yamauchi Toshiaki	Recovered 0650
1	3	2	Sea1 Yashiki Hiroshi	PO3c Nihei Sunao	Sea1c Shimayama Shinpei	Recovered 0650
1	2	1	PO1 Sakuchi Takashi	Lt. (jg) Satō Ryōzō	PO2c Anzai Michimori	Recovered 0650
1	2	2	Sea1 Takahashi Hiroshi	PO1 Nemoto Masao	PO2c Watanabe Suzuo	Recovered 0650
1	2	3	Sea1 Yamaguchi Shitago	PO2 Kobayashi Yoshihiko	PO3c Izumi Takeo	Recovered 0650
2	4	1	Lt. Samejima Hiroichi	PO1c Yoshihara Kaichi	PO2c Itō Kunio	Recovered 0645
2	4	2	Sea1c Oki Masayoshi	PO2c Kameda Minoru	PO3c Noda Kaoru	Recovered 0645
2	6	1	PO2c Kawahara Asao	PO1c Yamaguchi Shūichi	PO3c Ohata Hisatoshi	Recovered 0645
2	6	2	Sea1 Mizoguchi Yoshihiro	PO3c Shimada Yoshinari	Sea2c Nakajima Bunji	Recovered 0645
2	5	1	Ens. Shibata Mineichi	PO1c Itō Sadao	PO2c Kikuda Harasada	Recovered 0645
2	5	2	PO1c Oda Yasuo	PO1c Miura Isamichi	PO2c Kurahashi Kaname	Recovered 0645
2	5	3	Sea1c Motoyoshi Hideyoshi	PO2c Akiyama Hiroshi	Sea1c Takahashi Kazuo	Recovered 0645

Junyō Carrier Fighter Unit
Aircraft: 13 OK
Personnel: no casualties

Chūtai	Shōtai	Plane	Pilot	Observer	Radioman	Notes
1	11	1	Lt. Shiga Yoshio			*Junyō* pilot; aborted; recovered 0245
1	11	2	PO1c Yamamoto Ichirō			*Shōkaku* pilot; aborted; recovered 0245
1	12	1	WO Kitahata Saburō			*Junyō* pilot; joined *Ryūjō* attack group; recovered 0735
1	12	2	PO2c Sasakibara Masao			*Shōkaku* pilot; joined *Ryūjō* attack group; recovered 0735
1	13	1	PO1c Kubota Wataru			*Junyō* pilot; aborted; recovered 0245
1	13	2	PO2c Hasegawa Tatsukura			*Junyō* pilot; aborted; recovered 0245
2	14	1	Lt. Miyano Zenjirō			6th *Kū* pilot; aborted; recovered 0245
2	14	2	PO1c Ozeki Yukiharu			6th *Kū* pilot; aborted; recovered 0245
2	14	3	Sea1c Yoshida Ippei			*Ryūjō* pilot; aborted; recovered 0245
2	15	1	PO1c Okamoto Juzō			6th *Kū* pilot; aborted; recovered 0245
2	15	2	PO3c Tanaka Yoshizō			*Shōkaku* pilot; aborted; recovered 0245
2	16	1	PO1c Kamihira Keishū			6th *Kū* pilot; aborted; recovered 0245
2	15	2	PO2c Yotsumoto Chiune			*Ryūjō* pilot; aborted; recovered 0245

Junyō Carrier Bomber Unit
Aircraft: 15 OK
Personnel: no casualties

Chūtai	Shōtai	Plane	Pilot	Observer	Radioman	Notes
1	21	1	Lt. Abe Zenji		WO Ishii Masao	Aborted; recovered 0245
1	21	2	PO3c Takei Kazuma		PO1c Harada Yoshitarō	Aborted; recovered 0245
1	21	3	PO3 Nakatsuka Yasuichi		PO2c Kimura Haruo	Aborted; recovered 0245
1	22	1	PO1 Ōishi Yukio		WO Yamamoto Hiroshi	Aborted; recovered 0245
1	22	2	PO3 Okada Tadao		PO2c Sugie Takeshi	Aborted; recovered 0245
1	22	3	Sea2 Ikeda Hiroshi		PO2c Miyawaki Kōzō	Aborted; recovered 0245
1	23	1	PO1 Numata Kazutoshi		PO2c Takano Yoshio	Aborted; recovered 0245

Junyō Carrier Dive Bomber Unit (*cont.*)

Chūtai	Shōtai	Plane	Pilot	Observer	Radioman	Notes
1	23	2	Sea1c Nagashima Zensaku		PO2c Nakao Tetsuo	Aborted; recovered 0245
2	24	1	PO1c Kawabata Hiroyasu		Lt. Miura Naohiko	Aborted; recovered 0245
2	24	2	PO3c Yamakawa Shinsaku		PO2c Nishiyama Tsuyoshi	Aborted; recovered 0245
2	24	3	Sea2c Murakami Yasuhiro		PO2c Shibaoka Yoshiharu	Aborted; recovered 0245
2	25	1	WO Harano Nobuo		PO1c Tajima Ichirō	Aborted; recovered 0245
2	25	2	PO3c Kosemoto Kunio		Sea1c Nakata Katsuzō	Aborted; recovered 0245
2	26	1	PO1c Miyatake Yoshiaki		WO Tajima Kazuo	Aborted; recovered 0245
2	26	2	PO2c Gotō Tōjūrō		PO2c Yamanoi Hiroshi	Aborted; recovered 0245

Makushin Bay Strike Force

Launch time: 0945, 3 June

Overall commander: Lt. Shiga Yoshio

Ryūjō Carrier Fighter Unit
Aircraft: 6 OK
Personnel: no casualties

Chūtai	Shōtai	Plane	Pilot	Observer	Radioman	Notes
1	1	1	Lt. Kobayashi Minoru			Aborted; recovered OK
1	1	2	PO1c Kurihara Hiroshi			Aborted; recovered OK
1	1	3	PO1c Tomoishi Masateru			Aborted; recovered OK
1	2	1	PO1c Yoshizawa Tomio			Aborted; recovered OK
1	2	2	PO1c Miyauchi Yukio			Aborted; recovered OK
1	2	3	Sea1c Ishihara Shōji			Aborted; recovered OK

Ryūjō Carrier Attack Unit
Aircraft: 6 OK
Personnel: no casualties

Chūtai	Shōtai	Plane	Pilot	Observer	Radioman	Notes
1	4	1	Lt. Samejima Hiroichi	PO1c Yoshihara Kaichi	PO2c Itō Kunio	Aborted; recovered OK
1	4	2	PO1c Oda Yasuo	PO1c Miura Isamichi	PO2c Kurahashi Kaname	Aborted; recovered OK
1	4	3	Sea1c Oki Masayoshi	PO2c Kameda Minoru	PO3c Noda Kaoru	Aborted; recovered OK
1	6	1	PO2c Kawahara Asao	PO1c Yamaguchi Shūichi	PO3c Ohata Hisatoshi	Aborted; recovered OK
1	6	2	Sea1c Tamai Yoshiichi	PO1c Motohashi Hisayoshi	PO2c Mogi Ichirō	Aborted; recovered OK
1	6	3	Sea1c Mizoguchi Yoshihiro	PO3c Shimada Yoshinari	Sea2c Nakajima Bunji	Aborted; recovered OK

Junyō Carrier Fighter Unit
Aircraft: 6 OK
Personnel: no casualties

Chūtai	Shōtai	Plane	Pilot	Observer	Radioman	Notes
1	11	1	Lt. Shiga Yoshio			Aborted; recovered OK
1	11	2	PO1c Kubota Wataru			Aborted; recovered OK
1	11	3	PO1c Yamamoto Ichirō			Aborted; recovered OK
1	12	1	Lt. Miyano Zenjirō			Aborted; recovered OK
1	12	2	PO1c Okamoto Takashi			Aborted; recovered OK
1	12	3	PO1c Kamahira Keishū			Aborted; recovered OK

Junyō Carrier Bomber Unit
Aircraft: 15 OK
Personnel: no casualties

Chūtai	Shōtai	Plane	Pilot	Observer	Radioman	Notes
1	21	1	Lt. Abe Zenji		WO Ishii Masao	Aborted; recovered OK
1	21	1	PO3c Takei Kazuma		PO1c Harada Yoshitarō	Aborted; recovered OK
1	21	3	PO3c Nakatsuka Yasuichi		PO2c Kimura Haruo	Aborted; recovered OK
1	22	1	PO1c Ōishi Yukio		WO Yamamoto Hiroshi	Aborted; recovered OK
1	22	2	PO3c Okada Tadao		PO2c Sugie Takeshi	Aborted; recovered OK

Junyō Carrier Bomber Unit (*cont.*)

Chūtai	Shōtai	Plane	Pilot	Observer	Radioman	Notes
1	22	3	Sea2c Ikeda Hiroshi		PO2c Miyawaki Kōzō	Aborted; recovered OK
1	23	1	PO1c Numata Kazutoshi		PO2c Takano Yoshio	Aborted; recovered OK
1	23	2	Sea1c Nagashima Zensaku		PO2c Nakao Tetsuo	Aborted; recovered OK
2	24	1	PO1c Kawabata Hiroyasu		Lt. Miura Naohiko	Aborted; recovered OK
2	24	2	PO3c Yamakawa Shinsaku		PO2c Nishiyama Tsuyoshi	Aborted; recovered OK
2	24	3	Sea2 Murakami Yasuhiro		PO2c Shibaoka Yoshiharu	Aborted; recovered OK
2	25	1	WO Harano Nobuo		PO1c Tajima Ichirō	Aborted; recovered OK
2	25	2	PO3c Kosemoto Kunio		Sea1c Nakata Katsuzo	Aborted; recovered OK
2	26	1	PO1c Miyatake Yoshiaki		WO Tajima Kazuo	Aborted; recovered OK
2	26	2	PO2c Gotō Tōjurō		PO2c Yamanoi Hiroshi	Aborted; recovered OK

Dutch Harbor Strike Force
Launch time: 1430, 4 June
Overall commander: Lt. Shiga Yoshio

Ryujō Carrier Fighter Unit
Aircraft: 2 damaged, 1 lost
Personnel: 1 KIA

Chūtai	Shōtai	Plane	Pilot	Observer	Radioman	Notes
1	1	1	WO Uemura Haruichi			Recovered OK
1	1	2	PO1c Sugiyama Teruo			Recovered OK
1	1	3	PO2c Hōjō Hiromichi			Recovered OK
1	2	1	PO1c Endō Makoto			Hit. Recovered OK
1	2	2	* PO1c Koga Tadayoshi			Damaged by antiaircraft; emergency landing on Akutan Island, pilot killed
1	2	3	PO1c Shikada Tsuguo			Hit. Recovered OK

Ryūjō Carrier Attack Unit
Aircraft: 9 OK
Personnel: no casualties

Chūtai	Shōtai	Plane	Pilot	Observer	Radioman	Notes
1	1	1	PO1c Nishimura Hiroshi	Lt. Yamagami Masayuki	PO2c Endō Shōji	Recovered OK
1	1	2	PO1c Ōshima Tsuneo	PO1c Yamano Ichirō	PO2c Morita Hiromi	Recovered OK
1	1	3	Sea1c Shimada Kazue	PO2c Satō Yoshitomi	PO2c Hoshino Seiichi	Recovered OK
1	2	1	PO2c Horiuchi Tsutomu	PO3c Yamauchi Toshiaki	WO Uchimura Kahei	Recovered OK
1	2	2	PO2c Okuyama Iwao	PO2c Ikehara Toshiyuki	PO1c Ohashi Shin'ichi	Recovered OK
1	2	3	Sea1c Yashiki Hiroshi	Sea1c Shimayama Shinpei	PO3c Nihei Sunao	Recovered OK
1	3	1	PO2c Kawahara Asao	PO3c Ohata Hisatoshi	PO1c Yamaguchi Shūichi	Recovered OK
1	3	2	Sea1c Tamai Yoshiichi	PO2c Mogi Ichirō	PO1c Motohashi Hisayoshi	Recovered OK
1	3	3	Sea1c Mizoguchi Yoshihiro	Sea2c Nakajima Bunji	PO3c Shimada Yoshinari	Recovered OK

Junyō Carrier Fighter Unit
Aircraft: 5 OK
Personnel: no casualties

Chūtai	Shōtai	Plane	Pilot	Observer	Radioman	Notes
1	11	1	Lt. Shiga Yoshio			Recovered OK
1	11	2	PO1c Yamamoto Ichirō			Recovered OK
1	12	1	Lt. Miyano Zenjirō			Recovered OK
1	12	2	PO1c Ozeki Yukiharu			Recovered OK
1	13	1	WO Kitahata Saburō			Recovered OK

Junyō Carrier Bomber Unit
Aircraft: 4 shot down, 5 damaged, 1 aborted
Personnel: 4 KIA, 4 MIA

Chūtai	Shōtai	Plane		Pilot	Observer		Radioman	Notes
1	21	1		Lt. Abe Zenji			WO Ishii Masao	Hit; recovered OK
1	21	2		PO3c Takei Kazuma			PO1c Harada Yoshitarō	Hit; recovered OK
1	22	1	*	PO1c Ōishi Yukio		*	WO Yamamoto Hiroshi	Shot down by American fighters
1	22	2	*	PO3c Okada Tadao		*	PO2c Sugie Takeshi	Shot down by American fighters
1	23	1	*	PO1c Numata Kazutoshi		*	PO2c Takano Yoshio	Damaged by American fighters; ditched
1	23	2		Sea1c Nagashima Zensaku			PO2c Nakao Tetsuo	Hit; recovered OK
2	24	1		PO1c Kawabata Hiroyasu			Lt. Miura Naohiko	Hit; recovered OK
2	24	2		PO3c Yamakawa Shinsaku			PO2c Nishiyama Tsuyoshi	Hit; recovered OK
2	25	1	*	WO Harano Nobuo		*	PO1c Tajima Ichirō	Damaged by American fighters; ditched
2	25	2		PO3c Kosemoto Kunio			Sea1c Nakata Katsuzō	Recovered OK
2	26	1		PO1c Miyatake Yoshiaki			WO Tajima Kazuo	Engine trouble

Appendix 11: Aleutians Force Distributions

The Aleutians Operation anticipated three major force organizations ("Distributions"), to be undertaken at various points in the operation. In the event, neither the second nor third distributions were undertaken, owing to the turn of events around Midway itself. The three distributions are defined in tabular format below, as taken from Japanese Monograph No. 88.

First Distribution	Second Distribution[1]	Third Distribution[1]
Main Body	**Main Body**	**Main Body**
Nachi (CA)	*Nachi* (CA)	*Nachi* (CA)
Nenohi (DD)[2]	*Abukuma* (CL)	*Hibiki* (DD)
Hatsuharu (DD)[2]	*Kiso* (CL)	*Ikazuchi* (DD)
	Tama (CL)	*Inazuma* (DD)
	Nenohi (DD)	
	Wakaba (DD)	
	Hatsuharu (DD)	
	Hatsushimo (DD)	
	Hibiki (DD)	
	Ikazuchi (DD)	
	Inazuma (DD)	
2nd Mobile Force	**2nd Mobile Force**	**1st Support Group**
Ryūjō (CVL)	*Ryūjō* (CVL)	*Kongō* (BB) ❹
Junyō (CVL)	*Junyō* (CVL)	*Haruna* (BB) ❹
Takao (CA)	*Zuihō* (CVL) ❶	*Tone* (CA) ❹
Maya (CA)	*Takao* (CA)	*Chikuma* (CA) ❹
Ushio (DD)	*Maya* (CA)	*Akigumo* (DD) ❹
Oboro (DD)[3]	*Ushio* (DD)	*Yūgumo* (DD) ❹
Akebono (DD)	*Oboro* (DD)	*Makigumo* (DD) ❹
Teiyō Maru (AO)	*Akebono* (DD)	*Kazagumo* (DD) ❹
	Arashi (DD) ❶	*Kyokutō Maru* (AO) ❹
	Nowaki (DD) ❶	
	Hagikaze (DD) ❶	
	Maikaze (DD) ❶	
	Teiyō Maru (AO)	

First Distribution	Second Distribution	Third Distribution
Attu-Adak Invasion Force[4]	**Attu Defense Force**	**2nd Support Group**
Abukuma (CL)	*Kinugasa Maru* (AP)	*Hiei* (BB) ❹
Wakaba (DD)		*Kirishima* (BB) ❹
Hatsushimo (DD)		*Myōkō* (CA) ❺
Magane Maru (minelayer)		*Haguro* (CA) ❺
Kinugasa Maru (AP)		*Abukuma* (CL)
		Kiso (CL)
		Tama (CL)
		Nenohi (DD)
		Wakaba (DD)
		Hatsuharu (DD)
		Hatsushimo (DD)
		Genyō Maru (AO) ❻
Kiska Invasion Force[5]	**Kiska Defense Force**	**2nd Mobile Force**
Kiso (CL)		
Tama (CL)	**Coastal Defense Unit**	**1st Raiding Group**
Awata Maru (aux. cruiser)	Kaiho Maru *(minesweeper)*	*Ryūjō* (CVL)
Asaka Maru (aux. cruiser)	*Shinkotsu Maru* (minesweeper)	*Junyō* (CVL)
Hibiki (DD)	*Hakuho Maru (minesweeper)*	*Takao* (CA)
Ikazuchi (DD)[6]	Sub Chasers No. *25, 26, 27*	*Ushio* (DD)
Inazuma (DD)[6]		*Akebono* (DD)
Hokaze (DD)		*Oboro* (DD)
Hakusan Maru (AP)	Land Defense Unit	*Urakaze* (DD) ❹
Kumagawa Maru (AP)	*Hakusan Maru* (AP)	*Tohō Maru* (AO)[7] ❹
Kaihō Maru (minesweeper)	*Kumagawa Maru* (AP)	
Hakuhō Maru (minesweeper)		
Kaihō Maru (minesweeper)		**2nd Raiding Group**
Shinkotsu Maru (minesweeper)		*Zuikaku* (CV) ❺
Sub Chasers No. *25, 26, 27*		*Zuihō* (CVL)
		Maya (CA)
		Arashi (DD)
		Nowaki (DD)
		Hagikaze (DD)
		Maikaze (DD)
		Fujisan Maru (AO) ❼
Submarine Force	**Submarine Force**	**Attu Defense Force** ❽
6 *I*-type	6 *I*-type	
	7 *I*-type ❷	
Seaplane Tender Force	**Seaplane Tender Force**	**Kiska Defense Force** ❽
Kimikawa Maru (seaplane tender)	*Kimikawa Maru* (seaplane tender)	
Shiokaze (DD)	*Kamikawa Maru* (seaplane tender) ❸	
	Shiokaze (DD)	
	Hokaze (DD)	
Scouting Force	**Scouting Force**	**Submarine Force** ❽
Patrol Yachts	*Awata Maru* (aux. cruiser)	
	Asaka Maru (aux. cruiser)	

First Distribution	Second Distribution	Third Distribution
Ogasawara Force	**Ogasawara Force**	**Seaplane Tender Force** ❽
7th Base Force	**7th Base Force** *Magane Maru* (minelayer)	
Base Air Force 6 Flying Boats *Kamitsu Maru* (AP) *#2 Hino Maru* (AP) *#5 Seiji Maru* (AP) *#2 Kishi Maru* (AP)	**Base Air Force** 6 Flying Boats *Kamitsu Maru* (AP) *#2 Hino Maru* (AP) *#5 Seiji Maru* (AP) *#2 Kishi Maru* (AP)	**Scouting Force** ❽
		Ogasawara Force ❽
		Base Air Force ❽

Notes

❶ To be part of reinforcement from Midway Invasion Force.

❷ Under maintenance at time of planning.

❸ To be part of reinforcement from Midway Invasion Force.

❹ To be part of reinforcement from Southern Force.

❺ To be part of reinforcement from Submarine Force.[8]

❻ There was no change contemplated.

❼ To be part of reinforcement from Submarine Force (6th Fleet).

❽ Same as for 2nd Distribution.

Classification of Vessels

AO – Oiler

AP – Transport

CA – Heavy Cruiser

CL – Light Cruiser

CV – Fleet Carrier

CVL – Light Fleet Carrier

DD – Destroyer

Notes

Chapter 1: Departure

1 Throughout the text, we render Japanese names in their Japanese form of family name first, given name second.

2 For the sake of convenience, we will often render such terms as Battleship Division and Carrier Division in their shorter, Westernized abbreviations—BatDiv, CarDiv, CruDiv, DesDiv, and so on. It should be noted that the Japanese Navy did not use this nomenclature, referring to Battleship Division 1 simply as Division 1.

3 It should be noted that many authors refer to *Kidō Butai* as if there were no other mobile striking forces in the Imperial Navy. In point of fact, *Kidō Butai* was a term of convenience rather than a formal organizational title. The Battle of Midway would also witness the services of *Dai-ni* (Second) *Kidō Butai*— the force centered on *Ryūjō* and *Junyō,* which operated in the Aleutians. However, when we use *Kidō Butai* in the text without further specification, it will always be in reference to Nagumo's force.

4 As originally laid down, *Akagi* and *Kaga* were to have cost ¥24.7 million and ¥26.9 million, respectively. Each had completed roughly a third of their construction cycles before work had been suspended on all capital ships as a result of Japan's signing the Washington Naval Treaty. As a result, these two ships had likely consumed about ¥8 million apiece before work was stopped. In 1922 the Diet voted the staggering additional sum of ¥90 million to complete *Akagi* and her sister, *Amagi* (and later *Kaga*), as aircraft carriers. As a result, it is likely that each of the two big carriers of CarDiv 1 cost roughly ¥53 million ($36.45 million) to complete. This figure does include the very substantial sums later allocated to refit and modernize each of these vessels in the mid-1930s. Sources: Eric Lacroix in *The Belgian Shiplover, Showa Zosenshi.* By way of comparison, HMS *Nelson,* built in 1922 at a cost of £7.5 million, cost about ¥47 million in adjusted 1928 prices. We are grateful to Dr. Warren Bailey for his help in supplying pertinent economic data via his unpublished, "How Important Was Silver? Some Evidence on Exchange Rate Fluctuations and Stock Returns in Colonial-Era Asia," Cornell University, February 25, 2002.

5 *Akagi* had been laid down six months after *Kaga,* but was commissioned almost a year sooner.

6 Abe Zenji, in e-mail to Michael Wenger, 5/6/2002.

7 Fukui Shizuo, *Japanese Naval Vessels Illustrated, 1869–1945,* vol. 3 (Tokyo: KK Best Sellers, 1982), p. 66.

8 Indeed, it is arguable whether the Pearl Harbor raid could have even been attempted had they been absent from Japan's force structure. Mark Peattie, *Sunburst: The Rise of Japanese Naval Air Power, 1909–1941* (Annapolis, MD: Naval Institute Press, 2001), p. 61.

9 The first invasion attempt, launched by a distinctly second-string Japanese naval flotilla, had ended in a humiliating retreat, because the tiny Marine garrison sank two old Japanese destroyers.

10 *Kaga* had run aground at Palau on 9 February 1942. Although she had participated in the operations around Java, as well as the Port Darwin raid, her damage was considered serious enough that she was sent back to Japan for a proper dry-docking at Sasebo on 27 March. It is very likely that she had her bottom scraped and repainted at this time, thereby ensuring her ability to operate at her best speed in the upcoming Midway operation.

11 Arthur Marder, in the second volume of his *Old Friends, New Enemies,* makes it clear that the effects on the morale of the Eastern Fleet were far reaching and pervasive throughout the entire chain of command. Arthur Marder, *Old Friends, New Enemies, The Royal Navy and the Imperial Japanese Navy, Volume II: The Pacific War, 1942–1945,* Oxford, UK: Clarendon Press, 1990, pp. 148–49.

12 Robert Barde, *The Battle of Midway: A Study in Command,* Ph.D. Thesis, University of Maryland, 1971, pp. 15–16.

13 For characterizations of Nagumo, we draw primarily on Mitsuo Fuchida, *Midway: The Battle that Doomed Japan* (Annapolis, MD: Naval Institute Press, 1955); Gordon Prange, *Miracle at Midway* (New York: Penguin Books, 1982); Matome Ugaki, *Fading Victory* (Pittsburgh: University of Pittsburgh Press, 1991); David Evans and Mark Peattie, *Kaigun: Strategy, Tactics and Technology in the Imperial Japanese Navy, 1887–1941* (Annapolis, MD: Naval Institute Press, 1997); Tameichi Hara, *Japanese Destroyer Captain* (New York: Ballantine Books, 1961); and John Prados, *Combined Fleet Decoded* (New York: Random House, 1995). We are also extremely grateful to Mr. Daniel Rush, U.S. Navy, for his reminiscences of personal conversations with Nagumo's youngest son, Dr. Nagumo Shinji, in a series of e-mails to Jonathan Parshall dated 5/27–6/3/2001.

14 Barde, p. 52.

15 For characterizations of Kusaka, we draw primarily on Fuchida, Prange, and Ugaki.

16 Donald Goldstein and Katherine Dillon, *The Pearl Harbor Papers* (Dulles, VA: Brassey's, 1993), p. 151.

17 Hiroyuki Agawa, *The Reluctant Admiral* (Tokyo: Kodansha, 1979), p. 193.

18 Letter from Lt. Louis Poisson Davis (USN) to commander, Destroyer Squadron Eleven. 2 May 1923. Yamaguchi had visited Lieutenant Davis on board Davis's destroyer, USS *Woodbury* (DD309). Louis Poisson Davis Papers, Collection No. 309, East Carolina University Manuscript Collection, J. Y. Joyner Library. We are grateful to David Dickson for making us aware of this collection.

19 Goldstein and Dillon, p. 330.

20 Ugaki, p. 141.

21 Ibid.

22 Goldstein and Dillon, p. 144.

23 *Tone* has been typically credited with five aircraft—three E13Ns and two E8Ns. However, James Sawruk's examinations of the available records of the battle indicate that, in fact, *Tone* was missing one of her E13Ns. This loss apparently occurred around the time of the Indian Ocean operation in April 1942. E-mail from Sawruk to Parshall, 5/9/2001. Source: Japanese Operational Records, Microfilm Reel One, hereafter "JD-1."

24 The pronunciation of Hōdate's given name is unclear, and might have been Hōdate Takeshi. We are grateful to Jean-Paul Masson for his insights, derived from *Geneki Kaigun Shikan Meibō* (Active Navy Officer Register).

25 Casualty figures developed from Sawachi Hisae, *Midowei Kaisen; Kiroku* (Midway Naval Battle: A Record) (Tokyo: Bungei Shunjū, 1986).

CHAPTER 2: GENESIS OF A BATTLE

1   Willmott, *The Barrier and the Javelin: Japanese and Allied Pacific Strategies, February to June 1942* (Annapolis, MD: Naval Institute Press, 1982), p. 117; Barde, p. 43.

2   Prange, p. 28; Willmott, *Barrier and the Javelin,* p. 117.

3   Both H. P. Willmott's *Barrier and the Javelin,* and John Lundstrom's *The First South Pacific Campaign* (Annapolis, MD: Naval Institute Press, 1976), greatly inform this section. We also draw upon Willmott's preceding volume, *Empires in the Balance: Japanese and Allied Pacific Strategies to April 1942* (Annapolis, MD: Naval Institute Press, 1982), Fuchida's *Midway: The Battle that Doomed Japan,* Agawa's *The Reluctant Admiral,* and Ugaki, *Fading Victory.*

4   For characterizations of Yamamoto, we draw primarily upon Agawa; Fuchida; Prange; Ugaki; Willmott, *Barrier and the Javelin;* "Isoroku Yamamoto: Alibi of a Navy" in *The Great Admirals: Command at Sea, 1587–1945,* ed. Jack Sweetman (Annapolis, MD: Naval Institute Press, 1997); Evans and Peattie; and Prados.

5   Ugaki, p. 13; Prange, p. 285.

6   Ugaki, p. 36.

7   John Stephan, *Hawaii Under the Rising Sun* (Honolulu: University of Hawaii Press, 1984), p. 95.

8   Prange, p. 29.

9   Willmott, *Barrier and the Javelin,* p. 39.

10 Ugaki, p. 12.

11 Ibid., p. 40.

12 Lundstrom, *First South Pacific Campaign,* p. 41; Willmott, *Barrier and the Javelin,* p. 43.

13 Willmott, *Barrier and the Javelin,* p. 42.

14 Stephan, p. 82.

15 Ugaki, p. 75.

16 Ibid., p. 75.

17 Ibid., pp. 79–80.

18 Stephan, p. 81. Combined Fleet staff officers Kuroshima and Watanabe had been given responsibility for examining this possibility by Yamamoto.

19 Ibid., p. 82.

20 Ibid., p. 97.

21 Stephan, p. 98.

22 Barde, p. 29. Tomioka's father had been a vice admiral and chief of naval operations during the Russo-Japanese War. His grandfather had been a naval constructor. A 1917 graduate of Etajima, Tomioka had subsequently personally received a sword from Emperor Hirohito for being the top graduate in his class at the Naval War College in 1930. He was clearly destined for flag rank.

23 Stephan, pp. 98–99.

24 Ibid., p. 99.

25 Ibid., p. 99.

26 Ibid., p. 100.

27 Ibid, p. 100; Willmott, *Barrier and the Javelin*, p. 42.

28 Ugaki, pp. 79–80.

29 Ibid., pp. 79–80.

30 Willmott, *Barrier and the Javelin*, p. 42.

31 Ibid., p. 93.

32 Japan, *Bōeichō Bōeikenshūjō Senshibu* (originally, *Bōeichō Boeikenshūjō Senshishitsu*), also *Senshi Sōsho* (war history) series. Asagumo Shimbunsha. *Midowei Kaisen* (Battle of Midway), vol. 43, 1971, pp. 29–30.

33 Willmott, *Barrier and the Javelin*, p. 49.

34 Lundstrom, *First South Pacific Campaign*, p. 43.

35 Robert B. Edgertson, *Warriors of the Rising Sun—A History of the Japanese Military* (Boulder, CO: Westview Press, 1997), p. 275.

36 Lundstrom, *First South Pacific Campaign*, p. 43; Willmott, *Barrier and the Javelin*, p. 46.

37 Willmott, *Barrier and the Javelin*, p. 52.

38 Osamu Tagaya, *Mitsubishi Type 1 Rikko 'Betty' Units of World War 2*, Osprey Combat Aircraft Series, no. 22 (Oxford, UK: Osprey Publishing Ltd, 2001), pp. 35–37; Lundstrom, *First South Pacific Campaign*, pp. 33–34.

39 Willmott, *Barrier and the Javelin*, pp. 57–58.

40 Ibid., pp. 59–63.

41 Lundstrom, *First South Pacific Campaign*, pp. 41–42.

42 In fact, *Saratoga* (not *Lexington*) had been torpedoed on 11 January 1942, sending her stateside for repairs.

43 Japanese Monograph No. 93, p. 12. She was, in fact, operating with the British in support of the Home Fleet in the Atlantic.

44 Ibid., p. 12. *Ranger* was judged unusable for combat operations by the Americans.

45 Ugaki, p. 75.

46 Ibid., pp. 79–80.

47 Japanese Monograph No. 93. "Midway Operations May–June 1942." Washington, D.C.: Department of the Army, 1947, p. 11, states that the Americans were estimated to have fifty-six aircraft of various types there.

48 Ibid., p. 2.

49 At the height of their preparations for the battle, even the Americans never based more than about 125 aircraft (including flying boats) at Midway, which filled the base to bursting.

50 Stephan, p. 111.

51 Willmott, *Barrier and the Javelin*, p. 72.

52 Agawa, p. 297; Fuchida, p. 65.

53 *Senshi Sōsho*, p. 95; Stephan, p. 112; Ugaki, p. 109.

54 Willmott, *Barrier and the Javelin*, p. 73.

55 Barde, p. 34.

56 Japanese Monograph No. 88. "Aleutian Naval Operations, March 1942–February 1943," Department of the Army, 1947, pp. 6–7.

57 Ibid., p. 7.

58 Stephan, p 112.

59 Ibid., p. 112.

60 Ibid., pp. 112–13.

Chapter 3: Plans

1 American forces on the island of Corregidor, in the middle of Manila Bay, would hold out until May.

2 Willmott, *Barrier and the Javelin,* p. 169.

3 Ugaki, pp. 83–84.

4 Stephan, p. 114.

5 Prados, p. 289.

6 Stephan, p. 114.

7 Ibid., p. 115; Edgertson, p. 275.

8 *Senshi Sōsho,* pp. 92–95.

9 Stephan, p. 117. The original operational order (*Dairikushi* no. 1159) gave notification to Seventh and Second Divisions to prepare for the invasion. These two divisions were soon augmented with the Fifty-Third Division, an independent engineer regiment, and a tank regiment.

10 Fuchida, pp. 78, 83–84. Samuel Morison, *Coral Sea, Midway and Submarine Actions, May 1942–August 1942* (Edison, NJ: Castle Books, 2001), pp. 77–78.

11 Japanese Monographs No. 93 and No. 88.

12 Japanese Monograph No. 88, p. 7.

13 Japanese Monograph No. 93, p. 4.

14 United States Strategic Bombing Survey [Pacific], Naval Analysis Division. Interrogations of Japanese Officials, vols. 1 and 2, 1946, Nav-13, interview with Watanabe Yasuji.

15 *Senshi Sōsho,* p. 117.

16 For the remainder of this section, Tokyo time is used, which is a day later than the local time of the objectives themselves (which were all located across the international date line). To find Midway local time, twenty-one hours behind, simply subtract one day (i.e., twenty-four hours), then add three hours forward.

17 *Senshi Sōsho,* p. 96. We are grateful to John Lundstrom for pointing out this key fact.

18 Ibid., p. 121.

19 Japanese Monograph No. 88, p. 9

20 Ibid., p. 3.

21 Ibid., p. 32.

22 Ibid., p. 16.

23 Monograph No. 88, p. 10.

24 The proper designation of this aircraft is the Type 99 Carrier Bomber. However, for the sake of familiarity to American readers, we will use the term "dive-bomber" when describing this aircraft.

25 Monograph No. 88, p. 15.

26 Ibid., pp. 16, 20.

27 Ibid., p. 21.

28 Ibid., pp. 21–22.

29 Ibid., pp. 23–25.

30 It should be noted that the operational orders for Operation AL were issued after the Battle of Coral Sea; thus the anticipated use of *Zuikaku,* and not her more badly damaged sistership *Shōkaku.* It seems unlikely that the original AL plan included either member of CarDiv 5, as both carriers were originally designated for operations with Nagumo's First Striking Force at Midway.

31 *Senshi Sōsho,* p. 119. Given that the inclusion of CarDiv 5 in the attack formation would have raised the number of initial attacking aircraft in the dawn strike to more than 160, the anticipated need for a single strike may not have been far wrong.

32 Ibid., p. 119.

33 Barde, p. 28.

34 *Senshi Sōsho,* p. 186.

35 Japanese Monograph No. 93, p. 8.

36 Paul Dull, *A Battle History of the Imperial Japanese Navy 1941–1945* (Annapolis, MD: Naval Institute Press, 1978), p. 138.

37 *Senshi Sōsho,* p. 118.

38 Prados, p. 283; Willmott, *Barrier and the Javelin,* p. 88.

39 Willmott, *Barrier and the Javelin,* p. 93; Prange, p. 31.

40 *Senshi Sōsho,* p. 106; Monograph No. 93, p. 24.

41 This is not stated directly in *Senshi Sōsho,* but it is supported by the map of a subsequent Combined Fleet map exercise (pp. 117–18) in which the Red forces (American) were given a Main Body in addition to a mobile force of carriers. Given that it was Combined Fleet staff (likely Admiral Ugaki himself) that

scripted these exercises, it is reasonable to assume that the force allocations for the war game mirrored the Japanese vision of how the U.S. Navy would likely respond. We are grateful to Osamu Tagaya for his insights into these matters.

42 Fuchida, p. 79.

43 Lundstrom, *First South Pacific Campaign,* pp. 124–25; Willmott, *Barrier and the Javelin,* p. 82.

44 For a general discussion of prewar Japanese tactics vis-à-vis the decisive battle, see Evans and Peattie, pp. 273–98.

45 This figure includes CarDiv 5's two carriers.

46 "An Intimate Look at the Japanese Navy," Donald Goldstein and Katherine Dillon, *The Pearl Harbor Papers* (Dulles, VA: Brassey's, 1993), p. 325.

47 Sun Tzu, *The Art of War,* Samuel Griffith, trans. (Oxford, UK: Oxford University Press, 1963), pp. 97–98.

48 Ugaki, p. 100.

49 Monograph No. 93, p. 20.

50 The exact composition of CruDiv 7's air group at this time is unclear. It seems unlikely that any of the ships were operating more than one apiece of the newer E13A floatplanes, which were in short supply within the fleet as a whole at this time. Instead, CruDiv 7 was relying primarily on the older, slower Kawanishi E7K Type 94. However, while slower than the E13A, the E7K still had a very respectable range (over 1,000 nm), making it perfectly usable for long-range scouting missions. It was certainly a far superior platform to the short-ranged Type 95 spotting aircraft, which composed ten of the fourteen scouting aircraft carried by Nagumo's battleships and cruisers during the battle. Message from James Sawruk to Parshall, March 18, 2003. Source JD-1.

51 This includes the aircraft of the 6th Air Group (6th *Kōkūtai*), which were to be ferried by Nagumo's carriers to Midway. The composition of this unit is discussed in more detail later.

52 We are grateful to John Lundstrom for pointing this out.

53 *Kaga,* having been damaged in February, had returned to Japan for repairs during late March.

54 *Junyō's* sister, *Hiyō,* who shared her sister's limitations, would be available at the end of July 1942. However, the two ships were inferior in many ways to standard fleet carriers.

55 Again, the Japanese were assuming that *Lexington* had been sunk. The carrier USS *Ranger* was not considered combat worthy by the USN, but is included here for the sake of formality.

Chapter 4: Ill Omens

1 Lundstrom, *First South Pacific Campaign,* pp. 76–77.

2 Ibid., pp. 75–76.

3 *Ryūkaku* was considered to be a third unit of the *Shōkaku* class.

4 Lundstrom, *First South Pacific Campaign,* p. 84.

5 Ugaki, pp. 118–19.

6 Barde, p. 43.

7 Ibid., p. 43. It should be noted that Nagasawa was reporting this secondhand, as he was with Takagi's forces in the Coral Sea when these particular exercises were held.

8 Ibid., p. 44.

9 Ibid., p. 53.

10 Goldstein and Dillon, p. 348; *Senshi Sōsho,* p. 90. We are grateful to Osamu Tagaya for his insights into this matter.

11 Fuchida, pp. 91–92; also, Ugaki's diary divulges nothing but trivialities regarding the map exercises. No mention is made of any of the operational principles being played out or of his role in the exercises.

12 Prange, p. 35. This statement came to Prange via Watanabe's statement to him in 1964.

13 Willmott, *Barrier and the Javelin,* p. 112.

14 Ibid., p. 112.

15 Ugaki, p. 141; Prange, p. 36. This statement came to Prange via Watanabe's statement to him in 1964.

16 Prange, p. 36.

17 Ugaki, p. 122.

18 Walter Lord, *Incredible Victory* (New York: HarperCollins, 1967), p. 11.

19 *Shōkaku* was, in fact, only in dry dock until 27 June, and was operational by 12 July.

20 Willmott, *Barrier and the Javelin,* p. 101.

21 Lundstrom, *The First Team: Pacific Naval Air Combat from Pearl Harbor to Midway.* (Annapolis, MD: Naval Institute Press, 1984), p. 183.

22 E-mail from James Sawruk to Parshall, January 27, 2002. Source: JD-1.

23 Vice Admiral Mikawa Gun'ichi's stunning victory at the Battle of Savo Island (9 August 1942), for instance, was pulled off with a scratch unit composed of literally whatever units had been at hand in Rabaul and the Shortlands.

24 Japanese Monograph No. 93, p. 12.

25 Ibid. The basis for Japanese assumptions regarding "converted carriers" in the American inventory is far from clear, as there were none. The vast American shipbuilding program had yet to begin churning out carriers—converted or otherwise—in significant numbers.

26 Barde, pp. 49–50.

27 The Nagumo Report, p. 2, cites the Americans as having four squadrons at Midway. The American translation assumes that a squadron would be twelve planes, but it is by no means clear that this was actually the case, because the closest Japanese equivalent to an American squadron, the *hikōtai,* was at this point in the war usually eighteen aircraft, although unit composition varied. Source: *Nairei Teiyo* (Manual of Military Secret Orders). Translation of Captured Japanese Document, Item #613 (S-1193), July 20, 1943, National Archives, Washington, D.C., pp. 1–3. *Akagi*'s translated detailed action report, contained in "The Midway Operation: DesRon 10, Mine Sweep Div 16, CV *Akagi,* CV *Kaga,* CVL *Sōryū,* and CVL *Hiryū.*" Extract translation from DOC No. 160985B—MC 397.901, p. 4a, lists American strength as being two *chūtai* of patrol planes, two *chūtai* plus one plane of Army bombers, and two *chūtai* of fighter planes. The American translators of this report erroneously ascribed a *chūtai* as being four aircraft, which is too low. Depending on one's definition of a *chūtai*'s composition (usually nine aircraft), an estimate obtains of between thirty-seven and fifty-five aircraft, the latter being the most likely.

28 Japanese Monograph No. 93, p. 12.

29 Monograph No. 88, p. 11.

30 This was Northern Naval Force Order No. 24. Monograph No. 88, p. 32. The Nagumo Report is also explicit in its mention of the difficulties associated with orders being cut at the last minute.

31 Edwin Layton, *And I Was There* (New York: William Morrow, 1985), pp. 423–33.

32 Monograph No. 88, pp. 34–38.

33 Monograph No. 88, pp. 37–38; Monograph No. 93, p. 27.

34 *Senshi Sōsho,* pp. 117–18. We are grateful to Osamu Tagaya for his insight into these matters.

35 Ibid., pp. 119–21. We are grateful to John Lundstrom for his insight into these matters.

36 American Ultra intercepts of both *Akagi* and *Sōryū* indicate that the latter may have been involved in ferrying elements of the 23rd Air Flotilla (23rd *Kōkū Sentai*) at this time. Although not explicitly mentioned by the sources, it is possible that *Sōryū* was pressed into service as a replacement for the recently sunk seaplane carrier *Mizuho,* which was originally slated for the task. Ultra placed *Sōryū* in the vicinity of Truk as late as 22 May. Given the normal five-day transit time from Truk to Kure, it would not be surprising that she would not have been able to make it back to Kure in time to reprovision and then sortie for Midway as planned on the 26th. In a similar vein, on 16 May, Ultra also noted the change of CarDiv 2's flag from *Sōryū* to *Hiryū* the previous day, which may have been associated with *Sōryū*'s unanticipated ferrying duties. (Source: Ultra Intercepts—*Akagi* and *Sōryū,* May 16–22, 1942.)

37 Monograph No. 93, p. 27.

38 *Senshi Sōsho,* pp. 119–21.

39 Monograph No. 88, p. 38.

40 Goldstein and Dillon, p. 349.

CHAPTER 5: TRANSIT

1 Goldstein and Dillon, p. 211.

2 Ibid., p. 211.

3 Ibid., pp. 180, 213.

4 Ibid., pp. 186–95.

5 Fuchida, p. 104; Prange, p. 95.

6 John Keegan, *The Face of Battle* (London: Penguin Books, 1992), pp. 302–3.

7 Goldstein and Dillon, p. 328.

8 Tohmatsu Haruo's essay on Japanese perceptions of the Pearl Harbor attack, in H. P. Willmott's *Pearl Harbor* (with Tohmatsu Haruo and W. Spencer Johnson, London: Cassell, 2001), pp. 178–80, presents a perceptive treatment of this emotionally charged and internally contradictory topic.

9 Willmott is scathingly critical of this paradox. Indeed, the prospect of somehow "solving" the war in China by adding two vastly more widespread and complex conflicts to the docket is one that is difficult to comprehend.

10 Account of Kōzu Naoji, in Haruko Taya Cook and Theodore F. Cook, *Japan at War: An Oral History* (New York: The New Press, 1992), p. 318.

11 Sakai, Saburō, Martin Caidin, and Fred Saito. *Samurai!* (New York: Sutton, 1957; Reprint, Bantam Books, 1975), pp. 7–9.

12 Gordon Prange, *At Dawn We Slept* (New York: McGraw-Hill, 1981), pp. 280–81; Willmott, Haruo, and Johnson, *Pearl Harbor,* p. 60.

13 Prados, p. 137.

14 All of the oilers were relatively new units, capable of between 16.5 and 19.0 knots. Source: Roger Jordan, *The World's Merchant Fleets, 1939. The Particulars and Wartime Fates of 6,000 Ships* (Annapolis, MD: Naval Institute Press, 1999).

15 Bureau of Aeronautics, Air Technical Intelligence Group, Report #1, p. 2. This report, based on a postwar interview of *Akagi's* captain Aoki Taijirō, provided many unique insights on Japanese operations. Additional details on Japanese refueling techniques are found in the diary of Rear Admiral Chigusa Sadao, in Goldstein and Dillon, p. 177. Chigusa, who was executive officer of the destroyer *Akigumo* during the Pearl Harbor attack, kept a very detailed journal of the refueling activities made by that ship during that operation.

16 The U.S. Navy used side-by-side fueling almost exclusively by the late 1930s. Thomas Wildenberg, *Gray Steel and Black Oil: Fast Tankers and Replenishment at Sea in the U.S. Navy, 1912–1992* (Annapolis, MD: Naval Institute Press, 1996), pp. 31–38, 130–34. The drawbacks to in-line refueling were low pumping rates (since only one hose could be used), particularly if the fueling hose was brought in contact with the ocean, since the cool water had a tendency to increase viscosity of the oil in the fuel line, thereby creating difficulties. Given that Japanese warships were not apparently fitted with specialized tension engines to keep the guideline and fuel line above the surface of the water, it is likely that they suffered from this problem.

17 This is derived from *Sōryū's* detailed action report of the battle, which specifies that she had aerial patrol duty on May 27 and 31, i.e., every four days. *Sōryū* action report, WDC160985, p. 16.

18 A.T.I.G. Report #2, p. 4.

19 This is not true of the USN's new TBF Avenger, though, which was just being introduced into service.

20 There has been some speculation that there was a specially modified variant of the Type 97 that had greater range and that was used in the carrier reconnaissance role. However, research for this book has indicated that there was no such aircraft. Instead, it was standard practice for combat-loaded Type 97s not to fill the outboard 225-liter wing fuel tanks, so as to facilitate the aircraft's takeoff from the carrier. Type 97s on reconnaissance missions typically carried no ordnance, but they did carry the extra 450 liters of fuel, giving them a longer range. Source: Hyōdō Nisohachi monograph for Parshall.

21 It has usually been assumed that two D4Y were present on board *Sōryū,* and that one was lost en route to the battlefield, or shortly before *Sōryū* sortied from Kure, since it did not participate in the actions there. This is the opinion of *Senshi Sōsho.* However, it should be noted that there are no operational records for the second plane, so it is possible that the second aircraft was never shipped at all. Source: JD-1 reel, *Sōryū* detailed action report.

22 John Lundstrom's *The First Team,* pp. 182–85, and Mark Peattie's *Sunburst: The Rise of Japanese Naval Air Power, 1909–1941,* pp. 135–37, discuss these issues in greater detail than we will do so here. Lundstrom's work is also highly recommended for its comprehensive examination of air-to-air combat during the battle.

23 E-mail from Michael Wenger, February 2, 2002. According to Wenger, an expert on the Indian Ocean operations of *Kidō Butai,* this change may have been implemented between the raid on Port Darwin and the subsequent attack on Tjilatjap. Source: *Senshi Sōsho, vol. 26* (Indian Ocean Operations).

24 Many of our comments in this regard draw heavily from Wayne P. Hughes's *Fleet Tactics: Theory and Practice* (Annapolis, MD: Naval Institute Press, 1986), an enlightened, eminently readable, and highly recommended work on the matter of naval doctrine and tactics.

25 Ibid., p. 28.

26 Evans and Peattie's *Kaigun* remains the best source in English to date regarding these matters.

27 Peattie, p. 149.

28 Ibid., p. 151.

29 Kusaka remarked on the usage of two attack waves at Pearl Harbor as follows, "The reason for dividing the air attack force into two waves was the fact that all planes could not be launched in one wave due to the space and the take off range [*sic*] of the carriers." Goldstein and Dillon, p. 157. In our opinion, "take off range" is very likely a mistranslation of "takeoff length," referring to the limited run-off room forward on the carriers. The actual range of Japanese aircraft or carriers had no relation whatsoever to the number of aircraft in the deck spot.

30 Rear Admiral Murr Arnold, in a letter to John Lundstrom dated 9 April 1972, describes how USS *Yorktown,* in a training mission in the spring of 1941, spotted and launched her full air group of seventy-

three aircraft (four eighteen-plane squadrons plus the group commander) with full ordnance loads, i.e., torpedoes on the torpedo aircraft (TBDs) and 1,000-lb bombs on the dive-bombers (SBDs), and all in a single cycle. Arnold, who was CO of VB-5 at the time, was flying the lead SBD, which was spotted just behind the fighters. This exercise was done to achieve training for all pilots, even though it was realized that war requirements for search planes, combat air patrol (CAP), and antisubmarine patrol would probably never permit such a 100 percent launch of the air group.

31 Ugaki, p. 143.

32 It should be noted that at the Battle of Coral Sea, *Shōkaku* and *Zuikaku* in some cases apparently eschewed the usage of deckload strikes, instead spotting mixed strike packages. Their larger flight decks, particularly in comparison with the ships of CarDiv 2, apparently made this a more attractive option.

33 Nagumo Report, pp. 5–6; Japanese Monograph No. 93, p. 27.

34 *Senshi Sōsho,* vol. 26, pp. 591, 624. We are grateful to Michael Wenger for his insights on *Kidō Butai*'s training prior to the Indian Ocean operation.

35 The composition of the dive-bomber units was as follows:
      Akagi: Eighteen pilots (fourteen Pearl Harbor vets plus four new pilots)
      Kaga: Eighteen pilots (eleven Pearl Harbor vets plus seven new pilots)
      Hiryū: Eighteen pilots (thirteen Pearl Harbor vets plus five new pilots)
      Sōryū: Seventeen pilots (twelve Pearl Harbor vets plus five new pilots) plus two D4Y crew members, who presumably were veterans, because they had served with *Sōryū* previously.
   Grand total: seventy-two pilots, of which at least fifty (and probably fifty-one), were Pearl Harbor veterans. We are grateful to James Sawruk for his insights into these matters.

36 The composition of the attack plane units was as follows:
      Akagi: Eighteen pilots (all Pearl Harbor vets)
      Kaga: Twenty-eight pilots (twenty-one Pearl Harbor vets plus seven new pilots)
      Hiryū: Eighteen pilots (fifteen Pearl Harbor vets plus thee new pilots)
      Sōryū: Eighteen pilots (sixteen Pearl Harbor vets plus two new pilots)
   Grand total: eighty-two pilots, of which seventy were Pearl Harbor veterans. We are grateful to James Sawruk for his insights into these matters.

37 We are grateful to Allan Alsleben and James Sawruk for their insights on the arcane areas of Japanese aircraft production during the war. The following section regarding Japanese carrier air complements is drawn heavily from their e-mail communications to Jon Parshall, January 22–24, 2002.

38 Source: USSBS, Nav. 50, pp. 202–6, and supplemental figures provided by Allan Alsleben.

39 Figures on Japanese aircraft production are to be found in USSBS 22, Nav 50, and also wartime reports from the Japanese Munitions Ministry, which were forwarded to me by Allan Alsleben.

40 *Kidō Butai*'s Pearl Harbor actual aircraft complements are an arcane debate unto themselves, but for the purposes of argument, we use the following figures: *Akagi* eighteen plus three VF, eighteen VB, twenty-seven VT (sixty-three active aircraft plus three spare aircraft); *Kaga* twenty-one VF, twenty-seven VB, twenty-seven VT (seventy-five aircraft); *Sōryū* eighteen plus three VF, eighteen plus three VB, eighteen plus three VT (fifty-four active aircraft plus nine spare aircraft); *Hiryū* eighteen plus three VF, eighteen plus three VB, eighteen plus three VT (fifty-four active aircraft plus nine spare aircraft). Willmott, *Pearl Harbor*, pp. 185–89. Spare aircraft were normally kept disassembled and stowed in storage spaces on board ship. In the case of *Hiryū* and *Sōryū* this was mandatory—there was simply no place to put more aircraft in the hangars.

41 Determining the exact number of aircraft carried by *Kidō Butai* into battle in June 1942 is not an easy task. Much of the information contained in the older secondary accounts is grossly incorrect, and even the information found in the official Japanese war history series leaves much to be desired. However, on the basis of the original carrier action reports and other supporting documents, it is possible to present what we believe to be a definitive accounting of the matter that supersedes all previously published histories of the battle.

42 Recent research by James Sawruk has indicated that these two spare dive-bombers may have been two aircraft from *Sōryū* displaced to make way for the two prototype D4Y being carried. *Sōryū*'s hangars were the most cramped of the four carriers, and computer-generated stowage diagrams of her hangars strongly indicate that carrying twenty assembled dive-bombers, in addition to her augmented fighter group, was out of the question. Temporarily moving these two aircraft to *Kaga* would have allowed them to be carried fully assembled, making for an easier transfer back to *Sōryū* after the battle. It seems logical that this would have been seen as preferable to disassembling the aircraft and storing them on board *Sōryū*. However, it is likely that their aircrews were not on board *Kaga,* meaning that they could not have been used in the

battle (unless *Kaga* had spare aircrews). However, the possibility also remains that these two aircraft were not from *Sōryū* at all, but were merely Type 99s intended for usage by 6th *Kū* on Midway.

43 Experimental Model 13 Carrier Bomber (D4Y1) as reconnaissance aircraft. Preproduction aircraft models were not given a Type number until they were formally accepted into service. Until that time, they were referred to by their experimental *shi*-number, which indicated the date the initial contract for the aircraft was let. The D4Y was accepted for service as the Type 2 Carrier Bomber in July 1942.

44 *Senshi Sōsho,* p. 238.

45 6th *Kū*'s establishment on 20 May 1942 was composed of fifty-six Zero pilots, six C5M Type 98 reconnaissance plane pilots, and ten recon observers. Of the Zero pilots, twenty-five were classified as "Class A" pilots in terms of their training, with the remaining thirty-one being "Class C." All of them were probably capable of taking off from a carrier, but it is unknown how many could perform a carrier landing. The "Class C" pilots almost certainly could not have performed a carrier landing. Source: "Private Memo of Captain Shibata Fumio," held in personal collection of James Sawruk.

46 Willmott, *Pearl Harbor,* pp. 185–89.

47 *Junyō* and *Ryūjō*'s *kōdōchōshos* (detailed air group reports), located in JSDF Archives, held in private collection of James Sawruk. It is probable that there were additional 6th *Kū* aviators on board *Junyō* as well, but they may not have been carrier qualified, and hence were unable to participate in carrier air operations.

48 There is a certain amount of speculation involved in the numbers of aircraft carried on board ship, in that they are based on the numbers of pilots who are known to have actually flown a mission, according to the ship's *kōdōchōshos*. Given the already understrength nature of these air groups, it is likely that both *Junyō* and *Ryūjō* were operating every aircraft they had on board.

49 *Ryūjō* had gone to war with a fighter unit flying obsolete A5M4 Type 96 fighters. Despite having been heavily involved in operations in the southern region, she had been forced to fight with these for the first five months of the conflict. *Ryūjō* had finally replaced her Type 96s with new Zeros when she returned to Kure on 23 April, meaning that her fighter pilots had been using their new mounts for about a month. However, her attack aircraft were still a mixed bag of B5N2 and the older B5N1 Type 97 attack aircraft. At the time of Midway, against a nominal complement of forty-two aircraft, she had only thirty aircraft on board—twelve Zeros and eighteen Type 97s—and a similar number of pilots. This counts only the pilots named on her official rosters. However, her *kōdōchōshos* make it clear that she never operated more than nine Zeros and eighteen Type 97s at any one time during the battle—a strong indication as to her depleted air strength. Some sources list *Ryūjō* as carrying six aircraft of 6th *Kū* as well. However, noted researcher James Sawruk saw no evidence of this in her war records, and indeed such a total would raise the number of 6th *Kū* aircraft nominally involved in the battle to thirty-nine—an odd number not usually associated with standard air group organizational structures. Source: *Junyō* and *Ryūjō*'s *kōdōchōshos* (detailed air group reports), located in JSDF Archives, held in private collection of James Sawruk.

50 *Zuihō* was probably the worst off of the lot in terms of aircraft. She was also operating a mixed air group of six Type 96 fighters; six Zeros, which had just been put on board; and twelve Type 97 attack aircraft during Midway. Not only that, but her air wing at this time was composed of instructor pilots scraped up from various training commands. (*Maru Special* #38, March 1980, p. 8. We are grateful to Allan Alsleben for this insight.) Her sister, *Shōhō,* had been sunk the month before at Coral Sea, carrying just nine Zeros, four Type 96 fighters, and six Type 97 torpedo bombers—a pitifully small contingent for a carrier capable of carrying thirty aircraft. Source: Katsura Rihei, *Kubo Zuihō no Sogai,* p. 60. Courtesy James Sawruk.

CHAPTER 6: FOG AND FINAL PREPARATIONS

1 Lundstrom, *First South Pacific Campaign,* p. 150.

2 Layton, p. 408.

3 Lundstrom, *First South Pacific Campaign,* p. 150; Layton, p. 412.

4 Lundstrom, *First South Pacific Campaign,* p. 155.

5 Layton, pp. 421–22.

6 John Lundstrom, in *Quarterdeck and Bridge: Two Centuries of American Naval Leaders,* ed. James Bradford (Annapolis, MD: Naval Institute Press, 1996), p. 337.

7 Prange, p. 104; Willmott, *Barrier and the Javelin,* pp. 302–5, 337; Layton, pp. 409–25.

8 Layton, p. 425.

9 Lord, pp. 34–38.

10 We are grateful to U.S. Naval Historical Center historian Robert Cressman for his clarification regarding *Yorktown*'s entry into dry dock.

11 Some VF-42 pilots and maintenance personnel remained on board. E-mail from Robert Cressman, January 24, 2005.

12 *Yorktown* also carried three additional nonoperational aircraft; two F4F and one TBD triced up in the hangar overhead.

13 *Hornet* technically had thirty-seven dive-bombers, but one was left behind at Pearl Harbor, and another was lost en route to Point Luck.

14 Prange, pp. 65, 135.

15 We draw heavily on David Bergamini, *Japan's Imperial Conspiracy* (New York: William & Morrow Company, 1971), pp. 922–23.

16 Prange, p. 32.

17 Ibid., p. 32.

18 Orita Zenji and Joseph Harrington, *I-Boat Captain* (Canoga Park, CA: Major Books, 1976), pp. 62–66.

19 Ibid., p. 62.

20 Lord, p. 44; Fuchida, p. 128.

21 Bergamini, p. 923.

22 Ibid.

23 Ugaki, p. 142.

24 Ugaki, p. 131; Fuchida, p. 110.

25 Ugaki, p. 131.

26 Willmott, *Barrier and the Javelin,* pp. 347–49.

27 Prange, p. 137.

28 Ugaki, p. 131.

29 Fuchida, p. 116.

30 Nagumo Report, p. 3.

31 Fuchida, p. 113, asserts that *Akagi*'s radio reception capability was limited.

32 *Operational History of Japanese Naval Communications, December 1941–August 1945* (Laguna Hills, CA: Aegean Park Press, 1985), p. 104.

33 Ibid., p. 256.

34 Ibid.

35 Lacroix, p. 518. *Tone*-class cruisers had two transmitting rooms, two receiving rooms, two radio telephone rooms, and a radio direction-finding room equipped with an RDF unit mounted atop the foremast.

36 Ibid., pp. 200–201.

37 Fuchida, p. 111; Ugaki, p. 131.

38 Interestingly, the centralized communications model used by the Japanese at this point in the war was incapable of handling the increasingly heavy demands placed on it by the war and was shifted to a more decentralized model in June 1943. *Operational History of Japanese Naval Communications,* pp. 46–47.

39 *Akagi* detailed action report, p. 4a. Extract Translation from DOC No. 160985B—MC 397.901. JD-1 reel.

40 Ugaki, p. 131.

41 It is true that *Akagi*'s logs do not reveal any knowledge of the attacks against Tanaka's Invasion Force (described shortly) that were to occur the day before the battle. However, Kusaka indicated afterward that Nagumo was aware that the Invasion Force had been discovered. Prange, p. 176.

42 Ugaki, p. 131.

43 Ikari Yoshiro, *Kaigun Kugishō* (Tokyo: Kōjinsha, 1989), pp. 353–54. We are grateful to Osamu Tagaya for supplying us with the actual wording for these paragraphs.

44 Fog steaming conditions are described in Goldstein and Dillon, p. 185.

45 At least this is Fuchida's assertion (p. 115). We are not convinced that zigzagging would have been feasible as the weather continued to worsen.

46 Lord, p. 56. This practice may not have been as outlandish as it appeared, as the Japanese typically wear slippers indoors and keep their shoes near the entranceway of dwellings.

47 *Operational History of Japanese Naval Communications,* p. 41.

48 Fuchida, p. 116.

49 *Operational History of Japanese Naval Communications,* p. 41. Most accounts have the turn itself occurring at 1030. We prefer the message syntax given in this source, because it fixes a definite time for the turn, as well as giving all ships in the command adequate time to prepare for the maneuver, which necessarily had to be accomplished under very hazardous circumstances.

50 In fact, they were not. The Americans did not detect this transmission.

51 All Imperial Navy warships kept Tokyo time, regardless of what time zone they were operating in. Midway was three hours ahead of Tokyo.

52 Fuchida, pp. 131–33.

53 USF-74, the standard U.S. naval doctrine of the same period, is silent on the topic of two-phase searches.

54 "Research on Mobile Force Tactics" (Yokosuka #45, May 1943). This doctrinal study prescribes a search with the first wave launched two hours before dawn.

55 Message from James Sawruk to Parshall, June 1, 2001. Fuchida, p. 177, commenting on Nagumo's chances for a night battle, remarks, "It would take more than good luck for our Force, with no radar and only one night-scouting plane, to find and successfully engage this enemy." The night scout referred to is certainly *Nagara*'s, and other Japanese sources indicate that E11As were used in this role by light cruiser DesDiv leaders at this time.

56 Message to Parshall from James Sawruk, May 7, 2001. Japanese records seem to indicate that one of *Tone*'s floatplanes may have been either missing or out of service for some reason and was not used during the battle. While these records are somewhat sketchy, it appears that *Tone* only used four of her recon aircraft (counting both Type 95 and Type 0) on 4 June.

57 We are grateful to James Sawruk and Eric Bergerud for sharing their insights on this matter.

58 The reader will note that the American SBD scouting squadrons flew at much higher altitudes, as per USF-74 doctrine.

59 We are grateful to James Sawruk, the guru of PBY operations during the war, for his insights into these matters in an e-mail dated January 22, 2001.

60 Prange, p. 185.

61 Ibid., p 186.

62 Ibid., p. 176.

63 Goldstein and Dillon, p. 199.

64 Ibid, p. 212; USSBS Nav. No. 60, p. 252.

Chapter 7: Morning Attack—0430–0600

1 From this point forward, we will refer to *Kidō Butai*'s time in terms of Midway local, so as to facilitate the comparison of this narrative's events with those found in other Western accounts of the battle.

2 Civil twilight (the first moment when the horizon ought to be discernable) was at 0423 local that morning.

3 The wake-up time is somewhat speculative, based on working backward from the known task list that had to be accomplished before takeoff.

4 Goldstein and Dillon, p. 191.

5 Ugaki, p. 134.

6 Paul Kennedy, *The Rise and Fall of the Great Powers: Economic Change and Military Conflict from 1500 to 2000* (New York: Random House, 1988), p. 391.

7 There were exceptions to this practice. It is clear that the carriers of *Kidō Butai* used deck parks during their transit to the Pearl Harbor raid—their normal air wings having been strengthened to the point that it was impossible to stow all their aircraft below. In that case, the Japanese had carried those aircraft slated for their first-wave attacks on the flight deck. CarDiv 5 also used deck parks during the Indian Ocean raids.

8 Hasegawa Tōichi, *Nihon no Kōkūbōkan* (Japanese aircraft carriers) (Tokyo: Guranpuri Shuppan, 1997), p. 157.

9 The correct launching brackets had presumably been attached on the previous day as a result of the orders to the fleet. The same was likely true for the *tokaki* on the Type 97 aircraft aboard CarDiv 1—having been designated for the antiship strike, these planes would have been fitted with the mounting hardware necessary to carry Type 91 torpedoes.

10 Hyōdō Nisohachi, letter to Parshall, February 1, 2001.

11 The wings of its American counterpart, the SBD Dauntless, did not fold at all.

12 We are grateful to aviation historian Hyōdō Nisohachi for providing much of the detailed information on carrier spotting and launch procedures that is presented in this chapter.

13 David Dickson, "Fighting Flattops: The *Shōkakus*," *Warship International* 1 (1977): p. 18.

14 Three cycles. Japanese elevators were electrically driven. *Kaga*'s three elevators could move at thirty-five meters per minute at bow, at forty m/m at amidships, at forty-four m/m at stern. These were relatively slow speeds, compared to the fifty meters per minute of the *Shōkaku*-class carriers. Hyōdō, letter to Parshall, February 12, 2001, and Dickson, p. 18. The *Lexington* and *Saratoga*, contemporaries of Japan's CarDiv 1, suffered from similar problems with their lifts.

15 Unlike some American aircraft, early-war Japanese planes did not have powered folding wings.

16 Unlike the Americans, Japanese carriers, even at the end of the war, did not employ jeeps or other powered vehicles for flight deck spotting purposes.

17 *Senshi Sōsho,* p. 294; Kimata Jiro, *Nihon no Kōkūbokan* ("Japanese Aircraft Carriers"), p. 267. It should be noted that there is no universal agreement on the nature of this formation. ATIG Report No. 1, p. 2, and USSBS Nav. No. 4, p. 1 (interview with Captain Aoki of *Akagi*) describe a formation wherein the carriers are in two columns 2,000 meters apart, with division leaders separated from their division mate by 5,000 meters. Furthermore, *Kirishima* is reported to be leading the heavy units in the formation, with *Haruna* trailing. ATIG Report No. 2 and USSBS interview Nav. No. 1, p. 1, given by Amagai Takahisa (*Kaga*'s air officer) describes the same formation. However, it needs to be understood that these particular ATIG and USSBS interviews were, in fact, given on the same date, to a large group of USN officers. Thus, these latter two sources are in essence the same statement, although ATIG is more detailed in terms of its treatment of carrier operations. Similarly, *Sōryū*'s air officer, Commander Ōhara, describes a formation in Nav. No. 39, p. 167. However, both of the formations described in these sources are more consistent with day steaming formations, rather than those for conducting flight operations. It's worth noting, too, that both statements were confused with regards to which battleships were present in the force in the first place, making it not unlikely that their relative places in the formation may have been transposed as well. In addition, Ōhara's diagram also shows oilers in the fleet train, which had been detached well before reaching the objective. In the final analysis, we give precedence to *Senshi Sōsho* in this, as in most matters. It also jibes with the Hawaii and Coral Sea operations, wherein the Japanese typically kept a distance of at least 7,000 meters between their carriers.

18 *Akagi* battle report, pp. 8, 11, 25.

19 Willmott, *Barrier and the Javelin,* p. 372.

20 Conversation with Eric Bergerud, June 2, 2000; e-mail from Clint Bauer, June 7, 2000. It is important to note that the warm-up of aircraft engines occurred considerably before the aircrew manned their planes. This is a correction to the existing Western record extant in such books as Lord and Prange, as well as Fuchida's rendition of events.

21 American carriers, with their open-sided hangars, could warm up their planes below the flight deck. This was a major contributor to faster deck cycles aboard American carriers. In some cases, American aircraft were warmed up, loaded on an elevator with the engines still running, taxied under their own power onto the flight deck, and then took off directly. Such an abbreviated takeoff cycle was impossible on British and Japanese carriers.

22 Japanese carriers typically had only a single briefing room for their aircrews.

23 Lord, p. 90, says that Genda had a cold. Other accounts maintain that he actually had pneumonia.

24 The Japanese used the concept of a "Point Option"—the point in the ocean where the carrier ought to be at any given time—in the same fashion as the USN.

25 Many of the conventional Western accounts refer to the Japanese flight decks as being floodlit during the morning's launch, with the lights supposedly turning "night into day" (Fuchida, p. 135), but this is erroneous. While Japanese carriers did carry powerful searchlights, the only lights on the flight deck routinely used during flight operations were not "floodlights" per se, but rather lamps set flush with the flight deck. These were intended to outline the deck and indicate important features, such as the aft edge of the flight deck and the position of the landing barriers. Floodlights would have required elevation above the flight deck, and no such array of light platforms or fixtures are to be found on detailed plans of Japanese aircraft carriers. Obviously, illuminating oneself brightly in enemy waters hardly made good sense, hence the hooding of the flight deck lights. The intensity of these lights could be adjusted by a rheostat located at the air control station. ATIG Report No. 2, p. 5, and ATIG Report No. 5, pp. 2–3.

26 Each Japanese carrier aircraft carried an identifying tail code, the first two letters of which specified the carrier division to which the plane belonged. The issue of which tail codes were used by *Hiryū* and *Sōryū* at the Battle of Midway has been complicated by the change of CarDiv 2's flagship from *Sōryū* to *Hiryū* in April of 1942. These issues are more fully discussed in appendix 10.

27 While specifics of battle speeds for 1942 *Kidō Butai* doctrine are unavailable, according to *4sf* Doctrine (promulgated on 27 November 1941 and probably similar to *Kidō Butai*'s operational practices in this regard), battle speed 1 = eighteen knots; battle speed 2 = twenty knots; battle speed 3 = twenty-two knots; battle speed 4 = twenty-four knots; battle speed 5 = twenty-eight knots; maximum battle speed = maximum speed of which ship is capable. It should be noted, however, that by 1944, *Kidō Butai* doctrine gives the following battle speeds: 1 = twenty knots, 2 = twenty-four knots, 3 = twenty-eight knots, 4 = thirty knots, 5 = thirty-two knots, with no maximum battle speed listed. However, given the relatively brisk wind in evidence on the morning of 4 June, there would have been no need to launch at higher speeds than twenty-two knots. Therefore, during the remainder of this book, we use 1942 *4sf* battle speeds. We are grateful to David Dickson for his insights into these matters.

28 "Battle Report of Battle of Midway," p. 14. It is possible that the wind was gusting, because a wind of 160 degrees would place it 30 degrees from starboard on the force's nominal heading of 130. This would represent a rather large amount of crosswind for launch. It is likely that the carriers deviated from their base course briefly to put the wind fine across their bows during the few minutes needed for launching.

29 Japanese carrier action reports, WDC 160985B, pp. 6, 11, 14.

30 ATIG Report No. 5, p. 3.

31 Unlike their Western counterparts, Japanese carriers did not use catapults. An underdeck, air-propelled catapult design was apparently developed in 1935 (at about the time of *Kaga*'s refit), but was not adopted owing to its complexity, and the belief at the time that such gear was unnecessary. This lack of foresight would hamper Japanese carrier operations using heavier aircraft as the war went on. ATIG Report No. 1, p. 3, and ATIG Report No. 7, p. 1.

32 The authors learned a great deal about Japanese deck-spotting activities by building accurate computer-aided spotting diagrams for the four carriers. By scanning the photographic record and using the computer diagrams to account for such factors as propeller clearance and the creation of unbroken acceleration paths for the outboard planes to the centerline, it was possible to determine how and where individual aircraft were spotted on each of the carriers. Furthermore, the characteristics of the carriers came more clearly into focus. *Kaga*'s low speed was a real detriment to effective torpedo aircraft operation. Conversely, her expansive flight deck, 100 feet in width, made it possible for her to spot aircraft in comfort. *Hiryū,* whose island was relatively further aft, undoubtedly suffered from cramped conditions as strike sizes exceeded twenty-four aircraft. Zeros must have been crammed in all around her island, and the relative narrowness of the flight deck meant that the island and the mainmast just aft of it was a real hazard when a pilot spotted on the port side of the flight deck began his acceleration toward the centerline and then down the deck. In this sense, the *Sōryū* was actually superior to her larger sister, in that her island was well forward, and therefore created no complications for the spotting process.

33 ATIG Report No. 2, p. 5.

34 The exact number of planes spotted at this time remains speculation. It would not have been unusual for a *chūtai* of nine fighters to have been spotted on each carrier. At a minimum, a *shōtai* of three would have been spotted and readied by each, so as to be available for a speedy takeoff if needed.

35 PO1c Takahashi Toshio (pilot), Ens. Akamatsu Saku (observer), PO3c Koyama Tomio (radioman).

36 The U.S. Mk. 13, by contrast, was eight knots slower (33.5 knots), thereby ensuring that firing runs had to be made at short ranges and high angles of interception. (Indeed, the faster carriers of CarDiv 2 could literally outrun this weapon.) Worse, the American torpedo was limited to a maximum drop height of fifty feet at 110 knots, thereby ensuring a nearly suicidal attack profile for the American torpedo aircraft that would carry it. The Type 91, by contrast, could be dropped from as high as 1,000 feet or as fast as 260 knots, although the Japanese considered a drop height of 330 feet at 180 knots to be optimal. John Campbell, *Naval Weapons of World War Two* (London: Conway Maritime Press, 1985), p. 159; U.S. Naval Technical Mission to Japan, "Japanese Torpedoes and Tubes-Articles I, Ship and Kaiten Torpedoes," Report O-01-2 (Hereafter "NavTechJap O-01-2"), p. 8.

37 NavTechJap Report O-01-2, p. 12.

38 Letter from Hyōdō to Parshall, March 12, 2001.

39 Ibid. There is some degree of speculation in this assertion. Even though the Japanese did not expect enemy vessels in the area, they had to assume the worst, meaning that a capital-ship depth setting was most likely selected.

40 Confirmation of this point is to be found in the carrier records, which make it clear that the flight decks were in very heavy use during the morning, particularly from 0730 onward.

41 Yoshida Akihiko letter to Parshall, March 31, 2001.

42 Japanese doctrine of the time specified that capital ships (including heavy cruisers) could not be sunk by dive-bomber weapons, and that torpedoes were to be used (Tagaya, communication to Parshall, August 10, 2004). The torpedo aircraft were about to take off when word came back that the dive-bombers had, in fact, sunk the enemy cruisers. Given that torpedoes could not be brought back aboard the ship once their plane was launched, Egusa's timely message ended up saving CarDiv 5 from wasting thirty-six precious torpedoes. We are grateful to Michael Wenger for his insights on this matter.

43 Peattie, p. 145; Goldstein and Dillon, pp. 34-35.

44 Goldstein and Dillon, p. 35.

45 The pronunciation of Amari's first name is unknown, and may well have been Kiyoshi or Yoji. We appreciate James Sawruk's insights on this matter.

46 One of the reasons hinted at in some interviews with Japanese survivors related to the authors by James Sawruk, is that a matter of "face"—perhaps related to the incompetence of *Tone*'s catapult officer to

properly launch the craft, an unwillingness on the part of other enlisted members of the crew to assist him (and thereby embarrass him), and a consequent delay in making this failure known—may have been involved. However, neither Sawruk nor the authors have been able to verify these details, and they must therefore remain unsubstantiated, plausible as they may seem.

47 Interview with Iwao Konishi, former seaplane pilot aboard *Chitose,* courtesy of John Bruning Jr. Bruning Collection, Hoover Institute.

48 Prange, p. 185.

49 Ibid., p. 185.

50 Account of Lt. Yasukuni Nagatomo, *Hiryū* starboard gunnery officer, in *Shōgen Midowei Kaisen,* pp. 212–27.

51 This plane, flown by Lt. Howard P. Ady, had sent a sighting report at 0534, indicating the presence of two Japanese carriers. Robert Cressman, Steve Ewing et al., *A Glorious Page in Our History: The Battle of Midway* (Missoula, MT: Pictorial Histories Publishing Company, 1990), p. 59.

52 It remains one of the great mysteries of the battle as to what, exactly, *Tone's* No. 4 aircraft thought he was seeing when he made this transmission. *Senshi Sōsho* (p. 307) even goes so far as to aver that the message was logged incorrectly, and that it was *Tone's* No. 1 plane (flying search line No. 3) that was transmitted. However, *Senshi Sōsho* is wrong on this point, because American radio intelligence picked up *Tone* No. 4's signal, as well as Amari's particular call sign (MEKU 4), at exactly 0555. (HYPO Log, p. 499.) But even accounting for the fact that this aircraft appears to have flown a badly distorted search route, he still should have been some sixty to seventy-five miles north of whatever strike aircraft the Americans were currently sending after *Kidō Butai.* It is possible that he saw an American PBY search plane, or perhaps more than one, but he certainly didn't see fifteen of them grouped in such a manner.

53 Cressman et al., pp. 59–61.

54 Prange, p. 190.

55 Cressman et al., p. 60.

56 Prange, p. 190.

57 Cressman et al., p. 84.

58 Lundstrom, *First Team,* p. 332.

Chapter 8: A Lull before the Storm—0600–0700

1 Ugaki, p. 129; Lacroix and Wells, pp. 775–76.

2 Recent works on the Imperial Japanese Navy have suggested that *Hiryū* actually carried an experimental set at Midway as well. However, this is not true, and the topic is dealt with in appendix 7, "Japanese Radar at the Battle of Midway."

3 It is known that Japanese land-based Zero groups sometimes removed their radios altogether.

4 *Kaga* air group report, p. 19.

5 Peattie, pp. 147–48.

6 Research on Mobile Force Tactics, p. 15, a document issued by the Yokosuka *Kōkūtai* (which was the Imperial Japanese Navy's think tank for aerial doctrine) in August 1943, featured carriers protected by a circle of destroyers. No distances were specified between the escorts and the carrier, and there typically were six ships on the perimeter of the ring. Cruisers and battleships were still not part of the tactical AA mix, with the cruisers still being used in a scouting role.

7 The orders for her refit, according to her former gunnery officer in an article in *Maru* magazine in the 1970s, had already been cut. We are grateful to noted researcher and modeler Uchiyama Muttsuo for his insights into this matter in a series of correspondences dated November 25, 2003.

8 Much of this discussion is based on John Campbell's *Naval Weapons of World War II,* pp. 178, 192–94. At least one source cites *Sōryū* as having Type 91 as well, and that may well have been the case at the time of her launching. However, from the photographic record available, it appears that she was equipped with Type 94 by the time of the outbreak of the war.

9 At Midway, *Yorktown* and *Enterprise* were equipped with the older Mk. 33 fire-control system. The newer *Hornet* was equipped with Mk. 37. E-mail from Cressman, January 25, 2005.

10 Campbell, p. 178.

11 Hyōdō Nisohachi, essay on automatic weapons prepared for Jon Parshall, May 1, 2002.

12 The newer *Shōkaku* and *Zuikaku* had the ability to direct four batteries of two five-inch mounts apiece, which doubled the number of targets their five-inch guns could engage.

13 "IJN Diversion Attack Force Doctrine (1-1-44)." Courtesy David Dickson.

14 "USF 10A—Current Tactical Orders and Doctrine (2-1-44)."

15 These included an SBD lost while diving on *Kaga* and a B-26 shot down by *Akagi*.

16 The Americans lost a minimum of six aircraft from crash landings on June 4.

17 *Senshi Sōsho*, vol. 29, p. 653. We are deeply grateful to Michael Wenger, who shared excerpts from his forthcoming book on the Indian Ocean campaign, for his insights into these matters.

18 Four Blenheims were shot down by the CAP, another was lost when it ran into a returning Japanese air strike, one crash landed, and two more were damaged. Seventeen British aircrew were killed. One *Hiryū* Zero was shot down. We are grateful to Mark Horan for his insights into this action.

19 *Senshi Sōsho*, vol. 29, p. 653.

20 *Akagi* Action Report, p. 6.

21 We thank Alan Zimm for positing this explanation of Amari's actions.

22 Research by James Sawruk indicates that a VP-23 PBY piloted by James J. Murphy had an encounter with a Japanese floatplane. Given the search line of the PBY in question (336 degrees from Midway) and the time of the encounter, it seems likely that the plane was Amari's. The Japanese aircraft ducked into clouds to avoid the PBY, which likewise declined to pursue a fight. This evasive maneuver might also have disoriented Amari's pilot, causing him to fly his subsequent route incorrectly.

23 *Senshi Sōsho*, p. 309.

Chapter 9: The Enemy Revealed—0700–0800

1 Combat Intelligence Communications Intelligence Summary (hereafter referred to as "HYPO log"), Record Group 457, SRMN-012, p. 500.

2 Ibid. Imperial Japanese Navy ships kept Tokyo time wherever they were, so 0400 was 0700 local. We are grateful to John Lundstrom for his insights into this matter.

3 Ikuhiko Hata and Yasuho Izawa, *Japanese Naval Aces and Fighter Units in World War II*. Trans. Don Gorham (Annapolis, MD: Naval Institute Press, 1989), pp. 355–56.

4 The reader is advised to refer to Appendix 3 for details on the Japanese air unit launches and recoveries.

5 Kaneko, by the same token, was also given credit for two "large torpedo planes" this morning; clearly a reference to his actions against the B-26s. Hata and Izawa, pp. 355–56.

6 Fujita would be credited with seven kills this day (including partials), an exaggeration, but was clearly a prominent contributor to the CAP's activities during the morning's actions. Hata and Izawa, p. 326.

7 Account of Nagayasu Yasukuni, *Shōgen Midowei Kaisen*, pp. 212–27.

8 In fact, the pilot of this Avenger, Ens. Albert K. Earnest, managed to regain control of his aircraft—the only Avenger to return to base.

9 Mount No. 2 was the twin 25 mm farthest forward on the port side.

10 This aircraft was almost certainly piloted by 1st Lt. Herbert Mayes. It is likely that his aircraft had taken damage from both CAP fighters and AA. Mark Horan, e-mail to Parshall, March 31, 2002.

11 Prange, per Genda statement, p. 214.

12 Ibid., per Kusaka statement, p. 215.

13 Nagumo Report, p. 14.

14 Fuchida, pp. 136, 143. Why Fuchida recalled the reserve strike force being brought to the flight deck immediately after the morning launch is unclear. Every other Japanese source on the matter of rearming—ATIG reports, *Senshi Sōsho*, and letters from Japanese survivors such as *Hiryū*'s Arimura (a bomber maintenance chief)—make it clear that arming was performed in the hangars.

15 *Akagi* and *Kaga*, it will be recalled, had launched one *kankō* apiece for the morning's scouting missions, reducing the total number of aircraft in CarDiv 1's *kankōtai* from forty-five (twenty-seven on *Kaga*, eighteen on *Akagi*) to forty-three. *Akagi*'s B5N would return at 0740 and would have been rearmed as well. It is unclear when *Kaga*'s B5N, commanded by WO Yoshino Haruo, returned to the ship, but from Yoshino's accounts, it was likely later, during the American attacks on *Kidō Butai* that occurred after 0800.

16 The Type 91 torpedo was secured by widely spaced mounting brackets that kept the weapon at a slight downward incline to ensure a proper entry angle into the water. The *tokaki* that held the Type 80 general-purpose bomb, in contrast, were closer together. Not only that, but since the two weapons had different diameters, the hardware had to be differently curved to match their exteriors.

17 This is speculation, but it fits the evidence. The operation that consumed the majority of the time on the hangar decks during rearming was not removing or stowing ordnance, it was changing out the *tokaki*. The armorers had plenty of time to stow bombs below had they wished to. However, the bomb rooms were extremely cramped working spaces; stowing torpedoes while simultaneously retrieving bombs and sending them up would have been almost impossible. As a result the bottleneck in the stowage of munitions very likely resided in the bowels of the ship among the overworked magazine crews, not on the

hangars. Given this, the armorers would have little choice but to stow the munitions near the bomb lift and get on with their work, with the intent of passing the munitions below when the opportunity arose.

18 In point of fact, one can postulate arming models wherein the carts were used between more than one *chūtai* at a time. The authors constructed models of these much more complex process flows to optimize the use of the scarce resource in the process—the carts. However, the added complexity of this approach was hardly worth the effort, because it entailed additional internal elevator moves and wait times at the ordnance lifts. The authors consider it unlikely in the extreme that the Japanese would have taken this approach, or even have conceived of it. This was, after all, the 1940s, and sophisticated shop-floor flow management techniques were yet to be invented.

19 The fact that this plane landed a mere three hours after being launched is odd. The cruising speed of the Type 97 was 138 knots. Even accounting for the fact that *Kidō Butai* had moved to the southeast for the last three hours, thereby cutting perhaps sixty miles off Suzuki's return trip, there was no way he should have covered 600-some miles in just three hours. By all rights, he should have returned an hour and a half hence. Either *Akagi*'s records for the landing time of this aircraft are incorrect, or Suzuki had not flown his route correctly. In the absence of any additional evidence, it is impossible to know which.

20 Nagumo Report, pp. 7, 15.

21 Ibid., p. 15.

22 *Senshi Sōsho,* p. 313; Fuchida, p. 147, asserts that these rearming operations were merely "suspended," not reversed. However, given the lack of reliability of Fuchida, we hew to *Senshi Sōsho*'s version of events.

23 Dallas Isom, "The Battle of Midway: Why the Japanese Lost," U.S. Naval War College *Review* (Summer 2000).

24 Japanese Monograph No. 93, p. 38. It should be noted that a delay in communications was certainly conceivable. There had already been similar delays in transmission of other messages to the Japanese flagship this morning. There are good reasons for some of these delays. Incoming coded signals arrived by radiotelegraph, which had a rate of transmission of about seventy characters per minute at best (Peattie, p. 160). Thereafter, the message had to be decoded, transcribed, and taken to the bridge. As an example of this, Commander Ogawa's message that Sand Island had been bombed with "great results" had actually been sent *before* Tomonaga's signal announcing that a second attack against Midway was needed. But in the process of being translated (or perhaps even relayed from *Kaga*) over to the flagship, Ogawa's report had actually arrived on *Akagi*'s bridge seven minutes after Tomonaga's, and some twenty-seven minutes after it was first broadcast. Why Tomonaga's message, which presumably was also sent first to his mother ship—the *Hiryū*—made it over to *Akagi* first is unknown. It is likely that Tomonaga transmitted directly to *Akagi*. Alternately, *Hiryū*'s radio watch may have been speedier than *Kaga*'s in passing messages up the line.

25 HYPO Log, p. 500. We are grateful to John Lundstrom for pointing this out to us.

26 Isom, p. 18.

27 We are grateful to John Lundstrom for his insights regarding American carrier flag facilities, derived from his copious research on Admiral Frank Jack Fletcher.

28 Ryūnosuke Kusaka, *Rengō Kantai* (Combined Fleet) (Tokyo: Mainichi Newspaper Co., 1952), pp. 83–84; Prange, p. 223.

29 *Senshi Sōsho,* p. 282. We are grateful to Uchiyama Mutsuo for his insights into these matters.

30 Willmott, *Barrier and the Javelin,* p. 389.

31 Ibid, p. 388. Although Nagumo didn't know it, this was precisely what was happening, as TF 16 was in the middle of its launch.

32 Prange, per Kusaka statement, p. 217.

33 *Senshi Sōsho,* p. 282.

34 These were the oiler *Neosho* and the destroyer *Sims*. Both were sunk, although *Neosho* remained floating for some days before her ultimate demise at the hands of friendly vessels, allowing some men from both crews to be rescued.

35 Japanese fuel tanks were not self-sealing, meaning that even so much as a single bullet to a wing tank could lead to the loss of half of a plane's fuel load.

36 Depending on when WO Yoshino Haruo landed his Type 97 aircraft, which had been involved in scouting operations during the morning.

37 This number would have been eighteen aircraft, if not for the probable replacement of two of *Sōryū*'s squadron by the experimental Type 2 bombers being used in the reconnaissance role.

38 We assume that the absence of Yoshino's Type 97 would not affect the rearming of other *chūtai* during this period.

39 Fuchida, p. 203.

40 Ugaki, p. 144.

41 We are grateful to Commander John Kuehn, USN, an instructor at the Army's Staff College, for his insights into these matters, particularly with regards to modern U.S. carrier doctrinal approach to mixed fleet defense/strike operations.

42 Fuchida, pp. 149–50.

43 Isom, p. 14.

44 *Zuikaku* kōdōchōshos, JD-1 reel. We are grateful to James Sawruk for his insights on this matter. The same accident would occur later on board USS *Enterprise* in the Battle of the Eastern Solomons.

45 It might be argued that aircraft on the flight deck would be easier to set ablaze than aircraft in the hangar. However, as we shall see, the danger posed to the structure of the ship by explosive ordnance detonating in the confined spaces of the hangars was much greater than ordnance whose explosive power would be vented at least partially into the atmosphere.

46 Prange, per Kusaka statement, p. 233.

47 *Senshi Sōsho,* p. 282; Nagumo Report, p. 18. We thank Osamu Tagaya for clarifying this matter.

48 Fuchida, pp. 152–53.

49 Lundstrom, *First Team,* p. 336.

50 Willmott, *Barrier and the Javelin,* p. 397, notes this logical inconsistency in Fuchida's arguments as well.

51 In actuality, the task force centered around *Yorktown* was at this moment a bit closer—about 175 miles away. For the sake of argument, we will also set aside the fact that *Tone* No. 4's self-reported position would shortly be shown to be grievously in error, meaning that the Japanese aircraft probably would *not* have found the target directly in any case.

52 Isom, p. 18.

CHAPTER 10: TRADING BLOWS—0800–0917

1 Nagayasu account, *Shōgen Midowei Kaisen.* Nagayasu claims that one American aircraft "self-exploded" (i.e., made a suicide crash) near *Hiryū,* but this is not directly substantiated by the American records.

2 Cressman, p. 81.

3 Given the lack of any photographs taken of *Kaga* by B-17s at this juncture—which photographed the other three carriers of *Kidō Butai*—it may simply have been that *Kaga* was temporarily hidden by cloud cover and was able to hold her course without fear of attack.

4 *Kaga* Battle Report, p. 11.

5 Yoshino Haruo account, contained in interviews done for the game "Aces of the Pacific." We are grateful to John Bruning Jr. for supplying these accounts. Bruning Collection, Hoover Institute.

6 Cressman, p. 81.

7 Prange, per Kusaka statement, p. 215.

8 Isom, pp. 18–19.

9 *Nautilus* Battle Report.

10 Ibid.

11 Ibid.

12 The circumstances surrounding the disappearance of both these SB2Us are somewhat mysterious, in that none of their squadron mates saw them go down. However, it seems likely that Zeros accounted for both aircraft.

13 *Kaga* Battle Report, p. 19.

14 Fuchida, p. 150; Nagayasu account, *Shōgen Midowei Kaisen.*

15 Cressman, p. 113.

16 Naval War College Analysis, p. 125.

17 Lundstrom, *First Team,* pp. 339–40.

18 Ibid., p. 340.

19 Cressman, p. 89.

20 For night landings, this same information could be conveyed by a set of colored lights located aft of the island. In addition, a white light in the center of the landing array could be used to blink messages to the incoming pilot. A line of red, blue, and white lights aligned fore and aft just abaft the island were used to indicate relative wind over the deck. The outline and centerline of the flight deck were illuminated in white lights, while crash barriers and the aft edge of the deck were indicated by transverse rows of red lights. Each bank of lights could be dimmed independently by rheostats. ATIG Report No. 1: 5; ATIG Report No. 2: 2; and ATIG Report No. 5: 2.

21 Map in *Kaga* action report, WDC160985, pp. 9, 11. It should be noted that this conflicts with the generally accepted direction of the wind, which has it blowing from the southeast. However, these estimates were usually made by American pilots from their cockpits as a result of observing wave directions and other

atmospheric phenomenon. As such, we set them aside in favor of *Kaga*'s official records, whose aviators were in a better position to observe the weather in proximity to their ship. The morning's wind conditions were quite variable, however, and would shift to the northeast within the next hour and a half.

22 The track chart included in the Nagumo Report is probably that of *Nagara*. For one thing, it shows the fleet on an evasive figure-eight course at 0832, at a time when we know from *Akagi*'s air group records that she was landing aircraft, and therefore had to be holding a steady course into the prevailing wind. Interestingly, too, at 1025, after *Akagi* had been bombed, the Nagumo Report course chart shows the fleet apparently continuing to make progress to the north and then looping back to the south. In fact, this movement is quite consistent with *Nagara*'s known movements, as she doubled back to take Admiral Nagumo off of *Akagi*, which was dead in the water. Likewise, the peculiar "dogleg" to the northwest shown in the track chart between 1630 and 1700 corresponds to when *Nagara* was involved in investigating downed U.S. aviators, whereas *Hiryū* should have been going due west at this time. It must be admitted that attempting to re-create *Akagi*'s movements from the Nagumo Report require some educated guesswork at times, particularly regarding her evasive maneuvers against VT-8 from 0920 to 0930. Interestingly, though, despite the differences in course headings, the two course tracks converge in the same general region by about 1020. This reinforces the notion that the scene of *Kidō Butai*'s fatal attack was indeed near the area that the Nagumo Report chart has indicated, although our derived course would place her roughly four nautical miles west-northwest of that given in the chart. We don't consider this degree of error extreme, given the navigational methods of the era, the large size of the formation (probably around twenty miles across, including the screening units), and the battle conditions then pertaining.

23 USSBS interviews of both Captain Aoki (*Akagi*) and *Kaga*'s *hikōchō* Amagai confirm this.

24 This is based on a detailed examination of the sighting reports from these units, as well as those of the American units that attacked them.

25 Fuchida, p. 145.

26 The latter resulted from the prewar Japanese phonetic spelling of her name as "Sa-u-ri-yu." See the illustrations in appendix 6 for details.

27 Carl Snow, "Japanese Carrier Operations: How Did *They* Do It?" *The Hook* (Spring 1995). The similarity of this system to the optical "call the ball" systems developed postwar by the Americans and British is notable. Whether either force was influenced by this much earlier Japanese invention is unknown.

28 Ibid.; Hasegawa, p. 167; and USNTMJ, Report A-11, pp. 15–18.

29 ATIG Report No. 2: 2.

30 ATIG Report No. 1: 5; ATIG Report No. 2: 2; ATIG Report No. 5: 3.

31 ATIG Report No. 5: 3.

32 Kōjinsha, vol. 6, p. 35.

33 ATIG Report No. 1: 5.

34 Kōjinsha, vol. 6, p. 35.

35 It is likely that Tanaka had become involved in CAP activities over the fleet upon his return from Midway and was mortally wounded in this way.

36 Captain Eric Brown, *Duels in the Sky* (Annapolis, MD: Naval Institute Press, 1988), pp. 68–72.

37 In the early stages of the Pacific war, aircraft arresting hooks were controlled by the pilot (in single-seat aircraft) or the observer crewman (in multiseat aircraft). However, later in the war, the hook apparatus was modified so that the deck crew was made responsible for releasing the hook. This was because the decline in the quality of aircrew training had led to an increase in deck accidents caused by premature hook release. ATIG Report No. 3: 1.

38 Each arresting wire was controlled by enlisted crewmen, whose stations were staggered port and starboard down the length of the flight deck. All crash barriers were controlled by a single enlisted man stationed on the port side of the flight deck, who received signals to raise and lower the barrier from the *hikōchō*. ATIG Report No. 2: 2.

39 Nagumo Report, p. 16. Unlike thinly clad high-explosive (land attack) bombs, semi armor-piercing bombs had heavier casings that were capable of defeating at least some thickness of armor steel. They would therefore penetrate more deeply into a ship's vitals before exploding.

40 Prange, per interview with Kuroshima, 28 November 1964, pp. 235–36.

41 *Nautilus* action report.

42 Ibid.

43 While speculative, it is possible that the aggressive Yamaguchi had anticipated that his urgent suggestion to Nagumo to launch a counterstrike would be accepted. If so, he might have begun spotting his dive-bombers in anticipation of an attack. When such an attack was not forthcoming, Yamaguchi would have

had to clear his flight decks to recover Tomonaga and *Hiryū*'s aircraft. We are grateful to John Lundstrom for pointing this out.

44 Lord, p. 174.

45 They subsequently refused capture and were killed on Kure by American troops after the battle.

46 Maruyama account, Hoover Institution, Bruning Collection.

47 Prange, per Genda statement, p. 251.

48 This is speculation, but we know that the Japanese used *chūtai* in exactly such a manner so as to preserve some level of target selection capability for the subunits in the *hikōtai*, yet retain sufficient power to hit a target heavily.

49 WDC160985, p. 30.

50 Ibid., pp. 6–9.

51 Ibid., p. 13.

52 Ibid., p. 21.

53 Ibid., p. 29.

54 Cressman, pp. 67–68.

55 Ibid.

56 This plane, piloted by Lt. Kikuchi Rokurō, had forced landed near Kure. Rather than being taken prisoner when American troops showed up to collect them, the crew committed suicide.

CHAPTER 11: FATAL COMPLICATIONS—0917–1020

1 When arming for antiship strikes, standard Japanese practice was to equip dive-bombers with a mixture of one third HE weapons (for flak suppression) and two thirds semi-AP weapons, which would do the greater damage to the ship itself.

2 Fuchida, p. 153. He was clearly taking the Nagumo Report at its word in this regard.

3 Nagumo Report, p. 7.

4 Lord, p. 139.

5 Legend has it that Waldron and Ring had an acrimonious discussion involving hand signals just before Waldron's departure. However, this appears unlikely, given the vast altitude differences between the two commanders' formations. However, several members of *Hornet*'s air group, including Ens. Ben Tappan, Ens. Humphrey L. Tallmann, Ens. Troy T. Guillory, and ARM2c Richard T. Woodson, all recalled hearing a heated radio conversation between the two men after takeoff, despite the conditions of radio silence then pertaining. Midway Roundtable Forum, January 23, 2005.

6 Lundstrom, *First Team,* p. 341; Cressman et al., p. 91.

7 Thaddeus Tuleja, *Climax at Midway* (New York: Norton, 1960), p. 211; George Gay, *Sole Survivor* (Naples, FL: Midway Publishers, 1979), p. 113.

8 VT-8 action report, as written by Ens. George Gay.

9 Hata and Izawa, p. 291. Taniguchi graduated from the 51st Pilot Training Class of June 1940.

10 Ibid., pp. 295–96. Yamamoto graduated from the 24th Pilot Training Class of July 1934.

11 Ibid., pp. 345–46. Originally an engineering enlisted man, Suzuki graduated from the 28th Pilot Training Class in August 1935. Iizuka, Suzuki, and their wingman, PO1c Nagahama Yoshikazu, had all participated in the morning attack on Midway but were now back in action a mere half hour after landing.

12 Which three pilots remains unclear.

13 Cressman et al., p. 92.

14 The grim demise of Waldron's command illuminates an interesting side issue. Unlike the USN, the vast majority of whose pilots were officers, the Imperial Navy employed a mixture of enlisted men and officer pilots in its carrier groups. Often, the rigid social hierarchies prevalent in Japanese society were mirrored in the pilot ranks as well, with officers holding themselves apart from the rank and file. This often rankled the enlisted men, and not without good reason. The truth of the matter was that the enlisted men were often the better pilots. On average, they possessed substantially greater stick time than the lieutenants who led them into battle. By the war's end, nine of Japan's top ten naval aces would come from the ranks. VT-8's destruction was a microcosm of this larger reality, as Waldron's squadron found itself confronted by a group of NCOs who wore their Zeros like second skins, and were deadly triggermen.

15 VT-8 action report. Cressman et al., p. 92. The Nagumo log mentions that *Akagi* commenced AA action to starboard at this time after commencing evasive actions in reaction to the same attack, meaning that she must have turned to port to unmask her batteries against the targets to her northeast.

16 Lundstrom, *First Team,* pp. 335–36.

17 Ibid., p. 342.

18 Ibid., pp. 344–45.

19 Ibid., p. 343.

20 Testimony of Kanazawa Hidetoshi, a *kankō* pilot, as related to Hyōdō Nisohachi. Correspondence with Hyōdō, June 2001. It is even possible that Yamaguchi had begun to arm his *kanbaku* as early as 0830, when Nagumo's order to arm carrier bombers with 250-kg weapons had been received, despite the fact that takeoff was not imminent.

21 *Nautilus* action report.

22 VT-6 action report. *Sōryū* and *Hiryū*'s relative positions are less easy to fix, though it seems likely they were in a rough line abreast northeast of CarDiv 1. *Sōryū* should have been leading her sister, but her more convoluted evasive maneuvers in the face of Waldron's attack may have slowed her relative speed of advance.

23 VT-6 action report clearly states that the Japanese carriers were on a westward course at the time they were first sighted. This makes sense in light of the fleet having evaded VT-8 by running away from Waldron's flight.

24 VT-6 action report.

25 Ibid.; Cressman et al., pp. 93–94.

26 Nagumo Report, p. 17, speaks of *Akagi* maneuvering at thirty knots.

27 VT-6's chart makes it clear that the lower left corner carrier of a triangle of three carriers headed west was their target. Since we know that this ship was *Kaga*, this also supports the supposition that Kidō Butai's carriers had evaded VT-8's attack by turning on their heels, rather than turning in formation.

28 We are grateful to Mark Horan for his insights and wording regarding this attack, drawn on personal interviews with two survivors of VT-6—Lt. Robert Laub and MACH Walter A. Winchell.

29 U.S. Naval War College Analysis, p. 128.

30 Lundstrom, *First Team,* pp. 343–44.

31 Sano had declined to land with the rest of his CAP patrol at 0952.

32 One of VT-6's aircraft would ditch on the return flight; its crew would be rescued after seventeen days at sea.

33 VT-6 action report, 2nd endorsement to action report.

34 Prange, via Genda's statement, p. 252.

35 Cressman et al., p. 94.

36 Eric Bergerud, in his excellent *Fire in the Sky,* makes it clear that aerial combat in the Pacific theater operated under a completely different set of unwritten rules than were followed in Europe. Pilots on both sides in the Pacific routinely did everything in their power to kill enemy aviators. Eric Bergerud, *Fire in the Sky* (Boulder, CO: Westview Press, 2000), pp. 424–428.

37 Prange, via Genda's statement, p. 252.

38 CV-6 action report, p. 2.

39 VB-6 action report.

40 Cressman et al., p. 96.

41 Walter Lord Papers.

42 This notion is further reinforced by the fact that numerous witnesses on *Hiryū* describe the bombing of *Kaga* in great detail, and (according to one account), even tried to warn her of the impending dive-bombing. This is in contrast with the eyewitness accounts from *Sōryū,* which speak of *Kaga*'s attack in very vague terms and refer to the great distance from her. Additionally, diagrams in both VB-3's and VT-3's action reports clearly show VT-3's target as being the southwestern of the northern pair of Japanese carriers. Not only that, but that target is shown as lying closer to a more southerly carrier (which we will show to be *Akagi*), than it was to VB-3's target, which we know was *Sōryū*. These diagrams show VT-3's target (*Hiryū*) to be roughly on *Sōryū*'s port bow, southwest of her as both ships are on a northwesterly course. Thus U.S. and Japanese primary sources back the interpretation of *Sōryū* being the northernmost and calls the conventional interpretation of *Hiryū* being "way to the north" seriously into question. An additional piece of evidence to be considered in this matter is the known actions of *Chikuma*. By 1045, after the fatal attack, *Sōryū* was dead in the water and firmly ablaze. Shortly thereafter, at 1058, *Chikuma* observed *Hiryū* launching her counterstrike aircraft, meaning that she was in rough proximity to Yamaguchi's flagship. Yet we also know that *Chikuma* dispatched her No. 2 cutter with seven men and a doctor to assist the *Sōryū* at 1112. This would have required *Chikuma* to have come to a stop and lowered her boats shortly after 1100. The implication is clear: *Chikuma,* and therefore *Hiryū,* were both at least in the general area of *Sōryū* as late as 1100. Had *Hiryū* been north of *Sōryū* when the latter was attacked at 1025, this would be far less likely, as she would have presumably been increasing the degree of separation from her sister during the interval after the attack.

However, a scenario in which a more southerly *Hiryū* first turns south, away from *Sōryū* (so as to avoid the attack on her, much as *Akagi* did when she observed the attack on *Kaga*) and then circles around to head north again after the attack makes more sense. In this scenario, *Hiryū* would have taken a while to draw level with *Sōryū*, and would then have passed her by as she continued north. This would have allowed her escort *Chikuma* to be in a position to both aid *Sōryū* and still witness *Hiryū*'s launch. This is further supported by at least one vivid Japanese account from *Hiryū* (Oedi Hisashi, *Yamaguchi, Tamon*, p. 243) of what *Sōryū*'s appearance was shortly after the bombing. Yet the same eyewitnesses on *Hiryū*'s bridge had much less detail to share regarding *Akagi*'s and *Kaga*'s damage, since CarDiv 1 was by then far astern. The overall impression one gets, then, is that *Hiryū* was clearly in a position to observe her sister in minute detail after she was bombed, meaning that she most likely had to be south of *Sōryū* when she was attacked.

43 He may have ordered more than a *shōtai* warmed up; we simply do not know. In the face of a new attack, with the Americans being proximate, Captain Aoki could easily have spotted six new fighters on deck, whose numbers would have been more readily remarked upon by the Americans who would shortly be attacking her. However, this is speculation.

44 Agawa, p. 315.

45 See in particular John Lundstrom's *First Team*, pp. 362–63, and Cressman et al., pp. 99–100.

46 Cressman et al., p. 351. VT-6 survivors specifically mention seeing American Wildcats (most likely the two F4Fs flying close cover on VT-3) charging in to attack as they themselves were exiting the battlefield.

47 Nagumo Report, pp. 8–9. Amagai's account in USSBS also indicates that the carriers were all running to avoid this incoming attack.

48 Lundstrom, *First Team*, p. 360. This is based on the observations of the pilots of VT-3, who noticed all the Japanese ships running northwest at high speed with CarDiv 2's fantails toward them as they overhauled for attack.

49 Amagai account, USSBS.

50 Lord, "Riddles of Midway" appendix.

51 The Nagumo Report, p. 19, notes at 1020 that *Akagi*, steaming on course 300, sighted "bomber bearing 30 degrees directly over the *Kaga*" and thereafter went into a maximum turn. The English version left unclear whether "bearing 30 degrees" referred to a True bearing, or a relative bearing off *Akagi*'s bow, and if the latter, whether to port or starboard. However, Tully was able to verify that the original Japanese version of the report (JD-1 reel) plainly states the bearing as being 30 degrees to port, a discovery that cements the configuration of CarDiv 1 at the time of the attack.

52 Fuchida, p. 163.

53 Amagai account, USSBS.

54 HYPO log, p. 3, 0711 entry.

55 Lundstrom, *First Team*, p. 349; correspondence with Mark Horan, August 10, 2004.

56 Lundstrom, *First Team*, p. 352.

57 The identities of these Zero pilots are unknown, but it is likely that more than one came from *Kaga*. In addition, *Hiryū*'s fighter group mentions tangling with Grumman fighters. *Hiryū* lost three pilots during this time, including two very experienced first-class petty officers. Given *Hiryū*'s apparently numerous encounters with Grummans within this general time frame, it would not be surprising if one or more of her losses came at the hands of either Thach or the other pair of Wildcats in proximity with VT-3. See also Lundstrom, *First Team*, pp. 363–64.

58 We are grateful to Mark Horan for his insights into VT-3's attacks. His extensive interviews of the American Midway aviators proved crucial to our understanding of this matter.

59 VB-3 action report.

60 Prange, p. 255, via interviews with Fujita, 1964 and 1965. *Sōryū*'s operational records reveal that Fujita was only on board *Sōryū* for fifteen minutes between his second and third sortie of the day. As an officer and *chūtai* leader, he was expected to lead by example, and he certainly did so.

61 Hata and Izawa, p. 326.

62 Commander, VB-3 Report, June 7, 1942.

63 Ibid.; also communication from John Lundstrom, August 2, 2002.

64 Ibid., VB-3, and accompanying sketch.

65 Ibid.

66 VB-3 action report.

67 We are indebted to Mark Horan for his insights into this matter. Mark's interviews with many of the pilots involved in the dive-bomber attacks against *Kidō Butai* has helped confirm that all three dive-bombing squadrons attempted to take a position upwind against their targets, so as to increase their accuracy.

Enterprise's aircraft had the benefit of attacking out of the sun as well, which decreased the effectiveness of *Kaga*'s AA fire.

68 VB-3 action report, Mark Horan.

69 *Sōryū* report, p. 19.

70 USS *Enterprise* action report, June 13, 1942; Air Battle of the Pacific June 4–6, 1942, p. 2.

71 Prange, p. 261; Cressman et al., p. 101.

72 Cressman et al., p. 101.

73 Ibid.

Chapter 12: A Fallacious Five Minutes—1020–1025

1 Fuchida, pp. 155–156.

2 Nagumo Report, pp. 13–20, and translated JD-1.

3 *Senshi Sōsho*, pp. 372–78.

4 Best, in an interview with John Lundstrom, April 2000. Best stated that during the time of his attack, only six or seven aircraft were on *Akagi*'s deck, and they clearly were Zeros. Furthermore, they were spotted well aft and were using most of the flight deck for runoff room. As he attacked, a single Zero (Kimura's) was in the process of launching.

5 "Draft Report of Attack Conducted June 4, 1942, Prepared by Commander Bombing Squadron 3." This report is interesting in that it allows the historian to collect Leslie's immediate postbattle impressions, rather than reading the more polished official report. We are grateful to John Lundstrom for making us aware of this version of the report.

6 Lord, p. 169.

7 Walter Lord Papers.

8 Japanese pilots, of course, were often guilty of the same errors.

Chapter 13: The Iron Fist—1020–1030

1 Oide Hisashi, *Yūdan teitoku Yamaguchi Tamon* ("The Brash Admiral Yamaguchi Tamon") (Tokyo: Tokuma Shoten), 1985, pp. 222–23.

2 Yoshino Haruo and Maeda Takeshi accounts, Bruning Collection, Hoover Institute.

3 We know that *Akagi* noted that *Kaga* was just about to commence flight operations (Nagumo Report, p. 20). Since we are also certain that *Akagi* was trailing *Kaga*, and off her starboard quarter, a starboard turn to commence flight ops would have had the effect of bringing *Kaga* across *Akagi*'s bow and potentially onto a collision course—not a wise move. As such, we consider it probable that *Kaga* was turning to port. Cameraman Makishima saw this port turn (Walter Lord Papers), and may have mistaken it for an evasive maneuver.

4 *Senshi Sōsho*, pp. 376–77, indicates that *Kaga*'s evasive maneuver was to starboard.

5 Twenty-eight aircraft, to be exact. For the exact composition and ordnance carried by the American attack against *Kaga*, see appendix 5.

6 Yamazaki's death is confirmed in Sawachi, p. 378.

7 Some accounts assert that this hit also destroyed a *Kaga* fighter just taking off, but this is not substantiated in the ship's action report. *Senshi Sōsho*, p. 376, supports the ship's action reports in this matter.

8 It must be admitted that weaving Mitoya's and Amagai's (multiple) accounts into a coherent narrative is a frustrating exercise. These two men were apparently the only survivors from the catastrophe that befell *Kaga*'s bridge, yet neither was a direct witness to it, or they would have been killed as well. Mitoya's rendition of events (related in Howard Oleck, ed., *Heroic Battles of WW II* [New York: Belmont Books, 1962], pp. 150–58) actually places the destruction of the island much later, well after the initial American attacks were concluded. Indeed, he cites a mysterious *second* American attack as being the reason for the bridge's destruction. That he and Amagai—who were apparently standing not twenty feet apart at the initiation of the American attack—should have such a different account of subsequent events is extremely disturbing. Yet from a strict historical standpoint, Mitoya's account must be weighed as carefully as Amagai's, because he is one of the closest things we have to being a witness. This caution is compounded by Amagai's own faults as a source. His several accounts each contain internal inconsistencies of one sort or another, such that one wonders what his true role on board ship actually was that morning. Amagai, to be charitable, seems a bit flaky.
Mitoya also has his difficulties. He names *Kaga*'s gunnery officer, who was supposedly a close personal friend, as Lt. Cdr. Musumi Tadashi. Yet Sawachi Hisae's authoritative *Midowei Kaisen: Kiroku* names this same officer as Miyano Toyosaburō. Similarly, Mitoya mentions another officer, Lieutenant Fiyuma, who is apparently killed on the bridge. However, *Kaga*'s casualty returns show no such individual (and indeed, "Fiyuma" is not

a proper Japanese name.) Finally, Lt. Cdr. Mitoya describes himself as *Kaga*'s communications officer. Yet we know that Lt. Cdr. Takahashi Hidekazu, who was killed on board her, is named in Sawachi's account as having the job description that Mitoya claims for himself. All in all, we feel that Mitoya's account must be treated with great care. Indeed, he may be another charlatan along the lines of Ogawa Raita, a Zero pilot who gave his account of Midway to Walter Lord, despite not even being in the battle.

In the end, we incline toward accepting a synthesis of both accounts, with *Kaga*'s bridge being destroyed late in the initial attack by an actual bomb hit. This bomb hit may well have occurred later in the American attack sequence (which probably lasted about three minutes) than has been previously acknowledged, thereby giving Okada the time necessary to issue orders to the engine room and Mitoya before being killed. We discount the possibility of a gas cart destroying the bridge—the descriptions of damage to the bridge as put forth by Yoshino Haruo, Kunisada Yoshio, and *Senshi Sōsho* match more closely with a high explosive event directly on the island, rather than a simple pyrotechnic episode occurring outside its structure. Gasoline explosions are spectacular, but unless they occur within a contained space, they have less of a chance of generating the sort of blast overpressures that would have been needed to deform the island in the manner described by these various sources. Similarly, we reject the notion of the bridge being destroyed long after the 1022 attack—the very high fatality rate among the ship's senior officers suggests a "decapitating event" of some sort occurred at the outset of the attack, when several of them would logically have been grouped on the bridge. More important, there is no evidence that *any* American air attack occurred against *Kaga* after her fateful 1022 bombing.

9 The Nagumo Report's statement that Okada ordered emergency steering makes no mention if his order was actually acted on. While it is unlikely that *Kaga*'s engineering spaces were out of action this quickly, it is altogether possible that voice communications to engineering had been disabled through destruction of the sound tubes below.

10 Lord, p. 172.

11 This rendition of events originated with Fuchida, who did not witness them himself.

12 Yoshino Haruo, letter to Parshall, March 27, 2000. We are grateful to Ron Werneth for arranging this correspondence.

13 Yoshino Haruo account, Hoover Institute, Bruning Collection.

14 *Senshi Sōsho,* p. 376.

15 Sawachi Hisae's stunning *Midowei Kaisen: Kiroku* contains tabular data for every single casualty—Japanese and American—in the entire battle. This includes name, rank, term of service, province of birth, and age at time of death for each man. From this raw tabular data, it was possible to develop insights into the nature of *Kaga*'s damage profile, as well as that of the other carriers.

16 *Kaga* lost nine individuals of lieutenant commander rank and above; ten, if *Kaga*'s air group leader is included. By contrast, *Akagi*'s highest-ranking fatality was an engineering lieutenant (Lt. Sugiura Kyōzō); *Hiryū* lost her captain; and *Sōryū* lost her captain, chief engineer, and another lieutenant commander.

17 *Kaga*'s officer casualties are listed in Sawachi, pp. 364–404. Okada's death is listed on p. 368; Kawaguchi's on p. 387; Miyano, p. 372; Takahashi, p. 375; Monden, p. 402.

18 It is unlikely that the attack on *Kaga* was terribly well coordinated, seeing as it was composed of aircraft from two separate squadrons, one of which was not supposed to be diving on her at all. As a result, the attack probably lasted a little longer than prescribed in American dive-bomber doctrine, which specified dive intervals of six to seven seconds between aircraft. USF-74, p. 105.

19 Maeda Takeshi account, Hoover Institute, Bruning Collection.

20 Cho account, *Shōgen Midowei Kaisen,* p. 243.

21 VB-3 action report.

22 Kanao account, *Shōgen Midowei Kaisen.*

23 Lord, pp. 173–74.

24 As on most warships, *Sōryū*'s mounts were fitted with physical restraints to safeguard them from firing into the ship itself, or across the flight deck.

25 Kanao's account indicates that the American planes attacking from starboard were taken under fire by eight 25-mm guns, indicating that all three mounts on the bow, as well as the five mounts ranged down the starboard side, were committed to repelling this attack. This meant that very little was left to be used against the port and stern attacks, even if they had been detected, which apparently they were not.

26 Lord, p. 173.

27 Kanao account, *Shōgen Midowei Kaisen.*

28 Lord, p. 174.

29 This is something of a revision to the Nagumo Report, which places the forward hit more to the centerline of the ship.

30 There is conflicting evidence as to which bomb landed first, the one at the bow, or the amidships hit. Both came down within a minute of each other. It is interesting to note that the actual dive-bomber attack was apparently spread out over three minutes, even though three separate groups of aircraft were diving at approximately the same time. Normally, a three- or four-plane element would have completed their attack within thirty to forty-five seconds. It must be assumed, therefore, that the attacking groups were coming down separately. According to Mark Horan, the 1st Division (five aircraft plus one aircraft w/o bomb), the 2nd Division (three aircraft plus two aircraft w/o bomb), and Lieutenant Shumway of the 3rd Division all dove on *Sōryū*. One flier from the 2nd Division (who was armed), and two members of the 3rd Division (one aircraft armed plus one aircraft w/o bomb), dove on *Haruna* from widely divergent angles, while the two remaining members of the 3rd Division (both armed) dove on *Isokaze*. Given the dispersal of bomb hit times, it can be surmised that a hit on *Sōryū* was made by each attacking group. Lieutenant Holmberg almost certainly recorded the first hit, forward. Shumway delivered the amidships hit, but the rest of his division pulled out after seeing the third hit. This impact, astern, was most likely contributed by Lieutenant Bottomley, from the 2nd Division, which had swung around the farthest in their attack because of *Sōryū*'s evasive maneuvers.

31 The Nagumo Report states that *Sōryū* remained under power until 1040. However, it may well be that she was merely coasting to a stop between 1030 and 1040.

32 Naganuma account, *Shōgen Midowei Kaisen,* p. 133.

33 *Senshi Sōsho,* p. 379.

34 We are indebted to Mark Horan for specific information regarding Best's attack formation and results.

35 Nagumo Report, p. 20.

36 Japanese warships sometimes rolled the crew's hammocks into bundles and then wrapped them around the ship's island to serve as extra protection against splinters.

37 Makishima and Sasabe, as quoted in Lord's notes. Most American sources accept this interpretation as well. Hugh Bicheno's assertion in *Midway,* p. 148, that Kroeger's bomb "punched through [*Akagi*'s] deck and exploded close enough alongside to hole her hull" is not backed up by any of the primary or secondary Japanese sources available. Furthermore, given the American attack profiles, the drop angles of their bombs meant that any American weapons that hit *Akagi* would have been carried *in* toward the center of the ship, rather than away from her hull. Additionally, the likelihood that an American bomb would have hit the flight deck, traveled through some portion of the ship, hit and penetrated the ship's side, and then detonated nearer the waterline is extraordinarily low. In sum, Bicheno's claim is completely insupportable.

38 Sasabe, as quoted in Lord's notes.

39 Fuchida, Aoki, Kusaka, and Sasabe, in their various accounts, all say it did.

40 Makishima quote.

41 Lundstrom interview with Richard Best.

42 Nagumo Report, pp. 19–20. The report, referring to the two hits, states that the aft hit was "on the rear guard of the port flight deck. (Neither were fatal hits.)" Nagumo Report, p. 9. It should be noted, however, that a casual reading of the Nagumo Report would lead to the conclusion that it apparently contradicts itself regarding this hit. On *Akagi*'s damage chart, p. 52, the aft "hit" is listed as a fatal hit. Prange repeats this rendition in *Miracle at Midway.* However, we believe this to be a transposition error in the Nagumo Report, because the *center* hit is described as "fatal" in the more complete description of the damage earlier in the report (p. 20). Our view in this matter is further supported by Makishima's very detailed statements regarding the exact nature of the near miss, the deck spotting of the CAP fighters as observed by Best and inferred from *Akagi*'s operational records, and the known effects of the aft hit on the rudder.

43 It only stands to reason that earlier Western accounts, not having analyzed *Kidō Butai*'s CAP movements in detail, inferred the existence of strike aircraft on *Akagi*'s deck, and hence went to the "logical" conclusion regarding the existence of resulting explosions and fires.

44 We are grateful to Mark Horan for his insights into this attack, buttressed by his extensive interviews of Richard Best, Jim Murray, and other pilots in VB-6. E-mail to Parshall, March 6, 2003.

45 Lord, p. 173.

46 Statement of Wilhelm Esders, Harry Corl, and Lloyd Childers given to Mark Horan. Communication from Horan to Parshall, August 7, 2002. Japanese sources note attacks developing as early as 1013, although we are inclined to believe that these times note the beginning of taking the enemy aircraft under fire by the CAP, and not when they dropped their fish against *Hiryū*. It is worth noting, too, that Dick Best remarked that he saw VT-3's aircraft still closing on their target as he was exiting the battlefield *after* bombing *Akagi,* which surely meant sometime after 1030.

47 Nagayasu account, *Shōgen Midowei Kaisen.*

48 VT-3 2nd Section report by Capt. Esders.

49 Nagayasu account.

50 Prange, p. 256; Hata and Izawa, p. 326.

Chapter 14: Fire and Death—1030–1100

1   NavTechJap S-06-1, p. 69.

2   Japanese deck planking was 45-mm thick (Hasegawa, *Nihon no Kōkūbokan,* p. 143) and, unlike thicker timbers, would probably have burned relatively easily.

3   Figures given are for *Unryū*-class carriers, a late-war derivative of the *Hiryū,* and fairly representative of a late-model Japanese fleet carrier design. NavTechJap A-11. The density of the piping network aboard the older *Akagi* and *Kaga* is unknown, but it is likely that they had similar arrangements installed during their mid-1930's refits.

4   High-octane fuel was usually stored in separate portions of both the fore and aft aviation gasoline tanks. NavTechJap A-11, Figure 1, p. 11.

5   It should be noted that the U.S. Navy had begun to tackle these issues aboard its carriers within the first few months of the war. At the time of the battle, *Yorktown* was already draining her fuel lines and filling them with CO_2 when not in use—an important innovation in minimizing the dangers inherent in aircraft fueling systems.

6   We speculate that flashtight doors *were* fitted above the immediate level of the magazines. None of the carriers lost at Midway suffered magazine explosions, even after extensive fires, indicating that some level of protection existed in the ships' innards.

7   Letter from Yoshida Akihiko to Parshall, August 1, 2000.

8   It should be noted, however, that the particulars of the piping and segmentation used on older Japanese carriers is far from clear. NavTechJap Report S-01-3, pp. 36–37, contradicts the usage of cast-iron piping and port/starboard segmentation, stating that while segmentation was poor by American standards, it did exist, and that fire main piping was seamless galvanized stainless steel. However, NavTechJap's scope of interest was almost exclusively late-war Japanese design and practice, leaving it open to question as to whether the report's comments would have applied to the Midway carriers, two of which were among the oldest such vessels in the IJN and could not help but be designed well before the full hazards of hangar deck conflagrations were appreciated.

9   Many of the comments on carrier hangar deck construction in this section are derived from Peattie, *Sunburst,* pp. 52–77.

10 Noted Japanese naval aviation expert Osamu Tagaya speculates that one of the reasons the Japanese may have opted for enclosed hangar decks was because of the rougher sea conditions in the Western Pacific (communication to Parshall, August 20, 2004). This design practice may also have been continued as a result of the severe battering carrier *Ryūjō* suffered during a large typhoon off northern Honshū in September 1935 (the famous "Fourth Fleet Incident"), which led to widespread changes in Japanese naval design practice. See Evans and Peattie, pp. 243–45.

11 The flight decks of *Akagi* and *Kaga* were about sixty-five feet above the waterline. *Sōryū* and *Hiryū* were a more modest forty-two feet, but only by the expedient of reducing hangar clearance to an almost unusable figure of 15 feet in the upper hangar and less than 14 feet in the lower, as compared to 17.5 feet for all American fleet carriers from the *Yorktown* onward.

12 *Warships of the Imperial Japanese Navy,* vol. 6, *Shōkaku, Zuikaku, Sōryū, Hiryū, Unryū-class, Taihō* (Tokyo: Kōjinsha, 1996), p. 29.

13 Kunisada account, *Shōgen Midowei Kaisen.*

14 Bergerud, p. 536.

15 Sawachi, tabular data in *Midowei Kaisen: Kiroku.*

16 See appendix 5 for an analysis of the likely number of hits against *Kaga.*

17 *Senshi Sōsho,* p. 376, confirms that *Kaga*'s pumping capacity was destroyed at the outset, and this may have been why. The reasons for locating such a vital piece of damage-control equipment in such a vulnerable location defy understanding. Like as not, the need for such an emergency generator was not identified until *Kaga*'s 1935 refit, at which time no space for it belowdecks could be found. An exposed generator was certainly better than none at all, but its immediate destruction points out the difficulties in using converted warships as carriers—without a systematic, keel-up design, many aspects of the resulting warship were inferior to a purpose-built carrier.

18 *Senshi Sōsho,* p. 376.

19 Morinaga's account of the moments immediately following *Kaga*'s bombing are found in Lord, p. 181.

20 Kunisada account in *Shōgen Midowei Kaisen.*

21 At the time of the attack, *Kaga* had the following aircraft in her hangars:

Twenty-seven B5N (317 gallons apiece)
Seventeen D3A (285 gallons apiece)
Eleven A6M (114 gallons apiece)
Total: 14,658 gallons if all aircraft fueled.

Source for fuel figures: *Mechanic of World Aircraft*, vols. 5, 11, 14 (Tokyo: Kōjinsha), 1993, 1994, 1995, respectively.

22 This contains a degree of speculation, but fits with the evidence of *Sōryū*'s rapid loss of power and of steam emanating from her midships.

23 Kanao account, *Shōgen Midowei Kaisen*.

24 The Nagumo Report, p. 10, ascribes an explosion in *Sōryū*'s torpedo storage room as occurring at 1040, but this is unlikely. Such an explosion would surely have sunk *Sōryū* outright, or severely damaged her under water, leading to rapid flooding. Rather, we believe that the large explosions aboard the ship were the result of detonations of aviation fuel vapors and ordnance near the torpedo lift.

25 Naganuma account, *Shōgen Midowei Kaisen*.

26 Aimune account, *Shōgen Midowei Kaisen*; Interrogation of *Hiryū* survivors.

27 Lord, p. 174.

28 Nagumo Report, p. 20.

29 Ibid.

30 Contemporary USN damage-control practice, as cited in F.T.P. 170(B), is explicit on this point.

31 Kunisada account in *Shōgen Midowei Kaisen*.

32 The parallels between *Kaga*'s damage and that of the U.S. carrier *Franklin*, damaged off Japan in March 1945, are striking. *Franklin*, too, had been engaged in fueling operations when she was hit by two bombs. Her fuel lines had ruptured, and her hangar had rapidly filled with explosive vapor. Within a few minutes of the initial hits, she was convulsed by the first in a series of devastating fuel-air explosions. These heavy blasts served as catalysts to initiate further induced explosions in the ordnance lying on the hangar deck. The fact that *Franklin* survived her ordeal, albeit at a terrible cost of 724 dead (a number quite similar to *Kaga*'s losses of 814) is a testament to the superior survivability worked into the design of the *Essex*-class carriers and to the vastly superior damage-control technique of the U.S. Navy by that point in the war.

33 Account of Thomas Cheek, e-mail to Parshall, May 26, 2002.

34 Kunisada account, *Shōgen Midowei Kaisen*.

35 Amagai account, *Shōgen Midowei Kaisen*.

36 Amagai's account in *Shōgen Midowei Kaisen* states that at the time of his leaving the ship, he decided that he "would leave the vessel's fate to the more skilled actions of the crew, and her second in command officer, if alive."

37 Yoshino Haruo specifically commented that airmen knew nothing of the business of fighting fires, which is why the flyers were evacuated from their carriers as soon as possible. This was true for American aviators as well.

38 Both the chief engineer and chief of equipment were engineering lieutenant commanders.

39 This aircraft, described in the Nagumo Report as a torpedo plane, may have been a VT-3 TBD, or an SBD flying at low altitude trying to clear the area.

40 This last point is speculation but certainly would have occurred in the case of a major engineering casualty such as a loss of steering.

41 Commander Sasabe, as interviewed by Walter Lord in 1966. Personal notes of Walter Lord.

42 E-mail from William Garzke to Parshall, August 14, 2001. Garzke, a noted naval architect and marine forensics expert, gave credence to the theory that *Akagi*'s rudder was damaged by a near miss.

43 We are grateful to Nathan Okun for his insight into the matter of external bomb ballistics.

44 Specifics of the crew's efforts to fix the rudder are nonexistent, but it must be assumed that standard emergency methods would have been tried. Japanese emergency steering arrangements are described in detail in NavTechJap S-01-3, pp. 26–27.

45 Had this not been so, *Akagi* would have been able to correct her steering problems almost immediately by rigging emergency manual steering from below.

46 Nagumo Report, p. 20.

47 Japanese rudders were counterbalanced more heavily than Western rudders, which had the effect of requiring more force from the engines to turn them. NavTechJap S-01-2, p. 26.

48 It is possible that a repair party was left here to continue their efforts—restoring steering is a high priority in any DC situation. *Akagi* lost 115 engineers killed this day, its 36-percent casualty rate making it by far the most heavily hit department aboard the ship. While it is probable that the early (and apparently orderly) evacuation of the engine spaces meant that many engineers may have died topside fighting the fires, it is also known that a group of them died in the starboard aft engine spaces. Repair crews would have been prime candidates for becoming casualties as well.

49 Nagumo Report, p. 20.

50 Lord, p. 183; John Toland, *Rising Sun: The Decline and Fall of the Japanese Empire, 1936–1945* (New York: Random House, 1961), pp. 384–85.

51 Prange, pp. 265–66.

52 It must have been so, otherwise this would have been the quickest way for the bridge staff to have exited.

53 Prange, p. 266.

54 Lord, p. 184; Fuchida, p. 159.

55 Prange, p. 266; Fuchida, p. 159. It should be noted that Fuchida exited the ship permanently at 1130. As a result, all of his further comments regarding damage-control efforts aboard *Akagi* must have originated with other survivors and have been relayed to him after the battle, as none of his observations from this point on could have been firsthand.

56 Prange, p. 266.

57 Nagumo Report, p. 10.

58 *Senshi Sōsho,* pp. 376–77. White smoke would likely have been indicative of very high heat already being generated in the hangars and beginning to destroy the flight deck caulking and other sealants and adhesives in the ship. It is also indicative of high-order detonations, such as from exploding ordnance.

59 Lord, p. 180.

60 Nagumo Report, p. 10.

61 Nagumo Report, p. 20.

62 Lord, p. 187.

63 Lundstrom, p. 370.

64 Had Tomonaga's force been rearmed by this time, *Hiryū* would undoubtedly have gone with a combined strike of eighteen Type 99s, nine Type 97s, and six Zeros, for a total of thirty-three aircraft—a rather tight deck spot, but still feasible.

65 It is unlikely that this photograph was taken during *Hiryū*'s transit to the battle site for a number of reasons. First, *Hiryū* does not appear to have been the watch carrier on duty during 1 and 3 June, meaning that there was no reason for her to be launching any planes during this time, let alone the largish group seen on her fantail in the photo. Second, ASW patrols from the duty carrier were typically composed of either two or four aircraft, again in contrast to the group of around a dozen seen here. The Japanese, as we know, typically did not use deck parks, particularly with the normal-sized air groups they were currently operating from their carriers. The aircraft in this photograph are all in the process of being launched, making this too large a group for patrol purposes. These reasons make it seem likely that this photo, if it indeed was taken at Midway, was, in fact, taken on the day of the battle itself. Detailed examination of the photograph makes it clear that the aircraft on deck are Type 99 carrier bombers, recognizable by their fixed landing gear. *Hiryū* launched Type 99 aircraft only once during the day, during Kobayashi's strike. As a result, in the opinion of the authors, as well as other experts such as John Lundstrom and James Sawruk, if this photograph was indeed taken during the Midway operation, then this is most likely Kobayashi's force taking off.

66 See, for example, John Lundstrom's *First Team,* pp. 383–86, for particulars of the mixture of 242 kg HE and 250 kg semi armor-piercing bombs used against *Yorktown.*

67 Nagumo Report, p. 21.

Chapter 15: Up the Steel Steps—1100–1200

1 Oide Hisashi, p. 246.

2 Nagumo Report, p. 21.

3 Japanese signal practice specifically anticipated the usage of relay ships. Communication from Dickson to Parshall, August 20, 2004. Cruiser *Chikuma* was the oblique recipient of the first message along this rather attenuated chain of command. At 1130 Admiral Abe of CruDiv 8, signaled that he was "Dispatching one destroyer to each of the damaged carriers, and [then they are] to proceed towards the Main Body." *Chikuma* got the hint, getting underway and leaving her cutter and men behind with *Sōryū.*

4 Lundstrom, *First Team,* p. 392, gives the name of this *Akagi* pilot as WO Nishimori Susumu.

5 Lord, p. 184.

6 Ibid., p. 185.

7 Nagumo Report, p. 21.

8 Ibid., p. 22.

9 Ibid. Abe's curious mention of only having "part of CruDiv 8" at hand hints that perhaps *Chikuma* was still out of position owing to her delays around *Sōryū*.

10 This particular order was repeated at both 1146 and 1147, with the 1146 message detailing two destroyers per ship, whereas the 1147 message specifically mentions that only one tin can should be left, so that the others might be available for attack purposes.

11 Nagumo Report, p. 22.

12 Lundstrom, p. 369. A final torpedo bomber from *Akagi* was still airborne and would shortly deposit itself on *Hiryū*'s flight deck. Counting *Sōryū*'s Type 2 reconnaissance plane, this brought the actual Japanese total to sixty-six carrier planes.

13 Not to mention the fact that VMSB-241's earlier attack on *Hiryū* was also conducted with carrier-type aircraft, which should have heightened Japanese suspicions still further.

14 Ugaki, p. 141.

15 We draw heavily on John Lundstrom's *First Team*, pp. 345–47, for details concerning the actions of *Hornet*'s air group, as well as on the very extensive American aviator interviews conducted by Mark Horan.

16 We are grateful to Mark Horan for his insights into these matters.

17 Lundstrom, *First Team*, p. 365.

18 We are indebted to Mark Horan for his extensive help in reconstructing the movements of *Hornet*'s air group related in the next several paragraphs, related in a communication to Parshall, August 20, 2004.

19 Lundstrom, *First Team*, p. 368.

20 Ibid., p. 333.

21 The composition of this group was initially six aircraft. One was to ditch early, and its crew would be captured (and executed) by the Japanese. A second aircraft made a forced landing nearer home, and its crew was eventually rescued. But Ware's quartet simply disappeared without a trace.

22 Upon their return to *Yorktown*, the deck crews had wanted to get the fighters down as quickly as possible, since they would be running critically low on fuel. The SBDs were told to orbit. Just as Leslie was beginning his landing, Kobayashi's counterstrike was detected, and he was waved off.

23 Lundstrom, *First Team*, p. 390.

24 Ibid., p. 373.

25 Ibid., p. 369.

26 VS-6 (nine), VB-6 (seven), CHAG (one), VS-8 (fifteen), VB-8 (fifteen), VB-3 (fifteen), VS-5 (ten), for a total of seventy-two, ten of which were currently scouting. We are grateful to Mark Horan for clarifying these totals.

27 Lord, p. 182.

28 NavTechJap S-84(N), pp. 9–10. Naval aviators were among the first personnel ordered over the side of carriers *Sōryū* and *Kaga*, in the twofold knowledge that they knew little of fighting fires and were a valuable commodity worth preserving for future battles. This was the case in the USN as well—aviators were exempt from such duties.

29 For these remarks, we draw on NavTechJap S-84(N) as well as F.T.P. 170(B), which dates from 1944.

30 David Evans and Mark Peattie's *Kaigun: Strategy, Tactics, and Technology in the Imperial Japanese Navy, 1887–1941*, in reference to Japanese fire-control systems, notes on p. 507, that "the navy apparently did not discover modern systems engineering, the organizational technique of dividing large technological systems into subsystems with well-defined interfaces. That technique enabled U.S. engineers to create incredibly complex technical systems." This principle appears to have analogs in Japanese damage control, which failed to deal rigorously with the topic of how to subdivide and address the topics of flooding and firefighting.

31 NavTechJap S-06-1, p. 21. It is worth noting that the NavTechJap report detailing Japanese damage-control methods is a mere fourteen pages in length, strongly indicating that the U.S. Navy officers compiling it found little of value to relate.

32 USS *Franklin* BuShips Report, p. 26.

33 Fuchida, p. 159.

34 Morinaga's account is given in Lord, pp. 181–82. We interpret his movements on the basis of his description—although he does not explicitly state where he emerged from *Kaga*'s hangars, it seems clear that he exited the ship from the AA battery deck level, a level above the upper hangar deck, where the ship's boats were located.

35 Robert Ballard, *Return to Midway* (Toronto, Ontario: Madison Press Books, 1999), pp. 107–8. Akamatsu couldn't remember rightly whether it was *Hagikaze* that picked him up, but given his recollection of encountering other individuals that we know were rescued by *Hagikaze,* like Lieutenant Kunisada, we definitely place him on board this destroyer.

36 We are grateful to Jeff Palshook, whose intimate knowledge of USS *Nautilus*'s movements were crucial in re-creating *Kaga*'s course track for this time period. Mr. Palshook's expertise was instrumental in the discovery of some of *Kaga*'s remains in 1999.

37 The BuShips damage report for USS *Franklin,* p. 11, explicitly mentions that her having an armored deck acted as both a firebreak and a protection against ordnance fragments from above.

38 Mori's account of escaping *Sōryū* is given in Lord, p. 180.

39 A glance at combat photography from U.S. Navy carriers on fire often reveals a good many men apparently standing around doing little to directly combat the blaze. Only so many men can be fighting the fire at any given time.

40 See appendix 6 for exact figures on crew casualties.

41 Kanao account in *Shōgen Midowei Kaisen.*

42 Asanoumi apparently survived his ordeal. His name does not appear among the casualty lists compiled in Sawachi Hisae's *Midowei Kaisen: Kiroku.*

43 This is interesting, as Kanao was apparently near the area where a great many of the crew exited the vessel. The water, by all rights, should have been positively swarming with survivors. However, given his miserable circumstances, Kanao can hardly be blamed for perhaps feeling a bit abandoned.

44 Fuchida, p. 164, gives a much different account of Yanagimoto's end. According to him, a petty officer named Abe, a well-known Navy wrestling champion, was sent to the bridge to rescue the captain (apparently about midday), but his aid was refused by the skipper. It may well be that such an event transpired, but that Kanao and the other men in the water were unable to witness it. It is clear from both Dull, p. 153, and the Nagumo Report, p. 10, that Yanagimoto was burned during the attack and subsequently refused aid. Kanao's description of the captain's face as being bright red is consistent with this. Since Fuchida was not on board *Sōryū,* and did not directly witness the events, we opt for the unembellished eyewitness accounts of Yanagimoto's death.

Chapter 16: Japanese Counterstrikes—1200–1400

1 E-mail from Sawruk to Parshall, March 13, 2003, source: JD-1.

2 Nagumo Report, pp. 23–24.

3 Ibid., p. 23.

4 Ibid.

5 Ibid., p. 10.

6 It has been reported in some accounts (Lord, p. 202) that the plane that sent this message was the third plane in the 2nd *chūtai* but, in fact, that particular pilot (PO3c Kuroki Junichi) is known to have died during the attack. Nakazawa's plane was not only the third aircraft to make it out of the attack area, but his observer, Ens. Nakayama Shimematsu, was also the commander of the 2nd *shōtai* and the senior surviving aviator from Kobayashi's group. It would make sense that the duty of transmitting the results of the strike would have fallen on Nakayama's shoulders.

7 Shortly thereafter, at 1252, after a delay of more than half an hour, Kobayashi's original 0911 signal was finally sent to *Hiryū*'s bridge, belatedly echoing his anonymous subordinate's subsequent opinion that the enemy carrier was on fire. Kobayashi's message is logged in the Nagumo Report as having been sent at 1201. However, we adhere to John Lundstrom's opinion that Kobayashi would not have been in a position to observe *Yorktown* burning at this time, because, according to American records, the attack against her had only just begun and therefore she could not have been bombed yet. Furthermore, the syntax of the two messages—first the report that the squadron was attacking, followed by the specifics of initiating bombing runs—makes more sense if they are transposed. As a result, we subscribe to the theory that Kobayashi's communiqué was entered incorrectly in the communications log and was probably sent at 1211. Nagumo Report, p. 23; Lundstrom, *First Team,* p. 386.

8 Prange, pp. 316–17.

9 Ibid., p. 317.

10 Osmus would not live out the day. Later in the afternoon, by order of *Arashi*'s skipper, Commander Watanabe Yusumasa, Osmus was executed and his body thrown over the ship's side. Commander Watanabe rather blandly reported on 5 June that the prisoner had "died and was buried at sea" (Nagumo Report, p. 41), and it is unclear whether he ever made clear to his superiors the manner of Osmus's death.

Watanabe did not survive the war. Had he lived, it is likely that he would have met the hangman's noose as a war criminal.

11 Lundstrom, pp. 393–94; Lord, p. 214.

12 We know that at 1310 *Nagara* was able to blinker Nagumo's reconnaissance orders to *Haruna* and *Tone*, as one would expect. By the same token, at this very same time Yamaguchi on *Hiryū* sent Nagumo an important update, also by blinker. The fact that *Nagara* did not log it till 1345 suggests that it had to be relayed by one or more ships on the extremity of the formation.

13 Sometimes incorrectly given as Hara Iwai.

14 Either that, or he was flying a different plane.

15 Lundstrom, p. 393.

16 Hyōdō Nisohachi monograph prepared for Parshall.

17 Tomonaga may have been right. The Type 97's normal range was 528 nm, with a maximum range of 1,075. With only 30 percent of his normal fuel, he probably had a range between 160 and 320 nm. If so, it is conceivable that he might have made it home, if he had husbanded his fuel.

18 Lord, p. 215.

19 Ibid.; Lundstrom, *First Team*, p. 394.

20 Ibid., p. 372.

21 For details of this engagement in this and the following paragraphs, we draw from Lundstrom's *First Team*, p. 372, and Cressman et al., pp. 114–15.

22 In light of Minegishi's subsequent sortie, it is possible that he had simply shot off all of his ammunition, rather than receiving particularly heavy damage.

23 Cressman et al., p. 115.

24 Lundstrom, *First Team*, p. 376.

25 For the description of Kobayashi's attack, we draw heavily from the definitive account in Lundstrom's *First Team*, pp. 377–87.

26 Shot down and killed were PO2c Todaka Noboru, Sea1c Yoshimoto Suekichi, and PO3c Chiyōshima Yutaka.

27 The identity of this pilot is unknown. However, judging from his angle of attack, he was probably from Kobayashi's 1st *chūtai*. It should further be noted that the diagram in Hugh Bicheno's *Midway*, p. 157, which ascribes the identities of the first two aviators to attack as being PO3c Koizumi Naoshi and PO1c Imaizumi Tamotsu, is speculative and unsubstantiated in the Japanese records.

28 This photo is reversed in many publications, but is shown here as photographed from *Astoria*, which was off *Yorktown*'s port quarter during the attack.

29 Nakazawa's bomb had, in fact, penetrated the ship's stack uptakes and caused serious damage to her boiler spaces below.

30 This signal originated using Kobayashi's personal call sign. Lundstrom, *First Team*, p. 386. Given that Kobayashi's men had not actually commenced their attack until 0911, it is likely that 0901 was either a transmission or decoding error for 0911 (1211 local).

31 American aviator accounts make it likely that Kobayashi's plane had been forced to jettison his weapon while under attack from *Yorktown*'s CAP, prior to the commencement of the bombing runs by his men. An unarmed *kanbaku* at low altitude was spotted observing the progress of the attack at about this time. So preoccupied by the attack was this aircraft's crew that neither of the crew apparently observed an American fighter that approached undetected to within spitting distance, only to discover that his guns had jammed. This same Japanese aircraft was subsequently shot down by a pair of VF-6 pilots piloted by Lt. (jg) Thomas C. Provost III and Ens. James A Halford Jr. Lundstrom, *First Team*, pp. 386–87. The evidence suggests that this plane was that of Kobayashi.

32 Cressman et al., p. 121.

33 The large wreckage artifact from *Kaga* (comprising a large section of hangar wall and two 25-mm gun tubs) that was discovered off of Midway in September 1999, was almost certainly formed in this manner.

34 In fact, the portrait may have been moved forward already. The wardroom was located portside, just forward of amidships, on the same deck as the anchors but almost directly under the fires, and had been in danger for quite a while.

35 Based on *Nautilus*'s observations of her during this time.

36 Prange, p. 310.

37 *Senshi Sōsho*, p. 376.

38 Sawachi, p. 397. We are grateful to Jean-Paul Masson for his translations of Sawachi's casualty rosters, as well as his knowledge of the Imperial Navy's Register of Active Naval Officers (*Gen-eki Kaigun Shikan Meibo*).

39 Kunisada account, *Shōgen Midowei Kaisen*.

40 Kunisada's account contains interesting anomalies. He states that he made his way to the command spaces (which were generally abreast the No. 2 elevator well and higher up in the superstructure). But it is clear that he eventually found himself *below* the lower hangar deck levels, near the crew's quarters, from which he exited the ship onto her antitorpedo bulge. It can only be surmised that Kunisada began his account already on the lower hangar deck level and from there was unable to make his way higher in the ship.

41 It was the Japanese custom to refer to themselves by their rank or post, rather than in the first person.

42 Makishima Teiuchi, *Middoue no Higeki* ("The Tragedy of Midway") (Tokyo: Shosetsu, 1956), p. 188.

43 Ibid.

44 At this point in the war, U.S. Navy enemy ship recognition manuals still showed *Kaga* and *Akagi* as having their older triple flight deck configurations.

45 *Nautilus* action report.

46 Ibid.

47 Lord, p. 213.

48 Mitoya account, p. 155.

49 An analysis of the buoyancy of an Mk 14 Mod 3 with Mk 15 Mod 1 TNT warhead was performed for the authors by Fred Milford, a noted expert in WWII torpedoes. His computations reveal that Kunisada's and Mitoya's accounts of the American torpedo not sinking after hitting *Kaga* are credible from a buoyancy standpoint, provided the warhead did indeed separate from the afterbody of the torpedo.

50 *Nautilus* action report; "Report of First War Patrol, July 16, 1942," Serial 0801.

51 Samuel Eliot Morison is the most prominent example. It would appear that by some coincidence a new surge of the fires inside occurred about this time. Brockman's impression of many men abandoning ship by "going over the side" was certainly true enough, as *Kaga*'s alarmed survivors scrambled to get out of the way of the incoming torpedoes.

52 Kimata Jiro, *Nihon Kōkū Senshi* ("Japanese Carrier Battle History") (Tokyo: Kokusho, 1977), p. 292.

53 *Nautilus* action report.

54 Ibid.

55 Kunisada account in *Shōgen Midowei Kaisen.*

56 Ibid.

57 Yoshino Haruo account, Hoover Institution Archives, Bruning Collection.

58 Maeda Takeshi account, Hoover Institution Archives, Bruning Collection.

59 Ibid.

60 Maeda Takeshi account, Hoover Institution Archives, Bruning Collection.

61 Kanao account, *Shōgen Midowei Kaisen.*

CHAPTER 17: LAST GASP—1400–1800

1 Naval War College Analysis, p. 137.

2 Ibid., p. 140.

3 Ibid. She was actually at 31-40'N, 179-10'W.

4 VS-5 action, p. 1.

5 Nagumo Report, p. 26.

6 Ibid., 1202 entry.

7 Prange, p. 265. *Kaga,* for instance, had a total of nineteen medical personnel on board ship, and it must be presumed that some of them were killed or injured during the initial attacks. It is possible, too, that others died in the sick bay, much as happened on board the *Akagi,* where the ship's hospital was cut off by advancing flames and all the staff and patients perished. It should be noted, though, that the casualty records for *Akagi* contained in Sawachi Hisae's comprehensive *Midowei Kaisen: Kiroku* do not mention a senior medical officer being killed. It is likely, therefore, that the ship's surgeon survived.

8 Kunisada account, *Shōgen Midowei Kaisen.*

9 Monograph No. 88, p. 47; Fuchida, p. 183.

10 Monograph No. 88, p. 51; Fuchida, p. 183.

11 Nagumo Report, p. 26.

12 Ibid., p. 26.

13 Ibid., pp. 26–27.

14 Again, we refuse to accept Dallas Isom's assertion that the American carriers were steaming without escorts. Until such movements of the American carriers are substantiated in the American warship records from the battle, we will continue to dismiss these assertions.

15 Nagumo Report, p. 29.

16 Monograph No. 93, p. 46.

17 Not all of Tomonaga's surviving aircraft landed at this time. The pair of *Kaga* Zeros under PO1c Yamamoto Akira remained aloft to augment the ship's CAP.

18 We draw extensively from Lundstrom's *First Team*, pp. 398–411 and Cressman et al., pp. 128–32 for the details of Tomonaga's strike on *Yorktown*.

19 Lord, p. 217.

20 Lundstrom, p. 399. The roster for the 1st *chūtai* reveals the trailing aircraft likely would have been Ōbayashi's or Suzuki's.

21 However, both American pilots survived. Cressman et al., p. 130.

22 Lundstrom, *First Team*, p. 400; Cressman et al., p. 130.

23 Lundstrom, *First Team*, p. 401.

24 Ibid.

25 Ibid., pp. 401–2.

26 These were fighters being vectored from *Enterprise* in support of *Yorktown*. Lundstrom, *First Team*, p. 405.

27 Ens. John Adams. Lundstrom, p. 403.

28 Lundstrom, *First Team*, p. 402; Lord, p. 219.

29 Lord, p. 218.

30 These were flown by Ens. Mel Roach, and Lt. Elbert Scott McCuskey. Lundstrom, *First Team*, p. 404.

31 Lundstrom, *First Team*, p. 405.

32 Ibid., p. 407.

33 Ibid., p. 406; Lord, p. 222.

34 Nagumo Report, p. 26.

35 Lundstrom, *First Team*, p. 406; Lord, pp. 219–20; Cressman et al., pp. 131–32.

36 J. H. and W. H. Belote, *Titans of the Seas* (New York: Harper and Row, 1975), p. 125.

37 Cressman et al., p. 132.

38 Nagumo Report, p. 27. This message was not received by Nagumo until 1635.

39 Nagumo Report, p. 28.

40 Nagumo Report track chart; Nagumo Report, p. 28.

41 Nagumo Report, p. 27.

42 Ibid.

43 Cressman et al., p. 136; Lundstrom, *First Team*, p. 411.

44 Cressman et al., p. 136. As it developed, there were five additional SBDs that had been mechanical strikes or aborts from the morning mission, had been repaired, fully fueled, armed with 1,000-pound bombs, and were even manned, but were left on the hangar deck because Captain Browning failed to include them in the tactical organization—a rather glaring oversight. Horan, communication to Parshall, 23 August 2004.

45 Cressman et al., p. 136.

46 Ibid.; Lundstrom, *First Team*, p. 411.

47 Cressman et al., p. 136.

48 Lundstrom, *First Team*, p. 412.

49 Nagumo Report, p. 27.

50 We deduce from the fact that *Chikuma* was known to carry five aircraft, including three Type 0 recon floatplanes—her Nos. 1, 4, and 5 aircraft. By process of elimination, her No. 2 aircraft was a Type 95.

51 Nagumo Report, p. 27.

52 Ibid., p. 28.

53 Cressman et al., p. 135.

54 Lundstrom, pp. 413–14.

55 This would appear to explain the northward jog of *Nagara*'s track shown in the Nagumo Report at about this same time.

56 Both Flaherty and Gaido were tied to five-gallon kerosene drums filled with water and dumped overboard. Exactly when they were killed remains open to debate, although it was apparently well after the battle was over, the deed apparently occurring after *Makigumo* was ordered north to participate in operations in the Aleutians. *Makigumo* was assigned to these operations on 8 June and radioed on 9 June the full details of the intelligence gathered from the two prisoners (Prange, p. 253; Prados, p. 329; Cressman et al., pp. 114–15; Ultra Intercepts—*Makigumo* entries). No mention of the fate of these two American prisoners appears in the Nagumo Report.

57 Nagumo Report, p. 29.

58 Ibid.

59 Nagumo Report, p. 9.

60 Nagasuki account, *Shōgen Midowei Kaisen,* p. 325.

61 Ultra Intercepts, designated as "Orange Translations of Japanese Intelligence Intercepts," NARA (Archives II).

62 Nagumo Report, p. 9.

63 Kanao account.

64 *Senshi Sōsho,* pp. 376–77.

65 It must be noted that Lieutenant Naganuma's account, while fascinating, needs to be used with caution. Like many survivor accounts, Naganuma's contains few concrete time references, making the placement of his remembrances within the overall narrative a difficult proposition. Yet (as will be seen), Naganuma was quite clear that he escaped *Sōryū* only shortly before she sank. As such, despite the difficulty we have in comprehending how men could have actually survived eight hours in *Sōryū*'s engine spaces, we adhere to Naganuma's word in this matter, meaning that even as Kanao was abandoning *Sōryū* late in the day, Naganuma and some of the engine room crews were apparently still alive.

66 Lord, p. 232.

67 Photographs of *Hiryū* taken after her bombing make it clear that no planes were on deck when she was fatally attacked at around 1700.

68 Lord, pp. 232–33.

69 Nagumo Report, pp. 26–27.

70 *Enterprise* report.

71 Ibid., p. 137.

72 Nagumo Report, p. 29.

73 Monograph No. 93, p. 45, notes that it was *Hiryū*'s intent to launch this plane shortly. However, the photographic record of *Hiryū* after the attack makes it clear that this plane was most likely not on deck when the ship was bombed. Given that this aircraft would have needed several minutes to get warmed up before launch in any case, turning back to the east so early seems unnecessary.

74 USSBS 464, Nav. 106, p. 460.

75 *Enterprise* action report; Cressman et al., p. 137; Lord, p. 235; Lundstrom, *First Team,* p. 414.

76 Lundstrom, *First Team,* pp. 414–15, Cressman et al., pp. 137–38.

77 Gallaher noted that *Hiryū*'s turn completely threw off his aim. Horan, communication to Parshall, 24 August 2004.

78 VB-6 action report; Lord, p. 235; Cressman et al., p. 137.

79 Cressman et al., pp. 137–38.

80 The damage chart in the Nagumo Report indicates that bomb hits on *Hiryū* were received as far aft as the midships elevator, but this is not substantiated by the photographic record, which make it clear that no bombs landed further aft than *Hiryū*'s forward elevator.

81 Most accounts say that the entire elevator was lodged against the bridge, but a careful examination of the photographic evidence reveals that the fragment upended against *Hiryū*'s island is too small to have been the entire elevator. Whether the remainder fell back into the elevator well, or was hurled over the side, is unclear.

82 Lord, p. 236.

83 Account of Arimura Yoshikazu, letter to Parshall, January 27, 2002. We are grateful to Koganemaru Takashi and Alan Clark for their assistance in translating Mr. Arimura's account.

84 Lord, p. 236.

85 Lord, p. 236; Mandai account given in *Hiryū* prisoner interrogation.

86 Lord, pp. 239–40.

87 Prange, p. 290.

88 Lord, p. 236.

89 Arimura account.

90 Prange, p. 290.

91 Lord, p. 236. Other accounts say that her firefighting system was disabled. However, judging by Arimura's account, it would appear that *Hiryū* possessed some fire fighting capability, at least initially.

92 Arimura account; Naval War College Analysis, p. 142; Nagumo Report, p. 62.

93 Sweeney's flight of four had taken off from Midway at 1550, and had subsequently been caught up by two additional stragglers whose engine troubles had delayed their departure for half an hour. Cressman et al., p. 139.

94 Lord, p. 237.

95 Nagumo Report, p. 30.

96 Kawaguchi statement, USSBS, p. 4.

97 Blakey's B-17s would claim one hit on the CV, one on a destroyer, and two near misses on the CV, supposedly leaving her smoking and aflame. Sweeney's bombers claimed two hits on cruisers but did not observe all of their drops. Naval War College Analysis, pp. 118–19.

98 Nagumo Report, p. 34.

CHAPTER 18: SCUTTLINGS—1800–DAWN, 5 JUNE

1 Naval War College Analysis, pp. 140–41.

2 Cressman et al., p. 140; Lord, pp. 240–41.

3 Prange, p. 289; Cressman et al., p. 140; also, Lundstrom, unpublished Fletcher manuscript.

4 Lord, p. 256; Cressman et al., p. 146; Naval War College Analysis, p. 143.

5 In fact, these were merely the remnants of *Hiryū*'s CAP, which had been launched in the midafternoon.

6 Nagumo Report, p. 31.

7 Hyōdō monograph for Parshall; running depth for torpedoes intended for capital ships was five to seven meters.

8 Nagumo Report, p. 36.

9 The term "Long Lance" was never used by the Japanese, and was advanced postwar largely by Samuel Eliot Morison. However, Morison likely derived the phrase from a captured Japanese torpedo document that referred obliquely to the same term. "Battle Lessons Learned in the Greater East Asia War (Torpedoes)," JICPOA, vol. 6, Item 5782. We are grateful to David Dickson and Brooks Rowlett for their insights on this matter.

10 Kondō mentions the moonlight as an aid to his forces in his 1750 dispatch. Nagumo Report, p. 30.

11 bid., p. 34.

12 Ibid., p. 31.

13 Ibid., p. 34.

14 Nagumo Report, p. 30.

15 Ibid., pp. 29–30.

16 Prange, p. 308; Nagumo Report, pp. 9–10; Lord, pp. 245–46.

17 *Senshi Sōsho*, pp. 376–77.

18 USSBS, vol. 1, p. 2.

19 Note the various recollections of Amagai with regards to when he originally went into the water, as well as when he finally ordered the emperor's portrait removed. In particular, it is Commander Amagai who steadfastly maintained that *Hiryū* had radar during the battle, which is untrue.

20 *Senshi Sōsho*, p. 389. Paul Dull's account, p. 153, erroneously states that it was Nagumo preparing to reboard *Sōryū* from *Nagara*. This translation error, in turn, threw off H. P. Willmott's subsequent analysis of *Nagara*'s (and by extension, Nagumo's) movements at around this time.

21 Makishima, p. 191; Lord, p. 246.

22 Nagumo Report, p. 35.

23 Kanao account in *Shōgen Midowei Kaisen*.

24 It must be noted that Naganuma's account begs scrutiny. It is difficult to believe that he and his men were actually able to survive in the engine spaces, under such terrible conditions, for as long as they did. The possibility certainly exists that Naganuma managed to escape considerably earlier and spent a longer time in the water than he recalled later.

25 Kanao account in *Shōgen Midowei Kaisen*. It is worth noting that Kanao's recollection of "three" torpedoes jibes exactly with Executive Officer Ōhara's initial, albeit later recanted, claim that three torpedoes finished off *Sōryū*. Makishima, p. 183, also confirms the angle and details of *Sōryū*'s sinking, without explicitly mentioning scuttling.

26 See appendix 6 for details on *Sōryū*'s casualties.

27 Letter from Yoshino Haruo to Parshall/Tully, March 27, 2000.

28 Robert Ballard, *Return to Midway* (Toronto, Ontario: Madison Press Books, 1999), p. 111.

29 Yoshino Haruo's March 27, 2000 letter.

30 This description of *Kaga* draws on the recollections of Yoshino Haruo, made in separate statements to both Jon Parshall and Chuck Haberlein of the Naval Historical Center.

31 Kunisada account in *Shōgen Midowei Kaisen*.

32 Details on *Kaga*'s casualties can be found in appendix 6.

33 Ballard, p. 111.

34 We are grateful to Chuck Haberlein of the Naval Historical Center for providing us with a hand-drawn sketch from Yoshino Haruo depicting *Kaga*'s general condition at the time of her sinking.

35 Akamatsu's account states that it was *Maikaze* that did the deed, firing a single torpedo that broke *Kaga* in half. However, in our opinion, Akamatsu has clearly been shown to be an unreliable witness (among other things claiming to have been on combat flights during the morning that he never participated in), and, as such, his account must be used carefully. Given the agreement between Yoshino (in three separate accounts) and Kunisada regarding who was doing the firing, we tend to discount Akamatsu's account, although it is certainly possible that *Maikaze* fired as well. However, all accounts agree she sank upright and did not capsize.

36 Yoshino Haruo letter to Parshall, Kunisada account in *Shōgen Midowei Kaisen*; Ballard, p. 111; Maeda Takeshi and Morinaga Takayoshi, in separate accounts given to Ron Werneth, both stated explicitly that they witnessed *Kaga* being scuttled by torpedo.

37 Kunisada account, *Shōgen Midowei Kaisen*.

38 Ron Werneth, interview with Maeda Takeshi, e-mail to Tully, July 3, 2004. We are grateful to Mr. Werneth for providing us with excerpts of his extensive interviews taken from his forthcoming manuscript.

39 Ron Werneth interview with Takayoshi Morinaga, e-mail to Tully, July 3, 2004.

40 Commander Nakasugi Seiji account, *Shōgen Midowei Kaisen*.

41 Kunisada account, *Shōgen Midowei Kaisen*.

42 Japanese carrier air group operational logs, JD-1.

43 Cressman et al., p. 140.

44 Lord, pp. 239–40.

45 Nagumo Report, p. 34.

46 Ibid.

47 Monograph No. 93, p. 43.

48 Nagumo Report, p. 36. Ultra Intercepts—*Akagi*.

49 Ariga's message text specifies "1st section of DesDiv 4 [*Arashi, Nowaki*] is about 7 kilometers south of *Akagi*; 2nd section of DesDiv 17 [*Hamakaze, Isokaze*] is 7 kilometers north of *Akagi*, patrolling the E-W line. The second section of DesDiv 4 [*Hagikaze, Maikaze*] is patrolling within a 5-kilometer circle of *Akagi*." Ultra Intercepts—*Akagi*. The fact that this message listed Sixth Fleet as a primary addressee may also have communicated concerns on the part of Ariga that his ships, and the derelicts, might be endangered by their own submarines.

50 Dull, p. 155.

51 It is intriguing to speculate on whether Yamamoto's action regarding *Akagi* is perhaps a clue that Nagumo's earlier disposal of *Sōryū* and *Kaga* had added to the increasing perception of Combined Fleet's staff that the commander of *Kidō Butai* had prematurely given up hope.

52 Dull, p. 155.

53 Prange, p. 321.

54 Lord, p. 247. Aoki was retired from active service in October 1942 but was then recalled in October 1943 to command a series of air groups, before being demobilized in 1945.

55 Norman Polmar, *Aircraft Carriers: A Graphic History of Carrier Aviation and Its Influence on World Events* (New York: Doubleday Co., 1969), p. 224; Fuchida, p. 172. The Nagumo Report, p. 9, gives this time as being 2103, but this is likely a typo. This can also be inferred by the fact that at 2146 *Yūgumo* and the other destroyers were actively involved in fighting *Hiryū*'s fires, which could not have been accomplished had *Hiryū* remained underway at high speed. Nagumo Report, p. 36.

56 Nagumo Report, p. 36.

57 Ibid., p. 9. We can see no reason why *Hiryū* had developed a list, other than the temporary shipping of firefighting water—a phenomenon that occurred to other carriers during the war engaged in intensive firefighting activities. She sustained no known underwater damage, and subsequent photos of her show her on an even keel. Furthermore, those of her engineering staff who survived, who were surely in a position to comment on her watertight integrity prior to leaving the vessel, make no mention of pervasive flooding before she was scuttled.

58 Nagumo Report, p. 36.

59 At grid position HE E A 55 (28°-50'N, 179°-50'W). Ultra Intercepts—*Kaga*. National Archives. It is unknown if this signal was sent in response to an earlier inquiry by Yamamoto, but this appears likely.

60 Nagumo Report, p. 30. This report had been transmitted at 1755.

61 Nagumo Report, p. 34.

62 Ibid., p. 35.

63 Ugaki, p. 145.

64 Ibid., p. 151.

65 Ibid., p. 146.

66 Nagumo Report, p. 36.

67 Ibid.

68 Nagumo's subsequent messages reveal that he was probably still holding out hope for *Akagi* as well.

69 Naguma Report, pp. 36–37.

70 Ibid, p. 9.

71 Prange, p. 333, from an interview with Spruance, September 5, 1964.

72 Ugaki, p. 145.

73 Nagumo Report, p. 37.

74 Prange, p. 319, per interview with Watanabe, November 24, 1964.

75 Ibid.

76 Agawa, p. 321.

77 Prange, p. 319.

78 Ibid.; Ugaki, p. 145.

79 Nagumo Report, p. 38.

80 Monograph No. 93, p. 59, confirms DesDiv 8 was left behind because Kurita was making thirty-three knots. The destroyers were capable of similar speed, but it may well have been that they were concerned about having enough fuel to execute a sustained flank speed run to the east.

81 Nagumo Report, p. 37.

82 Dull, p. 147. The diagram in Dull's book shows Kurita breaking off to the northwest at 2245, but this doesn't jibe with the order log. Ugaki, p. 152, Monograph No. 93, and *Senshi Sōsho* (p. 477) all agree that it was 0230 when Kurita turned away. As a result, his force may well have gotten closer than fifty nautical miles to Midway.

83 *Senshi Sōsho,* p. 476.

84 *Senshi Sōsho,* pp. 475–77.

85 Prange, pp. 323–24.

86 Ibid., p. 324.

87 Theodore Roscoe, *United States Submarine Operations in World War II* (Annapolis, MD: Naval Institute Press, 1949), p. 131; Naval War College Analysis, p. 153.

88 Lord, p. 258.

89 War Diary of Sixth Fleet, Midway Operation, WDC 160268.

90 Prange, p. 322; Lord, p. 258.

91 Cressman et al., p. 142.

92 Ibid., p. 141.

93 Ibid.

94 Orange Translations, Crane Materials. Record Group 38, section 370 National Archives. This report, not reproduced in prior accounts because it was "omitted" from the Nagumo War Diary, was also intercepted by American radio intelligence units and subsequently decoded. Published here for the first time, its contents reveal valuable clues of the true state of Nagumo's thinking at this critical hour and even two near-final resting positions of some of the carriers:

> YAYO 2 # 566 (1-4) of 5 June, 2330
> 2330 5 June
> Striking Force Battle Report
> Part I:
> June 5 carried out air attack on Midway as scheduled. Shot down about 30 enemy planes and though inflicted considerable damage to equipment, details are not clear. Even after the attack, it seemed that the enemy was able to use the air field.
> Part II:
> From 0400—0730 more than 100 enemy planes attacked, among which more than 50 were shot down. Even though we avoided all the torpedoes, because of the attack of the shipboard bombers we received many direct hits. As it was impossible to continue the battle because of fires, I gave the order to retreat and with 6 destroyers in company shifted flag to the *Nagara*. With the remainder of this force, proceeded towards the enemy striking force and attacked. An aircraft carrier of the *Hornet* class received considerable damage with 2 torpedo hits. At 1430, because of an extremely serious attack by enemy shipboard bombers, we sustained great damage. It was a terrific battle. The air attack continued in succession until about 1600.

Part III:

After retiring to the northwest, we turned to attack. This force's 1800 position was TO A RU 32, course 320, speed 20 knots. The enemy's main force consisted of 3 *Hornet* type aircraft carriers (one of which was listing, burning and drifting), 2 aircraft carriers of uncertain type, 6 heavy cruisers and a number of destroyers. 1500 position of 10 ships TO SU WA 14, course 280, speed 24 knots. (30°-55'N, 176°-05'W).

Part IV:

Although the fire on the *Hiryū* has slackened a bit, she lies in the enemy's track and the fire cannot be brought under control. If it were possible to put out the fire, she might be able to get under way. She is under escort of two destroyers and retiring to the Northwest.

The *Sōryū* sank and the *Kaga* also sank. The *Akagi* is burning fiercely and is not expected to be brought under control. Getting under way is impossible. She is at approximate position TO E WE 43 under escort of two destroyers. (30°-40'N, 178°-50'W).

95 Dull, p. 158; Nagumo Report, p. 9.

96 This is an informed guess on our part, with the forward elevator slammed up against the front of the bridge, this is the only place on the island that such an address to the assembled masses could reasonably have been made.

97 Lord, p. 249.

98 Fuchida, p. 173.

99 Lord, p. 250.

100 Prange, p. 313.

101 Arimura account, *Shōgen Midowei Kaisen.*

102 Makishima, p. 193.

103 Japanese carrier air group records (JD-1 reel); Prange, p. 312.

104 Prange, p. 312.

105 Lord, p. 250.

106 Makishima, p. 195.

107 Makishima, p. 194; Prange, p. 313; Lord, p. 250.

108 Lord, p. 250.

109 Fuchida, p.173.

110 Lord, p. 250.

111 Makishima, p. 195.

112 Ibid.

113 Lord, p. 251.

114 Nagumo Report, p. 10.

115 Hisashi, pp. 291–94.

116 This is educated guesswork, but it fits the evidence at hand. *Hiryū* would take four hours to sink from this hit, meaning that whatever flooding occurred as a result was not sufficient to sink the vessel quickly. A direct hit amidships would have caused flooding radiating in all directions from the hit. A hit in the bow, by contrast, could only cause meaningful flooding through the comparatively smaller cross-section bulkheads immediately astern the hit. Indeed, when *Hiryū* was photographed an hour and a half later, she looked to be in relatively good shape—settling by the bow slightly, but on an even keel and in no great danger of foundering immediately.

117 Hisashi, p. 295.

118 Ibid. Several of these men would later be rescued by the Americans and would readily attest to their utter confusion as to what *Makigumo* intended by signaling them, and their disgust with their countrymen at being left for dead.

119 Prange, pp. 327–28.

120 Ibid., p. 328.

121 Ibid.

122 We are grateful to Dan Rush, U.S. Navy (Ret.), for his reminiscences of personal conversations with Nagumo's youngest son, Dr. Nagumo Shinji, in a series of e-mails to Parshall dated May 27–June 3, 2001.

123 Even had this transpired, the authors doubt highly whether *Akagi* would have been useful for anything other than scrapping in any case.

124 Ultra Intercepts—*Akagi.*

125 Prange, p. 320.

126 Ibid.; Ugaki, p. 148.

127 Prange, p. 320.

128 Ugaki, p. 148.

129 Prange, p. 320.

130 *Senshi Sōsho,* p. 378; Jiro Kimata, *Nihon Kōkū Senshi* (Japanese Carrier Battle History) (Tokyo: Kokusho, 1977), p. 294.

131 Kimata, p. 294.

132 Makishima, p. 199; Kimata, p. 295; and Commander Nakasugi Seiji account, *Shōgen Midowei Kaisen.* It should be noted that for the sake of simplicity, we have listed each carrier's complete toll of casualties, including aviators that may not have actually been lost on board ship, or who subsequently died aboard other vessels.

Chapter 19: Retreat

1 *Haruna* and *Kirishima* most likely put up Type 95s for ASW work as well.

2 Ugaki, p. 154; Monograph No. 88, pp. 40–42.

3 Ugaki, p. 154.

4 Naval War College Analysis, p. 150.

5 Ugaki, p. 164.

6 Ugaki, p. 153, mentions that the rendezvous process took as long as from 0800–1700. The majority of the force most likely did not rendezvous until around 1300, with some of the destroyers carrying survivors joining later.

7 Nagumo Report, p. 38.

8 We wish to thank Osamu Tagaya for his information regarding the aircrew involved.

9 Prange, p. 312.

10 Lord, p. 262.

11 Makishima, p. 197; Lord, p. 263.

12 CinCpac conf. let., File No A8/(37)/JAP/ (26.2), Serial 01848, of June 28, 1942, hereafter "Interrogation of *Hiryū* survivors," p. 3.

13 The B4Y1 sported spatted landing gear similar to the D3A.

14 Makishima, p. 197; Lord, p. 264.

15 Interrogation of *Hiryū* survivors, p. 3.

16 Ibid. Determining *where Hiryū* sank, as opposed to when, is more difficult. There is the official position that *Makigumo* reported scuttling her: 31°-27'N, 179° Pt-23'W. Yet, after this torpedo hit, the *Hiryū* drifted almost another four hours with the wind and current before she sank. The next and best fix is provided of course by *Hōshō*'s important sighting and photographs at 0720: 32° Pt-10'N, 178°-50'E. Finally, at 0820, scarcely an hour before she sank, U.S. fliers sighted her with bow pointed 245 degrees, bearing 335 degrees, 250 miles from Midway. In reviewing these, it is clear that the *Makigumo* position contains an error of 179 for 178 degrees, a discrepancy that had been noted before, but not resolved. The *Hōshō*'s sighting position allows a ruling strongly in favor of the 178 longitude interpretation. The *Hōshō* position also corresponds more closely with the chart position on the Nagumo chart, which is 31°-38'N, 178°-51'W, and implies that the chart positions were worked out retroactively (and are perhaps "more correct," as the American editors for Fuchida's book concluded).

17 Ibid.

18 Cressman et al., p. 175; Interrogation of *Hiryū* survivors, p. 3.

19 Interestingly, none of *Hiryū*'s POWs wanted it to be known that they had survived the battle or wished to be returned to Japan, preferring to let it be believed that they had perished in battle.

20 Willmott, *Barrier and the Javelin,* p. 483.

21 Prange, pp. 324–35.

22 Willmott, *Barrier and the Javelin,* pp. 483–84.

23 As recently as 1997, the Naval War College issued a report entitled "The Operational Failure of U.S. Submarines at the Battle of Midway—and Implications for Today," Naval War College Joint Military Operations Department, May 1996.

24 Cressman et al., p. 217; Lord, p. 262.

25 Cressman et al., p. 143.

26 Willmott, *Barrier and the Javelin,* p. 488.

27 Cressman et al., p. 146.

28 Nagumo Report, p. 38.

29 Orange Intercepts, *Hōshō.*

30 Nagumo Report, p. 38.

31 HYPO placed a sub just northwest of Midway, receiving an urgent message from Tokyo and Sixth Fleet at 2013.
32 Naval War College Analysis, p. 163.
33 Cressman et al., p. 143.
34 Ultra Intercepts—*Mikuma.*
35 Cressman et al., p. 143; Prange, p. 325.
36 Cressman et al., p. 144; *Mikuma* gives the time of the attack as 0800, and counted eight bombers involved. Ultra Intercepts—*Mikuma.*
37 Cressman et al., p. 144.
38 The message sent by *Mikuma* at 0905 after the Vindicator and B-17 attacks of 5 June clearly indicates that no damage was received by those attacks. *Senshi Sōsho,* p. 486, also denies it, as does the track record of movement (TROM) of *Mogami.* The popular folklore surrounding Fleming's attack was mainly based on the recollection of *Mogami*'s captain, Soji, as reported in postwar interviews that then found their way into the USMC monograph "Marines at Midway," by Robert Heinl. However, in time it was learned that Soji was speaking of a similar incident that occurred off of Guadalcanal in November 1942. A further contributing cause was a misinterpretation of debris atop *Mikuma*'s No. 4 turret in some of the photographs taken of her after she was bombed. Intriguingly, the claim never had much support even from the U.S. side, as neither the MAG-22 nor VMSB-241 action reports make any mention of it. Nor do wartime or immediate postwar publications mention the incident. We are grateful to Mark Horan for his insights on these matters, based on firsthand interviews with American crewmen in four of the participating aircraft, in a correspondence to Tully dated May 2, 2004.
39 Ultra Intercepts—*Mikuma.*
40 Ibid.
41 Morison, p. 148; Prange, p. 369.
42 Naval War College Analysis, p. 158.
43 "Significant PBY sightings of Japanese Carriers late 4–5 June [1942]," compiled by John Lundstrom, sent to Tony Tully, March 15, 2000.
44 Cressman et al., p. 146.
45 Cressman et al., p. 149; Prange, p. 331.
46 Cressman et al., p. 149; Lundstrom, *First Team,* p. 421.
47 Cressman et al., p. 149.
48 Ibid. Lundstrom, *First Team,* p. 421.
49 Cressman et al., p. 149.
50 Ibid.
51 *Hornet* action report, June 8, 1942.
52 Nagumo Report attack diagrams for *Tanikaze.*
53 Action Report, Bombing Squadron Three, 10 June 1942.
54 Ibid.
55 Cressman, et al., p. 151.
56 Naval War College Analysis, p. 164
57 Their position at 2130 was 31°-10'N, 172°-30'E; Ultra Intercepts—*Arashio.*
58 "Significant PBY sightings of Japanese Carriers late 4 June–5 June."
59 Some sources mention that *Chikuma*'s cutter was returned at this time as well, but we adhere to *Senshi Sōsho*'s interpretation (pp. 376–77) that the boat had been abandoned. It is unlikely that *Isokaze* would have been able to stow an extra cutter in addition to her own ship's boats.
60 Nagumo Report entries for afternoon 5 June.
61 *Senshi Sōsho,* p. 489; Ugaki, p. 153. Just exactly what American aircraft carried out this attack remains unclear.
62 Ugaki, pp. 153–54; also track chart in Nagumo Report.

CHAPTER 20: AND DEATH TO THE CRIPPLES . . .
1 Lacroix and Wells, p. 488.
2 Derived from scheduled rendezvous mentioned in previous radio signals (see chapter 18), and the fact the destroyers were already with the force when sighted in morning.
3 Some of these aircraft were from *Hornet,* having landed on *Enterprise* after the preceding evening's strike. Lundstrom, *First Team,* p. 422.
4 Cressman et al., p. 153.

5 Lundstrom, *First Team,* p. 422.

6 Cressman et al., p. 154.

7 Ibid.

8 Ugaki, p. 155.

9 Cressman et al., pp. 154–155.

10 The planes in question were Ens. Don Griswold, of VS-8, and Ens. Clarence Vammen, of VS-6. Ibid., p. 155.

11 Lacroix and Wells, p. 488.

12 This claim is based on inference from the fact that only one hit was scored on this pair of Japanese destroyers, namely on *Arashio,* at about 1450, hence no hits were scored during the attack in question. Furthermore, Bombing Eight's action report mentions heavy strafing of the destroyers.

13 Cressman et al., p. 155.

14 Ugaki, p. 155. As has been noted, the IJN claim was close to accurate, but only two, not three, aircraft had been splashed.

15 Cressman, p. 155; Lundstrom, *First Team,* p. 423.

16 Lundstrom, *First Team,* p. 423.

17 Cressman et al., p. 155; Lundstrom, *First Team,* p. 423.

18 Ugaki, p. 155.

19 *Enterprise* and *Yorktown* action reports; Cressman et al., p. 155; Lundstrom, *First Team,* p. 424.

20 Ibid.

21 *Mogami* TROM, Reel JD-1; Lacroix and Wells, p. 448.

22 *Enterprise,* "Air Battle of the Pacific," June 4–6, report of June 15, 1942.

23 Statement of Lt. (jg.) Kawaguchi Taketoshi, acting damage-control officer of *Mikuma* in War History Office files, letter to Walter Lord, January 22, 1966. Hereafter "Kawaguchi statement."

24 Lacroix and Wells, p. 488.

25 Ibid.

26 Ugaki, p. 155.

27 Cressman et al., p. 155.

28 Statement of Lt. Cmdr. Yamauchi Masaki, navigator of *Mogami* in War History Office files, letter to Walter Lord, January 22, 1966. Hereafter "Yamauchi statement."

29 Intriguingly, a similarly located explosion would doom *Mikuma*'s sistership, *Suzuya,* two years later at the Battle of Leyte Gulf.

30 Ugaki, p. 155.

31 Ultra Intercepts.

32 Ultra Intercepts—*Zuihō.*

33 Cressman et al., p. 157.

34 Naval War College Analysis, p. 161.

35 Prange, p. 346; Zenji Orita, with Joseph Harrington, *I-Boat Captain* (Canoga Park, CA: Major Books, 1976), p. 72.

36 Prange, p. 346.

37 Ibid.

38 Cressman et al., p. 157.

39 Prange, p. 347; Orita, p. 72.

40 Prange, p. 347; Cressman et al., p. 157.

41 Prange, p. 347.

42 Prange, p. 347; Orita, p. 73.

43 Prange, p. 347.

44 Lord, p. 275.

45 Prange, p. 348.

46 Orita, p. 74. Tanabe states explicitly that his boat was not then equipped with the more modern Type 95 torpedo—a smaller, pure oxygen-driven cousin of the Type 93 carried on board Japanese warships.

47 Prange, p. 350.

48 Cressman et al., pp. 157–58.

49 Ibid., p. 157.

50 Ibid., p. 159.

51 Orita, p. 74.

52 Prange, p. 351.

53 Orita, p. 75.

54 Prange, p. 351.
55 Ibid.
56 Prange, p. 351; Orita, p. 77.
57 Kawaguchi statement.
58 Yamauchi statement.
59 TROM of destroyer *Arashio,* courtesy Allyn Nevitt.
60 Yamauchi statement.
61 Saruwatari materials; Prange, p. 339.
62 Ugaki, p. 155.
63 Sawachi Hisae, *Midowei Kaisen Kiroku* tabular data. *Senshi Sōsho,* p. 503. It should be noted that we believe Sawachi's casualty figures for *Mikuma* to be authoritative. Likewise, we believe the figures given for the number of her survivors, which were derived by Lacroix and Wells from *Senshi Sōsho,* are likewise sound. The result, though, is to revise upward *Mikuma*'s likely complement from the 888 men nominally given in Sawachi and other sources, to a total of 940 (240 survivors + 700 casualties). This is not surprising—wartime complements were often somewhat larger than nominal peacetime manning. *Mogami*'s crew was known to be 932 at the time of the battle (842 survived + 90 casualties). The same overmanning is likely to have been true of Japan's carrier crews during the battle.
64 Ugaki, p. 157.
65 Yamauchi statement.
66 *Senshio Sōshō,* p. 497; Lacroix and Wells, p. 488.
67 Bombing Squadron Six, Report of Photograph Mission, June 6, 1942.
68 Ibid.
69 In an ironic coincidence, the same day *Mikuma* was officially removed from the Navy list—August 10, 1942—would also see the second go down, heavy cruiser *Kako,* which was torpedoed and sunk shortly after the Battle of Savo Island.
70 Bombing Squadron Six, Photographic Mission Report.
71 Sawachi Hisae, *Midowei Kaisen Kiroku* tabular data.
72 Fuchida, p. 197; Lacroix and Wells, p. 488.
73 Yamauchi statement.
74 CinCpac conf. let., File No A8/(37)/JAP/ (26.1), Serial 01753, of June 21, 1942. Hereafter "Interrogation of *Mikuma* survivors," p. 1.
75 Naval War College Analysis, p. 177.
76 Ugaki, pp. 156–57.
77 Naval War College Analysis, p. 171.
78 Ugaki, p. 157.
79 Ugaki, pp. 154–55; Naval War College Analysis, p. 171.
80 Ugaki, p. 157.
81 Ibid. Refueling was complicated by the fact that the seas were rough. The battleships of BatDiv 1 (*Yamato, Nagato,* and *Mutsu*) were evidently not as proficient in this exercise as the ships of BatDiv 3, who had presumably been doing more of this sort of thing during their frequent consorting with *Kidō Butai.*
82 Ugaki, p. 159.
83 Ibid, p. 157.
84 Ibid, p. 158.
85 Ibid.
86 In recent years there has been mistaken speculation that since *Yorktown* came to rest upright on the bottom, that she could not have capsized before sinking. This line of reasoning, however, takes no account of the hydrodynamic forces acting on a body falling through a liquid medium, which tend to reassert the object's original center of gravity. More crucially, the photographic record of *Yorktown*'s demise is ironclad in this respect.
87 Orange Intercepts: *Hōshō.*
88 Ugaki, p. 158. The ships in question were *Asagumo, Natsugumo,* and *Minegumo,* with *Chitose*; Dull, p. 166.
89 Monograph No. 93, p. 85.
90 Ibid, p. 159.

CHAPTER 21: A BITTER HOMECOMING

1 Bergamini, p. 933.
2 Ibid., p. 449.
3 Bergamini, p. 935.
4 Ugaki, p. 163. We are grateful to Bob Hackett and Sander Kingsepp for supplying additional details of the fleet's return. Source: tabular records of movement for BatDiv 1, JD-1 reels.
5 Ugaki, p. 163.
6 Lacroix and Wells, p. 393.
7 *Senshi Sōsho,* pp. 284–85.
8 Bergamini, p. 935.
9 Ugaki, p. 164; Fuchida, p. 12; Prange, p. 363.
10 Arimura letter.
11 Agawa, p. 322.
12 Lord, p. 286.
13 Prange, p. 362.
14 Ibid.; Lord, p. 286.
15 Bergamini, p. 935.
16 Maeda Takeshi account, "Aces of the Pacific" interviews. Hoover Institution Archives, Bruning Collection.
17 Prange, p. 361.
18 Ibid.
19 Crane Materials, Orange Translation Intercepts, Record Group 38, NARA.
20 The Navy was not alone engaging in such behavior; the Army and the government as a whole behaved in similar fashion.
21 Willmott, *Empires in the Balance,* p. 82.
22 NavTechJap S-84 (Report on Japanese Damage Control), p. 7.
23 Ibid., p. 8.
24 Ibid., p. 11.
25 Ibid., p. 12.
26 Peattie, p. 184; Communication from Osamu Tagaya to Parshall, August 25, 2004.
27 In particular, see Bergerud, pp. 320–31, and Peattie, pp. 183–86.
28 Peattie, p. 184.
29 Tokyo time.
30 Ugaki, p. 160.
31 Ibid., pp. 160–61.
32 Lundstrom, *The First Team,* pp. 92–93.
33 *Senshi Sōsho,* vol. 49, *Nantōhōmen Kaigun Sakusen, 1 Gato Dakkai Sakusen Kaishimade.* (Southeast Area Naval Operations, 1, To the Beginning of Operations to Recapture Guadalcanal) as translated by RADM Edwin T. Layton, USN (Ret.), and hereafter "Third Fleet Battle Plan," p. 545. U.S. doctrine evolved in similar directions.
34 Ibid.
35 Ibid., p. 546.
36 Ibid.
37 Ibid.
38 Ibid., p. 547.
39 We are grateful to David Dickson for his insights into this matter.

CHAPTER 22: WHY DID JAPAN LOSE?

1 Intriguingly, this is one of the first mentions of the notion of "functionalizing" the ships within a single carrier task force along task-specific lines—a trend that would shortly begin to manifest itself in Japanese carrier doctrine in the form of Third Fleet's battle plan.
2 Ugaki, pp. 160–62.
3 Ibid., pp. 138–39.
4 Ibid., p. 161.
5 Ibid., pp. 200, 203.
6 Ibid., pp. 201–2.
7 Ibid., pp. 205–9.

8 Ibid., p. 203.
9 Ugaki, p. 162.
10 Naval War College Analysis, p. 227.
11 Ibid., pp. 212–13.
12 Prange, p. 376.
13 Ibid, p. 382.
14 Ibid., p. 378.
15 Ibid., p. 381.
16 Ibid., p. 382.
17 Lord, p. 285.
18 Fuchida, pp. 210–11.
19 Goldstein and Dillon, p. 347.
20 John Prados, in *Combined Fleet Decoded,* p. 334, was one of the first contemporary American scholars to cast doubt on this as a credible explanation for Japan's defeat.
21 This is an error the Japanese took pains to correct. At the Battle of the Philippine Sea, for instance, the Japanese carrier force, which was similar in size to the one they used at Midway, would employ nearly forty search aircraft. Communication from David Dickson, August 25, 2004.
22 This failure has been commented on at length in the Naval War College analysis of the battle, among others.
23 See in particular Eliot Cohen and John Gooch, *Military Misfortunes: The Anatomy of Failure in War* (New York: Random House, 1990), pp. 5–28.
24 Evans and Peattie, p. 124.
25 Ibid., p. 129.
26 Ibid., p. 212. The Japanese were certainly not alone in their fixation on the big gun as the result of this encounter—Jutland had a calcifying effect on the doctrine of most of the major navies.
27 One might argue that given the Japanese expectation that the Americans would not be in the area, this was less a doctrinal failure than a simple misreading of the enemy. Conversely, the fact that we have shown that Nagumo had more information in hand than has been previously believed regarding the likelihood that "something was up" in the vicinity of Midway, and yet the scouting arrangements *remained* inadequate, argues that doctrine may have nevertheless been exerting a negative pressure on the force's scouting plan.
28 Barde, p. 292.
29 Cohen and Gooch, p. 121.
30 Evans and Peattie, p. 286.
31 Ibid., pp. 70–73.
32 Ibid., p. 150.
33 Ibid., pp. 238–39.
34 Ibid., p. 188.
35 Ibid., pp. 282–86.
36 Willmott, *Empires in the Balance,* p. 242.
37 Ibid.

CHAPTER 23: ASSESSING THE BATTLE'S IMPORTANCE

1 "Aircrew" refers to any crew member on board a combat aircraft—pilot, navigator, or radio operator/gunner. The Type 0 fighter carried a pilot, the Type 99 bomber a pilot/bomb aimer and radio operator, and the Type 97 torpedo attack plane carried a pilot, observer/navigator/bomb aimer, and a radio operator/gunner.
2 Richard Frank, *Guadalcanal* (New York: Penguin Books, 1990), p. 193. These figures include floatplane, flying boat, and ground-based naval aircrew as well as carrier aviators.
3 John Lundstrom, *The First Team and the Guadalcanal Campaign: Naval Fighter Combat from August to November 1942,* (Annapolis, MD: Naval Institute Press, 1994), p. 445.
4 Peattie, p. 134, estimates that there were approximately nine hundred carrier pilots available to the IJN at the outbreak. Assuming a roughly equal proportion of fighters, dive-bombers, and torpedo planes, this would mean roughly another nine hundred or so carrier aircrew as well. The Type 99 and Type 97 aircraft had crews of two and three men, respectively. The total naval pilot corps, including land-based air groups (of which there were many) numbered around 3,500 at the outbreak.

5 These costs were mitigated to a certain extent by the Japanese practice of placing ships on reserve status at various times. We are grateful to Osamu Tagaya for his comments on this matter.

6 The accounts of the rigors of training, as recounted by Sakai Saburō for instance, make it clear that the prewar Japanese naval pilot program was geared more toward finding excuses for washing candidates out than toward establishing reasonable benchmarks for developing high-quality pilots.

7 Bergerud, p. 668. These figures include carrier-based and ground-based naval aircraft, and are composed of both combat and operational losses. Losses over the following year—April 1943 to April 1944—sent the two-year total to 7,820 aircraft.

8 Cost figures derived from Wright Patterson Air Force Base Museum, http://www.wpafb.af.mil/museum/index.htm

9 John Ellis, *World War II: A Statistical Survey* (New York: Facts On File, 1993), p. 278.

10 The uniformity of Tōgō's battleships in terms of speed, gunnery, and handling characteristics, had paid handsome dividends in terms of unit cohesiveness and ability to maneuver more smartly than the opposing Russian squadrons.

11 Willmott, *Barrier and the Javelin,* p. 518.

12 David Dickson, noted expert on Japanese carriers and doctrine, has driven this crucial point home in numerous conversations with the authors over the years.

13 Willmott, *Barrier and the Javelin,* p. 169.

14 Stephan, pp. 117–18, specifies that Japanese plans formulated in September 1942 envisioned the use of the Second, Seventh, and Fifty-Third divisions, along with an independent engineer regiment and a tank regiment.

15 A battalion of Colonel Ichiki Kiyano's detachment, which had been slated to assault Midway, was destined to be annihilated by the Marine defenders at Alligator Creek just two months later in a display of superior American firepower.

16 Kennedy, pp. 428–29.

17 Mark Harrison, ed. *The Economics of World War II: Six Great Powers in International Comparison* (Cambridge, UK: Cambridge University Press, 1998), pp. 18–22.

18 Ibid., p. 11.

19 Willmott, *Barrier and the Javelin,* p. 519.

20 The recent more detailed evaluations of the gargantuan contributions of the Soviet Union during the war lend further credence to this general stance.

21 Willmott, *Barrier and the Javelin,* pp. 521–22.

22 U.S. Naval War College Analysis, p. 1.

23 Willmott, *Barrier and the Javelin,* p. 519.

CHAPTER 24: THE MYTHS AND MYTHMAKERS OF MIDWAY

1 Lord, pp. ix–x.

2 We're not the first to suggest this. John Prados's *Combined Fleet Decoded,* in a chapter entitled "Incredible Victories?" pp. 334–35, sharply calls into question the same conventional American wisdoms that we question here.

3 ATIG stands for Air Technical Intelligence Group, which comprised several naval officers tasked with gathering information regarding Japanese naval aviation via interviews with Japanese officers. Their interviews were sometimes conducted simultaneously with those of the USSBS, but they tended to drill down into naval technical matters more deeply than USSBS did.

4 Willmott, *Pearl Harbor,* pp. 143–57. Willmott's assessment of this famous incident presents compelling evidence that Fuchida "was engaged in blatant and shameless self-advertisement in his deliberately false representation of [the] episode" and even goes so far as to assert that Fuchida's version of events never took place.

5 Dull, p. 168.

6 However, it is also important to note that the Nagumo Report itself says nothing to directly promote such an idea—Yoshioka Chūichi apparently did his work honestly.

7 We are grateful to Osamu Tagaya for his insights into this matter.

8 Willmott, *Empires in the Balance,* p. 82.

9 Fuchida, p. 13.

10 Message from Hyōdō Nisohachi to Parshall, September 23, 2000, by Koganemaru Takashi.

Appendix 2: Japanese Order of Battle

1 Based on fragmentary records of *Kaga*'s manifest held in private collection of James Sawruk. Alternately, it is possible that these two aircraft were assigned to 6th Air Group for Midway.

2 Katsura Rihei, *Kubo Zuihō no Sogai*, p. 60.

Appendix 3: The Carriers of *Kidō Butai*

1 Although it is outside the scope of this study, it is worth remarking that a total of 11 floatplane crew members were also lost, bringing the total known aviator death toll in the battle to 121.

2 In wartime Japanese, *Sōryū* was written phonetically as "SA-U-RI-YU-U," but pronounced as "*Sōryū*." We are indebted to T. Katsuta for this clarification.

3 Two of these B-17 shots are well-known in the Western literature. The third, so far as we know, has only appeared in Japanese publications. There are also two photographs of *Hiryū* taken on the morning of 5 June by a plane from the carrier *Hōshō*. These shots do not reveal any details of her paint scheme, since much of *Hiryū*'s forward flight deck had been destroyed by the initial American attack and subsequent hangar deck explosions.

Appendix 4: The Aircraft of *Kidō Butai*

1 Information for this section is taken from Peattie's *Sunburst*, pp. 264–302. This data, which the author helped tabulate for Peattie's book, was originally derived from Mikesh and Abe; Francillon, *Japanese Aircraft of the Pacific War*; Hasegawa, *Nihon no Kōkūbokan*; and Nozawa Tadashi, ed., *Nihon Kōkū sōshū* [Encyclopedia of Japanese aircraft, 1900–1945]. 8 vols. Shuppan Kyōdōsha, 1958–1983.

2 The commonly used Allied code names for Japanese aircraft were introduced after the Battle of Midway, but are included here (even if not used in the text) for the sake of convenience.

3 At the time of the Battle of Midway, the D4Y was still experimental. Once accepted into service, this aircraft was known both as the Navy Type 2 Carrier Reconnaissance Plane, and the Navy Carrier Bomber Suisei (Comet).

Appendix 5: Japanese Amphibious Operations against Midway—An Analysis

1 Samuel Morison was a notable exception to this trend, declaring in his work that the Marines would likely have handed out a Tarawa-like defeat on the Japanese had they attacked.

2 Throughout this section, we are greatly aided by the insights of Messrs. William O'Neill, Eric Bergerud, Nathan Okun, Jim O'Neil, Byron Angel, Alan Zimm, Brooks Rowlett, Terry Sofian, Bill Schliehauf, Edward Rudnicki, Richard Worth, and Tim Lanzendorfer, all of whom contributed to our understanding in the course of a lively online discussion, April–May 2004.

3 Cressman et al., pp. 67–68.

4 Monograph No. 93, p. 14.

5 Morison, p. 86, tends toward the lower number. Marine histories tend toward the higher figure.

6 Cressman et al., p. 43.

7 1,500 Navy and 1,000 Army troops. The remainder of the 5,000 troops embarked were construction personnel, a survey detachment, and a weather detachment.

Appendix 6: Discovery of Carrier *Kaga*

1 For more details on the process used, see Parshall, Tully, and Dickson, "Identifying *Kaga*," U.S. Naval Institute Proceedings, June 2001, pp. 48–52.

Appendix 7: Japanese Aircraft Tail Codes at the Battle of Midway

1 This letter, dated November 1, 1999, was forwarded to Parshall from Mr. Allan Alsleben on March 1, 2001.

2 Osamu Tagaya, communication with authors, September 8, 2004.

3 Nagumo Report, p. 6. This may have been undertaken as a result of *Sōryū*'s being used for other duties during the run-up to the battle. Recent data concerning her movements during late May suggest that she may have been directly involved in moving elements of the 23rd Air Flotilla to Truk (Ultra Intercepts—*Akagi*), thereby putting her out of the loop during the important preparatory period before the battle. Admiral Yamaguchi would rightly have needed to shift his flag in order to be present at Hashirajima during this critical phase.

4 Tagaya notes as well that if the tail codes were changed, that the horizontal fuselage bands on the aircraft, which designated which ship within the given carrier division the aircraft were from, would all have to be changed as well.

5 We are grateful to Osamu Tagaya, James Sawruk, John Lundstrom, and Michael Wenger for their insights on this matter.

Appendix 8: Japanese Radar at Midway

1 *Hiryū* action report, p. 30.

2 Prados, p. 277.

3 We appreciate Michael Wenger's kindness in providing us with a copy of this document.

4 "Battle Report of CV *Hiryū*, No. 9, 26 March 1942—22 April 1942." WDC No. 160467, Group 25, Item 25A. A replacement copy of this report has since been provided to the Naval Historical Center by the authors.

5 These photographs were taken by a *Hōshō* scout plane on the morning of 5 June, while *Hiryū* drifted, after ostensibly being scuttled the night before. These photos, while somewhat indistinct, did not appear to have been tampered with by Japanese censors and were clear enough to determine that no bedspring antenna, or even remnants of one, was anywhere on *Hiryū*'s superstructure.

Appendix 9: Chronology of Japanese Fighter Operations

1 We are grateful to Mark Horan for providing the information presented in this appendix, which was originally translated by James Sawruk and Bob Cressman from the original Japanese carrier action reports.

2 Hata and Izawa, p. 410. We are grateful to Osamu Tagaya for his detailed comments regarding pilot training courses.

3 Ranks are as follows: Lt. = Lieutenant (*Chū-i*), WO = warrant officer (*[Hikō] Heisōchō*), PO1c = Petty Officer, 1st class (*Ittō [Hikō] Heisō*), PO2c = Petty Officer, 2nd class (*Nitō [Hikō] Heisō*), Sea1c = Flight Seaman, 1st class (*Ittō Hikōhei*), Ens. = Ensign (*Shō-i*).

4 The 6th *Kōkūtai* was being transported to Midway aboard the carriers of *Kidō Butai*. *Akagi*'s watch 4A is the only known incident where 6th *Kōkūtai* aircraft participated in the battle. 6th *Kōkūtai* aircraft were equipped with arresting gear, and some of the pilots were carrier-qualified aviators.

Appendix 10: Japanese Strike Rosters, Operations MI and AL

1 We are grateful to Mark Horan for providing the information presented in this appendix, which was originally translated by James Sawruk and Bob Cressman. It should be noted that not all information is complete, owing to the difficulties in translation and/or missing data in the original source documents, which are in handwritten Japanese. We are further grateful to Osamu Tagaya for his fact-checking and insight into Japanese names.

2 We are grateful to James Sawruk for his work in translating and tabulating these records.

3 Times and dates given in Midway local.

Appendix 11: Aleutians Force Distributions

1 Never implemented during the battle.

2 During the battle, *Nenohi* and *Hatsuharu* sailed with the Attu-Adak force. *Inazuma* and *Ikazuchi* took their place in the Main Body.

3 *Oboro* did not sail with 2nd Mobile Force during the battle. She remained in port, waiting to escort *Zuikaku* north to Ominato on June 15. Destroyer *Sazanami* sailed with Kakuta's force in her place.

4 During the operation, destroyers *Nenohi* and *Hatsuharu* sailed with the Attu-Adak force, thereby bringing its total destroyers to four (*Hatsuharu, Hatsushimo, Nenohi,* and *Wakaba*).

5 During the operation, destroyer *Akatsuki* was added to the screen of the Kiska Invasion Force. Nor did *Ikazuchi* and *Inazumo* sail with this force. Thus, in the event, the total number of destroyers with the Kiska Force was three (*Akatsuki, Hibiki,* and *Hokaze*).

6 Actually sailed with the Main Body.

7 Mistakenly listed as an AP in the original.

8 This is clearly a mistake on the part of the original author, as *Myōkō* and *Haguro* had nothing to do with the submarine force. Both cruisers were under repair in Japan at the time of the operational planning.

Selected Bibliography

Books

Agawa Hiroyuki. *The Reluctant Admiral: Yamamoto and the Imperial Navy.* Translated by John Bester. Tokyo: Kōdansha International, 1979.

Attack Force Pearl Harbor. Tokyo: Model Art Co. Ltd., 2000.

Ballard, Robert. *Return to Midway.* Toronto, Ontario: Madison Press Books, 1999.

Barde, Robert Elmer. "The Battle of Midway: A Study in Command." Ph.D. Thesis, University of Maryland, 1971.

Belote, J. H., and W. M. Belote. *Titans of the Seas.* New York: Harper and Row, 1975.

Bergamini, David. *Japan's Imperial Conspiracy.* New York: William Morrow & Company, 1971.

Bergerud, Eric. *Fire in the Sky.* Boulder, CO: Westview Press, 2000.

Bicheno, Hugh. *Midway.* London: Cassel, 2001.

Bix, Herbert. *Hirohito and the Making of Modern Japan.* New York: HarperCollins, 2000.

Boyd, Carl, and Yoshida Akihiko. *The Japanese Submarine Force and World War II.* Annapolis, MD: Naval Institute Press, 1995.

Bradford, James, ed. *Quarterdeck and Bridge: Two Centuries of American Naval Leaders.* Annapolis, MD: Naval Institute Press, 1996.

Brown, David. *Aircraft Carriers.* New York: Arco Publishing Co., 1977.

Brown, Captain Eric M. *Duels in the Sky.* Annapolis, MD: Naval Institute Press, 1988.

Campbell, John. *Naval Weapons of World War Two.* London: Conway Maritime Press, 1985.

Carpenter, Dorr, and Norman Polmar. *Submarines of the Imperial Japanese Navy.* Annapolis, MD: Naval Institute Press, 1986.

Chesneau, Roger. *Aircraft Carriers of the World, 1914 to the Present: An Illustrated Encyclopedia.* Annapolis, MD: Naval Institute Press, 1992.

Cohen, Eliot, and John Gooch. *Military Misfortunes: The Anatomy of Failure in War.* New York: Random House, 1990.

Cook, Haruko Taya, and Theodore F. Cook. *Japan at War: An Oral History.* New York: The New Press, 1992.

Cloe, John. *The Aleutian Warriors—A History of the 11th Air Force & Fleet Wing 4.* Missoula, MT: Pictorial Histories Publishing Co., 1991.

Cressman, Robert, Steve Ewing, Barrett Tillman, Mark Horan, Clark Reynolds, and Stan Cohen. *A Glorious Page in our History: The Battle of Midway.* Missoula, MT: Pictorial Histories Publishing Company, 1990.

Dickson, W. David. *Battle of the Philippine Sea, June 1944.* Surrey, UK: Ian Allen, Ltd., 1974.

Drawings of Imperial Japanese Navy Vessels, Vol. 3: Aircraft Carriers, Seaplane Carriers, Auxiliary Seaplane Carriers and Submarines. Tokyo: Model Art Co. Ltd., 1999.

Dull, Paul S. *A Battle History of the Imperial Japanese Navy 1941–1945.* Annapolis, MD: Naval Institute Press, 1978.

Edgerton, Robert. *Warriors of the Rising Sun: A History of the Japanese Military.* Boulder, CO: Westview Press, 1997.

Ellis, John. *World War II: A Statistical Survey.* New York: Facts on File, 1993.

Evans, David C., ed. *The Japanese Navy in World War II in the Words of Former Japanese Naval Officers.* 2nd ed. Annapolis, MD: Naval Institute Press, 1982.

Evans, David C., and Mark R. Peattie. *Kaigun: Strategy, Tactics, and Technology in the Imperial Japanese Navy, 1887–1941.* Annapolis, MD: Naval Institute Press, 1997.

Francillon, René J. *Japanese Aircraft of the Pacific War.* Annapolis, MD: Naval Institute Press, 1987.

————. *Imperial Japanese Navy Bombers of World War Two.* Windsor, UK: Hylton Lacy Publishers, 1969.

Frank, Richard. *Guadalcanal.* New York: Penguin Books, 1990.

Fuchida, Mitsuo, and Masatake Okumiya. *Midway: The Battle that Doomed Japan.* Annapolis, MD: Naval Institute Press, 1955.

Fukui, Shizuo. *Japanese Naval Vessels Illustrated, 1869–1945, Volume 3.* Tokyo: KK Best-sellers, 1982.

Gay, George. *Sole Survivor: The Battle of Midway and Its Effect on His Life.* Naples, FL: Midway Publishers, 1979.

Goldstein, Donald, and Katherine Dillon. *The Pearl Harbor Papers.* Dulles, VA: Brassey's, 1993.

Hanson, Victor Davis. *Carnage and Culture: Landmark Battles in the Rise of Western Power.* New York: Anchor Books, 2002.

Harrison, Mark, ed. *The Economics of World War II: Six Great Powers in International Comparison.* Cambridge, UK: Cambridge University Press, 1998.

Hasegawa, Tōichi. *Nihon no Kōkūbōkan* (Japanese aircraft carriers). Guranpuri Shuppan, 1997.

Hashimoto, Toshio. *Shōgen Midowei Kaisen* (Witnesses to the Midway Sea Battle). Tokyo: Toshio Optical Human Corporation, NF Library, 1999.

Hara, Tameichi, with Fred Saito and Roger Pineau. *Japanese Destroyer Captain.* New York: Ballantine Books, 1961.

Hata, Ikuhiko, and Yasuho Izawa. *Japanese Naval Aces and Fighter Units in World War II.* Translated by Don Gorham. Annapolis, MD: Naval Institute Press, 1989.

Healy, Mark, and David Chandler, eds. *Campaign Series, Midway 1942: Turning Point in the Pacific.* London: Osprey, 1993.

Hone, Thomas C., Norman Friedman, and Mark D. Mandeles. *American and British Aircraft Carrier Development, 1919–1941.* Annapolis, MD: Naval Institute Press, 1999.

Hughes, Wayne. *Fleet Tactics: Theory and Practice*. Annapolis, MD: Naval Institute Press, 1986.

IJN Photo File #5: Akagi, Kaga, Hōshō & Ryūjō. Tokyo: Kōjinsha, 1999.

IJN Photo File #6: Shōkaku, Zuikaku, Sōryū, Hiryū, Unryū-class & Taihō. Tokyo: Kojinsha, 1999.

Ikari, Yoshiro. *Kaigun Kugishō*. Tokyo: Kōjinsha, 1989.

Japan, *Bōeichō Bōeikenshūjo Senshibu* (originally, *Bōeichō Boeikenshūjō Senshishitsu*), also *Senshi Sōsho* (War history) series. Asagumo Shimbunsha.

——. *Midowei Kaisen* (Midway Naval Battle). Vol. 43, 1971.

——. *Nantōhōmen Kaigun Sakusen, Gato Dakkai Sakusen Kaishimade* (Southeast Area Naval Operations to the Beginning of Operations to Recapture Guadalcanal). Vol. 49, 1971. Excerpts as translated by RADM Edwin T. Layton, USN (Ret.).

Japanese Warships, No. 3, Aircraft Carriers Hōshō, Ryūjō, Akagi, Kaga, Shōkaku, Zuikaku, Sōryū, Hiryū, Unryū-class, Taihō. Tokyo: Kōjinsha, 1989.

Japanese Warships, No. 4, Aircraft Carriers Junyō-class, Zuihō-class, Chitose-class, Taiyō-class, Shinano, Seaplane carriers, etc. Tokyo: Kōjinsha, 1989.

Jentschura, Hansgeorg, Dieter Jung, and Peter Mickel. *Warships of the Imperial Japanese Navy, 1869–1945*. Annapolis, MD: Naval Institute Press, 1977.

Jordan, Roger. *The World's Merchant Fleets, 1939. The Particulars and Wartime Fates of 6,000 Ships*. Annapolis, MD: Naval Institute Press, 1999.

Katsura, Rihei. *Kubo Zuihō no Sogai* (Carrier *Zuihō*). Tokyo: Kasumi, 1999.

Keegan, John. *The Face of Battle*. London: Penguin Books, 1992.

Kennedy, Paul. *The Rise and Fall of the Great Powers: Economic Change and Military Conflict from 1500 to 2000*. New York: Random House, 1988.

Kimata, Jiro. *Nihon Kōkū Senshi* (Japanese Carrier Battle History). Tokyo: Kokusho, 1977.

Kusaka, Ryūnosuke. *Rengō Kantai* (Combined Fleet). Tokyo: Mainichi Newspaper Co., 1952.

Lacroix, Eric, and Linton Wells II. *Japanese Cruisers of the Pacific War*. Annapolis, MD: Naval Institute Press, 1997.

Mechanic of World Aircraft No. 5 (Zero Fighter). Tokyo: Kōjinsha, 1993.

Mechanic of World Aircraft No. 11 (Suisei / Type 99 Kanbaku). Tokyo: Kōjinsha, 1994.

Mechanic of World Aircraft No. 14 (Type 97 Kankō / Tenzan). Tokyo: Kōjinsha, 1995.

Mechanism of Japanese Warships No. 2: Aircraft Carriers. Tokyo: Kōjinsha, reprinted in 1999.

Layton, Edwin T., with Roger Pineau and John Costello. *And I Was There*. New York: William Morrow, 1985.

Lord, Walter. *Incredible Victory*. New York: HarperCollins, 1967.

Lundstrom, John. *The First South Pacific Campaign*. Annapolis, MD: Naval Institute Press, 1976.

——. *The First Team: Pacific Naval Air Combat from Pearl Harbor to Midway*. Annapolis, MD: Naval Institute Press, 1984.

——. *The First Team and the Guadalcanal Campaign: Naval Fighter Combat from August to November 1942*. Annapolis, MD: Naval Institute Press, 1994.

——. Unpublished manuscript on Admiral Frank Jack Fletcher.

Makishima, Teiuchi. *Middoue no Higeki* (The Tragedy of Midway). Tokyo: Shōsetsu, 1956.

Marder, Arthur. *Old Friends, New Enemies, The Royal Navy and the Imperial Japanese Navy, Volume II: The Pacific War, 1942–1945*. Oxford, UK: Clarendon Press, 1990.

Morison, Samuel Eliot. *History of United States Naval Operations in World War II. Volume Four: Coral Sea, Midway and Submarine Actions, May 1942–August 1942.* Edison, NJ: Castle Books, 2001.

Nihon Zosen Gakkai, ed. *Shōwa Zōsenshi* (A history of ship construction in the Shōwa Era). 2 vols. Tokyo: Hara Shobo, 1977.

Oide, Hisashi. *Yūdan Teitoku Yamaguchi Tamon* (The Brash Admiral Yamaguchi Tamon). Tokyo: Tokuma Shoten, 1985.

Oleck, Howard, ed. *Heroic Battles of WW II.* New York: Belmont Books, 1962.

Orita, Zenji, with Joseph Harrington. *I-Boat Captain.* Canoga Park, CA: Major Books, 1976.

Operational History of Japanese Naval Communications, December 1941–August 1945. Laguna Hills, CA: Aegean Park Press, 1985.

Overy, Richard. *Why the Allies Won.* New York: W.W. Norton & Company, 1995.

Pacific War Series # 4 (*Midowei Kaisen*—Midway Naval Battle). Tokyo: Gakken, 2000.

Pacific War Series # 13 (IJN CV *Shōkaku* Class). Tokyo: Gakken, 1999.

Pacific War Series # 14 (Carrier Strike Force). Tokyo: Gakken, 1999.

Peattie, Mark. *Sunburst: The Rise of Japanese Naval Air Power, 1909–1941.* Annapolis, MD: Naval Institute Press, 2001.

Plans of Ships of the Imperial Japanese Navy. Tokyo: Hara Shobo, 2000.

Polmar, Norman. *Aircraft Carriers: A Graphic History of Carrier Aviation and Its Influence on World Events.* New York: Doubleday Co., 1969.

Prados, John. *Combined Fleet Decoded: The Secret History of American Intelligence and the Japanese Navy in World War II.* New York: Random House, 1995.

Prange, Gordon W., with Donald Goldstein and Katherine Dillon. *Miracle at Midway.* New York: McGraw-Hill, 1982.

———. *At Dawn We Slept.* New York: McGraw-Hill, 1981.

Pugh, Philip. *The Cost of Seapower: The Influence of Money on Naval Affairs from 1815 to the Present Day.* London: Conway Maritime Press, 1986.

Random Japanese Warship Details. 2 vols. Tokyo: Tamiya, 1988.

Roscoe, Theodore. *United States Submarine Operations in World War II.* Annapolis, MD: Naval Institute Press, 1949.

Sakai, Saburō, with Martin Caidin and Fred Saito. *Samurai!* New York: Sutton, 1957. Reprint, Bantam Books, 1975.

Sawachi, Hisae. *Middowei Kaisen: Kiroku* (The Naval Battle of Midway: A Record). Tokyo: Bungei Shunjū, 1986.

Skulski, Janusz. *Anatomy of the Ship. The Battleship Yamato.* London: Conway Maritime Press, 1988.

———. *Anatomy of the Ship. The Battleship Fusō.* London: Conway Maritime Press, 1998.

Skwiot, Miroslaw, and Adam Jarski. *Akagi.* Gdansk, Poland: A. J. Press, 1994.

Smith, Peter. *Dive Bomber! An Illustrated History.* Annapolis, MD: Naval Institute Press, 1982.

Stephan, John. *Hawaii Under the Rising Sun.* Honolulu: University of Hawaii Press, 1984.

Sun Tzu. *The Art of War.* Translated by Samuel Griffith. Oxford, UK: Oxford University Press, 1963.

Sweetman, Jack, ed. *The Great Admirals: Command at Sea, 1587–1945*. Annapolis, MD: Naval Institute Press, 1997.

Tagaya, Osamu. *Mitsubishi Type 1 Rikko "Betty" Units of World War 2*. Osprey Combat Aircraft Series, No. 22. Oxford, UK: Osprey Publishing Ltd, 2001.

Toland, John. *The Rising Sun: The Decline and Fall of the Japanese Empire, 1936–1945*. New York: Random House, 1961.

Tuleja, Thaddeus. *Climax at Midway*. New York: Norton, 1960.

Ugaki, Matome. *Fading Victory: The Diary of Matome Ugaki, 1941–1945*. Translated by Masatake Chihaya; Donald M. Goldstein and Katherine V. Dillon, eds. Pittsburgh: University of Pittsburgh Press, 1991.

Warship Color. Tokyo: Model Art, 2000.

Warships of the Imperial Japanese Navy, Vol. 6—Shōkaku, Zuikaku, Sōryū, Hiryū, Unryū-class, Taihō. Tokyo: Kōjinsha, 1996.

Watts, Anthony J., and Brian G. Gordon. *The Imperial Japanese Navy*. Garden City, NY: Doubleday and Co., 1971.

Wildenberg, Thomas. *Destined for Glory: Dive Bombing, Midway, and the Evolution of Carrier Air Power*. Annapolis, MD: Naval Institute Press, 1998.

Wildenberg, Thomas. *Gray Steel and Black Oil. Fast Tankers and Replenishment at Sea in the U.S. Navy, 1912–1992*. Annapolis, MD: Naval Institute Press, 1996.

Willmott, H. P. *The Barrier and the Javelin: Japanese and Allied Pacific Strategies, February to June 1942*. Annapolis, MD: Naval Institute Press, 1982.

Willmott, H. P. *Empires in the Balance: Japanese and Allied Pacific Strategies to April 1942*. Annapolis, MD: Naval Institute Press, 1982.

Willmott, H. P., with Tohmatsu Haruo and W. Spencer Johnson. *Pearl Harbor*. London: Cassell, 2001.

Zenji, Orita, with Joseph Harrington. *I-Boat Captain*. Canoga Park, CA: Major Books, California, 1976.

Articles

Dickson, David. "Fighting Flat-tops: The *Shōkakus*." *Warship International* 1 (1977).

Hunnicutt, Thomas G. "The Operational Failure of U.S. Submarines at the Battle of Midway—and Implications for Today." Newport, RI: Naval War College Joint Military Operations Department, May 1996.

Isom, Dallas W. "The Battle of Midway: Why the Japanese Lost." *Naval War College Review* (Summer 2000).

_____. "They Would Have Found a Way." *Naval War College Review* (Summer 2001).

Itani, Jirō, Hans Lengerer, and Tomoko Rehm-Takara. "Anti-aircraft Gunnery in the Imperial Japanese Navy." In *Warship, 1991,* edited by Robert Gardiner. London: Conway Maritime Press Ltd., 1991.

Lengerer, Hans. "*Akagi* and *Kaga*." Parts 1–3. *Warship: A Quarterly Journal of Warship History* 22 (April 1982); 23 (July 1982); 24 (October 1982).

Parshall, Jonathan, David Dickson, and Anthony Tully. "Doctrine Matters: Why the Japanese Lost at Midway." *Naval War College Review* 54, No. 3 (Summer 2001).

Parshall, Jonathan, with Anthony Tully and David Dickson. "Identifying *Kaga*." *U.S. Naval Institute Proceedings* (June 2001).

Parshall, Jonathan. "What Was Really Happening on the Japanese Flight Decks?" *World War II* (Midway Issue, June 2002).

Schlesinger, James. "Underappreciated Victory." *Naval History* (October 2003).

Snow, Carl. "Japanese Carrier Operations: How Did *They* Do It ?" *The Hook* (Spring 1995).

Official Documents

Acting CO VT-6 (Lt. [jg] R. E. Laub), "Report of Action 4 June 1942."

U.S. Department of the Navy, Bureau of Aeronautics, Air Technical Intelligence Group, Advanced Echelon, Far East Air Forces, APO 925, 26 November 1945, Reports 1, 2, and 5.

Bureau of Ships, War Damage Report No. 56, USS *Franklin* (CV 13), September 15, 1946. Naval History Center, Washington, DC.

Bureau of Ships, War Damage Report No. 62, USS *Princeton* (CVL 23), October 30 1947. Naval History Center, Washington, DC.

CINCPAC to COMINCH, "Battle of Midway" (June 28, 1942).

CINCPAC to CNO(DNI), "Interrogation of Japanese Prisoners Taken after Midway Action 9 June 1942." Ser 01753 (June 21, 1942).

CINCPAC conf. let., File No A8/(37)/JAP/(26.1), Serial 01753, of June 21, 1942, interrogation of *Mikuma* survivors.

CO VB-3 (LCDR M. F. Leslie) to CYAG, "Attack Conducted 4 June 1942 on Japanese Carriers located 156 miles NW Midway Island, Narrative Concerning" (June 7, 1942).

CO VB-5 (Temporarily Designated VS-5) to CO USS *Enterprise*, "Report of Action June 4–6, 1942" (June 7, 1942).

CO VB-5, "Aircraft Action Report, 2000 5 June 1942."

CO VB-5, "Aircraft Action Report 1445 6 June 1942."

CO VB-6 to CO USS *Enterprise*, "Report of Action June 4–6, 1942" (June 20, 1942).

CO VB-8 to CO USS *Hornet*, "Action Report 5–6 June 1942" (June 7, 1942).

CO VS-6, "Aircraft Action Report, 1205 4 June 1942."

CO VS-6, "Aircraft Action Report, 1905 4 June 1942."

CO VS-6, "Aircraft Action Report, 1915 5 June 1942."

FTP-170-B Damage Control Instructions 1944. United States Government Printing Office, Washington, DC, 1944.

"Interview of Rear Admiral G. D. Murray, USN from the South Pacific," in the Bureau of Aeronautics, November 25, 1942. CINCPAC Box #101(1–40), Record Set 4797, File A4-31.

"Japanese Aerial Tactics," Special Translation Number 57, CINCPAC-CINCPOA Bulletin No. 87–45, April 3, 1945.

Japanese Monograph No. 88. "Aleutian Naval Operations, March 1942–February 1943." Department of the Army, 1947.

Japanese Monograph No. 93. "Midway Operations May–June 1942." Washington, DC: Department of the Army, 1947.

Kaigun Seido Enkaku (Naval Organization History), 1941. Contains nominal crew structures of carriers *Akagi, Kaga, Sōryū,* and *Hiryū.*

Lt. Arthur J. Brassfield to CO VF-3. "Report of Action 4 June 1942" (June 6, 1942); Wilhelm G. Esders, CAP, to CYAG, "Report of Action 4 June 1942" (June 6, 1942).

Lt. Sam Adams, "Aircraft Action Report, 1615 4 June 1942."

Nairei Teiyo (Manual of Military Secret Orders). Translation of Captured Japanese Document, Item #613 (S-1193), July 20, 1943. Defines aircraft squadron compositions for various periods. National Archives, Washington, DC.

Record Group 457, SRMN-012, Fleet Intelligence Summary, from May 27, 1942, to June 8, 1942. National Archives, Washington, DC.

"The Midway Operation: DesRon 10, Mine Sweep Div 16, CV *Akagi,* CV *Kaga,* CVL *Sōryū,* and CVL *Hiryū.*" Extract Translation from DOC No. 160985B—MC 397.901. (Contains translated carrier air group reports for *Akagi,*, *Kaga, Sōryū,* and *Hiryū.*).

Ultra Intercepts—Designated as "Orange Translations of Japanese Intelligence Intercepts." Intercept entries carded for *Akagi, Kaga, Hōshō,* etc. Crane Materials, National Archives II—Record Group 38.

USF-77 (Revised). "Current Tactical Orders Aircraft Carriers U.S. Fleet." Prepared by Commander Aircraft Battle Force, March 1941. Rec. No. 4756.

USF-75. "Current Tactical Orders and Doctrine U.S. Fleet Aircraft, Volume Two, Battleship and Cruiser Aircraft."

USF-74. "U.S. Dive-bomber Doctrine."

U.S. Naval Technical Mission to Japan reports, including:

"Aircraft Arrangements and Handling Facilities in Japanese Naval Vessels." Report A-11. Washington, DC; Operational Archives, U.S. Naval History Division, 1974.

"Characteristics of Japanese Naval Vessels—Article 2—Surface Machinery Design." S-01-2, Washington, DC; Operational Archives, U.S. Naval History Division, 1974.

"Characteristics of Japanese Naval Vessels—Article 3—Surface Warship Hull Design." S-01-3, Washington, DC; Operational Archives, U.S. Naval History Division, 1974.

"Characteristics of Japanese Naval Vessels—Article 4—Surface Warship Machinery Design (Plans and Documents)." S-01-4, Washington, DC; Operational Archives, U.S. Naval History Division, 1974.

"Effectiveness of Japanese AA Fire." Report C-44. Washington, DC; Operational Archives, U.S. Naval History Division, 1974.

"Japanese Anti-aircraft Fire-Control." Report O-30. Washington, DC; Operational Archives, U.S. Naval History Division, 1974.

"Japanese Damage Control." Report S-84(N). Washington, DC; Operational Archives, U.S. Naval History Division, 1974.

"Japanese Radio, Radar, and Sonar Equipment." Report E-17. Washington, DC; Operational Archives, U.S. Naval History Division, 1974.

"Japanese Submarine and Shipborne Radar." Report E-01. Washington, DC; Operational Archives, U.S. Naval History Division, 1974.

"Japanese Torpedoes and Tubes-Articles I, Ship and Kaiten Torpedoes." Report O-01-1. Washington, DC; Operational Archives, U.S. Naval History Division, 1974.

"Japanese Torpedoes and Tubes-Articles 2, Aircraft Torpedoes." Report O-01-2. Washington, DC; Operational Archives, U.S. Naval History Division, 1974.

U.S. Naval War College. "Battle of Midway, Including the Aleutian Phase of June 3 to June 14, 1942. Strategical and Tactical Analysis." Newport, Connecticut, 1948.

United States Navy Combat Narrative. "The Aleutians Campaign, June 1942–August 1943." Naval Historical Center Department of the Navy, Washington, DC, 1993.

United States Navy, Office of Naval Intelligence. *The Japanese Story of the Battle of Midway*. Washington, DC.: GPO, 1947. (Translation of parts of First Air Fleet, Detailed Battle Report No. 6, Midway Operations, 27 May–9 June 1942, in the *ONI Review*, May 1947).

United States Strategic Bombing Survey (Pacific), Naval Analysis Division. Interrogations of Japanese Officials, Volume 1 and 2, 1946.

War Patrol Report, USS *Nautilus*.

War Patrol Report, USS *Grouper*.

War Diary of 6th Fleet, Midway Operation, WDC 160268.

Japanese Microfilm Records—JD 1(a). Operational orders and records for the Battle of Midway June 1942. CVs *Akagi, Kaga, Sōryū, Hiryū*; Desron 10; detailed action report (DAR) CV *Kaga* 5 June; DAR CV *Sōryū,* 27 May–9 June (*sic*); DAR CV *Hiryū,* 27 May–6 June; DAR First Air Fleet, 27 May–9 June. Referred to in the text as "JD-1."

Second Fleet Ultra Secret Standing Order No. 16, May 1, 1944, "Diversion Attack Force Doctrine."

Private Papers

Excerpts from working notes of Walter Lord, received by Parshall and Tully, 2001.

Memo from Lt. Louis Poisson Davis to Commander Destroyer Squadron Eleven, May 2, 1923. Louis Poisson Davis Papers, Collection No. 309, East Carolina Manuscript Collection, J. Y. Joyner Library, East Carolina University, Greenville, North Carolina.

Mobile Force Doctrine. Collection of unpublished manuscripts regarding Japanese naval doctrine held in personal collection of David Dickson.

Plans of *Kaga* and *Sōryū*. Myco International, Japan.

Plans of *Akagi,* courtesy of Chuck Haberlein, U.S. Naval Historical Center.

Plans of Japanese carriers provided from private collection of David Dickson.

"Significant PBY sightings of Japanese Carriers late 4 June–5 June [1942]," compiled by John Lundstrom, sent to Tony Tully, March 15, 2000.

Tabulated American aircraft attack rosters and casualty figures, including cause of loss. Courtesy Mark Horan.

Translated carrier air group action reports, including flight rosters and mission times, of *Akagi, Kaga, Sōryū, Hiryū, Ryūjō,* and *Junyō.* Courtesy James Sawruk.

Bruning Collection, Hoover Institute. Contains interviews of IJN aviators. Courtesy John Bruning.

Private Correspondence

Letters to Jonathan Parshall from Hyōdō Nisohachi regarding Japanese naval aviation equipment, procedures, and technique; translated by Koganemaru Takashi; transmitted to Parshall, 2000–2002.

Letters to Jonathan Parshall from Capt. Yoshida Akihiko, JMSDF (Ret.) 2000–2004.

Phone interview with Arimura Yoshikazu conducted by Yoshida Jiro, transmitted to Jonathan Parshall, March 20, 2002.

E-mails from Daniel Rush, U.S. Navy (Ret.), to Jonathan Parshall, regarding reminiscences of Dr. Nagumo Shinji, June 3, 2001.

Magazines

Senzen Senpaku (Japanese Ships before the War). Private ship magazine published by Endo Akira and courtesy of same to Jonathan Parshall. Plans consulted and translated by Yoshida Akihiko include *Sōryū, Hiryū, Akagi,* and *Kaga.*

Index

About the Authors

Jonathan Parshall's interest in the Imperial Japanese Navy developed in childhood. He has written for the U.S. Naval War College *Review,* Naval Institute *Proceedings,* and *World War II* magazine, and has contributed to several books on the topic. In 1995 Jon founded www.combinedfleet.com, the foremost Internet site on the Imperial Navy, which currently attracts more than 50,000 visitors monthly. He was a consultant to the 1999 expedition by Nauticos Corporation and the Naval Oceanographic Office that discovered wreckage from the carrier *Kaga,* sunk at Midway. A graduate of Carleton College and the Carlson School of Management, he works in senior management for a Minnesota software company. He lives in Minneapolis with his wife Margaret, children, Anna and Derek, and cats Hiryū and Sōryū.

Anthony Tully's interest in the Imperial Japanese Navy is long-standing and wide-ranging. Like coauthor Jon, his interest began in childhood, and his interest in Midway, in particular, was inspired by Walter Lord's *Incredible Victory* and its careful attempts to reconstruct events. This attention to detail mentored the pattern of all of Tony's subsequent art and writing. A frequent contributor to journals and periodicals on matters both nautical and topical, Tony has been published in the U.S. Naval War College *Review,* Naval Institute *Proceedings, Naval History, Warship International,* the *Dallas Morning News, Today's Christian Man,* and *Kudzu* magazine. Likewise a consultant to the 1999 Nauticos/NAVO expedition, he has been an adviser to other undersea expeditions researching naval battle sites in the Philippines and elsewhere. Since 1996 Tony has been a major contributor to www.combinedfleet.com and other online resources on the Imperial Navy. A graduate of Texas Tech University, with extensive postgraduate studies, Tony works in the information technology and support field. He lives in Dallas, Texas.

Visit the authors at:
www.shatteredswordbook.com